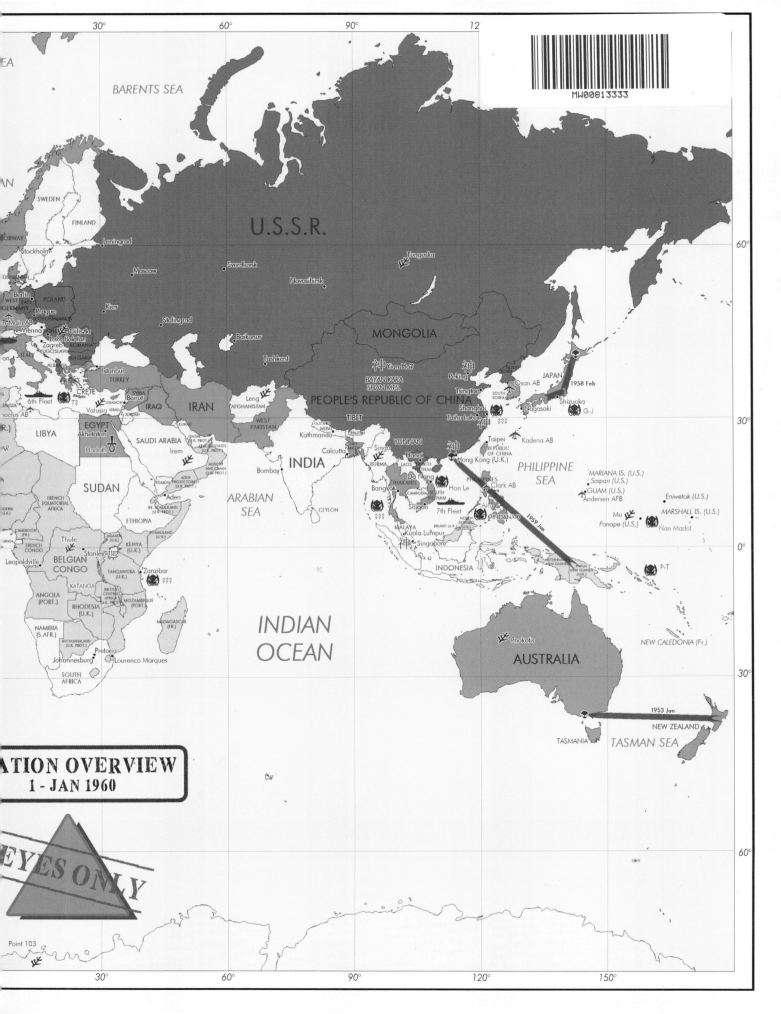

Based on **Delta Green: The Role-Playing Game**
by Dennis Detwiller, Adam Scott Glancy, Kenneth Hite, Shane Ivey, and Greg Stolze, with Gil Trevizo

Delta Green was created by Dennis Detwiller, Adam Scott Glancy, and John Scott Tynes

The Fall of Delta Green is published by arrangement with the Delta Green Partnership.
The intellectual property known as Delta Green is TM and © the Delta Green Partnership,
who has licensed its use here. The contents of The Fall of Delta Green are ©2018 Pelgrane Press Ltd.
excepting those elements that are components of the Delta Green intellectual property.
The Delta Green logo is a trademark of the Delta Green Partnership and is used with permission.
GUMSHOE system by Robin D. Laws

Includes material from **Ashen Stars** by Robin Laws, **Fear Itself** by Robin D. Laws and Gareth Ryder-Hanrahan,
and from **Trail of Cthulhu**, **Moon Dust Men**, **Majestic Overwatch**,
and **Night's Black Agents** by Kenneth Hite

Special thanks to Sheila Ralston for insights into Chicago police work.

The Fall of

DELTA GREEN

by Kenneth Hite

Publishers
Simon Rogers and Cathriona Tobin

Author
Kenneth Hite

Art Direction
Jen McCleary, Cathriona Tobin

Cover Art
Jérôme Huguenin

Interior Art
Gislaine Avila, Nyra Drakae, Kennedy C. Garza, Melissa Gay,
Quintin Gleim, David Lewis Johnson, Erika Leveque, Jen McCleary,
Anthony Moravian, Ernanda Souza, and Karolina Wegrzyn

Cartography
Ralf Schemmann

Design and Layout
Jen McCleary

Editing and Development
Colleen Riley, Simon Rogers, Cathriona Tobin

Additional Art Credits
The image on p. 025 is from the USMC Archives and is used under the CC BY 2.0 license
https://creativecommons.org/licenses/by/2.0/

All other images are in the public domain and taken from Wikimedia Commons.

Playtesters
Jack Anderson, William C. Bargo Jr, Jack Nicollas Baxter, Andrew Bestul, J. Michael Bestul,
Benjamin Brown, John Bryan, Leslie Camacho, Jordan Carroll, Taylor Carroll, Kane Cathain,
Karen Chan, Eric Chatterjee, Stephen Constantelos, Erik Coons, David Corrie, Bill Crosbie, Jim
D'Alessio, Neal Dalton, Michael Daumen, Dave, Rob Day, Steve Dempsey, Dimes, Colby Elliott,
Stephen J. Ellis, Keegan Fink, Ethan Fiset, Lauren Fram, Eric Franklin, Stephanie Franklin, Jeromy
French, Jérémy Ganivet, The Happy Fun Time Gamers, Michael Grasso, John Harford, Nathan
Henson, Morgan Hua, Chris Huth, Joshua, Rachel Kahn, Micah King, Zachary Kline, Shawn
Kowalski, Dani L., Moe Lane, Ed Laprade, Cyrus LeMoine, Andre LeMoine, Nick Levi, Bill Lynch,
Shannon Mac, Rob MacDougall, Nyssa Mackinnon, John WS Marvin, Jen McCleary, Lauren
McEwen, Timothy McGowan, Lara Milton, Toumy Misaysongkham, Aaron Morris, Andrew
Morrow, Andrew Murray, Debbie Norman, Emma Norman-Bargo, William C. Norman-Bargo
III, Erik Otterberg, Brian Overton, Aliénor Perrard, Marcelline Perrard, Michael Pfeiffer, Andrew
Pfeiffer, Keith Potter, Matthew Rapati, William Raynovich, Stephanie Ruehl, Wade Rockett, Ross
Rosenberg, Nat Roth, Liam Scanlon, Ross Sinodis, Jebadiah Smalls, John Smejkal, Kevin Smith,
John Robert Smith, Joshua Smolkin, Aaron Stultz, Robert Stutus, Matthew Sullivan-Barrett, Tiger
Swan, Alexx Swanson, Kamran Swanson, Brian Swisher, C. G. Swortwood, Bill Templeton,
Travis Thompson, Adam Thornsburg, Kyle Thorson, Megan Tolentino, Thomas Toynton, Blake
Tullo, Calliope Westbrook, Jeff Wikstrom, J. Yabuki, Michelle Zeigert, Andy Zeigert

Copyright © 2018 Pelgrane Press Ltd.
Pelgrane Press is co-owned by Simon Rogers and Cathriona Tobin.

Contents

INITIAL BRIEFING

"To a season of political and social upheaval was added a strange and brooding apprehension of hideous physical danger; a danger widespread and all-embracing, such a danger as may be imagined only in the most terrible phantasms of the night."

— H.P. Lovecraft, "Nyarlathotep"

A quagmire overseas chews up American forces.

Apocalyptic cults rise in the Middle East, riots paralyze Paris, and Russia moves aggressively into Europe.

The United States wages secret war around the globe while its social fabric shreds and its cities crackle with gunfire.

New technologies, new sciences, and new music revolutionize our lives.

The Earth's ecology teeters at the brink of toxic ruin.

The stars are coming right.

It is 1968.

What is DELTA GREEN?

DELTA GREEN is an authorized but unacknowledged black program of the United States national security establishment. Its personnel are tasked from all branches of the federal government, especially from the military, law enforcement, and intelligence communities. The program is classified Top Secret, with its existence and mission known only to holders of the DELTA GREEN clearance.

The program has a small permanent staff deep in the bowels of the Pentagon, but its agents operate in secret. The program buries DELTA GREEN missions inside other ongoing military operations, or disguises them as training exercises, liaison work, or entirely unrelated investigations. DELTA GREEN agents hold normal federal postings in the military, CIA, FBI, NSA, or some other agency. Their employers never understand the *real* mission of the program.

DELTA GREEN began with the raid on Innsmouth, Massachusetts forty years ago, in February 1928. That raid revealed a literally apocalyptic threat to the United States, and to the world. It gave the federal government a glimpse into a parallel physics and biology of alien gods and immortal monsters. Even the briefest contact with these phenomena destroys minds and lives; the touch of the unnatural corrupts and poisons those who study it and those who oppose it. Encounters with this implacably hostile, unutterably incomprehensible universe have leveled civilizations and sunk continents.

The mission of DELTA GREEN: Hunt and destroy any and all aspects of this unnatural reality at home and abroad. At any cost.

What is The Fall of DELTA GREEN?

This game adapts **Delta Green: The Role-Playing Game** from Arc Dream Publishing to the GUMSHOE rules system used by such Pelgrane Press games as **Night's Black Agents** and **Trail of Cthulhu.**

Arc Dream sets **Delta Green: The Role-Playing Game** in the "present day," the early 21st century. **The Fall of DELTA GREEN** is a "prequel" set in that game's back story: specifically in the 1960s, the decade when the DELTA GREEN program destroys itself in overreach.

On 24 July 1970, the Joint Chiefs of Staff officially disband DELTA GREEN, and it becomes an illegal conspiracy burrowing into the walls of the federal government.

Until that date, you have a warrant to save the country and the world.

Players take on the role of DELTA GREEN operatives, assets, and friendlies, in deadly one-shot adventures or in a campaign spanning the years from hope to madness. DELTA GREEN Agents might:

△ Hunt Deep Ones beneath the Atlantic or Mi-Go in the Himalayas
△ Investigate the dangerous visions of radical artists in New York, or of radical chemists in San Francisco
△ Search and destroy death-cults of alien gods in the dark heart of the Congo or Vietnam
△ Somehow contain and erase horrific manifestations and unearthly nightmares in the wide-open heartland and in the riot-torn cities of America
△ Preserve the secret of DELTA GREEN against investigative journalists, Communist espionage, and their own allies in the CIA and FBI
△ Investigate and covertly thwart MAJESTIC-12 and other secret technocrats who foolishly believe the unnatural can be exploited and weaponized

The decade begins in sunny optimism and ends in nighted disaster in the jungles of Indochina.

After the summer of the 1950s, now comes the fall – the fall of DELTA GREEN.

AGENTS AND HANDLERS

DELTA GREEN employs many officers, assets, analysts, and operatives - in a word, agents — all over the world. This game uses the capitalized term "Agent" for player-character DELTA GREEN personnel. Not all DELTA GREEN agents are Agents; only the ones you're portraying at your table.

Similarly, this game refers to the Game Master or GM (or Keeper, if you're familiar with *Trail of Cthulhu*) as the Handler, a contraction of "asset handler." Flavorful jargon notwithstanding, the characters she controls remain Game-Master Characters (GMCs).

Capital Letter Blues

While we're talking terminology, this book uses DELTA GREEN (in all capitals) when referring to the active black program and its clearance. It capitalizes other government projects and programs likewise.

Other works on the Delta Green setting, such as *Delta Green: The Role-Playing Game,* use mixed case (like that) to reinforce that even without federal authorization, Delta Green continues. This book uses mixed case when referring to the larger Delta Green setting created in 1992 and continuing even now.

A DAY AT THE RACES

A single unit of *The Fall of DELTA GREEN* play is called a *session*.

A single *The Fall of DELTA GREEN* mystery (what other games call a scenario or an adventure) is called an *operation*. In the game universe, DELTA GREEN operations have code names for security: Operation KURTZ, Operation OBSIDIAN, etc. Some operations take many sessions of play to complete. An "operation" for game purposes may only be a small part of a full DELTA GREEN Operation - Operation SOUTHERN HOSPITALITY went on for eight years!

DELTA GREEN agents sometimes call an operation a "day at the races," or a "Red Queen's Race," referring to an incident in Lewis Carroll's *Through the Looking Glass* in which Alice and the Queen run all day to stay in the same spot. Other, older agents sometimes claim the phrase "day at the races" comes from former DELTA GREEN Director Cook's habit at the beginning of an operation of holding confidential briefings at the Laurel Park thoroughbred racetrack, a location almost impossible to bug or to tail a target from.

TUMBLING DICE

GUMSHOE uses only one six-sided die for game resolution.

The abbreviation "d" stands for the result of rolling one die. The notation "d+1" for example means "the result of one die, plus 1." Most hand weapon damage in GUMSHOE falls between d-2 (fist) and d+1 (heavy firearm).

Occasionally this book uses "1d6" to mean the result of one die roll, or "1d3" to mean the result of one die roll divided by two. This is usually in main rules text where a simple "d" or "d/2" would be confusing.

What is GUMSHOE?

GUMSHOE games are about solving mysteries by accumulating clues. In GUMSHOE, if you have the ability, you get the clue. No roll needed.

Check your character sheet. Most of it is a list of abilities. You buy points in those abilities at the beginning of the game, and can add points to them after each adventure (or if you've saved some points to add in the middle of play). The total number of points you've bought in an ability is its rating, usually expressed this way: Athletics 5. As you spend points from that ability, you're spending from its pool. Your pool can go up or down as you spend and refresh: If you spend 2 points of Athletics to help scale a cyclone fence, your Athletics *pool* is 3, but your Athletics *rating* stays Athletics 5.

The **Investigative Abilities** listed there *always work*, even if you only have a rating of 1 and a pool of 0. History 1, for example, indicates you're well-trained and well-read; History 3 lets you play a world-class expert if you like. Whenever it seems relevant, all you need to do is tell the Handler you have the ability — she'll give you the clue you need from that scene. Sometimes, the Handler will even prompt you: "Who's got the best Astronomy?" For Interpersonal abilities like Intimidation or Negotiation, you may roleplay your ability a bit to get the information organically.

You can **spend Investigative points** to get special benefits: more information, better reactions from GMCs, a juicy roleplaying moment like a flashback, or even a bonus in a future contest if you spend well. Like using abilities for free, the Handler might offer a spend: "Who wants to spend a point of Astronomy?" Spends are story currency: when you spend, you're saying: "My character can add something cool to this scene"; when the Handler offers a spend, she's saying "There's something cool beneath the surface, if you want it." Spend if you want to: even if you spend your Investigative pool down to 0, the ability will still always get you a core clue. Your Investigative Ability pools usually refresh at the end of the scenario.

General Abilities, by contrast, might fail. They don't fail if you use them investigatively: Drive doesn't fail if you're identifying a car. But if you're trying to take a high-speed turn on a muddy Cuban cliff road in a Jeep, Drive can fail in any number of exciting ways. A General Ability rating of 0 represents, at best, bare civilian competence: with Drive 0 you can drive to the store and maybe even parallel park. Drive 8 represents serious mastery; you're the team's wheel artist.

To test a General Ability, if you have a rating in it, roll a six-sided die. Compare the result to a Difficulty set by the Handler, from 2 (very easy) to 8 (near impossible) or even higher. If you match or exceed the Difficulty, you succeed! An average, somewhat challenging task has a Difficulty of 4, so you succeed half the time. To try for a better result, you spend points from your pool. **Roll the die and add your spend.** Don't be shy about spending: the dangers facing DELTA GREEN are best stopped quickly. Your pool will refresh when your character has a chance to rest.

That's all! Welcome to *The Fall of DELTA GREEN.*

ALL THE AGENTS

Player characters in The Fall of DELTA GREEN are assumed to be realistically trained, capable operatives of the United States federal government. You may ring any number of changes on the above assumption in your own campaign of course: play older Agents well past their prime, or civilian assets brought in after their exposure to the unnatural, or foreign operatives allied with DELTA GREEN if not America per se.

But as a default, and to begin with, everybody gets their ticket punched by Uncle Sam.

"It was spookwar then, adventure; not exactly soldiers, not even advisors yet, but Irregulars, working in remote places with little direct authority, acting out their fantasies with more freedom than most men ever know."

\- Michael Herr, Dispatches

CHARACTER GENERATION SUMMARY

Determine your Investigative Ability point budget (p. 020).

You receive 65 General Ability points.

Take your free ability ratings:

- Agency 2
- Athletics 2
- Bureaucracy 2
- Health 4
- Network 5
- Sanity 5
- Stability 4

Determine your Military Service (p. 025) and apply the corresponding template, subtracting the points on that template from your point budget. Active duty personnel can skip the next step if they wish.

Select your Department (p. 030) and apply the corresponding template, again subtracting the points on that template from your point budget.

Go through the list of Investigative Abilities (p. 023) and see which ones remain unrepresented in your player group. Make sure that for each ability, at least one Agent has at least 1 rating point in it.

Finish buying your Abilities (p. 021) with your remaining points. As long as the player group as a whole covers all the abilities, you need not spend all your points.

If you're using Special Training (p. 072), select your free special training skill and purchase any further special training skills with build points.

Describe your Bonds (p. 045) and Motivations (p. 047).

Complete your Agent with personal details (p. 049).

If the Handler wishes, add damage consistent with prior service in DELTA GREEN and the Revelation of the truth (p. 050).

A WHITER SHADE OF PALE

The United States military officially desegregated in 1948, so combat-branch military Agents can be of any race. There are officially no women in combat positions: 90% of the female personnel deployed in Vietnam, for example, are nurses. That leaves ten percent: not just clerk-typists, but intelligence officers, electronics operators, and even trainers for South Vietnamese combat troops.

The CIA recruits heavily from military personnel – and even from foreign nationals – so their ranks also include more Black and Hispanic operatives than the governmental norm. As early as 1953, the CIA workforce was 40% female, but only one fifth of those women were in higher-level postings. (But perhaps what seems like a go-nowhere clerical job is actually ideal cover for covert action against the unknown.)

The FBI makes the CIA look like Woodstock: although a few Black police officers joined the Bureau (almost all before Hoover became Director), the first Black agents are only accepted to the FBI Academy in 1962. The first female FBI agents are not sworn in until 1972!

Homosexuals will not legally receive federal security clearances until 1995, which absolutely does not mean there are no gay or lesbian members of the national security community before then. Their sexual or gender orientation is hardly the biggest secret that bisexual, gay, lesbian, or trans DELTA GREEN Agents must keep, even in the 1960s.

In any given campaign, the players and Handler may decide to foreground the period's institutional discrimination or to ignore it. Choose what makes the drama tightest, and what improves your play experience, not necessarily what makes the most accurate history lesson.

Born Under a Bad Sign

Creating characters in the GUMSHOE system should be a collaborative process: you are building a team, not a pack of lone wolves. Each Agent should take point in some fields and bring up the rear in others. The whole group should cover each other's weak spots, and be able to bring any possible set of abilities to bear on an unnatural outbreak.

Build Points

To this end, **The Fall of DELTA GREEN** assigns an Investigative build point budget based on the number of regularly attending players in your group. Players who attend sporadically receive the same number of points as the regulars.

Investigative Build Points

Regularly Attending Players	Investigative Build Points for Each Agent
2	30
3	24
4	20
5+	18

Every Agent receives 65 General Ability build points.

After allocating free rating points (p. 018), **every rating point in an ability costs 1 build point.**

The exception: Buying rating points in a second Agency costs double.

Free Rating Points

Every Agent, being of sound mind and body (at least at first), receives the following rating points for free:

△ Agency 2
△ Athletics 2
△ Bureaucracy 2
△ Health 4
△ Network 5
△ Sanity 5
△ Stability 4

BRINGING IN NEW CHARACTERS

Your Agent is going to die, probably horribly. The program replaces dead Agents with new ones as soon as possible: sending an understrength team after the unnatural is often worse than sending no team at all.

The player of the dead Agent creates her new Agent as normal, but begins by placing 1 build point in each Investigative ability not covered by the other Agents on the Handler's Agent Tracking Sheet (p. 349). Give the new Agent enough extra build points to equal the experience earned by the other players.

Add Agents played by players newly joining the group during the campaign in the same fashion. They use the same number of Investigative build points as everyone else originally did, not the lower number applicable to the group's new size.

Players may always, if they wish, exchange their free rating points (at 1 to 1) for build points in other General Abilities, although this is likely unsafe. (Agency is an Investigative Ability, and points in it can be traded as above for build points in other Investigative Abilities.)

Background Templates

Determine your Military Service (p. 025) and apply the corresponding template. Active duty personnel can skip the Department step if they wish.

Select your Department (p. 030) and apply the corresponding template.

Each template lists abilities suited to (or required by) that background. The first line in a template lists the Investigative Abilities it buys; the second line lists the General Abilities it buys. (Further lines note their category.) The template buys your Agent rating points in those abilities as noted from her budget of build points.

As you go through Military Service and Department selection, subtract the points in those templates from your total point budgets.

These templates are not "balanced" against each other: some careers prove more costly, or more constrained, than others. If applying a Department template raises your Investigative total above the per-player maximum (which might happen with 5+ players), the Handler should either require you to trade a Bond for extra build points (see *Fewer Bonds, More Skill,* p. 045) or give the other players a higher maximum Investigative total to match yours.

If a template buys rating points in an ability you already have, add the template points to your pre-existing rating for a running total.

If applying two templates in succession drives any Investigative Ability (except Agency and Foreign Language) above 3, disregard that expenditure.

Example: Raina selects Medic for her Military Service, which includes Medicine 2. Later, she picks the CDC for her Department, which also includes Medicine 2. She raises her Medicine to 3 and saves the leftover 1 Investigative build point.

In many cases, the write-up provides some alternate abilities to select from as a means of customizing your Agent, or as recommendations for what to buy more points in further on in the character creation process. In almost all cases, feel free to buy more points in any ability given in the template; these are pointers, not restrictions. Keep in mind that buying more than 3 points in an Investigative Ability is a fairly dramatic expenditure.

The Handler and players then go through the list of Investigative Abilities (p. 023) to make sure that each one of them is covered by at least one Agent.

Leftover Build Points

Once all of the Investigative Abilities are covered, you can add any leftover Investigative or General build points to your various abilities.

If you're feeling short on build points, you can sell Bonds for build points: lose 1 Bond for an extra 2 Investigative or 6 General build points (see *Fewer Bonds, More Skill,* p. 045).

Saving Extra Build Points

You may, if you desire, save any **extra build points.** Keep your Investigative build pool separate from your General build pool, however.

You may use those saved points during the game as situations arise to assign yourself additional abilities, or to boost your ratings in the abilities you've chosen. When you choose to do this, you are not suddenly acquiring abilities on the spot, but simply revealing for the first time "on screen" what your Agent has been able to do all along.

SOME ABILITY TWISTS

Almost all the abilities work the same way, either as Investigative (p. 023) or General (p. 024) abilities.

Before you lock down all your points, you might want to look up the special rules for a few near-exceptions:

Agency (p. 052), **Art** (p. 053), and **Foreign Language** (p. 056) keep being useful even if you buy their ratings higher than 3.

Buying points in **The Unnatural** (p. 062) costs you potential Sanity (p. 070). In some campaigns, the Handler may not allow Agents to buy The Unnatural during character generation, or may insist that all Agents have 1 point in it to represent their previous introduction into the nightmare world of DELTA GREEN. (See *Revelation*, p. 050)

Agency (p. 052) and **Network** (p. 068) are extremely flexible in play.

Health (p. 066) and **Stability** (p. 071) are your "hit points," for physical and mental damage, respectively. Remember to buy them up if you intend your Agent to live a life of danger!

You can spend **First Aid** (p. 066) and **Psychotherapy** (p. 069) to restore lost Health and Stability points to yourself or your fellow Agents in a crisis.

Sanity (p. 070) is the ability to ignore the truth, for tactical purposes at least, and thus to continue operating against the unnatural. It is capped at 10 minus your rating in The Unnatural ability, but if you can you may want to buy it up to 9 for greater survivability.

TRADING POINTS

One optional rule to knit together a team allows players to swap points among themselves. If using this rule, a player may trade 1 Investigative build point for 3 General build points from another player. (Or, obviously, vice-versa.) Thus, the CIA analyst can give 6 General build points to the Green Beret (for example, for Melee Weapons and Demolitions), and get 2 Investigative build points from the soldier's pool to assign (for example, to Occult). Both players thus get to increase their Agents' "spotlight" abilities.

Buying Investigative Abilities

Having even 1 point in an Investigative Ability indicates that you're expertly trained, practiced, and well-read in that field. You are capable of broad leaps of intuition and brilliant insight; the sorts of deductions that, if you saw them in a movie, you might well dismiss as unrealistically rapid or complete. A rating of 2 or 3 points implies that your Agent is one of the top people working on the subject, or can hold her own with them. Abilities with a 3 rating define your Agent, in a way. Your concentration in them tells the other players (and you) something about his personality, life experience, and outlook.

Three Investigative Abilities — **Agency, Art,** and **Foreign Language** — give you more options and specific skills the more points you have in them. They still gather clues like normal Investigative Abilities, but you have a game-mechanical reason to buy them higher than 3.

Which Investigative Abilities Should I Buy?

All Investigative Abilities are important, and any one of them might be crucial in a given session. Rather than any given ability being vital for your Agent, however, it's far more important that the team as a whole have access to all of the Investigative Abilities. Ideally, someone on the team will have any needed ability, and everyone will have something cool that they can do.

That said, consider putting at least 1 point into each of **Notice** and **HUMINT,** two broadly useful skills in almost any scenario. You may want to bump up your **Agency** ability rating if your template doesn't do that already.

Every Agent should ideally have at least one **Interpersonal** ability, even if the Navy SEAL has just 1 point in Intimidation. If your Agent depends on Interpersonal abilities, you may want to take some points in **Foreign Language** so she retains her core skills on overseas missions.

Your highest rating among these four Interpersonal abilities determines your Bond values (p. 045), so you might want to buy one of them up: **Flattery, Inspiration, Negotiation, Reassurance.**

INVESTIGATIVE ABILITIES LIST

Investigative Abilities are divided into the following sub-groups: Academic, Interpersonal, and Technical. The main purpose of the sub-groups is to allow you to quickly find the best ability for the task during play, by scanning the most likely portion of the overall list.

Academic Abilities	Interpersonal Abilities	Technical Abilities
Accounting	Agency	Architecture
Anthropology	Cop Talk	Art
Archaeology	Flattery	Chemistry
Astronomy	HUMINT	Cryptography
Biology	Inspiration	Data Retrieval
Criminology	Interrogation	Forensics
Foreign	Intimidation	Fringe Science
Language	Negotiation	Notice
History	Reassurance	Pharmacy
Law	Streetwise	Photography
Medicine	Tradecraft	Physics
Military		SIGINT
Science		Survival
Occult		Traffic Analysis
The Unnatural		

Buying General Abilities

General Abilities come in handy at the sharp end; they help you survive whatever awfulness or mayhem your Investigative Abilities have uncovered. You get 65 build points to spend on them.

General Abilities use different rules than Investigative ones, which allow for possible failure: you spend ability points and roll a six-sided die to see if you succeed. When choosing General Abilities, you'll want to concentrate your points among a few abilities, giving your Agent comparatively higher ratings than you need in the Investigative category.

Where any points at all in any Investigative Ability implies impressive competence, spreads in General Abilities cover a wider range of capability levels.

△ **Rating 0:** Basic civilian competence, but useless in an emergency or a field situation.
△ **Rating 1-3:** A sideline. You trained in it after Basic or at the Farm, but you don't really rely on it in a pinch.
△ **Rating 4-7:** Very good, enough to beat many professionals.
△ **Rating 8+:** Impressively expert. At this level, the game mechanics allow you to guarantee yourself two or three automatic successes per day against most opposition.

Although there is no set cap on abilities, the second highest rating must be at least half that of the highest rating.

You want to have a Health rating of 30. This would require you to take at least one other ability at 15. That would leave you only 20 points to spend on all of the other General Abilities. You reconsider, opting for a lower Health rating so you can spend your other points more freely.

GENERAL ABILITIES LIST

Athletics
Bureaucracy
Conceal
Demolitions
Disguise
Drive
Filch
Firearms
First Aid
Health
Heavy Weapons
Mechanics
Melee Weapons
Network
Pilot
Preparedness
Psychotherapy
Ride
Sanity
Sense Trouble
Stability
Stealth
Unarmed Combat

Which General Abilities Should I Buy?

All General Abilities are important, and any one of them might be crucial in a given session.

That said, you're taking your life in your own hands if you don't boost **Athletics, Health, Stability,** and at least one combat ability (**Firearms, Melee Weapons,** or **Unarmed Combat**) to 5 or 6 at least. If you plan on regularly putting your character into harm's way (and into combat scenes), consider boosting **Athletics** to 8 (to raise your Hit Threshold) and one or more combat abilities to 8 or 10 or even higher.

If you plan on doing a lot of social engineering, you might want to buy a few more points of **Bureaucracy** and **Network.**

Preparedness and **Sense Trouble** are good, broadly useful abilities well worth a few points for most Agents. If you have the points to spare, putting 1 or 2 into **Disguise** and **Stealth** helps get past minor obstacles, although you'll want to leave full-on impersonation or black-bag jobs to your team specialist.

If you are the team specialist in something, try to get a rating of 8 or better in your specialty.

If you have a special training skill (p. 072), it's worth buying points in its most likely related ability or abilities.

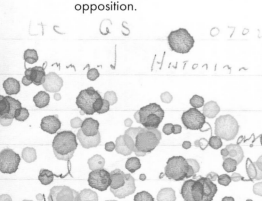

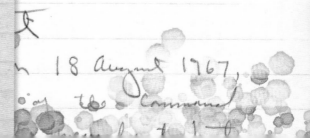

Military Service

Every male American aged 18 to 29 is subject to Selective Service conscription into the military. Depending on the exact date of the campaign, there is an excellent chance that some of the Agents will be veterans of Vietnam, Korea, or even the Second World War. An Agent who signed up just after Pearl Harbor (18 in 1941) is only 38 in 1961, after all. DELTA GREEN began in the military, and many of its agents are still servicemen and women on active duty.

Decide which category of military service best fits your Agent. Apply the listed template to your character sheet, adding the points to the various abilities as shown.

Ability ratings with asterisks add to the rating already in the template, if you pick that ability for your Agent.

If you pick an Active Duty template, you're done! Your military branch or unit is your Department (p. 030). That said, some Departments can include Active Duty military: AFOSI (p. 030), CIA (*SOD*, p. 033), DIA (*Military Attaché*, p. 035), and ONI (p. 039).

Feel free to build your own template along the lines indicated here, as long as your Handler clears it.

No Military Service

You were 4-F, or just weren't called up, or you were draft-exempt (a woman, a father, a college student, a worker in a critical industry), or you were a conscientious objector. You might have even dodged the draft, although your Agent needs to demonstrate the outré (and likely dangerous) reason he got a DELTA GREEN security clearance in such a case.

Either way, there's no template for this. Go on to pick your Department (p. 030).

Peacetime Conscription

Points: 2 Investigative, 3 General

You served your two-year hitch during peacetime, or at least not in a war zone.

Survival 1

Firearms 1, Unarmed Combat 1

Pick One Investigative: Inspiration 1, Foreign Language 1, Military Science 1

Pick One General: Drive 1, Mechanics 1

Chaplain

Points: 6 Investigative, 8 General

Active Duty: 10 Investigative, 16 General

You saw to the spiritual needs of the armed forces. You did not carry firearms.

Active Duty Chaplain: You are still serving in a combat zone, or at combat readiness. Double all ratings except Foreign Language. For the optional abilities, either double the selected rating or pick two.

Anthropology 1, Foreign Language 2, Inspiration 1, Reassurance 1

Bureaucracy 1, Psychotherapy 4

Pick One Investigative: Archaeology 1, Foreign Language 1*, History 1, Inspiration 1*, Interrogation 1, Military Science 1, Survival 1

Pick One General: Athletics 3, First Aid 3, Network 3, Psychotherapy 3*, Sanity 3, Stability 3

Medic

Points: 5 Investigative, 8 General
Active Duty: 10 Investigative, 16 General

Whether in combat, on ship, or on base, you served as a medic, corpsman, or nurse.

Active Duty Medic: You are still serving in a combat zone, or at combat readiness. Double all ratings. For the optional abilities, either double the selected rating or pick two.

Forensics 1, Medicine 1, Pharmacy 1, Survival 1

Bureaucracy 1, First Aid 4

Pick One Investigative: Biology 1, HUMINT 1, Military Science 1, Notice 1, Reassurance 1

Pick One General: Athletics 3, Firearms 3, First Aid 3*, Psychotherapy 3, Sense Trouble 3

Army Medical Corps

Points: 12 Investigative, 18 General

Build doctors with the Army Medical Corps as active duty Medics. Then add Agency 1, and increase Medicine to 3 and Bureaucracy to 4.

Psychiatrist

Points: 10 Investigative, 18 General

Approximately 25 military psychiatrists serve in Vietnam in any given year, either attached to a division or in a regional KO Team. Neurologists, psychologists, social workers, psychiatric nurses, and (enlisted) mental health corpsmen also serve in similar capacities.

Build a military mental health specialist as a regular (not active-duty) *Medic*. Reduce First Aid to 2, and increase Bureaucracy to 4. Then add:

Agency 1, HUMINT 1, Inspiration 1, Interrogation 1

Psychotherapy 7

Pick One Investigative: Medicine 1*, Pharmacy 1*

MILITARY RANK

Pick your Agent's rank, with your Handler's approval. Your Handler is unlikely to approve any rank higher than Major/Lieutenant Commander. (Naval ranks follow the slash mark.) DELTA GREEN is unlikely to recruit any active-duty personnel below NCO (corporal or sergeant/petty officer) rank, unless they have remarkable skills, or have encountered the unnatural and survived.

A Handler who wants players to feel the soul-crushing weight of military structure should mandate the following ability prerequisites for various ranks:

Non-Commissioned Officer (NCO): Intimidation 1, Military Science 1

Sergeant First Class/Chief Petty Officer or above: Inspiration 1, Intimidation 2, Military Science 2, Stability 6

2nd Lieutenant/Ensign: Military Science 1

1st Lieutenant/Lieutenant JG: Inspiration 1, Military Science 2

Captain/Lieutenant: Agency 1, Inspiration 1, Military Science 2, Stability 5

Major/Lieutenant Commander: Agency 3, Bureaucracy 5, Inspiration 1, Military Science 2, Stability 6

Sailor or Pilot

Points: 3 Investigative, 15 General
Active Duty: 6 Investigative, 30 General

You served on the sea or in the air. You may have been a helicopter pilot for the Army or Marine Corps.

Active Duty Personnel: You are still serving in a combat zone, or at combat readiness. Double all ratings. For the optional abilities, either double the selected rating or pick two.

Military Science 1, Survival 1

Athletics 1, Bureaucracy 1, Firearms 1, First Aid 1, Health 1, Mechanics 1, Pilot 3, Sense Trouble 2, Unarmed Combat 1

Pick One Investigative: Astronomy 1, Inspiration 1, Foreign Language 1, SIGINT 1

Pick One General: Athletics 3*, Demolitions 3, Heavy Weapons 3, Mechanics 3, Pilot 3*, Preparedness 3

U.S. Coast Guard

Use the *Sailor* template, but substitute Streetwise for Foreign Language and Conceal for Demolitions.

USAFSS Big Eye Operator

Under ACS/I, the USAF Security Service handles SIGINT and electronic security for the Air Force, and operates the Big Eye (College Eye after 1967) electronic warfare and early warning aircraft systems in Vietnam, over Cuba, and elsewhere.

Build a Big Eye operator with an *Active Duty Pilot*. To that template, add:

Cryptography 1, Data Retrieval 1, SIGINT 2.

Soldier or Marine

**Points: 4 Investigative,
20 General
Active Duty: 8 Investigative,
40 General**

You served in combat, on the ground, in World War II (1942-1945), Korea (1950-1953), or Vietnam (1965-present).

Active Duty Personnel: You are still serving in a combat zone, or at combat readiness. Double all ratings. For the optional abilities, either double the selected rating or pick four.

Military Science 1, Survival 1

Athletics 2, Bureaucracy 1, First Aid 1, Firearms 3, Health 2, Melee Weapons 1, Sense Trouble 2, Unarmed Combat 2

Pick Two Investigative: Anthropology 1, Inspiration 1, Intimidation 1, Foreign Language 1, Notice 1, SIGINT 1

Pick Two General: Conceal 3, Demolitions 3, Drive 3, Firearms 3*, Health 3*, Heavy Weapons 3, Mechanics 3, Melee Weapons 3*, Preparedness 3, Sense Trouble 3*, Stealth 3, Unarmed Combat 3*

INTELLIGENCE OFFICER

The intelligence officer in a military unit (usually company-sized or larger) is responsible for gathering and analyzing any and all relevant information about the battle space, and advising command authority. In a larger unit, there may be NCOs performing individual tasks such as prisoner interrogation, photo interpretation, or monitoring enemy communications.

Build intelligence officers using the template for either *Soldier or Marine* (p. 028) or *Sailor or Pilot* (p. 027), but add:

HUMINT 1, Military Science 1, Traffic Analysis 1

Pick One Investigative: Anthropology 1, Interrogation 1, Photography 1, SIGINT 1

Psychological Operations Group (U.S. Army)

Psychological warfare influences, and ideally alters, the mind and opinions of the enemy and his supporters. This includes propaganda and disinformation, operations intended to weaken morale or interfere with decision-making, and covert political action. The Army deploys the 2nd, 4th, and 7th Psychological Operations Groups to Vietnam in 1965; other Psychological Warfare Battalions remain attached to the major Army commands in Panama and Europe.

DELTA GREEN finds the loose operational constraints, experimental mindset, and deniability of PSYOP very congenial. With the front line in the war against the unnatural running through every human mind, DELTA GREEN also tries to develop genuine and effective PSYOP capability.

Prerequisite: Begin by building your Agent using the *Soldier* template (p. 028). You may be Active Duty.

Points: 10 Investigative, 10 General

Anthropology 2, Foreign Language 2, History 1, HUMINT 1

Bureaucracy 3, Psychotherapy 3, Stealth 4

Pick Two Investigative: Art 1, Foreign Language 1*, Fringe Science 1, HUMINT 1*, Interrogation 1, Occult 1, SIGINT 1, Traffic Analysis 1

Pick One Interpersonal: Flattery 2, Inspiration 2, Reassurance 2

USAIC Urban Intelligence Specialist

The wave of urban riots in the 1960s catches the military unprepared for domestic deployment. From 1967 to 1971, the U.S. Army Intelligence Command deploys a network of 1,200 agents in 300 cities across the country monitoring public gatherings of 10 or more people, and collecting militarily useful intelligence on transportation and urban conditions. Using a dedicated teletype network, agents can report events, suspicious characters, or anything else to AIC headquarters in Ft. Holabird, Maryland within 20 minutes.

Prerequisite: The *Soldier* or *Marine* background (p. 028). You are on active duty, but not at combat readiness: you need not take the Active Duty background.

Points: 6 Investigative, 10 General

Architecture 1, HUMINT 1, Notice 1, Streetwise 1, Traffic Analysis 1

Drive 4, Sense Trouble 3, Stealth 3

Pick One Investigative: Anthropology 1, Interrogation 1, Law 1, Photography 1, SIGINT 1

Special Forces

Points: 9 Investigative, 60 General

You are a warrior in an elite unit: Army Rangers, U.S. Army Special Forces ("Green Berets"), Long-Range Reconnaissance Patrol, Navy SEALs, Marine Force Recon, etc. You may still be on active service with your unit, or part of the CIA's Special Operations Division (p. 033).

Agency 1, Foreign Language 1, Military Science 2, Survival 2

Athletics 6, Bureaucracy 1, Conceal 4, Demolitions 2, Firearms 6, First Aid 3, Health 4, Melee Weapons 6, Sense Trouble 6, Stealth 6, Unarmed Combat 6

Pick Three Investigative: Anthropology 1, Inspiration 1, Interrogation 1, Intimidation 1, Foreign Language 1*, Negotiation 1, Notice 1, Photography 1, SIGINT 1, Survival 1*

Pick Two General: Demolitions 5*, Drive 5, Firearms 5*, Heavy Weapons 5, Melee Weapons 5*, Pilot 5, Preparedness 5, Stealth 5*, Unarmed Combat 5*

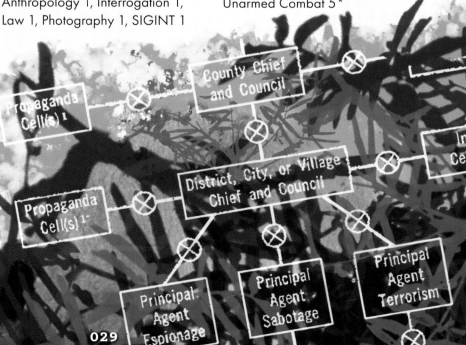

Departments

In addition to the military, DELTA GREEN draws personnel from many other agencies, branches, and offices of the federal government. Our general, if bureaucratically inexact, term for your Agent's ostensible employer is his Department, mostly because we already used Agency as an ability name (p. 052).

Each Department has a basic template of abilities associated with it. Feel free to build your own template along the lines indicated here, as long as your Handler clears it.

Ability ratings with asterisks add to the rating already in the template, if you pick that ability for your Agent.

Advanced Research Projects Agency

Part of the Defense Department, ARPA administers and plans research with military applications at laboratories all over the country. DELTA GREEN uses ARPA research (and researchers) to understand (or ideally, to thwart without understanding) the alien physics and technology it confronts.

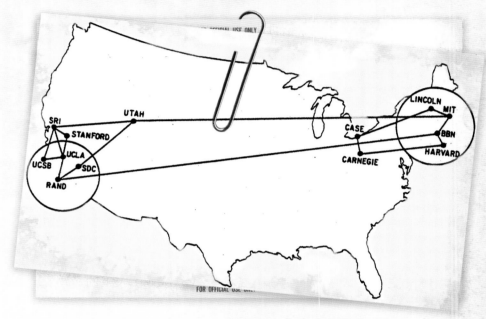

ARPA Researcher

Points: 10 Investigative, 17 General

Agency 1, Data Retrieval 1, Military Science 1, Physics 1

Bureaucracy 3, Mechanics 4

Pick Three Investigative:
Astronomy 2, Biology 2, Chemistry 2, Data Retrieval 2*, Foreign Language 2, Forensics 2, Fringe Science 2, Physics 2*, SIGINT 2, Traffic Analysis 2

Pick Two General: Bureaucracy 5*, Demolitions 5, Network 5, Preparedness 5, Sanity 5, Stability 5

Air Force Office of Special Investigations

The AFOSI investigates and thwarts criminal activity within the Air Force, and espionage against it. It also protects secret aircraft programs from outside interference, surveillance, and espionage. DELTA GREEN agents in AFOSI suspect that MAJESTIC has heavily penetrated the office, and therefore walk extra lightly.

AFOSI Investigator

Prerequisite: *Pilot* template (p. 027) for your Military Service. You may be Active Duty.

Points: 7 Investigative, 18 General

Agency 2, HUMINT 2

Add 3 to any three of these: Athletics 1, Bureaucracy 1, Sense Trouble 2, Unarmed Combat 2

Pick Three Investigative: Accounting 1, Criminology 1, Foreign Language 1, Inspiration 1, Interrogation 1, Law 1, Notice 1, Photography 1, SIGINT 1, Traffic Analysis 1

Pick One General: Athletics 3*, Conceal 3, Mechanics 3, Pilot 3*, Preparedness 3, Stealth 3

Atomic Energy Commission

The AEC is not part of the Defense Department, but a separate agency tasked with developing, maintaining, and protecting military and civilian nuclear facilities in the U.S. Other tasks under its wide and little-supervised remit include ecological analysis, nuclear threat detection and estimation (giving it access to intelligence about Soviet and Chinese nuclear programs, for instance), and anti-missile research.

AEC Investigator

Points: 7 Investigative, 14 General

Data Retrieval 1, Physics 2, SIGINT 1

Bureaucracy 2, Mechanics 4, Network 4

Pick Two Investigative: Biology 1, Foreign Language 1, Fringe Science 1, Medicine 1, Photography 1

Pick One Interpersonal: Agency 1, Intimidation 1, Negotiation 1, Reassurance 1

Pick One General: Bureaucracy 4*, Network 4*, Preparedness 4, Sense Trouble 4

Central Intelligence Agency

The CIA gathers and analyzes intelligence (both public and secret), runs assets to obtain secret intelligence from foreign countries, and conducts operations to destabilize foes and counter foreign operations. The CIA (and thus DELTA GREEN) has near carte blanche to operate overseas in the national interest.

Its Domestic Operations Division investigates foreign influence in American protest movements, stepping on the toes of the FBI and (some would say) violating the CIA's charter. DELTA GREEN thrives within such CIA operations, ones that even the CIA prefers not to examine too closely.

Directorate of Intelligence Analyst

Analysts sift through intelligence from all sources from newspapers to satellite photos, and apply their knowledge of specific countries and topics to produce the true picture. Which they can never tell anyone outside DELTA GREEN.

Points: 12 Investigative, 18 General

Anthropology 1, Agency 2, Data Retrieval 1, Foreign Language 2, History 2, Traffic Analysis 1

Bureaucracy 3, Firearms 1, Sense Trouble 1, Unarmed Combat 1, Stability 4

Pick Three Investigative: Accounting 1, Anthropology 1*, Criminology 1, Cryptography 1, Foreign Language 1*, Flattery 1, HUMINT 1, Military Science 1, Occult 1, Photography 1, Physics 1, SIGINT 1, Tradecraft 1

Pick Two General: Bureaucracy 4*, Drive 4, Network 4, Preparedness 4

Directorate of Plans Case Officer

Case officers recruit spies – foreign assets who inform on their own countries – and keep their intel coming by coddling or coercing them, whatever works.

Points: 14 Investigative, 39 General

Add 1 to any two of these: Agency 1, Foreign Language 1, HUMINT 2, Notice 1, Tradecraft 2

Add 3 to any three of these: Athletics 1, Bureaucracy 2, Disguise 3, Drive 3, Firearms 1, Melee Weapons 1, Network 5, Sense Trouble 4, Stealth 3, Unarmed Combat 3

Pick One Investigative: Criminology 1, Cryptography 1, Foreign Language 1*, Military Science 1, SIGINT 1

Pick Two Interpersonal: Flattery 2, Inspiration 2, Intimidation 2, Negotiation 2, Reassurance 2, Streetwise 2

Pick One General: Melee Weapons 4*, Network 4*, Preparedness 4, Psychotherapy 4, Stealth 4*, Unarmed Combat 4*

Directorate of Plans Operative

These are the CIA "cowboys," out in the real world doing what has to be done to save it. What has to be done is never easy, never pretty, and almost never right.

Points: 12 Investigative, 44 General

Anthropology 1, Foreign Language 1, Notice 2, SIGINT 1, Survival 1, Tradecraft 2

Add 3 to any two of these: Athletics 2, Disguise 2, Drive 2, Firearms 4, Health 3, Mechanics 2, Network 3, Preparedness 4, Sense Trouble 4, Stealth 4, Unarmed Combat 4

Pick Two Investigative: Architecture 1, Art 1, Cryptography 1, Foreign Language 1*, History 1, HUMINT 1, Military Science 1, Photography 1

Pick One Interpersonal: Inspiration 2, Interrogation 2, Intimidation 2, Streetwise 2

Pick One General: Athletics 4*, Bureaucracy 4, Conceal 4, Demolitions 4, Filch 4, Heavy Weapons 4, Network 4*, Pilot 4, Preparedness 4*, Sense Trouble 4*, Stealth 4*, Unarmed Combat 4*

Office of Research and Development Specialist

Part of the Directorate for Science and Technology (DS&T; 1962, Deputy Directorate of Research; 1963-1965, Deputy Directorate of Science and Technology). From 1963 to 1995, ORD researches intelligence collection by advanced technical or non-HUMINT means. These studies include new optics, chemical detection, acoustic and seismic research, electronic intelligence gathering (ELINT), and behavioral science including the MK-ULTRA and MK-SEARCH mind-control experiments. A government-funded front group, the Scientific Engineering Institute (SEI) conducts much of its research, along with MAJESTIC laboratories developing very advanced technical means.

Points: 13 Investigative, 18 General

Agency 2, Data Retrieval 1, Foreign Language 2, Notice 1, Tradecraft 1

Bureaucracy 3, Firearms 1, Mechanics 4, Sense Trouble 1, Unarmed Combat 1

Pick Three Investigative: Biology 2, Chemistry 2, Data Retrieval 2*, Foreign Language 2*, Fringe Science 2, Medicine 2, Pharmacy 2, Photography 2, Physics 2, SIGINT 2

Pick Two General: Bureaucracy 4*, First Aid 4, Mechanics 4*, Network 4, Preparedness 4, Psychotherapy 4, Stability 4, Stealth 4

Political Action Division Officer

The PAD specializes in propaganda and political change overseas, the equivalent of the Army's Psychological Operations Group (p. 029).

Points: 14 Investigative, 32 General

Add 1 to any two of these: Anthropology 2, Art 1, Foreign Language 2, History 1, HUMINT 2, Inspiration 1, Tradecraft 1

Add 3 to any two of these: Bureaucracy 3, Disguise 2, Drive 3, Firearms 2, Melee Weapons 2, Network 4, Psychotherapy 3, Sense Trouble 3, Stealth 2, Unarmed Combat 2

Pick One Interpersonal: Flattery 2, Inspiration 2*, Negotiation 2, Reassurance 2

Special Operations Division Operator

Model the CIA's paramilitary officers and SOD operators with the active-duty version of *Soldier or Marine* (p. 028) or with *Special Forces* (p. 029). To either template, add:

Foreign Language 1, HUMINT 1

Surreptitious Entry Specialist

Tucked into the Directorate of Plans is "The Shop," a small unit of "surreptitious entry" specialists: in a word, burglars. Their official specialty is black-bag jobs on foreign embassies to steal code books, but the complete deniability of their missions creates opportunities for rule-bending superiors and for DELTA GREEN.

Points: 12 Investigative, 30 General

Agency 1, Cryptography 1, Data Retrieval 1, Foreign Language 1, HUMINT 1, Notice 1, Photography 1, Tradecraft 1

Add 4 to any three of these: Athletics 2, Conceal 4, Filch 4, Mechanics 4, Stealth 4

Choose Four Investigative: Architecture 1, Art 1, Cop Talk 1, Criminology 1, Cryptography 1*, Foreign Language 1*, HUMINT 1*, Notice 1*, SIGINT 1, Tradecraft 1*

OSS

In 1941, President Roosevelt appointed William Donovan the Coordinator of Information (COI) in an attempt to establish an independent intelligence service under the Joint Chiefs of Staff. The next year, Donovan became head of the Office of Strategic Services (OSS), tasked with not only intelligence collection and analysis but also covert and special operations. In 1945, President Truman terminated the OSS - and a year later began transforming its remnants into what became the CIA in 1947.

Within the CIA, those able to trace a career back to the OSS claim and carry authenticity and authority that often exceeds their paper position. OSS veterans within DELTA GREEN have a similar affect; the clearance designation (if not the unit) originated with the OSS, after all.

An Agent with an OSS background must:

△ Have been born no later than 1923.

△ Spend 2 build points for 1 rating point in Agency (OSS), up to a maximum of 6 build points for 3 rating points.

That's all: you don't even need a Military Service template, as about 25% of OSS agents were civilians (and a third of OSS agents were women). This loose recruitment policy means almost any Department template - certainly any CIA or military template - can contain an OSS past.

Agency (OSS)

This Agency ability (p. 052) provides the regular Agency bonuses and benefits to investigating any OSS operations (mostly long forgotten, of course). Points spent from Agency (OSS) count *triple* for Bureaucracy tests against the CIA, and *double* for Interpersonal and Network spends involving CIA personnel. It does not necessarily grant other General ability (Stealth, etc.) bonuses against the CIA: routines change in two decades.

Agency (OSS) does not count as an additional agency for Multiple Agencies (p. 052).

Technical Services Division Designer

Under the Directorate for Science and Technology, the TSD supports field agents by developing and improving bugs and SIGINT, concealed and exotic weapons, disguises, and forged documents. TSD also handles many MAJESTIC initiatives, and runs MK-ULTRA and MK-SEARCH until 1963 when those programs spin off into the new Office of Research and Development (p. 032).

Points: 14 Investigative, 27 General

Agency 2, Data Retrieval 1, Foreign Language 2, Notice 1

Bureaucracy 2, Conceal 4, Firearms 2, Mechanics 4

Pick Four Investigative: Art 2, Biology 2, Chemistry 2, Data Retrieval 2*, Foreign Language 2*, Forensics 2, Fringe Science 2, Medicine 2, Pharmacy 2, Photography 2, SIGINT 2, Tradecraft 2

Pick Three General: Conceal 5*, Demolitions 5, Disguise 5, Mechanics 5*, Network 5, Preparedness 5

Communicable Disease Center

Begun as a malaria-control office in the U.S. Public Health Service, the CDC now studies the control and containment of epidemics, biological warfare, tuberculosis, venereal disease, and – for DELTA GREEN – unnatural infections of the body and mind.

The CDC becomes the National Communicable Disease Center (NCDC) in 1967, and the Center for Disease Control in 1970.

CDC Researcher

Points: 10 Investigative, 17 General

Add 1 to any two of these: Biology 1, Forensics 1, Medicine 2, Notice 1, Pharmacy 1

Bureaucracy 2, First Aid 4, Health 3, Network 4, Preparedness 4

Pick Two Investigative: Chemistry 1, Cop Talk 1, Data Retrieval 1, Inspiration 1, Reassurance 1, Traffic Analysis 1

Defense Intelligence Agency

Established in 1961, the DIA coordinates the efforts of the individual service intelligence agencies (Army Intelligence (G-2) Branch (Army Intelligence Agency after 1967), Office of Naval Intelligence (ONI, see p. 039), Marine Corps Intelligence (MCI), Coast Guard Intelligence (CGI), and Air Force Office of Assistant Chief of Staff, Intelligence (ACS/I)), specializing in research and intelligence gathering concerning foreign technical and military capabilities. The sprawling remit (the entire armed forces) and relatively small staff of the DIA make it a good posting for DELTA GREEN troubleshooters.

DIA Analyst

Intelligence about military technology extends into operational testing, especially at closed "foreign technology" sites such as Tonopah Test Range in Nevada and Wright-Patterson AFB in Dayton, Ohio.

Points: 11 Investigative, 18 General

Agency 1, Data Retrieval 1, Foreign Language 2, History 1, Military Science 2, Traffic Analysis 1

Bureaucracy 2, Firearms 2, Sense Trouble 1, Unarmed Combat 1, Stability 4

Pick Three Investigative: Architecture 1, Cryptography 1, Foreign Language 1*, Intimidation 1, Inspiration 1, Military Science 1*, Negotiation 1, Photography 1, Physics 1, SIGINT 1, Traffic Analysis 1*

Pick Two General: Bureaucracy 4*, Drive 4, Heavy Weapons 4, Network 4, Pilot 4, Preparedness 4

Military Attaché

The DIA takes over the Defense Attaché System from the separate services in 1965, providing it (and DELTA GREEN) with direct access to American embassies and diplomatic resources for intelligence gathering. Since military attachés serve openly as diplomats, they do less case-officering and more networking in foreign militaries.

Prerequisite: Either the *Soldier or Marine* (p. 028) or *Sailor or Pilot* (p. 027) background. Military attachés can be Active Duty personnel.

Points: 10 Investigative, 23 General

Foreign Language 2, History 1, HUMINT 1, Inspiration 1, Military Science 1, SIGINT 1

Bureaucracy 3, Network 4, Preparedness 4, Stability 4

Pick One Investigative: Agency 1, Anthropology 1, Foreign Language 1*, HUMINT 1*, Law 1, Military Science 1*, SIGINT 1, Traffic Analysis 1

Pick One Interpersonal: Flattery 2, Inspiration 2*, Intimidation 2, Negotiation 2, Reassurance 2

Pick Two General: Athletics 4, Drive 4, Firearms 4, Melee Weapons 4, Network 4*, Pilot 4, Preparedness 4, Ride 4, Unarmed Combat 4

PAGE 2 OF 4 PAGES

...PERMITTED TO WANDER AROUND HANOI UNACCOMPANIED.
...AID THAT HE WAS PARTICULARLY WELL TREATED SINCE
...DUATES
...CUPY INFLUENTIAL POSTS IN THE NVN REGIME.
...ZIM" AUTOMOBILE FOR HIS STAY.
...POSE OF
...AL SYSTEM. HE WAS IMPRESSED BY MEASURES
...GIME TO ELIMINATE ILLITERACY
...DICTIONARIES AND
...STANDARDIZING AND SIMPLIFYING
...MINSTRATION OF THE EDUCAT...
...VISIT WAS A SURVEY
NVN SCHOLARS

UNCLASSIFIED

INTELLIGENCE IS THE KEY

...NAM, THE SOLE BASIS FOR EFFECTIVE MEAN...
...RATION IS SPECIFIC INTELLIGENCE INFORMATION...
...LEFT GROPING ALMOST...

Defense Research Division (Library of Congress)

With 15 million books, journals, and pamphlets in its collection, along with 45 million miscellaneous other holdings from maps to recordings to film canisters, the Library of Congress is the single largest repository of human knowledge on the planet. DELTA GREEN researchers mine this mother lode of information within the Defense Research Division (Air Research Division before 1963), which is ostensibly tasked to provide research on any topic (especially military topics) for the Defense Department.

LoC DRD Researcher

Points: 15 Investigative, 10 General

Archaeology 2, Foreign Language 3, History 2, Occult 2

Bureaucracy 3, Filch 3, Network 4

Pick Three Investigative: Architecture 2, Art 2, Astronomy 2, Biology 2, Chemistry 2, Criminology 2, Foreign Language 2*, Fringe Science 2, Military Science 2, Physics 2, Traffic Analysis 2

Federal Bureau of Investigation

Under the watchful eye of Director J. Edgar Hoover, the FBI investigates federal crimes, and assists local police departments when criminals cross state lines. The Bureau also investigates espionage, sabotage, subversion, and treason against the United States. DELTA GREEN uses FBI agents – or FBI cover – to investigate and contain outbreaks of the unnatural inside the U.S.

FBI Laboratory Researcher

Points: 15 Investigative, 35 General

Add 1 to any three of these: Agency 1, Chemistry 1, Cop Talk 1, Criminology 2, Forensics 2, Law 1, Notice 1, Pharmacy 1, Photography 1

Add 3 to any two of these: Athletics 2, Bureaucracy 3, Drive 3, Firearms 4, Sense Trouble 3, Stealth 2, Unarmed Combat 4

Pick One Investigative: Art 1, Foreign Language 1, Medicine 1, Occult 1

Pick Two General: Bureaucracy 4*, Conceal 4, Firearms 4*, First Aid 4, Health 4, Network 4, Preparedness 4, Psychotherapy 4, Stability 4

FBI Special Agent

Points: 13 Investigative, 38 General

Add 1 to any two of these: Accounting 1, Agency 1, Criminology 1, HUMINT 1, Law 1, Notice 1

Add 3 to any three of these: Athletics 2, Bureaucracy 3, Drive 3, Firearms 4, Sense Trouble 3, Stealth 2, Unarmed Combat 4

Pick One Investigative: Art 1, Foreign Language 1, Forensics 1, Photography 1, SIGINT 1, Traffic Analysis 1

Pick Two Interpersonal: Cop Talk 2, HUMINT 2*, Interrogation 2, Intimidation 2, Streetwise 2

Pick Two General: Athletics 4*, Conceal 4, Disguise 4, Firearms 4*, Health 4, Preparedness 4, Sense Trouble 4*, Stability 4, Stealth 4*

FBI Undercover Agent

Much of the FBI's work involves in-filtrating G-men into criminal, subversive, or other illicit organizations. Such agents rely more on fast talk and fast thinking than on fast draws. From DELTA GREEN's perspective, an undercover FBI man reports in less often, and can take unauthorized leave to investigate cults or other unnatural phenomena.

Points: 14 Investigative, 38 General

Add 1 to any two of these: Accounting 1, Criminology 1, HUMINT 2, Law 1, Notice 2

Add 3 to any three of these: Athletics 2, Bureaucracy 1, Disguise 4, Drive 3, Firearms 4, Sense Trouble 4, Stealth 3, Unarmed Combat 4

Pick One Investigative: Foreign Language 1, Occult 1, Photography 1, SIGINT 1

Pick Two Interpersonal: HUMINT 2*, Intimidation 2, Reassurance 2, Streetwise 2

Pick One General: Athletics 4*, Conceal 4, Firearms 4*, Health 4, Preparedness 4, Sense Trouble 4*, Stealth 4*

Domestic Intelligence Division "Black-Bagger"

Between 1948 and 1966, the FBI carries out at least 238 "black-bag jobs" or surreptitious entries against domestic targets, plus at least 450 installations of concealed microphones. The files on these jobs are routinely destroyed after a year. In 1966, Hoover curtails black-bag jobs ... officially. Unlike conventional burglars, FBI black-baggers can often get keys or blueprints from the building's owner by "waving the flag under his nose."

Points: 14 Investigative, 38 General

Add 1 to any three of these: Accounting 1, Agency 1, HUMINT 1, Law 1, Notice 1, Photography 1, SIGINT 1

Add 1 to one Interpersonal: Cop Talk 1, Inspiration 1, Streetwise 1

Add 3 to any three of these: Athletics 2, Bureaucracy 1, Conceal 3, Drive 2, Filch 3, Firearms 2, Health 2, Mechanics 3, Preparedness 2, Sense Trouble 3, Stealth 4, Unarmed Combat 2

Domestic Security Division

Model FBI agents tasked with counterintelligence using the CIA *Directorate of Plans Case Officer* template (p. 032). Substitute Streetwise 1 for that template's Foreign Language 1.

Federal Bureau of Narcotics

Part of the Treasury Department, the FBN primarily investigates heroin and opium smuggling. It emplaces agents not just in the U.S. but also in France, Italy, Turkey, Beirut, Thailand, and other stops on the heroin connection. DELTA GREEN agents within the FBN investigate drug-cult activities including smuggled liao, black lotus, etc. and outbreaks from Inner Space (p. 216).

In 1968, it merges with the Bureau of Drug Abuse Control to become the Bureau of Narcotics and Dangerous Drugs; in 1970 the BNDD director requests CIA assistance in investigating rampant corruption in his bureau. DELTA GREEN is blamed – possibly justly – for using drug money stolen by its agents within BNDD as an off-books slush fund for its covert activities.

FBN Agent
Points: 12 Investigative, 25 General

Accounting 2, Agency 1, Criminology 1, Foreign Language 1, HUMINT 1, Law 1, Pharmacy 2, Streetwise 1

Athletics 3, Bureaucracy 2, Drive 2, Firearms 3, Pilot 3, Unarmed Combat 4

Pick Two Investigative: Chemistry 1, Cop Talk 1, Foreign Language 1*, HUMINT 1*, Notice 1, Pharmacy 1*, Photography 1, SIGINT 1, Streetwise 1*

Pick Two General: Conceal 4, Drive 4*, Firearms 4*, Health 4, Mechanics 4, Ride 4, Stealth 4

MACV-SOG

In 1964, the Joint Chiefs of Staff establish the Military Assistance Command Vietnam-Studies and Observations Group to carry out reconnaissance, covert action, and psychological warfare missions in Indochina, especially outside the borders of South Vietnam. MACV-SOG teams combine personnel from Army Special Forces, Navy SEALs, Marine Force Recon, USAF 56th Air Commando Wing, CIA SOD (p. 033), indigenous tribal fighters (p. 044), the South Vietnamese Strategic Technical Directorate (STD), and other specialized units as needed.

DELTA GREEN uses a similar principle, combining operatives from several different agencies and units both civilian and military. The two share so many similarities, including Top Secret classification and deniability, that it's quite possible that the Pentagon is deliberately attempting to replicate DELTA GREEN in a war-fighting context.

DELTA GREEN, of course, has penetrated MACV-SOG with its assets, over and above its official access to MACV-SOG intelligence product.

National Air and Space Administration

DELTA GREEN does not (usually) suborn astronauts, or even rocket scientists. It conceals ongoing research projects within the bottomless well of public money being hurled at the space program – and tries to monitor what its MAJESTIC rivals are doing in the next laboratory over.

NASA Engineer

Points: 10 Investigative, 16 General

Agency 1, Astronomy 1, Data Retrieval 2, Physics 1, SIGINT 1

Bureaucracy 3, Mechanics 5

Choose Four Investigative:
Accounting 1, Astronomy 1*, Biology 1, Chemistry 1, Foreign Language 1, Fringe Science 1, Inspiration 1, Medicine 1, Military Science 1, Photography 1, Physics 1*, Reassurance 1, SIGINT 1*

Choose Two General:
Demolitions 4, Drive 4, Mechanics 4*, Pilot 4, Sense Trouble 4

National Reconnaissance Office

The NRO is the most secret agency of the U.S. government. Established in 1960, it has never appeared in the newspapers or in open Congressional testimony. It operates the Corona reconnaissance satellite program and other even more secret missions. (The CIA operates the U-2 spy plane program.) Even more promisingly for DELTA GREEN, its budget is completely "black" and completely un-audited.

NRO Systems Engineer

Points: 12 Investigative, 8 General

Astronomy 1, Data Retrieval 2, Foreign Language 2, Physics 1, Photography 2, SIGINT 2

Bureaucracy 3, Mechanics 5

Choose Two Investigative:
Accounting 1, Agency 1*, Astronomy 1*, Foreign Language 1*, Fringe Science 1, Military Science 1, Physics 1*, Reassurance 1

National Security Agency

The defection of two NSA mathematicians to Moscow spectacularly blows the cover of the "No Such Agency" in 1960. Based at Ft. Meade in Maryland, the NSA analyzes and produces signals and electronic intelligence, a remit that includes computer science, electronics research, and cryptanalysis. (It also includes clandestine planting of bugs and wiretaps, and the monitoring of U.S. citizens' communications.)

Given the close relationship between higher mathematics and unnatural phenomena, DELTA GREEN works both with NSA mathematicians and within the NSA Office of Security, which watches the agency's mathematicians for signs of instability and subversion.

NSA Analyst

Points: 15 Investigative, 22 General

Cryptography 2, Data Retrieval 2, Foreign Language 2, Physics 1, SIGINT 2, Traffic Analysis 2

Add 4 to any three of these: Bureaucracy 1, Firearms 1, Mechanics 2, Network 2, Preparedness 1, Sense Trouble 2, Stealth 1

Choose Four Investigative: Agency 1, Cryptography 1*, Foreign Language 1*, Fringe Science 1, History 1, Physics 1*, SIGINT 1*, Tradecraft 1, Traffic Analysis 1*

NSA Security Specialist

Points: 12 Investigative, 22 General

Agency 1, Cryptography 2, Data Retrieval 1, Foreign Language 1, SIGINT 2, Traffic Analysis 1

Add 4 to any three of these: Conceal 2, Filch 2, Firearms 1, Mechanics 2, Stealth 2, Unarmed Combat 1

Choose Four Investigative: Architecture 1, Cop Talk 1, Criminology 1, Cryptography 1*, Foreign Language 1*, Fringe Science 1, HUMINT 1, Notice 1, SIGINT 1*, Tradecraft 1, Traffic Analysis 1*

Office of Naval Intelligence

Before the OSS assumed control and gave the program its code name, DELTA GREEN was the P4 Desk of the ONI. In a sense, the ONI remains the unofficial "home office" of the program to this day. While most of ONI concerns itself with assessing foreign naval capacity by technical means, since 1966 Task Force 157 (TF157) runs global networks of assets focusing on Soviet and Chinese shipping both military and merchant.

ONI Analyst

Prerequisite: *Sailor* template (p. 027) for your Military Service. You may be Active Duty.

Points: 10 Investigative, 16 General

Agency 1, Data Retrieval 1, Foreign Language 2, History 1, Military Science 1, Traffic Analysis 1

Bureaucracy 2, Firearms 1, Sense Trouble 1, Stability 4

Pick Three Investigative: Architecture 1, Astronomy 1, Cryptography 1, Foreign Language 1*, Fringe Science 1, Inspiration 1, Military Science 1*, Negotiation 1, Photography 1, Physics 1, SIGINT 1, Traffic Analysis 1*

Pick Two General: Bureaucracy 4*, Heavy Weapons 4, Network 4, Pilot 4, Preparedness 4

SECURITY AGENCY
NGTON 25, D. C.

OATH

id knowledge of operations of the National
(as an official, employee,
f the Agency in any other capacity) (though
company, business or commercial concern, or
department) subscribe to this oath freely,
the full intent to exercise meticulous care

TF157 Case Officer

Prerequisite: *Sailor* template (p. 027) for your Military Service. You may be Active Duty.

Points: 14 Investigative, 34 General

Add 1 to any two of these: Agency 1, Cryptography 1, Foreign Language 1, HUMINT 2, Notice 1, SIGINT 1, Tradecraft 2

Add 3 to any three of these: Athletics 1, Disguise 2, Drive 2, Firearms 1, Network 4, Pilot 4, Sense Trouble 2, Stealth 3, Unarmed Combat 3

Pick One Investigative: Astronomy 1, Foreign Language 1*, Military Science 1*

Pick One Interpersonal: Inspiration 2, Negotiation 2, Reassurance 2, Streetwise 2

Pick One General: Athletics 3*, Bureaucracy 3, Health 3, Mechanics 3, Melee Weapons 3, Network 3*, Preparedness 3, Psychotherapy 3, Stealth 3*

State Department

The official representatives of the United States government abroad, and the executors (or obfuscators) of its foreign policy. DELTA GREEN recruits friendly Foreign Service Officers in unnatural "hot zones," and plants its own where the heat is rising.

Foreign Service Officer

Points: 12 Investigative, 16 General

Anthropology 1, Foreign Language 3, History 1, HUMINT 2

Bureaucracy 4, Network 6, Preparedness 2, Stability 4

Pick One Investigative: Accounting 1, Agency 1, Data Retrieval 1, Law 1, SIGINT 1, Traffic Analysis 1

Pick Two Interpersonal: Flattery 2, Inspiration 2, Negotiation 2, Reassurance 2

INR Analyst

The State Department's Bureau of Intelligence and Research (INR) collates the raw intelligence product of U.S. embassies and subject-matter specialists to provide overviews of and up-to-the-minute briefings on regions, nations, or topics for the Secretary and for the rest of the federal intelligence community.

DELTA GREEN analysts inside INR sift the same product to develop briefings and threat warnings on un-natural outbreaks and other matters of concern.

Points: 14 Investigative, 16 General

Model such an analyst with the *Foreign Service Officer* (p. 040). Cut that template's two Interpersonal ratings from 2 to 1 and add:

Criminology 1, Traffic Analysis 1

Pick Two Investigative: Anthropology 1*, Fringe Science 1, History 1*, Occult 1.

SY Special Agent

The Office of Security (SY) protects diplomats, investigates passport and security clearance fraud, and works with the Marine Corps to maintain embassy security.

Points: 14 Investigative, 36 General

Add 1 to any two of these: Criminology 1, Foreign Language 2, HUMINT 1, Law 1, Notice 1

Add 3 to any three of these: Athletics 3, Bureaucracy 3, Drive 3, Firearms 3, Sense Trouble 3, Unarmed Combat 4

Pick Two Investigative: Accounting 1, Agency 1, Anthropology 1, Architecture 1, Foreign Language 1*, Military Science 1, Photography 1, Traffic Analysis 1

Pick Two Interpersonal: Cop Talk 2, Interrogation 2, Intimidation 2, Reassurance 2, Streetwise 2

Pick Two General: Conceal 4, Disguise 4, Drive 4*, Firearms 4*, Health 4, Melee Weapons 4, Preparedness 4, Sense Trouble 4*, Stability 4, Stealth 4, Unarmed Combat 4*

United States Marshals Service

Congress formally creates the Marshals Service in 1969, although the U.S. Marshals date back to 1789. Up to 1965, each U.S. District Court employs its own marshals; in 1965 the Justice Department establishes the Executive Office for U.S. Marshals.

Marshals track fugitives, provide protection for federal property and personnel (and civil rights volunteers), and handle federal prisoner transfers (including spy swaps). Marshals have almost no bureaucracy, little supervision outside federal court officers, and excellent relations with local police, making them ideal DELTA GREEN agents.

U.S. Marshal
Points: 12 Investigative, 45 General

Cop Talk 2, Criminology 2, HUMINT 1, Intimidation 1, Law 2, Notice 1

Athletics 4, Drive 4, Firearms 4, Health 4, Network 3, Preparedness 3, Sense Trouble 4, Stealth 3, Unarmed Combat 4

Pick Three Investigative: Cop Talk 1*, Forensics 1, HUMINT 1*, Inspiration 1, Intimidation 1*, Negotiation 1, Reassurance 1, Streetwise 1

Pick Three General: Athletics 4*, Conceal 4, Drive 4*, Firearms 4*, Melee Weapons 4, Network 4*, Ride 4, Sense Trouble 4*, Stealth 4*, Unarmed Combat 4*

DELTA GREEN ASSET PACKAGE

Any DELTA GREEN Agent inserted into another agency may well have developed the following abilities out of sheer self-preservation:

Notice 1: Make your generalized paranoia work for you!

Occult 1: Helps to spot potential unnatural spoor in reports or the field.

Tradecraft 1: Enables the asset to meet covertly with other DELTA GREEN personnel, or pass intel along.

Conceal 2+: Provides a quick hiding place for an unlicensed sidearm or false ID.

Filch 2+: Allows the agent to abstract reports (or artifacts) from theoretically sealed or restricted archives, to share them with DELTA GREEN or destroy them if they reveal too much.

Feel free to take any or each of these to match your idea of your Agent.

Other Backgrounds

DELTA GREEN being what it is (and players being who they are), not every single Agent is necessarily an employee of the federal government. Even in the case of CIA contractors such as Cuban pilots in the Congo or Norwegian boat captains in Indochina, their backgrounds may not necessarily mesh with the standard Military-plus-Department templates.

That said, when possible base non-USG Agent templates on the templates above. A Cuban exile working for the CIA might not have a military background, but can easily wind up becoming a Directorate of Plans Operative (p. 032) in game terms, if not on the books at Langley. A South Korean, South Vietnamese, or Australian soldier serving in Vietnam closely resembles the Active-Duty Soldier on p. 028, with an additional Foreign Language 1 for the South Korean and South Vietnamese.

Allied nations with Agents in your campaign generally have similar military service requirements and fairly closely related national-security organizations. Thus, they can be built as variants of U.S. DELTA GREEN Agents. For example, until 1984 the Royal Canadian Mounted Police (RCMP) is, within the limits of GUMSHOE resolution, functionally identical to the FBI (p. 036), with Ride 4 and Pilot 4 as optional General Abilities.

On a similar note, build British Agents from PISCES (p. 174) according to the U.K.-U.S. equivalent agencies table below.

Here are a few more non-federal backgrounds for non-federal Agents. With the exception of CIA contractors, non-federal Agents cannot have Agency ratings (unless the Handler decides to count the Mafia, for example, as an Agency). Put your 2 free Agency rating points into other Investigative Abilities.

U.K.–U.S. Equivalent Agencies

British Department	U.S. Department
Communicable Disease Surveillance Centre (CDSC)	CDC (p. 034)
Defense Research Establishments (various)	ARPA (p. 030), NASA Engineer (p. 038)
Government Communications Headquarters (GCHQ)	NSA (p. 038), NRO (p. 038)
Intelligence Corps	DIA (p. 035)
Microbiological Research Establishment (MRE)	CDC Researcher (p. 034) with Biology 2 and Military Science instead of Cop Talk
Naval Intelligence Department (NID)	ONI Analyst (p. 039) with Cryptography 1 and SIGINT 2
Public Records Office (PRO)	LoC DRD Researcher (p. 036) with Law 1 and Foreign Language 2 (not 3)
Secret Intelligence Service (MI-6)	CIA (p. 031) or DIA (p. 035)
Security Service (MI-5)	FBI (p. 036), esp. Domestic Security Division (p. 037)
Special Air Service (SAS) or Special Boat Service (SBS)	Special Forces (p. 029)
Special Branch	FBI (p. 036), esp. Undercover Agent (p. 037)

Activist

Just because you want a revolution doesn't mean you want Nyarlathotep. You work with the pigs because hey, at least you're both mammals.

Put your 2 free Bureaucracy rating points into other General Abilities.

Points: 10 Investigative, 14 General

Anthropology 1, Inspiration 1, Law 1, Streetwise 1

Conceal 1, Network 4

Pick Two Investigative: Art 1, Chemistry 1, Data Retrieval 1, Fringe Science 1, History 1, Law 1*, Occult 1, Pharmacy 1, Photography 1, Survival 1

Pick Two Interpersonal: Cop Talk 2, Flattery 2, Inspiration 2*, Intimidation 2, Negotiation 2, Streetwise 2*

Pick Three General: Bureaucracy 3, Demolitions 3, Disguise 3, First Aid 3, Network 3*, Sense Trouble 3, Stealth 3

Archaeologist

You dug up something best left buried. You want it reburied, and your new government associates have the biggest shovels around.

Points: 13 Investigative, 23 General

Anthropology 1, Archaeology 2, Architecture 1, Foreign Language 3, History 2, Notice 1, Photography 1

Athletics 2, Demolitions 2, Drive 3, Mechanics 4, Preparedness 3

Pick Two Investigative:
Anthropology 1, Archaeology 1*, Architecture 1*, Biology 1, Foreign Language 1*, Forensics 1, Negotiation 1, Notice 1*, Occult 1, Survival 1

Pick Three General: Athletics 3*, Demolitions 3*, Filch 3, Firearms 3, Melee Weapons 3, Pilot 3, Preparedness 3*, Ride 3

Engineer or Technician

You might have stumbled on something on a deniable MAJESTIC contract, or in independent investigation. Or perhaps DELTA GREEN called you in because you were in the closest lab that night.

Points: 10 Investigative, 19 General

Data Retrieval 1, Notice 1, Physics 1, SIGINT 1

Mechanics 4

Pick Three Investigative:
Astronomy 2, Biology 2, Chemistry 2, Data Retrieval 2*, Foreign Language 2, Fringe Science 2, Physics 2*, SIGINT 2*, Traffic Analysis 2

Pick Three General: Bureaucracy 5, Demolitions 5, Mechanics 5*, Network 5, Preparedness 5, Sanity 5, Stability 5

Gangster

You might be a Mafia contractor helping the CIA hit Castro, or a Mafia informant helping the FBI make a case. But now, you're in a wider turf war.

Put your 2 free Bureaucracy points into other General Abilities.

Points: 8 Investigative, 22 General

Interrogation 2, Intimidation 2, Streetwise 2

Firearms 3, Melee Weapons 3, Network 3, Sense Trouble 2, Unarmed Combat 3

Pick One Investigative:
Accounting 1, Criminology 1, Foreign Language 1, Law 1, Occult 1, Pharmacy 1

Pick One Interpersonal: Cop Talk 1, Flattery 1, HUMINT 1, Intimidation 1*, Negotiation 1, Streetwise 1*

Pick Two General: Athletics 4, Conceal 4, Demolitions 4, Disguise 4, Drive 4, Filch 4, Firearms 4*, Mechanics 4, Melee Weapons 4*, Network 4*, Sense Trouble 4*, Unarmed Combat 4*

Physician

You patched up some very peculiar wounds for some men with short haircuts — and then you saw what made those wounds.

For a psychiatrist, lower Medicine to 2, add Interrogation 1, switch First Aid with Psychotherapy in the template.

Points: 9 Investigative, 21 General

Forensics 1, Medicine 3, Pharmacy 2, Reassurance 2

First Aid 8, Network 2, Stability 2

Pick One Investigative: Biology 1, Forensics 1*, HUMINT 1, Notice 1, Reassurance 1*

Pick Three General: Athletics 3, Bureaucracy 3, First Aid 3*, Psychotherapy 3, Sanity 3, Sense Trouble 3, Stability 3*

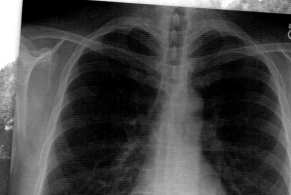

Pilot

You've been flying planes for the CIA's Air America or another deniable airline, or even flying combat missions in an even more deniable operation. Or perhaps you were just in the wrong sky at the wrong time.

Points: 5 Investigative, 24 General

Astronomy 1, SIGINT 1

First Aid 1, Mechanics 4, Pilot 6, Preparedness 2, Sense Trouble 4, Unarmed Combat 1

Pick Three Investigative: Cryptography 1, Inspiration 1, Foreign Language 1, Negotiation 1, Notice 1, Photography 1, Reassurance 1, SIGINT 1*

Pick Two General: Athletics 3*, Conceal 3, Demolitions 3, Mechanics 3*, Pilot 3*, Preparedness 3*, Sense Trouble 3*, Unarmed Combat 3*

Scholar

They needed someone who could translate Sumerian. You haven't dreamed in English since that night.

Points: 13 Investigative, 14 General

Foreign Language 3, History 2

Bureaucracy 1, Network 4, Stability 3

Pick Four Investigative: Archaeology 2, Architecture 2, Art 2, Astronomy 2, Biology 2, Bureaucracy 2*, Chemistry 2, Criminology 2, Data Retrieval 2, Foreign Language 2*, Fringe Science 2, HUMINT 2, Notice 2, Occult 2, Physics 2, Traffic Analysis 2

Pick Two General: Bureaucracy 3*, Health 3, Network 3*, Preparedness 3, Sanity 3, Stability 3*

Tribal Fighter

Hmong or Yao in Laos or Montagnard in Vietnam – you didn't want the Communists to take your village, so you helped the Americans. Then you found something even worse than the Communists to fight.

Put your 2 free Bureaucracy points into other General Abilities.

Points: 8 Investigative, 35 General

Anthropology 1, Foreign Language 1, Survival 2

Athletics 2, Conceal 2, Firearms 4, Melee Weapons 5, Sense Trouble 4, Stealth 4, Unarmed Combat 2

Pick Two Investigative: Biology 1, Foreign Language 1*, Military Science 1, Notice 1, Occult 1, Survival 1*

Pick One Interpersonal: Interrogation 2, Intimidation 2

Pick Three General: Athletics 4*, Conceal 4*, Demolitions 4, Firearms 4*, First Aid 4, Health 4, Melee Weapons 4*, Preparedness 4, Ride 4, Sense Trouble 4*, Stealth 4*, Unarmed Combat 4*

Bonds

Bonds describe your Agent's vital relationships: loved ones, family members and close friends. You can spend from your Bond pools on Stability tests – at a price (see *Burning Bonds*, p. 120).

Bonds are not abstracts or good feelings; they are your Agent's connection to humanity. An Agent with no Bonds is more susceptible to psychological trauma than one who has people waiting back home.

Your Agent begins with 3 Bonds.

Each Bond begins with a rating equal to one higher than your Agent's highest ability rating from among the following Interpersonal abilities:

- △ Flattery
- △ Inspiration
- △ Negotiation
- △ Reassurance

These abilities (unlike, say, Interrogation) at least pay lip service to understanding another person's needs. If you have no rating in any of these abilities, your Bond ratings begin at 1. If your rating in that ability drops (or raises if you put experience points into the ability (p. 127)), each Bond rating drops (or raises) by the same amount.

The maximum Bond rating is 4.

Bonds can weaken as you undergo the monstrous stresses of DELTA GREEN service. You can strengthen a Bond if you cultivate that Bond between operations (p. 128).

Defining Bonds

A Bond must be a real person or small group of real people who are alive, and who your Agent can interact with. Identify and name each Bond, for example:

- △ "My husband Carl."
- △ "My daughter Nancy."
- △ "My Grandma Earlene."
- △ "Mom."
- △ "My ex-partner in the Bureau, Greenbaum."
- △ "Father O'Malley."
- △ "Dr. Gestettner."

Bonds can be small groups of people:

- △ "My wife and kids."
- △ "My folks."
- △ "The squad."
- △ "Temple Beth-Israel."
- △ "My fellow survivors of the plane crash."

Whether with one person or a group, a Bond only has one strength. If the strength of your group Bond drops, your Agent's relationship with each member of that group suffers.

Raina is selecting Bonds for her Agent, Dr. Amanda Lincoln. She chooses Amanda's husband Jerome, her great-aunt Zorah, and her former fellow residents on the night shift at Cook County Hospital. Her highest rating in the Bond-relevant abilities is Reassurance 3, so she writes down the following on her character sheet under Bonds: Jerome (husband) 4, Zorah (great-aunt) 4, Chicago night shift (former fellow residents) 4.

Fewer Bonds, More Skill

If your Agent spends more time on the job than on his outside life, his Bonds dwindle to only the most vital.

During character generation only, you can trade 1 Bond for 2 Investigative build points, 1 Investigative and 3 General build points, or 6 General build points. You can do this twice, bringing you down to 1 Bond.

If Raina had wanted the extra points, she could have taken only two Bonds instead of the default three, and received: 6 extra points of First Aid, or 3 points in First Aid and 3 in Firearms, or 1 point in Pharmacy and 3 points in Unarmed Combat, or 2 points in HUMINT, or etc.

Or, if you'd rather, you can trade the other way: trade build points for Bonds at the same ratio. You can do this once, for a maximum of four Bonds.

Breaking Bonds

When a Bond deteriorates, the relationship it represents becomes strained. Just how is up to you and the Handler to decide or depict in play. The Handler may damage your Bond due to actions not involving your Agent's obsession and isolation: your squad might get ambushed by the Viet Cong, or your partner might get lung cancer. The Handler reduces that Bond's rating by 1.

If someone (or every member of the group) you have a Bond with dies or goes permanently insane, that Bond is destroyed. Cross it off your character sheet.

When a Bond's rating drops to *negative one* (-1), it is permanently broken. Cross it off your character sheet. The only way to regain a Bond with that GMC is to rebuild it from scratch (see *Establish a New Bond*, p. 129).

A SPECIAL BOND: DELTA GREEN

Powerful Bonds form between people who have to look out for each other to survive. Only fellow veterans understand what you've suffered. Sooner or later your Agent comes to rely on team more than family.

Each time someone in your Agent's DELTA GREEN team undergoes a catastrophic trauma, there's a chance your Agent develops or deepens Bonds with his teammates. Such traumas include:

△ A member of the team suffers temporary insanity.
△ A member of the team gains a new disorder.
△ A member of the team is incapacitated by injuries.
△ A member of the team dies or goes permanently insane.

Or anything else the Handler considers a severe enough stress.

After the crisis, when things are calm, your Agent must make a Difficulty 4 Stability test (p. 080). There's no effect if it succeeds. If it fails, your Agent gains a new Bond with each DELTA GREEN teammate (up to five) present for that disaster, and increases any Bonds with them that were already there.

For each teammate with whom your Agent doesn't already have a Bond, the failed Stability test adds a new individual Bond. Write that character's name and a note saying "DELTA GREEN" next to it. Its value is half your highest current Bond rating (round up). Your Agent immediately loses 1 point from one other (non-DELTA GREEN) Bond of your choice (if you have any left).

For each teammate with whom your Agent already has a Bond, the failed Stability test adds 1 to it and subtracts 1 from one other (non-DELTA GREEN) Bond of your choice.

On Dr. Lincoln's first mission, one of her teammates is killed. Raina makes a Stability test to see if Amanda forms new Bonds with Bob and Carlos, her surviving teammates. The Stability test fails, so she gains new Bonds with Bob and Carlos with a rating of 2 each (half her highest current Bond rating, 4). In turn, she loses 1 point from another Bond, dropping her bond with Zorah to 3.

After the next crisis, Amanda fails her Stability test again. Bob and Carlos survived, so she needs to add 1 to each Bond with her team mates and subtract 2 from her non-DELTA GREEN Bonds. Raina could take both losses off one Bond, but decides to weaken her Bonds with the Chicago night shift and with Jerome, dropping both Bonds to 3.

Motivations

What motivates an Agent? Why go back into the Outside, take point on the frontiers of reality, or pursue an investigation in which the truth is quite literally fatal? Because some people – perhaps not the best, and certainly not necessarily the brightest – are Motivated to do so.

Every Agent must have a **Motivation,** a core desire that impels him to answer the call to action from DELTA GREEN every time, at the cost of everything he values. Your Motivation is quite literally something more important to you than your life or sanity. Although many different psychological forces might motivate an Agent, and the player can roleplay her with such complexity, mechanically each character should only have one core Motivation.

Motivations in Play

If you don't tell the Handler when your Motivation impels your Agent to irrationally dangerous action, she will tell you. She might explain to you why your Motivation would spur you to action. Better yet, she could prompt *you* to explain it.

When invoking Motivations, Handlers should take care not to guide the player's specific response to the situation. The goal is to lead the player to move forward, not to force a particular choice. Avoid this by listing several viable choices, if the player has been stumped by his own caution.

You are never obligated to obey your Motivation. By exerting unusual force of will, you can control your behavior.

At a price, of course.

Stress Penalties

Refusing to follow your Agent's Motivation causes grave mental stress, and therefore costs Stability: between 2 and 5 pool points.

The Handler determines the level of stress damage depending on how hard the stimulus punches the Agent's buttons, and on how important taking dangerous action is to a satisfying and dramatic story.

The typical game unfolds without a single such stress penalty coming into play, as players willingly follow the path they themselves have chosen.

Certainty Refreshes

On the other hand, if the Agent really dives in and lives his Motivation, possibly at great risk to himself, the Handler may allow the agent to refresh 1 or 2 pool points in any General Ability, reflecting the inner certainty that comes of following deep-seated psychological motivations. This reward is limited to once per session per player.

Choosing Your Motivation

Choose your character's Motivation at the beginning of play, from the following list. Think of it as a key to her personality.

Some of these Motivations presume knowledge of the unnatural. A player might pick such a Motivation knowing that it will only come into play once his Agent confronts the Outside, or the Handler might agree that the Agent learned about the limits of the rational universe before the rest of the group (see *Revelation,* p. 050).

Feel free to propose to the Handler a custom Motivation that fills the same function as the ones given here. Write up an explanatory paragraph in the same shape as the supplied Motivations. If not immediately apparent, your Handler may ask you to supply hypothetical examples

of situations in which the Motivation will keep the Agent making active, interesting choices in solving a mystery or confronting the monstrous.

Altruism

You got into the game to protect innocents from Communism, or disease, or war, or tyranny. You're no innocent yourself now, but that only lets you know just how much innocence normal people have left to lose.

Atonement

You did something wrong: committed a crime, betrayed your friends, killed someone undeserving, allowed someone else to die or prosper who shouldn't. Maybe nobody else would think you need to atone, but maybe those are the things you most need to atone for. DELTA GREEN can never clear your name, but you need to clear your conscience.

You might specify your sin during character creation, or at the beginning of play, or leave it open for a dramatic revelation at any time during the game. You can tell the other players, or just the Handler, or keep it to yourself. If you choose to set up your past misdeed as a mystery, be sure to drop hints along the way, to increase the impact on the other players when the secret finally comes out. Alternatively, you could wait for an interesting possibility to arise during play, and then tie your past history into the current action. Clear it with the Handler first, to make sure that the facts you're adding to the narrative don't conflict with the plot you're investigating.

Comradeship

You might have been motivated by abstract or material concerns when you first signed up, but that fell by the wayside in Bien Hoa or Baltimore. The real reason to be part of a team, you realize, is for the intense bond between men and women who depend completely on each other for their lives and livelihoods. No value is more important than personal loyalty. No people matter more than your teammates. And for them to survive, you have to kill the things that want to kill them.

Duty

You know it's dangerous and ill-advised, but somebody's got to go down those steps or bust up that cult. And you're elected, because if you don't take care of things now, they're just going to get worse. If you don't, who is? Some time-serving goldbrick just counting down the days until their pension? Don't be ridiculous.

Mystery

You are driven to solve a mystery: this might be a personal mystery (What happened to my old partner? What happened during my missing week? Who leaked the intel that led to our ambush?) or an arcane mystery (Did Cthulhu's dreams inspire Ed Gein? What does the KGB know about the Outer Ones?). If you have a personal connection to the

mystery, your motives are relatively clear; otherwise, you have one of those brains so very attractive (and attracted) to intelligence agencies, a brain that cannot rest without solving a mystery or tearing itself apart.

Patriotism

These horrors threaten the United States, just as surely as does internal subversion or Communist aggression overseas. Therefore, they must be stopped by any means necessary so that decent Americans never discover their existence.

Revenge

The unnatural hurt or killed someone you cared about deeply. Although you weren't able to stop that tragedy — and you might not have even known what the chittering horrors were at the time — you resolved to hunt them down and destroy them.

Decide whether you have already succeeded in taking vengeance on the specific cult or creature, or (perhaps more interestingly) have so far been unable to find them. In the first case, still feeling empty inside, you resolved to take similar vengeance on behalf of the myriad other victims who can't do it for themselves.

In the second case, the Handler will look for opportunities to weave your hunt for the horrors into her scenarios. She may dole them out in stages, so that successful revenge against one of them puts you onto the trail of another cultist, and so on.

Thrill-seeker

You joined up thinking of Audie Murphy or James Bond. Maybe you just wanted to prove yourself at first, but now you know the truth: there's nothing better than surviving danger. You feel a new kind of alive when you're closest to death. Nothing beats live fire for high stakes; not sex, not sports, not gambling, not pills. Maybe your team calls you an "adrenaline junkie," but they're sure glad to have you take point. When you know where to aim, you go in guns blazing, pitying people who will never know the feeling.

CHANGING MOTIVATIONS

It's always possible that your character will shift and deform under the stresses of the game, or that some event or opportunity will crop up that invalidates your Motivation or makes another one particularly appropriate. In general, such an organic change of Motivation will be obvious to both you and the Handler, and changing your Motivation shouldn't be any problem. For more arbitrary "I don't like playing this Motivation any more" changes, consider seeking a glorious and informative death for your current Agent, and starting over with a character better suited to your new desires.

Personal Details

Don't obsess over the numbers on your character sheet. Engage with your Agent as a character, not an abstraction, and the terrifying catastrophes of **The Fall of DELTA GREEN** become human despite their cosmic scale.

To flesh out some details and make the Agent engaging, write the following notes on the character sheet:

△ The Agent's name.

△ A detail or two about the Agent's age, ethnicity, and appearance.

△ Where did your Agent grow up? Did he go to college or straight into the military?

△ A detail or two about the Agent's beliefs, hobbies, obsessions, tastes in music or sports loyalties. What does your Agent drink? What does she smoke?

△ Something you admire about the Agent.

△ Something you dislike about the Agent.

△ Why does DELTA GREEN trust your Agent to confront unnatural threats and keep them secret?

△ Why does your Agent agree that helping DELTA GREEN and keeping its secrets feeds her Motivation?

Your Personality

One interesting way to get a handle on your agent's personality is to look at her Interpersonal abilities: what does her point spread indicate she values the most? Not just the obvious signals of Intimidation or Flattery at 3; Cop Talk 3 might indicate gregarious professionalism; Negotiation 3 an openness to new experience; HUMINT or Tradecraft 3 might both signal incipient paranoia.

Conversely, an Interpersonal ability left at 0 implies the agent never uses that technique: why not? An Interrogation of 0 might indicate a gentle core that shrinks from breaking a subject, a clear sadism that reduces targets to babbling inanities or psychotic defiance, or psychological scarring from the agent's previous experiences being interrogated in Leavenworth or Lubyanka.

Your Past

Develop at least a sketch of your Agent's past. It doesn't have to be too detailed — you want to leave some room for skills and GMCs to get added to your dossier in play — but knowing your Agent's past can help you come up with Bonds, Network contacts, and other game events in an organic and natural-seeming fashion.

Your Agent's age will help answer a lot of these questions.

Check Wikipedia or other references for more details and possibilities once you decide your age. The possibilities below are only probabilities.

If you are in your 20s: Your military service is either Vietnam or an assignment you wangled to avoid Vietnam. Your covert work also likely focuses on Vietnam, or elsewhere in the Third World. You may have some sympathies with protesters and hippies; you likely have friends or fellow students among them.

Your mentor, if you have one, is in his 40s.

If you are in your 30s: Your military service was in Korea, or possibly unofficially in Indochina or the Philippines (or if you joined up young, WWII). This decade, the 1960s, is when your covert career will flourish – or vanish. You are the same age as the leaders of many of the protest movements, but don't necessarily see eye to eye with them.

Your mentor, if you have one, is in his 50s.

If you are in your 40s: Your military service was in the Big One, Dubya Dubya Two. You might have served in or out of uniform in occupied Europe or Japan. If you went to college, it was probably on the G.I. Bill in the late 1940s. You might have been involved in the overthrow of the governments in Syria (1949), Iran (1953) or Guatemala (1954), if you're a Company veteran. You remember when there wasn't a Company, but you might have been OSS. You probably feel these protests are taking things way too far way too fast.

Your mentor, if you have one, is in his 60s, possibly retired. Your protégé, if you have one, is in his 20s.

If you are in your 50s: If you were born in 1910, you could still join up (at age 31) after Pearl Harbor, but much older than that and you sat the war out on the sidelines or at best rode a desk somewhere. (Unless you were career military already when it started, of course.) If you're FBI, you were there for the war on the gangs and bank robbers that made the Bureau; if you're CIA you probably transferred from an officer's billet after 1947. These protesters are crazy if they're not just Commie dupes.

Your mentor, if you have one, is in his 70s, almost certainly retired. Your protégé, if you have one, is in his 30s.

Revelation

If your character is not yet part of DELTA GREEN, you're done.

But if you're playing a DELTA GREEN Agent, it's likely that some past experience with unnatural forces brought you to the group's attention, and made you willing to join them. You don't need to describe exactly what happened – save that for when you share terrible stories with your fellow Agents – but you need a sense of that past investigation or encounter.

You and the Handler may want to develop, or even play out, the Inciting Event (p. 315) that awakened you to the abhorrent truth.

Choose from one of four options and work with the Handler to build details around it. She might even run a quick no-dice flashback scene with you, one-on-one, to provide a proper moment of revelation for you both.

Changes to abilities are changes to rating points, not pools. They last until you use build points (unspent or from experience) to alter them again.

Extreme Violence: Add 1 to Occult, Military Science, or Criminology. Reduce Stability by 1. Remove 1 point from any Interpersonal ability, add 3 to Sense Trouble, and lower one Bond strength by 1. Your Agent is Adapted to Violence (see p. 120). Leave your pools and Bond strengths as they are now, but when you refresh them, refresh them only to the cap.

Captivity or Imprisonment: Add 1 to Occult or Streetwise. Reduce Health or Stability by 1. Shift 1 point from any Interpersonal ability to Intimidation or Interrogation. Your Agent is Adapted to Helplessness (see p. 120).

Hard Experience: Add 1 to Occult or Fringe Science, and 5 points to any General Abilities other than Health, Sanity, or Stability. Subtract 2 points from either Stability or Health or 1 from each. Remove one Bond.

Things Man Was Not Meant to Know: Add a rating of 1 in The Unnatural, and add 1 to either Occult or Fringe Science. Reduce Sanity by 1. Your Agent gains a new disorder caused by the Unnatural (see p. 125).

Abilities in Detail

Abilities in GUMSHOE break down into two main categories: the **Investigative Abilities** you use to gather the information you need to figure out what the opposition is up to and how to stop them; and the **General Abilities** that allow you to survive the investigation and win the confrontation.

The rules don't care whether your high Athletics rating comes from years of military training or just natural grace and speed. Similarly, whether you're an intuitive genius or a plodding, meticulous scholar is irrelevant in gauging your Archaeology ability. You can decide such things while personalizing your character. What matters is what you can accomplish; how you accomplished it is up to you.

Ability descriptions consist of a brief general description, followed by examples of their use in an operation. Creative players should be able to propose additional uses for their abilities as unexpected situations confront their characters.

Certain specific actions may overlap between several abilities, ideally providing many possible ways forward in the scenario and giving many players a shot at the spotlight. For example:

△ You can interpret an aerial photograph of a military base with Photography or Military Science, or with a corresponding military Agency ability.
△ You can analyze (or synthesize) a weird LSD variant with either Chemistry or Pharmacy. Or you can use Network to call a street-chemist contact and ask her.
△ You can identify a smuggled artifact with Anthropology, Archaeology, Art, or possibly Occult.

△ You can tell what gun made that exit wound with Criminology, Forensics, or Military Science — or with an investigative use of Firearms.
△ You can identify the general's mistress with HUMINT, Flattery, or by using Traffic Analysis on his phone records.
△ You can bluff your way into a hospital with your Agency (if you're from the CDC or similar), Intimidation, or Medicine, or with an investigative use of Bureaucracy or Disguise.

Some abilities, like Reassurance and Notice, are broadly useful, and will crop up constantly. Others may be called for many times in the course of one scenario, and not at all in others. When building your character, strike a balance between the reliable workhorse abilities and their exotic, specialized counterparts.

Investigative Abilities

If you have an ability relevant to the task at hand, you **automatically succeed** in discovering any information or overcoming any obstacles necessary to propel you from the current scene further into the story.

Each rating gives you a pool of points to spend in situations related to its base ability. You may ask to **spend points** to gain special benefits. Sometimes the Handler will offer you the chance to spend points. In other circumstances she may accept your suggestions of ways to gain special benefits. (See p. 078 for more on spends.) Use them wisely; spent Investigative points do not return until the next operation begins.

Interpersonal Use of Non-Interpersonal Abilities

Although some Investigative Abilities, like Flattery or Reassurance, are explicitly Interpersonal, every ability can be used as an Interpersonal ability on GMCs who have (or value) it. An Agent can use Art to look cool at a Greenwich Village happening, Physics to interact with atomic scientists as a professional equal, Medicine to chat up a doctor about the weird burns on the victim, or SIGINT to bluff the radiotelegrapher on the other end of the line that everything is fine here, no problem, thanks.

Accounting (Academic)

You understand bookkeeping and accountancy procedures; you can read and keep financial records. You can:

△ tell legitimate businesses from criminal enterprises
△ reconstruct financial histories from old records (uncovering, say, slave-trading or smuggling)
△ spot the telltale signs of embezzlement, bribes, blackmail, or shell companies
△ track payments to their source
△ launder funds and set up numbered accounts

Agency (Special)

Every DELTA GREEN Agent ostensibly reports to an agency of the federal government, or to a branch (or smaller unit) of the military. Civilian or military, the game mechanics call this your Agency. The Agency ability reflects your knowledge of, contacts within, and capacity to manipulate your Agency.

Assign your free Agency points (and any more points you buy) in this ability under the name of your specific Agency: CIA 3, AEC 2, Special Forces 3, USMC 1, etc. Your Agency may or may not be the same as your Department: you likely just have Agency (CIA) even if you took the TSD Department template on p. 034.

The Handler will help you determine how fine to grind your Agency: in a campaign in which all the Agents are MACV-SOG operators, each character's home corps or even division might be his Agency. In another game, one Agent might have "U.S. Navy" as her Agency to go with other Agents with "FBI," "CDC," and "State Department" as their Agencies.

You cannot assign points to an Agency you have not served in or worked for.

Agency is such a flexible ability that you may want to buy more than 3 points in it. You receive 2 rating points in your Agency for free.

Using Agency Interpersonally

Use this ability on another person in your Agency to schmooze them, convince them everything is copacetic, talk shop with them, or pump them for rumors and gossip. Consider this ability Cop Talk for your Agency, along with a pinch of HUMINT.

Using Agency Investigatively

Spend pool points from your Agency ability to know operating procedures, trade secrets, what time the guard shift changes, which personnel have a drug habit, etc. The ability acts as a dedicated point pool (p. 077) covering or equating to any Investigative Ability used *about* (not *by*) your Agency, even if you don't specifically have it: HUMINT, Military Science, Traffic Analysis, etc. plus all the little edge cases in between or on the margins.

Using Agency With a General Ability

Spend pool points from your Agency ability to get other things done involving that agency or its facilities: if you're trying to break into a CIA black site, you can spend from your CIA pool on the Stealth test. If you're tossing the apartment of an NSA cryptographer, you can spend from your NSA pool on the Conceal test. You cannot spend Agency on combat ability tests.

Agency pool points spent on tests or contests of Bureaucracy *within* your own agency *count double*.

Multiple Agencies

If your Agent has moved from one branch of government to another, possibly ahead of internal investigations into all those mysterious fires, she can buy points in more than one Agency. However, rating points in an Agent's second Agency cost double: spend 2 build points for 1 rating point. Rating points in an Agent's third Agency cost triple: spend 3 for 1. And so on.

AGENCY AND "THE AGENCY"

Don't confuse the game term "Agency" with "the Agency," meaning the CIA (or ARPA, or DIA, or NSA). Your Agency ability might refer to the CIA, the FBI, or the 101st Airborne.

In this book, when we mean "the CIA" we'll say so, or we might drop into spy slang and call it "the Company."

Side First

Use Other

Anthropology (Academic)

You are an expert in the study of human cultures, from the Stone Age to the Atomic Age. (Physical anthropology is covered by Forensics.) You can:

△ identify artifacts and rituals of living cultures

△ describe and predict the customs of a foreign group or local subculture

△ supply information about religious practices and beliefs

△ extrapolate the practices of an unknown culture from similar examples

△ develop a strongly appealing political or religious message for a given subculture or society

△ interact with very foreign cultures (e.g., Montagnard hill fighters) as an accepted insider

Archaeology (Academic)

You excavate and study the structures and artifacts of historical cultures and civilizations. You can:

△ tell how long something has been buried and date its construction

△ identify artifacts by culture and usage

△ distinguish real artifacts from fakes

△ navigate inside ruins and catacombs, including finding secret doors and hidden construction

△ describe the customs of ancient or historical cultures

△ spot well-disguised graves and underground hiding places

△ interpret site maps and archaeological dig records

△ estimate the market value of, and likely customers for, a smuggled artifact

Architecture (Technical)

You know how buildings (and infrastructure generally) are designed and constructed. You can:

△ guess what lies around the corner while exploring an unknown structure or sewer system

△ deduce or discover where sewer, electrical power, telephone, and gas lines enter or pass beneath a structure, and trace them within it

△ rough out a floor plan and interpret blueprints

△ judge the relative strength of building materials

△ identify a building's age, architectural style, original use, and history of modifications

△ deduce the existence of hidden rooms, bricked-over sewers, or secret crypts

△ construct stable makeshift structures

△ identify elements vital to the structural integrity of buildings, sewers, dams, or bridges

Art (Technical)

You are an expert on works of art (including the practical arts such as furniture and pottery) from an aesthetic, historical, and technical point of view. You can:

△ distinguish real works from fakes

△ tell when something has been retouched or altered

△ identify the age of an object by style and materials

△ accurately estimate the price of, and likely customers for, an *objet d'art*

△ call to mind historical details on artists and those around them

△ call to mind details of stolen or missing artworks

Regardless of your own gifts or medium, you can use Art to gain clues about any type of art.

Creating Art

You can also create some sort of art – music, painting, dance, sculpture, song, poetry, drama, and so forth. You can choose to focus on one medium or diversify: For each rating point in Art, you may select another type of art in which you are generally proficient. You may specify when you create your Agent, or choose opportunistically in the course of play, revealing that you happen to be, say, a gifted sculptor if circumstances suddenly require it.

Creating great (or even particularly notable) art requires spends (see p. 078); points allocated to such spends cannot be allocated to different art forms in the future.

Forgery

The federal government, either through your day job agency or DELTA GREEN, supplies you with any cover identities or false credentials it believes you require for an operation.

Your opinion may vary. In such cases, you can assign one or more Art rating points to Art (Forgery) and create forged documents or identification. Like other assigned rating points, you cannot reassign them to other art forms after spending them on a specific work.

Forging simple documents such as driver's licenses, checks, commercial security badges or ID, or military passes or ID requires a spend of 1 point of Art (Forgery); forging complex documents such as passports, federal security badges or ID, or military orders requires a spend of 2 points of Art (Forgery). Forgery also usually requires specialized paper or card blanks, a camera, and print-shop equipment.

None of your forgeries stand up to investigation ("I'll have to phone this in") unless you have used Bureaucracy or perhaps Data Retrieval to insert your forged records into the relevant files.

If you really, really want to put the Secret Service on your trail (and wind up in a shallow grave somewhere to boot if DELTA GREEN learns about it) you can assign Art rating points to Art (Counterfeiting).

The Handler may decide that Forgery (or Counterfeiting) requires Special Training (p. 072) in order to become an available category for the Art ability.

Astronomy (Academic)

You study celestial objects, including the stars and planets. You can:

△ decipher astrological texts
△ recall the phase of the moon and time of sunset and sunrise without looking it up
△ use a telescope, including large reflectors
△ plot the movement of stars and planets, including which ones are overhead at any given time
△ predict eclipses, comets, meteor showers, and other regular astronomical phenomena
△ calculate flight paths for ballistic missiles or rockets

Biology (Academic)

You study the evolution, behavior, and physical makeup of living organisms. You can:

△ determine whether an animal or plant is native to an area, and whether it is behaving strangely
△ tell whether the ecosystem in an area is healthy or diseased, and what might be ailing it
△ identify an animal from samples of its hair, blood, bones, or other tissue
△ analyze unknown ichor, scales, biological toxins, or slime
△ identify a plant from a small sample
△ isolate or detect natural poisons or venoms

Chemistry (Technical)

You're trained in the analysis and manipulation of chemical substances, and have a working knowledge of such related sciences as biochemistry, genetics, geology, and metallurgy. Given suitable lab facilities, you can:

△ create simple explosives, incendiaries, poisons, gases, and acids
△ analyze unknown substances, soil samples, minerals, alloys, compounds, etc.
△ match samples of dirt or vegetation from a piece of evidence to a scene
△ perform chemical document analysis on ink or paper
△ safely handle (or knowledgably advise against handling at all) hazardous materials

Cop Talk (Interpersonal)

You know how to speak the lingo of the police, and to make them feel confident and relaxed in your presence. You may be a current or former cop (or federal agent), or simply pose as the kind of person they immediately identify as a solid, trustworthy citizen. You can:

△ coolly ply cops for confidential information
△ get excused for minor infractions
△ imply that you are a colleague, authorized to participate in their cases
△ tell when a cop is lying to you or holding something back
△ interpret codes on a police radio
△ write a convincing police report
△ recognize an undercover cop in plain clothes by their body language or clothing

Criminology (Academic)

You study crimes, and the methods for solving crimes, from modern laboratory techniques to the nascent science of psychological profiling. You can:

△ recall details of past art thefts, bank robberies, serial murders, and everything in between
△ make accurate guesses as to the upbringing and pathology of criminals or killers based on their known modus operandi
△ predict criminals' future actions based on their past behavior, researched or observed
△ detail or predict the organizational structure, leadership, and activities of known organized crime rings
△ note blood spatter, relationships between objects, etc. at a crime scene, reconstructing sequences of events
△ transfer, take, and match fingerprints using the naked eye or microscopes; you are familiar with all major fingerprint record files
△ match typewritten materials to a given machine, handwriting to a known sample, tire tracks to specific models or vehicles, etc.

the computer you can often deduce the sort of data the tape or cards hold

△ recover data from erased or altered tape recordings or computer tapes

△ increase the clarity of audio recordings, zeroing in on or amplifying desired elements

△ rapidly and accurately transcribe an audio recording, or pull the salient details out of a recording with miraculous rapidity

With access and a spend, you can alter or forge a computer record, and insert, erase, or replace computerized records from a file or data bank.

Flattery (Interpersonal)

You are good at getting people to help you by complimenting them, as subtly or blatantly as they prefer. With subjects who might find you sexually attractive, you can turn flattery into flirtation — and perhaps into seduction!

On a susceptible target, you can:

△ quickly size up someone in conversation and discern areas of pride or of hidden shame

△ develop a notion of their specific romantic or sexual tastes

△ get them to reveal information, help you in small ways, or trust you

△ get them to date you or see you again socially, depending

△ spot romantic or sexual attractions or connections between other people by watching them interact

It's up to you whether a high rating in Flattery means that you are physically alluring, winning and charismatic, or simply have the gift of gab or a weird fascination.

△ bag and tag objects for forensic analysis without contaminating your samples

△ perform ballistics and gunpowder analysis of bullets or other residue

△ perform blood and fiber tests on crime scene evidence

Cryptography (Technical)

You are an expert in the making and breaking of codes in any language you can read. You can also:

△ identify known codes or reasonably infer who might be using a new type of code

△ create a one-time pad system requiring a super-computer to break

△ read and send in Morse and other common codes

△ puzzle out written foreign languages by brute force with time and a dictionary

Data Retrieval (Technical)

You retrieve data and information from non-print sources. You can:

△ use a computer to get information off its magnetic tape spools or punch cards; even without

Foreign Language (Academic)

For each rating point in Foreign Language, you are verbally fluent and literate in one language other than your native tongue.

You may elect to be literate in an ancient language that is no longer spoken, although the Handler may disallow occult, primordial, or inhuman languages such as Aklo (the tongue of the serpent-folk), Naacal (the language of Mu), or Pnakotic A (the Yithian language). The Handler may allow overlap between related languages — an Agent fluent in Norwegian may plausibly claim to be fluent (or at least "mostly able to get by") in Swedish, for example, without adding another rating point.

You may specify these when you create your character, or choose opportunistically in the course of play, revealing that you just happen to speak, say, Navajo when circumstances require it. You are not learning the language spontaneously but revealing a hitherto unmentioned fact about your Agent.

By and large, Interpersonal abilities are largely moot without a language in common.

Forensics (Technical)

You perform autopsies on deceased subjects to determine their cause and circumstances of death. You can use skeletal evidence to reconstruct the physical details (age, sex, medical condition, sometimes the occupation) of the deceased.

Among other things, your examination can discern:

△ the nature of the weapon or weapons used on the victim, if any

△ the approximate time of death

△ the presence of intoxicants or other foreign substances in the bloodstream or on the skin

△ the contents of the victim's last meal

△ a reconstructed sequence of events leading to the victim's death, based on the arrangement of wounds on the body

Fringe Science (Technical)

You're an expert in the experimental, eccentric, and just plain impossible reaches of science, from UFO lore to parapsychology to orgone. You can:

△ identify the fringe theory behind a research program from its scribbled notes and scrawled diagrams

△ guess the intended effect of an experiment from its physical aftermath

△ fake a psychic communication, UFO contact, or similar

△ conduct a rigorous parapsychological experiment if you have a rating in Psychotherapy

△ conduct a rigorous paraphysical experiment if you have a rating in Physics

△ supply historical facts and anecdotes concerning various fringe scientists, cryptids, UFO sightings, conspiracy theories, etc.

△ identify fringe spoor — UFO burn marks, crop circles, Bigfoot prints — as the work of hoaxers or as something so far unexplained

This ability does not encompass the alien gods and beings covered by the Unnatural (p. 062).

This ability does not allow you to use psychic powers or construct weird devices. You may believe in the fringe or not; the skill functions just as well in either case.

This ability covers the pseudoscientific; the supernatural falls under Occult. Some areas of weirdness, such as Atlantis or ley lines, may fall under both abilities at the Handler's discretion.

History (Academic)

You're an expert in recorded human history, with an emphasis on its political, military, economic, and technological developments. You are also an expert in the tools historians use: documents and books. You can:

△ recognize obscure historical allusions

△ recall important or relevant events in a given country, city, or region

△ identify ancient languages and scripts

△ perform textual analysis on a manuscript or book to date it or identify the author

△ determine the age of a document

△ tell where and when an object made during historical times was fashioned

△ identify the period of an article of dress or costume

HUMINT
(Interpersonal)

Technically, Human Intelligence (HUMINT) is intelligence gathered *from* a human source. This ability instead covers intelligence gathered *about* a human subject. To use HUMINT you must directly observe the target. This allows you to:

△ notice patterns of interaction and thus gauge potential Interpersonal susceptibilities

△ cultivate sources of information about the subject

△ deduce a subject's emotional makeup and physical confidence from their body language

If you speak to the subject, you can:

△ subtly pump them for information, if their suspicions are not already aroused

△ detect topics they would rather avoid

△ identify a bluff

△ cold-read a mark for fortune-telling scams, phony séances or mentalist acts, impersonations, and the like

△ recognize signs of nervousness, hostility, or suspicion, even if concealed behind a veil of courtesy or bland bureaucracy

△ recognize signs of brainwashing or coercion

△ recognize signs of dishonesty and evasion, and determine whether they are lying to you; with a spend, you can make a decent guess about their motives for lying

This ability does not allow you to determine what the subject is lying about, or to see through their lies to the underlying truth. It does not necessarily distinguish between someone telling the truth and someone who is honestly mistaken about the topic.

Certain individuals — con men, actors, expert deep-cover agents, professional gamblers, and similar — may be so adept at lying that they never set off your built-in lie detector, or overload it by being "always on." Some people believe their own falsehoods. Psychopathic and sociopathic personality types and brainwashed cultists lie reflexively and without shame, depriving you of the telltale tics and gestures you use to sense when a person is deceiving you. Many of those tainted by the unnatural will occasionally "read wrong," but will similarly fail to send any useful signals to a human watcher.

This ability replaces, and somewhat expands upon, the familiar GUMSHOE ability Assess Honesty/ Bullshit Detector.

Inspiration
(Interpersonal)

You gain assistance, cooperation, and information from your subjects by appealing to their better selves. After a few moments of interaction you intuitively sense the positive values they hold dearest, then invoke them in a brief but stirring speech. Depending on the subject, you might invoke her:

△ patriotism and love of country

△ religious beliefs

△ devotion to the scientific method

△ belief in peace, love, justice, or another abstract virtue

△ ideological predilections

△ team or unit spirit

This ability also broadly covers leadership, especially of a military unit, police squad, or team of federal agents. With it, you can gain their trust and disciplined obedience, at least until the tentacles come out.

WHY NO LYING ABILITY?

Unlike many other RPG rules sets, GUMSHOE does not treat lying as an ability unto itself. Instead characters employ it as a tactic while using any of the various interpersonal abilities. With Cop Talk, you tell detectives what they want to hear. A little Flattery convinces the attractive stranger that you admire her politics. Using Interrogation, you convince suspects that you're really just trying to help them out, and so on. There's a little bit of deception in nearly every successful interpersonal interaction — at least that's how it works for DELTA GREEN.

Interrogation (Interpersonal)

You extract information from subjects fearful of your authority, cruelty, or power. To fully use this ability, you must place the target in custody, or in a situation evocative of constraint and punishment. You might borrow an interrogation room from local cops, or construct a makeshift one in a jungle tent.

Through threats, persistence, and the occasional deception, you grad- ually establish a bond with your targets, convincing them to identify with you psychologically, and that giving up the information you seek — even if it's a confession — is their only remaining option.

As a trained interrogator, you can:

△ prepare a room for an interrogation session
△ assess what lines of attack might work best on an individual subject
△ recognize someone who's been professionally trained to resist interrogation
△ put someone on the defensive in an ordinary conversation
△ recognize an unwilling or accidental admission of the truth
△ recognize the signs of torture, both physical and psychological
△ know the laws regarding treatment of prisoners of war or criminal suspects

Intimidation (Interpersonal)

You elicit cooperation from targets by seeming physically imposing, invading their personal space, and adopting a psychologically commanding manner. Intimidation may involve implied or direct threats of physical violence, but is just as often an act of mental dominance such as a staredown or a well-directed taunt. You can:

△ gain information
△ inspire the target to leave the area
△ anger the target into involuntarily revealing information
△ quell a target's desire to attempt violence against you or others

Law (Academic)

You know the criminal and civil laws of your home jurisdiction well, and are broadly acquainted with foreign legal systems. At a rating of 2 or more, you may be (or impersonate) a bar-certified attorney. You can:

△ assess the legal risks attendant on any course of action
△ notice unusual or dangerous language in a legal document or contract
△ understand lawyerly jargon
△ argue with police, JAGs, and prosecutors

Medicine (Academic)

You study human illnesses of the body, and may be broadly acquainted with veterinary medicine as well. At a rating of 2 or more, you may have a medical license. You can:

△ diagnose diseases, poisonings, and other ailments
△ prescribe treatment for a treatable condition
△ deliver a baby or abort a fetus
△ identify the extent and cause of an unconscious person's trauma
△ detect when a person is suffering from a physically debilitating condition such as drug addiction, pregnancy, or malnutrition
△ establish a person's general level of health
△ use common medical equipment such as X-ray machines
△ identify medical abnormalities
△ understand medical jargon

At the Handler's discretion, you may be trained in a more complex specialty, as well as the sort of general practice indicated here. The Handler may or may not allow very elementary Forensics ("the killer used a blunt instrument; death was instantaneous") with this ability.

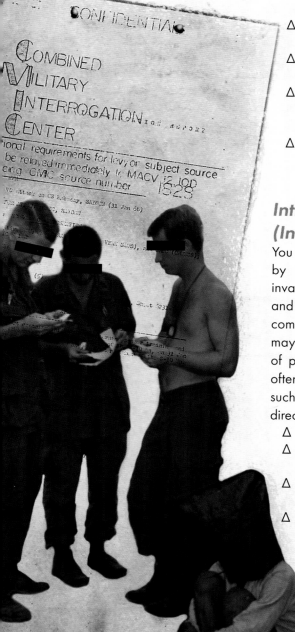

Military Science (Academic)

You are a student of warfare, probably trained as such in a military academy. This expertise includes knowledge of military history, strategy and tactics, and the weapons, technologies, and engineering techniques of the battlefield. You can:

- △ identify uniforms and insignia
- △ identify an unknown military or paramilitary force from the weapons or tactics they use
- △ deduce a soldier's training and assignment history from his demeanor and use of slang and jargon
- △ spot professional soldiers by their gait and posture, even in civilian clothing
- △ spot weaknesses in an enemy's fortifications or tactics
- △ write a convincing after-action report
- △ note relationships between objects and damage at the scene of a firefight or battle, reconstructing sequences of events

Negotiation (Interpersonal)

You are an expert in making deals with others, convincing them that the best arrangement for you is also the best for them. You can:

- △ haggle for goods and services
- △ gauge likely prices of items, including what someone else will pay for them
- △ successfully and politely bribe a corrupt official or policeman
- △ mediate hostage situations or diplomatic crises
- △ sell something to a potential buyer
- △ swap favors or information with others

Notice (Technical)

You are adept at casing a scene and at finding important clues. This is the generic ability for spotting a hidden clue, general situational awareness, or noticing a non-threatening visual anomaly. You can:

- △ spot hidden objects or objects of interest (including bullet casings under a car, or drops of blood behind the desk) at a crime scene or other investigation site
- △ case a location to spot guards, cameras, rear entrances, security procedures, potential police response, weapon mounts, etc.
- △ note entrances and exits from rooms you're in, and who's near them
- △ notice signs of a previous search of the location
- △ find and transfer fingerprints, fiber evidence, or other physical clues in a scene

Spotting enemy surveillance or monitoring a location uses Stealth; sensing a sniper lurking in the shadows uses Sense Trouble. Searching for a deliberately hidden object that is *not* a core clue uses Conceal.

Occult (Academic)

You're an expert in the historical study of magic, superstition, and sorcery from the Stone Age to the present. You can:

- △ identify the cultural traditions informing a ritual by examining its physical aftermath
- △ guess the intended effect of a ritual from its physical aftermath
- △ fake a fortune-telling session, séance, or other occult activity
- △ read and cast a horoscope
- △ supply historical facts and anecdotes concerning various occult traditions, cult groups, demons, and legends
- △ identify occult paraphernalia, grimoires, symbols, and codes
- △ identify occult activities as the work of informed practitioners or teenage thrill-seekers

This ability does not encompass the alien gods and beings covered by the Unnatural (p. 062).

This ability does not allow you to work magic or summon supernatural entities. You may believe in the occult or not; the skill functions just as well in either case.

Pharmacy (Technical)

You are able to identify and compound drugs and medicines. You can:

△ identify drugs and potions, and recognize their side-effects and contraindications

△ identify a drug addict after a brief interaction

△ identify poisons and determine antidotes

△ identify and successfully harvest hallucinogenic or narcotic plants and fungi

△ given the raw materials, manufacture morphine, heroin, cocaine, LSD, amphetamines, barbiturates, and other controlled substances

Photography (Technical)

You are proficient in the use of cameras, including still, television, and motion-picture photography. You can:

△ take useful visual records of crime scenes, surveillance targets, or riots

△ load and operate aircraft gun or spy cameras

△ take pictures covertly and plant hidden cameras for surveillance

△ develop film or plates, and blow up or enhance hidden details in photographs to a seemingly implausible degree

△ interpret aerial and satellite photography

△ use filters and lights to capture images only visible in infrared or ultraviolet

△ spot manual retouching or camera trickery in a photographic image or negative

△ take trick photographs using double exposures and other methods

△ realistically retouch and manipulate photographic negatives

Physics (Technical)

You study the fundamental forces of the universe: pressure, electromagnetism, thermodynamics, motion, gravity, optics, and radioactivity. You can:

△ design or refit experimental machinery to test, detect, or manipulate physical forces and energies

△ obtain and operate expensive or obscure pieces of laboratory equipment such as Geiger counters, lasers, cloud chambers, etc.

△ understand and apply advanced mathematics, including non-Euclidean geometries

△ attempt to comprehend advanced or alien technologies

△ calculate ballistic trajectories

Building experimental machinery is a matter for Mechanics, not Physics, although some such devices (especially reverse-engineered alien technologies) likely also require a Physics spend to construct.

Reassurance (Interpersonal)

You get people to do what you want by putting them at ease. This may involve fast talk, genuine sympathy, or just a calming presence. You can:

△ elicit information and minor favors

△ allay fear or panic in others

△ convince frightened or worried witnesses that they saw nothing unusual

△ instill a sense of calm during a crisis

SIGINT (Technical)

You can operate electronic communications devices and surveill electronic communications to gather SIGINT (signals intelligence). Given proper equipment, you can also:

△ trace telephone calls

△ plant and monitor secret listening devices

△ monitor and interpret radar and sonar signals

△ make high-quality audio recordings

△ send and read Morse and other common telegraphic codes

△ use scramblers, tight-beam equipment, and other complex radio gear

△ perform minor repairs and maintenance on communications equipment

△ recognize the "fist" of another radiotelegrapher

Sending a message in adverse atmospheric conditions may require a spend; gathering core clues by radio never does.

Discovering a bug on someone else is often a free core clue; discovering a bug planted on yourself or your fellow Agents usually requires a 1-point spend of SIGINT or a Conceal test (see *Bugs and Bug Detection*, p. 143).

Actually tapping a phone or telex line requires an Investigative use of Mechanics. Evading electronic surveillance systems is almost always a Stealth test.

Streetwise (Interpersonal)

You know how to behave among crooks, gangsters, druggies, hookers, grifters, and other habitués of the criminal underworld. You can:

△ deploy criminal etiquette to avoid fights and conflicts

△ identify unsafe locations and dangerous people

△ recall which gang or mafia claims a given area as turf

△ deal with fences, black marketeers, drug dealers, arms runners, and so forth

△ successfully price illegal goods such as drugs, stolen items, or weapons

△ get hired for a criminal operation

△ tell when practiced criminals and con men are lying, as with HUMINT

△ gather underworld rumors

△ navigate an unfamiliar urban street layout and locate buildings without looking like a rube

△ find open manholes, dangling fire escapes, and conveniently unlocked doors

△ interact on friendly terms with the local vagrant community

△ find (or avoid) a neighborhood where you can use Streetwise to good effect

Survival (Technical)

You can survive outdoors and in the wild, possibly thanks to a rural upbringing, military training, or extensive service "in country." You can:

△ notice unusual behavior or examples of flora and fauna

△ find edible plants, hunt, and fish

△ make fire and survive outdoors at night or in bad weather

△ navigate overland, albeit more easily with a compass and a map

△ find tracks, paths, and trails

△ predict the weather

△ plan an expedition or patrol

△ track people, animals, or vehicles; includes tracking with bloodhounds, assuming you have friendly dogs available

Tradecraft (Interpersonal)

You can utilize the techniques of espionage, and talk to spies if you must hold a meet. You can:

△ set up and check a dead drop

△ spot or conduct a brush pass or car toss

△ determine which agency trained a covert operative by examining his tradecraft, surveillance methods, etc.

△ identify good places for recognition signs, cleaning passes, etc.

△ recall notorious or relevant episodes of spying, covert ops, etc.

△ gather rumors in the clandestine world

△ make contact with spies, operatives, and assets without scaring them off

△ convey information or threats elliptically without tipping off eavesdroppers

Traffic Analysis (Technical)

You know how to boil down a mass of data — raw signals intel, a tranche of phone records, or days of surveillance tapes — and extract its meaning and patterns. Given the data, you can:

△ determine which numbers in a set of phone records are calling who, when, about what

△ determine which cars in a city's traffic pattern are driving where, when, and how long they're staying there

△ find patterns in the data flow, e.g., more murders in August, or the same museum guard on duty during all the incidents

△ work out the daily (and weekly, monthly, etc.) routine of an office, military base, museum, etc. and answer questions like: When is payroll made? Who takes delivery of parcels? When does the cleaning staff arrive?

△ find anomalies in the data flow, e.g., missing records or "dogs that didn't bark"

△ find weak spots in security that follows a regular pattern

△ identify the source of information (or disinformation) by tracking its route through the system

The Unnatural

You have begun to piece together the secret rules of the real world, rather than the ignorant scrim of physics and religion. You recognize the secret names, and the truths they conceal. If you've read a DELTA GREEN case file or a confiscated tome, using this ability lets you recall any specific hints or facts from it relevant to your current situation. If you're staring at an ancient alien bas-relief, using this ability lets you perceive, with a single shocking gestalt, the horrific history it unfolds.

Using this ability costs both Sanity and Stability (see p. 070).

The primary use of this ability in the course of an investigation is to "put together the pieces" and draw upon the terrible knowledge that you have been subconsciously suppressing, achieving a horrific epiphany. The Handler provides you with the result of your intuition, sketching out the impossible implications of the events you have uncovered. (See p. 121 for further Handler guidelines for this ability.) This may not be the "solution" to the mystery, although it should allow you to aim your efforts in the right direction; at the Handler's discretion, an actual spend might provide more specific (and potentially horribly dangerous) answers.

see p. 070

WHERE IS LIBRARY USE?

Or Research, as it's called in **Night's Black Agents.** As government employees, Agents are very familiar with endless archives and musty file rooms. Handlers and players use the subject matter to guide them: locate a dig report with Archaeology, a weird obituary with HUMINT or Medicine, a case file with Law, and so on. If there really doesn't seem to be a relevant ability to the research topic, use Traffic Analysis to sift through the files or shelves until the clue falls out.

*Consider "The Dunwich Horror" to be a **Fall of DELTA GREEN** adventure. Professor Armitage has read the Necronomicon, so when he uses his ability in the Unnatural he realizes that old Whateley somehow incarnated Yog-Sothoth on Earth. In the story, he then reads Wilbur's diary to learn that he needs both a special incantation and the Powder of Ibn-Ghazi to destroy Yog-Sothoth's spawn. Had he not managed to get hold of the diary, Armitage could use the Unnatural to "intuit" that Yog-Sothoth must be made visible before he could be fully banished, and spending a point might tell him that the Powder of Ibn-Ghazi would accomplish such a task. No spend would provide the formula for the Powder, except to suggest which eldritch tome might conceal similar truths.*

General Abilities

General Abilities use a different set of rules and are measured on a different scale than Investigative Abilities. Larger General Ability pools give you more options and power in an action scene. You **roll to succeed** in a General Ability against a target Difficulty. You may **spend points** from a General Ability pool to increase your die roll, giving you a better chance of success. General Abilities refresh during the operation, but you spend them faster when things get tense.

GUMSHOE handles the two ability sets differently because they fulfill distinct narrative functions. The goal of any **Fall of DELTA GREEN** operation is to investigate, hunt, or scout for the unnatural — and then confront the alien forces behind it, or at least their servitors or cultists. That confrontation must be suspenseful, which is why General Abilities have a possibility of failure.

But the confrontation must also occur for the story to satisfy, which is why investigating the problem — in order to get to the confrontation — must succeed. A well-designed **Fall of DELTA GREEN** operation rewards players for cleverly or dramatically solving the mystery by making the confrontation more exciting, more intellectually interesting, or even more (barely) survivable. (For more on operation design, see p. 317.)

Using General Abilities Investigatively

General Abilities can also function as Investigative Abilities when used to gather a clue rather than to overcome opposition. An Agent might use Unarmed Combat, for example, investigatively to identify an unusual fighting style or spot a rigged boxing match. She might use Drive to gauge the condition or rarity of an antique car, or deduce an escape route.

Like Investigative Abilities, they function as Interpersonal abilities with people devoted to those abilities' use. An Agent can use Unarmed Combat as an Interpersonal ability to infiltrate a dojo or gymnasium, and to gather information or gossip from the clientele or managers.

Athletics

You can perform general acts of physical exertion and skill: running, jumping, swimming, throwing grenades, rappelling down the side of a building, dodging (or catching!) dangerous objects, and so on. Any physical action not covered by another ability probably falls under the purview of Athletics.

Harder to Hit

If your Athletics rating is 8 or more, your Hit Threshold, the Difficulty number your opponents use when attempting to hit you in combat, is 4. Otherwise, your Hit Threshold is 3.

Bureaucracy

You know how to navigate a bureaucratic organization, whether it's a government office or a large corporation. You know how to get what you want from it in an expeditious manner, and with a minimum of ruffled feathers.

Make a test to get a bureaucracy to do something for you: re-task a spy plane, block an opponent's dangerous mission or funding probe, authorize the rescue of a captured asset, release a classified file to you (or bury one away from someone else), send in the Rangers, or anything else. In other tests, you may try to thwart or prevent your agency or branch from doing something it has decided on: trade a prisoner, investigate missing equipment, bug a laboratory.

Difficulty 4: A standard task that you have clearance or jurisdiction for.

Difficulty 6: Something you have to pull strings to get.

Difficulty 8: Something you have no business asking.

Raise Difficulties by +1 for state or local agencies or rival divisions of your own agency, +2 for other federal agencies or military branches, and by +3 for agencies of other governments. It will often be more convenient to build Network contacts (p. 068) in other governments than to actually go through channels.

The Handler may build GMC bureaucrats who oppose you often enough to get their own pools, and set the parameters for your operations based on the results of full contests of Bureaucracy. Such powerful GMCs may also help grease the

2	24	26	28	30	32	34	36	38	40	42
0	120	130	140	150	160	170	180	190	200	210
08	118	128	137	147	157	167	177	186	196	206
07	116	126	136	146	155	165	175	185	194	204
06	115	125	134	144	154	163	173	182	192	202
05	114	124	133	143	152	162	171	181	190	200
04	113	122	132	141	151	160	169	179	188	198
02	112	121	130	140	149	158	167	17?	86	195
	111	120	129	138	147	156	166	175	184	193

wheels for the Agents – in exchange for something unpleasant in return, of course.

Bureaucracy is an ideal ability for continuing challenges (see p. 082); you make one test per operation, with a bonus or penalty depending on your performance on the mission.

Bureaucracy only refreshes at the end of an operation; it cannot be refreshed during.

Investigative Bureaucracy

In other GUMSHOE games, Bureaucracy is an Interpersonal ability. Agents can use it that way as well, to:

△ convince officials to provide sensitive or inconvenient information
△ gain credentials on false pretences
△ find the person who really knows what's going on
△ locate offices and files
△ borrow equipment or supplies
△ convince third parties subject to a bureaucracy that you have a legitimate work order or request

In general, if you need information from the bureaucracy, use this ability Investigatively; if you need action, make a test.

As always, gaining a core clue from a bureaucrat may require a great deal of patience and firmness, but it does not require a spend or test.

Conceal

You can hide things from view and conceal them from search. Your methods might include camouflage, holding items out on your person, snaking things into drawers unobserved, building secret compartments into cars or briefcases, or even altering a thing's visual signature with paint or plaster.

Among other things, you can also:

△ discover things intentionally concealed, including microphones, cameras, and bombs
△ mask an infrared or scent signature, given suitable equipment such as insulated cloth or coffee grounds
△ efficiently pat down a target or, given time, conduct a thorough strip search
△ "clean" a crime scene or safe house of evidence indicating your presence there
△ detect signs of a previous careful, professional search
△ plant a listening device, hidden camera, or bomb

Wiring or building a bug or hidden camera uses SIGINT or Mechanics. Setting a bomb uses Demolitions. Discovering a camouflaged object in a reconnaissance photograph is Photography, or possibly Military Science. Tapping a telephone line is Mechanics.

Hiding yourself, even with camouflage, is Stealth.

Discovering a hidden clue (especially a core clue) comes under Notice.

You can also use SIGINT to detect bugs and cameras, especially those aimed at other targets.

Demolitions

You are an expert in bombs, incendiaries, and booby traps. You can:

△ defuse or trigger bombs and traps
△ handle nitroglycerine, napalm, or other dangerously unstable materials with relative safety
△ given time, blow open safes or vaults without damaging the contents
△ mix explosive compounds or napalm from common chemicals
△ safely construct and detonate explosive devices or booby traps of your own
△ implode, or selectively destroy one part of, a structure with explosives
△ set a reliably hot and destructive fire

Conventional "all-purpose" explosives, especially military explosive devices, are standardized for safety and ease of handling in stress situations. Using a standard weight of plastic explosive and a detonator, a satchel charge, or thermite requires a Difficulty 3 test of Demolitions. Building a booby trap or setting a specific charge with either grenades or dynamite is much harder (Difficulty 5+).

Tossing a grenade (or a satchel charge, or a stick of burning dynamite) is an Athletics test.

Investigative Demolitions

Demolitions doubles as an Investigative Ability when used to:

△ reconstruct exploded bombs or incendiary devices
△ for any bomb (exploded or unexploded) or incendiary, determine the method and materials of the bomb-maker or arsonist, and deduce his sophistication, background, and skill
△ reconstruct burn patterns of a fire

Disguise

You can alter your own appearance, posture, and voice to be unrecognizable or inconspicuous. Disguising others in anything more complex than a floppy hat or false mustache is good only for brief periods, as posture and body language are vital components in any successful disguise.

This ability also covers selling yourself as a different person: vocal mannerisms, altered body language, dress and motion sense, and realistic-seeming reactions. (Uniforms or ID obtained with Filch – or Unarmed Combat – help.)

Successfully disguising yourself as an actual person already known to those you're interacting with is extraordinarily difficult. (*Mission: Impossible*-style face masks do not exist except among the Mi-Go.) Brief voice-only mimicry pits you against a Difficulty of 4. Face-to-face impersonation requires a successful roll against a Difficulty of 7 for every five minutes of sustained contact between you and the target of your impersonation.

Investigative Disguise

Disguise doubles as an Investigative Ability when used to:

- △ create and maintain a cover identity among the unsuspecting
- △ impersonate a generic figure, such as a security guard, waiter, or messenger
- △ briefly misrepresent yourself, such as on the telephone or in a vestibule

This Investigative use of Disguise replaces the Impersonate ability in other GUMSHOE games.

Drive

You can achieve high performance from even the least promising cars. You can:

- △ evade or conduct pursuit
- △ avoid collisions, or minimize damage from collisions
- △ successfully drive off-road without bogging down or wrecking, assuming even minimally hospitable terrain
- △ maintain high speed under unfavorable weather conditions
- △ follow another vehicle inconspicuously
- △ perform jumps, drifts, reverses, and other driving stunts
- △ spot tampering with a vehicle
- △ hotwire a car
- △ conduct emergency repairs

With 1 rating point in Drive, you have such confident mastery in all makes and models of automobile, including Jeeps, vans, and pickup trucks.

For every additional rating point in Drive, you may add an additional motor vehicle type to your repertoire, such as: motorcycles, transport trucks and semi-trailers, tanks, buses, construction equipment, snowmobiles, hovercraft, or motorboats.

Like "new" Foreign Languages, a vehicle type added at an opportune moment does not represent suddenly learning to drive a bulldozer, but simply previous training or retroactive experience you've never had call to mention until now.

For aircraft and most watercraft, use Pilot (p. 068).

Filch

Your nimble fingers allow you to unobtrusively manipulate small objects. You can:

- △ pilfer small items from desks, counters, crime scenes, or museum displays, even under the supposedly watchful eyes of a guard or policeman
- △ walk out openly with a briefly unguarded bulky and low-value item as if you were entitled to it; e.g., steal a security guard uniform from the locker room
- △ given a diversion, lift almost anything you can carry under your clothing; e.g., cut a painting out of its frame and stuff it under your jacket
- △ pick pockets
- △ slip cell keys from guards' belts, lift ID badges from lapels, etc.
- △ plant objects on unsuspecting targets
- △ switch two similar objects (like two briefcases) without being noticed

Note that disarming alarms or picking locks requires a Mechanics or Stealth test.

Firearms

You are adept with rifles, submachine guns, pistols, and other personal small arms, including their field stripping, repair, and identification. This ability also, for game-mechanical simplicity, covers crossbows.

Crew-served weapons, machine guns, and artillery require Heavy Weapons.

You can spend 2 points from your Firearms pool to attempt to hit a target at Long range with a pistol, or at up to 500 yards with a rifle. This spend does not adjust your roll; it makes it possible in the first place. (See *Extended Range*, p. 098.)

First Aid

You can perform first aid on sick or injured individuals. For every 1 First Aid point you spend, you heal 2 points of damage to others or 1 point to yourself. Even with 0 points left in your First Aid pool, you can restore 1 Health point per scene to another character or yourself.

For other healing rules, see p. 126.

Health

Health is an abstract, general indicator of your survivability. It includes your ability to avoid lasting damage from a fight, and measures your ability to sustain injuries, resist infection, and survive the effects of toxins. When you get hit in the course of combat, your Health pool is diminished. A higher Health pool allows you to stay in the fight longer before succumbing to your injuries.

In game-mechanical terms, Health represents your ability to continue to act in a scene, often in a fight scene.

When your Health pool is depleted, you may be dazed, exhausted, wounded, or monster bait. For more about this, see *Injury and Death* (p. 094).

You begin with 4 free rating points in Health.

Heavy Weapons

You are trained on crew-served weapons: mortars, rocket launchers, machine guns, and artillery. You can aim, fire, and reload the guns on a fighting vehicle, tank, or aircraft, but without a slot in Drive or Pilot you cannot operate the vehicle itself.

Hypergeometry

Knowledge of the true structure of the universe, and the ability to manipulate it. In other words, "magic."

No Agent can begin the game with points in Hypergeometry. Hypergeometric potential (p. 197) and access to a source of hypergeometric knowledge are prerequisites for gaining points in Hypergeometry.

See *Hypergeometry* (pp. 197–207) for more details.

Mechanics

You're good at building, repairing, operating, and disabling mechanical, electrical, or electronic devices from catapults to hi-fis to key parts of a city's power grid. Given the right components, you can create jury-rigged devices, booby traps (see p. 140), or weapons from odd bits of scrap.

This ability also encompasses lockpicking, safe-cracking, and similar skills.

Investigative Mechanics

Mechanics doubles as an Investigative Ability when used to:

△ evaluate the quality of workmanship used to create an item

△ discover a hidden panel or compartment in a built object

△ determine the function of a given gadget

△ tap telephone lines

△ pick a lock to obtain a clue on the other side of it

△ spot junction boxes, transformers, or other elements of an electrical power system

△ spot non-fatal tampering with or sabotage of a device

△ use any mechanical, electrical, or electronic device in good repair as intended for an investigative (clue-gathering) purpose

Melee Weapons

You are skilled in the use of personal hand weapons such as knives, swords, axes, or nightsticks. This ability covers most thrown melee weapons such as spears, throwing knives, etc.

Throwing grenades falls under Athletics.

Using brass knuckles, a sap, or a roll of coins balled in your fist is an Unarmed Combat attack. Anything else (including cold-cocking someone with the butt of a gun) falls under Melee Weapons.

Network

This ability represents your network of professional contacts. At any time, you may reveal or remember the existence of a member of your network in a given city, firebase, or the like. Assign this contact his own pool of points taken from your unassigned Network pool; that contact's capacity to locate safe houses or guns, provide false papers, and so forth will resolve as a test of that contact's pool against a Difficulty generally dependent on the local jurisdiction. Finding an AK-47 assault rifle in Thailand is easier than finding one in Tribeca; crossing the border into Costa Rica is easier than crossing into Czechoslovakia.

Once assigned, those points remain with your Network contact. They do not refresh.

Your Network contacts are not necessarily DELTA GREEN friendlies, and may not even know that you work for the government. They are simply people from before the campaign started who owe you or are otherwise disposed to help you out.

Once a contact has exhausted his pool, you have exhausted your favors. If you had him do something dangerous, he may even be killed by the opposition. You may wind up using experience points to keep useful contacts alive.

Every player character begins with 5 free points in Network. Network does not refresh during an operation.

Investigative Network

Network contacts don't just do things for you; they can also *know* things for you. You might know someone fired from the Bureau but with a good memory for case files, or a specialist at Yale who briefed you on a topic, or a source you ran last decade who knows the Burmese heroin smuggling scene intimately. Think of investigative uses of Network as a "wild card" ability: the result might be a phone call, a face-to-face meet, or a physical copy of an asset's report routed through interoffice mail. Investigative uses of Network can also resemble investigative spends on Bureaucracy, HUMINT, Streetwise, Tradecraft, or even, in some campaigns, Fringe Science or Occult.

This is a great tool to use when you're stuck. You usually can't ask a Network contact "Who's behind these killings?" but you can ask "Who investigated these killings four years ago, and what did they find out, and what happened to them?" Decide what you need to know, determine how much of that kind of information might be available to anyone outside the opposition, and create a Network contact whose business it is to know such things. In general, an investigative Network contact provides a direction to search, another source to shake down, or otherwise narrows down the field of speculation.

If you tap a Network contact for information instead of action, spend 1 point from that contact's pool. If it's a real mother lode or red-hot intelligence, the Handler may charge you 2 points; use the difference between a 1-point and 2-point investigative spend as a guideline (see p. 078). The Handler will never charge you for a core clue delivered by a Network contact.

You can use the pool points of a single Network contact for both information and action, of course.

Pilot

Although almost anyone can paddle a canoe or even row a dinghy, you can pilot small boats (motorboats, sailboats, Zodiacs) or single-engine light aircraft (Cessna 172 or the equivalent) with professional aplomb and serene confidence. You can:

△ evade or conduct pursuit
△ anticipate bad weather
△ avoid crashes, or minimize damage from crashes
△ spot tampering with a vehicle
△ navigate by compass or the stars, read maps, and maintain a sense of direction
△ maintain high speed under unfavorable weather conditions
△ perform dives, spins, rolls, and other piloting stunts
△ land on an aircraft carrier or other confined space
△ conduct emergency repairs
△ A rating of 1 in Pilot allows you to select either small boats or single-engine light aircraft.

For every additional rating point in Pilot, you may add an additional air or water vehicle type to your repertoire, such as: small boats, single-engine light aircraft, barges and tugs, helicopters, yachts, multi-engine jets, hang gliders, cargo ships, and so on. You may choose exotic types, like airships, midget submarines, and fighter jets, although it's best to wait until you actually have access to one to fill the slot. Like the additional vehicles available with extra points in Drive, you may add them opportunistically in play if you have unassigned points.

Preparedness

You expertly anticipate the needs of any operation by packing a kit efficiently arranged with necessary gear. Assuming you have immediate access to your kit, you can produce whatever object the team needs to overcome an obstacle. You make a simple test (p. 080); if you succeed, you have the item you want. You needn't do this in advance of the adventure, but can dig into your kit bag (provided you're able to get to it) as the need arises.

Items of obvious utility to a covert operation or investigation do not require a test. These include but are not limited to: weapons, detonators, flashlights, binoculars, batteries, gloves, handcuffs, duct tape, rations, cigarettes and lighters, Swiss Army knives, pencils, and magnifying glasses.

Other abilities imply the possession of basic gear suitable to their core tasks. Agents with First Aid or Medicine have their own first aid kits or medical bags; Photographers come with cameras. If you have Firearms, you have a gun, Mechanics, you have a crowbar, and so on. Preparedness does not intrude into their territory. It covers general-purpose investigative equipment, plus oddball items — a Ouija board, a baseball, a tube of cyanoacrylate adhesive, a gas mask — that suddenly come in handy in the course of the story.

The traditional "rappelling line just long enough to get me down off this building" is a classic Preparedness feat of the spy thriller genre; having it in your pack might be Difficulty 3, while having it coiled, hooked on your belt with a carabiner, and ready to go with a jump is Difficulty 6.

The sorts of items you can produce at a moment's notice depend not on your rating or pool, but on narrative credibility. If the Handler determines that your possession of an item would seem ludicrous, anachronistic, or out of genre, you don't get to roll for it. You simply don't have it. Any item which elicits a laugh from the group when suggested is probably out of bounds.

Inappropriate use of the Preparedness ability is like pornography. Your Handler will know it when she sees it.

Scrounging

The Preparedness ability also covers scrounging, the gift for finding and liberating unlikely items nearby, especially in a military context. Most scrounged items are too large and bulky to be carried, unlike regular Preparedness items. Scrounging is a plausible way to get a retry (p. 081) on a Preparedness roll: "I didn't have a Ouija board *on me*, but I'll bet I can scrounge one up around here." Scrounging works best in a larger installation: a university, an air base, a laboratory campus, a warehouse, etc.

Make a Preparedness test to, e.g., remember where you saw a forklift (and its keys) on campus, or locate a 16mm film projector on a firebase. The test covers finding the item, securing it, and bringing it back to the rest of the team (unless, and only unless, active opposition moves the story forward). Depending on the environment, scrounging tests of Preparedness are at regular Difficulty or even one or two levels easier.

Psychotherapy

You can provide comfort, perspective, and solace to the mentally troubled. You can treat mental disorders in the short or long term, but you cannot use Psychotherapy on yourself. For specific rules mechanics, see p. 120 and p. 129.

Investigative Psychotherapy

Psychotherapy doubles as an Investigative Ability when used to:

△ diagnose mental illness
△ prescribe treatment for a treatable condition
△ identify the extent and cause of a mentally ill person's trauma
△ differentiate between an episode brought on by drugs and one brought on by a mental disorder
△ establish a person's general level of mental health
△ understand psychological jargon

Ride

Although staying on a walking horse (or mule or donkey) on flat terrain is relatively easy, you are a gifted equestrian. You can:

△ evade or conduct mounted pursuit

△ care for, groom, shoe, and stable mounts

△ maintain, prepare, and use riding gear such as saddles and bridles

△ safely and humanely load pack animals

△ calm a nervous riding animal

△ drive a horse-drawn wagon or cart

△ wield a weapon while riding

With 1 rating point in Ride you can expertly ride or harness a horse, mule, or donkey. For every 2 additional rating points in Ride you may add one additional animal: camel, water buffalo or ox, reindeer, yak, or elephant.

You may not add or ride monsters.

Sanity

Exposure to the truly unnatural shatters the core of the human psyche by stripping away all illusions of human significance, benign nature, and loving God, leaving nothing but the terrifying vistas of stark, cosmic nihilism. Your Sanity rating indicates the degree to which you can sustain belief in any fundamental human concerns whatsoever. Unlike other abilities, you never test your Sanity or spend points from your Sanity pool. They are leached away by the Outside.

Once your Sanity reaches 0, your beliefs – and what you used to consider your soul – have been

completely corroded beyond repair. In game terms, your Agent becomes a GMC under the Handler's control. He may be institutionalized, doped in an alley – or a willing servitor of the Great Old Ones.

Sanity and Stability are not correlated: you may barely cling to rationality by your fingernails (Sanity 1) but present a well-scrubbed, by-the-book image to not just your partners but yourself, or consider yourself inured to further shocks, or maintain a high Stability rating in any other way you decide to play your Agent.

The Unnatural Ability and Sanity

If you have any rating at all in the Unnatural ability (p. 062), your Sanity rating can never be higher than 10 minus your rating in that ability. (If you know nothing about the unnatural, your Sanity can be as high as you care to buy it.) For a longer-term, more survivable, or more highly colored game, the Handler may wish to adjust this ceiling upward, or shift it downward for a shorter, deadlier, or starker game. (Further rules for Sanity appear on p. 070.)

You get Sanity 5 for free.

Sense Trouble

This ability allows you to perceive (either with sight or other senses) potential hazards to yourself or others. For example, you can:

- △ hear the click of a safety being taken off
- △ see a flittering shape cross the moon
- △ smell the charnel reek of a ghoul's breath in the windowless warehouse
- △ notice the gill slits peeking out of the captain's uniform collar
- △ have a bad feeling about that clearing in the seemingly empty jungle trail

Players never know the Difficulty numbers for Sense Trouble before deciding how many points to spend, even in games where Handlers generously inform the players of other Difficulty numbers. Even a failed roll allows the group the sense that something is amiss; they just don't know exactly what this is. Think of it as the tabletop equivalent of eerie music in a horror movie.

The Handler should never require the use of this General Ability to find clues to the problem at hand. Instead, use Investigative Abilities, defaulting to Notice when no ability seems more appropriate. Sense Trouble is for a operation's action-oriented sequences. In short, if not seeing something will get you attacked, it's Sense Trouble.

Sense Trouble can also be used as the ability to specifically locate the source of an already-discovered problem: the ticking bomb, the concealed sniper, the soul-drinking rune.

Stability

Jarring or stressful events can exert a damaging, long-lasting psychological toll. Confrontation with monsters or other unnatural phenomena might provoke an outright mental breakdown, as might a night attack by the Viet Cong or a bad drug trip. Your Stability rating indicates your resistance to mental trauma and psychic attack, along with general willpower and self-possession.

Although losing Sanity can decrease Stability, the two are not directly correlated. A Sanity 0 cultist might be a gibbering backwoods cannibal (with a similarly low Stability) or an avuncular professor with a Stability higher than that of any of the Agents who seek to expose him.

All player characters start with Stability 4 for free.

See p. 113 for more on Stability loss and other mechanics.

Stealth

You can hide in shadows or cover, move silently, and enter places unseen by guards or alarms. You can also:

- △ pick small locks (including handcuff locks)
- △ deactivate or evade security systems
- △ find suitable places for forced entry, and use them
- △ conduct inconspicuous surveillance of a target, or guide a team of watchers
- △ follow a target on foot unnoticed
- △ blend into the background or into a crowd

- △ listen at doors or windows without being overheard yourself
- △ shake pursuers on foot or evade surveillance

Spotting a tail or other non-electronic surveillance of yourself might be Notice or Stealth (if spotting the tail probably won't lead to combat) or Sense Trouble (if it will lead to combat); the Handler should use her best judgment.

Picking a large, complex, or difficult lock uses Mechanics.

Following a target in a vehicle uses Drive. To outrun a pursuer, use Athletics.

This ability combines the Infiltration and Surveillance abilities found in other GUMSHOE games.

Unarmed Combat

Hold your own in a hand-to-hand fight, whether you wish to kill, knock out, restrain, or evade your opponent. This ability covers all sorts of unarmed combat, from judo matches to bar brawls to muy thai kickboxing bouts.

Using brass knuckles, a sap, or a roll of coins balled in your fist is an Unarmed Combat attack. Using anything else is a Melee Weapons attack.

① Grasp the opponent by his lapel

Optional Rule: Special Training

Some equipment or specific skills require specialized training that not everyone with a given ability can (or does) receive. With special training, your Agent can recognize specialized clues and do something new, unique, or technically complex with an existing ability.

The default rule for special training is that the special training ability functions both as an Investigative Ability on that subject and as a bonus to General tests of abilities while using that trained skill. For example, an Agent with SCUBA special training can recognize a Soviet aqualung or spot tampering with a dive set (Investigative), and get a +2 bonus on Athletics tests of swimming with SCUBA equipment (General).

In relevant General Ability contests, an Agent with special training takes contest advantage (p. 086) rather than the bonus.

In some cases – space suit use or cheating at cards, for example – characters *without* special training are at a +2 to Difficulty on tests, while those with special training make ability tests as normal. In a few cases – clinical hypnosis or surgery, for example – it might be sheerly impossible to do something without special training.

Where needed, the Handler should adjudicate specific cases for various special training skills.

Examples of Special Training

Here are a few examples of special training skills. The General Ability that special training likely modifies appears in parentheses.

△ Astronautics (Pilot)
△ Brush Pass/Pickpocket (Filch; -2 to observers' Alertness Modifier to notice)
△ Card Cheating (Filch)
△ Clinical Hypnosis (Psychotherapy)
△ Computer Programming (Bureaucracy, Stealth)
△ Deep knowledge of a particular subculture, tribe, or community (acts as Agency for, e.g., Montagnard tribesmen or the Mafia)
△ Electronic Surveillance Devices (Conceal, Mechanics)
△ Escape Artist (Athletics, Stealth)
△ Foot Surveillance (Stealth)
△ Forgery (Disguise, Network; makes many investigative approaches possible at all)
△ Freemasonry (Network)
△ Guard Dog Handling (Stealth, or perhaps Preparedness to have a sedative-laden steak)
△ Higher Mathematics (Hypergeometry, possibly Heavy Weapons and Mechanics)
△ Jungle Warfare (Sense Trouble, Stealth; combat ability on the first round of combat only)
△ Lockpicking (Mechanics, Stealth)
△ NATO Liaison (Bureaucracy)
△ Nuclear Weapons (Demolitions)
△ Parachuting (Athletics)
△ SCUBA (Athletics, Melee Combat)
△ Skiing (Athletics)
△ Space Suit (Athletics)
△ Surgery (First Aid)
△ Tanker (Drive, Heavy Weapons)
△ U-2 Spy Plane (Pilot)
△ Vehicular Surveillance (Drive)
△ Yale Degree (Network)

Note that some of these special training skills (e.g., Electronic Surveillance Devices, Lockpicking) are already listed as part of an ability's core competency (SIGINT and Mechanics, respectively) or as a possible specialization (Forgery and Art). Handlers can decide whether to require special training for such skills (removing them from the scope of "generic" ability) or simply allow the Agent with special training in such skills to take the spotlight and the bonus.

Note that vehicle special training skills still require an assigned slot in Drive or Pilot; Tanker requires the Agent assign a Drive slot to tanks; U-2 Spy Plane requires the Agent assign a Pilot slot to single-jet aircraft (not fighter jets).

SPECIAL TRAINING COURSE

If you can't justify already having special training in a skill, or the Handler wants to raise the cost of adding new special training skills in the game, you have to use your time between operations (p. 128) on a special training course.

This reduces one non-DELTA GREEN Bond by 1 as you neglect other responsibilities to focus your time on the course.

Gaining Special Training

Special training, by and large, comes from the Agent's military or federal service. An Agent with a Special Forces background (p. 029) might have Parachuting as an Army Ranger, or SCUBA as a Navy SEAL, for example. Handlers using special training skills should allow each Agent to take one special training skill for free, based on his Department or other background.

If the Handler decides to charge for special training, or an Agent wants a second special training skill, the cost for each special training skill is 2 build points. The Handler may allow an Agent to pick up special training between operations using experience points, either as a "refresher" of something she already knew or as a newly trained skill (see box).

Special Weapons Training

Getting special training in a weapon is a different matter. You may not take special weapons training for free; the Handler might not even allow special weapons training at all.

You can spend 6 build points to grant your Agent special training in one particular make of firearm: for example, a Walther PPK, M40 sniper rifle, or Uzi submachine gun. (When taking this option during character creation, these build points must come from your budget of General build points.) In your hands, this weapon increases its damage by +1. A light firearm carries a damage value of d+1, while a heavy firearm does d+2. Against that, only the first attack you make with it in any given combat gains a +2 Firearms special training ability test bonus.

This applies not only to the particular weapon you own, but to all other weapons of that exact make. If you have special weapons training in the Browning Hi-Power 9mm and your own weapon is confiscated by the Cuban militia, the replacement BHP you later acquire from an MI-6 contact in Mexico City still provides you the first-attack bonus and enhanced damage rating.

You may take special training in one light and one heavy firearm.

Melee Weapons and Special Weapons Training

You can also spend 6 build points to grant your Agent special training in one particular make of melee weapon: for example, a switchblade, recurve longbow, garrote, or a kukri. The rules above apply.

You may take special training in one type of knife and one other make of melee weapon.

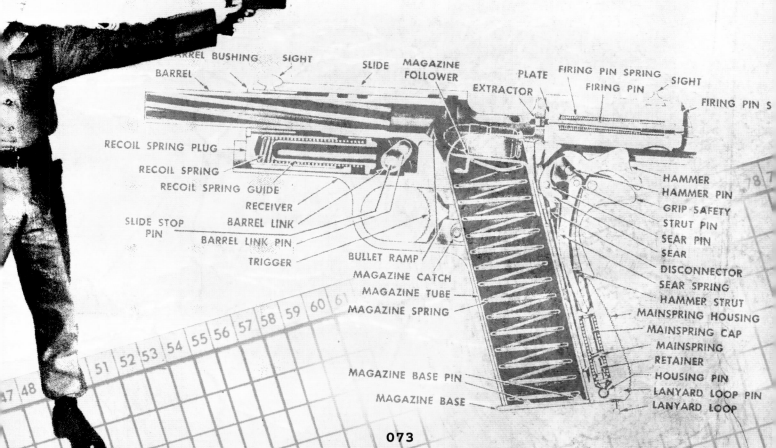

"It occurred to us, too, that our
venture was far from safe, for in
what strength the thing might appear
no one could tell. But we deemed the
game worth the hazard, and embarked
on it alone and unhesitatingly..."

— H.P. Lovecraft, "The Shunned House"

RULES OF THE GAME

The Fall of DELTA GREEN occurs in a world where everyone — not just the federal government — believes that problems have solutions, that the world means something, and that working together we are greater than we are alone.

This is a lie. The solutions, whether of science and schematics, or of samadhi and sinsemilla, all erode to the bedrock of true reality: a malign universe, which when discovered ushers in disintegration and chaos. Beneath the gray flannel suits, behind the tie-dye, humans are terrified primates aching to howl and glory in a holocaust of chaos. And worse things wait to feast on those squalling semi-apes, to eel through the dimensions and drown everything.

Welcome to the truth.

The dice represent this uncaring cosmos where plans and ideals, peace and love, matter less than a single atom drifting in the galaxy. All you can do is rage against doom, burn out your mind and body and damn your nonexistent soul keeping your family, your country, your planet, ignorant and safe for one more day.

Here's how the game works.

Clues, Spends, and Tests

The GUMSHOE engine, which powers **The Fall of DELTA GREEN** rules, separates finding information from confronting its usually horrific consequences. In law enforcement and intelligence work, agents are awash in facts and leads; they must piece them together to uncover the other side's operations and to plan a counter to them.

In a GUMSHOE game, information is only withheld when it makes the story more interesting – a stonewall from a State Department lawyer, or a witness dead when the Agents come back for another question, or a Viet Cong cadre camped at the temple site. In GUMSHOE terms, the Agents are not trying to get an available clue and failing, the failure itself is the clue: the diplomat's stonewall is a Bureaucracy clue that State is somehow involved, the dead witness provides information on his killers' methods via Forensics. The VC aren't even withholding information, just adding a little challenge: if you can get a photograph of the ruins by research or surveillance (or distract Charlie in a firefight), Archaeology still spots the squid-idol relief.

Of course part of the fun is saying things like "Karachi Station product shows unusual Soviet radar activity along the Afghan border" or "That chicken feed we planted at the NATO conference showed up in Prague today, so General Schemann's office is the leak" or "Word on the street is that something heavy is going down tonight in the park." You can still say, and do, all of those things in **The Fall of DELTA GREEN**. It's just that GUMSHOE doesn't make you roll to succeed in doing them: those are automatic successes with (in the above examples) SIGINT, Traffic Analysis, and Streetwise. But what do you do with that intel? What plan do you foil? What strike do you launch? The action really starts after the Agents gather the clues.

DELTA GREEN operations are not about trying to find clues. They are about correlating and interpreting the clues you will find.

Discovering the obscene truth behind the scenes is difficult and traumatic enough without someone hiding half the pieces from the players.

TALKIN' BOUT MY SPECULATION

Investigative scenarios often bog down into speculative debate between players about what *could be* happening. Many things *can* be happening, but only one thing *is*. If more than one possible explanation ties together the clues you have so far, you need more clues.

Whenever you get stuck, **get out and gather more information.**

As a Handler, meandering speculation is a sign that you need to throw more information at the players — don't be stingy about it, particularly for the first few operations of a campaign.

Gathering Clues

Gathering clues is simple. All you have to do is:

△ get yourself into a scene where relevant information can be gathered,

△ have the right ability to discover the clue, and

△ tell the Handler that you're using it.

As long as you do these three things, you will never fail to gain a piece of necessary information. *It is never dependent on a die roll.* If you ask for it, you will get it.

DEDICATED POOL POINTS

Occasionally, the Handler may give you extra pool points you can use in a given circumstance or on a given subject. These are called **dedicated pool points,** and usually come from reading books of lore, sudden communion with alien perceptions, mental illness, or other specialized stimuli. In most cases, dedicated pool points stack on top of your rating. For example, if you have an Archaeology rating of 2, and you read a tome granting you 2 dedicated pool points for Valusian ruins, you have 4 points you can spend on Archaeology, but 2 of them can only be spent investigating the relics and artifacts of that ancient serpent-folk kingdom.

In a way this is what the rules already do when, for example, they separate Cop Talk from Reassurance, but slicing abilities too thinly makes it hard to build competent Agents.

You can specify exactly what you intend to achieve: "I use Chemistry to test the blood sample for iridium."

You can ask in general: "I dissect the body." The Handler knows you have Forensics, and you get the clue.

You can speculate: "Is the witness on acid? I have Pharmacy."

You can prompt: "I have Art, is that painting weird?"

You can go fishing: "I use Anthropology to find a respected priest in the village who's worried about the disappearances." You sensibly guess that the town is infested, but you don't want to waste time going from GMC to GMC trying to read the Handler's mind and figure out which one contains the magic plot pellet. Nor should you. In this example, if the Handler planned on having the local police chief provide the info instead of the local priest, she can either change the information's source retroactively or tell you something like: "Before you can talk to Father Bernardo, a nervous fat man in a uniform pulls you aside. Fortunately, he's very concerned about the strangers in the desert and eager to get your help with them."

Passive and Inconspicuous Clues

Some clues would be obvious to a trained Agent immediately upon entering a scene: a fiber across the door frame, a witness who compulsively glances away during questioning. Other clues lurk in the background until an Agent's subconscious notices them: an occult sigil on a concert poster, or a concealed door in the base corridor. This often happens in places the Agent is moving through casually or doesn't regard as scenes in need of intensive searching.

The Handler provides these passive or inconspicuous clues without prompting, to the Agent with the highest pool in the relevant ability (usually Notice or HUMINT), or to the player who hasn't had a spotlight moment lately.

Simple Searches

Something even more obvious (a classified file taped to the underside of the desk, a bloodstain on the carpet) any Agent can find without any ability, just by saying "I look under the desk" or "I search the panel van."

If an ordinary person could credibly find a clue simply by looking in a specified place, the clue discovery occurs automatically. The Handler might even say something like "As a trained FBI man, you toss the mattress as a matter of routine, so of course you find the envelope under it."

The Core Clue

For each scene, the Handler designates a **core clue**. This is the clue you absolutely need to move to the next scene, and thus to complete the entire operation. Ideally, more than one Investigative Ability can provide the core clue. As a backstop, the character creation system ensures the team as a whole has access to all the Investigative Abilities.

Spends and Benefits

Certain clues allow you to gain special **benefits** by spending extra time or effort, as represented by 1 or 2 points from the relevant Investigative Ability pool. During your first few operations, the Handler will offer you the opportunity to spend additional points as you uncover these clues. After that, it's up to you to ask if there's anything to be gained by spending on a given clue. You can even propose specific ways to improve your already good result; if your suggestion is persuasive or entertaining, the Handler may award you a benefit not mentioned in her notes.

The act of spending points for benefits is called a **spend**. The Handler's operation notes may specify that you get Benefit X for a 1-point spend, or Benefit Y for a 2-point spend.

Benefits might give you:

△ **Extra information** about the situation: a Data Retrieval spend pulls up the sound of a signal knock before the conversation starts.

△ **Potential advantage** in a future contest of General Abilities: an Architecture (or Photography) spend notes a blank spot in closed-circuit camera coverage, making the Stealth test to break in that night easier.

△ **Extra time** when you speed up an action: a Forensics spend lets you run all of the blood samples you gathered in the barn in half a day, instead of half a week.

△ **Favorable reaction** from a GMC: a Flattery spend in an exclusive club lets you infiltrate a suspect's social circle and drop their name when talking to other targets.

△ **Less blowback** from a course of action: Cop Talk with the FBI agents on scene might get you a core clue for free, but a 1-point Negotiation buys the same information out of the bus driver without going into a file somewhere.

△ **Personal insight** from a flashback scene or other dramatic moment: you find the body of an old colleague; a Tradecraft spend lets you remember that he was a bulldog who never gave up on a file. Perhaps his records are still around here?

When asking you whether you want to spend for a given benefit, the Handler always tells you how much it will cost. Additional information gained provides flavor and options, but is never required to resolve the situation or move on to a new scene. It is always to your advantage to propose cool benefits to the Handler, even when she doesn't have anything specific written down or in mind yet.

Tyler's Agent, an NSA spook named Seabring, checks out the mysterious radar array in Laos. "I've got 3 points in SIGINT, I've got to have some idea what this thing does."

The Handler responds, "Well, you know it's not configured like a standard anti-aircraft array. The dishes' geometry is wrong, for one thing." The dish geometry is the core clue, representing a sigil of Yog-Sothoth the team will encounter later. She continues, "Would you like to spend 1 or 2 points of SIGINT to learn more?"

Tyler goes all in: "2 points." The Handler checks her notes and begins with the 1-point spend: "In fact, the way those dishes are set up, they create an interference pattern about 100 clicks to the northeast, over that range of hills. It's like a deliberate blind spot masking their signal." "Or like a hologram? Two waves interfering, and all?" Tyler asks. That's actually noted as a Physics spend, but the Handler gives it to him: "Yes, it could very well also create a hologram, in radio waves instead of light. But with your 2-point spend, you can also figure out the frequency the array transmits on: if you tune your field radios to it, you can get a few minutes' warning as they warm up the dishes."

"Oh, I definitely tune a set to that frequency, and I set up a reel-to-reel to record the transmission as well." That's good thinking, and the Handler rewards it by agreeing. Agent Seabring and Dr. Lincoln get ready for their expedition to those eerie hills.

If you wish to make a spend in a situation where the Handler has no special benefit to offer you, and neither of you can think of one that pertains at all to the operation, you do not lose the points you wish to spend.

Even if you spend all the points in your Investigative Ability pool, you still keep your rating in the ability; you still automatically succeed with it.

The mechanical role of Investigative pool points is to manage spotlight time, and as a method for the players and Handler to signal "oncoming cool" to each other. A player who says "Can I spend a HUMINT point here?" is requesting something cool for his agent to do or discover during the scene. When the Handler says, "Do you want to spend an Anthropology point here?" she's signaling that there's something cool available during this scene that she thinks the player (or players) would enjoy. This exchange eventually becomes almost seamless and automatic.

General Spends

Occasionally you'll want to create a task at which there is no reasonable chance of failure, but which should cost the characters a degree of effort. To do this, simply charge the character(s) a number of points from relevant General Ability pools. Where tasks can be performed by cooperative effort, multiple characters may contribute points to them. 1 or 2 points per character is a reasonable General spend.

Failsafe Clues

In the course of laying down clues for the Agents to follow, it might seem to the Handler that any reasonably competent cultist or Soviet officer would keep their secrets behind locked doors or land mines. In other words, that no plausible Investigative Ability could discover the trail; that some degree of opposed effort is required for a core clue.

But in GUMSHOE, the Agents never fail to gain a core clue. What to do?

In these circumstances, use a **failsafe test**. This is a General test (see *Tests*, p. 080) that never *entirely* fails. It's usually a test of Drive (following the VW microbus to the cult compound), Mechanics (opening a safe), or Stealth (breaking into an information-rich AEC laboratory), but there are no doubt others.

The Handler sets the Difficulty as normal. If the Agent fails the test, she still succeeds at the task. But she trips an alarm, shows up on the security camera, gets spotted by cultists, or otherwise increases the risk of danger *after* getting the clue.

Also use failsafe tests when success is dramatically necessary for the story to progress speedily or interestingly: jumping a fence into the compound, fixing a truck to escape a Cuban labor camp, or palming a card to win a high-stakes poker game against a Mafia don. In such cases a failed test accomplishes the task at a cost: the Agent clambers over the fence but cuts himself on the razor wire, the truck overheats and throws a rod in an isolated fishing village on the coast, the Mafioso's girlfriend saw you cheat.

Tests

A test occurs when the outcome of an ability use is in doubt. Tests apply to General Abilities only. Unlike information gathering attempts, tests carry a fairly high chance of failure. They may portend dire consequences if you lose, provide advantages if you win, or both.

Even in the case of General Abilities, the Handler should call for tests only at dramatically important points in the story, and for tasks of exceptional difficulty. Most General Ability uses should allow automatic successes, with possible bonuses on point spends, just like Investigative Abilities.

There are two types of test: simple tests and contests.

Simple Tests

A simple test occurs when an Agent attempts an action without active resistance. Examples include driving a treacherous road, jumping a gorge, sneaking into an unguarded building, shooting an idol, planting a bomb, remembering to bring a magnet along, or resisting a Tcho-Tcho toxin smeared on a dart.

The Handler determines how hard any given action is by assigning it a **Difficulty**, or Difficulty Number, ranging from 2 to 8 (occasionally even higher), where 2 offers only a slim chance of failure, 4 is the norm, and 8 verges on the impossible. The player rolls a single die; if the result is equal to or higher than the Difficulty, the character succeeds. Before rolling the die, the player may choose to spend any number of points from the relevant ability pool, adding these to the final die result. Players who forget to specify the number of points

TUMBLING DICE, PART II

All die rolls in GUMSHOE use a single ordinary (six-sided) die, or d6. One die roll is abbreviated "d". For example, "d+1" means roll the die and add 1 to the result. Die modifiers usually only apply to the roll on damage rolls (see p. 091).

More often, modifiers adjust the Difficulty of the test instead.

A **successful 6** is a test that succeeds, *and in* which the die rolled a result of 6.

A **failed 1** is a test that fails, *and in which* the die rolled a result of 1.

The total of the die roll, any points spent, and any modifiers applied to the die is the **total result.**

The difference between the total result and the Difficulty of the test is the **margin.**

they want to spend before rolling are stuck with the unmodified result.

As you spend points from your ability pool, your *pool* dwindles but your *rating* stays the same.

In the game world, expenditure of pool points in this way represents special effort and concentration by the character, the kind you can muster only so many times during the course of an operation.

The jungle floor beneath Sergeant Sanchez seems to open up, revealing a yawning pit below studded with sharpened bamboo stakes smeared with something that glows bluish in the darkness. Sanchez needs to jump for the edge of the pit or plummet to an unpleasant fate. He has 8 points in his Athletics pool. With the alternative certain maiming – or worse – Sanchez' player Carmen decides to go all out. She spends half her pool, 4 points, on the attempt. She rolls a 5, to which she adds the 4 spent

Athletics points, for a final result of 9. With a mighty leap, Sanchez' fingers close around a trailing liana vine. He pulls himself up and out of the pit, coming to rest at the base of a large banyan tree.

In the cruel universe of **The Fall of DELTA GREEN,** Agents are frequently tired and distracted, and often their merely human senses are unreliable. To truly evoke that feel, the Handler does not reveal Difficulty Numbers. For entirely conventional obstacles in the beginning of an operation – milspec fences, commercial burglar alarms, and the like – the Handler may choose to disclose the Difficulty of a test. More often, she may give a rough verbal indication of how hard a test seems to the naked eye:

△ "The elevator entrance is only a few feet above, so it should be in reach if you jump."

△ "You've jumped higher. And you've fallen short of lower."

△ "If you can get a finger hold, it'll be a miracle."

Regardless, the Handler never reveals the Difficulty of a Sense Trouble test (see p. 071).

Retries

The test represents the Agent's best chance to succeed. Once you fail, you've shot your bolt and cannot retry unless you take some other supporting action that would credibly increase your odds of success. If allowed to do this, you must spend more pool points than you did on the previous attempt. If you can't afford it, you can't retry.

The basement Marxists didn't seem to have any connection to the Hastur cult, but they did have a homemade bomb ticking in the sink of their squat. Sanchez' only hope is to disarm the bomb with his Explosive Devices ability. The Handler describes it as "built by amateur hop-heads, and it's kind of a miracle it hasn't gone off already," and decides the sloppiness hazard balances out the lack of sophistication involved. She thus sets the Difficulty at 4. Fortunately, Sanchez has bought Demolitions up to 5, and spends 2 points on the attempt. Sadly, Carmen rolls a 1, and the Handler describes the alarming fizzing sound emerging from the device.

Sanchez has one more shot before the witches' brew goes up taking the building and himself, though not the whole capitalist state structure, with it. To qualify for this attempt, he must spend at least 3 Explosive Devices points. Since that's all he has left, Carmen burns them all. She

says *"If it's in the sink, let's see if it's a waterproof bomb" and says "Sanchez twists the faucet wide open." She rolls a 2, for a total result of 5 and a success! The bomb emits a kind of squelching noise and a cloud of caustic smoke. Sanchez, and the capitalist state structure, live to fight another day.*

Piggybacking

When a group of Agents act in concert to perform a task together, they designate one to take the lead. That Agent makes a simple test, spending any number of his own pool points toward the task, as usual. All other Agents pay 1 point from their relevant pools in order to gain the benefits of the leader's action. These points are not added to the leader's die result. For every character who is unable to pay this piggybacking cost, either because he lacks pool points or does not have the ability at all, the Difficulty of the attempt increases by 2.

Sanchez, Lincoln, and Seabring plan to break into the sealed wing of the Sandia Laboratories to find out more about the design of those radars. With her Stealth of 6, Lincoln takes the lead. Sanchez has Stealth 4, and Seabring has Stealth 0. ("I'm used to having clearance to break into things," he grouses.) Sanchez pays 1 point of Stealth, dropping his pool to 3. Because Seabring has no points to spend, the Difficulty of the job increases from 5 to 7. The team can't leave him behind — he's the one who knows what a radar experi-

ment should look like! Lincoln spends 4 points and rolls a 3 for a total result of 7 — exactly what she needed.

In many instances a group cannot logically act in concert. Only one Agent can drive a car at one time. Two Agents with Preparedness check their individual kits in sequence, rather than checking a single kit at the same time.

Cooperation

When two Agents cooperate toward a single goal, they agree which of them is undertaking the task directly, and which is assisting. The leader may spend any number of points from her pool, adding them to the die roll. The assistant may pay any number of points from his pool. All but 1 of these is applied to the leader's die roll. Some tasks (lifting a heavy stone sarcophagus lid, or repairing a tank engine) can logically allow more than two Agents to cooperate.

The new radar prototype is behind a heavy aircraft hangar door. Seabring and Sanchez need to open it by main strength, since powering the door up might send an alarm somewhere. Sanchez' Athletics pool is 6 and Seabring's pool is 3. Dr. Lincoln has only 1 point left in her Athletics pool, so there's no point in her assisting, because her single point would go to the cooperation cost instead of adding to the die roll.

Sanchez spends 4 points, all of which add to the die roll as usual. Seabring spends all his

3 remaining points, but adds only 2 to the result. Sanchez' roll is a 3, to which 4 and 2 are added for a result of 9. This beats the unrevealed Difficulty of 7, and the door swings upward, revealing a bizarre tangle of metal gridwork and wire that seems to float above the concrete floor.

Continuing Challenges

Some tasks, such as battering down a stone wall or driving a military convoy all night across the Algerian desert, simply take more time than a single test represents, whether that test takes a round or a scene of effort. Or from another angle, multiple tests more accurately and dramatically represent productive, repeated effort. For these continuing challenges, assign the obstacle a pool representing the base Difficulty of doing it all at once unaided: this will generally be 8 or higher, often much higher. The tests per se use the standard Difficulty of 4. The Handler also decides how often the test can happen: once per round for the wall, once every two hours for the convoy, for example.

The players may take turns, co-operate on each action, or use any other means at their disposal in a series of tests: Athletics to batter down that wall, or Drive to safely and stealthily get the Jeeps and trucks across the desert. The points they roll and spend accumulate; when they have enough points to overcome the initial Difficulty, the task is done. No points or rolls spent on a failed test add to the total.

GENERAL TESTS WITHOUT ABILITY RATINGS

If you don't have any *rating* in a General ability, you can't make a test in it. (Don't confuse this with *pool* points – you can always make a test in a General ability you have a rating in, even if your current pool is 0.) This standard GUMSHOE rule exists to allow players to build generalists, with 1 or 2 points in a broad variety of abilities, at the cost of two or three spotlight abilities.

To avoid being caught short, players can hold back a few build points or experience points to put at least 1 into General abilities that suddenly come up during play (see p. 021).

If the Handler is feeling *extraordinarily* generous, here's an *optional* rule:

If you are making a General test *with a 0 rating* in the ability, a roll of 1 is an automatic, damaging, failure: a 1 on a Firearms test means you hit a fellow Agent, a 1 on Stealth means you lose the target you were following and get made, a 1 on Drive means you wreck the vehicle, etc.

Furthermore, in any General test involving damage, such as combat or Demolitions, if you succeed, you still do less damage: a −2 penalty.

The team is trying to get the CIA station in Tokyo to redirect a U-2 flight over that range of hills in Laos – without telling Langley or the CIA station in Laos about it. This is a tricky and necessarily subtle contest of Bureaucracy. The Handler sets the Difficulty of retasking a national intelligence asset and crossing turf boundaries in the bargain at an arbitrarily high 20, and says that in the interest of keeping a low profile the team can only pull strings or ask favors every two days.

Lincoln spends 3 points from her Bureaucracy pool of 4, and rolls a 6. That's a 9 total, and Lincoln's friend

agrees to talk to someone in the U-2 program about it. Sanchez doesn't have much Bureaucracy, but spends his 1 and rolls a 2. This failure adds nothing to the total, which remains 9. Seabring, feeling the time pressure, blows his whole 5 point pool and rolls a 3; he adds that result of 8 to the total, for a total of 17. Lincoln has 1 point left in her pool, and 3 to go before the bird can lift, and the new radars are going to be installed any day now...

Some tasks are just impossible no matter how many tests you make: tearing open a vault door barehanded, for example.

Contests

Contests occur when two characters, often a player character and a supporting character controlled by the Handler, actively attempt to thwart one another. In the GUMSHOE system, the Handler can escalate between three separate types of contest, depending on how dramatic the scene should be.

△ **Player-facing contests** are for quick, active, "one and done" sorts of contests: i.e., using Athletics to toss a grenade into a Volkswagen.

△ **Full contests** amp up the drama; they're "showdowns" or "main opponent" sorts of contests: i.e., using Athletics to beat a rival skier to the bottom of the mountain.

△ **Chase contests** fall between those two types; they provide more suspense and last longer than player-facing contests, but don't take over the story: i.e., using Athletics to run away from a Cuban patrol on the way to the real mission.

In theory, any contest of General Abilities can use any of these three layers of contest, but in practice some contests just work better at different levels or as simple tests. Preparedness, for example, is almost always going to be a simple test; Filch will almost always be a player-facing contest; Bureaucracy might be a simple test (getting access to a dossier), a player-facing contest (getting access to a dossier when you've been officially ordered off the case), or a full contest against Internal Affairs trying to trace the mysterious rash of dossier leaks. As the examples above indicate, Athletics might be any sort of contest, in addition to simple tests like jumping over a fence.

Combat abilities (Firearms, Melee Weapons, and Unarmed Combat) use the Combat rules in the next section (see pp. 089 – 107) to overcome violent or intelligent opposition. Hitting a nonliving target with a pistol or a thrown knife, for example, is a simple test — but a marksmanship competition against an important opponent is likely to be a full contest.

Player-Facing Contests

Player-facing contests work exactly the same as simple tests: you roll against a Difficulty, and spend ability pool points to add to your die roll. The one exception: there are no "retries" against active opposition. If you fail, you either suffer the consequences immediately or kick the contest up to a full contest as your opponent gets a chance to counter your failed move.

It's called a "player-facing" contest because the Handler doesn't roll. To see if an Agent is surprised, the player makes a Sense Trouble test. To see if an agent surprises an NPC, the player makes a Stealth test. The player character's fate — the die roll and any spent points — is entirely in the player's hands. The Difficulty in a player-facing contest is usually 4, unless the Handler shifts it up or down. Often, this shift appears in her notes as either an Alertness Modifier or a Stealth Modifier. Note that these modify the player character's Difficulty in the contest.

Alertness Modifier

An opponent's **Alertness Modifier** represents its ability to sense your activities, whether through standard senses like sight and hearing, or exotic ones like echolocation or telepathy. When you try to sneak past it, the Alertness Modifier is applied to your base Stealth test Difficulty, which is usually 4. If you're trying to call in favors to breach security around a document, you might instead oppose Bureaucracy or a test of Network (p. 068) against an office's Alertness Modifier. It also applies to Stealth tests when you're trying to observe the opponent without being observed in turn, or when you're trying to slip their surveillance of you.

The Handler might also apply an Alertness Modifier to tests of Conceal, Disguise, Filch, or any other activity the agents covertly attempt under potential observation.

The Alertness Modifier reflects all of the opponent's sensing capabilities: natural, supernatural, and technological. A drug-addled guard, or a torpid Deep One, might have a *negative* Alertness Modifier, making your Difficulty lower and your contest easier.

Stealth Modifier

An opponent with a **Stealth Modifier** is either significantly harder or easier to spot with Sense Trouble or Stealth. It alters the Difficulty number for that or similar tests. In keeping with GUMSHOE's

DARKNESS

Much of DELTA GREEN's activity happens in not just the metaphorical darkness, but in the literal dark. GUMSHOE considers only three levels of darkness worth measuring.

- **Night:** This is the level of darkness of a normal, modern city at night, an interior room during daytime with its lights off, or the countryside in bright moonlight.
- **Dark:** This is the level of darkness of a city street at night with no streetlights, a building at night with its lights off, or the countryside at night with no moon.
- **Pitch Black:** This is total darkness, with no light source anywhere: a sealed shipping container or an underground crypt, for example. The Difficulty of all Stability tests increases by +1 in pitch blackness.

Darkness Effects

Darkness Level	Opponent's Stealth Modifier	Opponent's Alertness Modifier	Hit Thresholds	Visual Task Modifiers
Night	Up by +1	Down by -1	+1 at Near or longer range	+1 Difficulty
Dark	Up by +2	Down by -2	+1 at Close range; +2 at Near or longer range	+2 Difficulty
Pitch Black +1 to Stability test Difficulty	Up by +3	Down by -3	+1 at Point-Blank; +2 at Close; +3 at Near or longer	+3 Difficulty

Apply bonuses and penalties only to abilities and tests with a primarily visual component (e.g., bomb disposal, car repair). Sense Trouble, for instance, depends more heavily on sound and combat reflexes than it does on visual acuity, it might only increase in Difficulty by 1 in pitch blackness. Similarly, dogs depend primarily on smell: darkness will have no effect on their Alertness bonus or on the Hit Threshold of their foes.

No level of darkness makes getting a core clue require a spend, although if the core clue is in a book (for example), the Agent may have to wait for a light to read it.

Flashlights

In general, flashlights lower the darkness by one level: Pitch Black becomes Dark, for instance. However, anyone carrying such a brightly lit target gains *no* Hit Threshold advantage from the darkness: they're the easiest thing to hit!

EXHAUSTION

An Agent who works too long, or faces extreme danger without resting, becomes exhausted. The Handler determines when this happens, but going a night without sleep, or continuing strenuous activity after losing Stability or Health, likely leads to exhaustion.

Regardless of her Health pool, an exhausted Agent counts as *Hurt* (p. 094). The Difficulty number of all tests and contests, including Hit Thresholds, increases by +1. To spend points on an Investigative Ability requires a Consciousness roll (p. 094).

An exhausted Agent cannot refresh General Abilities that automatically refresh after 24 hours (Athletics, Drive, Firearms, Heavy Weapons, Melee Weapons, Pilot, Unarmed Combat).

A full night's sleep cures exhaustion.

Stimulants

Coffee, pep pills, or chain-smoking stave off the exhaustion penalty for 1-6 hours. Amphetamines, cocaine, and other harder drugs offset it for 2-12 hours. An Agent can take more stimulants to keep going, but every dose after the first costs d-2 points (minimum 1) of either Health or Stability.

---

player-facing approach, the Stealth Modifier appears in lieu of an opponent's Stealth ability. Instead of rolling Stealth (or Conceal, or Filch, or...) for an opponent, have an observing player character make a Sense Trouble (or Conceal, or Stealth, or...) test against a Difficulty of 4, adjusted by the Stealth Modifier.

Full Contests

In a full contest, each character acts in turn. The first to fail a roll of the contested ability loses. The Handler decides who acts first based on the contest's logic and circumstances.

For example, in a chase, the character who bolts from the scene acts first. Where the characters seem to be acting at the same time, the one with the lowest rating in the relevant ability acts first. In the event of a tie, supporting characters act before player characters. In the event of a tie between player characters, the player who arrived last for the current session goes first in the contest.

The first character to act makes a test of the ability in question. If he fails, he loses the contest. If he succeeds, the second character then makes a test. This continues until one character loses, at which point the other one wins.

Stealth and Alertness modifiers apply as normal.

Typically each character attempts to beat a Difficulty of 4:

On her way to meet a contact in the Thai ministry of health, Dr. Lincoln catches sight of teeth filed sharp in the face of what she thought was just a boy in the Bangkok crowd: a Tcho-Tcho? Lincoln's Stealth pool is 6; her tail's is 10. The only saving grace is that here in the unfamiliar city, the jungle hominid's normal Alertness Modifier doesn't come into play.

As the eluding character initiating the contest, Lincoln acts first. Raina spends 1 point, dropping Lincoln's pool to 5. Her ensuing roll is a 4, for a result of 5. This beats the standard Difficulty of 4.

Raina describes her success: "Sidling into a sidewalk café, I pick up a newspaper and use it to hide my face in the crowd."

On behalf of the Tcho-Tcho, the Handler spends 3 and rolls a 3, for a result of 6. It's still stalking the doctor. The Handler narrates accordingly: "Although it never seems to look directly at you, it oils through the crowd toward you as though following an invisible thread."

Raina spends another point, taking Lincoln's Stealth pool down to 4. She rolls a 6, for a final result of 7. The Handler invites Raina to explain what she's done to dry clean her trail. "I duck down an alley and really run the length of it, hoping Lincoln's longer legs can get me a lead over this thing. The first place I see cooking pork, I dive in and sit down fast upwind of the grill."

The Handler rolls for the Tcho-Tcho, spending 2 points and rolling a 1. That's a failure. "The goblin-thing comes out of the alley and for the first time you see its distorted face crinkle in confusion... and what looks like disgust at the smell of spoiling good meat by cooking it."

Lincoln has shed her tail, but she can't leave the cookshop without walking right in front of the fiend. Raina's choice of narration has hemmed her in; she can use an Interpersonal ability on the stall-keeper to see if there's a back exit, send a messenger to call for help or a diversion, or dig through the baskets of herbs to see if there's something here that can thwart the Tcho-Tcho's sense of smell more permanently.

Throughout the contest, Handler and players should collaborate to add flavor to each result, explaining what the characters did to remain in the contest. That way, instead of dropping out of the narration to engage in an arithmetical recitation, you keep the fictional world verbally alive.

Contest Advantage

Where the odds of success are skewed in favor of one contestant, the Handler may assign different Difficulties to each. A character with a significant advantage ("contest advantage") gets a lower Difficulty Number. A character facing a major handicap ("contest disadvantage") faces a higher Difficulty. When in doubt, the Handler assigns the lower number to the advantaged participant.

An Agent scrabbling without gear up a rock face finds it harder to move quickly than the well-equipped climber he's pursuing. In this case he might face a Difficulty of 4, while the mountaineer gets the lower Difficulty of 3.

Chase Contests

Full contests can drag out, and they can drain Agents' ability pools. Often, that's the point: full contests are supposed to be important scenes of drama and danger. For a quick dose of both, in a scene that perhaps involves simple thugs or cultists rather than monsters, or that you intend to be a palate-cleanser or spicy action nugget in a longer series of investigative scenes, consider a chase contest.

Chase contests resemble Full Contests, with four specific differences:

△ Both sides reveal their spends simultaneously
△ The contest only lasts for three rounds
△ The winner of two out of three rounds wins the contest
△ The "runner" can raise the Difficulty for all contestants

As the name implies, this contest usually applies to a chase, on foot (Athletics), on horseback (Ride), or in vehicles (Drive or Pilot). But the Handler can apply it to any contest she wants to spotlight but still end quickly:

△ Can the NSA black-bagger get in and out of the office before the security guards find her? (Stealth vs. Stealth)
△ Can the psywarrior surface a witness' personality against a possessing sorcerer? (Psychotherapy vs. Hypergeometry)
△ Can the CIA handler get through Prague unnoticed? (Disguise and Stealth vs. Stealth)
△ Can the Ranger deal with the two guards without an alarm sounding? (Unarmed Combat or Melee Weapons vs. Unarmed Combat)

The ability tested is the **chase ability**; points in that ability are the **chase pool.** In some cases, Agents can change their chase ability: e.g., diving out of the burning car changes the chase ability from Drive to Athletics.

Decide which side is the "pursuer," and which is the "runner." This is usually obvious; if not, consider the Agent the "runner."

Simultaneous Reveal

Both the pursuer and the runner select and record their spends, if any, in secret and then reveal them simultaneously. You can use notes on pieces of paper, poker chips, coins, pips on a die, or any other agreeable method of recording a spend.

Once the spends are revealed, the runner rolls first and adds his spend; the pursuer then rolls and adds hers.

Compare the margins of the tests: the side that succeeded by the most (or failed by the least) wins. If time or pacing is an issue, ties go to the runner; otherwise, ties don't count as victories for either party.

As in a full contest, the players and Handler should improvise and narrate the specific events that shaped the chase: "I drop from the window onto the van's roof," or "You skid and swerve to avoid a woman pushing a baby carriage," or "Both cars smash through the bazaar; chickens and vegetables fly everywhere, reducing visibility to stir-fry and nothing."

This constitutes a **round.**

Contest Advantage in Chases

Only apply contest advantage (p. 086) if one side is clearly faster (helicopter vs. Jeep; car vs. bicycle), or clearly outnumbers the other, or has a major advantage like secured (or telepathic) communication or aerial overwatch.

Best Two Out of Three

A chase contest lasts only three rounds.

The side that wins two out of the three rounds wins the chase contest: the players and the Handler decide what that result looks like in the game world, based on the margin of victory. Two victorious rolls of 6 and 5 in a row paint a decisive, accelerating victory; three contests decided by a point each way represent a taut struggle.

If the runner loses a chase and doesn't surrender, a combat likely begins (p. 089). The pursuer gets the choice of going first in that combat, regardless of ability ratings.

The runner also wins if other actions (by other Agents, for example) have killed, crashed, or disabled all the pursuers.

Raises

Turning into oncoming traffic, speeding up on those Riviera mountain curves, or charging out onto a projecting girder in an unfinished apartment block: when you're running for your life, anything looks like a good idea.

Before the next round of the chase starts, the runner can raise both sides' Difficulty Numbers by 1. For example, if the Difficulty of the last chase round was 4, the runner can raise it to 5. This represents trying to throw off the pursuer by changing the ground rules of the chase, if only for a little while.

This raise applies to the final Difficulty set by any special circumstances: if the pursuers have radio cars coordinating the dragnet (Difficulty 3) while the runner has only her native wits (Difficulty 4), a raise changes the pursuer's Difficulty to 4 and the runner's to 5.

The runner (player or Handler) should describe the specific action she's taking to set up the raise: "She cuts through the railway yards, the clangs and whistles of oncoming trains nearly deafening you," or "I jump for the fire escape and swing up it," or "The smuggler's boat heads toward the wake of that docking freighter."

If the runner fails at the raised Difficulty, the Difficulty drops back to its previous level for the next encounter.

If the runner succeeds, and the pursuer fails, the runner may choose between keeping the Difficulty raised or lowering it for the next encounter.

If both succeed, the runner may choose to raise the Difficulty again, or keep it raised. The pursuer must agree to lower the Difficulty for the runner to lower it in this circumstance.

Multiple Pursuers

Since the Agents' opponents in a Chase Contest are often nameless grunts or faceless thugs, the Handler should assemble all their (usually weak) relevant abilities into one pool to pit against the active Agent (usually the driver or pilot). Killing or crashing one pursuer should lower the pursuers' chase pool by a set amount.

Use the Cooperation rules (p. 081) to simplify chase contests involving multiple Agents.

The most complex chase contest you will likely want to play out is a "three-handed chase": e.g., the Cuban military are chasing the Agents, who are chasing a shape-shifting alien. Resolve this as two simultaneous and overlapping chase contests: the Agents do not roll twice in a round, but compare their result against that of both of their foes.

Making Things Messy

A chase contest can get as hairy as the Handler wishes. She should consider these to be optional rules, or apply them on an ad hoc basis when the story demands a mechanical echo.

Attacking During Chases

Passengers in (or unruly strangers climbing onto) a vehicle involved in a chase use their combat abilities at +1 to the target's Hit Threshold (see p. 090). Remember, someone in a car likely has the equivalent of full cover (see p. 096), unless you're shooting at the driver from the car's hood.

Pursuers and runners must pay 3 pool points to attack during a chase, which can come from either Firearms or the chase pool or a combination. Their target's Hit Threshold increases by 1, as does the Difficulty of their chase test in the round they attack.

Shooting out tires requires a Called Shot (p. 102) at +3 to Hit Threshold. Losing one tire raises the Difficulty of all Drive rolls by 1; losing two tires results in a crash.

See p. 110 for damage from a crash.

Investigative Abilities and Chases

Before the chase begins, or between rounds in a chase, any Agent — not just those directly involved in the chase — can try to influence the contest by calling on a rated Investigative Ability. This requires a spend if the Agent is not present on the scene.

An Agent might: use Architecture to recall the layout of the office building she's running through, or use Military Science to predict the Viet Cong search pattern, or use Cop Talk on the police frequency to misdirect the pursuers, or Intimidate a shopkeeper into locking the door he just burst through.

In any given chase, each ability can only be used once: if Sanchez has used his HUMINT for this chase, Lincoln can't use hers.

Invoking an ability might:

△ increase your side's roll by +1 (tactical or positional advantage)

△ force the other side to reveal its spend first; your side may then adjust your spend (slows the enemy down)

△ allow a 3-point refresh of the chase ability (opportunity for respite)

Players should narratively justify their use of such abilities; the Handler should assign the effect based on that narrative.

Ramming

If one side rolls a successful 6, it can make a ramming attempt, ending the chase in their favor immediately. (In foot chases or other non-vehicular contests, apply the equivalent sudden, dangerous, dramatic end.) The rules depend on whether the Agents are the rammers or the ones being rammed.

On the defensive (avoiding being rammed): The player adds his vehicle's Maneuver *to the die roll* (against a Difficulty of 4), plus any other spends he makes.

If he succeeds, the rammer must spend 2 points immediately from her chase pool.

If he fails, he is crashed (or the equivalent) and loses the chase.

On the offensive (ramming): The player adds her vehicle's Maneuver *to the Difficulty* of 4, and adds any other spends she makes to the die roll. Note that vehicles with a negative Maneuver will lower their Difficulty on a ram attempt: less maneuverable vehicles are usually heavier, which is an advantage when trying to force someone off the road.

If she succeeds, the chase ends in victory and at least one foe has crashed.

If she fails, she must spend 2 points immediately from her chase pool. If she cannot, the Difficulty of her next chase test increases by +1.

Thriller Chases

A more complex and cinematic set of chase rules appears as the Thriller Chase Contest in **Night's Black Agents.**

Combat

Fights are terrible and chaotic, frightening and fast. Skill, weapons, and tactics help, but even the most elite warrior can fall to a random bullet or blow. Don't let the game mechanics below turn combat into something predictable or boring; Handlers and players alike should look for opportunities for horror in this oldest of human pursuits.

Standard Combat

Combat is a specialized sort of contest, usually involving any of the following combat abilities:

△ Unarmed Combat vs. Unarmed Combat, Unarmed Combat vs. Melee Weapons, or Melee Weapons vs. Melee Weapons: the characters are fighting at close quarters.

△ Firearms vs. Firearms: the characters are apart from one another and trying to hit each other with guns.

△ Heavy Weapons are a special, usually lethal, case (see p. 099).

△ Animals and some monsters (p. 221) use a generic Fighting ability rather than human-style Unarmed Combat. The rules are the same.

As with full contests, the combatants take turns using their abilities. The other guy may swing first, but the fighter with the highest rating seizes the **initiative.** Unlike an ordinary contest, in a fight it is usually advantageous to strike first.

Surprise

Characters are surprised when they suddenly find themselves in a dangerous situation.

Surprise GMCs by sneaking up on them with a successful Stealth test. The basic Difficulty is 4, which may increase for especially vigilant foes (see *Alertness Modifier*, p. 083). A sudden, surprising combat move, such as triggering a concealed

QUICK-DRAW

A combatant without ready weapons can spend 3 points of the relevant combat ability to "quick-draw" a carried weapon and make it ready. This only applies if one combatant is ready and the other unready, obviously: if both fighters are unready, both draw their weapons and then resolve initiative ranking as above.

Claymore mine, or a seemingly helpless victim pulling a .38 Special, may require a different test: Demolitions (to set off the charge at the right psychological moment) or Disguise (to seem helpless until too late), for example. Usually "surprise" tests during a combat or confrontation begin at Difficulty 5; foes are just naturally more alert at such times.

Agents avoid being surprised with a successful Sense Trouble test. The basic Difficulty is 4, which may increase for especially sneaky foes (see *Stealth Modifier*, p. 083).

Surprised characters go last in combat, and suffer a +2 increase to all General Ability Difficulties for any immediate subsequent action. In a fight, this increase applies to the first round of combat.

Sanchez (usually Hit Threshold 4) and Seabring (usually Hit Threshold 3) have surprised the guards at the LZ by climbing a tree nearby (with Athletics) and then each succeeding at a Stealth test. For the first round of combat, the guards' combat Difficulties increase by +2, making Sanchez' Hit Threshold 6, and Seabring's Hit Threshold 5.

The Handler may rule that very badly surprised characters (GMCs when the Agents made their Infiltration test by 4 or more points; the Agents, if they failed their Sense Trouble test by 4 or more points) may also forfeit one or more rounds of action. The +2 Difficulty penalty then applies to the first round in which they can act.

Initiative and Combat Order

Training beats aggression, and the first punch thrown may not control the combat. Surprise aside, initiative depends on two things: combat ability rating, and having a weapon ready.

The standard order of combat is as follows:

△ Combatants with weapons drawn and ready go before combatants without ready weapons. Unarmed Combat "weapons" are always "ready," as are animal or monstrous talons, fangs, tendrils, etc.

△ Combatants with guns act before combatants using melee weapons. (See *One Gun, Two Combatants*; p. 096)

△ Combatants act in descending order of their combat ability rating.

△ Surprised combatants (p. 089) act last.

In case of a tied combat ability rating, the combatant with the higher *pool* goes first.

If the relevant pools are tied, Agents win **ties** against human foes, and lose ties against inhuman foes: an Agent with an Unarmed Combat rating and pool of 5 goes before a GMC with an Unarmed Combat rating and pool of 5, but after a ghoul with a Fighting rating and pool of 5.

Sanchez (Firearms rating 6) has a .45 Colt, Seabring (Melee Weapons rating 3) has a switchblade, Lincoln (Unarmed Combat rating 4) is unarmed. They face two Tcho-Tcho, Apoh (Melee Weapons 7) with a kris, and Bhat (Unarmed Combat 7) with a mouth full of blue toxic drool and razor-sharp filed teeth. The ranking order for their donnybrook would be: Bhat, Sanchez, Apoh (gun trumps kris), Lincoln, Seabring. If Apoh's kris was hidden in his robes instead of ready, he would go last.

The time it takes to go through the ranking order once, with each character taking an action, is called a **round**. When one round ends, another begins.

Don't bother recalculating ranking order every round; for speed of play, ranking order *stays where it was at the beginning of the combat* even if pool values have changed, or even if one combatant drew a knife or dropped his gun.

Hit Thresholds

Each character has a Hit Threshold of either 3 (the standard value) or 4 (if the character's Athletics rating is 8 or more). The Hit Threshold is the Difficulty Number the fighter's opponent must match or beat with a combat ability test in order to harm him.

Creatures both natural and supernatural may have Hit Thresholds of 4 or higher, regardless of their Athletics ratings. Extremely large creatures will usually have a Hit Threshold 1 lower than roughly man-sized beings of the same sort; cat-sized or smaller creatures will have higher Hit Thresholds.

Between cover (p. 096), darkness (p. 084), Called Shots (p. 102), and other modifiers, Hit Thresholds can escalate. Try to rebalance those values if you can: if one combatant has a Hit Threshold of 7 and one has a Hit Threshold of 9, run their combat as if they had Hit Thresholds of 3 and 5, respectively. This keeps fights shorter and more dangerous, and therefore more exciting.

Action in Combat

When called upon to act, each character may strike at any opponent within range of his weapons (see *Range*, p. 097). Some unnatural creatures may strike more than once per round. They make each attack in succession, and may divide them up between opponents within range, or concentrate all of them on a single enemy.

Once the fight has begun, if a combatant wishes to do something else besides fight — run away, get a manuscript out of their pack, throw a grenade — they move immediately to the last position in the ranking order as they turn to expose their vulnerable back to the foe, crouch to go through their duffle bag, fumble for the pin, or whatever.

Monsters, thugs, and similarly callous foes may choose to use their actions to deal additional damage to downed or helpless opponents rather than engage active opponents. They automatically deal one instance of damage per action. Shooting the wounded calls for a 4-point Stability test (see p. 080) for Agents.

Fighters who join a combat in progress come last in the ranking order. If more than two characters join during the same round, the Handler determines their relative precedence using the combat order rules (p. 090).

The fight continues until one side capitulates or flees, or all of its members are unconscious or otherwise unable to continue.

Running Away

Fleeing from an ongoing melee requires an Athletics test. The Difficulty is 3 plus the number of foes you're fleeing from: to flee one enemy is Difficulty 4, fleeing two enemies is Difficulty 5, fleeing four enemies is Difficulty 7. On a success, melee ends and you flee; if they intend to chase you, your foes must roll first in the ensuing full contest of Athletics. If you fail, the opponent with the highest damage value automatically deals one instance of damage to you. Melee still ends, but you must roll first in the ensuing chase.

If the Handler decides your attempted escape sets up a chase contest scene (see p. 086), a success on the flight test of Athletics gives you contest advantage in the first round of the chase. A failure on the flight test gives your pursuer contest advantage in that round.

In situations where it seems appropriate to make flight more difficult, on a failure, any directly engaged opponent might spend 3 Athletics to block you from fleeing—interposing himself between you and the exit, tackling you, slamming the hangar door, or whatever the narrative description warrants. In this case, your enemies forgo the damage they would otherwise deal.

Dealing Damage

When your total result matches or exceeds your opponent's Hit Threshold, you deal damage to him. To do so, you make a damage roll, rolling a die modified according to the relative deadliness of your weapon.

Characters do not spend points from their combat pools to increase their damage rolls. (Except indirectly, with Autofire (p. 100) and Called Shots (p. 102)).

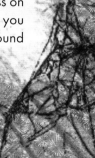

Weapon Damage

Weapon Type	Damage
Fist, kick	d−2
Blackjack, brass knuckles, small improvised weapon, pistol butt, nightstick, punji stake, knife	d−1
Machete, baseball bat, rifle butt, heavy club, large improvised weapon, crossbow bolt, light firearm (.32 pistol or smaller, 6.5mm rifle or smaller, assault rifle, 20-gauge shotgun or smaller)	d+0
Sword, fire axe, fixed bayonet, arrow, bed of punji stakes, heavy firearm (9mm pistol or larger, .30 rifle or larger, submachine gun, 12-gauge shotgun or larger)	d+1
Very heavy firearm (.50 MG, anti-materiel rifle)	d+2

Unnatural creatures often exhibit alarmingly high damage modifiers.

The final damage result is then subtracted from your opponent's Health pool. When a combatant's Health pool drops to 0 or less, that combatant collapses from exhaustion or blood loss and is unable to continue fighting. (Agents, and some fanatical or extra-important GMCs, may make a Consciousness roll and continue fighting; see p. 094.) Any combatants currently engaged with him in a close quarters fight can then freely deal another instance of damage to him.

Extra Firearm Damage

For firearms, add an additional +2 when fired at Point-Blank range. All shotguns add an additional +1 to damage at Close range. (See *Range*, p. 097)

Treat all Hurt results (p. 094) to humans from firearms as Seriously Wounded results. Where bruising or even hacking damage might be "shaken off," any gunshot that drops your Health pool to 0 or below does an additional +6 points of damage.

Ghouls and other once-human monsters don't suffer any such extra damage from gunshots unless the Handler explicitly rules that they do.

SPECIAL AMMUNITION

Armor-Piercing: Reduces all Armor ratings by half, rounding down: e.g., −2 or −3 Armor becomes −1 Armor; −1 Armor becomes −0.

Hollow-Point: Soft-nosed bullets that mushroom on impact; they do more damage to unarmored targets (+1 to normal damage). They can be hand-loaded to contain poison, mercury (to cause tumbling), or any other liquid or particulate. Increases all Armor ratings by one: e.g., Armor −1 becomes −2.

Incendiary: Contains a small amount of white phosphorus. If an incendiary round hits a fuel tank, ammo dump, or gas leak, it can trigger an explosion (L2 or L3; see p. 099). They do not ignite flesh or clothing under normal circumstances. Firing an incendiary ("tracer") round also leaves a bright streak pointing right at your own position: Your Hit Threshold drops by 1 against incoming fire for the next 2 rounds, but so does that of your target if you hit.

Rubber: Used by riot police; doubles all Armor ratings. Does normal damage, but cannot reduce any target below Hurt.

Shotgun Slugs: Instead of a traditional cased round full of pellets, shotguns can fire solid rifled slugs. These increase damage by +1 and range to Long. Armor protects against shotgun slugs as normal bullets, not at −2. Shotguns no longer gain additional damage at Close range, however.

Lethality

Certain attacks inflict damage well beyond the possibility of survival. A burst of heavy machine gun fire or an artillery shell – or a shoggoth pseudopod – makes fast work of human anatomy. Such attacks have a Lethality rating.

If an attacker hits with a weapon that has a Lethality rating, there's a chance it simply kills the target outright. Compare the result of the damage die roll to the weapon's Lethality rating, indicated by a number after the letter "L": L2, for example. If the result is equal to or lower than the Lethality rating, a human target immediately drops to -12 Health. If the result is higher than the Lethality rating, add that result to five times the Lethality rating as damage:

A 60 mm mortar shell has a Lethality rating of L2. If the damage roll is 1 or 2, the target dies. If the roll is 3, the target loses 13 (2x5 = 10 + 3 = 13) points of Health. And probably dies anyway.

Some weapons denote their Lethality rating with an asterisk: L1*, for example. In those cases, a damage roll one above the Lethality rating reduces the target to -6 Health (Seriously Wounded). If the target is already Hurt or worse, the attack kills them.

A grenade has a Lethality rating of L1. If the damage roll is 1, the target dies. If the roll is 2, the target becomes Seriously Wounded. If the target was Hurt and the roll is 2, the target dies. If the roll is 3, the target loses 8 (1x5 = 5 + 3 = 8) points of Health.*

NON-LETHAL DAMAGE

Players may always announce that their Agents are using their Unarmed Combat attacks to do non-lethal damage: choke holds, arm locks, body blows, and the like. Such attacks never lower a target's Health pool below -11, but merely force yet another Consciousness roll if successful.

Similar conditions can apply to non-bladed Melee Weapons attacks.

Bringing a knife or gun into a fight is a declaration of willingness to kill. There is no such thing as a non-lethal Firearms attack.

Grappling

Using this optional rule, an Agent who declares a non-lethal Unarmed Combat attack can describe it as a grappling attack. Once a grappling attack reduces a foe's Health to 0 or below, the grappler may force a one-round contest of Athletics or Unarmed Combat (the target may resist with either). If the grappler wins, their foe is pinned or otherwise unable to continue fighting. If the grappler loses, the foe can escape to Close range. GMCs can use grappling attacks if the player Agents do.

Unnatural creatures may be immune to all or some of a weapon's Lethality. If so, roll the damage die and add that result to five times the Lethality rating; this base damage may be modified still further by armor or other defenses.

Many explosives do additional damage depending on the target's location downrange. (See *Explosives*, p. 098.)

Some damage (impact, electricity, shock in general) has a special kind of Lethality notation: an "H" means you are Hurt (reduced to Health 0) if the die comes up on the indicated number.

A damage roll of 2, for example, means the character:

Is Hurt by a Lethality of L1H.

*Is Seriously Wounded by a Lethality of L1*H.*

Is dead from a Lethality of L2H.

If the target is already Hurt, he becomes Seriously Wounded by an H result; if already Seriously Wounded, an H result kills him.

Weapon Lethality

Weapon Type	Lethality Rating
Assault rifle or submachine gun on full auto, WP grenade	L1
Light machine gun or squad automatic weapon (.30 cal, BAR, M60), hand grenade, rifle grenade, M79 shot-shell, flamethrower	L1*
Heavy machine gun (.50 cal), RPG (M72 LAW, RPG-7), helicopter-mounted rocket (2.75-inch FFAR), light mortar shell (up to 60mm), autocannon (20mm or 40mm), WP shell	L2
Claymore mine, heavy mortar shell (61mm+), canister shell, automatic grenade launcher (M75, M129) burst, vehicle-mounted flamethrower	L2*
Tank main gun, recoilless rifle, satchel charge	L3
HE artillery shell, air-dropped napalm strike	L3*
Air-dropped general-purpose bomb	L4*

Injury and Death

Unlike most abilities, your Health pool can drop below 0.

When it does this, you must make a **Consciousness** roll. Roll a die with the absolute value of your current Health pool as your Difficulty. You may deliberately strain yourself to remain conscious, voluntarily reducing your Health pool by an amount of your choice. For each point you reduce it, add 1 to your die result. The Difficulty of the Consciousness roll is based on your Health pool *before* you make this reduction.

Ghouls are chasing you through a burned-out church in Maine, after a surveillance attempt that did not go your way. They hit you with a harpoon, dropping your Health pool to −3. You would really rather not gather first-hand intel on ghoul feeding habits, so you must remain conscious. The absolute value of −3 is 3, so this is the Difficulty of your Consciousness roll. You spend another 2 Health points you don't have, pushing yourself on toward the sunlight outside where you left the car. That spend gives you a bonus of 2 to your roll. You roll a 4, for a final result of 6. You remain conscious and get away, but now your Health pool is down to −5.

If your pool is anywhere from 0 to −5, you are **Hurt**, but have suffered no permanent injury, beyond grazes, cuts, and bruises, or "through-and-through" gunshot wounds. You must make a Consciousness Roll.

However, the pain of your injuries increases the Difficulty Numbers of all other tests and contests, including opponents' Hit Thresholds, by +1. To spend points on Investigative Abilities, you must make a Consciousness roll.

A character with First Aid can still restore your Health points with first aid while you are Hurt.

If your pool is between −6 and −11, you have been **Seriously Wounded**. You must make a Consciousness roll.

Whether or not you maintain consciousness, you are no longer able to fight. Until you receive first aid, you will lose an additional Health point every half hour. A character with the First Aid ability can stabilize your condition with a Difficulty 3 test of First Aid. However, she can't restore your Health points.

Even after you receive first aid, you must convalesce in a hospital or similar setting for a period of days. Your period of forced inactivity is a number of days equal to the positive value of your lowest Health pool score. (So if you were reduced to –8 Health, you are hospitalized for 8 days.) On the day of your discharge, your Health pool increases to half its maximum value. On the next day, it refreshes fully.

When your pool dips to –12 or below, you are **dead.** Time to create a replacement character.

Combat Conditions

This section sets guidelines and boundaries for firefights and other standard sorts of combats. Combat can be as complex as you want to make it, and numerous RPGs have decided to do so. The GUMSHOE rules, and *Fall of DELTA GREEN* specifically, set out to promote drama first, which usually means keeping action fast and rules minimal.

The next section, *Combat Options*, adds more rules, though still in the spirit of adding more terror and drama rather than becoming a straight exercise in military simulation.

Armor

Armor may reduce the damage from certain weapon types. If you're wearing a form of armor effective against the weapon being used against you, you subtract a number of points from each instance of damage dealt to you before applying it to your Health pool.

DEATH AND CONSEQUENCES

Killing people hardens the killer, and not in a good way. The operative word is "sociopath." But if you don't harden yourself to your acts, your guilt tears at you; you see their faces at night.

Every time you kill a human being, you lose 1 rating point of Stability, 1 point from a Bond, or 1 rating point of any Interpersonal ability. Your choice: haunted, hidden away, or hardened?

You can rebuild a Bond in your down time (see p. 128). You can rebuild the lost Stability and Interpersonal points with experience points (see p. 127); if so, you're consciously dedicating effort that could have gone into other pursuits to remaining human. Congratulations.

A very few police tactical units begin using nylon-and-steel "Barrier Vests" in 1969; Kevlar does not enter production until the 1970s. The only practical armor against bullets is a fragmentation vest, made of ballistic nylon. The U.S. military's M55 and M69 vests can hold heavy (7.5 lb.) boron-carbide or aluminum-oxide plates, called "chicken plates" by helicopter aircrew.

Ballistic nylon: reduces damage from bullets by 1 point, explosive damage by 2 points.

Vest with chicken plate insert: reduces damage from bullets or stabbing weapons by 2 points, explosive damage by 3 points.

M1 "steel pot" helmet: reduces damage from bullets by 3 points (head only).

The U.S. military designs body armor to resist shrapnel, not direct bullet fire. Body armor removes the asterisk from the Lethality rating (see p. 093) of a weapon used on the wearer.

All armor subtracts 2 more points from shotgun damage at any range greater than Point-Blank, as the individual pellets spread out. E.g., a vest with chicken plates reduces shotgun damage at Close or Near range by 4 points.

Body armor cannot be concealed under normal clothing. It is hot, heavy, obvious, and uncomfortable. Difficulty for almost all tests except Firearms or operating military vehicles while wearing body armor increases by 1. Wearing body armor in a hot climate such as Vietnam, Cuba, or Africa increases the chance of exhaustion (see p. 085).

Creatures often have high armor ratings. They may possess bony hides or monstrous anatomies that can take greater punishment than ordinary organisms. Most unnatural creatures are more resistant to bullets and other missile weapons than they are to blunt force trauma, slashes, and stab wounds.

Cover

In a typical gunfight, combatants seek cover, hiding behind walls, furniture or other barriers, exposing themselves only for the few seconds it takes them to pop up and fire a round at their targets. The GUMSHOE rules recognize three cover conditions:

Exposed: No barrier stands between you and the combatant firing at you. Your Hit Threshold decreases by 1.

Partial Cover: About half of your body is exposed to fire. Your Hit Threshold remains unchanged. This is also the condition if you have full cover, but only behind thin or flimsy materials like foliage, drywall, or canvas. A smoke screen provides partial cover.

Full Cover: Except when you pop up to fire a round, the barrier completely protects you from incoming fire. Your Hit Threshold increases by 1. If your cover is between you and the impact, you subtract 1 from the Lethality rating of successful attacks, both for the Lethality roll and the final damage calculation (see *Lethality,* p. 093).

Ammo Capacity

Characters need reload only when dramatically appropriate, or if the Handler feels they've used a lot of full-auto bursts lately. Otherwise, they're assumed to be able to refill the cylinders of their revolvers or jam magazines into their automatic weapons between shots.

When reloading is an issue, Handlers may request a Firearms test (Difficulty 3) to quickly reload. Characters who fail may not use their Firearms ability to attack during the current round.

ONE GUN, TWO COMBATANTS

If your opponent has a gun well in hand and ready to fire, and you charge him from more than 2 yards away, he can empty his entire magazine or cylinder at you before you get to him, badly injuring you. You are automatically hit. He rolls one instance of damage, which is then tripled. Yes, we said *tripled*. And, yes, the tripling occurs after weapon modifiers are taken into account. This is why few people charge when their opponents have the drop on them.

If your opponent has a pistol but it is not well in hand and ready to fire, you may attempt to jump him and wrestle it from his grip. If he has a pistol well in hand but is unaware of your presence (for example, if he is Surprised; see p. 089), you may also be able to jump him, at the Handler's discretion. The characters engage in an Unarmed Combat contest to see which of them gets control of the gun and fires it. This is a generalized wrestling match with the gun as the prize; it doesn't involve a Called Shot. The winner has the pistol, and may make a damage roll against the loser, using the pistol's damage modifier, including the +2 for Point-Blank range.

If you jump an opponent with an unready rifle, run the Unarmed Combat contest as before; the winner may immediately use the rifle as a heavy club with Melee Weapons or spend one round (or 3 Firearms pool points; see p. 066) readying the rifle to fire.

Special forces, FBI agents, and the like are trained to take advantage of less-skilled foes holding them at gunpoint. This involves getting inside the gunman's reach and immediately striking for the gun. The Handler may call for a 2-point Reassurance spend against civilians or untrained foes, or a player-facing contest of Firearms (at Difficulty 5 plus the enemy's Alertness Modifier) to let the Agent get into position for either an Unarmed Combat contest as above, or a Disarm attempt (see p. 104). Well-trained gunmen don't allow this to happen: the Handler can simply say something like: "He backs up a step and levels the gun at your torso meaningfully." Then, you're back to that triple damage routine.

Handlers may also request a Preparedness test (Difficulty 3) if it seems a character has run through a lot of ammunition recently. Characters who fail have one magazine (or cylinder) left.

Range

Although painstaking calculations of windage and angles of fire are all very well and good, to keep the focus in **Fall of DELTA GREEN** on horror and action, we only utilize four ranges.

Point-Blank

You are literally face-to-face (or face-to-back-of-head) with your opponent, within easy arm's reach. All brawls, knife fights, and scuffles occur at this range. At this range, all firearms do an additional +2 points of damage, and all shotguns are considered heavy firearms, with a base damage modifier of +1.

For most fights and most fighters, moving into Point-Blank from Close range moves your action to the end of the round.

Close

You are in the same room with your opponent, or within no more than 10 yards or so. A melee or a karate match might happen at this range, but no farther; this is about the size of a boxing ring, for instance.

At this range, all shotguns do an additional +1 point of damage. This is as far as you can throw an object directly at a target unless the object is specifically designed for throwing (i.e., a grenade, a javelin).

Near

You can see your opponent distinctly, perhaps across a warehouse or across the street, no more than 30 or 40 yards away. At this range, all shotguns are considered light firearms, with a base damage of d+0, and do no extra damage. This is the farthest range at which you can hit a target with a shotgun at all, or with a pistol or submachine gun unless you spend 2 Firearms points (see *Extended Range*, p. 098).

This is as far as you can throw any object, either in a general direction (like a stick of dynamite) or at a specific target (like a baseball). Thrown weapons at Near range do -2 damage, and the target's Hit Threshold is 1 higher.

Long

Your opponent is within 100 yards. Opponents farther away cannot be reliably targeted at all, and are out of the combat. This is the farthest range at which you can hit a target with a rifle or assault rifle, unless you spend 2 Firearms points (see *Extended Range*, p. 098).

EXTENDED RANGE

You can spend 2 points from your Firearms pool to attempt to hit a target at Long range with a pistol or submachine gun, or at up to 500 yards with a rifle or assault rifle. If the rifle is specifically designed as a sniper rifle, and you have a bipod and scope, the Handler may allow you to extend its range up to 1,000 yards.

This spend does not adjust your roll; it makes it possible in the first place.

Using a weapon with a scope removes 1 point from the cost of Extended Range.

Using Sniping (see p. 104) with a scope allows shots at Extended Range without paying extra points.

Extended Range never applies to shotguns.

Explosives and Explosions

Seemingly inert matter that flashes into chaos, probably killing someone in the process: if there's a better metaphor for the Lovecraftian universe, let's hope nobody deploys it against you.

Using Explosives

Setting an explosive charge merely requires using Demolitions; assuming the victim is on the spot when the charge is triggered, the explosion automatically goes off at Point-Blank range. To conceal a charge (e.g., in a booby trap or car bomb) requires a Conceal test (see p. 064). If the Agents are the targets of a bomb, allow them a Sense Trouble test (Difficulty 4 or higher, depending on the skill of the bomber) to dive (or pull their slower teammates) away to Close range.

Grenades

Throwing a grenade is an Athletics test with the Difficulty set by range: 2 for Point-Blank targets, 3 for Close targets, 5 for Near targets. Rifle grenades (p. 139) use Firearms, at the next range increment up: 2 for Close targets, 3 for Near targets, 5 for Long range targets.

If you are attempting to hurl a grenade at a specific spot (such as through a car window), the Difficulty number increases by +1 at Point-Blank or Close range targets, and by +2 for Near range targets. Rifle grenades are already fired at specific targets using the rifle's sight, although the Handler may assess a Called Shot modifier (see p. 102) for tricky shots.

All Difficulties are +1 for throwing non-balanced explosives such as sticks of dynamite or Molotov cocktails (see *Burning*, p. 108).

Agents and alert GMCs get an Athletics test (Difficulty 6) to halve the damage from hand grenades or dynamite tossed at them; this represents diving for cover, knocking the grenade away, etc. A successful Athletics test turns a lethal result (e.g., rolling a 1 or 2 on a grenade with an L1* rating; see *Lethality*, p. 099) into normal (d+5) damage.

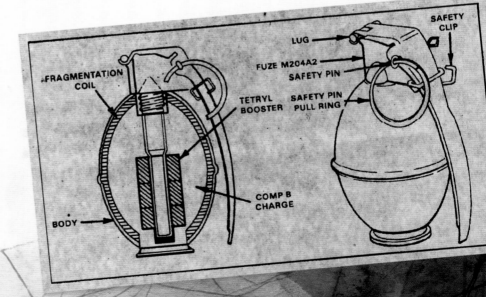

Heavy Weapons Attacks

Rockets, mortars, artillery, etc. use Heavy Weapons tests, with a base Difficulty of 7 to land the charge within Point-Blank range of a target, 6 to land it within Close range, 5 to land within Near range, etc. A spotter who can see the target, and who can communicate with the firer, can spend his own Heavy Weapons points on the test. (If the spotter has a gridded map, he can also spend Astronomy, Pilot, Physics, or Survival on the second attack and all ensuing attacks from the same weapon.)

This does not apply to machine gun attacks, which resolve as normal Firearms tests but use the Heavy Weapons ability.

Explosion Damage

Explosive damage divides by *Lethality* rating (see below). Artillery shells often land in barrages; the Handler may add +1 to the Lethality rating of a barrage rather than roll multiple damage dice.

If you are within a bomb's **lethal range** when it detonates, you apply Lethality to the damage die as normal.

If you are within a device's **damage range** (but outside its lethal range) when it explodes, you take a die of damage, plus a modifier equal to five times its Lethality rating.

If you are outside of its lethal or damage range but within its **debris range,** make an Athletics test with the explosion's Lethality rating times 3 as the Difficulty. If you fail, you take a die of damage, plus a modifier equal to its Lethality rating.

Some explosives, like fragmentation grenades, Claymore mines, or pipe bombs packed with nails, may be designed to deliver especially damaging debris, with a damage modifier equal to twice the device's Lethality rating within the debris range.

Suitable protection (inside a tank, a military bunker, etc.) moves you one range class out: e.g., if you're inside a tank hit by an RPG rocket, take damage as if you were at Close range rather than Point-Blank. Subtract any armor as normal. Inferior protection (such as being inside

Explosives Range and Damage

Lethality Rating	Examples	Lethal Range	Damage Range	Debris Range
L1*	grenade, pipe bomb, stick of dynamite	Point-Blank	Close d+5	–
L2	RPG rocket, helicopter-mounted rocket, brick of C-4 or Semtex, 2 yd. of Primacord, light mortar (up to 60mm) shell, propane tank	Point-Blank	Close d+10	Near
L2*	Claymore mine, land mine, canister shell	Point-Blank	Close d+10	Near
	Heavy mortar (81mm) shell, gas main	Close	Near d+10	Long
L3	Anti-tank artillery shell, recoilless rifle shell, satchel charge, light air-to-ground missile (AGM-12, AGM-22)	Close	Near d+15	–
L3*	High-explosive artillery shell, cluster bomb, truck bomb	Close	Near d+15	Long
L4	Heavy air-to-ground missile (AGM-65)	Near	Long d+20	–
L4*	Air-dropped general purpose bomb	Near	Long d+20	240 yd

a car) still allows you to subtract any armor against damage, assuming there's a damage roll for you to survive.

Combat Options

These rules add more options and more dramatic possibilities to standard GUMSHOE combat. They also advantage tactically minded players, as in practice players are always more interested in wringing advantage from the system than Handlers are. With the extreme potential lethality of **Fall of DELTA GREEN,** we see this as more a virtue than a problem.

Admit these combat options to your game on a case-by-case basis. You may feel the need for Called Shots without wanting to open the door to Suppressive Fire, or vice versa.

For more (and wilder) combat options, see **Night's Black Agents.**

Autofire

Fully automatic firearms – especially assault rifles, submachine guns, and machine guns – fire multiple shots with one trigger pull. Most assault rifles can fire single shots, or three-round bursts, or "rock and roll," spraying "full auto" fire as long as the shooter keeps the trigger down. For such selective fire weapons, declare what rate you fire at before you spend or roll the die.

Single shots work as normal Firearms tests.

To fire a **three-round burst,** declare your action, spend at least 3 extra Firearms points and roll the die. For each 3 points in the margin of your result, you do one extra instance of damage to a maximum of three.

Raiding an Oakland cult compound, Sanchez unlimbers his assault rifle and opens fire on a guard at the top of a stairwell. He decides to fire a three-round burst, and spends 3 points to augment his Firearms roll against the guard's Hit Threshold of 3. He rolls a 5 for a total result of 8.

Sanchez' margin of 5 over the guard's Hit Threshold means that one extra bullet hits. (If Sanchez had spent 4 points, his margin would have been 6, and two extra bullets would have hit.) Sanchez rolls two damage dice, getting a 5 and a 3; the M16 does d+0 damage. The guard's Health is 6; the first hit drops him to 1 and the second hit to -2, increased to -8 (Seriously Wounded and out of the fight) by the effect of gunfire on humans (p. 092).

To fire a small arm (assault rifle, SMG, etc.) on **full-auto,** declare your action, spend at least 5 extra Firearms points, and roll the die. You may also spend Stability or Athletics points for this purpose, although only spent Firearms points add to the total Firearms result. Your damage becomes L1 (see *Lethality,* p. 093). Roll a damage die for each target downrange (within 2 yards either way of your point of aim). On a roll of 1, that target dies.

Sanchez charges down the now cleared stairwell into a cellar full of cultists. He decides to rock and roll, firing on full auto. His Firearms pool is only 3, so he spends 1 of those points, and 2 each from

Stability and Athletics. He rolls a 2, for a total result of 3, enough to hit the cultists.

The Handler randomly decides that of the eight cultists in the cellar, six were inside the firing radius; Sanchez rolls six damage dice (or one die six times) for 1, 1, 2, 3, 3, 5. Two of the cultists are dead; the next four lose 7, 8, 8, and 10 points of Health. All of them had Health 7 to make the Handler's job easier; the three dropped to 0 or worse lose 6 more to become Seriously Wounded. The last three cultists standing probably scatter or drop to the ground in panic.

Actual machine guns (e.g., BAR, M60) are always full-auto weapons. You do not need to spend extra Heavy Weapons points to "activate" Lethality or full autofire from a machine gun.

Walking Fire

When firing a spray of bullets, it is possible to "walk your fire" toward a particular target. When firing on full auto, by spending either 2 points of Firearms (or Heavy Weapons) or 1 Firearms (or Heavy Weapons) and 2 Athletics, you can hit a target standing within 3 yards of your previous target, provided that the original result would have hit him. In theory, you can keep "walking fire" until you are out of targets, out of pool points, or out of ammunition.

Sanchez wants to nail the cult leader Aquarius X, who is running from the massacre. He spends 1 Firearms and 2 Athletics, tugs his gun up and left, and hits Aquarius in the back. He could not walk his fire to hit Virgo, the survivor cowering behind the altar, as the cover gives Virgo a Hit Threshold of 4, higher than Sanchez' original Firearms result of 3.

You can also walk your fire with a three-round burst, but you still cannot fire more than three bullets.

At the Handler's discretion, foes with ready guns can shoot back during the "walking fire" segment, assuming they act next in the combat round ranking order.

Shot Dry

On a Firearms or Heavy Weapons roll of 6 with full-auto fire, you have shot the weapon dry, and you must reload (see *Ammo Capacity*, p. 096). However, you can roll two instances of damage for any two targets (or three times for one target), with extra chances for Lethality.

Undisciplined firers (civilians, most terrorists, many irregular or Third World opponents) shoot themselves dry on a Firearms or Heavy Weapons roll of 1 or 6. A roll of 1 does not allow extra damage, however, even if it hits. The player decides if her Agent is "undisciplined"; the Handler decides if the Agents' opponents are.

Weapon Jams

Two "1" ability test rolls in a row with any full-auto weapon indicate that the gun has jammed. It requires a Firearms (or Heavy Weapons) or Mechanics test (Difficulty 4) to fix in one round. Fixing it in two rounds is a Difficulty 3 test; fixing it in three rounds is a Difficulty 2 test.

ROCK AND ROLL WILL NEVER DIE

Veterans of other GUMSHOE games may notice that these autofire rules are extremely deadly. (For softer, or at least more expensive, autofire rules, see **Night's Black Agents**.) This is because fully automatic weapons, especially against nearby targets, are extremely deadly: there's a reason doughboys called the Thompson submachine gun the "trench broom" in World War I.

Handlers worried about game balance in a game using autofire rules should consider the following:

- Fully automatic weapons are not standard issue for anyone except combat arms personnel. Getting issued a tommy gun is a tough Bureaucracy test for an FBI agent, much less for a researcher at the Library of Congress. (But see *Buying Guns*, p. 137)
- Enforce the *Shot Dry* (p. 101) and *Weapon Jams* (p. 101) rules.
- Tell the players that she'll be counting ammo expenditure, and a full-auto burst counts as at least 10 shots. An M16 comes with a standard 20-round magazine.
- Enforce the *Death and Consequences* rule (p. 095).
- Fully automatic weapons fire is very very loud, which does not often match up with DELTA GREEN operational rules of engagement calling for covert action and deniability. Even when fired off in the middle of nowhere, or of Vietnam, autofire makes the Agents very noticeable to their foes.
- And those foes very likely have AK-47s... which are also capable of fully automatic fire.

Called Shots

In certain situations simply hitting an enemy isn't enough: you need to get him in a particular spot. You may need to shoot a foe in the unarmored leg, stab a monstrosity in its burning three-lobed eye, blast a detonation trigger out of a terrorist's hand, or sever a hideous proboscis currently draining a comrade's blood.

To specify the location of a hit is to make a called shot. Called shots are harder to make than ordinary strikes. If you're using Firearms, the target is smaller than the enemy as a whole. With Unarmed Combat or Melee Weapons, you forfeit the opportunity to take opportunistic shots when your opponent lets down his defenses against you.

When taking a called shot, you specify the desired location of the strike. If you are trying to achieve an effect other than damage to the opponent, specify this now. The Handler decides whether this is a likely outcome of such a hit. If it is clearly not a likely outcome, and your Agent would logically know this, the Handler warns you in advance, so you can do something else instead.

The Handler then adds points to the target's Hit Threshold, depending on the additional difficulty entailed. Use the following table as a guideline. Body locations assume a human of ordinary size. Hit Threshold modifiers for ordinary body parts of extraordinary creatures are left as an exercise for the Handler. *Vehicle locations are in italics.*

Called Shots Modifiers

Desired Location	Modifier to Hit Threshold	Additional Damage
Large carried object (rocket launcher, suitcase, backpack)	+1	
Torso, *windshield*	+1	
Target in a crowd: at Near range, or in a small, dense group (3-6)	+1	
Chest (if attacker is facing target)	+2	+2 (weapon)
Gut, *specific window, tail rotor*	+2	
Head or limb	+2	+2 (weapon; head only)
Target in a crowd: at Long range, or in a large, dense group (7+)	+2	
Hand or foot, joint, groin, *tire*	+3	+2 (unarmed; joint or groin only)
Throat, mouth, or face	+3	+3 (weapon; throat only) +2 (unarmed)
Heart	+3	+3 (weapon)
Weapon or other hand-held object	+3	See Disarm, p. 104
Eye, *headlight*	+4	+2 (weapon, blind for 2 rounds) +3 (unarmed)

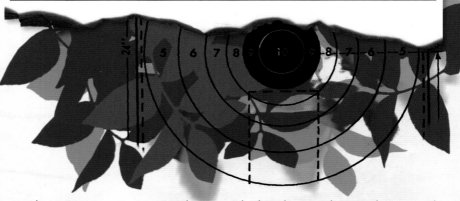

Shooting one target in a dense crowd is a Called Shot depending on the range and the size of the crowd.

With the new Hit Threshold determined, you then make a combat ability test, as per the standard rules. If you succeed, your specified effect occurs as desired.

Called shots to some locations do extra damage, depending on whether the attacker used Unarmed Combat or a weapon (melee or firearm), as indicated on the table. This extra damage may or may not apply to unnatural beings; it does not apply to vehicles, other than the mechanical result of losing a tire or headlight.

Extra damage does not apply to a point-blank gunshot, which is already assumed to hit a vital location.

Deep in the London Underground, Lincoln spots Anwar, an Algerian terrorist and arms dealer. Rather than draw a gun in the crowd and risk spooking him, Lincoln tries to bring him down with a crippling throat strike. Anwar's normal Hit Threshold is 4, and a throat strike increases the Difficulty by 3, for a total Hit Threshold of 7. She spends 3 Unarmed Combat points and rolls a 4, smashing him in the larynx. She rolls a 3 on the damage die. A punch normally does -2 damage, but she adds +2 for the throat strike, for a net total of 3 points. Anwar's Health goes from 7 to 4.

This assumes a trained, targeted strike intended to disable or cripple. You may narrate some other crippling strike to suit your own specific martial arts idiom, but the modifiers remain the same if you want to do the extra damage.

GARROTES

Using a strangling cord, or garrote, requires surprise and an attack from behind: Agents get a Sense Trouble test to notice a garrotiste approaching. Sneaking up on a victim is a Stealth test; getting close enough to loop a garrote over the neck adds +2 to the target's Alertness modifier.

The actual garrote attack is a Melee Weapons attack using a Called Shot to the throat (+3 to Difficulty; see p. 102). After the first hit, consecutive attacks on the same target automatically succeed, assuming the attacker isn't thrown off with Unarmed Combat or otherwise discouraged. (The Handler may assess a Hit Threshold penalty for strikes on a target directly behind you.)

A regular garrote such as a thong, electrical cord, or the like does d+0 to the throat. This includes the bonus for a throat attack.

A razor-sharp metal wire garrote (used with wooden handles) does d+3 to the throat or d+0 to any other body part.

Disarm

A disarm attack is a special kind of Called Shot that targets a foe's weapon, either in-hand or holstered.

If you make a successful Called Shot to a weapon in-hand, the result depends on how you did it:

△ If you used Firearms, the weapon is probably damaged, and certainly knocked free.

△ If you used Melee Weapons, and your weapon is heavier, you disarm your foe. On a successful 6, you disarm your foe even if your weapon is lighter or flimsier.

△ If you used Unarmed Combat, your foe cannot use that weapon against you. Instead, the two of you are wrestling for control of the weapon in an Unarmed Combat contest as described in *One Gun, Two Combatants* (see p. 096).

If you make a Called Shot to a short, one-handed weapon (such as a pistol or combat knife) worn in a foe's holster or scabbard, the Difficulty is still +3. But if you hit at all, you can spend 3 Filch or Melee Weapons points and take it for yourself; you can use it on your next attack. No matter how many points you spend, you can't take a long, unwieldy weapon (such as a sword or rifle) from a foe even by surprise.

These rules may not apply in combat against creatures with superhuman strength, of course.

Critical Hits

When you roll a successful 6, *and* your total margin over the target's Hit Threshold is 5 or more, you score a critical hit, rolling two instances of damage and adding them together.

Seabring punches a surprisingly tough rocket engineer (Hit Threshold 4) at the pad in Leopoldville. He spends 3 Unarmed Combat points on the attack, then rolls a 6, for a final result of 9. The roll of 6 and the margin of 5 allows a critical hit. Seabring deals damage equal to two punches, each with a -2 damage value. He rolls a 5, for a modified result of 3 damage, and a 6, which modifies to 4 damage. The engineer loses 7 Health, going from 6 to -1 and slumping unconscious.

If Agents can score critical hits, their enemies can, too.

Evasion

By going evasive, you can opt to fight defensively, decreasing both your chance of being hit and your chance of hitting anyone else. While evasive, you duck, weave, backtrack, and otherwise concentrate on not being hit. Announce that you're going evasive at the beginning of your action for the round; doing so does not cost an action itself.

For every 2 Athletics points you spend, your Hit Threshold increases by 1, for a maximum increase of 3. When you try to hit anyone else, their Hit Thresholds against you increase by 2 for every 1 point your Hit Threshold increased. The effects last until the beginning of your next action, at which point you can renew them (provided you can afford the cost).

Badly pressed and running out of Unarmed Combat points, Seabring attempts to fend off the serpent-man while waiting for other members of his team to run across the tarmac to his rescue. He declares evasive action and spends 4 Athletics on a 2-point Hit Threshold increase, taking his threshold from 3 to 5. The reptilian's Hit Threshold increases (against Seabring's attacks only) from 4 to 8. When Lincoln shows up, she attacks the serpent-man against its normal Hit Threshold of 4.

Sniping

If you have a Firearms rating of 8 or more and are armed with a rifle, you may decrease the Hit Threshold of a target for a single Firearms attack by taking at least one round to aim. If the target is aware of your presence, his Hit Threshold decreases by 1. If he is unaware of your presence, it decreases by 2.

If your rifle has a scope, you may make a Sniping attack at Extended Range without paying the normal 2 point cost (see p. 098).

Suppressive Fire

If you are armed with a gun and have a Firearms *rating* of 8 or more, you can lay down suppressive fire, preventing opponents from crossing a line drawn by your weapon's bullets. Although creating a line of suppressive fire prevents you from hitting your opponents, it also prevents them from firing directly at you. It is most useful for preventing enemies from advancing or pursuing.

Laying Down Suppressive Fire

When you first lay down a line of suppressive fire, make a Firearms test against a Difficulty determined by the approximate length of the line you're drawing. The line must be within your weapon's range. Note the final result of your test: if you spend more points on the roll, you raise your opponent's Difficulty to cross that line.

Suppressive Fire Difficulty

Length of Line	Difficulty
Alleyway width, door-way	3
Road (1 lane), drive-way	4
Road (2 lanes), ware-house doors	5
Road (3 lanes), hangar doors	6

You may then maintain the line of bullets with no further effort, provided you do nothing else, for either 2 rountds (if using a semi-automatic pistol or rifle) or 5 rounds (if using a fully automatic weapon like an assault rifle or submachine gun). Once this period elapses, you must take an action to reload, dropping your suppressive fire for one round. Then you must retake the test.

Opponents can see the line of fire; only the reckless or desperate will try to cross it.

Crossing Suppressive Fire

To cross an established line of suppressive fire requires an Athletics test with the result of the gunman's suppressive fire test as the Difficulty. On a failure, the character suffers an instance of damage for the weapon type and falls back to his previous position on the far side of the fire line. (Fully automatic weapons use Lethality for this roll; see p. 093.) If he succeeds with a margin of 0 to 4 between result and Difficulty, he crosses the line but suffers an instance of damage. On a margin of 5 or more, he crosses the line without taking damage.

As his comrades rush a rescued civilian to safety, Sanchez stays behind on a Saigon street to delay her former captors. He blazes away with his sidearm, laying down a line of suppressive fire across the mouth of the alleyway he expects them to emerge from. Spending 3 Firearms points against a Difficulty of 3, Sanchez rolls a 1, for a result of 4. This is enough to lay down a line of fire across the alleyway.

The lead kidnapper, Apoh, has no respect for human weapons. It charges through the suppressive fire. The Handler makes Apoh's Athletics test, spending 3 points on the attempt, and rolls a 4, for a final result of 7. This overcomes the Difficulty, which is Sanchez' result of 4, by 3 points. This is enough to cross the line but not enough to avoid damage. Sanchez rolls damage (d+1) for his Colt .45; a 5! Apoh loses 6 Health (5 + 1) from a bullet hit... but keeps coming. If Sanchez had been firing an M16, he would have rolled against its Lethality rating of 1; a 1 would have killed a human... but not necessarily Apoh.

By acting in tandem with other team members, you can increase the size of your line of fire, and keep the bullets flying when one of you has to reload.

In some cases, especially for civilian characters unused to combat, the Handler may also call for a Stability test (at the same Difficulty) to even try to cross a line of suppressive fire, before the Athletics test.

Opposing Forces

Here are a few quick examples of human foes (and one canine) that might get in between the Agents and their goals. The Handler may alter these ratings as she sees fit; they are benchmarks, averages, and guidelines, not hard-and-fast absolutes.

For further variety, pick one member of the opposing group and add 1 or 2 to Athletics, Health, and various combat abilities: this will be the senior NCO, commander, the tough guy in the mob, or other boss figure.

Bodyguard

Specialized security for a wealthy or important figure: political, criminal, or financial.

General Abilities: Athletics 8, Drive 6, Firearms 6, First Aid 4, Health 7, Melee Weapons 6, Unarmed Combat 10

Hit Threshold: 4

Alertness Modifier: +2

Stealth Modifier: +0

Attack: fist/kick (d-2), blackjack (d-1), Colt Detective .38 Special revolver (d+1; +1 Difficulty at greater than Close range)

COMBAT OPTIONS SUMMARY

Autofire

Three-Round Burst: Spend at least 3 extra Firearms points, which add to your roll. For each 3 points of margin over target's Hit Threshold add one more damage roll.

Full Auto: Spend at least 5 extra Firearms points, which add to your roll. You may spend Athletics and Stability to get to 5, but they do not add. Damage becomes L1 to all targets in your firing radius (2 yd. from aim point).

Walking Fire: Spend 2 Firearms (or 1 Firearms and 2 Athletics) to hit another target up to 3 yd. from your previous target. Your first result must hit all walking fire targets.

Shot Dry: On an unmodified roll of 6 you shoot the weapon dry and must reload. You can roll two instances of damage for two targets or three instances of damage for one target.

Jam: Two unmodified Firearms rolls of 1 jams a full-auto weapon. Firearms or Mechanics test (Difficulty 4) to fix in one round; Diff 3 in two rounds; Diff 2 in three rounds.

Heavy Weapons: Use Heavy Weapons instead of Firearms for machine guns. Machine guns fire on Full Auto without spending 5 extra points.

Disarm

Called shot to a weapon (+3 to Difficulty). Effect depends on ability used:

- Firearms: Target disarmed.
- Melee Weapons: Target disarmed if his weapon was lighter; on a successful 6, target disarmed even if his weapon was heavier.
- Unarmed Combat against carried weapon: One-round Unarmed Combat contest, winner gets the weapon.
- Unarmed Combat against holstered weapon: Spend 3 Filch or Melee Weapons to take weapon for yourself.

Critical Hit

Roll a successful 6, exceed Hit Threshold by 5+, do two instances of damage.

Evasion

Declare evasion, spend 2 Athletics to increase your Hit Threshold by +1, maximum +3. Your foes' Hit Threshold against you increases by +2 per spend, maximum +6.

Sniping

Prereq: Firearms 8+; using a rifle.
Take at least one round to aim, decrease foe's Hit Threshold.
- Aware foe: Hit Threshold -1.
- Unaware foe: Hit Threshold -2.
- **Extended Range:** spend 2 Firearms; free if your rifle has a scope.

Suppressive Fire

Make Firearms test at Difficulty depending on width of area suppressed (Diff 3 [doorway] to 6 [three lane road]).

Maintain fire for up to 2 rounds (semi-auto) or 5 rounds (full auto).
Cross suppressed area with Athletics test at Difficulty equal to result of suppressive fire Firearms test.

Civilian

Just another bystander. For a low-life bystander or roughneck (or a civilian in good shape with recent military training), raise Unarmed Combat to 4, and add Melee Weapons 2 (club or knife, d-1 damage).

General Abilities: Athletics 3, Health 2, Unarmed Combat 1
Hit Threshold: 3
Alertness Modifier: -2
Stealth Modifier: -1
Attack: fist (d-2)

Guard Dog

Untrained dogs have lower abilities: Athletics 6, Fighting 4, Health 3. Dogs trained to sniff out drugs, smuggled humans, etc. have Conceal 5, plus their Alertness Modifier.

General Abilities: Athletics 8, Fighting 6, Health 5
Hit Threshold: 4
Alertness Modifier: +3 (keen smell and hearing)
Stealth Modifier: +1 (if trained to keep silent; otherwise, -1)
Attack: bite (d+0 plus worry)
Pack Attack: Up to three dogs can attack a single target in one round. The foe's Hit Threshold drops by 1 against the third attack.
Worrying Bite: If two bites in a row succeed against the same target, the dog's teeth clamp down, and the second attack thus does double damage. The dog need not roll to hit that target thereafter, but will continue to worry the foe, doing normal damage to him each round until killed or driven off. The dog's Hit Threshold is only 3 against an enemy clamped in her jaws.

Militia

Unorganized soldiers (and some "regulars") in the Third World; warlord troops; guerrillas; hireling guards; aroused locals with pitchforks and torches.

Guerrillas in long-running insurgencies such as the Viet Cong have Alertness Modifier +0 and Stealth Modifier +1; they may also have Firearms 4 or 5.

General Abilities: Athletics 3, Drive 1, Firearms 3, Health 3, Melee Weapons 3, Unarmed Combat 3
Hit Threshold: 3
Alertness Modifier: -1 (distractible)
Stealth Modifier: -1 (undisciplined)
Attack: fist (d-2), pitchfork or machete (d+0), 7.62mm AK-47 assault rifle (d+0 [L1 on full auto])

Police

Street cop, plainclothes or uniform; use for private security forces. Add +1 to Athletics and Firearms for gendarmerie in France, Spain, Italy, and other nations with a quasi-military national police force.

Add +2 to Drive, Health, Firearms, and Unarmed Combat for security police such as KGB, Special Branch, or FBI.

For border guards and customs police, add +2 to Conceal.

General Abilities: Athletics 5, Conceal 2, Drive 4, Firearms 4, Health 6, Melee Weapons 4, Unarmed Combat 6
Hit Threshold: 3
Alertness Modifier: +1
Stealth Modifier: +0
Attack: fist (d-2), nightstick (d-1), .38 S&W Model 10 Police revolver (d+1), 12-gauge Remington 870 pump-action shotgun (d+1)

Soldier

Regular soldier from NATO or Warsaw Pact military or equivalent. Lower all ratings by -1 for conscriptees or national guard. Increase Firearms by +1 for soldiers on active combat operations.

Increase all ability ratings by +2 (and thus Hit Threshold to 4), and add +1 Stealth Modifier for special forces and other elite troops.

General Abilities: Athletics 6, Drive 3, Firearms 6, Health 5, Melee Weapons 4, Unarmed Combat 5
Hit Threshold: 3
Alertness Modifier: +1
Stealth Modifier: +0
Attack: fist (d-2), combat knife (d-1), 5.56mm M16 assault rifle (d+0 [L1 on full auto]), grenades (L1*)
Armor: helmet (-3 vs. bullets, head only)

Thug

Muscle for a criminal organization, random guards. Add +3 to Firearms for a dedicated triggerman and change the pistol to an M1911 .45 automatic pistol (d+1) or a .45 Thompson SMG (d+1).

For a made man or other underboss, change Stealth Modifier to +0, Athletics to 8, and Hit Threshold to 4. A made man expecting trouble may also wear a multi-layer cotton and silk "bulletproof vest" (-1 Armor against bullets or stabbing weapons).

General Abilities: Athletics 4, Drive 2, Firearms 3, Health 5, Melee Weapons 5, Unarmed Combat 6
Hit Threshold: 3
Alertness Modifier: +0
Stealth Modifier: -1
Damage: fist (d-2), blackjack or knife (d-1), club (d+0), Beretta M1935 .32 ACP (d+0)

A Life of Danger

A DELTA GREEN Agent walks into a world full of many hazards besides fists and firearms.

Burning

Acids (and caustic alkalines) and fire both do damage depending on the area of your body exposed to them. Acid and fire continue burning until countered, although acid eventually neutralizes itself as noted in the table. Roll a die for damage in the first round of exposure (or first few seconds, outside of combat), then automatically apply that result each round thereafter until the burning stops.

The damage table assumes a strong acid such as sulfuric or nitric acid. Weaker acids do less damage; subtract a further -1 or even -2 from the damage die for such substances.

Characters surrounded by fire also run the risk of smoke asphyxiation, which uses the drowning and suffocation rules (p.110).

Put it Out!

Counteract acid with proper materials and a 1-point spend of Chemistry or Medicine. (First aid does not prepare you for acid casualties.)

If your clothes are simply on fire, the flames are easier to put out (Difficulty 3 Athletics test; roll instead of taking other actions; fire out in 1 round) than if you are covered in accelerant like jet fuel (Difficulty 5 Athletics test; fire out in 2 rounds). Quick action with a fire extinguisher puts out a fire in 1 round. The Handler may call for a Preparedness test or a Notice spend to have spotted where the nearest fire extinguisher is.

Napalm and Co.

Military incendiaries such as napalm, thermite, or white phosphorus (WP) burn for 2-12 rounds without smothering or chemical suppression, and cannot be put out with water.

Napalm clings to its target; flaming napalm has a Lethality rating of L1* for each round after the first. (For napalm strikes or explosions larger than a portable flamethrower, use the listed Lethality on p. 093 for the first round, then drop to L1* for successive rounds.)

Thermite (p. 141) burns much hotter than regular fire; roll three instances of damage.

White phosphorus smoke doubles the rate of suffocation (p. 110).

Burning Damage

Exposure	Acid Damage	Fire Damage	Notes
Minor (an extremity, a quick splash) Molotov cocktail miss by 1	d-2 each round for 2 rounds	d-2 each round	
Partial (face or up to half of body) Molotov cocktail hit	d+0 each round for 4 rounds	d+0 each round	Might also blind victim until healed
Extensive (full immersion, swallowing)	L1 each round for 6 rounds (swallowed acid each 3 rounds for 18 rounds)	L1 each round	Might also blind victim until healed

IN GIRUM IMUS NOCTE ET CONSUMIMUR IGNI

M9 FLAMETHROWER

The standard-issue US military flamethrower, the M9 weighs 50 lbs. filled with 4 gallons of napalm and 25 lbs. empty. Firing it is a Firearms test. It can hold and fire conventional gasoline (-1 to damage, and only burns for 1d6 rounds) if napalm is not available.

Fired at Close range, it inflicts d+2 damage (extensive exposure) on a hit, and d-2 damage (minor exposure) on a miss by 1. A second consecutive hit on the same target at Close range does L1* damage.

At Near range, it only does d+0 damage on a hit.

Firing a flamethrower at Point-Blank range is a great way to get set on fire yourself while carrying a tank of napalm — not recommended.

Impact

The human body is not designed to take impacts well: joints deform, bones break, brains concuss. It's enough to make one believe that whatever altered tree-dwelling monkeys into humans did so as a joke.

Calculate damage based on the distance fallen or the speed of impact (being hit by or hurled out of a moving car, for example) using the table.

On any final damage result of Hurt or worse, you have automatically broken a limb or joint.

Modifiers

Depending on what you hit, or what hit you, you may take more (or even less) damage from an impact.

Where the table mentions adding one more H or asterisk to the Lethality rating, add the H at the end; add the asterisk after the numerical Lethality rating. For example: A fall onto concrete from 20 yards becomes L1HH; a fall onto a jagged surface from 20 yards becomes L1*H.

Impact Damage

Distance Fallen	Speed of Impact	Damage
5 yards	10 mph	d+0
10 yards	20 mph	d+1
20 yards	25 mph	L1H
30 yards	45 mph	L1*H
40 yards	65 mph	L2H
50 yards	85 mph	L2*H

Impact Modifiers

Circumstances of the Impact	Damage Modifier
fall through branches, awnings, or other slowing obstacles	-2; ignore result of 1 on Lethality roll
fall into water, if you can dive in (make an Athletics test Difficulty 5)	minus margin of Athletics test success; no Lethality roll
fall or roll onto normal soil	+0
fall into water, if you can't dive in	+2
fall onto or hit by hard surface (asphalt, concrete, ice, moving car)	+2; add one more H to Lethality rating
fall onto jagged surface (rocks, icy crevasse); hit by heavy vehicle (truck, bus) or armored surface (tank, armored truck, train)	+3; add one more * to Lethality rating
fall onto or hit by spikes (from any height)	d+2 plus impact damage

Crashes

If you are in a vehicle crash, you suffer damage equal to the Difficulty Number of the Drive (or Pilot) test attempt you or the driver missed (if there was no test, the base damage is 5).

Then:

△ Add the speed modifier from the table for the faster vehicle.

△ *Subtract* the vehicle type modifier for *your* vehicle.

△ Add the vehicle type modifier for the other vehicle.

Aircraft crashes simply do the damage indicated. Add one more * to the Lethality rating if the aircraft is on fire (most likely from enemy action) before the crash. The pilot can make one more Pilot test at the Difficulty she missed before to crash-land, avoiding the Lethality roll.

A motorcycle crash damages the rider as impact damage based on the speed the motorcycle was going (p. 109). If the rider is wearing a helmet, do not add the extra H from an impact on a hard surface.

If you hit a structure rather than another vehicle, use the italicized examples in the table to gauge damage. The Handler determines any damage to the vehicles based on the circumstances, both physical and dramatic.

Crash Protection

If you were wearing seat belts or had other crash protection, divide damage in half (rounded up).

Personal armor protects as though the crash were explosive damage. Vehicle armor does not apply.

Collision Modifiers

Collision Circumstances	Damage Modifier
average city driving speed	+2
highway speed	+4
VW Beetle, open Jeep, light sports car	-1
limousine, van, *reinforced post or gate*	+1
armored limousine, truck, *normal building, crash barrier*	+2
semi-trailer, APC, heavy truck, *abutment, bunker*	+4
Motorcycle crash: as impact damage for motorcycle speed (p. 109)	
helicopter crash	d+2; L1H
plane crash	d+6; L2*H

Drowning and Suffocation

If you have advance warning before being immersed in water or an unbreathable atmosphere, you can hold your breath for five rounds, or two minutes out of combat. (This may involve a Sense Trouble test.)

After that point, you start suffocating; you lose 1 Athletics every round, as you struggle to hold your breath. After that you lose 1 Health every round as you start inhaling water, smoke, or gas.

Up to half these lost Health points (minimum 2 Health) can be restored with a 1-point First Aid spend if you are rescued and resuscitated before you die. You cannot resuscitate yourself with First Aid.

Acting Underwater

Agents fighting or otherwise attempting to move with precision underwater suffer a contest disadvantage (p. 086) vagainst foes with superior underwater equipment or conditioning. In a few cases, they may receive a contest advantage against less-prepared enemies.

For example, Navy SEALs or (after 1967) Soviet PDSS combat frogmen have contest advantage underwater against regular foes. Deep Ones have contest advantage underwater against any human.

The easiest way to model this in combat is to simply adjust the more capable contestant's Hit Threshold upward by +1. For player-facing contests or similar, raise the Difficulty by +1 for underwater actions.

Electricity and Other Shocks

Damage from exposure to electricity varies according to voltage. You can suffer:

Mild shock, equivalent to briefly touching an ungrounded wire or damaged electrical appliance. You lose 1 Health and are blown backward for a couple of yards.

Moderate shock, equivalent to a jolt from a cattle prod. You lose 2 Health and (if in combat time) your next four actions. You always lose at least one action, but may buy off the loss of other actions by paying 3 Athletics points per action.

Extreme shock, equivalent to a lightning strike, has a Lethality rating of L1H.

Temperature Extremes

In intense heat or cold, it can be difficult to move or think. Treat characters suffering from extreme heat or cold (in the Sahara Desert in summer, for example) as Hurt.

Freezing

The amount of time you have before beginning to freeze to death in subzero temperatures (or freezing temperatures combined with high winds) depends on how well prepared you are for the cold.

Unprepared, e.g., wearing shirtsleeves: twice your Health in minutes.

Somewhat prepared, e.g., wearing warm clothes but not Arctic gear: 10 times your Health in minutes.

Prepared, e.g., decked out for mountaineering or an Antarctic expedition: twice your Health in hours.

You (or anyone with you) may spend 2 Survival to double this span.

Once freezing sets in, you lose 1 Athletics every five minutes. After that, you can no longer move, and lose d-1 Health every five minutes.

Exposure to warmth and shelter restores 1 point of Athletics per minute; lost Health heals normally.

Heat

In a tropical environment such as the Congo or Vietnam, strenuous activity during the heat of the day (noon to 3 p.m.) demands a Health test at Difficulty 4. Agents who fail become Hurt until the next day (or until nightfall, if they can somehow rest in a cool environment). Use this same guideline for deserts or other very hot environments.

Toxins

Toxins are either inhaled, ingested (including by contact or exposure), or injected directly into the bloodstream. They vary widely in lethality and in nature. A dose of household cleanser may impose damage of d−2, where a sophisticated nerve gas might range from d+3 to high Lethality.

Inhaled toxins tend to take effect right away. Injected and ingested toxins take delayed effect, anywhere from rounds to minutes to hours after exposure. Diseases usually take effect days after exposure. Their damage might be parceled out in increments, and almost always prevents you from refreshing Health points until somehow neutralized.

Note that basic poison control *is* an aspect of first aid: an Agent using First Aid may be able to restore lost Health points (if the poison was weak or easily purged), or at least stabilize the victim until he can get to a hospital.

The Handler may give you a chance to avoid exposure, likely via Chemistry, Pharmacy, or Sense Trouble. If you are exposed, consult the table for the effects.

Onset: How soon the toxin takes effect. Toxins take effect in rounds instead of minutes, hours, etc. during combat.

Test: Health test Difficulty. +L means add the Lethality rating to the Difficulty.

Minor: Result on a successful Test. A result here of Hurt *does not* reduce Health pools by itself.

Severe: Result on a failed Test. Even a lethal result takes at least two rounds to occur, enough time for a last-minute First Aid test (usually Difficulty 4) to resuscitate the victim to Seriously Wounded (Health -10).

The sample toxins in the table are only a tiny shadow of the vast and glorious universe of plagues and poisons. All of their effects might be weaker in lower dosages, or worse in higher ones.

Toxins

Toxin	Onset	Test	Minor	Severe
Anthrax	inhaled; 2-8 days	6	d+0	Hurt (p. 094); d+3 damage and -3 Athletics every day
BZ nerve agent	inhaled or ingested; 30 minutes to 4 hours	6+	-3 Athletics, Shaken (p. 113); lasts 10 minutes (or 3 rounds)	totally incapacitated by hallucinations, Shaken, Hurt; lasts 1-4 days
Curare	injected; 15-30 mins (5-10 rounds)	7	d+3	L1; total paralysis for 1-6 hours
Cyanide	inhaled or ingested; 1-6 rounds	7	d+2	L4
Fentanyl	Injected; 10-45 mins (5-10 rounds)	5	-5 Athletics, Shaken; lasts 2 hours	d+0; unconsciousness for 1-6 hours
Halogenous gas (chlorine, mustard gas, phosgene)	inhaled; 1-6 hours	6	d+0	L2*; blinded as tears turn to hydrochloric acid
Heroin	injected or inhaled; 1 minute (or 2 rounds)	7	Shaken for 1-6 hours	totally incapacitated by ecstasy; lasts 1-6 hours; Addiction (see p. 123) until cured even if you already have a Disorder
LSD	injected or ingested; 30-90 mins	6+	-3 Athletics, Shaken; lasts 10 mins (or 3 rounds)	sensory distortion and distraction; Shaken, +3 to all Difficulties; lasts d+5 hours
Nerve gas (sarin, VX)	inhaled or absorbed; 2-12 rounds	7+	d+3, Hurt; lasts until treated	L3*
Plague	inhaled or flea bite; 1-6 days	4	Hurt, fever for 3 days	Hurt; d+0 damage and -2 Athletics every 3 days
Radiation (100-800 rads)	exposure; 1-6 hours	4+	d-2	d-4; every 3 days, -2 Athletics and damage increases by +2 (d-2 on Day 4, d+0 on Day 7, etc.)
Snake venom	contact or injection; 15 mins (or 5 rounds)	4+L	d+2, Hurt; lasts until treated	L1 (rattler), L2 (cobra), L3 (mamba or krait); -2 Health and -1 Athletics every hour
Spider venom	bite; 1-6 hours	4	d-1	Hurt; d+2
Tear gas	inhaled and eye contact; 1 round	5	-2 Athletics; all tasks requiring vision take 1 extra spend; lasts until exposure ends	-4 Athletics, Hurt, all physical spends only half as effective, blindness (+2 to all visual Difficulties including Hit Thresholds); lasts until 5 mins after exposure ends

Stability and Sanity

"If you can keep your head when all about you are losing theirs, perhaps you have misjudged the situation."

— PFC Gustav Hasford, USMC, The Short-Timers

As noted in the abilities lists, Stability and Sanity refer to two different, but related, qualities. Stability is your resistance to mental and emotional trauma of any kind, natural, human, or unnatural. Think of it as your mental and emotional Health pool. Your Stability pool is quite likely to dwindle rapidly over the course of a single operation, but it is also likely to completely refresh between operations. Consider Stability a short-term measure of your current mental health.

Sanity is the ability to believe in, fear for, or care about any aspect of the world or humanity as we know it: religion, science, family, natural beauty, human dignity, even "normal" immorality. The horrible truth of the unnatural is that Sanity measures your ability to believe a comforting lie — but a lie necessary in order to live as a human being rather than a soulless tool or plaything of alien gods. Your Sanity will probably erode slowly over the course of many missions. You may lose none at all in some operations. But Sanity is slow to return. Consider Sanity a long-term measure of how close you are to fully realizing the bleak and awful reality of the cosmos.

In short, your Stability pool measures how close you are to snapping today; your Sanity pool measures how close you are to seeing the Truth forever.

Losing Stability

Like Health, your Stability pool can drop below 0.

If your Stability ranges from 0 to –5, you are **Shaken.** You can still do your job, but seem distracted.

△ You can't spend points from the pools of your Investigative Abilities.

△ Difficulty Numbers for all General Ability tests (including Stability) increase by +1.

△ If you already have a mental disorder, you must make a Stability test at Difficulty 4 to avoid an acute episode (see *Acute Episodes,* p. 123).

△ If an Unnatural shock rendered you Shaken, you lose 1 Sanity rating point.

If your Stability ranges from –6 to –11, you are **Shattered.** You have snapped, and are visibly deranged.

△ The only actions you can take are *panicked flight* or *frenzied all-out attacks* on any perceived dangers.

△ You may also choose to *do nothing* colorfully: babble incoherently, chant Bob Dylan lyrics, freeze into catatonia, faint dead away, etc. (See also *Fainting,* p. 122.)

△ You continue to suffer the effects of being Shaken.

△ You permanently lose 1 point from your Stability *rating*. The only way to get it back is to purchase it again with build points.

△ If an Unnatural shock rendered you Shattered, you lose 2 Sanity rating points.

△ You acquire a mental disorder, which stays with you even after your Stability pool is restored to normal (see *Mental Disorders,* p. 123).

△ If you already have a mental disorder, you must make a Stability test at Difficulty 6 to avoid one of: an acute episode, a relapse of a cured disorder, or acquiring another disorder.

△ Each time you are Shattered after the second, the Difficulty of all directly mental illness-related Stability tests increases by +1, including the tests to resist an acute episode or relapse.

When your Stability reaches –12 or less, you are **Gone.** You may commit one last desperate act, which must either be self-destructively heroic or self-destructively destructive. Or your mind might cease to function and you withdraw into yourself. Assuming you survive, DELTA GREEN quietly ships your Agent off to a discreet facility upstate, never to be seen again. Time to create a new character.

ROLEPLAYING INSTABILITY

Although there is no mechanical effect to losing Stability until your pool goes below 0, many players enjoy roleplaying the shocks and edginess of a terrifying encounter. It also helps build mood if you describe how your Agent reacts to the shock: does he jump and startle, does she go pale and wipe sweat from her brow? It helps you build your own sense of your character if you take a minute to think about how coming unstuck feels to her.

Here are a few possibilities:

1-2 point loss: You might twitch, or stutter. Your voice could rise a bit, or you could Very. Explicitly. Stay. In. Control.

3-4 point loss: You might have to stop a bit and hyperventilate. You're blinking a lot, and maybe sweating, too. If you talk, you might run away with your own words. Keep doing something comforting - rack the slide on your shotgun, hum "Boola Boola," that kind of thing. That will see you through this.

5-6 point loss: This is serious. You may go into a little fugue state; déjà vu comes over you, or you get "frame drop" and miss a couple of seconds. Nothing fatal, no, you're still good. Nope. If you're talking, you might call out some encouragement to your mates! They're probably not doing near as well as you! If you've got a pre-existing disorder, you're hyper-aware of anything that might trigger it.

7-8 point loss: How are you not shaken yet? You've almost certainly gone into adrenaline shock; your peripheral vision is gone, and your hands and feet are cold. You may babble personal confessions ("I've always loved you, Tom") or just shout incoherent threats. If you can make Interpersonal abilities work at all, they work more through fear of what you might do next than anything else.

The three major threats to Stability are **Violence, Helplessness,** and the **Unnatural.**

These categories can overlap. Being tied up and tortured might trigger both Violence and Helplessness. It's up to the Handler to decide which aspect affects the Agent.

Violence and Helplessness

When shocked or confronted by extreme Violence or Helplessness, make a Stability test against a Difficulty Number of 4. As with any other test of a General Ability, you are always permitted to spend Stability points to provide a bonus to your roll. However, it's never a good bet to spend more points than you stand to lose if you fail. You can "spend yourself negative," if you think you absolutely have to keep it together in these tunnels, although you can not voluntarily reduce your Stability pool below -11.

Unless the stimulus is primarily visual, Stability tests in pitch blackness (p. 084) are at +1 to Difficulty.

If you fail, you either suffer some negative result (usually, giving in to your own mental illness) or you lose a number of points from your Stability pool, in addition to any points spent on the test itself. The severity of the loss depends on the stimulus.

When an operation calls for a Stability test, it describes a Stability test with a potential loss of 4 points as "a 4-point Stability test."

If multiple horrific stimuli occur during one scene, you only test Stability when the potential Stability loss *increases*: if you made a 3-point Stability test, you don't have to roll again during that scene unless a 4-point (or worse) trigger shows up.

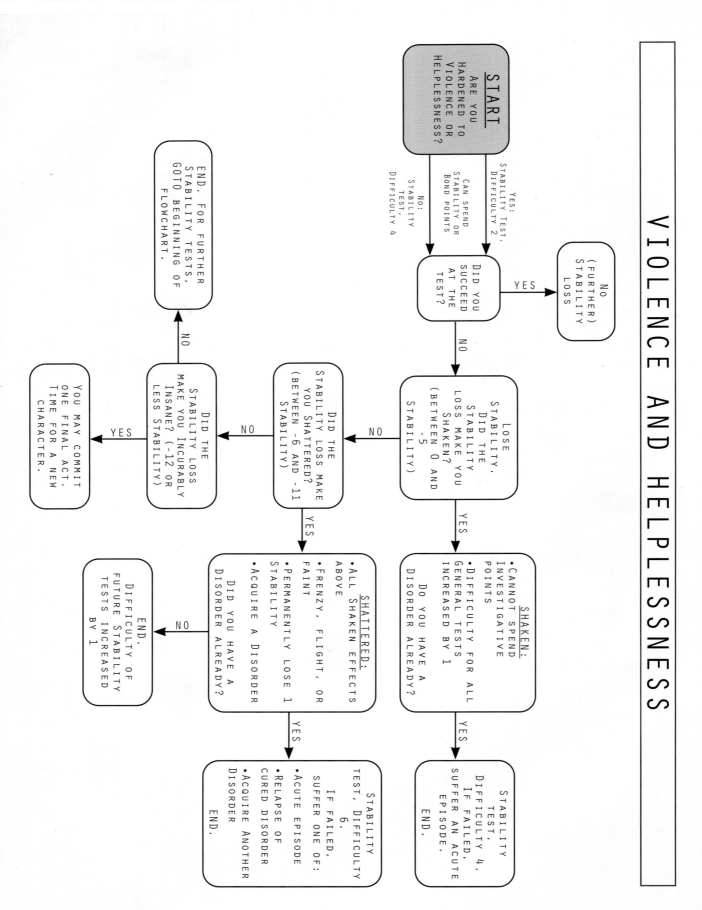

VIOLENCE AND HELPLESSNESS

START
ARE YOU HARDENED TO VIOLENCE OR HELPLESSNESS?

YES: STABILITY TEST, DIFFICULTY 2

NO: STABILITY TEST, DIFFICULTY 4

CAN SPEND STABILITY OR BOND POINTS

DID YOU SUCCEED AT THE TEST?

YES → NO (FURTHER) STABILITY LOSS

NO

LOSE STABILITY. DID THE STABILITY LOSS MAKE YOU SHAKEN? (BETWEEN 0 AND -5 STABILITY)

SHAKEN:
• CANNOT SPEND INVESTIGATIVE POINTS
• DIFFICULTY FOR ALL GENERAL TESTS INCREASED BY 1

YES → DO YOU HAVE A DISORDER ALREADY?

YES → STABILITY TEST, DIFFICULTY 4. IF FAILED, SUFFER AN ACUTE EPISODE. END.

NO

DID THE STABILITY LOSS MAKE YOU SHATTERED? (BETWEEN -6 AND -11 STABILITY)

SHATTERED:
• ALL SHAKEN EFFECTS ABOVE
• FRENZY, FLIGHT, OR FAINT
• PERMANENTLY LOSE 1 STABILITY
• ACQUIRE A DISORDER

YES → DID YOU HAVE A DISORDER ALREADY?

NO → **END.** DIFFICULTY OF FUTURE STABILITY TESTS INCREASED BY 1

YES → STABILITY TEST, DIFFICULTY 6. IF FAILED, SUFFER ONE OF:
• ACUTE EPISODE
• RELAPSE OF CURED DISORDER
• ACQUIRE ANOTHER DISORDER
END.

NO

DID THE STABILITY LOSS MAKE YOU INSANE? (-12 OR LESS STABILITY)

YES → YOU MAY COMMIT ONE FINAL ACT. TIME FOR A NEW CHARACTER.

NO → **END.** FOR FURTHER STABILITY TESTS, GOTO BEGINNING OF FLOWCHART.

Violence Stimuli

Incidents of Violence	Potential Stability Loss
You see a fresh corpse; you witness a killing; you are ambushed by gunfire	1
A human opponent attacks you with evident intent to do serious harm; you mutilate or desecrate a stranger's corpse	2
You witness acts of torture	2
You cripple an innocent	2
A human opponent attacks you with evident intent to kill; you burn your friends' bodies or otherwise desecrate their corpses	3
You kill someone in a fight	3
You see a particularly grisly murder or accident scene	3
You are set on fire or mutilated; you are reduced to 0 Health or below	4
You see hundreds of corpses; you witness a large battle	4
You kill someone in cold blood; you torture someone; you accidentally kill an innocent	5
You are tortured for an hour or longer	6
You kill a friend, loved one, or Bond	8

Helplessness Stimuli

Incidents of Helplessness	Potential Stability Loss
You get fired	1
You nearly get a Bond or team mate hurt or killed	2
A Bond score is reduced to -1	3
You are pinned or caught in a trap in a dangerous place (e.g., punji stake pit, minefield)	3
You learn that one of your Network contacts has been violently killed	3
A Bond or team mate is badly wounded or hurt	3
You spend a week in solitary confinement	4
You are suddenly paralyzed or blinded	4
You learn that a friend, loved one, or Bond has been violently killed	4
You discover the corpse of one of your Network contacts	4
You are flung into a pit of corpses	5
You discover the corpse of a friend, loved one, or Bond	5
You are attacked by a friend, loved one, or Bond	5
You see one of your Network contacts killed	5
You see a friend, loved one, or Bond killed	6
You discover that you have committed cannibalism	6
You see a friend, loved one, or Bond killed in a particularly gruesome manner, or in a way you accidentally caused or abetted	7

The Handler should feel free to assess Stability losses for other incidents, using the examples provided as a benchmark.

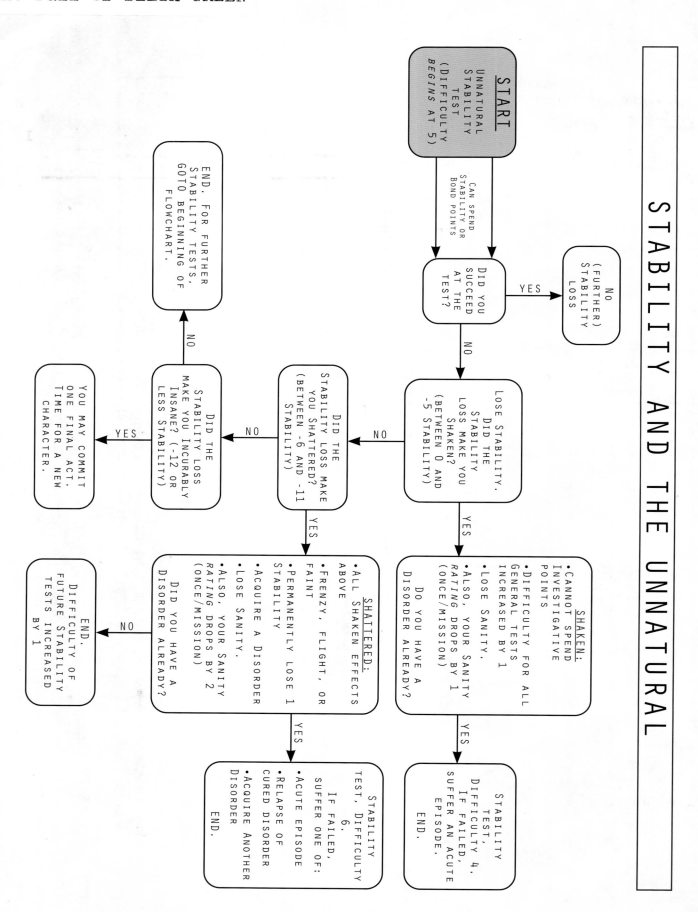

STABILITY AND THE UNNATURAL

START
UNNATURAL STABILITY TEST (DIFFICULTY *BEGINS* AT 5)

CAN SPEND STABILITY OR BOND POINTS

DID YOU SUCCEED AT THE TEST?

— YES → NO (FURTHER) STABILITY LOSS

NO ↓

LOSE STABILITY. DID THE STABILITY LOSS MAKE YOU SHAKEN? (BETWEEN 0 AND -5 STABILITY)

— NO → DID THE STABILITY LOSS MAKE YOU SHATTERED? (BETWEEN -6 AND -11 STABILITY)

— NO → DID THE STABILITY LOSS MAKE YOU INCURABLY INSANE? (-12 OR LESS STABILITY)

— YES → YOU MAY COMMIT ONE FINAL ACT. TIME FOR A NEW CHARACTER.

— NO → END. FOR FURTHER STABILITY TESTS, GOTO BEGINNING OF FLOWCHART.

SHAKEN:
• CANNOT SPEND INVESTIGATIVE POINTS
• DIFFICULTY FOR ALL GENERAL TESTS INCREASED BY 1
• LOSE SANITY.
• ALSO, YOUR SANITY RATING DROPS BY 1 (ONCE/MISSION)

DO YOU HAVE A DISORDER ALREADY?

— YES → STABILITY TEST, DIFFICULTY 4. IF FAILED, SUFFER AN ACUTE EPISODE. END.

SHATTERED:
• ALL SHAKEN EFFECTS ABOVE
• FRENZY, FLIGHT, OR FAINT
• PERMANENTLY LOSE 1 STABILITY
• ACQUIRE A DISORDER
• LOSE SANITY.
• ALSO, YOUR SANITY *RATING* DROPS BY 2 (ONCE/MISSION)

DID YOU HAVE A DISORDER ALREADY?

— NO → END. DIFFICULTY OF FUTURE STABILITY TESTS INCREASED BY 1

— YES → STABILITY TEST, DIFFICULTY 6. IF FAILED, SUFFER ONE OF:
• ACUTE EPISODE
• RELAPSE OF CURED DISORDER
• ACQUIRE ANOTHER DISORDER
END.

The Unnatural

Stability tests against the Unnatural are qualitatively different from those against Violence or Helplessness. While humans recoil from bloody danger, and strain against inaction, they cannot even begin to guess at responses to stimuli from outside the edges of existence. The unnatural literally short-circuits human cognition, because it is utterly alien to human experience, and it opens huge gaps in our connection to the world.

All Stability tests against the Unnatural *begin* at a Difficulty of 5. They otherwise behave mechanically like other Stability tests. Agents may make such tests to resist psychic attacks or hypergeometric influences, as well as in response to potentially deranging incidents.

Here are two Stability tests in action:

Seabring's current Stability pool is 8. While staking out a dismal warehouse on the Cleveland waterfront, he sees a cadaverous figure the color of bleached bone materialize in the warehouse's dim interior. He must make a Stability test against the standard Difficulty for an Unnatural incident of 5. Seabring spends a sensible 2 points of Stability on the test. Alas, he rolls a 1, for a result of 3, two lower than the Difficulty Number. Having failed, he suffers a Stability loss of 3. ("You see an unnatural creature from a distance.") Having spent 2 points on his bonus and lost another 3 to the failure, Seabring's new Stability pool value is 3.

Unnatural Stimuli

Incidents of the Unnatural	Potential Stability Loss
You attempt a Psychotherapy test (not merely a spend) on a character tainted or damaged by the unnatural	2
You experience a strong unnatural sensation such as intense déjà vu, "missing time", or hallucinations	2
You see an unnatural creature or phenomenon from a distance	3
You witness an obviously unnatural, but not necessarily threatening, omen or magical effect – a wall covered in horrible insects, a talking cat, or a bleeding window	3
You see an unnatural creature or phenomenon up close; you see a corpse walk	4
You witness a clearly unnatural or impossible killing; you are attacked by the unnatural	5
You witness or experience an obviously unnatural, and threatening, omen or magical effect – a cold hand clutches your heart, a swarm of bees pours out of your mouth	5
You are attacked by a single human-sized or smaller unnatural creature	6
You are possessed by some outside force, but conscious while it operates your body unspeakably	7
You speak with someone you know well who you know to be dead	7
You are attacked by a single gigantic unnatural creature or by a horde of unnatural creatures	7

Seabring has a mental disorder, a phobia of white things caused by his experiences in Greenland. Because he lost Stability from the sight of a white shape, he has to resist an acute episode of his phobia. (If he were Shaken, he would have to resist an acute episode regardless of the current trauma.) He makes a Stability test to resist fleeing and remain on watch, at a Difficulty of 4. Putting 2 points into the test, he rolls another 1, for a result of 3, another failure. Seabring turns and runs, but loses no additional Stability for failing, only the 2 points he spent on the test. His new Stability pool value is 1.

PULL YOUR OWN TRIGGER

With players who are really enthusiastic about the personal-horror side of the setting, the Handler may want to try this more intense option: let the player decide when some emotional crisis or damage in play triggers a 2-point Stability test for her Agent. Such players will sense when the pressures of constant warfare, lying, and existential terror grind their Agents hardest.

Psychological Triage

A character with the Psychotherapy ability can spend points from that pool to help another character regain lost Stability points. For every 1 Psychotherapy point spent, the recipient gains 2 Stability points.

If a character is Shaken, entering an acute episode, or otherwise acting in an erratic manner due to mental stress, you can spend 2 points of Psychotherapy (and a few minutes) to talk him down into a state of temporary lucidity. He can then act rationally unless something worse happens.

You can use psychological triage only during the same operation in which the subject character lost Stability.

Adapting to Trauma

People can become hardened to traumatic stimuli. What sends one Agent fleeing may seem mundane to an individual who has survived it often enough. Adaptation to Violence or to Helplessness means your Stability test Difficulty lowers to 2 for that type of trauma.

Adaptation to Violence or adaptation to Helplessness occurs after your Agent has lost Stability from that kind of trauma three times in a row without becoming Shaken. The character sheet has spaces to mark your Agent's progress toward adaptation.

Adapting to Violence: Unfortunately, your Agent's empathy suffers. Her ratings in Flattery, Inspiration, Reassurance, and Negotiation are capped at 1, meaning all her Bond strengths are capped at 2. She can spend any excess pool points remaining in those categories but they will not refresh.

Adapting to Helplessness: Your agent's individuation and will to succeed suffers. He gains 1 fewer pool point from any refreshes (p. 126) during the operation (except from *Burning Bonds*, see below), and loses 1 extra point of Stability to any Stress Penalties (p. 047) during the operation.

Adapting to the Unnatural: Is impossible.

Burning Bonds

You can spend points from any Bond on any Stability test, as though they were Stability pool points.

You can also spend Bond points *immediately* after losing Stability to refresh Stability pool points you just lost. This costs 2 Bond points per 1 Stability point refreshed. This exchange rate remains the same whether or not you are Adapted to Helplessness (p. 120). You can "undo" becoming Shaken or Shattered this way.

In both cases, this represents your Agent drawing strength from normal human relationships, or possibly projecting her worries and fears onto them. In either case, it damages your Agent's relationship with the object of the Bond. Make a note of the damage, and the next time your Agent interacts with that person, decide and demonstrate the shape his damage takes: hostile acting out, getting drunk, irrational blame, cheating, sullen withdrawal?

The burden of DELTA GREEN does not only weigh on those who volunteered to shoulder it.

MOTHER'S LITTLE HELPERS

Taking any of the new tranquilizers such as Valium and Librium can give you either 1 or 2 points (Agent chooses) to spend on a Stability test to resist an acute episode of a disorder. They raise the Difficulty for all other actions (except Stability tests) in this scene and the next by +1 or +2, respectively. Using such drugs frequently may lead the Handler to award you a pill Addiction as a new disorder, which among other things means the tranquilizers stop boosting your Stability tests.

Heavy drinking or marijuana use gives your Agent 1 point to spend on such a Stability test. Getting wasted raises further Difficulties by +1 or +2 (Handler rolls or decides) as above. Alcohol Addiction is a likely next disorder in such a case; frequent marijuana use is grounds for dismissal from the federal government or military.

Losing Sanity

Your Sanity is affected by directly experiencing the unnatural and by piecing together its truths from the evidence you uncover during your investigations. You cannot make a test to avoid losing Sanity.

You lose Sanity in one of four main ways:

△ An Unnatural shock drops your Stability pool to 0 or below.

△ You use the Unnatural ability (p. 062).

△ You perform a hypergeometric ritual (see *Hypergeometry*, p. 197).

△ You behold one of the gods or titans behind the scrim of the universe (see *Encountering Entities*, p. 282).

A few other specific hypergeometrical or unnatural stimuli can also cost you Sanity. Such happenings usually appear in a given scenario or operation; the designer or Handler should tailor the specifics to the story.

When your Sanity reaches 0, you have accepted the complete reality of the unreal. You are a willing puppet of hideous outside forces: in other words, you have become a GMC.

Unnatural Shocks

Each time you are Shaken by an Unnatural encounter or attack (when your Stability drops to between 0 and -5), your Sanity *rating* drops by 1 point.

Each time you are Shattered by an Unnatural encounter or attack (when your Stability drops to between -6 and -11), your Sanity *rating* drops by 2 points.

You can only suffer one such Sanity rating loss (the most severe) in a given mission or operation.

Unnatural Ability Use

Using the Unnatural ability (see p. 062) to "piece together fragments of dissociated knowledge" and gain insight into an adventure invites the loss of both Stability and (if the discovery is terrifying enough) Sanity. You cannot make a test to avoid this loss. The degree of loss does not depend on the number of pool points in the Unnatural you spent (if any), but on the nature of the revelation.

The Handler should not enforce losses if the player deduces the horrible truth without actually using the Agent's ability in the Unnatural. This is merely heads-up thinking, and should be rewarded. Any player can, of course, request such a loss for her Agent, but it's easier to just use The Unnatural to earn one and confirm your deduction.

Any Sanity loss from the Unnatural use cannot be denied away — such knowledge comes from within, and the Agent knows it to be accurate.

Use the nearby chart as a guideline, but the Handler should take care to hand craft really powerful revelations to the individual Agent.

Agents who suffer a revelation that proves their Motivation to be meaningless can no longer gain Certainty Refreshes from following it. They can still lose Stability by not following their Motivation, raging helplessly at the mechanical fate that enmeshes them within its toils. This is an excellent opportunity for role-playing.

Unnatural Ability Revelations

Revelation or Intuition	Stability Pool Loss	Sanity Pool Loss
Some aspect of the unnatural is behind this mystery; any specifics are either comfortably distant in space or time, or not immediately relevant to your larger concerns	2	0
This unnatural truth poses a clear and present danger to innocents; this truth goes deeper, reaches back farther, or has wider implications, than you previously believed	3	1
This unnatural truth poses a clear and present danger to you or your loved ones	4	1
This unnatural truth poses a clear and present danger to your country; this truth is global or epochal in scope	6	2
This unnatural truth could destroy the world or is doing so right now, probably inevitably; this truth proves your Motivation to be meaningless or doomed	8	3

Clawing Sanity Back

The mind rejects its own destruction. It's possible to cushion the blows of reality and remain in ignorance for a few precious weeks or months longer.

Δ If you cannot prove it happened, you can seek refuge in **denial**.

Δ If your brain shuts itself down, you can miss the true horror by **fainting**.

Δ If you **destroy the unnatural** horror before you, you can fool yourself into believing that you've restored reality.

Denial

If, at the end of the operation, there is absolutely no proof of your horrible experience – samples, photographs, recordings, eerie artifacts – then your Sanity rating recovers by 1 point. This may lead to conflicts with other Agents (or DELTA GREEN higher-ups) who wish to save such things for future study.

The Handler may require your Agent to take a mental disorder or at least provide an excellent "cover memory" describing what you believe "actually" happened. If your Investigator acts on unnatural knowledge gained from the mission, the Handler may immediately charge you 1 Sanity rating point as the traumatic memories force their way back to the surface.

You cannot recover Sanity without losing it first.

If your Sanity was driven to 0 or lower by the shock, you can no longer deny the terrible beauty of the unnatural.

Fainting

If the player wishes, he may declare that his Agent faints dead away rather than fully absorbing a given unnatural experience. Such an Agent loses only 1 Sanity pool point, and does not necessarily become Shaken or Shattered, but may play no further part in the scene. Agents cannot "faint away" the consequences of using the Unnatural ability.

If the Agent faints while alone, or his partners flee the scene without his body, the Handler may maltreat the fainted Agent in any number of ways. She should try to adhere to the following two guidelines, however:

Δ First, if the fate of the fainter is a mystery, she should be prepared to offer clues to its solution, just as she would any other occult horror in the game.

Δ Second, the Handler should avoid just killing the fainter outright. It's weak narrative, it's bad drama, and it's just plain counter-productive game play. Horror role-playing is a constant collaboration; by fainting, a player is offering a valuable resource – and considerable trust – to the Handler. Don't squander either.

Destroying the Unnatural

The unnatural represents such an affront to the human mind that exhibiting any sort of control over it is a "victory." At the Handler's discretion, any destruction of the unnatural by an Agent can restore hope, and in the process, Sanity.

Destroying an unnatural creature, neutralizing an unnatural phenomenon, or destroying an object known to contain otherworldly power restores an amount of Sanity rating points equivalent to the amount that would be lost by deducing its nature using the Unnatural (see table, p. 121). Destroying a danger to innocents restores 1 Sanity; destroying a danger to the entire United States restores 2 Sanity.

You can never restore more than 3 Sanity during or after any one operation.

Destroying the unnatural can never bring Sanity higher than its maximum, usually 10 minus your rating in the Unnatural ability (p. 062).

Each Agent who was directly involved in putting the threat down gains this Sanity recovery.

If your Handler is running a Bright and Shining game (*These Are the Lonely Times*, p. 130) you refresh Stability pool points equal to your restored Sanity rating points.

If your Handler is running a Harrowing game, you cannot restore Sanity to above your current Sanity rating. You refresh Sanity pool points instead of rating points.

Mental Disorders

A human mind can only cope with so much stress. Traumatic events such as contact with the supernatural, witnessing violent acts and a life of deception take their mental toll, and eventually, an Agent can develop a disorder as a coping mechanism. An Agent who becomes Shattered (p.113) gains a disorder. A disorder is like a release valve for intolerable stress. Indulging in it helps your Agent cope. It's possible to suffer from multiple disorders at the same time. There is no game-mechanical difference between mental illness caused by mundane trauma and mental illness caused by unnatural phenomena, and possibly no medical difference detectable by contemporary science.

Whatever the source of the disorder, it takes the form of an adaptation to the stimulus that produced it. It may manifest a few hours after the trauma, or it might take days, weeks, or months to appear.

The Handler and the player determine which disorder your Agent receives and when, if the circumstances or trigger event do not make the choice obvious. (Since each type of stress has six sample disorders, Handlers with a firm belief in the randomness of the universe can roll a die.) If Deep Ones swarmed your Agent, she might suffer thalassophobia (the fear of the ocean), but ailurophobia (the fear of cats) is unlikely. Consider the sample disorders just that: examples, not restrictive requirements.

Acute Episodes

A disorder is a chronic, ongoing condition. It lurks under the surface, threatening to erupt when things get bad.

Any time your Agent becomes Shaken, or any time your Agent loses Stability from a trigger that pertains directly to his disorder, you must make a Difficulty 4 Stability test. (Difficulty 5 if your Agent is Shattered.) If it succeeds, your Agent masters his disorder, for now. If it fails, the disorder takes over. If he suffers from more than one, the Handler decides which comes to the fore. As long as the Agent is in crisis or in the presence of the trigger, he succumbs to the disorder's internal logic and must act accordingly.

The Handler always decides the exact repercussions, and whether it happens immediately or builds gradually, in the aftermath of the trauma.

When your Agent is going through an acute episode, it is obvious to everyone that something is wrong. The Psychotherapy ability can diagnose your Agent's particular disorder.

Sample Disorders from Violence

Violent stresses tend to produce behavioral disorders: alterations of action or behavior, or a return to the source of the trauma.

Addiction

You develop a serious addiction, most likely to alcohol or drugs. When you do not have a supply available, you must make a Stability test (Difficulty 4) to proceed with the current operation rather than chasing your fix. When presented with an opportunity to gratify your addiction, you must make the same Stability test to resist the opportunity. Being drunk

WITHDRAWAL

Going through withdrawal from a physiologically addictive substance such as heroin or alcohol takes four weeks. During this time, you are Shaken. You must make one Stability test per week, at whatever Difficulty level your addiction was when you began withdrawal. Failure drives you to relapse — if you absolutely cannot get a fix, reduce your Health by the amount of your failure. Any relapse restarts the four-week clock.

or high is game-mechanically the same as Hurt (p. 094).

Acute Episode: Your addiction distracts you from the job; to make an Investigative spend or a General test requiring concentration (most non-combat tests) you must also spend 1 Stability point.

Aggressive Tendencies

You react impulsively, and usually angrily, to any sign of disrespect, neglect, or crowding. You have sudden mood swings, ranging from fear of being left alone to chronic boredom to rage against yourself or your so-called friends. You must spend 1 additional point to use any Interpersonal ability besides HUMINT, Interrogation, Intimidation, or Streetwise.

Acute Episode: You lash out in irrational rage; if you are Shattered, you attack in all-out frenzy.

Fixation

You fixate on an object associated with your trauma and credit it with your salvation: a weapon, a helmet, a Bible, etc. You cannot be without your object; if it's destroyed or lost, you immediately lose d+3 Stability.

Acute Episode: You can do nothing except protect your fixation-object from harm.

Gross Stress Reaction

You are haunted by dreams of the incident, and spend your days in a constant state of anxiety and alert, as if prepared for it to repeat itself at any moment. Loud noises especially unnerve and terrify you, or any sensory input reminding you of the incident. You must spend 2 Stability pool points to take the first action in a combat.

Acute Episode: You freeze up, unable to take any action for fifteen minutes, and remain Shaken for 24 hours after that.

Nightmares

Every time you try to sleep, make a Stability test (Difficulty 4). If it fails, you wake repeatedly in terror, losing the possibility of rest or pool point refreshment (p. 126), and becoming Exhausted (p. 085).

Acute Episode: Sleeplessness leads to hallucinations as your nightmares unfold before your waking (?) eyes. You are Shaken, and suffer +3 to all Difficulties.

Paranoia

Your fear of unseen enemies, looming danger, and betrayal by your own side has surpassed occupational hazard levels. Not just

the Handler but the other players can call for your Stability test to resist an acute episode at a stressful moment. On the bright side, you can now spend Stability on Stealth tests to avoid surveillance.

Acute Episode: You take ridiculous and time-consuming counter-measures, accuse allies of betraying you to Them, or otherwise give your fears full rein. Add 1 to the cost of all Academic and Interpersonal spends.

Sample Disorders from Helplessness

Helplessness causes anxiety, which typically relieves itself in neurotic and psychoneurotic defenses.

Addiction

See the description on p. 123.

Anxiety Neurosis

You suffer uncontrollable worry manifesting in fatigue, restlessness, headaches, panic attacks, and compulsive behavior. You may insist on cleaning or ordering your surroundings, e.g., staying behind to straighten up all the shell casings.

Acute Episode: You can only spend points on Conceal, Notice, or Preparedness. You add +1 to all test Difficulties.

Conversion Reaction

Superficially you seem fine, if distant and tense or nervous and high-strung. Choose one form of this disorder: blindness, deafness, or paralysis.

Acute Episode: The disorder strikes and leaves your Agent blind, deaf, or paralyzed with numbness and tremors until the source of stress goes away.

Depressive Reaction

You fall into dull, deadened melancholia. You have trouble sleeping, getting out of bed, motivating yourself, and thinking optimistically. You feel sluggish, drained of energy. You are increasingly haunted by suicidal thoughts, and by feelings of utter worthlessness and guilt.

Acute Episode: You can never act as the aggressor in a contest; in group combats or chases, you are always last to act. Your Hit Threshold is 1 lower than normal, to reflect both your sluggishness and your carelessness in danger.

Dissociative Reaction

You suffer periods of detachment from yourself and the world, feeling helplessly disconnected from your body or from physical existence itself. It's as though you're watching it happen to someone on television, or in some kind of game.

Acute Episode: You have no interest in taking any action, including self-preservation in combat.

Phobia

You have an irrational terror of some object, color, state of being, or activity that your mind relates to your trauma. Enclosure-related phobias (claustrophobia or agoraphobia) are most common, but many others exist.

Acute Episode: You must flee in terror from the phobic object. If you cannot flee, you collapse into a fetal position.

Sample Disorders from the Unnatural

How does the mind – an organ evolved to decipher reality – respond to the stress of perceiving that which cannot be understood? Often, with psychosis.

Amnesia

You forget everything about the traumatic experience. This disorder works like Denial (p. 122) if applicable. Make a note of all Stability and Sanity lost to the traumatic incident.

Acute Episode: Either you recall your trauma and immediately lose the Stability and Sanity cost associated with it the first time; or you enter an amnesiac fugue state and begin wandering around not knowing anything about yourself, including how to fire a weapon.

Megalomania

What does it mean to pass through the very mirror of reality? Are you chosen by the hidden gods, or are you humanity's last best hope against them? Either way your exalted viewpoint exempts you from mere human concerns.

Acute Episode: You cannot use Interpersonal abilities, or Stealth, or do anything else involving leaving the spotlight for one minute.

Multiple Personality

Most of the time, you seem fine, but when under stress you take on an alternate identity with its own personality, memories, and subset of your abilities. The longer you suffer multiple personality (or the more acute episodes you undergo), the more alternate identities may surface. The Handler decides when and whether you keep control of your Agent's behavior.

Acute Episode: You shift into an alternate identity.

Nightmares

See the description on p. 124.

Paranoia

See the description on p. 124.

Schizophrenia

You are plagued by hallucinations, both visual and auditory — "hearing voices" is the classical symptom of schizophrenia. You may also suffer from delusions ranging from confusion of identity ("I am Jackie O!") to mind control. ("The computer was drinking my thoughts, so I smashed it.") Your speech can be slurred and disorganized, even breaking down into completely aphasic "word salad." Your social affect is flat and you scare people, either by inappropriate giggling or jerking, or for no apparent reason.

Acute Episode: All that, except worse. You are Shaken, and suffer +3 to all Difficulties.

Refreshment and Recovery

Agents wear themselves down over the course of an operation, drawing on reserves of inner strength and focus built up over years of training and life-or-death decisions. And assuming they make those decisions correctly, what does not kill them may make them stronger.

Regaining Pool Points

Spent points from various pools are restored at different rates, depending on their narrative purpose.

Refreshing Investigative Ability Pools

Investigative Ability pools are refreshed only at the end of each operation, without regard to the amount of time that passes in the game world. Players seeking to husband their resources may ask you how long cases typically run, in real time. Most groups finish operations over 2-3 sessions. Players may revise their sense of how carefully to manage point spending as they see how quickly their group typically completes an adventure.

Handlers running extremely long, multi-stage operations may designate certain story events as breakpoints where all Investigative pools are refreshed. For example, a thorough investigation tracking an artifact smuggling ring from New York galleries to Greek shipowners to Beirut bazaars to Iraqi archaeological sites might allow refreshment of Investigative pools after each layer of the organization is rolled up.

Refreshing General Ability Pools

At the Handler's discretion, you may be able to refresh 1 or 2 pool points from any General Ability by following your Motivation into danger or story complication (see *Certainty Refreshes*, p. 047).

Tactical Fact-Finding Benefits (see p. 146) and other special circumstances may also allow refreshes during play.

Pools for the physical abilities of Athletics, Drive, Firearms, Heavy Weapons, Melee Weapons, Pilot, and Unarmed Combat fully refresh whenever 24 hours of game-world time elapses since the last expenditure. If the Agent got no sleep during that period, the Handler may not allow full (or any) refreshes.

Bureaucracy and Network cannot be refreshed during an operation.

Health and Stability have their own refreshment rules (p. 126).

Sanity does not refresh after the operation, although Agents can recover lost Sanity by *Denial* (p. 122) and *Fainting* (p. 122), and by *Destroying the Unnatural* (p. 122).

The remaining General Abilities (and Network) refresh at the end of each operation, like Investigative Abilities. General Ability points spent investigatively (see p. 063) still refresh just like General Abilities.

Havens

Whenever the Agents are able to reach a temporary haven — a bar, an all-night diner, a car trip, a church, a safe house — in which they're free from danger and horrific manifestations for an hour or more, they may fully refresh up to three General Abilities, except for Bureaucracy, Health, Network, Sanity, and Stability. (Think about the next scene: if it's likely to be a fight or a chase, refresh Athletics or Drive and two combat skills.) They lose all refreshed points if their supposed place of safety is penetrated or reveals itself as a place of hazard.

The Agents get only one opportunity for accelerated Haven refreshment per session.

Refreshing Health

The Health pool refreshes over time, at a rate of 2 points per day of rest. (*Seriously wounded* characters heal at a different rate, over a period of hospitalization; see p. 094.)

Use of the First Aid ability (see p. 066) can restore some health in the course of a session.

Refreshing Stability

Stability does not refresh automatically.

If you suggest a spend for your Agent, and the Handler and other players agree that the result was especially impressive, you may roll one die and refresh that many Stability points to reflect your Agent's restored confidence in herself. This rule does not apply if your Handler is running a Harrowing game (*These Are The Lonely Times*, p. 130).

In a Bright and Shining game (p. 130) you recover some Stability by destroying the unnatural (*Destroying the Unnatural*, p. 122).

Another Agent can spend Psychotherapy pool points to permit you to recover some Stability in the course of a session (see *Psychological Triage*, p. 120).

If you have an Addiction (see p. 123), you can refresh 2 points of Stability by engaging in your addiction between operations.

Otherwise, you refresh Stability by engaging in your Personal Life (p. 128) between missions.

Improving Your Character

At the end of each operation, each player gets **2 experience points** for each session they participated in. (This assumes a small number of 3-4 hour sessions; if you play in shorter bursts, modify accordingly.) Players who had Agents die in the course of the investigation only get points for each session involving their current Agent.

These experience points can be spent as build points to increase either Investigative or General Abilities. You can also save them as unattached build points, and assign them to abilities in play as mentioned in *Saving Extra Build Points* on p. 021.

You may acquire new abilities or bolster existing ones. If necessary to preserve credibility, rationalize new abilities as areas of expertise you've had all along, but never really had reason to demonstrate before.

You can increase Stability or Health with experience; you increase your pool along with your rating.

You *can not* increase your Sanity rating with experience. The only way to increase your Sanity rating is by *Destroying the Unnatural* (p. 122).

Reassigning Points

You may also reassign 1 or 2 build points from one ability to another, justifying it as skill atrophy: "I've let my Photography become quite rusty, what with all the Demolitions I've been setting off." This may reflect in-game experiences, or just your changed priorities for the character.

OPPOSITION POOL REFRESHES

In accordance with GUMSHOE's narrative-based style, opponents refresh ability pool points according to how often they appear. A foe not encountered for 24 hours or more may replenish all of his ability pools, with the exception of Health, which he recovers at a rate of 1d6 points per day.

If the Agents encounter a foe later in the same day, such as by tracking her to a safe house, she can refresh all her ability pools to a maximum of half their total rating, again with the exception of Health, which she can not refresh at all.

The Handler may refresh such a foe's Health with a narrative explanation (she stopped off at an emergency room, she had a medic on her squad), but in general, player initiative in harrying a foe should be rewarded with that opponent's weakness.

Many unnatural creatures regenerate Health in special (and unsavory) ways, or at an accelerated rate, or both. They use their own rules (see p. 268) rather than these general guidelines.

Back in the World

The Fall of DELTA GREEN features occasional vignettes that focus on the Agents' regular lives. These short scenes last no more than a few minutes. You likely play them out between missions, but the Handler can set them whenever she thinks is appropriate: cross-cuts, flashbacks, and responses to a brain wave are all possibilities. Other players may take the roles of the GMCs in vignettes, if your group tends toward dramatic play.

Vignettes let you explore the human things in your Agent's life – and often track their slow destruction by DELTA GREEN.

What Changed

In a home vignette, take stock of what changed for your Agent in the last operation.

Bonds Damaged or Broken: How have these relationships deteriorated?

Permanent Injuries: What do they look like?

Disorders Gained: If you and the Handler haven't determined your new mental disorder yet, do so. Maybe play out a (mostly) "safe" acute episode at work or home.

Work: Is there blowback on your official cover job from the last operation? Did you abuse your authority, lie to superiors, steal or destroy government property? Can anyone prove it? See *Discipline* (p. 131) and *Prosecution* (p. 131).

Personal Life

For the vignette, the player chooses one of the following pursuits. Describe how your Agent is pursuing it, and roll the appropriate test to resolve it.

All points spent during inter-operation vignettes come after the normal post-scenario refreshes of Investigative and General Abilities.

Some pursuits damage non-DELTA GREEN Bonds. *This does not apply if an Agent has no Bonds outside of DELTA GREEN.*

Rebuilding Bonds

You focus on your daily life or work. Describe what you do to support a Bond other than one with DELTA GREEN. Make a Difficulty 4 Stability test. You can spend Interpersonal points on this test, but they do not refresh before your next mission.

If you succeed, play a brief happy or hopeful vignette, increase the Bond by 1, and refresh d-2 Stability (minimum 1).

On a successful 6, increase the Bond by 2, and refresh d+0 Stability.

If you fail, play a hurtful or bleak scene; on a failed 1, reduce that Bond by 1.

One With Nature

You spend time alone, away from stress, distraction, and obligation. This is not time with family or loved ones; it's physical activity without thought or commitment. Perhaps it somehow nourishes your Motivation (p. 047). It might be a weekend in the mountains or in Vegas, as long as it's not a work trip. Make a Difficulty 4 Stability test. You can spend points from an appropriate Investigative Ability (e.g., Streetwise, Survival) on this test, but they do not refresh before your next mission.

If you succeed, describe how you refreshed d-1 Stability.

On a successful 6, refresh d+1 Stability.

If you fail, reduce the non-DELTA GREEN Bond you selfishly neglected by 1 and play the scene that way.

Establish a New Bond

You meet someone special, or realize that someone you've already met is truly important to you. Spend 1 Interpersonal point and roll a die. Do not refresh the Interpersonal point before your next mission. Also, reduce one non-DELTA GREEN Bond by 1 point as you neglect them for the new person in your life.

On a 1, they reject the Bond. Lose 1 Stability pool point.

On a 2-5, you Bond successfully. Subtract 2 from the die result; that is your new Bond's rating. (Yes, you can begin with a Bond rating of 0.)

On a 6, you Bond successfully, with a rating of 3. Refresh the Interpersonal point you spent.

Play out the scene to reflect the result.

Head Games

You seek help for your mental stress through therapy. The character administering the treatment makes a Psychotherapy test (Difficulty 4). Alternately, you might use Network to recruit a GMC psychologist, or Bureaucracy to find a government therapist on the q.t. A GMC psychologist makes the test using her point pool (either your Network spend or your Bureaucracy test margin) at Difficulty 3.

If you tell your therapist the truth (and spend 1 Reassurance), her roll is at -1 to Difficulty, but you may have exposed her to danger (or Stability loss) or yourself to DELTA GREEN discipline for violating operational secrecy. You do not refresh your Reassurance point before the next mission.

If you lie about your experiences, her roll is at +1 to Difficulty.

Each successful session refreshes d+0 Stability, or d+2 on a successful 6.

A failed session does nothing but waste time and points. On a failed 1, you lose 1 Stability.

After three consecutive successful tests, *and* three consecutive operations in which the patient's Stability pool remains above 0 at all times, all mental disorders suffered by the patient go away. Players may still adopt quirks and features of their illness into the roleplaying and characterization of their Agents, even if cured.

Stay on the Case

You spend your nights and weekends poring over an old operation's case files and evidence. Reduce one non-DELTA GREEN Bond by 1 as your obsession drives them away.

Spend 1 point of either Criminology, Fringe Science, or Occult, which does not refresh before the next mission.

You uncover some pertinent fact, significant insight, or valuable clue to an ongoing investigation or operation, though perhaps not one you're immediately tasked for. The Handler will come up with something good, or she may ask you to wait to follow up until she can think of something really good.

Refresh d-3 Stability as you come to terms with the horror of the past. And yes, this means you might lose 1 or 2 Stability if you roll low: your obsessive focus on the horror of the past costs you.

Study the Unnatural

You pore over a grimoire, study an inscription, sleep with an artifact under your pillow, or camp out in a standing stone circle. Reduce one non-DELTA GREEN Bond by 1 as your obsession drives them away.

You gain 1 Hypergeometric Potential point (p. 197) or learn one ritual (p. 200).

Make a Difficulty 5 Stability test. If you succeed, nothing else happens; if you fail, lose 2 Stability. On a failed 1, lose 3 Stability and gain 1 rating point in the Unnatural.

The Handler narrates a brief vignette of your unnerving experience.

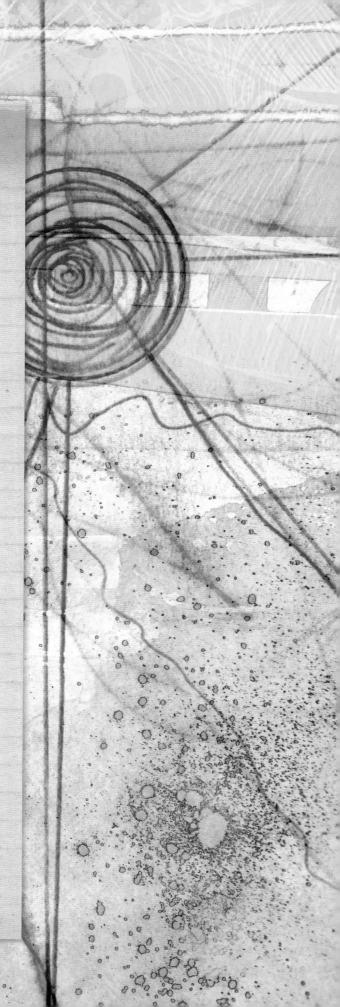

THESE ARE THE LONELY TIMES

For a long-running campaign intended to follow an arc from the Kennedy Summer to the Nixonian Fall, consider these optional changes to the Stability recovery rules.

Regaining Stability through interaction with the outside world works best when that world is not itself disintegrating. As distrust of the United States government increases throughout the decade, its employees find it harder and harder to remember why they risk life and sanity, and why it matters that they live a lie every night.

Apply the following changes to the Personal Life vignettes, depending on the campaign mode. Campaign modes by default hold true during given campaign years, as follows.

Bright and Shining (1960-1963): Increase all Stability rewards from Personal Life vignettes by 2 points. In addition, if you recovered any Sanity from a mission by *Destroying the Unnatural* (p. 122), recover an equal number of Stability points. Character generation does not need to include a *Revelation* (p. 050).

Stabilizing (1964-1967): Apply the rewards as written.

Harrowing (1968-1970): Decrease all Stability rewards from Personal Life vignettes by 1 point. The minimum reward remains 1 point, except for *Stay on the Case* (p. 129). Also, you cannot get Stability refreshes for spends (p. 078), and you cannot increase your Sanity *rating* (though you can still refill your pool) by *Destroying the Unnatural* (p. 122).

The Handler can use these modes outside a chronological context. She might decide she values character continuity in her game over psychological horror, and thus "set" her game at Bright and Shining regardless of the campaign year. Contrastingly, a game intended to focus on human disintegration in the face of the Outside might begin (and stay) at Harrowing. In a Harrowing game, Agents will likely put most of their experience build points into Stability, just trying to keep themselves together for one more mission.

Discipline

If the Agents have violated protocol, flashed badges under a flimsy pretext, left their post without explanation, misused agency funds, shot off ammunition without reporting it, and finally show up with unexplained injuries two weeks later ... there may be consequences.

If an Agent has pushed his luck or Uncle Sam's patience too far, the Handler might say his job is on the line. The Agent may resort to Interpersonal spends to stay sweet, Accounting or Law spends to fudge the paperwork, Agency spends to work the system, Bureaucracy tests to avoid too much real punishment, and so on.

If the mission was a big success for DELTA GREEN, regardless of its impact on the Agents or their cover jobs, higher-ups in the program may put a word in and lower the no-doubt dizzyingly high Difficulty of that last Bureaucracy test. Wise Agents have built up lots of favors with MAJESTIC, the CIA, or other offices known for quashing inconvenient internal investigations.

At the end of the process, a failed Bureaucracy test results in suspension or other disciplinary action. A badly failed Bureaucracy test results in dismissal.

Getting Fired

If you're fired, reduce your Bonds (including DELTA GREEN Bonds) by d+3 total points.

Getting fired from a cover job doesn't have much impact on being in DELTA GREEN. You may get transferred to a new, more DELTA GREEN-friendly (but inconvenient and worse paid) desk somewhere. Or you may technically be a fired civilian with even less access to resources. But you will still get the call and be expected to join the next operation. The mission is everything.

Prosecution

The Agents routinely violate state law, federal law, military procedure, and every other code they swore to uphold. Sometimes they do it where other people find out about it. Sometimes DELTA GREEN can't cover it up for them.

If your Agent is prosecuted for such crimes, determine the result in a between-missions vignette. A legal drama-minded Handler could bring the other Agents in as witnesses and play out a brief (TV episode trial-sized) courtroom sequence and cross-examination.

Given that the Agent is surely actually guilty, the team must make a Difficulty 8 (or higher!) Preparedness test to have pre-salted the record with falsely exculpatory evidence. Agents can Cooperate on this test: the defendant is the leader.

Any Agents may spend points from Law, Interrogation, or other relevant abilities on this test. Make sure they explain how that ability helps build the phony case for their partner's innocence.

They may also attempt to get DELTA GREEN to pull strings behind the scenes; this is usually a Bureaucracy test at Difficulty 5 or 6 depending on how valuable the Agents are to the program. A success lowers the trial Difficulty by 1, or by 2 on a successful 6.

No points spent on the trial refresh before the next mission.

A successful Preparedness test results in acquittal. The stress of the trial still reduces your non-DELTA GREEN Bonds by d+0 total points.

If the Preparedness test fails, your Agent is convicted or admits guilt in a plea bargain. See the consequences of *Getting Fired* (p. 131). Whether the Agent winds up in prison, on probation, or the target of a bankrupting civil suit is up to the Handler, as is the DELTA GREEN reaction to his fate.

TOOLS OF THE TRADE

This chapter covers the tools that Agents (and their players) can use during *The Fall of DELTA GREEN*. Some of these tools are physical items: sniper scopes, bug-sweepers, or Huey gunships.

Some of them are tactics and techniques for in-game action and player strategies.

Some of them might even be effective against the unnatural and its manifestations.

"They carried all they could bear, and then some, including a silent awe for the terrible power of the things they carried."

— Sgt. Tim O'Brien, U.S. Army, "The Things They Carried"

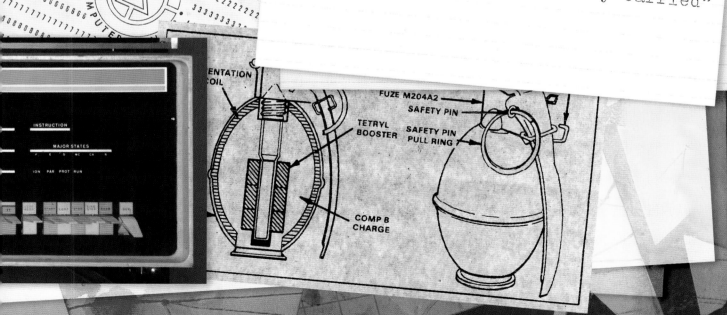

How to Get It

DELTA GREEN Agents are federal employees or contractors, at least theoretically on assignment by their employing agency or seconded to another. Thus, the government provides most of their mission requirements – vehicles, papers, weapons, etc. – ahead of time. Problems arise when the Agents' notion of the mission's requirements departs from that of their federal supervisors, or at least from that of whoever checks their expense reports afterward.

While incidental expenses can be ignored or handwaved as personal funds or cash socked away from an earlier operation, bigger purchases may have to show up in the story.

The Agents can model those bigger purchases with tests of Preparedness (when they already have it), Bureaucracy (when requisitioning it from their supervisors), or sometimes Network (if they just need access from someone who's already got one). Although the Difficulty numbers for any given test should respond to the specific game events first, use the Difficulty number in the Expense table as a guideline.

Expenses

Expense	Example	Difficulty
Incidental (Up to $20)	Meal, liquor, tank of gas, phone call, Kodak, shoes, taxi fare, low-level bribe, ammunition, not-fancy hotel room	1
Standard ($20-$100)	Firearm, suit or dress, medical exam, good camera, train ticket, week's hotel stay	4
Unusual ($100-$600)	Color TV set, new furniture, refrigerator, excellent rifle, used car, airplane ticket, fancy hotel for a week, fake papers	6
Major ($600-$5,000)	New car, rented villa, professional forgery	8
Extreme ($5,000+)	New house, your pay for a year (~$10,000)	10+

You Already Have It

This is not your first rodeo. The Agents have been on the job for years; they already have footlockers or duffel bags with their names written on tape on the side sitting in the corner of some federal office or firebase.

Active-duty military have their kit, including personal small arms and grenades. FBI agents have standard-issue pistols, handcuffs, walkie-talkies, binoculars, cameras, and other surveillance gear with a shotgun in the trunk. CIA field agents don't usually carry guns, but have one stashed somewhere just in case.

They have relatively easy access (Bureaucracy test Difficulty 4) to small transmitters, miniature cameras, and other spy tech.

CIA analysts and other federal office worker types might know where the weapons locker is, but don't have anything more dangerous than a fountain pen... unless they took a gun back home with them after their military service and kept it quietly in the closet.

Assume the Agents already have any conventional item appropriate to their agency and "day job." For unconventional items, there's the Preparedness ability.

Green Boxes

Not everything gets reported, even to the higher-ups within DELTA GREEN. Agents who question General Fairfield's "burn everything" doctrine ("we went through a lot to get that book"), or who just don't want to explain a glowing idol made of bloodstone to their CO, occasionally drop their finds in hides known as "Green Boxes." Some Green Boxes nestle in vast government depots; others lurk in prepaid, anonymous civilian storage lockers. A Green Box also makes a great place to stash extra guns, rolls of twenties, and files or gear you're not technically cleared for.

You may have set up the Green Box yourself, or inherited it from a retired (or missing) partner. You may merely have picked up its location in program gossip, or your case officer might have slipped you a tape-wrapped key in a deniable handshake. Locating a Green Box takes a Difficulty 6 Preparedness test: you can spend Agency pool points on this test as well.

The Green Box may be full of unnatural spiders, monitored by another less-forgiving government agency, or simply in a very bad neighborhood if the Handler thinks the game could use a little challenge: "When we set this dump up, Laos was a friendly government." Alternately, it could be clear sailing if the important thing is to get gear in a hurry.

When you open the Green Box, every player can spend 1 Preparedness pool point to name one piece of equipment stashed there: you may name two pieces of equipment

for free. If plausible, the Green Box cache can include one vehicle, or keys and a map to it at least. This equipment may or may not be top of the line, fully reliable, or well maintained: a roll of 1 while using cached equipment might cause a malfunction or jam at the Handler's discretion. (A day's repair or maintenance work by an Agent with Mechanics, Firearms, Drive, or other appropriate ability removes this disability.) Like other Preparedness tests, the Handler may veto a suggested piece of cached equipment on the grounds of ridiculousness.

Requisition It

DELTA GREEN Agents are, theoretically, on government assignment unless the operation is deeply off-book. Thus they can requisition needed equipment from their theoretical superiors, local liaison, or at worst from their DELTA GREEN case officer.

It can be risky. An official investigation means oversight and a paper trail. In the best-case scenario, the cover investigation itself is highly classified, and its details and funding sources are beyond the reach of ordinary auditors. But the Handler determines just what "classified" and "beyond the reach" mean: the bigger the item, the more intent the questions... questions the Agents likely don't want to answer.

Requisitioned equipment is on loan to the Agent. It must be returned at the end of the operation. Misusing or damaging a requisitioned item may be a cause for Discipline (p. 131).

For a requisition, an Agent makes a Bureaucracy test using the Difficulty number in the Expense table (p. 134). Use the modifiers from the Bureaucracy ability (p. 063) and from the table below to adjust the Difficulty:

Requisition Modifiers

Circumstance	Difficulty Modifier
High-priority mission (imminent threat)	−1
Low-priority mission (routine)	+2
Immediate turnaround and delivery (12-48 hrs) of Unusual+ item	+2 or more
Weapon, narcotics, explosives, or other controlled item	+1
Classified item	+2
In war zone (military gear or action)	−1

Remember that *the issuing agency* determines the circumstances based on the operation's cover story. The Agents aren't likely to convince the FBI that a seemingly routine surveillance operation involves an imminent threat to national security — unless they make up a good cover story for their cover story!

Requests through DELTA GREEN rather than official channels use the same numbers, but since no Agent has an Agency (DELTA GREEN) ability, it's practically harder to get a good result. After all, every outside resource that DELTA GREEN brings to bear must be justified in a report, which by definition risks exposing the horror the Agents are supposed to cover up. Which is why DELTA GREEN already deployed its most important asset: the Agents themselves.

Borrow It

Agents can use Network to borrow an item, or approach a non-DELTA GREEN Bond to call in a favor. Such borrowing and favor tests use the Difficulties from the Expense table (p. 134).

For favors from Bonds, the Agent needs to spend at least 1 Bond or Interpersonal pool point and role-play the interaction. Roll a die and add the number of points spent: if the result equals or exceeds the Difficulty number given, the Agent gets the item or favor. If the result is under the Difficulty, the Bond strength drops by 1 due to the stress of the request and the Agent gets nothing from that contact.

For Extreme expenses or equivalently impossible requests, the Bond strength drops by 1 regardless of the die result. On a failure, the Bond strength drops by 2.

ILLICIT FUNDS

It's up to the Handler whether DELTA GREEN makes embezzled black funds, heroin trafficking profits, looted Axis gold, or other tranches of illicit cash available to the Agents. Agents who keep their eyes open in the seedier reaches of federal operations may stumble on any or all of these activities on their own, of course.

If so, they can deal themselves in. Once they've done so, they can spend time they should be Back in the World (p. 128) in illicit operations.

Illicit Operations

You spend your off-hours managing your criminal enterprise. Reduce two non-DELTA GREEN Bonds by 1 as your suspicious behavior, stress, and distraction alienate those who know you.

Spend 1 point of Accounting, Agency (if your own agency is involved in the corrupt activity), Bureaucracy, or Criminology, which does not refresh before the next mission. Then roll a die.

On a 1 or a 2, you merely maintain your position.

On a 3 through 5, you successfully rake off substantial funds: enough to raise one Bond by 1 (thanks to a convenient windfall) and fund several Unusual expenses, or to fund one Major expense.

On a 6, you successfully make a big score: raise two Bonds by 1 and keep enough cash on hand for several Major expenses or one Extreme expense. A big score also attracts the attention of the relevant law-enforcement agency or its internal affairs division.

Steal It

Of course, some Agents prefer to "borrow" gear — especially weapons — from the Viet Cong, the Mafia, or other mundane opponents who can't report the loss. Or they may decide to knock over a gun shop or filch items from the evidence locker.

This is the sort of requisition that winds up in a Green Box at the end of the operation. The paradigmatic "raid to get guns for our raid" can take as much or as little screen time as the Handler feels it deserves.

Buy It

Use the Expense categories given to determine whether your Agents can just buy something. Lots of mission-useful items simply sit on store shelves: incendiaries, sporting ammunition, horse tranquilizers, you name it.

Illegal or borderline equipment requires a Streetwise spend along with a cash expenditure.

Making an Unusual expense from personal funds means the cash-strapped Agent cannot Re-build Bonds, be One With Nature, or Establish a New Bond during the next Back in the World session (p. 128). She probably has to pull over-time hours or otherwise make up the shortfall.

Making a Major expense from personal funds automatically reduces all of an Agent's non-DELTA GREEN Bonds by 1 due to financial stress.

Buying Guns

In most of the United States, buying any firearm except sporting rifles and shotguns is functionally impossible. Even where local or state law allows handgun purchases, for instance, the required permit (usually issued on a political basis by the local sheriff) is very difficult to get. (Firearm ownership remains unrestricted in Vermont, and Washington state passes a "must-issue" ordinance for gun licenses in 1961.) Buying fully automatic weapons such as submachine guns is illegal without a federal firearms certificate, which the Agents likely do not have, and cannot use without blowing their cover.

In short, Agents who need extra unregistered firepower also need extra Streetwise points. An illegal gun purchase is an Unusual expense at least, unless you have a black-market gun dealer as a Network contact.

Make It

Assuming you have the correct tools (which can be bought or handwaved for Agents with Mechanics), materials (see *Buy It*, p. 136) and workspace (likely through Network), you can build or upgrade most of your needed gear: even hand-making a firearm's bolt from scratch takes time, knowledge, steel, and a drill press, but it's not impossible.

Most things — from silencers to surveillance equipment to silver bullets — are considerably easier to knock together from parts. An Agent with a few tools and an hour or so of work can uprate a semi-automatic AR-15 rifle (for sale after 1964) into a fully automatic assault rifle (Firearms test at Difficulty 6 or Mechanics at Difficulty 5).

Agents may need to make just a Mechanics test against a set Difficulty (given pre-existing parts), or to also spend points from related pools (Chemistry, Drive, SIGINT, Firearms, etc.) to modify or scratch-build gear. A test of Demolitions is all that's needed to make a bomb; merely possessing Pharmacy lets an Agent concoct common drugs, with quantity, specificity, or rapid production possibly requiring a pool point spend.

As a very general rule, making things takes hours (napalm, silver bullets, silencers, jury-rigged surveillance gear from transistor radios or other electronics), days (specialized surveillance or communications gear, identity documents, stable explosives, single-action "zip gun" style pistols, flamethrowers), or weeks (vehicles, firearms, complex machines). These are just guidelines: it's possible to assemble an entire 9mm Sten submachine gun from scrap metal in six hours, given tools, a bolt, and a barrel.

MONEY (THAT'S WHAT I WANT)

Resist the temptation, no matter how realistic in the context of career federal bureaucrats, to itemize expenses. Treat major expenses (or wind-falls) as story beats, not accounting entries. If you are one of those rare players who genuinely enjoys bookkeeping, go ahead and do it for the group, but nobody (especially the Handler) should force players to care about the quotidian at the expense of the cosmic.

That said, feel free to mention amounts of money from the ten-dollar bribe for a wharf cop to the "three-million-dollar warplane you cowboys just destroyed" to provide flavor and grounding in the world of the 1960s. Specifically, $1 in 1960 equates to $8-10 in 2017; by 1970, inflation reduces that dollar to about $6 in 2017 purchasing power.

Equipment

Agents of DELTA GREEN have access to some of the most advanced technology in the world. But most government work is done with government-issue equipment: military radios, FBI reel-to-reel tape recorders, CIA miniature cameras.

Under each general heading, **Standard Equipment** lists gear that Agents almost certainly already have. It might be standard issue, openly bought, or supplied with Preparedness. Specific entries call out characteristic equipment, or gear that might need special justification in the course of an operation.

NEW THIS DECADE

A few things invented, patented, or first marketed in the 1960s:

Contraceptive pill (FDA approval 1960)
Halogen lamp (1960)
Laser (1960)
Weather satellite (1960)
IBM Selectric typewriter (1961)
Non-dairy coffee creamer (1961)
Hand-held TV camera (1962)
Industrial robot (1962)
Running shoes (New Balance 1962, Tiger (Nike) 1964)
Audiocassette tape (1962)
Communications satellite (1962)
CAT scanner (patent 1963, first used 1971)
Polaroid self-developing film (1963)
Pull-tab aluminum beverage can (1963)
ASCII (1964)
Cray CDC 6600 supercomputer (1964)
Moog synthesizer (1964)
Olivetti P101 desktop calculator (1964)
Astroturf (1965)
Stereoscan scanning electron microscope (1965)
PDP-8 minicomputer (1965)
Super 8mm film (1965)
Digital transmission over telephone lines (1966)
Xerox Magnafax fax machine (1966)
Overseas direct dialing (1967)
Amana Radarange microwave oven (1967)
Live-virus measles vaccine (1967)
Computer mouse (1968)
ARPANET (1969)
Compound bow (1969)
Boeing 747 jumbo jet (1970)
Intel 1024-bit memory chip (1970)

Communications

Vehicular communications gear falls under Drive or Pilot; an Agent with SIGINT or Mechanics can use most other communications gear effortlessly and effectively. Intercepting police or other communications may require a SIGINT spend, except for core clues.

Standard Equipment: Walkie-Talkie, shortwave radio, frequency-switching gear, car telephone, wristwatch, headphones, reel-to-reel tape recorder, microphone, notebook, xerographic photocopier, pen or pencil, permanent marker, signal mirror, strobe light.

Field Radio

Agents most likely have access to a PRC-25 ("Prick-25") field radio. Rugged and nearly waterproof, it weighs about 25 lbs. With a short antenna, it can transmit about 3-4 miles; from a height, it can transmit line-of-sight up to 18 miles. It plugs into a vehicle or other power source, or runs off batteries good for around 3 hours of continuous use.

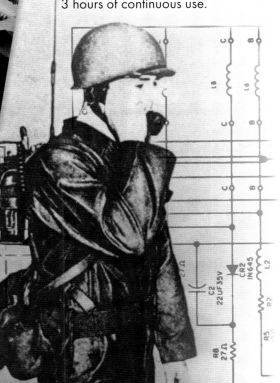

Lineman's Handset

This combines a telephone dial and headset into one piece, connected to two alligator clips and usually a piercing spike and punch-block connector. The user can hook into any telephone lines or switching system and place calls indistinguishable from conventional phones. With a SIGINT spend, an Agent can monitor a specific phone line.

Demolitions

Simply pushing the plunger takes no special skill. Using anything more sophisticated than that requires at least minimal Demolitions (Difficulty 2 for conventional military equipment) or a generous Handler.

Building detonators is relatively simple (Difficulty 4 Demolitions test), with or without blasting caps. Blasting caps and dynamite are openly for sale at farm and hardware stores until 1971. Sourcing plastic explosives or grenades definitely requires Streetwise or a military connection (Network or Agency). Once sourced, however, assume that an Agent with Demolitions has some in his pack on an operation without resorting to Preparedness.

Standard Equipment: Blasting caps, bleach, blowtorch, candles, chlorine, detonators, duct tape, dynamite, electrical tape, fertilizer and fuel oil, fireworks, gasoline, hand or road flare, lighter, matches, smoke bombs, wire cutters, wires of many colors.

Flare Gun

This single-shot weapon shoots a bright-burning flare that does d+0 damage on impact and burns for d-2 damage for 1d6 rounds. It can only reliably hit a target at Close range, but you can spend 2 Firearms points to fire it at a Near-ranged target, and 4 points to fire it at a vehicle-sized target at Long range. (As with other Extended Range options, these points do not add to the Firearms roll.) Fired into the air, the flare flies about 300 yards, hanging and burning for a minute or so, and removing all darkness penalties (see p. 084) for 3 rounds, and lowering them only to Night for 5 more.

Primacord

Detonating cord, or Primacord, is a half-inch-thick cable made of high explosive under a fiber-and-plastic sheath. When ignited, it detonates nigh-instantaneously. It can be used to connect multiple charges for simultaneous implosions, to cut through a girder, to booby trap a stretch of road, or to open a really stubborn crypt.

Specialized "cutting cord" has a shaped charge inside the cord; its primary use is to blow openings in walls or to blow open heavy doors or vehicles.

Rifle Grenades

The term "rifle grenades" is something of a misnomer, since they aren't fired from the barrel of a rifle but from a dedicated launcher (usually the reliable M79 or "Thumper" single-shot 40mm grenade launcher), but it differentiates weapon-launched grenades from hand grenades.

The touchy, fragile, and failure-prone XM148 underbarrel grenade launchers fitted for use with the M16 assault rifle come into service in 1967; the more rugged M203 comes on line in 1969.

Rifle grenades can only fire at Close, Near, or Long range; Extended Range applies (p. 098).

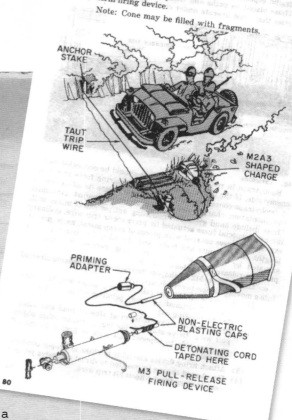

(6) Screw priming adapter and nonelectric blasting cap into threaded cap well.
(7) Conceal boobytrap.
(8) Arm firing device.
Note: Cone may be filled with fragments.

BOOBY TRAPS

To set a booby trap for an opponent requires two tests. You roll both of them when the enemy encounters the booby trap: a Conceal test to see if he notices the trap (modified by the foe's Alertness Modifier), and a Mechanics (or Demolitions) test to see if the trap worked. Damage is at the Handler's discretion: a trip wire might do no actual damage, but allow a round of surprise (see p. 089) or tumble the target down a flight of stairs (d+0 damage or more). A really good result on the Mechanics test should generally create a more effective, or more damaging, trap.

Agents expecting a booby trap can make a Conceal test to spot the trigger mechanism; agents not expecting traps make a Sense Trouble test (usually at a higher Difficulty). The Handler modifies the Difficulty based on the abstract skill of the opposition (akin to a Stealth Modifier) and rolls damage based on trap type as above. Agents can disarm a trap with a quick flick of the combat knife, a thrown brick, or with Mechanics or Demolitions; the Handler should tell the players of Agents with those abilities which option is safe.

Some traps can use alternative tests: Agents planting or disarming a bomb use Demolitions rather than Mechanics. To spot a car bomb, for example, an agent could make either a Drive, Conceal, or Demolitions test.

Haste in setting, disarming, or checking for traps raises the Difficulty by +1 (in a hurry) or +2 (in a chase or combat).

Punji Sticks

This Viet Cong specialty is a nest of sharpened bamboo stakes rammed into the bottom of a pit or, worse, pointing downward along the sides of a narrow leg-trap pit. The G.I. steps in, can't pull his leg out, and thus pins his unit in place for an ambush, or at least removes two men from the patrol (the victim and the man needed to carry him out).

The average punji pit requires a Difficulty 4 Conceal to spot, or a Difficulty 5 Sense Trouble to avoid instinctively. If caught by a punji trap, the target takes d+1 damage (plus any falling damage, p. 109) and must make an Athletics test at a Difficulty of 1 plus the stake damage inflicted to get off the stakes without crippling his leg.

For extra effect, the VC sometimes (and the Tcho-Tcho always) rub the stakes with feces, toxic plants, or poison frogs (use spider venom with an Onset of 15-30 mins (5-10 rounds); p. 112).

In addition to regular high-explosive fragmentation grenades (L1*), rifle grenades come in other varieties.

M31 High-Explosive Anti-Tank (HEAT): Fired from the barrel of an M14 carbine, not from the M79. Against soft targets, damage is L1. Negates 1d3 points of metal armor, or penetrates up to a foot of concrete.

Illumination: Effects similar to a flare gun (p. 139).

Silent: Not the explosion, but the shot: the grenade "shoots itself" out of the barrel without smoke or flash. Range is Near, not Long. Issued to Navy SEALs in 1967.

Smoke: Colored or black smoke that lasts 4-6 rounds and covers an 8-yard radius. Targets on either side are effectively concealed (+3 to Hit Threshold and to attempts to locate).

Tear Gas: Cloud of tear gas (p. 112) lasts 4-6 rounds and covers an 8-yard radius.

White Phosphorus: Sets a WP (p. 108) fire at the detonation point; the first round burn does double damage.

Thermite

An aluminum-based pyrotechnic that, when activated, burns incredibly hot (over 4,000°F) for a brief period (2-12 rounds). It cuts through steel, slags iron, burns underwater, and ignites anything flammable nearby. Set on a car hood, it burns through the engine in six or seven seconds.

Stealth

Most standard infiltration equipment requires either Stealth or no special ability to use. Vigorous use of ropes, grapnels, etc. often requires an Athletics test.

Standard Equipment: Bolt cutters, bridges and bypass circuits (for electrical alarms), caltrops, camouflage clothing, compass, crowbar, duct tape, fingerprint powder, flashlight, gas mask, glass cutter, grapnel, industrial cleanser, lockpicks, map or blueprint, parachute, rappelling kit, rope, rope ladder, spray paint, wire cutters.

Liquid Freon

As an aerosol spray, liquid Freon turns paper transparent, allowing the Agent to read the contents of a sealed envelope without opening it. It evaporates in minutes, leaving no visible trace (a Chemistry spend and a lab test can detect it, however).

Lockpick Gun

Uses brute force to open a lock by pushing small metal rods into the pins and tumblers. Works on most commercial locks; high-grade, specialized, or custom-built locks thwart its relatively clumsy mechanism. Without a Mechanics or Stealth spend, it may destroy the lock leaving evidence of forced entry.

Rebreather

The US Navy's Emerson rebreather (issued to SEALs starting in 1963) weighs 35 lbs. and resembles a bulbous backpack and vest combination connected to a mask and mouthpiece. Its 12.7 cu. ft. of oxygen allow 2 hours of dive time to a maximum depth of 40 feet. The Soviet equivalent is the IDA-64. The CIA uses the smaller and less conspicuous Westinghouse Min-O-Lung; it weighs 15 lbs. and provides one hour of dive time.

Using a rebreather is tricky and exhausting, adding +2 to the Difficulty of the swimming Athletics test. But it means no trail of telltale bubbles: -1 to the Difficulty of the Stealth test to swim past an observer. A human observer, anyway.

Silencer

Firearm sound suppressors do not silence gunshots. A .38 gunshot normally audible 500 yards away can still be heard from 60 yards. A suppressor reduces the sound of a gunshot to something closer to a loud clap or motorcycle engine; more importantly, it also deforms the sound and makes it less recognizable as a gunshot.

In game terms, using a silencer means you haven't automatically ruined a Stealth test. When you fire a silenced weapon, the Handler adds +1 to your Stealth test Difficulty, or +2 if the opposition has a positive Alertness Modifier. If that's enough for your roll to have failed, the enemy has heard you.

For Agents, a silenced gunshot anywhere in Near range lowers the Difficulty of their Sense Trouble test by -2.

Silencers don't work at all on revolvers.

Agents with Mechanics and Firearms can build sound suppressors in a few hours' time from a few common parts (rubber washers and PVC pipe, mostly). Hand-built suppressors are bulky and burn out after several shots.

Tranquilizer Gun

This is an air rifle (or pistol) chambered in .50 caliber loaded with anesthetic darts (use Fentanyl, p. 112). The darts can, of course, contain other toxins.

Air guns have shorter ranges than normal firearms: Close for pistols, Near for long arms.

Surveillance

Using most surveillance equipment requires either the SIGINT or Mechanics ability, although anyone with Conceal can plant a device.

Surveillance gear needs to be requisitioned or built from parts; it's not common enough to be available with Streetwise. Once sourced, however, an Agent with SIGINT has such equipment on hand without Preparedness.

Standard Equipment: binoculars, camera, closed-circuit camera (live only), directional microphone, headphones, high-speed film, map, parabolic microphone, reel-to-reel tape recorder, replacement license plates, metal detector, radio direction finder, stop watch, tape measure, telephoto lens, tracking beacon.

Fibroscope

Invented in 1957, this yard-long bundle of fiberoptic cables can snake under doors, through holes drilled in the wall or baseboard, inside safes, or even into an Agent. Attached to a video screen at the user's end, it allows the observation of an interior space, although the attached filament lamp is quite dim.

Minox III Camera

Built in West Germany for commercial sale, the CIA uses this 3-inch long camera for most covert missions. An even smaller camera the size of a cigarette lighter, the Suzuki Echo 8, is also commercially available.

The CIA's Technical Services Division also conceals cameras in seemingly innocuous objects such as cigarette packs, lighters, briefcases, wristwatches, purses, and the like. Agents with access to CIA equipment might have such things, or be able to hand-build their own versions. It's easier to train agents to use a regular camera from a pocket or from inside a jacket: a Difficulty 3 Filch test suffices if the Agent has a rating in Photography.

Night Vision Optics

The PAS-4 assembly deploys in 1962, combining an infrared light source with an IR scope, weighing 28 lbs. including the battery. (The Soviet equivalent is the NSP-2.) It functions in total darkness, but renders Agents highly visible to foes who see in the infrared.

Improved "passive" light intensifiers such as the PVS-1 and PVS-2 "Starlight Scope" begin development in 1961, and are in common use in Vietnam after 1965. (The Soviet equivalent is the 1PN-27.) They require moonlight or bright starlight; they cannot function in pitch blackness.

Against a foe without night vision, using NVO (night-vision optics) gives Agents the possibility of surprise, and a likely team pool to boot (see p. 146). NVO is likely to lower Difficulties for Stealth and Sense Trouble tests at night.

SRT-3 Transmitter

Introduced by the TSD in 1959, this all-transistor transmitter is about the size of a pack of cigarettes. Its signal has a range of a third of a mile, but its battery has only a week of continuous use. The SRT-3 can be remotely activated and deactivated, to save battery power.

After 1966, the SRT-3 becomes increasingly rugged and masked from audio and radio detection.

Tracking Beacon

This small (8 oz.) radio transmitter can be clipped or magnetically attached to a target such as a vehicle or object. Once activated (when attached, or remotely by radio) its signal can be detected up to 25 miles away.

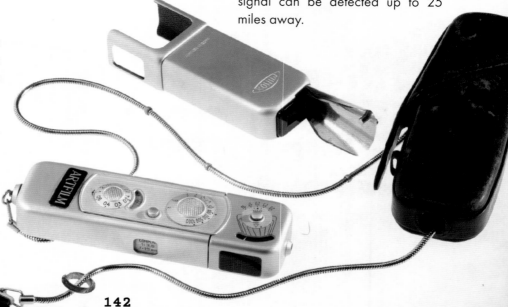

BUGS AND BUG DETECTION

Any covert audio surveillance device is a "bug," although the FBI can covertly eavesdrop through a normal telephone receiver. A bug combines a microphone receiver with a radio transmitter, although a room fully under clandestine control (like a Soviet-bloc hotel room) may simply be "wired for sound" with a simple hidden microphone wired to a tape recorder. In an age without video recording, covert video surveillance requires constant monitoring or a human cameraman; thus, it's less common outside secured facilities or the occasional KGB honey-trap nest.

Most bugs are attached (usually physically) to an existing audio pickup in the target area: a telephone receiver, an intercom system, or the like. Phone taps are specialized bugs designed only to monitor telephone calls on a given line. They can be installed anywhere along the line, possibly even blocks away at the phone junction box.

With an antenna (any non-grounded metal on site, such as a curtain rod, couch spring, or filing cabinet), bugs can transmit farther than the half-mile or so that they can unaided. Some bugs smuggle their transmissions alongside a normal, expected signal in the room: a television or radio, for example.

Detecting a bug is far easier when it is active; this usually involves using RF gear to find any radio transmissions in the area. Some active bugs can even be detected by moving a normal radio near them; their transmission interferes with the radio's tuner, resulting in a squeal of distortion.

Successfully planting a bug can be done with **SIGINT** or (for self-contained bugs that do not need any local wiring or receiver to work) with a test of **Conceal**; the Difficulty for the latter will vary with the type of bug (e.g., a higher Difficulty to conceal an active bug for long) and the type of location to be bugged. A bug dramatically needed to provide specific clues for one operation uses SIGINT; planting a long-term bug in a "fishing expedition" requires a spend or a Conceal test or both.

Successfully detecting a bug requires either a Conceal test or a 1-point spend of SIGINT along with any necessary equipment. Usually, if SIGINT gives a core clue in this context, it tells the Agent that someone else is being bugged; finding bugs planted on yourselves is often useful, but is almost never a core clue. Thus, finding a bug on another target may not require a spend; finding a bug on yourselves almost always does.

Vehicles

This game handles vehicles, as GUMSHOE does most things, with abstractions intended to promote drama rather than simulations intended to promote gritty realism.

Even on-duty military Agents can't just borrow a tank, helicopter, or other combat vehicle. They may need to make an Agency spend or a Bureaucracy test to pull strings, or come up with some other plan in the heat of the moment.

Speed

The speeds in the Vehicle Table are top road speeds; cruising speed is normally two-thirds, or even half, that amount. Off-road speeds are halved. These figures are for purposes of comparison; maintenance, rebuilt engines, and driver skill can vary them in practice.

Maneuver

Applies during ramming attempts in Chase Contests (p. 086). Apply it as a modifier to Drive or Pilot tests to make dangerous swerves and other sudden changes of direction. (If you'd prefer, apply the negative of the Maneuver to the Difficulty.)

Off-Road Capacity

A vehicle with an "OR" designation in the Vehicle Table has off-road capacity. Their speed is only reduced by one-fourth, not halved, when not on roads. In an off-road chase between ground vehicles, off-road vehicles have contest advantage (p. 087) over conventional ones.

Vehicle Armor

A conventional civilian ground vehicle provides armor as follows against bullets:

Windshield, tires: -0
Doors or panels: -1
Engine block: -4

Hiding behind the whole body of a car provides Full Cover (see p. 096).

Remember to apply the additional -2 to damage from shotgun shells at Close range or farther.

The Armor listing in the Vehicle Table adds to the above: e.g., a Humvee door has -4 Armor against bullets. Windshield and tire armor increases only with specially reinforced windows (Armor -2) or solid "run-flat" tires (no additional Armor, but the only effect of a bullet is +1 to Drive difficulties).

See Attacking During Chases (p. 087) and Called Shots (p. 102) for rules about shooting out tires and other specific attacks on vehicles.

Vehicles

Vehicle	Speed (mph)	Maneuver	Notes
Harley-Davidson motorcycle	100	+1	OR
VW Beetle	70	+0	
Ford Galaxie LTD sedan	90	+0	Police car
Ford Mustang GT muscle car	105	+1	Steve McQueen's police car
Maserati Mistral sports car	145	+1	
VW Microbus	80	-1	Holds up to 10 hippies
Cadillac Series 70 limousine	120	+0, -1 if armored	Ambulance or hearse; can be armored to -4 (lower Speed by 10 mph per point of Armor)
Fire truck	70	-2	Armor -1
Armored truck	70	-1	Armor -5
M35 2.5-ton cargo truck	55	-1	OR; rated for 2.5 tons of cargo
Mack R series big rig truck	70	-2, -3 fully loaded	Standard 53' semi-trailer can carry 22 tons of cargo
Jeep	65	+0	OR; mount for a light machine gun (L1)
M113 armored personnel carrier	40	-1	OR; amphibious (4 mph swimming); 2 crew + 11 troops; M2 and M60 machine guns (L1*), possible TOW anti-tank missile (L2); Armor -2
M60 Patton battle tank	30	-3	OR; 4 crew; 105mm gun (AT L3 or HE L3*), .50 machine gun (L1*); Armor -7
Sailboat or sampan	2-10	-1 or -2	Speed varies with wind and boat length
Zodiac inflatable boat	5-20	+0	Holds 7 crew + 1,000 lbs cargo; speed varies with oars, outboard motor
Fairey Huntress 23 speedboat	30	+0	The longer (28') Fairey Huntsman has a top speed of 50 mph
PCF Swift Boat	30	-1	6 crew + 6 passengers; three .50 M22 machine guns (L2), 81mm mortar (L2*)
Piper PA-18 Super Cub	130	+0	Single-engine prop plane; 1 pilot + 1 passenger
Boeing 727 jet airliner	540	-3	3 crew + 131 passengers
Bell UH-1 Huey helicopter gunship	135	+0	1-4 crew + 2 tons cargo (14 troops); 2 M60 machine guns (L1*) plus other weapon mounts depending on mission; Armor -3 (pilot seats only)
F-4 Phantom jet fighter-bomber	1400	-2	2 crew; Vulcan autocannon (L2) plus varying loads of missiles, bombs, napalm; Armor -2
C-130 turboprop transport	360	-3	5 crew + 22 tons cargo (64 airborne troops)
B-52 jet bomber	650	-3	5 crew; Vulcan autocannon (L2) plus 70,000 lb. bomb load

Tactical Fact-Finding Benefits

Tactical Fact-Finding Benefits (TFFBs) allow Agents to blend their investigative and combat abilities to produce tactically useful (and game-mechanically significant) results. TFFB opportunities can occur during interstitial investigative sequences, or during the fight scenes themselves.

Each TFFB has the following four elements:

△ the Investigative Ability used to gain the advantage

△ the action required to find the information

△ the tactical circumstance under which the benefit comes into play

△ the nature of the benefit

Although the most obvious ability to yield a TFFB is Military Science (p. 059), the other Investigative Abilities can also yield plenty of useful information.

△ Interpersonal abilities can elicit (or wring) valuable tactical data from allies, witnesses, shady middlemen, prisoners, and enemy operatives.

△ HUMINT can predict where the enemy will make a stand, or indicate likely key personnel.

△ Forensics and Criminology can determine an unknown monster's attack pattern.

△ Traffic Analysis can estimate the reaction time of any off-site reinforcements, or even the size of the current garrison.

△ Cryptography cracks the tactical information in encoded enemy communications.

△ A Stealth exercise might secure a floor plan of the site to be raided — as might Bureaucracy.

△ Architecture could discover possibly unguarded entry points such as sewer mains.

These clues may be garnered in a scene previous to the fight in which they become relevant. Alternately, the players may get the chance to gather a clue in the middle of a fight.

Sometimes they get the benefit simply by taking part in the battle. On other occasions they may have to do something to trigger the benefit — wear magnets, blow up a load-bearing column, set a strobe light in place.

Benefits of tactical investigation may take the following forms:

△ **Refreshes:** one or more Agents gain a refresh of a set number of pool points in a designated ability or abilities; points that would put their pools higher than their ratings are ignored. Refreshes are best used when the benefit's triggering circumstances occur in mid-fight, and when the benefit is abstract and hard to quantify.

△ **Team pool:** the whole team gains access to a shared pool of points in a designated ability or abilities. Any player can spend them as though they were her own; once expended, they do not refresh. If the scene ends with team points unused, they disappear. Team points are best used for situations of broad and abstract benefit, where the Agents enjoy a tactical advantage from the outset of the armed conflict.

△ **Difficulty adjusts:** The Difficulty of a specific action decreases for the team, or a team member, or increases for an enemy or enemies. The most obvious example is an decreased effective Hit Threshold for one's enemies, or an increased effective Hit Threshold for oneself. Changes in difficulty can apply to many circumstances; Hit Threshold adjusts best reflect positional advantages, where the Agents are better able to conceal themselves from incoming fire, or force enemies to expose themselves to it.

△ **Enemy pool reductions:** When the benefit's triggering circumstance comes into play, the opposition loses a particular number of points in one or more pools. Pool reductions are best used to reflect a change in battlefield conditions putting the enemy at a sudden and dramatic disadvantage.

△ **Surprise:** The Agents are able to surprise the enemy (see p. 089). In some cases, they can also begin the fight with one or more rounds during which the enemy is unable to return fire or perform other actions. This applies to situations where the Agents are able to leverage tactical information to suddenly launch an attack against unprepared adversaries.

Some situations may warrant a combination of advantages — a Difficulty reduction plus a number of team points, for example. The Handler should be prepared to substitute more appropriate benefits when creative players wring different and unexpected tactical circumstances from their tactical fact-finding.

In general, a single, effective TFFB should provide 3 or 4 points to each Agent, either together as a team pool, individually as a refresh, or toward a reduction for foes. If it also provides battle-useful intelligence (such as a monster's weakness in magnetic fields), the award may be less. However, feel free to reduce those numbers to 1-2 per Agent for an unlikely or transient advantage ("I use Art to shoot the vase the cultist likes best, making him angry") or increase them to 5-6 points per Agent for a very complex, impressive, or dangerous TFFB.

In a standard GUMSHOE scenario, an opportunity to enhance later tactical success with an Investigative Ability generally requires a spend, because it confers an advantage that is only tangential to the solution of the central mystery. In some **Fall of DELTA GREEN** operations, the acquisition of tactical advantage *is* the central mystery. In those cases, gaining TFFBs should not require spends. Whether a given TFFB requires a spend in the specific case is a Handler's call; since every campaign has a different rhythm, we don't lay down hard-and-fast requirements.

Fact-Finding and Combat Sequence

Prevent tactical fact-finding during a fight from slowing the action to a crawl by integrating it with the turn sequence.

Right before the fight, each player gets the chance to query a single Investigative Ability. When an appropriate ability is named, the Handler supplies the tactically beneficial information. Invoking a particular ability yields all information arising from it; there is never any benefit to repeating an already-used ability.

Except in odd circumstances where it is possible to meaningfully interact with enemy combatants while they're trying to kill you, and the occasional "taunt him into revealing his position" Intimidation test, Interpersonal abilities are typically of little use in mid-fight fact-finding.

Each player also gets to invoke another ability at the top of each action during the fight. Drawing on an Investigative Ability does not cost an action. Players should spend their off-turn time picking the ability they want to use. The Handler may well rule that a player who dithers over his ability choice can't attempt tactical fact-finding that round, but should not penalize him by also skipping over his combat action, or making it more difficult.

As with Investigative Ability use during chase contests (see p. 088), the Handler may pre-plan these options into her operational notes, or simply roll with player creativity. As players become more familiar with the game system and with the specific metaphysics of the campaign, most combats will eventually involve a combination of the two.

Example TFFBs

From surveillance photos, the Agents can use **Photography** to locate the refrigerated railroad car holding the MAJESTIC mobile surgery. With a Difficulty 4 test of Mechanics to switch the junctions and tracks in the proper sequence, they can send the car onto a remote siding. If they succeed in isolating the car from assistance or escape, the team gains a pool of 12 points to be used for any General Ability during their inevitable break-in, not to mention diminishing the number of their foes.

Note the triggering action (photo surveillance), ability (Photography), tactical circumstance (rerouting the car) and benefit (team pool).

Having located a cult center, the group may assess the site using **Archaeology**. If so, they discover signs of a Maya tunnel complex underneath it. If they attack through the tunnels, they can, on a Difficulty 3 Demolitions test, blow a hole in its ceiling — which is the cultists' floor. The targets come raining down into the tunnel, injured and unready, their Health pools reduced by 4 apiece, ceding the team one round of surprise.

The triggering action is the decision to assess the site's history, the ability Archaeology, the tactical circumstance is blowing the tunnel ceiling, and the benefit is the lowered Health pools plus one round of surprise.

Using **Streetwise** to mingle with peripheral members of a Corsican drug ring, one agent can discover that the ring's leader calls himself Lupin, and that he can be recognized by his long-jawed, wolf-like features. When they engage his gangsters, every agent can gain a 4-point refresh of any combat ability when Lupin is killed, demoralizing his men.

Triggering action: asking the right questions of the gangsters; ability: Streetwise; circumstance: killing the leader; benefit: refreshes.

Having determined that some unknown monster is preying on the docks at San Pedro, the team uses **Criminology** to reconstruct the killings. By analyzing the evidence, they can determine the thing's capacity for damage — and perhaps some potential weaknesses. ("It seems to have stayed out of the street light. Does it hate light? Sodium? Electrical fields?") When they actually go after the thing, they will start out with a team pool of 8 points to use for any General Ability during the upcoming combat, along with an estimated Athletics and Fighting value for it, some notion of its Hit Threshold, and leads to potential weaknesses if any.

Triggering action: getting the police records or going over the scene; ability: Criminology; circumstance: going after a scouted creature on scouted ground; benefit: team pool and information.

Training Flashbacks

Flashbacks to training and briefing provide a fun way to convey information to the players as if their characters already know it. This allows everyone to jump into the operation and skip the usual overdose of introductory exposition.

In early fight scenes, especially those conducted *in media res*, training flashbacks can allow the Handler to provide TFFBs to players without putting them through prior investigative sequences. These might grant benefits for free, simply to add interest to a fight scene, without an ability use or triggering action.

The Handler begins the session with a "bug-hunt" encounter against a ghoul. As the action begins, DELTA GREEN assets have already located the thing's lair in the cemetery. Now the Agents are here to clean up the manifestation.

The Handler says, "As you watch through your gunsights, you remember your briefing from a veteran of the Special Subway Police in the Thirties. Old Cap said the only thing that saved him was the things' appetite for dead meat, that sometimes they'd rather eat than fight. Flashing back to the graveyard, the players are now given a chance to realize that they can probably find a fresh corpse to distract it with. If the Agents dig a body up and leave it out, when the ghoul comes sniffing around they get a reduction in its Hit Threshold and a round of surprise against it.

Alternately, it might occasionally be dramatically appropriate for training flashbacks to require abilities and thoughtful use of triggering actions. The later in the operation a training flashback occurs, the more the players should have to work for its benefits.

Tradecraft

Unlike standard FBI counter-intelligence and CIA intelligence work, DELTA GREEN operations are typically short and intense. Once an unnatural outbreak manifests, the Agents have no time to establish networks of informants, and probably couldn't trust the testimony of anyone in a position to provide inside information.

DELTA GREEN actions are "stovepiped," insulated from existing CIA and FBI networks and operations for obvious security reasons. Unless it's unavoidable, the Agents don't use CIA safe houses or FBI surveillance posts. (Of course, Agents with Bureaucracy and the relevant Agency ability sometimes disregard this sensible policy.) They are on their own, out of communication not only with any existing clandestine network but with their own superiors, and that's exactly how DELTA GREEN likes it.

Staying Clean

Thus, rather than handling assets or making dead drops, DELTA GREEN Agents focus on operational security: staying out of sight and out of contact, solving the problem in the darkness, then tying off loose ends and providing an acceptable cover story. The Handler decides which abilities those tasks involve, and which tasks she wants to handle with a quick spend and which she wants to devote a scene to playing out in more detail.

In most cases, DELTA GREEN provides a cover mission complete with orders and budget authority to the Agents' home agency ("seconded for training in interagency operations" is always popular). In some cases, the team's DELTA GREEN tasking officer provides cover stories, advance clearance with active military or law enforcement in the target zone, or even the name of a local asset already tagged as a DELTA GREEN "friendly."

For missions inside the United States, DELTA GREEN often provides cover-identity FBI credentials; for missions outside the United States, DELTA GREEN provides false DIA credentials. DELTA GREEN cannot always supply enough pre-cleared sets of ID for all the Agents.

Every once in a while, though, the Agents have nothing but a hastily transcribed report, a set of grid co-ordinates, and a Monday morning deadline.

If DELTA GREEN hasn't already taken care of things, or you don't want DELTA GREEN to know your plans, here's how to do it yourself.

Cover Mission

Use **Agency** or **Law** to come up with a "cover mission," or even secure a prosecution or other official federal action as a pretext for your team's presence at the scene of the investigation.

Use **Bureaucracy** to arrange a designation, orders, and a budget for the cover mission. Difficulty depends on the plausibility of the cover mission pretext.

Use **Cop Talk, Inspiration, Military Science,** or a spend from the appropriate **Agency** ability to convince local police, the Army, or another agency to supply manpower, vehicles, equipment, or other resources for the cover mission. Or go through channels with **Bureaucracy** (p. 063; also see *Requisition It,* p. 135).

Use **Bureaucracy** to avoid taking the blame when the cover investigation doesn't get enough

results to keep headquarters happy (Difficulty 5) or when an operation gets police or bystanders killed (Difficulty 8).

Create an Agent's cover and a "legend" with **HUMINT** or **Tradecraft**. You may have to use **Art (Forgery)** to falsify papers or ID to bolster your cover.

Use **Cop Talk, Military Science,** or **HUMINT** to predict when an investigator, witness, or suspect is likely to look into the team's credentials, cover story, or jurisdiction. That may offer a chance to talk them out of it or take other steps.

To alter a case file without arousing suspicion, spend **Accounting** or **Law,** or use **Bureaucracy** (Difficulty 5) to simply bury it.

Safe Houses

You shouldn't use one already tasked to another mission: for one thing, the FBI or CIA always has their safe houses bugged to the rafters. Maybe you can con your way into one with **Agency** or a strong cover mission and just stay quiet, but then you leave tracks, or holes, in the record.

Find your own safe house with **Network** (to know someone who has an out-of-the-way place suitable for hiding out or dissecting aliens);

build the contact and roll. Difficulty varies by the size and density of the city they're hiding out in: Difficulty 4 for a large city or tourist destination; Difficulty 5 for a medium city or large town; Difficulty 6 or more for a small town. Agents may have to spend Investigative Ability points to find one on their own: **Architecture** (to determine multiple exits and lines of sight), **Streetwise** (to know where cops avoid), **Tradecraft** (to assess isolation and anonymity), or **Notice** (to find an abandoned or otherwise anonymous building). The spend total should equal the Difficulty above. It may just be easier to check into a motel with fake ID.

Suppressing Evidence

If clues pointing to the unnatural wind up in police or other local hands, use **Filch** or **Stealth** to intercept it before it leaves the scene. If it's already in an evidence locker, things get more complicated. That may require **Law** or **Cop Talk** to get access, or **Bureaucracy,** but that leaves a paper trail. Either way, you likely need Bureaucracy to falsify the chain of custody so it doesn't set off a hunt for corruption (Difficulty 6 minimum).

Surveillance

DELTA GREEN Agents may not routinely make brush passes with foreign assets, but they do spend a lot of time watching or following suspects while trying to avoid being followed or watched themselves.

Plant microphones with **Conceal, Mechanics,** or **SIGINT.** Break into the target area with Stealth to plant the bug, and to retrieve the recording.

Go through the lock with **Mechanics** or **Stealth** or a lockpick gun (p. 141). Rewire the alarm with Mechanics or Stealth.

Use **Athletics** to climb the wall and enter through the roof entrance or skylight.

Use a **Criminology** spend or **Conceal** to obscure the marks of your breaking and entering.

Stakeout

Find a good place for a stakeout with **Architecture, Notice,** or **Tradecraft.** Gain access with lockpicks (**Mechanics**), a quickly flashed badge and a line of patter (**Cop Talk** or **Inspiration**), by knowing the landlord already (**Network**), or with a week's rent in advance (see *Buy It,* p. 136). Or park across the street, using **Drive** or **Tradecraft** to keep the car in sight of the target, but not continuously and thus conspicuously so.

Take pictures with **Photography,** get parabolic mike coverage with **SIGINT.**

Spot the suspect leaving the scene with **Stealth** or a spend of **Notice.** If the suspect's movements are a core clue, spotting her leaving requires no roll or spend. If the suspect leaves from a rear entrance or somewhere else the Agents don't have covered, perhaps Notice gets them a helpful tire track or footprint, or **Streetwise** finds a bum who might have seen something while sleeping one off.

Tailing

Multiple tailing Agents use Cooperation (p. 081). Having three trained tails (Stealth 4+ or Tradecraft 1+) provides contest advantage

(p. 087), through the "ABC" technique: Shadower A (closest to the rabbit) has the eye. Shadower B follows behind A so the eye can pass between them as necessary; the rabbit doesn't keep seeing the same face behind him. Shadower C follows in a parallel course along the street. If the rabbit turns or doubles back, then A leaves the tail and C falls in behind B who moves up to tail the rabbit. A then becomes the new C.

Often, the Handler will prefer treating a tail as a Chase Contest (p. 086) rather than a full contest.

Foot Tails

Agents use **Stealth** for foot tails of a rabbit, or for evading a tail on foot as the rabbit. If the Handler agrees, a tailing Agent may also spend from **Disguise** on one Stealth roll (or on a *Raise,* p. 087) if he can quickly change appearance (pull off a wig, reverse his coat) or has pre-planned a uniform or other costume designed to blend in.

Followers with walkie-talkies look conspicuous; the rabbit can spot them, so they don't gain contest advantage despite the benefits of coordination.

Explain a rabbit's success on foot or a tail's failure:

△ The rabbit stopped suddenly, making a U-turn or looking into a reflective surface.

△ The rabbit went into a large, crowded building with multiple exits: a train station, department store, or the like.

△ The rabbit went into a large, leafy public park.

△ One of the tails made eye contact with the rabbit, who made the tail.

△ The rabbit got into public transportation, a cab, or another vehicle.

△ The rabbit changed her appearance suddenly: put on or took off a coat or hat, for example.

Explain a foot tail's success or a rabbit's failure:

△ The street was crowded and the tail blended in.

△ The rabbit was physically attractive: passersby looked at the rabbit, allowing the tail to blend into the gawkers or watch them instead.

△ The tail got a higher vantage point and followed the rabbit by eye.

△ The tail successfully passed the eye to a partner or fellow Agent.

Vehicular Tails

Use **Drive** for vehicular tails, of a rabbit on foot or in a car.

Following a target in a car from your own car (or evading the nondescript sedan following you) becomes a contest of Drive.

Multiple cars with radio communication with partner vehicles or an overwatch or dispatch station have contest advantage (p. 087) against targets (or pursuers) without it. The Agents need to use **Cop Talk** to get local police to dispatch cars to follow suspects, and probably need a pretext or cover mission to boot (p. 149).

Explain a rabbit's success or a vehicular tail's failure:

△ Their car went through a choke point such a tunnel or bridge, letting her identify the tailing vehicles.

△ Their car went down a road with no traffic; she spotted the tail easily.

△ The rabbit made an unexpected U-turn or ran a red light.

△ The tail got caught in traffic.

△ The rabbit got onto or off of public transportation suddenly.

Explain a vehicular tail's success or a rabbit's failure:

△ The tail set up a new follow car on the other side of the choke point.

△ Traffic was steady, the tail car blended in well.

△ The rabbit got caught in traffic, or canalized by police road-blocks or other government action.

△ The tail deduced the rabbit's destination using HUMINT or other methods (see Investigative Abilities and Chases, p. 088).

△ The rabbit had a conspicuous vehicle.

Progressive Surveillance

A "progressive tail" intended only to map the target's usual daily or weekly routine is easier because you don't need to maintain continuous coverage, and can switch up over the longer period of the search. Of course, you don't always have a week or two for a progressive tail.

For tailing Agents, a player-facing test of Drive or Stealth modified by the target's Alertness Modifier (p. 083) is enough to establish a routine after a week. Difficulty numbers go up for shorter-term progressive tails: +1 for 4 days, +2 for 2 days, +4 for a one-day tail intended to map the target's whole daily routine.

Tailed agents test **Stealth,** modified by their follower's Stealth Modifier.

The Human Element

When surveillance is not feasible, detectives and intelligence officers must cultivate human sources. These might be your fellow law enforcement officers – who might graduate to full DELTA GREEN "friendly" status if they survive – or they might be slightly less degenerate cultists terrified at their own power. Cops, soldiers, witnesses, suspects, cultists: DELTA GREEN Agents may have to lie to any of them... or worse.

Finding out who to investigate might be as simple as picking the target off the surveillance photo (**Photography, Criminology, Cop Talk** with other investigators) or asking around with **Streetwise.** If the Agents have access to telephone records, **Traffic Analysis** can focus on the numbers most often dialed from a suspicious location. **HUMINT** can identify jilted lovers or business rivals; an **Agency** or **Network** contact might know someone who knows something about someone.

Use the correct Interpersonal ability to convince an unwilling investigator, witness, or suspect to co-operate, or to allay suspicions. Use **HUMINT** to determine the likeliest Interpersonal ability to use on the approach.

Turning a contact into an informant is the tricky part. Traditionally, assets flip for one of four MICE: Money, Ideology, Coercion, or Ego. A Money turn requires a Major expense at least; **Inspiration** works for Ideology; Ego strokes need **Flattery.**

For crash-turning an asset, Coercion gives the best results fastest: figure out something to hold over your asset's head, show him his weakness, and twist. Those three steps can be three quick scenes in a mini-operation that nets you an inside man.

Asset Running

Once you've got an asset, you can spend 1 Interpersonal pool point (of whatever sort you and the Handler agree is appropriate) to get information from him; you can spend 2 Interpersonal pool points to make him do something risky for you. If you spend Tradecraft, you can gain information or cooperation covertly (although if your asset is under pressure, you may need to make a Stealth test to avoid blowing his cover). If your asset has a core clue, getting that information from him never requires a spend.

The difference between an asset and a Network contact is that an asset might betray you, lose his nerve, screw up, or otherwise turn things interesting and dangerous. Network contacts are more reliable: but then, they cost Network points to create, and assets don't.

Search and Arrest

Many Agents are law-enforcement officers with the power to arrest and detain suspects and to obtain search warrants from courts. And often an operation has the pretext of a criminal case. Sometimes placing a suspect or witness under arrest can be useful, even if prosecution for a crime is not the ultimate goal. And often the authority of a warrant is the easiest way to get into a site and look around.

Spend **Law** to come up with a convincing pretext for making an arrest if one isn't obvious, or to convince a judge that there's enough reason to suspect criminal activity to justify a search warrant.

But never forget the risk of blowback. Placing someone under arrest or executing a search warrant means scrutiny, and paperwork, and a trail back to the Agents. With truly bad luck, the Agents can find themselves named in a wrongful arrest suit if the suspect is not prosecuted.

Interrogation

To interrogate a target, the Agents have to get custody of him. The actual interrogation requires an isolated or controlled space and a secure hold on the prisoner. This might require a warrant, or just a **Cop Talk** or **Agency** favor from the agency or police department that currently holds him. It might even require a kidnapping, which definitely requires a temporary safe house (p. 149) or at least a remote motel room.

Using the **Interrogation** ability automatically extracts a core clue, if any are available, although it might take hours or even days if the subject is trained or conditioned to resist. (If a subject had a core clue, other Interpersonal abilities can often get it faster without arrest.) For information the Handler doesn't deem "core," spends still probably turn up something actionable — a name or two, for instance — unless the target actually doesn't know anything, thanks to compartmentalization, or psychic clouding, or the Agents grabbing the wrong guy.

Polygraph

The polygraph, or "lie detector," detects changes in heart rate, blood pressure, and electrical potential on the skin of an interrogated subject.

Whether it actually detects any lies remains an open question; it certainly does not reliably detect spies.

If the subject is psychologically vulnerable to a polygraph, using the device (a test of Mechanics at Difficulty 6 or Psychotherapy at Difficulty 5) offers the equivalent of a 1-point spend of Interrogation. Simply being strapped into the thing can inspire a nervous subject (or one with a lot to hide) to respond to other Interpersonal approaches.

Torture

Some subjects – especially those in "tough guy" milieus like the military, police, or organized crime – won't talk without a pro forma beating, a broken finger or two, or at least a casual smash of their head into a car hood. This comes after a quick combat, or through Intimidation. This "tuning up" period might also set up the subject for the "good cop" using a softer Interpersonal ability.

For game purposes (though not by legal definition), torture goes beyond arm-twisting and into measured, continuous infliction of pain and stress. Witnessing or engaging in torture triggers a Stability test (*Violence*, p. 115). Pain and panic often leave torture victims unable to discern the truth from whatever lie they must tell to make it stop. The Handler always gets the final word on whether this yields information worth having.

Truth Drugs

The CIA and other intelligence agencies use barbiturate cocktails, including scopolamine and sodium thiopental, to assist interrogation. These drugs induce a general sense of well-being, lowered inhibitions, and (under proper guidance by an interrogator) a tendency to rattle off anything and everything on their mind, truthful or not. In effect, "truth serum" acts just like getting someone really, really drunk or high.

Using truth serum requires a 1-point spend of either Medicine or Pharmacy to judge dosage, and a test of Psychotherapy to guide the questioning. The Difficulty depends on the subject's conditioning and training.

Agents resist truth serum like a toxin. After injection, the Agent makes a Difficulty 6 Stability test. On a success, he is Shaken for 1-6 hours, but doesn't talk. On a failure, he is still Shaken, but also trusts his interrogator and spills.

The Pharmacy ability does not cover mixing truth drugs from scratch, and they cannot be bought on the open market. If the Agents want truth drugs, they need to source them with Agency, Bureaucracy, or a really recondite Network contact.

Medical Treatment

If Agents get hurt, they ideally want to get to a nearby military hospital with a DELTA GREEN friendly on staff, but this is not always possible. If not, they should avoid hospitals entirely. Going to a hospital means the best possible care, but it also means questions and paperwork that can blow a covert operation wide open. Agents who wind up in a hospital may need to use Law to come up with a pretext for the emergency and point the police and their own agencies in the wrong direction, an Interpersonal ability (or **Medicine** used Interpersonally by an un-wounded Agent) to convince hospital staff to keep things quiet, or fight a **Bureaucracy** rear guard action to bury the report.

Agents with medical backgrounds can break into a veterinarian's office, smaller clinic, or dentist's office to use the facilities. Or more likely have the FBI black-bag specialist use **Stealth** while you stabilize your gut-shot partner with **First Aid.**

Use **Streetwise** to quietly ask around for a doctor or veterinarian who provides off-the-books medical treatment to the local underworld. First aid is a Standard expense; surgery is a Major expense; life-saving immediate surgery is an Unusual expense. Cash only, up front.

Disposing of a Body

DELTA GREEN operations seem to always leave bodies behind. Often it's better to get rid of one than to try explaining it to the authorities.

Mutilating or desecrating a corpse triggers a 2-point Stability test against Violence, or 3-point if you knew the deceased.

Leaving no traces behind requires a 1-point **Forensics** spend or a **Conceal** test (Difficulty 5).

In a pinch, remove the head. If investigators are looking for a missing person that might match the body, the lack of a head (and therefore dental records) delays the identification by 24 to 48 hours. If other investigators find the body but have no idea who it belongs to, it may never be identified unless the fingerprints are on record. Saw off the hands to make sure!

For more thorough disposal, consider the following:

△ Carve the corpse into manageable pieces; wrap them in plastic and bury them in dispersed locations or leave them in the wilderness to be eaten by animals.

△ Dissolve the corpse in a polypropylene barrel filled with acid. This requires a Difficulty 4 Athletics test (Difficulty 3 with a Chemistry spend) to avoid being splashed with acid (p. 108). The supplies are an Unusual expense. Transfer everything into a steel drum and bury it deep: Criminology may turn up an illegal dumping site.

△ Dissolve the corpse in quicklime with a 1-point Forensics spend.

△ Burn the corpse to ash in an industrial incinerator or a crematorium. This takes 1-6 hours,

and access: breaking and entering or a stiff bribe (Major expense and a Negotiation spend).

△ Melt the body into metal in an industrial crucible. This is a Difficulty 6 Mechanics test (you can spend Drive on it if you have a Drive slot for heavy machinery) to avoid being splashed by molten metal (d+2 damage, then minor fire damage for 1-6 rounds). Access is the same as for an industrial incinerator.

△ Dump the body in a deep lake or swamp to deteriorate. First, perforate the body deeply to prevent bloating and floating.

△ Dump the body at sea, if you can take a boat out deep enough. Unless you want it to wash ashore, dump it in a sealed, heavy metal drum more than 20 miles offshore.

Advice to Players

The purpose of playing **Fall of DELTA GREEN** is to collaborate in telling a horror technothriller. In this collaboration, it's the players' job to feel the horror, to use the tech, and to help keep it all thrilling. It's the Handler's job to make the players' jobs possible in the first place. Both the Handler and the players benefit from agreeing on and internalizing what the game is supposed to look and play like.

Although every operation holds the chance to go horribly wrong, a standard **Fall of DELTA GREEN** operation goes something like this:

Δ DELTA GREEN learns of a possible incursion of the unnatural. Intelligence analysts do their best to confirm the incursion, so the Executive Committee doesn't waste time and resources sending a team of Agents where they're not needed.

Δ The Executive Committee, or a member of it, establishes the new operation, gives it an internal name, and assigns a case officer to send a team of Agents.

Δ DELTA GREEN assets in the relevant agencies or military branches establish bureaucratic cover for the operation and secure whatever resources are necessary and available. The Agents may or may not also be responsible for this part of their mission.

Δ The case officer assembles the team of Agents and provides their instructions, an intelligence briefing, and resources.

Δ The Agents investigate the manifestation and develop a plan to defeat or otherwise end it. They carry out their plan, which usually involves a physical confrontation with the manifestation or its cause.

Δ Throughout the operation, the Agents maintain operational security, providing a cover story or other disinformation to explain any portion of the operation that attracts outside attention.

Δ The Agents undergo whatever debriefing the case officer requires, and then return to their homes and their normal jobs.

Δ DELTA GREEN assets in the relevant agencies disseminate disinformation as needed to cover up the Agents' activities and reinforce their cover story.

Δ Other loose ends – prisoners, evidence, alien artifacts – vanish into the federal bureaucracy or DELTA GREEN research facilities.

If an operation follows this pattern, no matter how ichor-stained and shriekingly insane things get along the way, DELTA GREEN and the players can count it as a success.

GUMSHOE Best Practices

To ensure thrills and horror, the players should keep these GUMSHOE best practices in mind.

You Can Win

Yes, this is a game of horror, in which your Agent might well be slaughtered, forcibly injected with Yuggothian spores, or buried in a Cambodian swamp. That will *definitely* happen if you do nothing, so you might as well do *something*.

Take the initiative: pick the most appealing offense and execute it. Will something horrible happen? Of course it will — it's a horror game! Something horrible will happen no matter what your plan is. At best, you'll find one that requires desperation and daring, and might still cost you your lives. But no fun whatsoever will happen unless you choose something to do and do it.

So be bold and seize the initiative. Pick the type of terrifying risk you're most able to confront and go after it with both hands. Who knows? Maybe you'll surprise the Handler, if not the opposition. As in any game, the Handler will allow any halfway credible approach you come up with a good chance of success, and will place nasty obstacles in your way to make your success more exciting. Pick something quickly, grit your teeth, and send your Agent into that Cambodian swamp.

Read Your Character Sheet

If you're stuck for an approach or a plan, think about how to use your best abilities to make what you want to happen, happen. Look at your highest ability scores, both Investigative and General. Play those high numbers right, and you play to win; and better yet, to a win

155

where you risk fewer talon wounds. Got a Marine rifleman with Firearms 10? What gets easier with a sniper involved? Got a NSA infiltrator with Stealth 9? Maybe the plan should involve a break-in. What's your highest Interpersonal ability? What GMC seems like they would respond to it? Have you analyzed the evidence with your highest Technical or Academic abilities? Something might well pop out at you when you do.

If you still find yourself unable to justify some near-suicidal plan, think of your Motivation. Come up with some reason to drive yourself into danger, and maybe pick up a nice refresh for doing it along the way. Look to your Motivation as a source of action and inspiration, and use it to decide which near-suicidal plan is right for your Agent.

When in Doubt, Get More Information

If you are legitimately stuck, and not just rejecting perfectly viable courses of action, don't just stick close to home hashing over your options. Whenever you get stuck, **get out and gather more information**. Ask yourself what you need to know in order to formulate a plan. Then figure out how to get that information, and go out and get it.

HUMINT is Key

Many groups are reluctant to use their Interpersonal abilities, figuring that they can get into less trouble by sticking purely to physical clues at the scene, or by poring over records in a safe government archive. This is a disastrous mistake. Talking to assets, witnesses, experts, and informants

is by far the best way of gaining information about the situation. With information, access, and assets, you can find that coveted way in that will set up a kill shot for you. Remember to use Investigative Networking (see p. 068) in a pinch if you're stuck.

Keep Moving Forward

Expect to find only one major clue per scene. Although you shouldn't be too quick to abandon a scene for the next one, most groups make the opposite mistake, returning endlessly to the same few places or witnesses, hoping to scrape more info out of them. If you find a clue that leads you somewhere else — go there! Chances are, once you're there, you'll find another clue, that will in turn lead you to a new scene, with a further clue that takes you to a third scene, and so on. Unsuccessful groups endlessly re-sniff the same ground. Successful ones follow a trail, just like successful federal agents.

Remember, You're the Protagonist

When you created your Agent, you cast a character, a protagonist — a hero — in a story. A story about a federal agent who fights the unnatural. Sure, some people curl up into a ball and whine that Cthulhu doesn't exist. Those people are called "game master characters." Or "lunch."

Paralysis is boring. When you create your Agent, or develop her personality during play, think about realistic ways to portray her as proactive and resourceful and dangerous — as, in a word, heroic — even in the face of non-Euclidean nightmares.

Players in horror games — and spy games! — often make the mistake of thinking solely about how realistic their responses are. Instead, make interesting choices and then find a way to make them seem plausible. An interesting choice is one that keeps your Agent, and the operation, moving fast.

The Innsmouth Rules

While DELTA GREEN very carefully does not print up field manuals or provide clear-cut rules of engagement, the survivors and veterans of its operations have their own list of life savers. Agents who refer to the list at all call it the "Innsmouth Rules," after the CIA's famous "Moscow Rules" for Company men in the Kremlin's backyard.

As might be expected, the best practices for DELTA GREEN Agents are slightly different.

Thou Shalt Not Get Caught

This is Rule One and Only. You do not have a "Get Out of Jail Free" card or a license to kill. You have a job to do, and that job includes doing it in the dark. If you do get caught, say nothing and take your lumps. The program will get you out unless keeping the mission quiet calls for you to do hard time for it, which it very well might. So don't get caught.

Live Your Cover

Don't refer to the program or the unnatural in public or private. Always have another story, another mission, another identity in mind. Ideally, have the papers to back it up.

Always Lie, Except To Us

Make sure your lies are consistent. Never lie to your partners or your case officer, and never ever lie to the program. We will find out and then nobody will ever find out what happened to you. Because we will lie to them.

Friendlies can know the truth about an operation. They can never know the truth about the program.

Intelligence is Your Weapon

Scout the manifestation, research it, watch it. Then go out and talk to the locals, to witnesses, to bums and inbreds and hop-heads and anybody human. You *really* can't learn about your enemy from books alone, so don't try.

The Minimum Size of a Team is Two

Do nothing alone. Our enemy can replace you, take over your mind, or simply remove you from existence and memory. Don't give them the opportunity. If you need to approach a contact solo, bring a partner for backup and overwatch.

Don't Kick In the Door

Not the front door, anyway. Make your own entry point. This rule applies to much more than entering buildings.

In the worst case, burn down the building and ambush them when they flee.

Don't Wait For the Whites of Their Eyes

Too many of your enemies don't die when you shoot them. Don't wait until close combat to find that out. (Absolutely do wait until you have confirmed that they are targets, not bystanders.) Similarly, give no warning shots, or warnings of any kind. Surprise is your only advantage.

A Successful Retreat is a Victory

When the opposition attacks you, you are part of their plan and they have the initiative. Don't be part of their plan: break contact and retreat to the rally point. (You *did* select a predetermined rally point, right?) Then analyze their attack and plan your counterstrike at their weak point, for a time and place where you have the initiative.

Never go in without a line of retreat. Always know where the exit is.

Trust Your Gut

If it feels wrong, it is wrong. Back off and get more information. If it feels really, really wrong, back way off and call for reinforcements. They might even come!

ON THE EVE OF DESTRUCTION

HANDLER'S EYES ONLY

In 1960, as journalist I.F. Stone put it, the world feels like "a bar-room on the verge of a brawl." The United States government means to win the brawl and clean up the bar-room at the same time. This is the decade that the government declares war on poverty and sends half a million troops to Indochina; desegregates voting booths and infiltrates Black movements; shoots rockets at the moon and not quite at the Soviets. If we put our mind to it and our backs into it, there is nothing we can't do to make the world better, for America and for everybody else.

Even DELTA GREEN believes that. For the time being.

"The time would be easy to know, for then mankind would have become as the Great Old Ones; free and wild and beyond good and evil, with laws and morals thrown aside and all men shouting and killing and revelling in joy. Then the liberated Old Ones would teach them new ways to shout and kill and revel and enjoy themselves, and all the earth would flame with a holocaust of ecstasy and freedom."

— H.P. Lovecraft, "The Call of Cthulhu"

Inside DELTA GREEN

The project that would become known as DELTA GREEN began with Operation PUZZLEBOX (the name given to it by DELTA GREEN during a reclassification in 1942), a federal raid on the decrepit fishing town of Innsmouth, Massachusetts on 23 February 1928. The ONI handled overall planning and coordination of this unusual multi-agency, civilian-military operation.

The ONI already had a desk devoted to unusual investigations: the Parapsychology, Paranormal, and Psychic Phenomena Desk, abbreviated to P4. A dismal assignment, P4 was where the Navy buried the cryptographers, Marines, Treasury agents, and sailors who survived both the Innsmouth Raid and its bureaucratic backlash. P4 took over the YY-I facility at Camp Fly in Arizona, where they held the Deep One-human hybrid prisoners taken at Innsmouth, and eventually dissected them as they died in the desert heat. As evidence accumulated from autopsies and archives, P4 re-opened PUZZLEBOX on a covert "need-to-know" basis.

Navy expeditions took P4 personnel across the globe searching for colonies like Innsmouth. They soon found them: in Greenland, the Philippines, Nicaragua, and elsewhere. They also discovered something of the larger picture at home, conducting operations in the continental U.S. against groups that P4 determined were engaged in "unconventional dangerous activities."

Overworked and underfunded, P4 investigators often arrived after action by local authorities had already taken place, and could only cover up the mess. The cults and madmen they found worshipped a dizzying variety of beings, corresponding to indications in medieval grimoires and to certain archaeological findings in that decade. By the end of the Thirties, P4 realized that PUZZLEBOX might hold far more than Deep Ones and their cultists.

The OSS Era

Domestic adventures dropped off the map for P4 after Pearl Harbor. In early 1942 Lt. Commander Martin Cook, the head of P4, briefed Major General William J. "Wild Bill" Donovan, the commander of the new OSS, on the Karotechia (see p. 286) though not on the larger unnatural picture. Donovan was convinced to bring in P4 as specialists who could exploit the Axis high commands' weakness for the occult. He promoted Cook to Commander and incorporated P4 into the OSS, giving it a special security clearance: DELTA GREEN.

Cook turned his DELTA GREEN teams loose on the Karotechia, capturing or destroying books and artifacts sought by Himmler's agents, while devoting as many air raids and depth-charge bombardments as he could to secondary targets P4 had identified. Soon, the program added the Genyosha (see p. 285), the Japanese occult apparat, to its priorities.

As Germany collapsed, DELTA GREEN agents moved into the falling Reich seizing or "denying to the enemy" books, artifacts, and Karotechia personnel connected with the unnatural. This Operation SUMMER BREEZE raced against not only various apocalyptic dead-end Nazi plans but against at least two sets of Soviet counter-occult operations specialists, within SMERSH and the GRU. Operations LUNACY in Germany, and SOUTHERN HOSPITALITY in South America and elsewhere, seemingly stamped out the Karotechia threat for good.

DELTA GREEN Reborn

On 1 October 1945, President Truman disbanded the OSS – and DELTA GREEN along with it. On 24 June 1947, the Roswell saucer crash reanimated the program inside the MAJESTIC Special Studies Group (see p. 166). Many analysts with DELTA GREEN clearance found themselves recalled to duty, sworn to secrecy, and attached to MAJESTIC.

Other DELTA GREEN veterans saw an opportunity to provide legal cover to their various off-the-books investigations, and lobbied the White House to reorganize DELTA GREEN itself within the U.S. military "to deny the use of unorthodox technologies by any foreign power." Truman agreed, and directed the Joint Chiefs of Staff to establish DELTA GREEN as an interservice military intelligence unit specializing in psychological warfare, under the command of now-Commodore Martin Cook.

Monitored by an Executive Committee of senior officers and JCS deputies, Cook would report directly to the Joint Chiefs of Staff, bypassing (in theory) the individual armed services and their bitter rivalries. Truman expected that DELTA GREEN would track UFO incidents overseas, to keep the U.S. ahead of the intelligence curve.

Cook and his veterans had other ideas. Deep Ones, Nazi occultists, and the Black Ocean were very terrestrial. Flying saucers seemed like a distraction; those agents interested in "Buck Rogers stuff" ultimately joined MAJESTIC, which finally relieved DELTA GREEN of its UFO-related duties in 1953 to the delight of both programs. From that point forward, the two organizations kept out of each other's way. This early division further compartmentalized intelligence that, if seen as a whole, might have revealed much about the nature of the unnatural.

In May 1959, DELTA GREEN lost the services of Rear Admiral Cook, when he was confined to the psychiatric wing of Bethesda Naval Hospital for complete mental and physical collapse due to exhaustion and overwork. In 1963, Cook is released and retires quietly to his ranch in Montana, where he lives until his death in 1968. During the last years of his life he declines to participate in DELTA GREEN operations, even in an advisory capacity.

DELTA GREEN Now

Cook's retirement leaves the top of the DELTA GREEN table of organization empty. His adjutant, Captain David Payton, had survived Operation BRISTOL (p. 215), and now lacks the ambition (and some suggest, the energy) to replace him. The Joint Chiefs don't want to think about DELTA GREEN, and certainly don't want to doom some able officer's career by assigning him to a program that seemingly produces nothing but the occasional disastrous body count. Captain Payton continues to coordinate ongoing DELTA GREEN operations, but the program drifts during the election year of 1960.

Robert S. McNamara — Re-Organizer

In 1961, newly appointed Secretary of Defense Robert S. McNamara re-organizes a number of Pentagon systems, including DELTA GREEN. President Kennedy (Massachusetts native and lifelong sailor) enthusiastically embraces the DELTA GREEN mission after receiving a briefing from MAJESTIC-12. Rather than restoring the direct military command structure, JFK and McNamara pull responsibility for DELTA GREEN upstairs to the National Security Council, which reconstitutes the Executive Committee ostensibly charged with its oversight.

McNamara and the NSC increase civilian involvement on the ExComm and in the program. Throughout the 1960s, DELTA GREEN recruits from academia and taps civilian intelligence and law-enforcement agencies for personnel,

adding investigative brainpower to the program's raw firepower. When an unnatural event comes to DELTA GREEN's attention, the case officer provides relevant personnel with a temporary clearance, briefing them on the essential, "need-to-know" details of the mission.

After participating, the survivors receive a small, green delta (Δ) attached to their files. Once marked, these DELTA GREEN "friendlies" can be mobilized again if they are in the general vicinity of a crisis, or if their particular talents are needed. DELTA GREEN grows less centralized, with individual members of the Executive Committee, and even individual veteran case officers, possessing the de facto authority to mount operations without the foreknowledge of the program's leadership.

As a rapid-response strategy for a rapidly disintegrating world, this method has its advantages. As a survival strategy, it costs DELTA GREEN greatly.

Facilities

By and large, DELTA GREEN prefers to work within other federal government facilities rather than maintaining its own specialized establishment. For one thing, this makes it harder for observers to track program operatives by their movements; for another, it avoids needless reduplication of radio telescopes or mainframe computers.

The program subcontracts physical security for non-governmental DELTA GREEN facilities (and some federal ones) to the firm Wackenhut Security, which also provides security for NASA and other federal agencies. This saves manpower and promotes operational security; the Wackenhut guards know nothing about the buildings and random stretches of wasteland they protect.

Headquarters

DELTA GREEN has no headquarters building, not even a dedicated floor. The Executive Committee has their individual offices, and meets in an anonymous, windowless third-floor conference room in the C Ring of the Pentagon. What little permanent staff DELTA GREEN has (by 1969, 78 staff officers, secretaries, case officers, and analysts) operates out of Wing Five, a remote stretch of the increasingly decrepit Munitions Building on Constitution Avenue. This staff organizes cover missions, logistics, and funding for program operations.

Another team of nine analysts works from a compartmentalized office in the Langley, Virginia headquarters of the CIA, mostly for ease of access to open-source and raw intelligence. Finally, 22 researchers with DELTA GREEN clearance work in the Defense Research Division of the Library of Congress (p. 036), but in theory none of them know any of the others.

There is an ad hoc headquarters office for the use of the program in the Military Assistance Command Vietnam HQ at 137 Pasteur Street in Saigon. The program also sets up temporary field headquarters both overseas and at home for any given operation, some of which last long enough to seem permanent. The field office in Boston, for example, was established in 1927 in the Custom House Tower to coordinate PUZZLEBOX, and closed in 1937; it then reactivates for RIPTIDE in 1963 and remains open until 1970.

The Annex

After Freis' fire burned out the original DELTA GREEN archives in 1955 (see p. 195), the question arose not just of where, but *whether*, to store the program's records and the various items of unnatural salvage taken in the field. Some DELTA GREEN analysts and officers (the "burn the books crowd," as their opponents labeled them) insisted that Freis was not insane but had instead done humanity, and the program, a great service.

Having no records of any DELTA GREEN mission vastly improved operational security, but it made planning and strategic vision nearly impossible or at best dependent entirely on unreliable human memories. Accumulating unnatural artifacts and tomes clearly carried considerable, and unknowable, risks – but without studying them, could DELTA GREEN plan future operations?

For five years, the debate smoldered in memos and meeting rooms. Active members of the Executive Committee and even some case officers set up their own files and sometimes even their own storage facilities in various government buildings and basements, or in their homes. This very bad habit continues, even after the typically bureaucratic solution eventually emerges from the McNamara reorganization.

In 1961, DELTA GREEN re-establishes its operational records system, including a library for confiscated hypergeometric and occult works, but its location remains classified. No researcher, or any program staffer at all, is allowed direct access to it. This is the Annex, or as some veterans call it, the Barn (since its door was firmly closed now that the horses had escaped).

The Annex is a building in Baltimore owned by a CIA front company using a Mafia front company as a shell. It appears to be a "fireproof storage" facility, one very unwelcoming to would-be clients. A small security and courier unit maintains the Annex without ever studying or reading its contents, which are individually sealed before being sent to the facility. If a member of the Executive Committee wants a record or resource from the Annex, he sends the file or shelf number on a dedicated teletype; the desired item arrives within four hours. Every member of the Committee has a personal code number (changed weekly) for requests; any other number triggers a security investigation. All records so requested must be returned to the Annex, resealed, within 24 hours.

The Ward

The Ward is a secure wing of Naval Hospital Portsmouth in Portsmouth, Virginia. Although many large US military hospitals have at least one DELTA GREEN friendly on staff, the program intervenes as soon as medically possible (and sometimes before then) to transfer all patients with DELTA GREEN clearance to the Ward. All such patients wind up in the Ward for any needed longer-term recovery and ongoing psychiatric care.

The primary reason is security: delirious with pain or pain-killers, patients have been known to babble all manner of revealing things. As a secondary concern, the medical staff in the Ward have seen enough strange phenomena that they can often guess which symptoms are life-threatening and which ones are weird but distracting.

The Executive Committee

Since its establishment in 1947, DELTA GREEN has operated under the supervision, at least, of an Executive Committee. Sometimes called the ExComm or the 9895 Committee (after the Executive Order establishing the program), it is appointed by the President and by the Joint Chiefs of Staff. Under Truman and Eisenhower, the 9895 Committee mostly acted as a rubber stamp and occasional facilitator for Rear Admiral Cook's plans, only rarely refusing its imprimatur for an operation.

Secretary of Defense McNamara reasserts White House control over the process by appointing 26 new members to the Executive Committee, many of them civilians from intelligence, other departments, and even academia. At Kennedy's insistence, at least one representative of the Special Forces is added, Army Brigadier General Reginald Fairfield. After a thorough briefing by DELTA GREEN staff (including on-site examination of a Deep One prisoner), the new Committee sets about its work.

During the 1960s, the Executive Committee includes:

Dr. Joseph Camp (b. 1918)

Recruited out of Harvard's Far Eastern Studies Department by DELTA GREEN in 1942, Camp served with the OSS in the China-Burma-India Theater. Camp is currently officially Deputy Chief for Country Studies of the Defense Research Division, but spends a great deal of time as a Pentagon adviser on Vietnam and China. He has a remarkably stable and clear analytical mind, and supports the "know thy enemy" faction of the program, urging the salvage of books and artifacts.

Brigadier General Reginald Fairfield (b. 1914)

As an OSS commando, Fairfield served in France, Italy, and the Mediterranean. After spending the 1950s working on Operation GLADIO in Europe training stay-behind guerrillas to resist Communist invasion, he transferred to Vietnam in 1959. Martin Cook read him into the program that year; his aggressive "burn the books, dynamite everything" policy (and his right-wing political views) sets some of the Committee against him. He is promoted to Major General in 1968, when he becomes the head of the Executive Committee on Rear Admiral Payton's retirement. Most of the missions he organizes are major operations like KURTZ (p. 180), involving platoon- or company-sized units from many branches.

Colonel Michael Keravuori (b. 1919)

A veteran of the Russo-Finnish War, Keravuori became a naturalized American citizen in 1946 and served in Korea as an Army Ranger. He commanded Operation SIC SEMPER TYRANNIS (December 1952), which destroyed an MGB laboratory outside Novosibirsk attempting to use Karotechia re-animation research to make Stalin immortal. The most puzzling aspect of the operation was that the GRU had captured the DELTA GREEN infiltrators *before their raid*, but, after interrogation, inexplicably released them and allowed them to complete their mission. Then, the GRU attempted to assassinate the survivors; only Keravuori made it back, walking over the frozen Bering Straits.

After Operation SKUNKED in Colombia (May 1956) he received a transfer to the 9895 Committee. He pays consummate attention to every detail of his operations; his staff says it's as if he doesn't need to sleep. In fact, he can't sleep. He hasn't slept at all since Colombia. But he still has dreams. Some day, he will remember them.

Colonel Marcus Mitchell (b. 1920)

Sergeant Mitchell served with the all-Black 92nd Infantry in Italy, where he salvaged the DELTA GREEN Operation THRENODY in Bordighiera (April 1945) and was read into the program. After SUMMER BREEZE, LUNACY, service in Korea, and OCS at Ft. Benning, the program transferred Lt. Mitchell to domestic operations, often against suspected unnatural cults within the civil rights movement. (Aside from Operation SUDDEN SAM in 1967 (p. 183), most of these turn out to be false alarms.) Promoted to Colonel and elevated to the Executive Committee in 1963, he believes the oblique approach and overwhelming firepower solve most problems.

Rear Admiral David Farragut Payton, USN (b. 1904)

An Annapolis graduate, Payton joined ONI in 1929 and P4 in 1932. Stationed in Mexico, Japan, and the Philippines, he uncovered the Black Ocean and its ties to Dagon; during WWII he worked as a codebreaker at Station S on Bainbridge Island, Washington. In 1947, he became Commodore Cook's adjutant in the new DELTA GREEN. His last field assignment was Operation BRISTOL in 1955; he has been listless and unfocused since then. But as one of the few surviving P4 veterans in the program and its titular commanding officer (promoted to Rear Admiral in 1961), he retains considerable potential influence until he retires in 1968.

Brigadier General Michael Stillman, USAF (b. 1921)

Stillman was in the original class of DELTA GREEN OSS recruits; in December 1942, he captured the Donnerschlag sonic cannon plans from the Karotechia station at Fécamp in France in Operation UPROAR. He transferred to the USAF and rejoined the program in 1947 studying UFOs (Projects SIGN, GRUDGE, and BLUE BOOK). When MAJESTIC took over all UFO research, Stillman remained at DELTA GREEN. He still believes in weaponizing the unnatural and in cooperation with MAJESTIC. If he hears about surviving prehuman science or an encounter with the Mi-Go, he mounts an operation immediately.

Dr. Augusta Warren (b. 1919)

Her father, occultist Harley Warren, disappeared in Florida before Augusta was born. She tried to stay well out of his shadow, studying sociology at the University of Chicago. Unfortunately, her researches kept turning up strange patterns in the data, unsettling conclusions about human mass behavior. After Kennedy's win in 1960, Warren uses her father's surviving protégés (and her political connections with the Daley machine in Chicago) to get onto the Executive Committee. She ignores the pervasive sexism, militarism, and resentment of her string-pulling, and goes ahead with her research: tasking trained investigators with on-the-ground, first-hand fieldwork on anomalies she notices in the data. Teams sent on these "Warren Reports" tend to encounter nothing – or phenomena indescribably weird even by program standards.

Historical Figures

The Handler may also want to add a few historical figures to the DELTA GREEN Executive Committee, such as:

△ **Miles Copeland, Jr. (b. 1916):** Joined the CIA in 1947, running operations throughout the Middle East. He was a major player in Operation AJAX (the 1953 overthrow of Mossadegh in Iran), and plans other coups d'etat from Syria to Ghana. In 1954, he set up the Occultism in High Places (OHP) program to plant CIA-backed astrologers and other occultists on receptive foreign leaders. He lives in Beirut under non-official cover (NOC).

△ **Dr. Sidney Gottlieb (b. 1918):** The "Black Sorcerer" of the CIA, so called because of his expertise in poisons and hypnosis. He heads the chemical division of the TSD (p. 034) and runs the CIA's MK-ULTRA mind control program. (Gottlieb also makes an excellent MAJESTIC sub-director, and likely works with both programs in any case.)

△ **Virginia Hall (b. 1906):** Served with both the SOE and OSS during WWII, operating in Nazi-occupied Europe as agent "Artemis." She and her husband both work for the CIA's Political Action Division running operations behind the Iron Curtain; she keeps a very low profile and officially retires in 1966.

△ **Major General Edward Lansdale, USAF (b. 1908):** OSS veteran and psychological warfare expert, Lansdale managed elections and counterinsurgencies in the Philippines and Vietnam for the CIA. He heads the anti-Castro Operation MONGOOSE for the Department of Defense until 1963, then returns to Vietnam on a vague posting until 1968, when he retires.

△ **General Nathan Twining, USAF (ret.) (b. 1897):** Commanding officer of the Air Materiel Command at the time of the Roswell crash, he recommended the creation of Project GRUDGE to study UFOs. He served as Chairman of the Joint Chiefs of Staff until his formal retirement in 1960.

COLONEL SATCHEL WADE, USMC

Born in Pittsburgh, Pennsylvania in 1932, Satchel Grange Wade joined the Marine Corps at the beginning of the Korean War and rapidly racked up an impressive combat record, including a Bronze Star and two Purple Hearts. After the armistice, he moved into the officer track; in Vietnam, he receives a Silver Star and his third Purple Heart, rising to Colonel by 1968.

He was one of the survivors of the Hwasun ambush in 1950, during counterguerrilla operations against the Olaegodae ("very old") mountain tribes; his experiences there led him into DELTA GREEN. He urges constant, relentless military action against the unnatural, his motto being: "They seek to cause us fear, and our response must be to cause them fear."

Wade wants to be on ExComm, but he doesn't have the bureaucratic connections to ascend. So instead, he plans and carries out mission after mission in Southeast Asia, hoping to earn a spot by sheer guts and hard work. Unfortunately, his ambition leaves him open to manipulation by his Khmer mistress Li. He begins using more and more unnatural means to fight the war on the unnatural: by 1968, reports of Tcho-Tcho guards – and worse – at his jungle command post trickle in. In 1969, Wade plans Operation OBSIDIAN (p. 186), which results in the release of an unnatural entity and in DELTA GREEN's disbandment the next year.

On 7 January 1970, Staff Sergeant Donald Poe and Sergeant Adolph Lepus, two of the few survivors of Operation OBSIDIAN, assassinate Wade and Li at their command post in Binh Thuy province.

Analysts

DELTA GREEN analysts, at Headquarters or in position at the CIA, NRO, NSA, FBI, or other federal intelligence bureaucracies, sift reams of data and reports to detect possible unnatural incursions or activity worldwide. Satellite and surveillance photographs, human intelligence reports, signals interception, local police reports: any or all of these might cross a program analyst's desk. Some analysts work for the Geological Survey, the Department of the Interior, or even for the Smithsonian seeking ARCHINT: archaeological intelligence that indicates prehuman or other unnatural activity in the past.

Analysts may task researchers or even friendlies in the field to determine if a given report is a hoax or error, then pass the most likely paranormal incidents up to the Executive Committee. Analysts are not supposed to take the field themselves, but sometimes they're the only ones handy who know that particular Eskimo dialect.

Case Officers

Case officers manage teams of agents, ideally acting on authorization from the Executive Committee, or from one member of it. Case officers organize and facilitate operations; they rarely participate. Almost all case officers are former agents, experienced and tough enough to motivate agents and offer suggestions. But many are so badly damaged, physically or psychologically, that smart agents do not want them out in the field.

Case officers are responsible for maintaining active communication with the agents and for keeping Headquarters informed. There are few hard and fast rules. Some case officers are hands-on; others prefer not to interfere as long as they're kept in the loop. Some high-priority or high-visibility operations require more active management than others.

For deniability's sake, case officers always go by false identities, even with their agents. A team of agents may work with the same case officer for years under a particular name and title, never hearing any of the case officer's many other pseudonyms.

MAJESTIC

Let DELTA GREEN root around in swamps and sewers for monsters to kill. MAJESTIC will take America to the stars.

On 24 June 1947, an extraterrestrial flying disk crashed near Roswell, New Mexico, triggering a renewal of U.S. government interest in the unknown. President Truman ordered the creation of a special off-the-books unit under the entirely theoretical supervision of the National Security Council to analyze the wreckage, cover up the crash, and erase all public knowledge of the event.

This new unit, headed by Presidential Science Adviser Vannevar Bush, assembled a committee of twelve of the finest scientific, military, and intelligence minds in the world to respond to the saucer crash at Roswell: the MAJESTIC Twelve Special Studies Group, MAJESTIC-12 or MJ-12 for short. (MJ-12 also, confusingly, refers to the Project DELPHI subsection of MAJESTIC.) Their deputies and permanent staffs became heads of the various working groups beneath the MAJESTIC clearance umbrella. "MAJESTIC-12" now refers to the Steering Committee that runs the MAJESTIC program.

The examination of the Roswell saucer and its crew of four Grey aliens demonstrated that America's military technology was barely beyond the flint spearhead on a galactic scale. A 30-foot craft could travel interstellar distances, powered not by some atomic pile but by a series of sigils carved into clay tablets: pure hypergeometric manipulation of the fabric of spacetime. MA-JESTIC-12 removed the "Bucket," as the saucer became known, to the Air Materiel Command headquarters at Wright Field (Wright-Patterson AFB after 1948) in Dayton, Ohio.

MAJESTIC-12 brought DELTA GREEN back to life, mostly to pick the brains of those with previous hy-pergeometric experiences, and to gain access to the only other known xenobiological specimens: the Deep One prisoners and corpses captured at Innsmouth. The project consolidated the Grey and Deep One specimens in a new facility inside the AEC Los Alamos Scientific Laboratory, YY-II, codenamed the ICE CAVE.

As MAJESTIC-12 correlated two decades of research into the unnatural with the new findings from the Roswell saucer, they rapidly recognized the absolutely critical need for total secrecy. The project divided into "white-badge clearance" (code word MAJESTIC) – which merely provided its various researchers with a cover story about ultra-technology and crashed UFOs – and a more limited "black-badge clearance" (code word MAJIC) that revealed as much of the truth as MAJESTIC-12 knew about the unnatural. That wasn't too much, but it was more than they could handle.

Mission and Structure

The mission of MAJESTIC is the same as it was in 1947:

△ To determine the truth about extraterrestrial life.

△ To recover, control, and exploit alien and paranormal technology and artifacts.

△ To keep the project totally secret.

That second mission statement results in oceans of black budget money from the military and top-secret science establishments flowing into MAJESTIC programs. The third one sometimes leads to the death of witnesses – or even unreliable officials who know too much. In 1949, an MJ-3 team threw former Secretary of Defense (and former MJ-2) James Forrestal out of a 16th-floor Bethesda Naval Hospital window; his psychological breakdown posed a clear security risk to MAJESTIC.

The need for secrecy is real: revealing that the United States is defenseless against alien attack would at best cause nationwide panic and at worst trigger an arms race or even a pre-emptive nuclear strike. No foreign nation, no matter how close an ally, knows anything except that the United States is covertly investigating UFOs. In fact, no U.S. President since JFK knows about MAJESTIC.

The need for secrecy also makes direct organization of MAJESTIC difficult at best. Instead, its original twelve working groups have become twelve self-sustaining projects, each worming tentacles into the federal bureaucracy to siphon off resources and personnel. Any one of the twelve might have scientists, engineers, shooters, investigators, or an-

THE GREY TRUTH

MAJESTIC does not know, although MJ-10 head Gordon Gray theorized it during the initial 1947 meetings, that entirely different aliens constructed the Greys and their craft in order to provoke a specific psychological response. The Greys are bioroids psychically controlled by the real aliens, and the living Grey specimen continues to telepathically explore (and possibly subvert) every highly placed expert or official who comes near it.

The real aliens, the Mi-Go (p. 244), want to create addicts to hypergeometry among powerful humans while testing their competence to hide the truth and their ruthlessness in doing so. They require human pawns to assist them in mining Earth's resources, both mineral and biological (human brains fascinate them). The fungi from Yuggoth are auditioning the U.S. government for the role of servitor cult, and MAJESTIC is performing well.

The Mi-Go do not reveal the next step of their agenda - a phony "treaty" with the United States - until 1980. Until then, their spy lies in the ICE CAVE astrally exploring humanity's best technology, and their slow harvest of human brains and wills continues.

alysts on call. Many MAJESTIC personnel are fringe theorists, loners or the alienated: the project fakes their deaths and moves them into the ICE CAVE or Area 51 facilities full-time. Others live in protected apartment complexes in Las Vegas, Dayton, and Albuquerque, shuttled to and from work on unregistered aircraft or in buses with polarized windows.

The twelve projects are numbered MJ-1 through MJ-12, designations also used to refer to the project heads on the MAJESTIC Steering Committee. For added confusion, the personnel and staff of the MAJESTIC Steering Committee and the DELTA GREEN Executive Committee overlapped throughout the 1940s and 1950s; even now, unofficial back channels and dual-clearance officers continue to exist. In 1970, after DELTA GREEN disbands, the new MJ-1 Lucas Graves finally clears out the last of the overlap, laying off staffers and transferring officers away from the gaze of a briefly curious Joint Chiefs of Staff.

The MAJESTIC Steering Committee meets even less frequently than the DELTA GREEN ExComm; MJ-1 and MJ-3 exercise some control by managing information and security, but do not direct the other teams in a meaningful fashion. MJ-1 and MJ-3 don't mind, because this provides deniability and compartmentalization if one part of MAJESTIC is exposed.

MJ-1: Project AQUARIUS

Officially organized under the NSA, Project AQUARIUS (Project GLEEM until 1966) acts as the coordinating body for MAJESTIC as a whole, providing logistics and basic financing for all projects. AQUARIUS also serves as MAJESTIC's personnel and scientific scouting office, reviewing files and records of every scientist or engineer with a government grant, looking for talent and technologies that any part of MAJESTIC can use. It also conducts background checks in conjunction with MJ-3.

Its cover mission is information security, giving it access to a wide net of government facilities and archives. Behind that outer cover is its "white-badge" cover: that AQUARIUS exists to coordinate all federal research into UFOs.

The current director of MJ-1 and Chairman of the MAJESTIC Steering Committee is **Rear Admiral Joseph Wenger, USN (ret.),** following the 1961 death by lung cancer of the previous Chairman, Horace Gaither. Admiral Wenger was Vice Director of the NSA until 1953 and MJ-4 until 1961; patriotic and no-nonsense, he believes implicitly in the MAJESTIC mission. Ill health forces his final retirement in 1969; his replacement is Lucas Graves, Deputy Director of the NRO.

MJ-2: Project PLATO

The original task of MJ-2 (Project GERONIMO) was to develop a defense posture against alien attack, which rapidly proved impossible. Established in 1954 to instead open diplomatic relations with aliens, Project PLATO has little to do until MJ-4 (Project SIGMA) deciphers the alien signals. It maintains the COUNTRY CLUB, a secret facility in Maryland accessible only by air, where it brainstorms about hypothetical contact scenarios and drafts provisional treaties. The infrequent face-to-face meetings of the twelve members of the MAJESTIC Steering Committee occur at the COUNTRY CLUB, which also serves as MAJESTIC's de facto archive and records facility.

The current MJ-2 is **Arthur K. Tallmage,** a deeply frustrated State Department "lifer." Bored and out of his depth, he is something of a loose cannon on the Steering Committee, launching occasional investigations on his own recognizance. He is one harebrained scheme away from a visit from MJ-3.

MJ-3: Project GARNET

Project GARNET is MAJESTIC's counterintelligence and security arm, responsible for control of, and accountability for, all information and documents regarding the Greys, and of all MAJESTIC projects. Project GARNET is deeply involved with the CIA's mind control research program, MK-ULTRA: like the CIA, MJ-3 covets the ability to erase memories, program assassins, and force truthful testimony.

With the creation of the National Reconnaissance Office in 1960, GARNET has a perfect source of deniable operatives and black funding. Although GARNET assets in the CIA's Domestic Operations Division still do most of MJ-3's investigating, security teams working for NRO's "Section DELTA" under deep cover are bureaucratically invisible: their parent agency officially doesn't exist! MJ-3 security teams thus automatically have secondary cover as employees of the Air Force or FBI.

NRO DELTA teams use disinformation, blackmail, burglary, threats, and force (very much including deadly force) to keep MAJESTIC's secrets. A visit from MJ-3's "Men in Black" is a harrowing experience, even for DELTA GREEN agents. More often than not, NRO DELTA operatives do not know what it is they are guarding or covering up; there are layers of disinformation between NRO DELTA and the MAJESTIC-12 Steering Committee.

The rest of GARNET's cover in the federal bureaucracy is Project BLUE BOOK, the Air Force unit assigned to "investigate" UFOs. The current MJ-3 is **Colonel John Douglass, USAF,** aggressive head of security for Nellis Air Force Base in Nevada and the Nevada Test Range, which includes MJ-6 and MJ-7's facilities at S-4/Area 51.

MJ-4: Project SIGMA

In October 1953, NSA listening posts around the world began picking up oddly patterned signals. In 1954, MJ-4 established Project SIGMA to analyze them, and by July determined they were systematic communications from deep space. SIGMA's remit now is detecting, decrypting, and establishing extraterrestrial communications. The SIGMA messages inspired President Eisenhower to centralize UFO research under MAJESTIC and increase its budget, and to greenlight construction of the Arecibo radio telescope.

In 1961, President Kennedy suggests launching manned missions to the Moon to search for the source of the signal. This gives SIGMA a power base within NASA, as well as the NSA.

The current MJ-4 is **Captain Thalia Brewster, USNR,** the cyberneticist and cryptographer who picked the alien signal out of the hash of NSA intercepts. A protégé of original MAJESTIC-12 committee member Donald Menzel, she works at the Computation Center at Harvard University. Owlish and intensely focused, she sees alien codes as just another pattern to crack. She works closely with MJ-7, as the nearly forgotten hyperspatial mathematics of Carl Upham prove relevant to both projects.

MJ-5: Project MOON DUST

MOON DUST was formed in 1953 to intercept, shoot down, and recover any extraterrestrial craft, occupants, or evidence of visitation. The precursor to Project MOON DUST was the Air Force Materiel Command's BLUE TEAM, based at Wright-Patterson AFB. In 1954, MAJESTIC-12 permanently detached the USAF BLUE TEAM personnel to Project MOON DUST. The crash-recovery unit, called Operation BLUE FLY, is staffed by USAF personnel, and operates in the field under the cover of the 39th Aerospace Rescue and Recovery Squadron. (In Indochina, BLUE FLY works through MACV-SOG's SOG-80 "Recovery Studies

Division.") Project MOON DUST turns over all recovered materials to MJ-6 Project PLUTO and MJ-8 Project DANCER.

BLUE FLY and MOON DUST are based at MAJESTIC-restricted facilities at Wright-Patterson AFB; Ft. Belvoir, Virginia; Edwards AFB in California; and Nakhon Phanom RTAFB in Thailand. However, MOON DUST and BLUE FLY detachments can stage from secure hangars on 19 air bases in the U.S. and 25 overseas. In theory, a MOON DUST team can get anywhere in the U.S. within six hours – and anywhere in the free world within 24.

The current MJ-5 is **Brigadier General Rudolf C. Kohler, USAF,** commander of the 1127th Field Activities Group, the cover unit for the Project. He eagerly seeks opportunities to try his planes and airmen against "little gray men."

MJ-6: Project PLUTO

MJ-6 comprises teams from the Air Force's Foreign Technology Division at Wright-Patterson AFB and Air Force Weapons Laboratory at Kirtland AFB near Albuquerque, the Naval Scientific and Technical Support Center in Suitland, Maryland, the NSA's Office of Research and Engineering, the CIA's Directorate for Science and Technology, and ARPA. They work on a sub-project, compartmentalized basis, with only a few key Project PLUTO personnel knowing how the whole enterprise interacts.

PLUTO evaluates, studies, and attempts to reverse-engineer all advanced technology from recovered crash debris or associated with any unnatural event or irruption. Project PLUTO stores its master techni-

cal data archive at the COUNTRY CLUB, and runs MAJESTIC-restricted laboratories at NASA, and at private contractors and universities throughout the military-industrial complex. In 1961, PLUTO establishes its primary MAJIC-restricted fabrication and experimental facilities at the S-4 laboratory at Area 51 in the Nevada Test Range.

PLUTO research sounds like science fiction: antimatter, aircraft-killing lasers, time machines and teleportation, new kinds of light, materials that absorb radar or deflect energy, anti-gravity, miniaturized computer circuits, and cancer control. Each field has one or more Sub-Projects at one or another stage in it, many of them designed to weaponize the unnatural. Sub-Project GABRIEL investigates low-frequency sound weapons for use against the Greys; MJ-1 kills that project in 1966 as "unhelpful."

Vannevar Bush set up PLUTO in 1949, but is forced into mandatory retirement in 1962. His replacement as MJ-6 is **Edwin Forbes Cavanaugh,** former head of research at Raytheon. Cavanaugh wants to conquer space travel for the United States, of course, but he also wants to make an obscene amount of money selling black technology to defense contractors and, eventually, to the civilian market.

MJ-7: Project REDLIGHT

Originally established in 1947 for the purpose of repairing and flying the "Bucket," by 1954 REDLIGHT had widened its remit to reverse-engineering the saucer and its components. During the 1950s, REDLIGHT analyzed the Bucket at Wright-Patterson AFB; grappling with its alien physics kills or mentally cripples three dozen researchers. In 1961 MAJESTIC begins monitoring the researchers more intensively, cutting back opportunities to study the equations and sigils obsessively. For increased security and monitoring capabilities, MAJESTIC transfers the "Bucket" to the Nevada Test Range, specifically to a top-secret section of the range known as Area 51, previously nicknamed "the Ranch" and "Dreamland."

Located on 90,000 acres of desert near the dry bed of Groom Lake, Area 51 served as the site of Lockheed and the CIA's U-2 test flights in the 1950s; it currently also hosts the A-12 and D-21 test projects and (from 1968) the HAVE DOUGHNUT evaluations that fly captured Soviet bloc aircraft in mock combat. The S-4 laboratory is the MAJIC-restricted facility at Area 51 where REDLIGHT attempts to apply alien technologies to terrestrial aircraft, and to repair and operate the antimatter reactor and anti-gravity propulsion system on the "Bucket."

The current director of MJ-7 is **General Harlan Tate, USAF,** who replaces Johns Hopkins biophysicist Detlev Bronk in 1960. Tate served under Nathan Twining (p. 164) during the original Roswell flap; he sees REDLIGHT as crucial to national security and drives his subordinates to take ever more dangerous risks. In 1972, he dies in the antimatter explosion resulting from an attempt to restart the "Bucket."

MJ-8: Project DANCER

Project DANCER analyzes alien biology. Its specimens include not just the three dead Greys and the survivor, but the remaining Innsmouth

hybrids and Deep Ones taken over from DELTA GREEN. (The latter have all been catatonic for decades, owing to their lack of contact with the ocean.) Samples of ghoul flesh, further xenospecimens acquired by Project MOON DUST, and other biological curiosities complete the unholy menagerie in the ICE CAVE facility beneath Los Alamos.

With the modeling of DNA structure in the 1950s, research possibilities for DANCER seem endless. Altering human genetics to create super-soldiers, unlocking psychic abilities, grafting alien DNA into humans, and other sub-programs advance boldly into the unknown.

Dr. Olivia Jackson McKay currently heads MJ-8. Formerly deputy director of the CIA's Office of Scientific Intelligence and a trained

surgeon, McKay sees her alien charges as the next natural stage of human evolution. There can be no blasphemy in hurrying the process along. She only needs a few more specimens...

MJ-9: Project OVERVIEW

MJ-9 performs long-range, nonterrestrial reconnaissance, with the goal of creating a deep-space early warning system. While Project MOON DUST monitors the atmosphere and near-orbital space for incoming or outbound alien craft to intercept or track, OVERVIEW is tasked with carrying out a detailed survey of the solar system to determine if the Greys have established a base anywhere. OVERVIEW analysts believe an active underground base exists

THE ONION AND THE WHITE SHEET

MAJESTIC-12 began analysis of the "Bucket" hoping it would provide insights into anti-gravity and the unified field. Instead, it held clay tablets engraved with sigils, while the exterior of the craft bore subtle, larger glyphs etched into its indestructible metal skin. Detlev Bronk, the top-level bio-physicist on the MAJESTIC-12 committee, had received a PUZZLEBOX clearance to study the Deep Ones and their artifacts.

The Onion

Put in charge of Special Study Group 2 (which became MJ-7 REDLIGHT), Bronk ordered tracings made of the similarly engraved stones from the Innsmouth raid, along with the glyphs and sigils from the saucer. Bound into a single oversized volume, the book of alien etchings became known as "the Onion," because it held layers and layers of truth on onionskin paper. There are currently four copies of the Onion in existence: in the ICE CAVE, S-4, the MAJIC-cleared facility at Wright-Patterson, and the archive at the COUNTRY CLUB. Only MAJIC-cleared individuals know the Onion exists at all.

Studying it for several hundred hours provides a Hypergeometric potential of 2 or more (p. 197) and 1 rating point each of Unnatural and of Fringe Science; it also triggers a series of 4-point (or worse) Stability tests against the Unnatural.

The Gravity Sigil

The sigil from the "Bucket" seems to project gravity - with no apparent counter-force - in a way that human science cannot even begin to decide how to understand. MAJESTIC-12 threw the best minds on the planet at the sigil, and destroyed many of them. Project REDLIGHT has replicated the sigil in rote copy, using it to propel objects and even kill. (Access to a copied sigil requires MJ-3 approval *and* two MAJESTIC-12 directors' personal signature.) But after over a decade of effort, humanity has not moved an inch toward understanding how it works.

The White Paper

Bronk assigned the young, brilliant mathematician Dr. Stephen Courtis to study the sigils. His startling research led to the restoration of power within the vehicle, and various other breakthroughs, but in that time he grew withdrawn and secretive. On 12 December 1949 Wright-Patterson security found Courtis crushed beneath a sigil of his own design (similar to those found in the alien craft) carved into a four-foot wooden beam. The sigil was somehow exerting 190 gravities of force - with no equivalent counter-force.

All that remained of Courtis besides his shattered corpse was a single sheet of typing paper on which he had written 34 equations and one word: "escape." Since then, the White Paper has driven twelve mathematicians into breakdowns or full insanity. When Dr. Sylvia Garcia simply disintegrates while studying it in 1964, MJ-7 regretfully restricts the White Paper to "joint access by Director's hand only." MJ-7 has not been able to squelch the rumors that Dr. Garcia's last words were "Of course. It's all so simple."

on the dark side of the Moon. With the launch of the OAO-1 satellite in 1966 (its "failure" was MAJESTIC disinformation), OVERVIEW gains a much better observational platform – and disturbing evidence of very widespread alien activity from Mars to Pluto.

The director of MJ-9 is **Dr. James H. Kellaway,** head of the NASA Planning Office. His paranoia about the Greys and other aliens is justified, but the increasingly extreme security and disinformation measures he takes indicate an incipient breakdown.

MJ-10: Project SIDEKICK

MJ-10 is responsible for meeting with foreign military and civilian intelligence services in NATO and U.S.-allied countries to co-ordinate world efforts to address UFO phenomena. SIDEKICK keeps in contact with other government UFO investigation agencies such as the "H Traffic" Office in the Brazilian Air Force, the British Air Ministry's AI3 Desk in the Deputy Directorate of Intelligence (the Defence Ministry's DI55 from 1967), the Project BOLIDE of Australia's Joint Intelligence Bureau, and the relevant UFO desks in Canada's Department of National Defence and France's CNES. SIDEKICK guides the NATO Supreme Headquarters Europe's UFO "Assessment" in 1964. It also monitors quasi-governmental and independent UFO investigation groups in America and elsewhere, such as MUFON, NICAP, SaucerWatch, and BUFORA.

In practice, this amounts to spying on other government and civilian UFO investigation groups. SIDEKICK does not utilize MAJESTIC assets for this espionage, instead relying on collecting their information through regular sources within the U.S. intelligence community. Knowledge of the Greys, the Roswell saucer, and even MAJESTIC-12's existence has never been revealed to a foreign power, whether enemy or ally.

Gordon Gray remains MJ-10, the only holdover from the original MAJESTIC twelve still on the Steering Committee. While he served as Eisenhower's National Security Adviser from 1958 to 1961, Gray's deputy ran SIDEKICK; Gray remains on the President's Foreign Intelligence Advisory Board. A veteran Washington knife-fighter, Gray cannot be budged from MAJESTIC-12; an expert in psychological warfare, he cannot easily be fooled or outmaneuvered. He suspects the Grey story is a psychological warfare gambit, but agrees the United States has no option but to continue the MAJESTIC project and hope for more intelligence.

MJ-11: Project LOOKING GLASS

LOOKING GLASS has the remit of determining how much Communist and other unfriendly nations know about the Greys and UFOs, and assessing the possible alien technological resources of such nations. Tactics range from traditional espionage to imagery analysis to supporting front groups encouraging "global cooperation in UFO research." Although MJ-11 has assets in other technical intelligence agencies from the NRO to the Air Force's Foreign Technology Division, the project operates primarily through the DIA.

The head of MJ-11 is Army **Brigadier General Isaac Coleman,** who served as a tanker under Patton and still wishes he'd turned north for Berlin in 1945. He transferred into the Counter-Intelligence Corps (CIC) during the occupation, and was tangentially involved in SUMMER BREEZE and LUNACY though he never received DELTA GREEN clearance. (His file still marks him as a DELTA GREEN friendly.) When the Pentagon folds the CIC into the Army Intelligence Branch in 1961, MJ-1 taps Coleman to take over LOOKING GLASS. He is promoted to Major General in 1967.

MJ-12: Project DELPHI

DELPHI compiles the intelligence reports collected from the other MJ-12 projects, as well as sources in the military, intelligence, journalistic, and academic communities, and produces an up-to-date picture of the current situation and projects estimates for the future. DELPHI's staff works with the enormous and isolated archive at the COUNTRY CLUB. There, DELPHI runs various "alien invasion" scenarios through their mainframe computers, attempting to determine how an armed confrontation with the Greys would turn out. DELPHI also directs Sub-Project ARCHINT, or Archaeological Intelligence, to examine ancient terrestrial civilizations for evidence of contact with alien civilizations. DELPHI doesn't conduct archaeological expeditions itself, but instead collects data from scholars and archaeologists around the world.

Its cover is the Pythia Group, a "blue-sky" think tank developing outré wargame and political modeling scenarios for the Defense and State Departments. It hires academics, especially those whose theories and research are too radical for tenure.

The current MJ-12 is **Dr. Benson MacAllan,** a CIA veteran; he sees no contrast between loyalty to the CIA and to MAJESTIC. His staff and investigators may turn up anywhere the unnatural does; he almost certainly has "inside men" in DELTA GREEN.

MAJESTIC and DELTA GREEN

Until 1953, MAJESTIC and DELTA GREEN were technically part of the same covert bureaucracy. DELTA GREEN agents went along on MOON DUST missions, and vice versa. Scientists and spies with DELTA GREEN clearance helped build MAJESTIC, and the pull of MAJESTIC's saucer helped revive DELTA GREEN. In quiet corners of the Pentagon basement, you can even hear it whispered that Martin Cook served as MJ-2 after Forrestal's breakdown. (Good luck finding that in any records, though.) Their rivalry back then, and even now, resembles a "Yale vs. Annapolis" scrimmage more than a "heroes vs. traitors" dynamic.

MAJESTIC sees DELTA GREEN as knuckle-dragging cowboys whose response to the greatest potential advance for humanity since fire is to set it on fire. DELTA GREEN sees MAJESTIC as pointy-headed intellectuals who won't admit they don't understand the unnatural until they've accidentally blown up a mountain with it, or a city. But only a minority of each group really thinks of the other as anti-American, much less as evil.

MAJESTIC has not yet sold out America and the human race to the Greys. There are certainly corrupt and ambitious men on the MAJESTIC Steering Committee – but the same could be said for the DELTA GREEN ExComm.

MAJESTIC In Your Game

In your campaign, consider MAJESTIC as not just the dark mirror of DELTA GREEN but also the spoiled rich antagonists: the ones with the bigger budget, the nicer offices, the better equipment. NRO DELTA Men in Black should be deadly, competent, and dangerously insistent on taking some fragment of monstrous unreality into the bosom of America's national scientific establishment. Build their ability ratings as slightly (or significantly) better than those of the Agents.

MAJESTIC assets are also opponents the Agents can't just kill their way past. If a MAJESTIC employee (even an unknowing one) dies suddenly, MJ-3 absolutely investigates, and it does the job thoroughly. MJ-3 doesn't just write a mysterious death off to the cost of doing business; it keeps going until the mystery is solved, or at least explained.

MJ-3 brings in any needed federal resources: the FBI crime lab, NSA communications intercepts, military logs and records. If MJ-3 smells the Agents' involvement, it flips their Network contacts, and pressures their day job supervisors. At the very least the Agents should only eliminate MAJESTIC foes deep in the jungle with no witnesses, at night, and use subsonic rounds. And even then they may need bulletproof alibis and an ironclad frame on someone else.

A LITTLE HELP FROM OUR FRIENDS

The United States is not the only Western nation officially investigating the unnatural. DELTA GREEN personnel know of at least two more such programs, in Canada and the United Kingdom.

M-Section

Formally created in 1946 as part of the Special Branch (the Directorate of Security and Intelligence since 1962) of the Royal Canadian Mounted Police, M-Section traces its founding back to investigations of wendigo attacks and Sila cults by Northwest Mounted Police Superintendent John Moodie in 1903. Superintendent David Wainwright, a "by the book" cop, took over M-Section in 1953, which faces not just ancient wind gods but Sasquatch attacks, cannibals, witches, and occult murderers linked to the FLQ terrorist movement in Quebec.

DELTA GREEN operators encountered M-Section investigators in 1956 during a hunt for the Hungarian sorcerer János Hegedus in Edmonton, Alberta. Each team recognized the other as aware of the unnatural, but the secrecy imposed on both agencies means that cooperation remains informal and personal. Project MOON DUST encounters M-Section while attempting to recover the UFO crashed in the ocean near Shag Harbour, Nova Scotia on 4 October 1967; thanks to Pentagon pressure on the Canadian government, M-Section backs off the case and allows MAJESTIC free rein.

PISCES

The Paranormal Intelligence Section for Counter-Intelligence, Espionage and Sabotage (PISCES) is an inter-agency task force under Britain's MI-5 and MI-6 security and intelligence organizations. Created in 1940 as a reorganization of the WWI-era British psychic intelligence group MI-13, PISCES battled the Karotechia during WWII, the Black Ocean in India, the Tcho-Tchos in Malaya, and a hundred other occult foes throughout the fading Empire. The Section keeps a substantial occult library at its headquarters in Kilmaur Manor, Scotland, and maintains a Medieval Metaphysics research facility codenamed Magonia on the island of Hirta beyond the Outer Hebrides.

PISCES agents use hypergeometric rituals developed there in their battles against the unnatural; PISCES by and large has a more pragmatic and less apocalyptic response to the unnatural than DELTA GREEN. "By and large" is not "always," however. Brigadier Charles Balfour takes over as director of PISCES in 1961; in 1968 he launches an Innsmouth-style eradication raid on an alien-infested town on the Severn Estuary in Gloucestershire. Unfortunately, the aliens - psychic, Azathoth-worshiping insects - infested two PISCES agents who discovered their pyramidal spacecraft. This decade, PISCES also begins to fall. Balfour retires in 1969, replaced by Alan Hopkinson of MI-5.

DELTA GREEN and PISCES got off on the wrong foot in February 1943 when the then-director of PISCES, Colonel David Cornwall, tried to have a DELTA GREEN team assassinated in Australia during Operation TARQUIN. (A similar occurrence marred the PISCES/DELTA GREEN Operation KLINGSOR the next month in the Belgian Congo.) PISCES planned to utilize prehuman records of future events - weaponizing the unnatural was something Commander Cook already had no interest in.

Concerns about such priorities, and (post-Hiss and post-Philby) about security on both sides keep official contact and cooperation to a minimum. Although usually at loggerheads on the Executive Committee, both Generals Stillman and Fairfield advocate for closer ties between the two organizations, as does Group Captain James Starkweather of PISCES, a veteran of Antarctic exploration and of Malaya.

No Chance No Untried Operations

DELTA GREEN conducts hundreds of operations during the 1960s on every scale from single-target breaking and entering to the battalion-sized sweeps of Operations RIPTIDE and OBSIDIAN. The player Agents can take part in any of them, at the discretion of their case officers, which is to say the whim of the Handler.

This section provides some example operations from the decade. For the larger missions, it adds suggestions for the role of a smaller player-group-sized team. Some of these operations are part of the "canon" background of the DELTA GREEN universe, but the Handler should not feel constrained by them. If she or the players want to try to prevent Operation OBSIDIAN, that can be an excellent ongoing goal for the campaign – but big missions have their own inertia. Dozens of people in very high places predicted disaster in Indochina, after all, and none of them could prevent it.

Each year also includes a few touchstones and major events to orient the players historically. They focus on political and security developments, and on the United States, because that is what DELTA GREEN also focuses on. For a few characteristic technological developments in the 1960s, see *New This Decade*, p. 138.

This section does not attempt to replace a good history book, or even Wikipedia. If anyone wants to know more about the Kennedy assassination or the Tet Offensive, there are fifty books this size plus a whole Internet full of rich, gameable details.

1960

The President of the United States is Dwight D. Eisenhower.

U.S. troops in Indochina: 900; U.S. military deaths in Indochina: 5

Best-selling album: Original Broadway cast, *The Sound of Music*; Highest-charting single: Elvis Presley, "Are You Lonesome Tonight?"

△ After savage Chinese bombardment makes them untenable, the CIA's Special Operations Division relocates its Chushi Gangdruk guerrilla camps from Tibet proper to Mustang on the Nepalese border. The ST-BARNUM program of arming Tibetan anti-Communist fighters began in 1951 and continues until 1965; Nixon shuts the ST-CIRCUS Tibetan training program down completely in 1971.

△ The CIA begins arming Meo and Hmong tribes in Laos for its Armée Clandestine, with U.S. air and advisory support based in Thailand. The U.S. "Secret War" in Laos continues until 1973.

△ Peak year of Mao's Great Leap Forward famine, which starves 40 million Chinese to death between 1959 and 1962.

△ **22 Jan:** Lt. Don Walsh, USN, and Jacques Piccard descend to the bottom of the Marianas Trench in the bathyscaphe *Trieste*.

△ **1 Feb:** Sit-ins by Black students begin at the Woolworth's lunch counter in Greensboro, North Carolina.

△ **1 May:** Soviets shoot down a U-2 spy plane over Sverdlovsk and capture its pilot, Francis Gary Powers.

△ **11 Aug:** The botch-plagued Corona satellite imagery program finally succeeds with Discoverer 13; the first payload successfully retrieved from orbit.

△ **24 Oct:** Prototype R-16 ICBM explodes on the launch pad at Baikonur Cosmodrome in the USSR, killing 90 people including many top Soviet rocket experts.

175

Operation MALLORY

From 1956 to 1965, DELTA GREEN hunts yeti and follows up on reports of uncanny alien sightings in the Himalayas, burying its activities within the CIA's ST-CIRCUS and ST-BARNUM Tibetan resistance programs.

Your Agents' team might:

△ Mount a raid into Tibet to close down a newly opened gateway into Leng.

△ Attempt to divert a MAJESTIC team sent to measure gravitic and other anomalies emitted from the temple of Dza-nGar Phan in the Ü-Tsang Plateau.

△ Rescue a DELTA GREEN friendly captured by the Chinese and held in a Kuen-Yuin torture garden for interrogation and conversion to a Xin servitor.

△ Encounter Tcho-Tchos in eastern Tibet, and recognize them with horror years later in Vietnam and Cambodia.

△ Survive enough encounters with the metoh-kangmi (p. 247) to deduce their commonality with the Mi-Go.

Operation HOUND DOG

On 21 May a Richter 8 earthquake strikes Concepcion, Chile; two more Richter 7 quakes hit the next day. Fifteen minutes after the third quake, a fourth shock (Richter 9.5) destroys 40% of the city of Valdivia. Fragmentary reports from Chile describe "dog-headed men" and "mermaids" amongst the chaos. DELTA GREEN inserts teams into the 7th Field Hospital from Ft. Belvoir and the 57th Medical Air Ambulance Company from Ft. Meade. Both arrive in Santiago on 27 May and become fully operational at Valdivia on 1 June.

Your Agents' team might:

△ Investigate rumors of human sacrifice in coastal fishing villages, leading them into combat with Deep Ones.

△ Be tasked to capture a ghoul alive.

△ Discover, while on patrol, books from the library of the Jesuit University of Concepcion – books lost in the earthquake that destroyed the city and the university in 1751. One of the books is half of a hypergeometric text.

△ Escort the U.S. Geological Survey team mapping the geology of Valdivia – and discover an immense worm of some kind burrowing into the liquefied earth near the epicenter.

AIR POUCH
PRIORITY

UNCLASSIFIED
(Security Classification)

DO NOT TY

031.00

FOREIGN SERVICE DESPATCH

FROM : American Embassy, Katmandu

DESP. NO.

TO : THE DEPARTMENT OF STATE, WASHINGTON.

November 30, 19
DATE

REF : Embassy, New Delhi, Despatches 1473, June 22, 1959 and 374, Sept

	ACTION	DEPT.
For Dept. Use Only	NEA-4	RM/R-1, IRC-8, L-2, M/O-1, M/OP-1, IES-5, 10
	REC'D	OTHER
	12/7	CIA-10, USIA-10, OSD-4, OCB-1, ARMY-4, NA

SUBJECT: REGULATIONS GOVERNING MOUNTAIN CLIMBING EXPEDITIONS IN NEPAL – RELATING TO YETI

There are, at present, three regulations applicable only to expeditions searching for the YETI in Nepal. These regulations are to be observed in addition to the 15 clauses as listed in Mountaineer and Scientific Expeditions in Nepal.

The three regulations are as follows:

1. Royalty of Rs. 5000/- Indian Currency will have to be paid to His Majesty's Government of Nepal for a permit to carry out an expedition in search of "Yeti".

2. In case "Yeti" is traced it can be photographed or caught alive but it must not be killed or shot at except in an emergency arising out of self defence. All photographs taken of the animal, the creature itself if captured alive or dead, must be surrendered to the Government of Nepal at the earliest time.

3. News and reports throwing light on the actual existence of the creature must be submitted to the Government of Nepal as soon as they are available and must not in any way be given out to the Press or Reporters for publicity without the permission of the Government of Nepal.

FOR THE AMBASSADOR:

Ernest H. Fisk
Counselor of Embassy

JRClingerman:ld
REPORTER

UNCLASSIFIED

INFORMATION COPY

1961

The President of the United States is John F. Kennedy.

U.S. troops in Indochina: 3,205
U.S. military deaths in Indochina: 16

Best-selling album: Original Broadway cast, *Camelot*; Highest-charting single: Chubby Checker, "Let's Twist Again"

△ Attorney General Robert Kennedy personally oversees the inter-agency campaign against organized crime, expands FBI wiretap authority.

△ CIA establishes JM-WAVE, an anti-Castro covert ops and intelligence headquarters station on the South Campus of the University of Miami, Florida.

△ **17 Jan:** In his Farewell Address, President Eisenhower warns of the power of the "military-industrial complex."

△ **12 Apr:** Soviet cosmonaut Yuri Gagarin aboard Vostok 1 becomes the first human in space.

△ **22 Apr:** Failed coup d'etat against Charles de Gaulle in Algeria and France.

△ **14 May:** Ku Klux Klan firebombs a Freedom Riders bus in Anniston, Alabama.

△ **13 Aug:** Soviets begin construction of the Berlin Wall.

△ **18 Sep:** UN Secretary-General Dag Hammarskjöld dies in a plane crash en route to the rebel province of Katanga in the Congo.

Operation LIBRETTO

In mid-January, sometime CIA consultant Dr. Lewis Strater of the OUTLOOK Group (a think-tank based in Bountin, Maryland) predicts total success for an anti-Castro brigade landing near Trinidad in Cuba. The OUTLOOK Group's record of uncannily accurate prediction already has Strater on the program's radar. The OUTLOOK report suggests making the landing at Casilda Bay, a name that triggers Rear Admiral Payton's memories of the disastrous Operation BRISTOL in 1955. He orders a full-court investigation.

Your Agents' team might:

△ Investigate the OUTLOOK offices and uncover evidence of Yithian penetration or other unnatural influence.

△ Attempt to trace any connection between Strater and the 1955 performance in New York of the play *Her Grey Song*. This might put your Agents onto the track of the original *King in Yellow*, for good or ill.

△ Be covertly inserted into an increasingly alert (not to say paranoid) Communist Cuba to scout the Casilda Bay landing site first-hand.

LIBRETTO apparently uncovers something uncanny. On 11 Mar President Kennedy rejects the Casilda landing plan. The CIA moves the invasion site to the less militarily suitable Bay of Pigs; on 19 April the hastily planned operation ends in disaster. The OUTLOOK Group is disgraced and its supporters transferred. Strater dies during an apparent home invasion in 1963, after which the CIA takes over OUTLOOK as a front.

CUBA
SELECTED SOVIET FORCES AND INSTALLATIONS
⊗ Airfield with MIG aircraft
⊡ Armored group
★ Surface-to-Air Missile (SAM) site

SECRET

1962

The President of the United States is John F. Kennedy.

U.S. troops in Indochina: 11,300
U.S. military deaths in Indochina: 53

Best-selling album: Soundtrack, *West Side Story*; Highest-charting single: Ray Charles, "I Can't Stop Loving You"

- △ The political rifts that have been building between Mao and Khrushchev since 1959 culminate in a definitive Sino-Soviet split and the severing of diplomatic relations.
- △ Algeria wins its war for independence from France; hardline OAS terrorists continue attacks into 1963.
- △ **8 Feb:** Military Assistance Command (South Vietnam) created.
- △ **20 Feb:** John Glenn aboard Friendship 7 becomes the first American to orbit the Earth.
- △ **9 Jul:** STARFISH PRIME U.S. nuclear test detonates 1.4-megaton device 400 km above Hawaii.
- △ **30 Sep:** U.S. Marshals escort James Meredith, the first Black student at the University of Mississippi, onto campus.
- △ **26 Oct:** U.S. forces placed at DEFCON 2 during the Cuban Missile Crisis; the next day the U.S. Navy drops depth charges on a nuclear-armed Soviet submarine.
- △ **21 Nov:** China unilaterally declares a cease-fire in the month-long Sino-Indian War after occupying a stretch of Himalayan borderland.

Operation OVERDUE

On 11 December Massachusetts State Patrolman Michael Myrlo is discovered turned inside-out on State Highway 133 nine miles outside Innsmouth. DELTA GREEN investigates.

The Agents discover a break-in at the abandoned Ephraim Waite house in Innsmouth, realize a diary was taken, and fight off whatever things remain behind. They then track the book thief and murderer from Massachusetts to Kern, Wisconsin to discover the isolated house of the flesh-alchemist Tomas Banner.

A collector of the paintings of Robert Harrison Blake, Banner has discovered how to consume human pineal glands and commune with the alien dimension Blake called "Shaggai." Using Waite's androgyne magicks, Blake seeks to turn him-her-self into a perfected being of Shaggai.

1963

The President of the United States is John F. Kennedy.

U.S. troops in Indochina: 16,300
U.S. military deaths in Indochina: 122

Best-selling album: Soundtrack, *West Side Story*; Highest-charting single: Elvis Presley, "(You're the) Devil in Disguise"

△ Attorney General Robert Kennedy authorizes FBI wiretaps on associates of Martin Luther King as part of the Bureau's ongoing COINTELPRO program. From 1956 to 1971 COINTELPRO monitors, infiltrates, disrupts, and sabotages movements of which J. Edgar Hoover disapproves, including the civil rights movement, Black Panthers, Nation of Islam, KKK, and various anti-war, Communist, and "New Left" organizations. It also provides domestic political intelligence to JFK, LBJ, and Nixon.

△ **23 Jan:** Kim Philby defects to the Soviet Union.

△ **4 Jun:** British Secretary of State for War John Profumo resigns in a scandal that brings down the Macmillan government.

△ **28 Aug:** Martin Luther King, Jr. delivers his "I have a dream" speech during the Freedom March on Washington.

△ **15 Sep:** Bombing of a Black church in Birmingham, Alabama kills 4 and injures 22.

△ **2 Nov:** South Vietnamese President Diem assassinated during a U.S.-backed coup d'etat.

△ **22 Nov:** President Kennedy assassinated in Dallas.

Operation RIPTIDE

On 10 April, the USS *7Thresher* nuclear attack submarine sinks with all hands, 100 miles east of Innsmouth, Massachusetts. The next day, DELTA GREEN initiates Operation RIPTIDE, a week-long assault using airdropped anti-submarine warfare weapons and depth charges to utterly destroy the Deep One city of Y'ha-nthlei, which had only been damaged by the submarine attack of 1928.

Your Agents' team might:

△ Supervise Navy vessels close inshore to Devil Reef, keeping a watch out for shoggoths.

△ Scout the shore for observers human and inhuman alike.

△ Direct the Marine Corps company deployed in Innsmouth to prevent any retreat or counter-attack.

△ Encounter and isolate the horrifically mutated survivors of the *Thresher*, transferring them to the Ward or to the ICE CAVE.

△ Investigate any of the many unnatural sightings in the Manuxet and Miskatonic valleys over the next few years once RIPTIDE stirs everything up.

1964

The President of the United States is Lyndon B. Johnson.

U.S. troops in Indochina: 23,300
U.S. military deaths in Indochina: 216

Best-selling album: Original Broadway cast, *Hello, Dolly!*; Highest-charting single: The Beatles, "I Want to Hold Your Hand"

△ **30 Jan:** General Nguyen Khanh leads a bloodless military coup d'etat in South Vietnam.

△ **21 Jun:** The KKK murders three civil rights workers in Philadelphia, Mississippi.

△ **2 Jul:** Congress passes the Civil Rights Act.

△ **7 Aug:** Congress passes the Gulf of Tonkin Resolution, giving the President broad war powers in Vietnam.

△ **15 Oct:** Leonid Brezhnev and Alexei Kosygin depose Nikita Khrushchev and take power in the Soviet Union.

△ **24 Oct:** Britain deploys specialist counter-insurgency units to Aden to combat Soviet-backed rebels.

△ **16 Oct:** China detonates its first atomic bomb at Lop Nor.

Operation PARIAH

In January, DELTA GREEN person of interest Stephen Alzis (p. 288) appears in his old mansion in Tsingtao, China. ONI chatter indicates that a CIA aircraft registered to Civil Air Transport (later Air America) will pick Alzis up somehow and fly him to Taiwan. Joseph Camp orders Alzis assassinated, ideally by destroying the aircraft in flight: simply revealing Alzis' plan to the Chinese has far too much potential for disaster.

Your Agents' team might:

△ Infiltrate Tsingtao on the old ONI ratlines (the city, now a Communist naval base, was the headquarters station of the U.S. Western Pacific Fleet until 1949) and find out how Alzis plans to board a CIA craft and fly out of Red-controlled airspace.

△ Infiltrate the CIA station in Taipei to sabotage the plane (a PBY-5A seaplane), while avoiding the uncanny attention of the Khmer "stewardess" Li.

△ Stage a Douglas A-1 Skyraider out of Osan AFB in Korea to intercept Alzis' plane and shoot it down – without attracting Japanese, Korean, or Chinese attention.

The plane disappears over the Yellow Sea on 22 Jan; Stephen Alzis reappears three months later in Brussels, none the worse for wear.

Operation KURTZ

Throughout 1964 Congolese government forces, backed by the CIA, harry the Marxist Simba rebels in the eastern Congo. Some of the Simba commanders turn to Soviet and Cuban advisers; others turn to an older evil. On 23 September a Simba cadre unleashes the god Mauti to slaughter a unit of CIA-backed mercenaries in the upper Maranga valley, and General Fairfield of DELTA GREEN launches an annihilating reprisal.

The force devoted to Operation KURTZ is almost battalion-strength: two companies of CIA paramilitaries from the SOD and three companies of deniable European mercenaries out for revenge, all on river craft; and a hard core of helicopter-mounted DELTA GREEN operators. Air support comes from T-28 ground-attack fighter-bombers of the Congolese Air Force, flown by CIA-paid Cuban exile pilots. D-Day for KURTZ is 29 October – if Mauti survives until Halloween, very bad things happen.

Your Agents might:

△ Command uncleared units against the Simbas' bulletproof, drug-crazed suicide fighters and cannibalistic white apes.

△ Rescue DELTA GREEN friendlies taken hostage by radicalized Simba fighters.

△ Encounter Cuban Palo Mayombe sorcerers looking for nkisi (wooden fetishes containing powerful spirits) to bind to the Revolution.

△ Scout upriver searching for the main temple compound of Mauti, and try to escape the god's sight.

△ Provide on-the-ground radio guidance and spotting for the air strike on the temple of Mauti. Accuracy is vital!

△ Escape the apocalypse on the river, the closing dimensional rift, and the frenzied attacks of former allies.

1965

The President of the United States is Lyndon B. Johnson.

U.S. troops in Indochina: 184,300

U.S. military deaths in Indochina: 1,928

Best-selling album: Soundtrack, *Mary Poppins*; Highest-charting single: The Rolling Stones, "(I Can't Get No) Satisfaction"

△ A CIA secret army in Peru, trained and led by Green Berets, eliminates the Marxist MIR rebels.

△ An abortive military coup in Indonesia triggers the rise to power of CIA-backed General Suharto, and the targeted killings of 1 million Indonesian Communists, Chinese, and others.

△ **21 Feb:** Malcolm X assassinated in Washington Heights, New York City.

△ **7 Mar:** Bloody Sunday in Selma, Alabama; state troopers attack civil rights marchers, hospitalize 17.

△ **8 Mar:** First officially acknowledged U.S. combat forces land in Vietnam at Da Nang.

△ **30 Apr:** U.S. forces land in Santo Domingo (withdraw 26 May), ending a civil war in the Dominican Republic.

△ **19 Jun:** South Vietnamese Air Force head Nguyen Cao Ky takes power in a coup d'etat.

△ **6 Aug:** Congress passes the Voting Rights Act.

△ **11 Aug:** Beginning of the six-day race riot in Watts, Los Angeles that leaves 34 dead and 1,032 injured.

△ **23 Sep:** UN ceasefire agreement ends the Indo-Pakistani War after two months of inconclusive fighting.

△ **9 Nov:** Massive electrical power blackout in the Northeast.

Operation GOBLIN MARKET

As the American intelligence and assistance program in Indochina ramped up, and reports of all kinds flooded into Washington, DELTA GREEN analysts began noticing the familiar spoor of the unnatural in the jungles and along the coasts.

Program analysts had long suspected the coastal Cham people of having ancient Deep One ties: they practiced ocean burial, carved batrachian "temple guardians," and inspired fervent hatred in all their neighbors. And indeed, in 1958 DELTA GREEN identified a Deep One hybrid colony on the island of Hòn Mò (Tomb Island) near Da Nang. However, wantonly destroying a Vietnamese fishing town, even a Cham one, was not politically possible.

Once U.S. forces deploy into Da Nang, the situation changes. Your Agents' team might:

△ Be tasked with planting false evidence indicating that Hòn Mò is a Viet Cong listening station (early March).

△ Be tasked with scouting and photographing the Cham Islands by air and water to locate the Deep One city under the ocean, working with local fishermen who hate the islanders (March-early April).

△ Accompany the Marines sent ashore to wipe out the "Communist spy station" on the island, and retrieve any artifacts, scriptures, or other ARCHINT (20 Apr).

△ Accompany or direct the depth-charge and submarine torpedo assault on the Deep One city using operational research data from RIPTIDE (20-24 Apr).

△ Analyze the ARCHINT, interrogating prisoners and interviewing locals from competing traditions; uncovering leads to the Tcho-Tcho, the Dao Sâm cult in Vietnam and Cambodia, and to Angka in "Funan" (Cambodia).

1966

The President of the United States is Lyndon B. Johnson.

U.S. troops in Indochina: 385,300
U.S. military deaths in Indochina: 6,350

Best-selling album: Herb Alpert & the Tijuana Brass, *Whipped Cream & Other Delights*; Highest-charting single: Frank Sinatra, "Strangers in the Night"

- △ Mao launches the Cultural Revolution in China. Over the next five years of deliberate radicalization of Party cadres and destruction of Chinese traditional society, Red Guards purge or imprison 36 million people and kill 3 million.
- △ France removes its forces from NATO military command; USAF bases in France closed; U.S. forces in France redeployed to Italy and West Germany.
- △ **11 Jan:** The SR-71 Blackbird reconnaissance plane enters service.
- △ **24 Feb:** CIA-backed coup overthrows President Nkrumah of Ghana.
- △ **1 Mar:** Soviet Venera 3 probe crashes on Venus, the first spacecraft to reach another planet.
- △ **13 Jun:** In *Miranda v. Arizona*, the Supreme Court rules that police must read individuals in custody their rights before interrogating them.
- △ **15 Oct:** Bobby Seale and Huey Newton found the Black Panther Party in Oakland.

Operation PORLOCK

On 12 November, three people die and two disappear during a "Cosmic Experience Acid Test" held in the closed fairground outside Escabacogan, Illinois. The sheriff arrests as many of the "drug freaks" and "Chicago element" as he can, but DELTA GREEN needs to find out what happened.

Was it a release of ultraviolet entities during the cosmic light show? Was it creatures from Innerspace? Was it a connection to some other plane? Is there something about the town, built on a Potawatomi battlefield, that the music and lights awakened? And where has the "Head Trickster," acid-show impresario M.G. Drake, disappeared to?

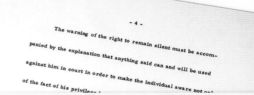

- 4 -

The warning of the right to remain silent must be accompanied by the explanation that anything said can and will be used against him in court in order to make the individual aware not only of the fact of his privileg...

1967

The President of the United States is Lyndon B. Johnson.

U.S. troops in Indochina: 485,600
U.S. military deaths in Indochina: 11,363

Best-selling album: The Monkees, *More of the Monkees*; Highest-charting single: Procul Harum, "A Whiter Shade of Pale"

△ The "Long Hot Summer" of 159 race riots in U.S. cities includes Cincinnati (1 dead, 63 injured), Milwaukee (4 dead, 100 injured), Newark (26 dead, 727 injured), and Detroit (43 dead, 1,189 injured).

△ CIA begins Operation POPEYE weather control missions over the Ho Chi Minh Trail. POPEYE cloud-seeding missions continue until 1972.

△ **14 Jan:** "Human Be-In" rally in San Francisco introduces hippie and psychedelic culture to the mass media.

△ **27 Jan:** Fire on board Apollo 1 during a launch pad test kills three astronauts.

△ **11 Mar:** First uprising by the Khmer Rouge in Cambodia, beginning the Cambodian Civil War.

△ **10 Jun:** Israel wins a decisive victory over Egypt, Syria, Jordan, and other Arab states in the Six-Day War.

△ **3 Sep:** General Nguyen Van Thieu elected President of South Vietnam.

△ **9 Oct:** A Bolivian Army unit trained by U.S. Army Rangers and accompanied by CIA agents captures and executes Che Guevara.

Operation SUDDEN SAM

On 4 May, local astrologer, UFO contactee, radical activist, and Africana retailer Abdullah Evers predicts that Cleveland will burn to the ground during the partial solar eclipse predicted for 9 May. The prediction makes national news (cast as the threat of a Black riot), and DELTA GREEN notices that Evers' mentor in astrology, Emmett Cobb, resides in the Lima State Hospital for the Criminally Insane.

Evers lives in the Glenville neighborhood. He is protected by his gun-toting guards of the African Nation of New Carthage and by Mayor Ralph Locher, who doesn't want to spark a riot, especially during an election year.

If Evers serves or channels the entity Qu-tugkwa (p. 273) he knows it as "Great Malik" (cognate with Moloch); he might also have discovered or re-contacted Charybdis (***Trail of Cthulhu,*** p. 226). Or something else the Handler wants to introduce into her campaign might be going on.

The Agents have to find out whether Evers is trying to warn the authorities, accidentally or purposely channeling unnatural entities, attempting to manipulate those beings, or just suffering from his diagnosed personality disorder. And ideally, find out before the eclipse.

1968

The President of the United States is Lyndon B. Johnson.

U.S. troops in Indochina: 536,100
U.S. military deaths in Indochina: 16,899

Best-selling album: Jimi Hendrix Experience, *Are You Experienced?*; Highest-charting single: The Beatles, "Hey Jude"

△ MACV-SOG begins coordinating the PHOENIX program in Vietnam to identify, capture, interrogate, and execute Viet Cong cadres. Provincial Reconnaissance Units composed of CIA and Special Forces operators, along with South Vietnamese security, hunt and sometimes assassinate VC figures in cities and villages across South Vietnam. Along with an intensive interrogation and HUMINT program, PHOENIX PRUs neutralize 81,000 VC operatives and informants, killing over 26,000 of them before the program ends in 1972.

△ The CIA's Office of Research and Development begins Project OFTEN. An extensive study of narcotic, paralytic, and hallucinogenic drug effects on human physiology and behavior (building on the Defense Department's 1967 Project CHICKWIT), it reportedly branches into the occult: black magic, voodoo, and psionics. OFTEN ends in 1973.

△ **21 Jan:** Siege of Khe Sanh begins.

△ **23 Jan:** North Korea captures the spy ship USS *Pueblo*.

△ **24 Feb:** South Vietnam recaptures Hue, ending the Tet Offensive; on 27 Feb Walter Cronkite reports the war is stalemated.

△ **4 Apr:** Assassination of Martin Luther King, Jr. in Memphis triggers riots in over 100 cities over the next week, leaving 43 dead and over 2,500 injured.

△ **13 May:** Situationist-inspired student occupation of the Sorbonne touches off two weeks of street demonstrations, strikes, and riots in Paris.

△ **5 Jun:** Robert F. Kennedy assassinated in Los Angeles the day he wins the California Democratic primary.

△ **17 Jul:** Baath Party coup in Iraq.

△ **20 Aug:** 250,000 Soviet and Warsaw Pact troops invade Czechoslovakia, ending the Prague Spring.

△ **28 Aug:** Police attack protestors in Chicago during the Democratic National Convention; hospitals treat 160 injured over the week of protests.

△ **6 Sep:** Robin Morgan leads a feminist protest of the Miss America pageant in Atlantic City; "women's liberation" gains mass media currency.

△ **24 Oct:** Possession of LSD becomes illegal in the United States.

Operation NORTHERN LIGHTHOUSE

Program assets in AFOSI report the quashing of an investigation into possible subversion within the 6594th Aerospace Test Wing, now part of the Air Force Satellite Control Facility. What little evidence AFOSI retains points to the BMEWS radar station at Thule Air Base in Greenland as the target of the conspirators. With Greenland playing a major role in two major unnatural mythologies, DELTA GREEN assigns a team to investigate.

A cult of Air Force and NRO radar operators has discovered (or contacted) Yog-Sothoth, and MJ-3 has spiked the official investigation to pursue it on their own. One possible coloration of MJ-3's activities: they intend to allow the cult to contact Yog-Sothoth and record its signal traffic, providing incredible raw hypergeometric data for MAJESTIC use.

The cult has a copy of the Dho-Nha Formula, used to reveal the "hidden city at the magnetic poles." If transmitted over the enormous radars at Thule, who knows what could happen?

For what does happen on 21 January, see p. 211 or look up the "Thule Air Base B-52 Crash" on Wikipedia.

Operation POMPEY

It looks like the Deep Ones don't know they're losing the war. Four submarines vanish in 1968:

△ 24 Jan: Israeli attack submarine INS *Dakar* disappears east of Crete.

△ 27 Jan: French missile-carrying submarine *Minerve* vanishes just south of Toulon.

△ 8 Mar: Soviet ballistic missile submarine *K-129* vanishes 600 miles north of Midway Island.

△ 22 May: U.S. nuclear attack submarine USS *Scorpion* disappears between Spain and the Azores.

Your Agents' team might:

△ Investigate any of the disappearances and uncover Deep One or Cthulhu-cult activity in Scotland (where the *Dakar* fit out), Crete, Cyprus, France, Spain, or the Azores.

△ Investigate the disappearance of the German submarine *U-29* near the Azores on or about 20 August 1917 – WWI British Admiralty records indicate possible unnatural "Atlantean" influence.

△ Infiltrate the covert U.S. Navy tracking of *K-129*, and discover what else the SOSUS sonar network has been picking up.

DELTA GREEN plans a massive anti-Deep One operation in the Mediterranean to coincide with the NATO fleet exercises in 1970, but POMPEY is cancelled when the Joint Chiefs disband the program.

1969

The President of the United States is Richard M. Nixon.

U.S. troops in Indochina: 475,200
U.S. military deaths in Indochina: 11,780

Best-selling album: Iron Butterfly, *In-A-Gadda-Da-Vida*; Highest-charting single: The Archies, "Sugar Sugar"

△ The CIA coordinates its multiple domestic intelligence operations under one program as Operation CHAOS. The Domestic Operations Division monitors and infiltrates anti-war, dissident, radical, and other groups potentially in contact with foreign intelligence services, including the B'nai B'rith. The CHAOS operations begin in 1964 and run until 1973.

△ Between January 1969 and April 1970, there are 4,330 domestic bombings in the U.S.; 370 of them in New York City.

△ **2 Mar:** Chinese troops ambush Soviet forces on the Ussuri River, beginning seven months of border conflicts.

△ **22 Jun:** Weatherman faction takes over the Students for a Democratic Society, championing urban resistance and terrorism.

△ **28 Jun:** Riot at the Stonewall nightclub in New York City catalyzes gay rights activism.

△ **20 Jul:** Apollo 11 lander touches down on the Moon.

△ **14 Aug:** Britain deploys troops to Belfast and Derry in response to riots; beginning of the "Troubles" in Northern Ireland.

△ **15 Aug:** Beginning of the Woodstock Festival.

△ **Autumn:** "Hot Autumn" strikes and student protests roil northern Italy.

△ **4 Dec:** Chicago police fire 80 bullets into Black Panther leader Fred Hampton and his bodyguard, killing them.

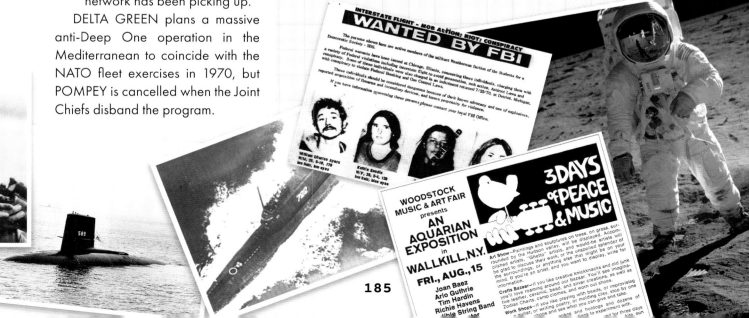

Operation LOOKING GLASS

Satellites detect strange patterns in the weather conditions over the Vaupes River valley in southeastern Colombia. On 18 January, DELTA GREEN airdrops 45 Army Rangers and 23 CIA officers into the valley. The team is entirely wiped out except for its commander, Major Walter J. Greyman. He reports parachuting into a mile-wide black sphere in the valley, wherein he and six survivors found a sailing yacht named *Templo Mayor* partially encased in pack ice, and the remains of the rest of the LOOKING GLASS troops. Greyman alone escapes the cult of genital-sacrificing Shub-Niggurath worshippers in the area.

Your Agents' team might:

△ Have been the other team that, unknown to Greyman, entered from the river. Do they survive?

△ Investigate the whole operation as an after-action tiger team, dedicated to finding out what went wrong and how to repair the damage.

△ Infiltrate the U.S.-Colombian archaeological team that discovers an impossible Olmec temple ("Casa de Xibalba") on the site on 9 March.

△ Be sent back into the Vaupes valley to destroy the cult on the ground, because launching a B-52 airstrike on an allied nation is not possible.

Operation OBSIDIAN

On 23 November Colonel Satchel Wade (p. 165) launches the hastily planned Operation OBSIDIAN. Three Marine companies (and an unknown number of convicts recruited from Long Binh Jail) parachute into the Cambodian jungle with orders to destroy a Dao Sâm temple at Ban Talat devoted to summoning the Khmer Rouge god-principle Angka to Earth. From the beginning, the mission is a disaster. Whistling, invisible Things destroy half the aircraft carrying the strike force; a double agent on the raid uses the deaths of 100 or more Marines and DELTA GREEN operatives to summon the "Black Buddha."

Wade reports the men he sent to their deaths as deserters and covers up the operation. A diverted bomber flight during the USAF Operation MENU secret bombing of Cambodia obliterates the Ban Talat temple and the entity on 6 January 1970. Official DELTA GREEN mythology later holds that this was Wade's plan all along: set the mission up as bait to lure Angka out to be destroyed. Two survivors of OBSIDIAN assassinate Wade and his mistress on 7 January 1970.

Your Agents' team might:

△ Be part of the OBSIDIAN debacle, and fight their way back to Vietnam in the aftermath.

△ Investigate Wade's increasingly erratic behavior and stumble on the vast approaching disaster that is OBSIDIAN. The Executive Committee doesn't seem to be acting on their warnings: what can the Agents do to avert catastrophe?

△ Desperately try to divert the MENU bombings – possibly the most closely held secret of the War at the time – to cauterize the Ban Talat rift.

△ Testify against Wade in the inevitable hearings.

△ Melt into the Golden Triangle of opium warlords, like Wade's killer Adolph Lepus does.

1970

The President of the United States is Richard M. Nixon.

U.S. troops in Indochina: 334,600
U.S. military deaths in Indochina: 6,173

Best-selling album: Simon and Garfunkel, *Bridge Over Troubled Water*; Highest-charting single: The Beatles, "Let it Be"

△ On 24 July 1970, the Joint Chiefs of Staff officially deactivates the DELTA GREEN classification and program. Pentagon clerks remove the green triangles from hundreds of personnel files.

△ Various Maoist and Muslim revolutionary movements begin armed struggle in the Philippines, especially in Mindanao and the south.

△ **15 Jan:** The Biafra War ends in Nigeria after two and a half years with 100,000 war dead and 1 million starved to death by famine.

△ **13 Apr:** Apollo 13 mission aborted.

△ **29 Apr:** U.S. and South Vietnamese forces invade Cambodia.

△ **4 May:** Ohio National Guard kills four students at Kent State University during an anti-war protest.

△ **24 Jun:** The U.S. Senate repeals the Gulf of Tonkin Resolution.

△ **21 Nov:** In Operation IVORY COAST, Special Forces raid the Son Tay prison outside Hanoi but find no POWs.

Operation BINGO

In December, the disbanded program launches its first unofficial operation. Generals Fairfield and Stillman pull strings to retask B-52s from the ongoing Operations ARC LIGHT (in Vietnam), GOOD LOOK (in Laos), and FREEDOM DEAL (in Cambodia). Over the last two weeks of the month, U.S. air strikes obliterate every known Tcho-Tcho village and religious site, hitting some locations dozens of times. Individual program veterans in ONI and USAF follow up on targets of opportunity, redirecting Operation BARREL ROLL napalm strikes by F-4s from the USS *Kitty Hawk* and A-1s out of Thailand.

Your Agents' team:

△ Goes back into Indochina for one last mission.

△ Pulls strings and calls in favors to get one more bombing run redirected illegally.

△ Roots out Tcho-Tcho infiltrators in Saigon and other rear areas, then turns them over to Project PHOENIX teams (p. 184) for assassination – or does it themselves.

△ Discovers that you never leave DELTA GREEN, even when the program stops existing.

Strange Days Have Found Us

It's not all war and politics on the desks of the Executive Committee. Throughout the decade, program analysts monitor *Fate* magazine and the *National Enquirer* just as assiduously as they do the *Washington Post* and *The Economist*.

This section gives a few of the highlight moments from the weirder side of the 1960s. As with the other events in the previous section, the Internet provides far more information (of varying reliability) on any of these incidents than this book possibly can. For still more, Google "UFO" or "cryptid" or a similar keyword and any year. Handlers interested in turning these events (or something like them) into DELTA GREEN operational hooks should privilege strangeness over fidelity to the letter of a report. Remember, the report is what made it past the DELTA GREEN disinformation cover-up.

1960

△ 557 UFO sightings reported to Project BLUE BOOK; 14 remain "unexplained."

△ Maharishi Mahesh Yogi begins his meditation campaign in London.

△ **Mar:** Diminutive alien captured near New Paltz, N.Y., turned over "to the CIA."

△ **Summer:** Anthropologist Carlos Castaneda meets the brujo "Don Juan."

△ **Aug:** 20' long blob covered in hair washes ashore, Tasmania.

△ **15 Sep:** Former BLUE BOOK head Edward Ruppelt dies of a heart attack at age 37.

△ **6 Oct:** Thule Air Base tracks UFO by radar.

1961

△ 591 UFO sightings reported to Project BLUE BOOK; 13 remain "unexplained."

△ Antiquarian book dealer Hans Peter Kraus purchases the Voynich Manuscript.

△ **10 Jan:** UFO tracks a Polaris missile launch from Cape Canaveral.

△ **Spring:** Chinese government investigates sightings of yeren ("wild man") in Yunnan border zone.

△ **Spring:** National Science Foundation drills the first shafts of the Mohole Project off the coast of Yucatan.

△ **18 Apr:** Eagle River, Wisconsin close encounter.

△ **9 Jun:** USAF/NASA flight test of the Avro Canada VZ-9 flying disk.

△ **19 Sep:** Barney and Betty Hill abducted by Greys, Lancaster, N.H.

△ **Nov:** UFO sighting in Minot, N.D. followed by Men in Black visit.

△ **Nov 1:** "Order of the Dolphin" formed at the Green Bank Conference on SETI.

1962

△ 474 UFO sightings reported to Project BLUE BOOK; 15 remain "unexplained."

△ **5 Feb:** Grand Conjunction of Mercury, Venus, Jupiter, Saturn, and Mars; total eclipse over New Guinea and the Pacific.

△ **18 Apr:** UFO seen over Oneida, N.Y., lands in Nephi, Utah, crashes north of Las Vegas.

△ **31 May:** Underwater "wheel of light" seen by *SS Telemachus*, Gulf of Siam.

△ **Sep:** Sea monster seen off Bribie Island, Queensland.

1963

△ 399 UFO sightings reported to Project BLUE BOOK; 14 remain "unexplained."

△ John C. Lilly builds his "Dolphinarium" in St. Thomas, V.I. with NASA funding; studies dolphin communication with sensory deprivation tanks and LSD.

△ **Summer:** "Devas" aid spiritual explorers in Findhorn, Scotland, to grow miraculous vegetables.

△ **3 Jun:** Humped water monster seen in Lough Bray, Ireland.

△ **12 Jul:** Third mysterious metal sphere found north of Broken Hill, Australia.

△ **13 Nov:** Explosion at AEC facility, Medina AFB, San Antonio.

1964

△ 562 UFO sightings reported to Project BLUE BOOK; 19 remain "unexplained."

△ **24 Apr:** Close encounters in Tioga, N.Y. and Socorro, New Mexico.

△ **29 Aug:** USNS *Eltanin* photographs an underwater antenna in the Antarctic Ocean west of Cape Horn.

△ **15 Sep:** UFO tracks and crashes an Atlas F missile launched from Vandenberg AFB.

△ **10 Dec:** UFO crash near Ft. Riley, Kansas.

1965

△ 887 UFO sightings reported to Project BLUE BOOK; 16 remain "unexplained."

△ Paul Twitchell founds Eckankar in Las Vegas.

△ Latvian psychologist Konstantine Raudive investigates supernatural voices caught on tape recordings.

△ **5 Jan:** Electrical fire destroys USAF space tracking radar at Eglin AFB, Florida.

△ **8 May:** Ionospheric physicist Carl Robert Disch vanishes outside Byrd Station, Antarctica.

△ **3 Jul:** Chilean and Argentine scientists in Antarctica sight a UFO.

- △ **3 Sep:** "Exeter Incident" UFO wave, Exeter, N.H.
- △ **27 Nov:** Ken Kesey conducts his first LSD "Acid Test" happening in Soquel, California.
- △ **9 Dec:** Project MOON DUST handles UFO crash in Kecksburg, Ohio.

1966

- △ 1,112 UFO cases reported to Project BLUE BOOK; 32 remain "unexplained."
- △ USAF funds a committee headed by physicist Edward Condon at the University of Colorado to study UFOs; the Condon Report is released in 1969.
- △ Process Church of the Final Judgement founded in London.
- △ New Orleans District Attorney Jim Garrison begins investigating the JFK assassination.
- △ **4 Feb:** Russian Luna 9 probe photographs "runway markers" in the Oceanus Procellarum on the Moon.
- △ **6 Feb:** Close encounter in Madrid, beginning of the UMMO wave.
- △ **March:** UFO wave over Michigan.
- △ **23 Mar:** Cigar-shaped UFO seen on the ground, Temple, Okla.
- △ **26 Apr:** UFO sighting over Tashkent precedes devastating earthquake.
- △ **30 Apr:** Anton Szandor LaVey founds the Church of Satan.
- △ **Jul:** UFO blacks out power at Nha Trang Air Base.
- △ **31 Jul:** Silicon monster and UFO seen in Erie, Pa.
- △ **1 Aug:** Charles Whitman shoots 16 people from a tower at the University of Texas, Austin.
- △ **11 Oct:** UFO sighting at Wanaque Reservoir, N.J. followed by encounters with Men in Black, mysterious helicopters, "grinning man."
- △ **Nov:** Mothman sightings in Point Pleasant, West Virginia.

- △ **Nov:** Cattle mutilations begin in southeastern Ohio near Wright-Patterson AFB.
- △ **20 Nov:** NASA Orbiter 2 probe photographs eight 50' pyramids in the Sea of Tranquility on the Moon.

1967

- △ 937 UFO cases reported to Project BLUE BOOK; 19 remain "unexplained."
- △ **23 Mar:** UFO disintegrates a MiG-21 over Cuba.
- △ **17 May–28 Oct:** Wave of sickle-shaped UFOs sighted between Crimea and Volgograd.
- △ **17 Aug:** Project MOON DUST deployed to Sudan.
- △ **9 Sep:** Horse mutilation discovered near Alamosa, Colorado.
- △ **20 Oct:** Roger Patterson films a Sasquatch on Bluff Creek in California.
- △ **21 Oct:** Yippies attempt to levitate the Pentagon.
- △ **17 Dec:** Australian Prime Minister Harold Holt disappears while swimming off Point Nepean, Victoria.

1968

- △ 375 UFO sightings reported to Project BLUE BOOK; 3 remain "unexplained."
- △ **12 Feb:** UFO crash at Orocue, Colombia.
- △ **25 Mar:** Project MOON DUST recovers four objects from Kathmandu.
- △ **15 Jun:** UFO sighting over the Ben Hai River in Vietnam leads to friendly fire attacks on HMAS Hobart.
- △ **2 Jul:** Mysterious skyquake and explosion at al-Kazimiyah north of Baghdad.
- △ **Aug:** Arthur Folden films Ogopogo lake monster at Lake Okanagan, British Columbia.
- △ **7 Aug:** Buff Ledge Camp UFO abduction in Vermont.
- △ **2 Sep:** Bimini Road discovered underwater in the Bahamas.

- △ **24 Oct:** B-52 spots a UFO on radar; also seen by ground observers at Minot AFB.
- △ **20 Dec:** First confirmed murders by the Zodiac Killer.

1969

- △ 146 UFO sightings reported to Project BLUE BOOK; 1 remains "unexplained."
- △ Hans Peter Kraus donates the Voynich Manuscript to Yale.
- △ **6 Jan:** Former Georgia State Senator Jimmy Carter sees a UFO in Leary, Ga.
- △ **11 May:** UFO leaves crop circles behind in Pembroke, Ontario.
- △ **13 Jul:** UFO leaves crop circle behind in Van Horn, Iowa.
- △ **Summer:** Submersible Pisces makes sonar contact with large, fast-moving object beneath Loch Ness.
- △ **Aug:** Glowing, bat-winged "bird woman" appears to U.S. Marine Earl Morrison near Da Nang.
- △ **9-10 Aug:** Charles Manson's "Family" cult kills seven people in the Tate-LaBianca murder spree.
- △ **24 Oct:** Chilean Navy destroyer tracks UFO on radar 350 miles south of Valparaiso.

1970

- △ **Jan:** Rash of skinwalker sightings in New Mexico.
- △ **30 Jan:** USAF terminates Project BLUE BOOK.
- △ **Apr:** Underwater UFO seen by USCGC Mellon, Gulf of Siam.
- △ **4 Apr:** On orders from KGB Director Yuri Andropov, the KGB burns the bodies of Adolf Hitler and his entourage in Schoenebeck near Magdeburg, scattering the ashes into the Ehle River.
- △ **24 May:** Soviets begin drilling the Kola Superdeep Borehole.
- △ **Jun:** Mountaineer Don Whillans sees a yeti on Annapurna.
- △ **7 Oct:** Project MOON DUST recovers wreckage in Chad.

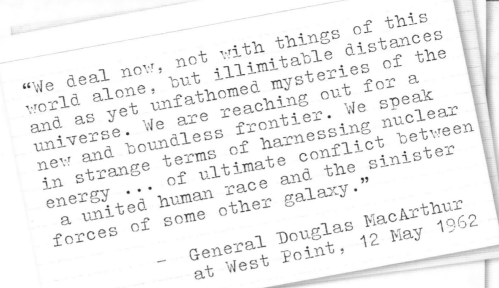

"We deal now, not with things of this world alone, but illimitable distances and as yet unfathomed mysteries of the universe. We are reaching out for a new and boundless frontier. We speak in strange terms of harnessing nuclear energy ... of ultimate conflict between a united human race and the sinister forces of some other galaxy."

— General Douglas MacArthur
at West Point, 12 May 1962

THE UNNATURAL

The unnatural incorporates, and transcends, the "supernatural" and the "paranormal." Both religion and science are crippled tools, incapable of perceiving the cosmic truths of real existence: comfortable superstitions about morality and human value have no meaning in or to the universe, and ancient demons can violate the so-called "laws of nature" for any reason or none at all. A monstrous calculus — or a non-Euclidean pantheon — directs and delimits everything from quantum effects to quasars to the questions you can ask about either.

Any attempt to systematize the unnatural fails at the first hurdle: the cosmos is not a system. Quantum theory comprehends only a tiny fragment of the irrationality, perversity, and inexpressibility of the physical universe — and there is far more to the universe than the mere physical. Full-fledged flight into medieval occultism is no better: Alhazred is just as human, and therefore just as blind, as Einstein.

4 of 10

Names in the Pages

Knowledge of the unnatural comes not just from experience but from books — and from field reports, psychiatric records, obsessively scrawled manifestos, carefully typed site analyses, and any other way the infection of language spreads.

A WORD ABOUT TRUTH

Since human brains are inadequately evolved to even comprehend the universe, much less respond intelligently to it, nothing we ordinarily say or do to it makes any difference. Speaking the names of Great Old Ones does not bring down damnation from Heaven or invoke non-Euclidean curses from Outside. Cthulhu, Hastur, Yog-Sothoth, and the rest appear in a few dusty demonologies, and a few more even dustier anthropological or archeological papers, alongside names like Baalberith, Glasya-Labolas, or Volturnus. The now-obscure novelist Randolph Carter mentions some of the Great Old Ones' names in his works (1919-1928), intermingled with theosophical entities such as Morya, Choronzon, Oaeohoo, Savitar, and so on. In short, a character with 3 points in Anthropology, Archeology, or Occult might well recognize a name like Nyarlathotep ("a syncretized demon-figure mentioned in a few Ptolemaic papyri, and in later Arabic grimoires as a type of anti-Christ") while a DELTA GREEN agent who busted a Crawling Chaos cult might never have heard the name.

In a *Fall of DELTA GREEN* game especially, the feeble scratchings of even the believers uncover only a tiny fragment of an entity's reality. Nodens might manifest within a dispersed conspiracy of dog-owning serial killers - he anciently guided hunters, after all. Meanwhile, devout believers in Cthulhu calve stones from high desert mountains to reveal Its impossible materia - It "seeped down from the stars," you know.

Reading the Unnatural

If a work is in a foreign language, the reader needs a rating in that language to make sense of it at all.

Agents can either skim a work or pore over it. Skimming is for finding the clue or ritual needed right now for the operation; poring over a work takes time (sometimes months) but provides hateful knowledge and horrid comprehension.

Skimming

Skimming takes 30 minutes per 100 printed pages, or 5 minutes per handwritten page. Particularly tangled or convoluted texts may take longer. A 1-point spend halves (at minimum, at the Handler's discretion) this time; a 2-point spend immediately discovers the vital fact, spell, etc. in the text with a few minutes' search.

What to spend depends on the work:

△ The appropriate Language (Foreign) for a work in a foreign language
△ Bureaucracy or the appropriate Agency for a government report
△ Cryptography for a coded text
△ Psychotherapy for a psychiatric report, transcribed session, madman's ranting manifesto, etc.
△ Art or Archaeology for a bas-relief, wall painting, inscription, etc.
△ Anthropology for a cult scripture, or for a primitive or non-traditional text
△ Occult for a grimoire or other "magic book"

△ Fringe Science (or Physics or other relevant scientific ability) for a scientific paper, experiment record, etc.

Skimming a work provides no Unnatural or other Hypergeometry potential points, and does not necessarily count as using the Unnatural ability.

It may grant dedicated pool points (p. 077). Unless explicitly stated otherwise, a benefit gained by skimming a tome can only be gained once per adventure, but can be repeatedly gained in multiple adventures.

Unless otherwise described, skimming texts only provides dedicated Investigative pool points. If no ability is specified, the dedicated pool points may be split between abilities or used on one.

Poring Over

Poring over an Unnatural work takes place between operations, and can take as long or as little time as the Handler desires. (Shorter works likely take 1-6 weeks of study; longer or more abstruse ones 2-12 months.) Poring over an unnatural tome grants you a basic understanding of its contents, possibly including rituals or other secrets.

The Handler is always allowed to retroactively insert spells or secrets into a work if she needs it to function as a clue later: "Suddenly, that cryptic quatrain in the *Livre d'Ivon* makes a horrible kind of sense to you."

If the work grants Hypergeometry potential points (p. 197), or Unnatural or other ability points, you gain them all at your first pore-over; repeated porings-over do not add further points.

Ninety Percent of 'Em Gotta Be Burned

Handlers should custom-design any tomes or other compendia of unnatural lore that might fall into the Agents' hands. Rituals should never just be stuffed into a book to make weight or because a story or supplement implied they had to be there. Books vary by edition, condition, and marginal notes: many of them are hand-written originals full of cryptic codes, indecipherable scrawls, and unpleasant stains.

In short, this shelf of unnatural tomes is only meant as a guideline. DELTA GREEN does not have access to all the tomes on this list; perhaps nobody does. Likewise, change the values given here just as readily as you change the rituals included in a given text.

Poring over a tome can increase the reader's rating in the Unnatural ability or provide Hypergeometry potential points or both.

The Necronomicon

Core text of the unnatural, the "Black Book" may be anti-scripture, drug-fueled metaphysics text, diary of nightmare, poetic revelation, or all of the above.

Al Azif

Abdul Alhazred (c. 730 A.D.; Arabic).

The original, and most complete, copy of the *Necronomicon*. No copies are known to exist.

Unnatural: 4
Hypergeometry Potential: 5

Necronomicon

Translated by Olaus Wormius (1623; Latin).

The most common surviving text of the black book, based on a very rare Latin version of 1228 and the lost Greek translation of 950 A.D.; there are possibly a dozen copies extant, though only six are definitely known and catalogued.

Unnatural: 3
Hypergeometry Potential: 4
Dedicated Pool Points: 1-4 for any specific investigation, based on the Handler's judgement.

Dauthsnamjansboka

Unknown trans. (ca. 800 A.D.; Gothic).

The prize of the Karotechia library, much bleaker and less allusive than other versions. DELTA GREEN destroyed most of the copies and German translations during Operation LUNACY; the only known remaining copy (the original) lies untranslated in the GRU SV-8 archive under Khodinka Airfield in Moscow.

Unnatural: 4
Hypergeometry Potential: 7

Other Tomes

Awake Awake Awake

The Whippoorwills (1963; English).

A weirdly discordant and psychedelic folk-rock album recorded by four Children of Chorazin (p. 304) and an unknown flautist (credited only as "Jägare") in Anningley Hall, Essex. According to urban legend, playing it in a haunted house awakens ghosts; it sold poorly and original pressings are rarities. Later recordings grant no bonuses, but may still awaken ghosts.

Unnatural: 1 if the listener already has a rating in that ability, and is high.
Hypergeometry Potential: 1

Azathoth and Others

Edward Pickman Derby (1919; English).

A collection of the Arkham poet's early works, it weaves local legendry and startling insights into lyrics of surprising power. It takes only an hour or so to pore over.

Unnatural: 1 if the reader already has a rating in that ability.
Dedicated Pool Points: 1 to Sense Trouble during any operation taking place in Arkham or the Miskatonic valley.

Book of Dagon

Black Chamber translation (1929; English).

Transcription and translation of conical stone tablets recovered from Innsmouth, carried out by the WWI-era SIGINT office, the Black Chamber. 44 pages, marked P4 EYES ONLY. Contains Call of Dagon (p. 204).

Unnatural: 1 if the reader has no rating in that ability already.
Hypergeometry Potential: 2

Cultes des Goules

Francois-Honore Balfour, Comte d'Erlette (1703; French).

A necromantic work describing a ghoul cult throughout Europe. Contains Charnel Meditation (p. 204).

Unnatural: 1
Hypergeometry Potential: 1
Dedicated Pool Points: 2 for any investigation involving ghouls.

De Vermis Mysteriis

Ludvig Prinn (1543; Latin).

Prinn, a Flemish wizard who claimed to have been born in the 13th century, smuggled this work out just before being burned at the stake by the Inquisition in 1542. The next year, it appeared in print at Cologne.

Unnatural: 2 (1 for later editions)
Hypergeometry Potential: 3 (2 for translations)
Dedicated Pool Points: 2 for any investigation involving Egypt, Arabic lore, or the undead.

Eltdown Shards

Translated by the Rev. Arthur Brooke Winters-Hall (1917; English).

In 1882, two Cambridge scholars excavated 23 pottery shards from unmistakably Triassic strata at Eltdown, Sussex. Rev. Winters-Hall, a local antiquarian and fairy-lore enthusiast, privately printed his prolix, murky "translation" of the shards' oddly regular markings.

Unnatural: 1 (2 if you have already encountered either the Elder Things or the Great Race of Yith)
Hypergeometry Potential: 1
Dedicated Pool Points: 1 Occult.

Freis, Daniel M., Case File

Captain Robert Feitelberg, supervising psychiatrist (14 Jan 1955-1 Oct 1970; English).

On 13 January 1955 Dr. Freis, one of the original Black Chamber cryptographers who had translated the *Book of Dagon*, and DELTA GREEN's most gifted researcher, suffered a mental collapse and went on a rampage. After attacking several personnel with an axe, he set fire to the central archives. The resulting blaze destroyed all the materials seized during the Innsmouth raid, along with most of the captured Karotechia materials from the Second World War and SUMMER BREEZE. Freis even smashed the original incised conical stones of the *Book of Dagon* to bits.

The program captured him and had him committed to the psychiatric ward of the San Diego Naval Hospital. He dies there in 1970.

Freis' case file eventually swells to 221 pages of medical forms, personnel files, and session transcripts in four accordion files. The diagnosis is depressive complex and paranoid schizophrenia.

Unnatural: 1 if the reader has no rating in that ability already.

Dedicated Pool Points: 1 for anything involving a previous DELTA GREEN operation between 1928 and 1955.

Geheimes Mysterium von Asien

Gottfried Mülder (1847; German).

Mülder accompanied von Junzt on his 1818-1819 journey to Inner Asia and used hypnotic recall to dictate this memoir of their journey. A pirated American version was published in Baltimore in 1849 as *Secret Mysteries of Asia, With a Commentary on the "Ghorl Nigral,"* referring to the blasphemous text (only one copy of which exists in the world) that von Junzt studied in a lamasery in Yian-Ho. Gottfried Mülder's descendant Hermann Mülder published a new limited edition for the Karotechia in 1939.

Unnatural: 1

Hypergeometry Potential: 2

Dedicated Pool Points: 1 for any investigation involving Asia, Leng, Mu, the Xin, or the Tcho-Tcho.

The King in Yellow

Unknown playwright (c. 1895; English or French).

This play, suppressed in France, cannot be skimmed, but it only takes an hour or so to pore over. Once opened, you must make a Stability test against Difficulty 5 (Helplessness) to avoid reading it completely. Once you read it, you will begin to encounter a number of unnatural phenomena with increasing Stability costs, at least once per operation.

You see the Yellow Sign manifest where Hastur has irrupted. (This grants you 2 dedicated pool points to Sense Trouble for Hastur-related phenomena; they refresh immediately after use. Seeing the Sign is a 3-point Stability test.) After four such encounters, things get really intense – you may become attracted to Hastur, rotate into Carcosa, or develop a mental disorder.

Unnatural: 2; it also adds 1 to your Art ability rating.

Liber Damnatus

Attributed (falsely) to St. Lazarus (1570; Latin).

Supposedly a narrative of dying, being damned, experiencing Hell and resurrection, likely written by an unknown sorcerer in Germany. It contains lengthy disquisitions on means of preserving and animating the dead. Its rituals likely involve the creation of zombies or even Raise From Essential Saltes.

Unnatural: 1 if the reader has no rating in that ability already.

Hypergeometry Potential: 3

Dedicated Pool Points: 2 for any investigation involving the dead or necromancy.

Livre d'Ivon

Translated by Gaspard du Nord (1240; Occitan French).

Based on C. Philippus Faber's 9th-century Latin *Liber Ivonis* and du Nord's own occult researches, this purports to be the work of the legendary Hyperborean wizard Eibon.

Unnatural: 1 (2 if you have already encountered Tsathoggua or its minions)

Hypergeometry Potential: 3

Dedicated Pool Points: 1 for Anthropology, Astronomy, or Occult.

Pnakotic Manuscripts

Unknown authors (various; Koiné Greek).

The *Pnakotika*, Greek magical papyri from around the time of Christ, draw oracular and mythical meanings from a set of indecipherable runes and hieroglyphics supposedly discovered in Ultima Thule. Various interpretations of it became part of the Western magical tradition; since about 1485, explorers, occultists, philologists, and archaeologists have added further texts, steles, and inscriptions in similar alphabets (as well as forgeries, honest mistakes, and trance writing) to the Pnakotic corpus, along with their commentary.

There are no complete editions of all the "Pnakotic manuscripts" or "Pnakotic fragments." A three-volume set of the commonly accepted corpus at that time was printed in London in 1768 (now prohibitively expensive), but handwritten copies, academic conference proceedings, and other partial versions can be found in most top-rank university collections.

With a 2-point Anthropology or Occult spend and privileged library collection access, an Agent can assemble enough Pnakotic material for her own research purposes.

Unnatural: 1 for each poring-over per year (maximum 3)

Hypergeometry Potential: 1 for each poring-over per year (maximum 4)

Dedicated Pool Points: 2 for any ability; the Handler chooses which during the operation: "Your study of the Pnakotic manuscripts tells you..."

PUZZLEBOX After-Action Report

ONI Capt. Alphonse Dumars (1928; English).

Accordion case-file stuffed with field reports and photographs of the Innsmouth Raid carried out on 23 February 1928. Also includes reports from the 42nd Battalion of the Marine Corps, the Coast Guard cutter *General Greene*, the Navy submarine *O-9*, the Bureau of Investigation (a report written by J. Edgar Hoover), and the Treasury Department intelligence summary including the testimony of Robert Olmstead.

Unnatural: 1 if the reader has no rating in that ability already.

Dedicated Pool Points: 3 for any operation involving the Deep Ones.

Seven Cryptical Books of Hsan

Ascribed to "Hsan the Greater" (ca. 180 B.C.; Chinese).

The *Ch'i Pen Shu Hsieh Le Tsui An*, or *Seven Books Written in Darkness*, are ascribed to "Hsan the Greater," a legendary sage variously dated as far back as 4200 B.C. The oldest known version is a redacted text on bamboo strips, prepared from scraps that survived the book burnings of 213 B.C. by the first Ch'in emperor. The confirmed existence of Tibetan copies implies that Hsan originally translated the *Seven Books* from some other unknown Asian language. The "Polyglot Hsan" printed anonymously in Shanghai in 1920 as *The Seven Cryptical Books of Earth* includes French and Russian translations.

Unnatural: 1 (2 for Tibetan)

Hypergeometry Potential: 1 (2 for Tibetan)

Dedicated Pool Points: 2 for any investigation involving China or dreams; the Tibetan version grants 3 for any investigation involving Leng or dreams.

Unaussprechlichen Kulten

Friedrich Wilhelm von Junzt (1839; German).

A travelogue of the horrific, providing ample details of many unnatural cults, conspiracies, and activities.

Unnatural: 2 (1 for the bastardized *Nameless Cults* editions in English: Bridewall (1845) and Golden Goblin (1909))

Hypergeometry Potential: 3 (1 for later versions)

Dedicated Pool Points: 1 for any investigation involving cults.

Hypergeometry

What most human cultures call "magic" DELTA GREEN knows as hypergeometry: the study of the hyperspatial interrelation of forces, dimensions, and entities across and above the observable Euclidean universe. Hypergeometric operators – "magi" – visualize and manipulate hyperdimensional energy fields by means of acoustic control tones (words of power), geometric matrices (sigils, runes, and physical actions such as gestures), and pre-tuned vertices or foci (artifacts or "enchanted" items). Transdimensional energy flows often depend on specific patterns of stellar or cosmic radiation. They also depend on specific mental conditioning by the operator: one person might "cast a spell" to no effect, where another might destroy the Earth.

Learning Hypergeometry

Hypergeometry is a General Ability. Agents can use it as an Investigative Ability to figure out what a given spell or item might do (or cost to use), what deities or cosmic forces it invokes, or what grimoire tradition it comes from.

You cannot use character build points to buy Hypergeometry rating points at character creation.

Specific experience of the unnatural must awaken your hypergeometric potential: reading unnatural books, communing with vast entities, or visiting cosmically touched locations. Hypergeometric Potential points quantify such experiences.

Reading Unnatural Tomes: A given work might provide between 1 (a madman's diary) and 3 (a major grimoire) Hypergeometric Potential points; a good translation of the *Necronomicon* provides 4. Although the Handler can always vary this for dramatic purposes, as a rule each potential point requires either one period of between-mission down time (*Study the Unnatural*, p. 129) or one month of poring over the tome in question.

Communing With Entities: Each exposure to a cosmic entity provides 2 Hypergeometric Potential points; a "more magical" being such as Tsathoggua, Yog-Sothoth, or Nyarlathotep might provide 3. With some entities, gaining Hypergeometric potential might require conversation, or unsavory favors. Whether a given entity teaches or inspires Hypergeometry (or has no effect other than a brief, mind-blasting rapport), and how much, is up to the Handler.

Entering Unnatural Places: A cosmically touched location provides Hypergeometric Potential only on a character's *first* visit, and usually only 1 point. Only the most unhallowed and tainted places – the Nameless City in Arabia, the chambers beneath the Great Pyramid, the Moon-Pool of Ponape – provide 2 points. R'lyeh itself, dread Carcosa, or the inner city at the Magnetic Poles would provide 3 Hypergeometric Potential points.

Regardless of which method you use, you must spend experience build points on the Hypergeometry ability just like any other – it doesn't come "free" with a horrific vision of Yog-Sothoth, or by reading the *Book of Eibon*. You can only raise your Hypergeometry ability to the current total of your Hypergeometric Potential. Thus, it's up to the Agent (and his player) to exploit that potential if he wishes.

After wisely buying up Firearms, Raina has only 2 build points left over at the end of the operation, but she wants her Agent, Dr. Lincoln, to read Nameless Cults to get some Hypergeometry as well. Even though von Junzt's black book allows a gain of 3 Hypergeometric Potential points, Raina can only add 2 to Lincoln's Hypergeometry rating. However, after the next operation, she can use 1 of her new build points to "finish studying" Nameless Cults and get Lincoln 1 more Hypergeometry point.

PSYCHIC POWERS

The CIA researches psychic powers within MK-ULTRA; Project DANCER and various MAJESTIC sub-projects also investigate psionic phenomena. Additionally, brushing up against the unnatural can break the natural defenses humans have against psychic contamination from outside and inside, triggering a psychic "bloom" or awakening in some survivors. It's up to the Handler whether player Agents can use psionic abilities, and which ones: each psychic ability is a separate General Ability.

Build points for psychic General Abilities come from the pool of General build points. The first rating point in any paranormal ability costs 5 build points; after that, build points for that ability become rating points as normal.

Sarah wants to get Pyrokinesis (starting fires at a distance). She spends 7 build points, and gets Pyrokinesis with a rating of 3. The first rating point costs 5 build points; the next two each cost 1 build point.

Using a paranormal ability is like any other General Ability use: roll a die, add any points you spend, and compare the result to the Difficulty. However, you *must spend* at least 2 points from your ability pool if you can. If you have insufficient points in that pool, you must spend points from your Stability pool instead. Points spent from your Stability pool do not add to the die roll, however. Using a psychic ability is a 3-point Stability test of the Unnatural; shocking revelations or other uncanny phenomena almost certainly accompany paranormal ability use, triggering further Stability tests.

While using a paranormal ability, you cannot use any other ability. You cannot use any paranormal ability while in combat or in immediate physical peril.

After using a paranormal ability, you must make a Difficulty 5 Health test or immediately lose 2 Health *and* become Hurt for the rest of the scene. (If you are already Hurt, you become Seriously Wounded.) This represents a profound, bone-deep exhaustion approaching shock, not an actual injury.

Paranormal abilities do not refresh until after an operation.

Psychic powers are the first fumblings at hypergeometric perception: as such, they are always dangerous and potentially horrible. Difficulties should be high, and particularly dramatic ability use should come with physical deterioration (-1 Health per paranormal ability point spent). The Handler can and should visit psychic Agents with visions, uncontrollable outbreaks, nosebleeds, or anything else, especially in the presence of powerfully psionic beings like Deep Ones, K'n-Yani, and Mi-Go.

GMC Psionics

The Soviets have extensive ongoing "psychotronic" technology research programs, as well as conventional parapsychological institutes at Kharkov and Leningrad. DELTA GREEN may assign a psychic or "special talent" to the Agents' team on an ad hoc basis – or they may be tasked with eliminating him!

GMC psychic power use is entirely player-facing (with the exception of Telekinesis, below).

First, the psychic spends *at least* 2 points from a General pool: usually Athletics, Health, or a combat ability. Then the Handler rolls a die and adds the result to the spend. If her total is greater than 4, the attack occurs. The Handler then describes the sense of the attack to the player: "You feel like you're sleepwalking, or in a waking dream" or "You feel icy fingertips rifling through your thoughts" or "You find your memory of the last hour fading" or "Your gun seems impossibly heavy." If the player decides to resist, he makes a Stability test with the Difficulty equal to the total result of the GMC's roll plus her spend. If he fails the test, the psychic attack succeeds.

GMC psionic use on other GMCs succeeds or not as the Handler decides the drama dictates.

Telekinesis: TK uses the same rules, but resolves the attack as a Firearms or Unarmed Combat attack for a psi blast or telekinetic punch. (The actual attack ability remains Athletics, Health, or Telekinesis.) Telekinetic attacks cannot be resisted by Stability. Damage is d+0; the psychic may increase that damage by +1 per 2 additional points spent to increase damage. These points *do not* modify the roll; if the blast misses, those points are wasted. For a psionic Athletics test to throw, crush, or break an inanimate object, set the Difficulty by how hard it would be for *that psychic* to cause the effect – a Grey might throw a car at Difficulty 4 while a mutant child might need Difficulty 7 to manage it.

Alien Psionics

The various alien races DELTA GREEN faces, of course, have a vast panoply of psionic abilities, the product of millions of years of evolution in entirely different dimensional states.

If not detailed in their writeup, alien abilities either use Hypergeometry or the GMC rules above, at the Handler's discretion.

Using Hypergeometry

Sotlving a hypergeometrical equation, or incrementing an alien rote, or casting a spell – in game terms, this is a **ritual.** Every ritual is different: even two versions of the Elder Sign may have different requirements, costs, effects, and associated sigils. This preserves both mystery and the Handler's dramatic freedom in a given operation.

One important subset of rituals is **objects:** informational representations of a solved equation, sometimes a scroll or bas-relief, often an "enchanted item" or similar artifact. Triggering such an object may not require any knowledge of the underlying ritual at all, or just a code phrase or two as a lemma. Some objects, such as the Shining Trapezohedron, solve or contain several rituals; inhuman cults and desperate sorcerers seek such things at all costs.

Each ritual has four components: its name, its elements, its effects, and its Cost.

Name: What does the grimoire call the ritual? What does the archaeologist who committed suicide after deciphering it call it?

Elements: Items, actions, conditions, or the like required to perform the ritual. It might require a knife, a specific chemical compound, or a blood sacrifice; it might need to be performed near the ocean or while Aldebaran is above the horizon. One very important element is the time needed to perform the ritual: one round, several rounds, or many minutes or even hours.

Effects: The outcome of a successfully performed ritual. These should never be empty things like "lose d+1 Health" but rather "d+1 Health sublimes away as your flesh turns to sand." Define the duration of the effect as well: most ritual effects should last only a few rounds, or perhaps minutes. Permanent effects require more energy and effort, as they warp conventional geometry more severely.

Cost: The cost in points (usually from Hypergeometry, Health, or Stability) the operator must pay to perform the ritual. Some very powerful rituals require expenditure of Sanity points.

Learning a Ritual

Given a copy of the ritual in a language the Agent can read, the time needed to learn a ritual depends on its complexity. This usually, but not always, corresponds with the power of its effects.

Most objects have Simple activation rotes.

An Agent can spend 1 pool point of the Unnatural to speed up study: an Elaborate ritual becomes Complex, a Complex ritual becomes Simple, and a Simple ritual can be grasped in minutes instead of hours.

Learning a ritual requires a 2-point Stability test at Difficulty 5.

Ritual Complexity

Ritual Complexity	Learning Time	Activation Time
Simple	5+ hours	rounds
Complex	20+ hours	minutes
Elaborate	100+ hours	hours

Using a Ritual

To use a ritual or object, the operator must:

△ know the ritual or the activating rote for the object.

△ fulfill any necessary elements and carry out any required actions, such as chanting, gestures, etc.

△ pay the Cost of the ritual.

△ make an activation test of Hypergeometry or Stability against a Difficulty equal to her current Sanity pool. If the test fails, she pays only half the Cost.

Many objects "pre-pay" some portion of the Cost, or reduce the Difficulty of the activation test, or both.

Ritual Cost

To perform a ritual, the operator pays its Cost in points (called "Cost points" as an abstraction); these can come from a number of different abilities.

△ **Hypergeometry:** 1 pool point of Hypergeometry equals 1 Cost point.

△ **Health or Stability:** 2 pool points of either ability equals 1 Cost point. The operator should describe the mental or physical damage he does to himself in the process of performing the ritual.

Depending on the ritual, the operator might be able to lower the Cost by 1 by spending 1 point of an Investigative Ability: Art, Physics, or even Occult. This is always up to the Handler or mentioned explicitly in the ritual description.

For some rituals and some effects, the operator can choose to sacrifice 1 *rating* point of Sanity; this pays the entire Cost to activate most objects or to perform more subtle rituals. Sacrificing rating points of Sanity is required for the Cost of other, more powerful, rituals.

An operator with a Sanity rating of 0 (a GMC, in other words) no longer needs to sacrifice Sanity to perform a ritual.

Performing a ritual in a place of power, or at a significant time, may lower the Cost. Or, of course, the ritual may only be possible at all at such a point — the normal Cost would be literally astronomical.

Activation Test

To manifest a ritual's effects, the operator makes a Stability test against a Difficulty equal to her current Sanity pool. Thus, as she loses Sanity, working hypergeometric rituals becomes easier and easier...

She can "spend herself negative" on this test, spending more Stability than her current pool contains.

The operator can also spend Hypergeometry on this test, but cannot spend more points than she has in her pool.

If this test fails, the ritual does not take effect; the operator pays only half the Cost.

Distorted or flawed rituals may increase the Difficulty of the activation test by +1 or even more.

The ritual effect itself always imposes an Unnatural (Difficulty 5) Stability test on the caster, the target, and any witnesses. The severity of the test depends on the effect, but performing or being targeted by a ritual likely requires a 4-point test or worse; witnesses may get away with only a 3-point test.

Assistance

Some rituals and objects allow assistance in fulfilling the Cost. Sometimes, this assistance is willing (a second chanter at a ritual who

RITUAL ADDICTION

Manipulating the true geometry of the universe folds the mind of the percipient and creates a link that can become naked dependency. Hypergeometric power is a better high than cocaine, a more wondrous trip than LSD, a purer bliss than heroin.

If the operator's Stability drops to 0 or below while casting or using a hypergeometric ritual or object, he develops an Addiction (p. 123) to it. The next time a problem arises which might be "solved" by the application of that hypergeometrical power, that Agent must make a Difficulty 4 Stability test to resist the urge to use it. On a failure, he tries using the hypergeometric effect to solve the problem. Smashing or otherwise destroying an object cures object-oriented Addiction, but ritual addiction is incurable.

may expend points with the operator), and sometimes it is unwilling (the sacrificial victim who expends his Health upon his death or injury).

Human sacrifice by Agents always incurs an additional 7-point Stability test against Violence (for the caster) and two additional Stability tests against Violence and Helplessness (for the victim, if he survives).

Each ritual and object defines whether such assistance is possible.

Designing a Ritual

The Handler sign the feel and flavor of a ritual to suit the immediate dramatic needs of the game, with special attention to the grotesque, eerie, and cosmic. But despite these player-facing, story-focused details, the Handler usually builds a ritual from a standard menu of effects, with a Cost roughly comparable with the degree of change it works on the Euclidean world.

Hypergeometric effects vary wildly in operation time, scope, and effect. They are balanced not in the details, or against each other, but only on the highest level of the game.

Specifically, using rituals drains Stability and (eventually) Sanity until the would-be magus is either a GMC or a casualty or both. The inevitable decline of an Agent using hypergeometry is thus guaranteed.

The main effect of the ritual sets the core Cost. If the Handler believes it requires it, and a hypergeometrical ritual achieves multiple effects at the same time (such as movement and damage) the Handler may assign a +2 point cost increase per category added.

The Handler defines a new ritual she calls "the Touch of Saval". It allows the operator to reach out, across any distance, and attack a target with inhuman tentacles for d+2 damage for d-2 rounds. The Handler determines the main effect of the ritual is Damage, so the Cost is 5 points (or 1 Sanity), but since the tentacles also scry (they can find a target remotely), she adds a +2 operator cost, so it costs 5+2 = 7 points (or 1 Sanity).

Damage

The effect lowers (or increases) an ability pool as noted in the Ability column. The ability affected is usually Athletics, Health, or Stability. However, any ability might be fair game: a ritual to grant clairvoyance might effectively add points to Sense Trouble or Preparedness, for example, or an Aklo rite might grant points in Foreign Language. Permanent crippling (rating point loss) usually carries double the Cost; permanent enhancement almost always counts as an ongoing effect.

No ritual increases Sanity; very, very few rituals actually increase Stability (as opposed to freezing mental activity or otherwise counterfeiting social cues).

Some very terrible rituals cause Lethality (p. 093) effects, for the noted Cost.

Move

The effect transports entities, objects, or the operator according to the Distance column.

Ritual Parameters

Ability	Scope	Distance	Cost
d-2	Minor	Close range	2 (or 1 Sanity)
d-1		Near range	4 (or 1 Sanity)
d+0	Substantial	Long range	5 (or 1 Sanity)
d+2		In sight	7 (or 1 Sanity)
L1	Major	Continental	10 (or 1 Sanity)
L2		Global	15 (or 1 Sanity)
L3	Sweeping	Interplanetary	20 (or 1 Sanity)
L5*	Cosmic	Interstellar or interdimensional	40 + 1 Sanity
L5*		*Permanent, ongoing effect*	50 + 2 Sanity

Permanent or Ongoing Effect

Not an effect in itself, but a characteristic of the ritual. This establishes a continuous, "self-solving" ritual without further attention by the operator: a gate to Yuggoth, or tattoos that grant -3 Armor. This is how objects are created.

Scry

The effect provides information at a distance (see the Distance column for Cost). Usually this involves direct sensory stimulation: an ecstatic vision, auditory hallucination, etc. This effect also includes contacting entities, but not summoning them.

Summon

The effect brings an unnatural creature into the operator's presence. "Summoning a monster" creates a pinpoint wormhole, or rotates the monster from its dimension into ours. Merely "calling" a creature – dropping incised stones into the ocean to contact Deep Ones, for example – has the same Cost as a scrying effect.

The Cost of a true summoning equals the creature's Hypergeometry rating, or *half* its Athletics or Health, whichever is higher. For transcendent entities, the summoning Cost is likely in the dozens or even hundreds: such rituals must be performed at specific times and places that lower the Cost for that moment, or after many ceremonies if the ritual allows the operator to build and store expended Cost points over time. Or, of course, mass slaughter might do it.

Some rituals allow the expenditure of 1 Sanity to summon a creature; some objects summon creatures with only minimal Cost to the wielder (before the Stability hit from seeing the thing, of course).

Once present, the entity invariably attempts to resist and destroy the operator. If the operator has become Shattered due to the summoning, or after beholding the creature, or simply has no points left, she cannot control it. Instead, the entity attempts to destroy the operator and then escape.

If the operator remains compos mentis, each round he may expend 1 point (Stability or Health) to maintain control of the entity, or must expend another 1 Sanity point and be able to control the entity for the length of the summons.

Controlled entities may be commanded to perform actions consistent with their intelligence level. Most entities understand "kill X target". Once this action is complete, the entity may return to its point of origin, having fulfilled the summons.

Most (but not all!) summoning rituals also contain the relevant banishment ritual, for half the Cost.

Sample Rituals

Each of these rituals presents a "default" form – but don't adhere to anything too rigidly. Hypergeometry is chaos and irrationality; customize or ignore these rituals at will. A given ritual may have a much lower or higher Cost than another with similar effects, or more subtle or powerful consequences. It may just be an inexplicable effect of a moment of insanity or of reading the wrong glyph off the wall.

Call Forth Those From Outside

Elaborate ritual, Cost varies

This ritual summons unnatural entities from outside our world. It involves a strange mixture of medieval and classical invocations and calls to unnatural powers in inhuman tongues, often accompanied by thunderous releases of energy and strange behavior by dogs, birds, and other nearby animals.

The Cost depends on the entity summoned (see *Summon*, p. 203). This cost can be paid by assistants, who need not know the ritual themselves as long as they follow the operator's instructions, or by human sacrifice.

The core of this ritual is the same regardless of the entity. Applying the ritual requires learning techniques peculiar to the entity being summoned, which must be found in various sources requiring long research. Learning a new entity's secrets requires its own study time.

Whether a ritual applies to any given entity is up to the Handler. Make a note of the particular summonings an operator knows. For example: "Call Forth Those From Outside" (Dimensional Shambler), "Alert the Hosts of the Airs" (Mi-Go), "Benefit the All-In-One" (Yog-Sothoth).

The Call of Dagon
Simple ritual, Cost 4

This ritual requires the five-hour creation of a clay tablet, which is then thrown in the sea, in an area known to be populated by Deep Ones. It calls Deep Ones to the surface for "communion." The normal Stability test for seeing Deep Ones applies. After decades of DELTA GREEN using this ritual to ambush them, modern Deep Ones are less trusting than their predecessors, as well as less forgiving. It should be noted that this is not a summons or a command, but a "call." A request. It does not in any way compel them to respond or control the Deep Ones who answer — though the text may be misread to imply that.

Charnel Meditation
Simple ritual, Cost 4

At a graveyard frequented by ghouls, the operator enters a reverie and utters a litany of strange meepings. Enacting the ritual on a moonlit night lowers the Difficulty of the activation test by -2. If the activation test succeeds, a few ghouls arrive within the hour. This ritual exerts no control over them whatsoever.

The Closing of the Breach
Complex ritual, Cost varies

This ritual breaks a connection with the unnatural. This could be the banishment of a Great Old One, one of their servitors, the ending of an ongoing hypergeometric effect, or the destruction of a gate. Knowledge of the ritual is usually not enough; the operator must extensively research the thing to be banished. Whether the ritual affects any given situation is up to the Handler.

In most cases, the Cost is half that of summoning the entity being banished or the enacting the effect being stopped. The Cost can often be shared with assistants, or paid by human sacrifice. The Handler always decides which costs must be paid to banish a particular effect or entity.

Performing the ritual usually takes about an hour and requires strange gesticulations and chanted invocations in unknown languages, and must be performed near the effect to be stopped. The operator makes the activation test and pays the Costs as soon as the ritual has begun. Usually, the thing being assailed cannot come near or interfere with the ritual once the activation test succeeds — unless the Handler decides otherwise.

Create Stone Gate
Elaborate ritual, Cost 20 + 2 Sanity + 40 Health

This powerful but flawed version of the hyperspace gate ritual requires an arch of carved stone. The structure can be built by anyone with Architecture 2+. The operator (and any assistants who know the ritual) must spend days or weeks inscribing the carvings that give it power and then succeed at the activation test.

A character with a rating in Architecture can lower the Cost by 1 with a 1-point spend of Physics.

The operator and assistants must pay the Cost and Sanity between them, and ritually inflict 40 Health damage upon unwilling sacrifices. (Or even a single sacrifice over time, if the victim is allowed to heal between injuries.) Once the gate has been successfully crafted and infused with power, it may be opened at a Cost of 1, by anyone who knows any Create Hyperspace Gate ritual, with an activation test. It can open onto anywhere on Earth the caster knows; the activation test is +1 Difficulty if they destination is only somewhat familiar, or +2 Difficulty if the operator has only a photograph or detailed description to work from.

Once the gate is open, anyone may pass through at a Cost of 1, and may return through the same spot at the same Cost. Passing through the Gate triggers a 4-point Unnatural Difficulty test. Each time the gate is opened, roll a die twice. If the result comes up "1" twice, the operator must make a second activation test (or pay 1 Sanity) to avoid some deadly repercussion, such as unnatural cancerous growths in a user or a sudden explosion of energy at the far end.

The Elder Sign
Simple ritual, Cost varies

The Elder Sign is a mystical sigil either drawn in the air by gesture or inscribed upon a sturdy surface. It commands respect from many of those from Outside. When gestured in the air (Cost 3) it prevents such beings from coming within about 10 yards of the gesturer for 2d6 rounds, provided the gesturer takes no hostile action against them. If an entity is somehow physically forced into that radius, it loses d+0 Health or Hypergeometry. As a gesture, the Elder Sign affects a given entity only once in 24 hours.

The Elder Sign may be inscribed permanently in a surface (preferably some especially long-lasting stone or metal; the inscriber must have an appropriate Art specialty) at a Cost of 2 Stability rating points. Beings from Outside cannot come within about 10 yards of it unless the sigil is broken, and they lose 1 Health per round if somehow forced to come that near. For any except a Great Old One, this loss can be fatal.

The most potent engraving of the Elder Sign carries a Cost of 99 by the engraver (who must sacrifice at least 2 Stability and 1 Sanity rating point of their own, and who must have an appropriate Art specialty), ritual chanters, or human sacrifices over the course of 24 hours. Beings from Outside cannot come within 100 yards of it, and lose d+0 Health per round if somehow forced to come that near. Even coming within 6 miles saps such an entity of 1 Health per hour, until the entity vanishes — banished or destroyed — upon reaching 0 Health. Rituals to summon such entities always fail within that radius.

Unbeknownst to many operators, the Elder Sign suggests that the operator is allied with a specific group of powerful beings from Beyond. Some say those beings lend power to the Elder Sign and perhaps feed upon the unnatural energies that it saps from its victims. It has even been reputed to summon those entities or embody them in the dead. The exact nature and implications of such allegiance, if it's true, is up to the Handler. As inhuman, unnatural entities, they would certainly be inimical to humanity.

The Handler should decide beforehand if any particular monster will be warded off, ignore, or be encouraged by the Sign. An Unnatural ability spend can usually tell the operator whether the Elder Sign would be efficacious.

Exchange Personalities
Simple ritual, Cost varies

Mastered by some cults of Shub-Niggurath, this ritual transfers the mind and "life-glow" of the operator to another character's brain. The operator must gaze hypnotically at the target, although some scrying or other magical visions may also allow Exchange Personalities.

Targets of this ritual absolutely get a Sense Trouble roll, which manifests as a jolt of detached perspective. ("It's as though you were looking at yourself from different eyes.") A success lets the target pinpoint the operator, if he can see her.

Operator and target engage in a contest of Hypergeometry vs. Stability. If the caster wins, she rolls an Erosion die at a -2 modifier, keeping a running total. Unless the target also knows the ritual, nothing happens if the target wins. (If the target knows the ritual and wins, the spell ends.) Once the running Erosion total is higher than the target's Stability, the caster can trade minds with the target. Being mind-switched causes a 5-point Stability test (Unnatural) for the target. Every subsequent switch *also* causes a 4-point Stability test (Helplessness) for the target.

Costs and effects of the ritual depend on how often the operator has targeted the same victim.

Exchange Personalities Invasions

Invasion	Duration	Cost	Erosion Die Modifier	Stability test (Unnatural)
First	1 round	2	-2	2-point
Second	1 minute	4	-1	3-point
Third	1 hour	5	+0	4-point
Fourth and subsequent	1 day	7	+1 and higher	4-point

On the fifth invasion, the Erosion die modifier is +2, and so on. At this point, the operator can make the switch from far away, and may come to sense the thoughts and actions of the host even when not intruding.

Once the Erosion die modifier is higher than the target's Stability rating, the operator can make the switch with a strong act of will, paying only a Cost of 1.

At this point, the operator can make the exchange permanent with a Cost of 1 Sanity and a human sacrifice to Shub-Niggurath. Tradition (and the ritual, if the Handler so dictates) dictates this sacrifice be performed on Halloween.

A body slain while hosting an exchanged "life-glow" may stir and move, rotting but animated, in some cases long after death. Whether this happens, and when, remains up to the Handler.

Infallible Suggestion
Simple ritual, Cost 5

Taking two rounds to implement, this ritual requires strange gestures and a quiet chant in some prehuman tongue. The chant is alien to any linguist, but those with the Unnatural ability may recognize a form of Aklo.

The operator must overcome the target in a contest of Hypergeometry vs. Stability. For one round, the target willingly obeys any command given by the operator. Commanding a target to commit murder, suicide, or some other awful act triggers the same Stability test in the operator as it does in the victim.

Meditation Upon the Favored Ones
Complex ritual, Cost 4

Must be cast outside the Earth's atmosphere, via a powerful radio broadcast, or in a mountain range currently mined by the fungi from Yuggoth. Suitable mountain ranges include the Appalachians, Adirondacks, Andes, Himalayas, and Balkans.

Typically, a few mi-go appear after less than an hour of chanting. Assistants may contribute by echoing the operator's speech, even if they don't know the ritual.

One Who Passes the Gateways
Elaborate ritual, Cost 4

This ritual consists of a litany that must be intoned within five concentric circles of fire or phosphorus. The operator's spirit leaves its sleeping body and travels alien realms where much wisdom may be gained, though such experiences may incur further Stability tests. On a failed 1 on the activation test, the operator strays and severs the link between spirit and body. Her body remains comatose.

Pentagram of Power
Elaborate ritual, Cost 6

The operator inscribes in chalk or paint a pentagram in a circle surrounded by four circles, then imbues the design with power by animal or human sacrifice. The process takes about two hours and requires a 4-point Stability test against Violence (for animal sacrifice; 7-point for humans). If the ritual activation test succeeds, the pentagram reduces the cost of controlling a summoned entity to 1 pool point of Health or Stability per 3 rounds, or 1 pool point per minute with a human sacrifice.

The Powder of Ibn-Ghazi
Elaborate ritual, Cost 3 per vial

Whether blown from a tube, sprayed from an insecticide gun, or sprinkled by hand, this grayish powder attracts ultra-terrene matter-energy into the four-dimensional universe. Its primary use is to make invisible beings visible, but (at the Handler's discretion) it also allows some spells of banishment or dismissal to work more effectively. One vial of the powder works on one being, object, or monster, regardless of size. It lasts for d+2 rounds, and must be delivered from no farther than Close range. Compounding this powder requires mummy dust, powdered silver nitrate, and other chemicals available in a good laboratory.

Raise From Essential Saltes

Elaborate ritual, Cost 10 (render) or 4 (raise or reduce)

This spell ("*Y'ai' ng'ngah, Yog-Sothoth, h'ee-l'Geb, f'ai thro-dog, uaaah!*") raises up the body and soul of a corpse that has been reduced to a bluish-gray powder of its essential salts by an alchemical process. The reverse of this spell ("*Ogthrod ai'f, Geb'l-ee'h, Yog-Sothoth, 'ngah'ng ai'y, zhro!*") returns such a revenant to its essential salts.

It is important that the entire corpse is available for rendering. An ancient, dessicated body is usually acceptable, as is a body that has been dismembered, as long as it is complete. But if the corpse has been too much eaten away by vermin or has rotted badly, what is revived is not a living, intelligent person but a gibbering, horrifying monstrosity (see *Ye Liveliest Awfulness*, p. 244).

That said, as long as the coffin is intact, and the necromancer has taken sufficient care to scrape together all the fragments and dust within, the spell is possible. Rendering a corpse into its essential salts requires 3 months of work in an alchemist's laboratory or the equivalent, a Cost of 10, and a total Occult and Chemistry rating of 8.

Restoring "essential saltes" to life is a somewhat simpler process, though it requires strange incantations and great quantities of human blood. It has a Cost of 4. A revived subject suffers an 8-point Unnatural Stability test from the memory of death and the incomprehensibly unnatural experience of awakening from it, and must feed on human blood for days afterward to survive.

A revived subject may be reduced back to "essential saltes" by reciting the restoration incantation in reverse. That takes a few minutes and has a Cost of 4. The subject is helpless to resist, unless the operator can be physically stopped.

The Voorish Sign

Simple ritual, Cost 3

An operator who makes this strange series of hand gestures can briefly see things that are invisible due to their extradimensional or otherworldly nature: unseen entities, unnatural gates, indications of ongoing hypergeometric effects, and so on. Using the Voorish Sign grays out or distorts some wavelengths of visible light.

Withering

Simple ritual, Cost 7

This chanted ritual blackens and twists the flesh of a target regardless of armor. It inflicts 1 Health damage on the operator and d+2 damage on any living target at Long range or closer that the caster can see or smell.

The operator can enact the ritual on a target who is not in sight by burning a small effigy that contains a sample of the target's blood, hair, semen, or other bodily matter. This carries an additional Cost of 7, but the operator may spend that cost over any amount of time while constructing and ritually consecrating the effigy.

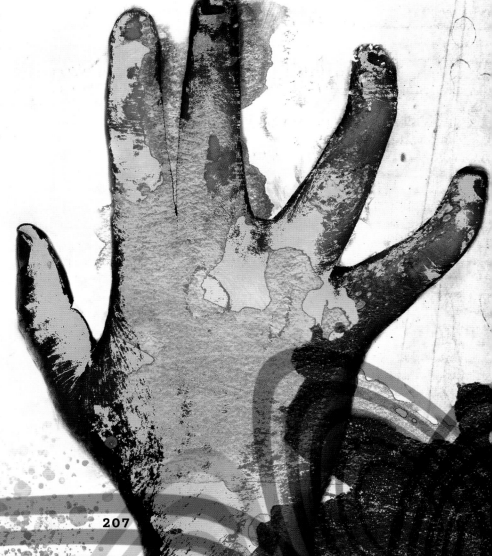

The Hidden World

Despite camera-carrying satellites and deep-diving submarines, humanity knows almost nothing of its world.

The Earth is older than we know, older perhaps than we can know given the strange behavior of the aeons around the Great Old Ones. It holds dead secrets that could snap the globe back to the methylated snowball it was a billion years ago, or leave it a scattering of cosmic gravel in a new asteroid belt.

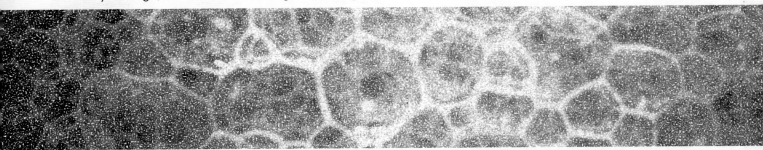

The place humans can live – the dimensional construct we call "the present" or "space-time" – is a soap bubble. Outside the bubble's walls, endless and infinite varieties of Hell stretch forever around it and through it. Fortunately, we can barely perceive these Outside dimensions, and could not remain sane, or solid, in any but the nearest and most traveled of them.

There are humans, however, who have touched these pasts and these futures and these planes, and been twisted by their unearthly gravity or irradiated by their impossible radiances. They seek to bring the hidden things into light, to uncover the true past or open the way to the real outer space.

DELTA GREEN exists to stop those madmen, those cultists, those sages. It fights to neutralize – to blind and kill and eradicate the very memory of – the explorers and dreamers and scientists who would doom and damn the Earth for the sake of power or knowledge or glory.

Other Times

The past isn't dead, Faulkner wrote. It's not even past. DELTA GREEN knows better than most how unwittingly true that is, and it knows very little.

The program's analysts can only apply human knowledge, after all, and do not willingly apply very much of that.

Humans must perceive time as a sequence, believe in cause and effect, see past and future as separate countries and not as two doors of the same cavern. Modern science must believe that erosion and evolution are processes, and not the lies and scar tissue reality uses to protect itself from itself.

DELTA GREEN has no choice but to believe that alien gods and races ruled the world before humanity did. After all, the program's soldiers have fought both. And DELTA GREEN knows that They shall rule again when it loses the fight.

That doesn't mean the program knows very much about any of this hidden history, especially since those who correlate such knowledge often find themselves setting the fires to destroy it.

The Prehistory of Unhistory

With all that said, however, here's what a paleontologist and an occultist might piece together if DELTA GREEN or MAJESTIC were ever foolish enough to allow such a team access to the Annex or the COUNTRY CLUB archives.

Dates derive from 1960s paleontological and paleogeological research; they are necessarily approximate.

△ **5 billion years ago:** The accreting spheres of the planets force the Hounds of Tindalos into the angles of time. (Moon and Earth form)

△ **2 billion years ago:** The spectral, polypous Muuruup arrive from space, dominating Earth and three other planets in the Solar System. (Basalt upthrust by a series of orogenies in Australia; red shales begin to appear indicating sudden presence of free oxygen)

△ **600 million years ago (m.y.a.):** The crinoid Elder Things arrive on Earth, seeding millions of species with their experiments. (Cambrian speciation)

△ **500 m.y.a.:** Great Race of Yith arrive and possess conical super-lichen species; war with the Muuruup. (Edicaran fossils vanish, evidence of severe storms in shallow ocean silts)

△ **450 or 345 m.y.a.:** Cthulhu and its spawn arrive from Zubeneschamali (Beta Librae) or Sothis (Sirius). (Silurian extinction of trilobites; Late Devonian black shale deposits)

△ **300 m.y.a.:** R'lyeh sinks, Cthulhu trapped; N'Kai founded by refugee servitors of Cthulhu. (Pangaea forms)

△ **230 m.y.a.:** Serpent people evolve, or are created by Yig; they rule empires in Laurasia (North America + Eurasia) the greatest of which is Valusia roughly where the Mediterranean is now. (E.C. Case excavations of Late Permian tropical reptiles in Oklahoma)

△ **225 to 220 m.y.a.:** The shoggoths rebel against their Elder Thing masters, unleashing a global war fought with cosmic weapons in which the crinoids are victorious at great cost. (Pangaea breaks up, massive tectonic uplift, Permian marine extinction)

△ **200 m.y.a.:** Possibly fleeing the shoggoth war, serpent people migrate underground to Yoth. (Late Triassic reptile hyperspeciation in new environments)

△ **145 m.y.a.:** Mi-Go arrive on Earth in force from Yuggoth, bring Ghatanothoa to a Pacific subcontinent ("Mu"), use it as a weapon to defeat the Elder Things and restrict them to the Antarctic. (Morrison Formation, increase in Pacific volcanism, breakup of Gondwanaland)

△ **70 m.y.a.:** The Muuruup escape from their underground prison, drive the Great Race from their rugose cone-bodies and into the future. The cataclysm destroys most Elder Thing cities, leads Mi-Go to reduce their presence on Earth. (Cretaceous land extinction)

△ **50 m.y.a.:** Black, formless beings from Kythamil build K'n-Yan. (Great Plains form)

△ **5 m.y.a.:** Flooding of the Mediterranean ends final serpent kingdom of Valusia. (Zanclean flood)

△ **4 m.y.a.:** Elder Things create hominid servant-pets. (Australopithecus)

△ **3 m.y.a.:** Rhan-Tegoth rules in what is now Alaska; Tsathoggua arrives in Hyperborea from N'Kai or Saturn.

△ **1.5 m.y.a.:** Furry hominid Tsathoggua-worshipers, the Voorii, establish the civilization of Hyperborea in Greenland. (Aftonian Interglacial)

△ **1 m.y.a.:** Hominid white apes construct the ward-city "Thule" in central Africa. (Tchadanthropus)

△ **800,000 years ago:** Xin rule in Mu.

△ **700,000 years ago:** Tcho-Tcho evolve in southeastern Asia. (Java Man)

△ **173,148 B.C.:** Worship of Ghatanothoa becomes supreme in Mu.

△ **130,000 years ago:** Human civilization first (?) rises in Hyperborea and Lomar, drives the Voorii south. (Neanderthal Man)

△ **70,000 years ago:** Itla-shua destroys Hyperborea and the final Elder Thing city with ice; Lomarians retreat into K'n-Yan, except for those in the capital city of Olathoë. (Wisconsin Glaciation)

△ **28,000 years ago:** Lomarians bring worship of Tsathoggua out of K'n-Yan, re-establish his cult across the North. (Farmdalian glacial retreat)

△ **26,000 years ago:** Final destruction of Olathoë by the hairy Gnophkehs.

△ **10,000 years ago:** Rise of Cimmeria under Crom-Ya. (Last glacial maximum)

△ **9,500 years ago:** Sinking of Atlantis. (Plato, end of Ice Age)

△ **9000 B.C.:** Tcho-Tcho found Ai-Lao-Žar on the Plateau of Singu.

△ **8000 B.C.:** The Doom comes to Sarnath in the land of Mnar. (Flooding of the Persian Gulf seafloor.)

△ **6000 B.C.:** Last kings of Stygia carve the Sphinx.

△ **4400 B.C.:** Destruction of Irem of the Pillars (Fission-track dating of Wabar meteorites)

△ **2980 B.C.:** Nephren-Ka, the Black Pharaoh, rules in Egypt. (Confused and fragmentary records of the Pharaoh Nefer-ka (2nd Dynasty) or Nefer-ka-re (3rd Dynasty))

△ **2700 B.C.:** The Yellow God-Emperor rules China.

△ **2475 B.C.:** Ghoul queen Nitocris rules in Egypt. (Turin King List)

△ **5000 A.D.:** The cruel empire of Tsan-Chan flourishes.

△ **50 million years from now:** Great Race of Yith returns to incarnate into a hardy coleopteran species, reconquers the Earth.

Other Lands

Paleontology and geology provide only chance glimpses of the primordial past, but shadowy countries and unknown gateways persist even in the modern Earth. A few rolls of satellite film and a few dives by a bathyscaphe pinprick the shroud of mystery, but can hardly – and may never – pull it aside to reveal the true geography of our planet.

The oceans blanket monstrous civilizations and archaean ruins as inaccessible as if they were on Mars; the depths of the earth and ice caps likewise despite the occasional mine shaft or crevasse. The jungles and deserts mask dead cities of mankind and his predecessors; mountains confound compass bearings and starve those who climb them of oxygen. When alien physics, distorted perception engines, time slips, and unnatural geometries enter the picture, the picture blurs to impenetrability.

For every Akhetaten or Macchu Picchu discovered by science there may be a dozen monolithic temples or necropoleis buried beneath snow or sand. The labyrinthine gullies of the Hoggar in Algeria, or the mist-shrouded chasms of the Andean altiplano, could easily hide ruined cities of the Garamanteans or Tihuanaco.

Those tribesmen or peasants who know of such structures say little, and stay away from them themselves save on certain significant nights. Such a place is a curse or a resource, and in either case seldom to be revealed to outsiders. Even closer to home, towns close themselves off, isolated farms go silent, settlers instinctively turn away from the unnatural. Fifty or a hundred miles in the direction no one goes from any city in the world, and you can walk ground untrodden for decades... by human feet.

The folklorist Albert Wilmarth sums up the effect of the unnatural on human geography in his monograph "Folkloric Pathways in the Settlement of Vermont":

> "Once their habitual paths and dwellings were established according to a certain fixed plan, they remembered less and less what fears and avoidances had determined that plan, and even that there had been any fears or avoidances. Most people simply knew that certain hilly regions were considered as highly unhealthy, unprofitable, and generally unlucky to live in, and that the farther one kept from them the better off one usually was. In time the ruts of custom and economic interest became so deeply cut in approved places that there was no longer any reason for going outside them, and the haunted hills were left deserted by accident rather than by design."

Those blasted heaths, haunted hills, and uncanny valleys connect to the domains of the unnatural. Sometimes just a thread of perception allows the horror to trickle through; other times a door opens wider, on Walpurgisnacht or Candlemas Eve for example. Sometimes the unnatural has fixed itself in one location, immobile ruins waiting for their masters to revive them: the Nameless City in Arabia, the City of the Great Race in Australia, the shoggoth necropolis in Antarctica below the Mountains of Madness.

Other times, the unnatural suffuses a whole district, rising and clotting where towers might suddenly loom out of the murk or towns be ineluctably drawn into it:

△ Upper Miskatonic Valley and Quabbin Reservoir, Massachusetts
△ Severn Estuary, Britain
△ Singu Plateau, Burma
△ Parts of the Ü-Tsang Plateau, Tibet

Still other times, the unnatural country remains constant, but its boundary in human space shifts and diverges: wizards and pilgrims have seen and even entered Leng, Kadath, and N'Kai from different continents over the millennia.

This, then, represents an impossible accumulation of strange, far places encroaching – at one or another time, at least – on the perimeter of reality guarded by DELTA GREEN. An agent who once enters Leng may see it on a combat tour, in a desert mirage, or in his nightmares thereafter, its border no longer geographical but psychological.

Dho-Nha

The name of this "inner city at the magnetic poles" comes from the ritual that grants access to it – the city revealed by the Dho-Nha ritual may have another name to its builders. The *Necronomicon* and other texts describe only a single city, implying that Dho-Nha occupies a pocket dimension tangent to both magnetic poles. Alternately, there may be two cities (Dho and Nha?), one at each pole. The city has some connection with Yog-Sothoth, and may act as a gateway to other dimensions or times. Its location on Earth shifts with the magnetic poles, but until the immanentization of Yog-Sothoth it can only be reached using the ritual, or possibly from the air.

Captain Curtis Criss, USAF, is the only DELTA GREEN asset known to have seen Dho-Nha without using the ritual. On 21 January 1968, he joins a B-52 airborne alert flight out of Thule Air Base in Greenland under cover as a substitute navigator. When his bomber crashes near the airbase six hours later, one man is dead, the cockpit burned out, and one nuclear weapon is missing. In his later debrief, Criss describes "a kind of angled chaos" with "pointed towers" and "things in the gardens." (See Operation *NORTHERN LIGHTHOUSE*, p. 184.)

Irem and the Nameless City

The legendary pre-Islamic Arabian city "Irem of the Pillars" appears in the Koran and the *Thousand and One Nights*, both of which describe its sudden destruction by Allah for the impiety of its inhabitants. Later mythographers located Irem variously in the interior of Saudi Arabia, Yemen, or Oman: Harry St.-John Philby mounted an expedition into the Rub al-Khali in 1932, and discovered a meteor crater at Wabar that he identified with the remains of Irem.

Alhazredic legend connects Irem to a prehuman "Nameless City" inhabited by ghostly reptiles, implying that the Adites of Irem somehow destroyed it. Alhazred supposedly composed the first couplet of the *Necronomicon* ("That is not dead," etc.) dreaming of the Nameless City while in the ruins of Irem.

Irem and the Nameless City may be the same place, or two different haunted Arabian ruins: the Rub al-Khali is the size of Texas and even the Bedouins avoid entering it. Alternately, they might be separate but overlapping dimensional extensions – the Nameless City could be Irem's extension into the Dreamlands, or vice versa.

△ Prisoner testimony from the 1907 St. Bernard Parish raid places Irem near or at the center of the global Cthulhu cult.

△ Nathaniel Wingate Peaslee may have entered Irem or the Nameless City in 1911, while under Yithian possession.

△ The writings of the occultist Randolph Carter describe Irem as a city on the Border between reality and the Outside, with a mighty Hand sculpted on the keystone of its main arch. Carter implies that Yog-Sothoth indwells there.

△ The 19th Baron Northam mounted an expedition to the Nameless City in 1921 and returned to London a shattered wreck, seemingly decades older.

△ A 1930 letter by Harry St.-John Philby recounts his conversation with an old man in Yemen who had seen Irem in the al-Dahna desert in central Saudi Arabia, and worshiped there at underground shrines of Nug and Yeb.

△ Philby's son Kim may have compromised a PISCES mission (Operation CALDERA) to the Wabar/Irem site in 1948.

Kadath

The Pnakotic manuscripts describe "Kadath in the Cold Waste" as "beyond Leng" and as the "home of the gods of Earth." Classical and medieval authors placed it either in the icy mountains of inner Asia or in the Dreamlands. It is mystically connected to the sacred mountains Hatheg-Kla and Ngranek (most likely Nanga Ranik, in the Hindu Kush), which serve as "pillars to Heaven" in Pnakotic lore and the theosophy of Randolph Carter, respectively, much like the Mount Meru of Hindi mythology.

△ Pánfilio de Zamacona mentions "the mountain Kadath" as being "near the South Pole" in his *Narrative Concerning the Subterranean World* (c. 1545).

△ Geologist William Dyer speculated that the impossibly high mountain range he observed in the interior of Wilkes Land on the 1930 Miskatonic Antarctic Expedition might have been the origin of the myth of Kadath. In this context the *Necronomicon*'s mention of the "ice desert of the South," where the seal of the Old Ones is engraved, may likewise refer to Antarctic Kadath.

△ Thomas Danforth, a survivor of that expedition, identified the primordial city of the Elder Things itself as Kadath, the "home of the gods of earth."

△ The Karotechia may have established their Point 103 research station in Queen Maud Land in an attempt to locate Kadath on their own. The Point 103 complement disappeared in 1945 while looting an elder city.

△ Aided by Karotechia specialists, Argentine dictator Juan Peron attempted to reactivate Point 103 in 1952. In April, DELTA GREEN agents (and a company of Army paratroopers) eliminated the Karotechia explorers and their Argentine escort force. After a deadly firefight on the site, only a handful of U.S. paratroopers survived to seal the excavations with high explosives. The program reported the American dead as killed-in-action in Korea.

△ In December 1957, the Second Soviet Antarctic Expedition established Vostok Station 290 km from the coordinates for the Elder Thing city at Kadath given by Dyer's report.

△ In 1958, the Third Soviet Expedition discovered the Gamburtsev Mountains, a range the size of the Alps, buried 600 meters below the ice cap.

K'n-Yan

K'n-Yan, or Xinaián, is a subterranean realm filled with an eerie blue light located beneath Oklahoma, although (possibly hypergeometrical) entrances to it can be found in Vermont among other places. Below it is the red-litten cavern of Yoth, and below that, the black abyss of N'Kai.

Everything known about K'n-Yan comes from the *Narrative Concerning the Subterranean World* purportedly written by a Spanish conquistador, Pánfilio de Zamacona y Nuñez (1512-1545?). The ethnologist Z.L. Bishop published Zamacona's tale in 1930 after finding it buried in the so-called "Ghost Mound" near Hydro, Oklahoma, describing it as a 19th-century hoax or social satire.

Operation ADVANCE MAN in Oklahoma in August 1955 pitted DELTA GREEN agents against the Xinaián, and left 22 dead (including one agent) and three insane.

See the K'n-Yani (p. 242) for the inhabitants of the hidden city.

Leng

The "icy desert plateau" of Leng slides between Earth and other dimensions, including the Dreamlands. Its geographical location on (or tangent to) Earth varies by occult source.

△ In his *Unaussprechlichen Kulten* (1839), Von Junzt locates "inaccessible Leng" in Central (or "Inner") Asia.

△ The kingdom of Ling in Tibetan legend, and the traces of necrophagy in some Bön rites, may descend from Leng and its "corpse-eating cult," placing Leng in Tibet.

△ The common association of the Tcho-Tcho people with Leng argues for a possible connection with the "Lost City of Gelanggi" or Linggiu in Johor state, Malaysia.

△ William Dyer identified Leng as the central Antarctic plateau in his 1931 report.

△ Perhaps the last word on the topic belongs to Randolph Carter: "Men reached Leng from very different oceans."

The ruler of Leng is a monstrous high lama wearing a yellow silken robe and veil. He dwells in a windowless lamasery in the middle of a circle of crude (or aeon-eroded) monoliths. Leng's other landmark is the "Elder Pharos," a lighthouse that shoots a glowing blue beam up into the skies, attracting foolish wanderers both mundane and occult.

According to the *Necronomicon*, the lamas of Leng wear a winged hound as their soul-symbol. Despite this, occult lore seldom associates them with Nodens of the Hounds, but rather with Itla-shua, Hastur, Azathoth, or Nyarlathotep. Von Junzt even repeats rumors of a cult of Ghatanothoa on the plateau of Leng, possibly a holdover from its Lemurian-era golden age.

Lomar and Hyperborea

The arctic continent of Lomar rose during the Miocene Era. Initially peopled by the Voorii, a fur-bearing hominid species, after millennia of warfare it became the home of the first known human culture, Zobna, near the current North Pole. The humans pursued the Voorii south into lower Lomar (what would become northern North America) and Hyperborea (even then slowly glaciating into Greenland), founding the cities of Olathoë in Lomar and Commoriom in Hyperborea.

The Hyperboreans learned hypergeometric magic from their god Tsathoggua, and from the prehuman Pnakotic manuscripts they copied and utilized. Hyperborean sorcerers opened time gates into the warm, lush Miocene and built the Vault of Souls to imprison and weaken Itla-shua, creating a temperate (if temporary) paradise. Using their own set of Pnakotic fragments, the lords of Lomar mastered Yithian telepathy, sending their minds into other species and centuries. Their great foe was Rhan-Tegoth, who ruled to their west.

Eventually, Itla-shua had its revenge and buried both civilizations under the ice. The last remnant of Lomar, Olathoë fell to the anthropophagous Gnophkehs and to the humans who followed them.

△ A Puritan chronicle (c. 1700) mentions the "old Tribes of Lamah, who dwelt under the Great Bear, and were antiently destroy'd for their wickedness." It implies they could control or contain "Ossadagowah."

△ In 1936, the Royal Canadian Mounted Police discovered stone ruins 260 km south of Baker Lake, Northwest Territories. Before the site could be analyzed, a band of Eskimo angakok shamans destroyed the ruins they called "Lamah."

△ DELTA GREEN assets at Thule Air Base in Greenland (and in the NRO) regularly examine overflight IMINT for signs of Hyperborean ruins exposed by melting ice. The program maintains similar watch lists for the much larger volume of Alaskan air photos and Lomarian ruins.

Pnakotis and Thule

After a series of wars against the invisible, polypous Muuruup, the Great Race eventually sorted itself into four fascist-socialist megastates, each centered on a large campus city and its Great Library.

Following their Cretaceous-era defeat by the Muuruup, the Yithians impelled (and perhaps forcibly evolved) a race of hominid white apes to construct an immense stone structure near Itoko in the Congo. The Yithians designed this African complex to keep the Muuruup in check while terrestrial life evolved the Yithians' new coleopteran hosts.

△ In 1935, the Miskatonic Geological Australian Expedition uncovered one of those cities near Pilbarra in Western Australia, dubbing it Pnakotis after the Pnakotic manuscripts thought to have originated there.

△ In 1942, SS-Standartenführer Stephan Andries leads Aktion PARSIFAL, the Karotechia investigation of a white proto-human creature. PARSIFAL eventually discovers the Itoko time colony, naming it "Thule" after the mystic homeland of the Aryan race.

△ In February 1943, Operation TARQUIN destroyed the Great Library at Pnakotis to keep knowledge of the future out of enemy hands.

△ In March 1943, Dr. Thomas Arnold of DELTA GREEN prevents an attempt to destroy the Itoko complex but obliterates any Yithian records at the site (Operation KLINGSOR).

△ Some elements of DELTA GREEN Operation KURTZ encountered the white apes (p. 258), though not Itoko-Thule, in Fall 1964.

Yian-Ho

This primordial Lemurian (or Lengi) city in the mountains of western China (or of Sinkiang) is the Earthly reflection, or the true form, or the anchor, of the dream-city of Yian, "where the great river winds under the thousand bridges — where the gardens are sweet scented, and the air is filled with the music of silver bells."

Yian may also be a memetic construct built by the Yithians or the Kuen-Yuin (p. 294) and impressed onto human minds as a "back door" into the Dreamlands.

△ Chinese lore says the "Maker of Moons" Yue-Laou dwells in Yian-Ho, where he commands the sorcerous Kuen-Yuin cult and the hideous Xin (p. 259). Yue-Laou and the Kuen-Yuin are immortal; their emblem is a golden globe engraved with reptiles.

△ The Dutch sorcerer Claes van der Heyl reputedly entered Yian-Ho around 1570.

△ The magician Dirck van der Heyl may have opened a gateway to Yian-Ho in upstate New York around 1760, near the town of Chorazin.

△ Von Junzt's traveling companion Gottfried Mülder entered Yian-Ho in 1818, where he read the *Ghorl Nigral*.

△ In the 1880s, Colonel Franklyn Barris (U.S. Army, ret.) travels extensively in China, reportedly in search of Yian. In 1893, he joins the U.S. Secret Service; he disappears in 1896 while investigating the Kuen-Yuin.

△ Informants captured in the 1907 St. Bernard Parish raid claim that "deathless Chinamen" direct the cult of Cthulhu from the "mountains of China."

△ The Polish mystic Ossendowski (1922) describes the scarlet-robed Tchortcha guardians of Yian-Ho, and their "Song of Thirty Thousand Calamities."

△ P4 Lieutenant Lester Dean and 22 men disappeared into the wilds of Kansu province in February 1933 during Operation THIMBLE, attempting to locate Yian-Ho based on ARCHINT from Agua Verde in Nicaragua. In October 1934, Dean stumbled into a Yangtze valley village babbling about a secret city in the mountains. Committed to a madhouse in Hong Kong, he died in 1938 raving about "gray men from the future."

Other Dimensions

The mathematical and physical laws that govern most other dimensions eliminate humanity, removing us from their equations. Other species such as the Mi-Go are more robust, or less falsifiable. But in some cases some parts of us continue to hold some small value in those dimensional equations.

Sometimes those dimensions merely alter and distort our senses, in dreams or visions or hallucinations. Sometimes, the laws and equations there shift us to more smoothly fit their math, or transfer us into a new column or multiply us by some unguessed-at constant to derive a new value. Those values rarely fit within our old three- and four-dimensional math, however. Some remainder is generally lost.

Based on the Operation BRISTOL catastrophe among others, DELTA GREEN treats other dimensions as toxic, nightmarish, and schizophrenogenic. To enter another dimension is to literally derange yourself. MAJESTIC, by contrast, treats other dimensions as potential weapons: to be understood, defended against... and harnessed. DELTA GREEN believes the MAJESTIC approach typifies the insanity caused by exposure to other dimensions.

Carcosa

Carcosa appears to be a sewer of human thought, drained off into the void by hydraulic attraction from the Great Old Ones. Poems, thoughts, and ideas incarnate themselves, usually in impossibly contradictory forms. Occultists refer to its ruler or guardian spirit or daemon as the King in Yellow, the Pallid Mask, or sometimes Hastur (p. 281).

Carcosa seems to act and react to human thought, to change and direct itself, harmonizing with human fear and disorder and chaos. These harmonic resonances prove extremely corrosive to sanity.

Carcosa envelops and digests humans like a slug, burning away their minds even as their mind changes the world. All that remains behind are their thoughts and perceptions, which sometimes echo in this backwater of reality forever.

Perceptions strongly associated with Carcosa for the last two centuries (and possibly longer) include:

△ Twin suns setting in the cloud-covered Lake of Hali

△ The moon passing in front of the city's towers

△ Black stars in a white sky

Occultists and others have located – and possibly encountered – Carcosa:

△ In primordial Mongolia under the rule of Mu; its coming created the Gobi Desert. It lent its name to the medieval Mongol city Khar Khota ("black city").

△ In the city of Carcassone, France; a cult of Tsathoggua may have opened a portal to Carcosa there during the Albigensian Crusade of the 13th century.

△ On the island La Certosa in the Lagoon of Venice.

- △ The residence of the British High Commissioner for Malaysia in Kuala Lumpur, called Carcosa House. Designed in 1896 by the architect A.B. Hubback, it is known to DELTA GREEN as the main PISCES station in Southeast Asia.
- △ Absorbing and incorporating the planet Yhtill somewhere in the constellation of Taurus, possibly orbiting Aldebaran.
- △ Anywhere the play *The King in Yellow* (suppressed in France in 1895) is read or performed.
- △ This includes Greenwich Village in 1955 under the name *Her Grey Song*; seventeen people died during the ensuing Operation BRISTOL, which involved a dimensional portal to Carcosa opening in New York.
- △ In the distant future as a ruined city of what is now California.

Dreamlands

DELTA GREEN's understanding of the Dreamlands derives equally from the theosophical fiction and poetry of the writer Randolph Carter, and from Carl Jung's theories of the "collective unconscious." Most of the dangerous tinkerers with this dimension have lurid paperback editions of both Carter and Jung on their shelves; the really dangerous ones have critical editions of both, usually heavily underlined and stolen from the campus library.

The Dreamlands comprise the dreams of all humanity – and of some other species, including cats and ghouls. Powerful "Dreamers" can create or design portions of the Dreamlands to their whim; artists and magicians likewise, although it's unclear where art, dreaming, and magic diverge. Some Dreamers are lucid dreamers or practitioners of Yoga Nidra or Tibetan Nyilam, while others retain no knowledge of their Dream selves when awake.

On the surface, the Dreamlands seem to be highly colored: like something out of the *Arabian Nights* or French Symbolist and Surrealist art. Beneath the surface, they are (like dreams themselves) often unutterably horrific. Cults and wizards of the Dreamlands sometimes demonstrate awareness of the waking world, doubtless to its detriment.

Entering the Dreamlands usually requires a specific dream of the "700 Steps of Deeper Slumber," depositing the dreamer in the Enchanted Wood. Powerful Dreamers can enter the dimension at other locations, or can dream themselves into it from specific places on Earth such as Kingsport, Massachusetts or Zagreb, Yugoslavia.

Physical entry to the Dreamlands may be possible through certain tangent realms: the lost city of Sarnath, the Plateau of Leng, and Mount Kadath exist both on Earth and in the Dreamlands. More horribly, French works on necromancy and lucid dreaming both mention tunnels from human graveyards to a vast Dreamlands boneyard, the Vale of Pnath, traveled by ghouls in vast numbers.

Hyperspaces

There is not just one "hyperspace," but many. Dozens, possibly millions, of potential solutions exist to the massive hypergeometries interpenetrating and overlapping our own Euclidean experience. And in a few of them, mankind can survive... after a fashion, and for a measurable amount of what we call time.

Translating a human into such a solution usually involves a hyper-geometric gate, a perception-altering ritual, or a brute-force technological application.

△ The European witch-cult learned enough of the mathematics underpinning existence to enter an "astral plane" full of violet light, folding space and time, and tangent to many other dimensions.

△ Between 1933 and 1939, Dr. Carl Upham published a number of papers on the mathematics of hyperspace taking certain constants and geometric relationships from "phases of magical lore transmitted from antiquity." Dr. Upham's work was classified retroactively when he was recruited into the Manhattan Project in 1942.

△ The physicist Crawford Tillinghast invented a resonator that allowed those exposed to its "T-radiation" to perceive higher dimensions, one of which he called "the Ultraviolet" or "the Beyond." The Ultraviolet hosts a viciously predatory ecology, which killed Tillinghast and two others in April 1920.

△ A Tillinghast resonator (code named MIRAGE III) installed on the *USS Eldridge* on 28 October 1943 shifted the destroyer into N-space (or null space), a featureless gray superdimension tangent to the Beyond.

△ The ONI investigation of the *Eldridge* incident, Project PUZZLE, involved DELTA GREEN-cleared physicists. The PUZZLE report is not even cleared for internal review until 1969, but MAJESTIC has gained access to it.

Inner Space

If position in space-time is relative to perception, as Einstein grudgingly admitted and quantum theory gingerly maintains, then altering perception potentially alters the perceiver's dimensionality. The so-called "Inner Space" opened up by hallucinogenic and perception-altering drugs begins as an overlay or bleed-through into normal space-time, later becoming a shared hallucination with culturally common symbolic features much like the Dreamlands, and quite likely connected to them somehow. Past that, the use of certain drugs, meditative states, and other stimuli such as the Ganzfeld solid-color effect opens gateways to other mentalities and other dimensions.

The CIA experiments with LSD between 1951 and 1973 under Project ARTICHOKE, later renamed MK-ULTRA, then MK-SEARCH in 1964. Their goal: develop a mind-control drug. DELTA GREEN (and possibly MAJESTIC via Project OUTLOOK) piggybacked on much of the MK-ULTRA material to explore those dimensions. Other DELTA GREEN operators enter Inner Space while operating undercover infiltrating hallucinogenic and entheogenic cults.

Other Worlds

The unnatural does not manifest solely on Earth, of course. Earth is only one world among trillions, all of them haunted. Everywhere in the universe is tangent to the horrors of Outside.

To Yuggoth and Beyond

The archives of occultists, visionaries, and UFO contactees burgeon with alien worlds often barely described: Yekub probes for planetary death with telepathic cubes, Shonhi and the triple-star Nyhon draw sages from many galaxies, Yaddith is home to the wise Nug-Soth and the burrowing bhole-worms, the living god-planet Nemesis rolls in deep space bearing the song of destruction. At the center of it all lies the court of the Daemon Sultan, blind and howling Azathoth.

Our own solar system shows the stigmata of the unnatural:

△ Mi-Go mine the dark side of the Moon.

△ Alien races have left cyclopean ruins on Mars.

△ In 1904, alienist Giles Fenton transcribed the dream-statement of the insane murderer Joseph Slater describing a race of insectile aliens on Callisto. Yithian records confirm Slater's account; they reached their cultural and philosophical apex six million years ago.

△ In 1884 Oskar Reichenbach proposed that the Earth once orbited Saturn, called the "sun star" in Chaldean records. Pnakotic and Hyperborean inscriptions depict Tsathoggua, at least, moving easily between the two worlds. Malevolent quasi-felines dwell in Saturn's Dreamland, implying a sapient race in the Saturnian system to dream.

△ Wind-fed intelligent fungi – possibly Mi-Go creations – inhabit the atmosphere of Neptune.

△ The Wilmarth report identifies Pluto with Yuggoth, the home (or local staging area) of the Mi-Go. Mi-Go camouflage or disinformation conceals Yuggoth's warm seas and metal bridges beneath Pluto's craters and nitrogen ice fields. The Mi-Go also extensively colonize and mine Pluto's moon Kynarth.

Other stars likewise:

△ Algol (Beta Persei), from the Arabic for "the Ghoul," represents a monstrous force in some upstate New York cults, as well as to peoples such as the ancient Greeks (who called it *Gorgo*) and Chinese (who called it *Dà Líng*, "the Mausoleum").

△ The Pnakotic manuscripts identify the double planet orbiting Arcturus (Alpha Boötis) as Kythamil. A cult of Tsathoggua's black, plastic worshippers flew to Hyperborea from Kythamil, perhaps explaining why the Greenland Eskimos call Arcturus *Sivulliik* ("the First Ones").

△ Occult lore connects Aldebaran (Alpha Tauri) and the "mystery of the Hyades" to Hastur. Mystics allude to the Hyades as the location for the enigmatic Great Library, possibly a backup archive left by the Yithians.

△ According to prophecy, Nyarlathotep will "come down from the world of Seven Suns." This may refer to the Pleiades or Ursa Major.

DELTA GREEN in Space

DELTA GREEN agents might well find themselves climbing the Plateau of Leng, or drawn into Carcosa, but how likely are interplanetary adventures going to be for federal employees? Even NASA employees go no farther than the Moon – unless MAJESTIC has an entire covert space program it has failed to mention.

Other worlds in **Fall of DELTA GREEN** games might never be more than dropped names and cosmic elements found in cult rituals, or in the rants of deranged astrophysicists. Or in more mundane circumstances yet:

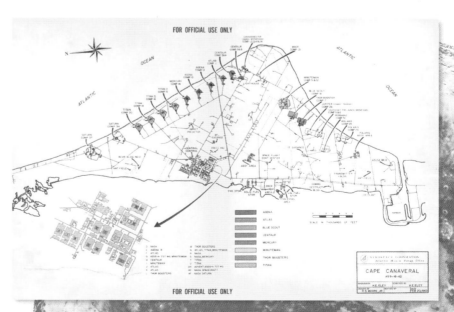

217

a seemingly straightforward operation against white slavers or stock fraudsters suddenly turns unnerving when a tattoo or faded file tab depicts or labels Kynarth on the Rim. Slightly more intense: if the traffickers insist that they shipped girls to Kynarth (although the odometer shows they never left the tri-state area) or the boiler-room con artists swear they picked their stocks by consulting an ephemeris for the non-existent planet.

Now put an unknown mineral in the truck's tire treads, or open a banker's box to reveal a crumbling 1881 *Ephemeris of Kynarth* – that nonetheless tracks Project OVERVIEW research into a new trans-Neptunian planet. The next step is, of course, off world: the Agents actually walk in their targets' tracks, onto the surface of an alien and inimical planet. The key here is to combine as much scientific realism as you can with, to quote Lovecraft's words on interplanetary fiction, "stark outrageous monstrousness." Be prepared with red- or blue-shifted stars, or weird gravity effects, or entirely unknowable skies.

If possible, even if the cultists call it Shargoth or The World of Violet Skies, give your world a horribly boring name from a star catalog: a string of numerals followed by the genitive for a constellation: e.g., 4436 Persei. This heightens the contrast with its malevolent abnormality. An alien world should feel entirely different from even Leng or Carcosa – humans did not evolve there, and do not belong there, and "there" tells them so on every wavelength they can perceive and on many that humans can't.

Keep the encounter short: if cosmic rays or the toluene compounds in the atmosphere don't kill the Agents in minutes, the gateway is closing or the alien natives are coming, or both. There should not be enough time for the Agents to do everything they want to do, or for the players to get used to the world. They should carry damage and terror back to Earth, and be haunted for months or years by their steps into the literally alien.

Creating and Customizing Places

The advantage to Handlers of Lovecraft's teasing uncertainty about locations like Kadath and Leng is that you can put them almost anywhere: maybe there's a mist-shrouded peak in the Andes named Cadáta Desconocida, or a high and inhospitable Lang County in Idaho. This works even better if your Agents have already entered Leng in Malaya, or seen Kadath in dreams.

Lovecraft's sleight-of-hand shifting of Sarnath from prehistory to Dreamland and back again accomplishes the same thing: if the Agents wander into Sarnath from a mission in the Tigris swamps, did they travel in time or in dreams or both? Uncertainty is one key to Lovecraftian horror: the questions "Where are we?" and "When are we?" always bring up not just the specific awful answer but even worse questions like "Were we always here and just not know it?" and perhaps just: "Are we?" Keep boundaries fluid, even as you drive specific horrors into the Agents' lives and the players' minds.

Devil's Island is in the Details

Because the other key to Lovecraftian horror, uncannily enough, is as many specific, realistic – ideally actually researched – details as you can manage. Its technothriller heritage positions **The Fall of DELTA GREEN** ideally for lots of map coordinates, "115 klicks north-northwest of the firebase," falling barometric pressure, Archulean arrowheads, and so on.

Don't worry about pinning yourself down: two absolutely reliable details that totally contradict each other produce just as much uncertainty as "you got lost in the fog" does. Lovecraft maintained that no story could truly terrify unless it was produced with the "care and verisimilitude of an actual hoax." Every detail that can be, should be accurate and grounded in the real world: costumes of the natives, what the high altitude feels like, anthropological or geological trivia, and anything else an hour or so with Google can turn up.

Into the Mood

Blending uncertainty and detail gives you the outline of the setting, or at least of the doorway the Agents walked through to get there. But past the outline comes the actual place, and its job in the scenario. An unnatural place serves two functions at the table: to convey mood, and perhaps even to drive the story.

The first task argues for starting with Lovecraft where you can. By dropping a name like "Leng" into the dialogue, or by pointing the team's Huey into the Arabian desert and slowly revealing a sand-covered

ruin, you channel the tone and mood Lovecraft has already established directly into your game. That ability to piggyback on pre-existing horror is the best reason to customize a pre-existing unnatural location rather than invent a new one.

New Lands From Old

You needn't restrict yourself to Lovecraft's imaginary lands. Lovecraft certainly didn't, adapting such legends as Irem, the hollow earth, Atlantis, and Mu for his specific story-hoaxes, adding them to his gazetteer alongside fictional places mapped by Robert W. Chambers, Robert E. Howard, and Clark Ashton Smith. Even if the pre-existing material is as jejune as the theosophists' Mu, the contrast between that anodyne legend and the horrific events you unveil at the table adds depth and resonance to the adventure. Think of it as the equivalent of taking the plastic wolf mask off the serial killer.

The Feel of Nowhere

Don't worry about your version of Lomar contradicting a detail in Lovecraft: he did that himself, too. (Was Lomar destroyed by the "squat, yellow Inutos" or the "hairy cannibal Gnophkehs"?) Instead, concentrate on the mood your version of Lomar creates or intensifies: cosmic deep time, terror of identity loss, civilizational disintegration, something else, or all of the above?

Begin driving tone with the landscape and weather of your weird place, just like the Gothics that Lovecraft modernized do. Then start creeping the players out with shifts of perception, unnatural spoor and phenomena, or, sure, a Tcho-Tcho ambush. Almost any weird location can trigger a hallucination (or is it a brief transference in space-time?) of its true cosmic colors for the Agent who wanders off the path or foolishly has the lowest Stability.

This pays dividends when you recuperate the cosmic horror in seemingly mundane occurrences: a little more violet in a rainbow, or a cave mouth that looks too much like the long-vanished temple guardian for comfort.

New Dimensions

Other dimensions, from storied Carcosa to a new plane you just invented, depend even more fully on mood, since that's often all they have. A new dimension doesn't need to keep to a single mood any more than Leng needs to stay in one time zone; re-read Lovecraft's "Dreams in the Witch-House" and note the changes he rings on Gilman's astral plane. But unless chaotic input is itself the intended mood of your dimension, changing tones and horror palettes too much risks untethering the player from the story: you don't have the geographical hoax on which to anchor them.

Here Be Narrative

How does your imaginary place serve the story? In addition to presenting terror and wonder in its mood and incident, it should also drive the narrative: something in the story can't happen without that place. The place is the goal of the antagonist, or holds a crucial clue for the protagonist Agents, or provides the culmination of the mood and tone developed in the "hoaxed" but (mostly) natural and material world.

Thus, you have to build the location into the clues and incidents that point the Agents there; another reason to use a "pre-built-in" location out of Lovecraft or Chambers, as those links already exist. For a location of your own invention, of course, you can custom-build those links for your current adventure – and then

come back to that location in another operation to both reinforce and batten off them.

Escape From A-Lao-Zar

Every so often, of course, the weird location begins the story: the narrative then becomes "How do we escape this baleful place/ dimension/nightmare?" For this to work, you have to have a very deep bench of terrors and dangers to drive the Agents forward and (hopefully) outward to the transient safety of Euclidean space-time.

Again, a location with multiple signifiers, ideally one developed over several stories, works better for the escape story than a completely arbitrary mystery spot. Hyperborea, Carcosa, or Leng symbolically outweigh the relatively unmapped K'n-Yan or Shaggai, or just plain have more weird stuff you can rip off from earlier works.

Discovering the Undiscovered Country

So after all that, if you are bound and determined to invent a new unnatural place, what should you do? First, come up with a name that you can work seamlessly into your hoax: if you're planning an operation in the Philippines, for example, tool around the Google map of Luzon or Mindanao and see if you spot a name redolent (or almost redolent) with Yog-Sothothery. Or, if you're inventing a new dimension, pick a name that sounds plausible in the mouth of an occultist or theoretical physicist or whoever the Agents' unfortunate (or malign) tour guide will be.

Establish your location's mood and tone, and come up with three or four reliably creepy manifestations, phenomena, or landmarks to reinforce them. Invent at least one story that requires your new location to work – even if you just mean to drop this uncanny planet or lost city into a ritual, it never hurts to have something deeper and more developed to draw on for imagery.

Once you've seeded your new location into the backdrop of one operation, you can work on building up the hoax surrounding it, and laying pipe for another brush with its malign presence.

Unwelcome Tenants

Besides "what does it feel like" and "how does it reveal itself," the final big question about an unnatural location is "who or What dwells there?" Lovecraft's suggestive canvas lets you put almost anything in Leng, as long as it feels desolate and cold. Other settings such as Pnakotis and Yuggoth are more constrained, or at least more characteristic of one or another alien or god.

The question of inhabitants also goes to the role of the location in the story: the patron deity or hideous indigenes have their own goals and agendas, ones almost certainly in conflict with those of the Agents. The setting may be one of their weapons in achieving such a goal, or just the initial battlespace in which DELTA GREEN discovers the eons-long war.

Whoever or whatever else lurks there, it almost certainly knows the dimension or planet or plateau better than the Agents. Even if they don't urgently need to escape Leng, they almost certainly have to escape the spectral pursuer behind them.

Alien Intelligences

Monstrous entities pollute our world, clinging to it, buried beneath it, or plotting to rule it. Some of them are extra-terrestrial, or not even native to this dimension. Some were created by mightier entities, some have chosen to serve them, and still others remain independent or unaware of the cosmic monstrosities that blight the universe.

DELTA GREEN knows a few of them, some of them even by their correct names. But as Handler, you should do everything in your power to create that confusion among your players! Never give a clear enough description that a veteran player recognizes the threat. Never use a name that players can recognize from prior games or fiction. Change the sensory impressions that these entities create. Change their abilities and weaknesses if you must. Familiarity kills the sense of cosmic weirdness that this game is meant to evoke. Never let players think that they know exactly what looms before their terrified Agents.

General Rules for Creatures

Unnatural creatures may not follow the rules of physics, but they follow the rules of GUMSHOE. They have General Abilities, spend and roll to succeed at tests and contests (such as eviscerating the Agents), and so on.

However, they are almost without exception more powerful than humans, so they can do more damage and suffer less.

The Handler should not tie herself down to a given portrayal of a creature: one tribe of ghouls might be able to outrun a Jeep, while another can only run down a fleeing human on foot. In such matters, the dramatic needs of the adventure take priority. This includes rewarding player effort; if the Agents spend Drive points in a panic and roll well to escape the ghouls, their Jeep puts on a sudden burst of speed and leaves the slavering pursuers behind. Of course, it's likely to overheat and stall out if they try that again...

Ability Names

Most of the unnatural creatures have acidic ichor, razor-sharp talons, or mouthfuls of cutting teeth, making "Unarmed Combat" something of a misnomer; thus, most creatures have an equivalent Fighting ability instead. Those that use weapons also have Melee Weapons ability ratings or, occasionally, an equivalent to Firearms: Archery for Tcho-Tcho, for example (which includes blowguns), or Energy Weapons for the Mi-Go.

Alien Hypergeometry

Some alien creatures fuel their strange powers with Health or Athletics, translating their terrestrial manifestation into unearthly energies.

Others actually use hypergeometric formulae, although the difference in play is minimal: their casting time is much shorter than humans can manage, unless the specific scenario calls for the Mi-Go to take all night on a certain ritual.

Unless the description explicitly says differently, assume that alien powers take only one round to use, and that hypergeometric formulae take only a few minutes. Unlike human sorcerers, most alien creatures can perform rituals or cast formulae in combat, and unless noted otherwise can do so in 1d6 rounds.

Alien entities often cast hypergeometric rituals at a lower Cost than humans pay, indicated in parentheses.

Psionic Attacks

Many alien creature attacks use the GMC Psionics attack rules from p. 199, even if they are not technically psychic powers. Use these rules if the attack mostly or entirely affects the Agent's mind or perceptions, is mostly non-physical, or if the attack mode is especially injurious to the Agent's mental health.

To recap the rules:

△ The creature spends at least 2 points from its psionic attack ability.

△ The Handler rolls a die and adds the result to the spend.

△ If her total result (roll plus spend) is greater than 4, the attack occurs; the Handler describes what the Agent perceives about the attack: "You feel cold" or "The walls seem to fold in on you."

△ If the Agent decides to resist, he makes a Stability test at a Difficulty equal to the creature's total result.

△ If he fails the test or does not resist (an effective roll of 0), the attack succeeds, with results as described in the individual creature or power description.

Ability Pool Refreshment

Creatures refresh ability pool points according to how often they appear. A creature that is not encountered for 24 hours or more may replenish all of its ability pools, with the exception of Health, which it recovers at the rate of 1d6 points per day.

If the Agents encounter a creature later on in the same day, such as by tracking it to its lair, it can refresh all of its ability pools to a maximum of *half* their total rating, again with the exception of Health, which it cannot refresh at all.

Creatures that have special rules for recovering Health, such as regenerating creatures, follow their own rules rather than those given here.

Health Loss

To save the Handler extra bookkeeping, creatures die, or return to their home dimension, or disintegrate, or whatever, when their Health is reduced below 0. Some creatures have exceptions in their own rule text, and the Handler can always keep monstrous entities alive until they reach Health -12 if she thinks it dramatically necessary.

Monstrous Grappling

Many creatures grab their prey with tentacles, talons, or similar extrusions. Use these general rules for monstrous grappling attacks:

△ The creature must spend at least 2 points from Fighting or another appropriate attack ability.

△ The Handler rolls a die and adds the result to the spend.

△ If her total result (roll plus spend) is greater than the target's Hit Threshold, the grappling attack hits.

△ The target is grappled. The creature's Hit Threshold against the target drops by -1; the target's Hit Threshold drops by -2. The grapple may do damage; if so, further squeezing or grappling attacks automatically hit the target.

△ On his turn, the target may either try to break free or attack if the Handler rules he has a potentially usable weapon.

△ To attack, the grappled target must spend 2 Athletics (or more for extremely strong creatures) to writhe into position. This spend does not add to the attack roll.

△ To break free, the target must make a Difficulty 5 player-facing Athletics test; the creature may spend Athletics or Fighting to increase the Difficulty by +1 for every 2 points spent.

△ Some creatures require two (or more!) consecutive successful escape tests to break free from.

Humans cannot use these rules, although humanoid creatures such as ghouls or Deep Ones might if the Handler so chooses.

Special Defenses

Some creatures have more than rugose hide and squamous armor to protect them from human wrath.

Out-of-Phase

Entities of this kind weave in and out of our physical space, moment to moment. Only attacks that roll an odd number hit this type of entity. Attacks that roll an even result simply pass through it as if it were Transcendent.

Reduced Lethality

Human (and conventional terrestrial) Lethality has less effect on some unnatural creatures, as denoted at the end of the Armor entry by a negative Lethality rating, e.g., [L-1]. Some natural, but enormous, creatures also gain reduced Lethality thanks to sheer bulk: an M16 spray is unlikely to kill a blue whale.

The Handler subtracts the given number from the Lethality of the attack. For example, a creature with [L-2] treats L3 attacks as L1. This approach holds for more complex Lethality ratings, too: a creature with [L-2] treats an L3*H attack as L1*H. When L reaches 0 – e.g., if a creature with [L-1] is attacked by a normally L1 attack – treat the attack as a regular attack inflicting d+5 damage. A normally L1* or L1H attack reduces an [L-1] creature to Seriously Wounded or Hurt on a result of 1, rather than killing it, while an [L-2] or tougher creature would take d+5 from such a roll. The creature's Armor may reduce this further.

A black winged one has [L-1] so Sanchez' M16A1 does only d+5 damage even on full auto. He rocks and rolls anyway, and rolls a 3, for a total of 8. The creature's carapace (Armor -2) further reduces the damage to 6. Sanchez' tossed grenade (normally L1) renders the thing Seriously Wounded if he rolls a 1, but does only d+5 damage on any other result, again reduced by its armor.*

Resilient

Entities of this kind are made of non-terrene matter, have advanced and resistant biologies, or are inured to dimensions that inflict more punishment than human technology can unleash. On a Resilient target, physical attacks do the minimum possible damage. Resilient creatures often also have Reduced Lethality.

A creature listed as Resilient (type) such as Resilient (bullets) or Resilient (electricity) takes minimum damage from that specific attack type.

Transcendent

Entities of this kind are immune to broad categories of attack. Transcendent (fire) would mean the entity would suffer no damage from fire or flame. The Handler makes the final call as to what this defense does or does not cover.

Some beings are Transcendent (matter) or Transcendent (energy) or entirely Transcendent. Unless specifically mentioned, all creatures are vulnerable to hypergeometric formulae and rituals.

Stability Loss

This entry indicates the *additional* Stability loss (as a modifier to the standard Stability loss) to the Agents caused by sighting, fighting, or witnessing the attacks of the creature in question.

Investigation and Creatures

Each creature has an Investigation section describing some possible clues – either to its approach or to its traces – the Handler can provide the

Agents. These clues are organized by the likely abilities that would uncover them. (Other abilities that might provide the same clue are in parentheses.) Even more than usual, the Handler should change these descriptions around to suit herself. That said, here's where she might start.

NOW IN CINEVISION

By and large, the creatures in *Fall of DELTA GREEN* are more powerful than their equivalents in *Trail of Cthulhu*. This is because the *Delta Green RPG* generally gives its monsters higher attack skills and statistics than *Call of Cthulhu* does, and because the Agents likely have access to heavier weapons than do *Trail of Cthulhu* Investigators.

Feel free to substitute the *Trail of Cthulhu* values if you prefer a less dangerous game.

If you want to use a *Trail of Cthulhu* monster not appearing here at the higher danger level, increase its Athletics by around two-thirds, and its Fighting (Scuffling) and Health by around half.

Avatar of the Headless One

In 1944, DELTA GREEN agents accompanying the liberation of Provence encountered a bloated, headless monstrosity in the old medieval tower above the town of Sanary-sur-Mer. Slavering mouths opening in the palms of its hands, it eviscerated three men before sustained machine-gun fire knocked it over and grenades finished it off. Before the five surviving agents could report the encounter more fully, they were dead – apparently shot by each other to stop a burgeoning possession. The ranking NCO, Sergeant Dov Goldstein, killed himself and burned most of the squad's equipment and records upon returning to the OSS base in Aix.

The program has had further encounters with the Headless One since then, most notably in 1955 when it apparently possessed a DELTA GREEN researcher in the Library of Congress. She, too, transformed into the hulking, acephalic, and priapic image of the god. Despite the apparent hazards involved in knowing too much about the entity, analysts have pieced hints together from von Junzt, Alsophocus, and other scholars of the unnatural. For more details on this headless god, see The Headless One, p. 275.

Headless One Avatar

Abilities: Athletics 13, Fighting 20, Health 24

Hypergeometry: 13; many rituals including Call Forth Those From Outside and all rituals related to the Headless One.

Hit Threshold: 3 (huge)

Alertness Modifier: +3 (only for those in a state of self-abasing sin or those who seek or know the Headless One)

Stealth Modifier: -2 (enormous and glowing)

Attack: biting hands (d-1 unhealing), hurl and smash (L1H); the Avatar may either hurl and smash or attack once per round with each hand

Armor: Resilient (metals, including bullets)

Stability Loss: +1

Biting Hands: The Avatar has biting, slavering mouths in its hands. The damage they do cannot be healed or refreshed.

Human Form: In its human suit, the Avatar merely seems neurotic and flabby. Its abilities are those of its host. It can change between shapes at will, but its growth into gigantic Avatar form usually destroys its human host's clothing.

Hurl and Smash: With a successful Fighting attack, the Avatar can pick up a target and hurl it up to 20 yards away, usually into the worst or most painful place or object around.

Invasive Name: The Avatar can transmit the name of the Headless One by skin contact. (If it touches a victim by Fighting, this touch does not deliver a biting hands attack.) Treat this as a psionic attack (p. 221) using Hypergeometry. Those who learn the name of the Headless One (from this attack, or by reading even a page of his scriptures) lose 1 Sanity immediately and receive an Addiction (p. 123) to pornography and sexual stimulation; within 1d6 x Sanity hours they become potential hosts of the Avatar.

Investigation

Forensics: One man's back was simply broken, possibly due to impact against the tree. The other has large bite marks on his left cheek, ribcage, right armpit and forearm, and groin. Death was due to shock and blood loss. The bite marks look human, although I'm not sure how the biter could orient his head for some of them.

Sense Trouble: You see a shadow cast on the windowpane – looks like someone weirdly hunched over with his arms akimbo.

Streetwise: We've trailed this guy to the storefront of a "book and film society" that provides very specific pornography to a justifiably furtive clientele.

Black Winged Ones

These semi-insectile, semi-humanoid entities carry out murder at the behest of Cthulhu or Its cult masters.

Their true appearance is a mystery; their outer form seemingly drinks light or at least sheds perception like an oil slick. The few surviving witnesses don't generally mention eyes or even number of limbs, but they all mention the black wings. Some carry knives or scimitars, or make use of bayonets or razors found nearby.

When not carrying out abductions, killings, and ritual mutilations for a cult, the black winged ones dwell in the closest waste place: a still lake in the bayou, a rocky outcrop in the desert, an abandoned warehouse in the city's worst neighborhood. Three or five usually service any given cult; a solitary madman makes do with a single black winged one. No DELTA GREEN agent has ever seen more than five in one place, or perhaps none have survived to report the sighting.

Black Winged One

Abilities (on land/in air): Athletics 8/12, Fighting 8/12, Health 9, Melee Weapons 6/12

Hypergeometry: 2-3; only formulae connected with Cthulhu or their own race (Cost 3).

Hit Threshold: 4/5

Alertness Modifier: +1

Stealth Modifier: +0/+1

Attack: improvised weapon or claw (d+1), neck snap or killing pressure-point blow (L1); a Black Winged One can make two weapon/claw attacks or one neck snap attack per round.

Armor: -2 vs. any (inhuman carapace) [L-1]

Stability Loss: +0

Investigation

Forensics: The victim died instantly of a snapped neck; the various mutilations were all done post-mortem. The cuts are clean and sure, but seemingly random: a psychopath with no knowledge of human anatomy, perhaps.

Intimidation: Even after everything you've threatened to do, he refuses to name the cult meeting place or identify the high priest, only the next target. You've done this enough to know that he absolutely fears the threat of death by his cult, and that he's seen it carried out. *1-point spend:* When he names the next target, he pretends he's broken – but you can tell he expects you to die when you try to save her. (Interrogation)

Sense Trouble: You have an overpowering sense of déjà vu: You dreamed of doing exactly this activity, in exactly this spot, just before you died.

Ai-Apa

DELTA GREEN has encountered this black winged creature many times, most often as the servant (or nightmarish steed) of some sorcerer. The name comes from the Peruvian Mochica (meaning "decapitator"). The creatures flock in high mountainous regions, and according to occult lore, travel through interstellar space. Its less humanoid appearance recalls something not unlike an ant or a vulture.

Their speed has been reported as anywhere from 45 to 600 mph; they may fly partially through hyperspace rather than exclusively through the terrestrial atmosphere.

Ai-Apa

Abilities (on land/in air or space): Athletics 6/20, Fighting 8/13, Health 13

Hypergeometry: possibly as high as 5-9; the alpha of a flock can summon more ai-apa or create hyperspace gates (Cost 3).

Hit Threshold: 4

Alertness Modifier: +1

Stealth Modifier: +0/+1

Attack: claw (d+1), bite (L1)

Armor: -2 vs. any (fur and hide, absence of vitals) [L-1]

Stability Loss: +1

Grasp: The ai-apa can seize a foe in its claws (d-1 damage) using *Monstrous Grappling* (p. 222). The target can struggle free – but of course, the ai-apa can

simultaneously fly thousands of feet into the air during the round.

Investigation

Forensics: The body is slashed and torn almost to rags, and the blood spatter pattern indicates it was carried around the area *during* the struggle. The head was severed from the body, as though snipped off with immense, dull shears.

Outdoorsman: The jungle brush around the tent has been beaten down, as if by very large wings. From the pattern of dead foliage – killed as if by a sudden frost, unlikely in Vietnam – the wings were roughly bat-like. (Notice)

Sense Trouble: A waft of icy air seems to rush past you, and an astringent smell like rotting juniper stings your nostrils.

Colour Out of Space

Colours are immaterial beings of unknown origin, using our dimension as a nesting ground. A larval Colour falls to Earth inside a meteorite and germinates, splitting its metallic shell and nestling into the ecosystem as coruscating incandescence matching nothing in the Earthly spectrum.

It is not a gas or plasma, but an insubstantial light. (That said, if its light touches human flesh, it feels like a brush of slimy vapor.) Bright light inhibits a Colour. It spends daylight hours in dark, cool hideaways, preferably underwater: cisterns, wells, lakes, reservoirs, and oceans all are suitable. If it moves, it resembles nothing so much as a weird moonbeam pouring across the ground, moving anywhere any light whatsoever can go, occasionally flashing into eye-blink flight.

As the Colour pupates, it filters into the local vegetation; plants grow unnaturally, glisten oddly, and taste bitter. Then insects and animals are born deformed, their eyes glowing with the Colour. At night, all plant life shines with it, twisting and writhing as in a strong wind. As it grows, the Colour feeds. Animals and humans deteriorate mentally and physically, then die.

When it has enough energy, it departs the planet for space and adulthood, leaving a ruined, barren heath 5 to 20 acres (depending on the area's initial richness) in extent. And possibly another larva...

Colour Out of Space

Abilities: Fighting 1-30, Health 1-30

Hit Threshold: N/A

Stealth Modifier: +2

Armor: Transcendent (material attacks, fire, electricity)

Stability Loss: +0 to see a Colour; +1 to see the victim of a Colour.

Drain: The Colour gains 1 point of Health and of Fighting each month for the first year it drains a living ecosystem, and 2 points of each per month thereafter. At Fighting 20, it can melt iron by spending 2 Fighting. When it reaches 30 Health points, it departs.

Iridescent Attack: When the Colour reaches Fighting 12 it can "attack" as a floating globe of light once per night. Treat this as a psionic attack (p. 221); damage is the Colour's margin of success, which it can take from the target's Health or Stability or a combination. The target drops unconscious. It gains 1 Health and 1 Fighting if the target dies. If its attack fails, it returns to its nesting spot until the next sundown.

Malaise: Someone living in the area a Colour drains automatically loses 1 rating point of Stability and Health each month of residence there, as their mind weakens and their body erodes. They must also make a 2-point Stability test to leave after the first night.

Investigation

Chemistry: Under spectroscopic analysis, samples from the meteor display bands in unknown spectra, indicating very strange, possibly transuranic, chemical makeup. They are not volatile at any temperature, but are very ductile. An acid-solvent test reveals Widmanstätten lines similar to meteoric iron.

Forensics: The flesh is dry, brittle, scaly, and sunken in, giving off noisome odors upon dissection. The fat is congealed and bloated, with strange iridescent effects. Parts of the body are shriveled or compressed disproportionately, but there is no sign of pressure damage or bruising. The eyes bulge, with high air pressure distending the orbits; the soft parts of the face are likewise distended. All parts of the body are gray or grayish.

Physics: This looks like nothing so much as radiation poisoning, but this many rads should have cooked us all already. (Medicine)

Sense Trouble: That reflection is an odd color...

Deep Ones

The amphibious species known as the Deep Ones moves with alarming speed on land, and with predatory grace and power under water. Their teeth and claws are razor-sharp, and their skin combines scales with a thick subdermal layer for efficient protection against injury and cold. Ducts and nictitating membranes keep their bulging, unblinking, black eyes moist.

Chinless, hunched, batrachian humanoids with fish-like gills, they sport webbing and talons on their hands and feet. Ridges of scales along the spine and joints erupt from gray-green, scaly skin. They are at least as intelligent as the average human, and the oldest Deep Ones far more so than the greatest primate minds. They dwell in cities on the continental shelves, and (until DELTA GREEN began its worldwide campaign against them) in hybrid colonies along the coasts.

For at least the last 100,000 years they have preyed on humans as breeding stock, sacrificial victims, and food. Deep Ones interbreed with humans, creating hybrids such as the folk of Innsmouth. Innsmouth's "Esoteric Order of Dagon" also provided them with cultists and victims, drawn in (as are so many Deep One servants) by the promise of gold, rich fisheries, and immortality.

Deep Ones are effectively immortal unless killed violently, a common occurrence within their own society. Their response to human meddling or activity of any kind is likely to be similarly violent and lethal. Deep One and human aesthetics are not completely separate: Deep One art (usually metalwork or jewelry) captivates and intrigues some human artists, even those without Deep One hybrid ancestry.

Deep One Hybrids

Humans with Deep One lineage but not yet fully metamorphosed into Deep One form act as agents, procurers, and cultists on land. They use normal human game statistics. An Agent who has faced hybrids before can detect the "Deep One taint" or "Innsmouth look" with a 1-point HUMINT spend or success on a Difficulty 6 test of Sense Trouble (depending on the scene type).

Hybrids refresh 3 pool points of Athletics or Unarmed Combat per scene after being submerged in seawater; they have Contest Advantage (p. 086) underwater against normal humans. Hybrids farther along in their transformation may suffer Athletics penalties on land as their hopping, shuffling gait slows them down.

Many Deep One hybrids, of course, are unwitting carriers of the Deep One gene. Some might even be unwitting double agents inside DELTA GREEN, slipping through the inevitable holes in the genealogical screening.

Lesser Deep One

Abilities (on land/in water): Athletics 8/12, Fighting 10/15, Health 9, Melee Weapons 6/4, Speargun 3

Hypergeometry: 7; for them, most spells connected with Cthulhu or their own race have a Cost of 3.

Hit Threshold: 4/5

Alertness Modifier: +0/+1

Stealth Modifier: +0/+1

Attack: claw or bite (d+1), trident (d+1), speargun (d+1), thrown harpoon (d+2; up to Near range)

Armor: -1 vs. any (scales and skin)

Stability Loss: +0

Frog-like Leap: Deep Ones can leap up to 10' vertically and 20' horizontally for 2 Athletics points.

Investigation

Biology: These frogs are breeding far out of season. Something has completely disrupted their natural cycle, some toxic taint or huge predatory pressure. (Survival)

Forensics: The neck is neatly slashed by four parallel wounds, like razor blades mounted on a frame of some kind. There are similar four-wound patterns on his arm, and on his leg, which was twisted nearly backwards.

HUMINT: This man doesn't sweat. Or blink.

Plan Silent, Plan Deep

DELTA GREEN believes that the United States (and perhaps Britain and the Soviet Union) is at war with an underwater civilization whose attempt to infiltrate America the program thwarted at Innsmouth in 1928. This is, at best, only slightly true.

Innsmouth was only the Deep Ones' second-largest colony in North America: DELTA GREEN does not even suspect the existence of Al'hu Ai, off the shore of Black Cod Island in southern Alaska. The Black Cod hybrids (who superficially resemble the Haida Indians they claim to be) maintain the worship of Cthulhu and the enormous progenitor Deep One Shaurash-Ho, who they call He-Who-Swims-With-Corpses.

The Deep Ones have already sunk their talons deep into the American establishment through the Exalted Circle cult (p. 301), just as they had in Japan through the Black Ocean Society (p. 285). Most Deep One "planning" and "infiltration" comes from such cults and their hybrid or cultist leaders, who retain human interest in such things as political power or subversion.

KEEPING DEEP ONES SCARY

The Deep Ones become boring when they become familiar. A predictable threat is not a threat. Something understood and quantified cannot play upon your fears. As a Handler, you must breathe new life into the old fish-men to make them something to fear.

Begin by changing up their appearance and behavior. Deep Ones have the genetic material of the whole ocean to draw on, not just fish-frogs. They might resemble, or attack like, sharks, orcas, moray eels, piranhas, snapping turtles, or barracudas. Liberally add hypergeometric rituals, or thicker armor, or extra powers, to the Deep Ones your team faces.

Finally, use ruthless tactics against the Agents: Deep Ones can see in inky blackness and are superbly efficient and terrifying attackers (even in familiar fish-frog shape) underwater. Enforce penalties for darkness and wet equipment. Agents in boats should be made to understand their own vulnerabilities, and they should always have to go out in a boat to stop the Deep One menace.

Remember that Deep Ones have no size limit: the Agents may plan to ambush a hunchbacked Innsmouth type and wind up facing a 20-foot tall giant. The Greater Deep Ones are even worse, and totally unknown foes to boot. At any size, Deep Ones resort to shocking, horrendous violence to solve any problem expediently.

By contrast, Deep One hybrids are people. They readily use guns, vehicles, and the Agents' sympathies. They are as cunning, sneaky, and dangerous as any cornered human. Play up their humanity to keep the players guessing, and to emphasize the true horror of the Deep One taint.

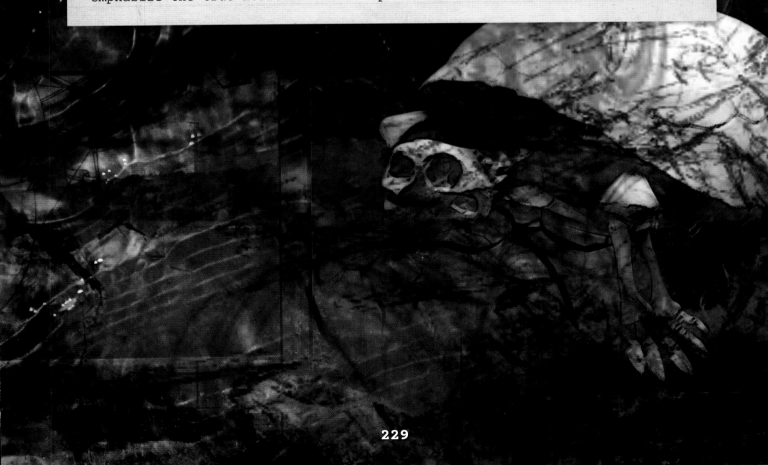

The Deep Ones occasionally respond to provocations: they sank the submarines USS *Squalus* in 1939 and O-9 in 1941 after Innsmouth, and attack USS *Thresher* in 1963 and USS *Scorpion* in 1968. But aside from such seemingly random responses, the Deep Ones shrug off the worst that humanity can muster.

Their actual plans run long, operating not in years or decades but in epochs. Immortal entities have patience, and time to reconsider something hasty or risky. What might appear to be their main goal — such as interbreeding with humanity — could be nothing but a ten-thousand-year feint to cover their true, unknown, much more terrible purpose.

Greater Deep Ones

Unbeknownst to most (including DELTA GREEN), the Deep Ones are divided into two classes: Greater and Lesser Deep Ones. Humans most often encounter the batrachian, humanoid Lesser Deep Ones. They seldom survive the sight of the monstrous, completely inhuman Greater Deep Ones. Greater Deep Ones have no fixed physiology; one might have chitinous, prehensile crablike limbs encircling its jaws while another sports an enormous tentacle surrounded by four eyes and two bony-ridged mouths.

Large, fanlike scales and razor-sharp spikes cover their gorilla-sized (or larger) bodies. They swim at 40 knots or more. Their huge, globular eyes see through the ocean murk and in complete darkness. They are oceanic, and only venture onto land briefly for ritual purposes. Internal self-regulating gas bladders allow them to move from the surface to the abyssal depths.

Greater Deep Ones reproduce asexually, injecting a parasitic gene complex into the unfortunate (usually human) host. This complex mutates the human into a Deep One hybrid, and a carrier of the Deep One gene complex in their own chromosomes. Thus the Deep One taint spreads through humanity much like a sexually transmitted disease. (This is what happened in Innsmouth, and in all the Deep One hybrid colonies.) After more than two generations, the Deep One complex ceases to breed true, remaining recessive in the hybrid until stress or some other cross-mutation triggers the metamorphosis to Lesser Deep One form.

Greater Deep One

Abilities (on land/in water): Athletics 13/19, Fighting 13/19, Health 14

Hypergeometry: 10+; for them, most spells connected with Cthulhu or their own race have a Cost of 1.

Hit Threshold: 4/5

Alertness Modifier: +1 (noisy targets)/+2 (echolocation)

Stealth Modifier: +0/+1

Attack: talons (d+2), bite (L1*)

Armor: -2 vs. any (scales and skin); Resilient (bullets, stabbing weapons) [L-1]

Stability Loss: +1

Injector: Greater Deep Ones can attack prone targets with a barbed stinger (d-2) that, on a successful Fighting test, injects the target with the Deep One genetic complex. If the target survives the encounter, remembering the attack or noticing the symptoms triggers a 4-point Stability test against Helplessness. The target may also eventually transform into a Lesser Deep One.

Progenitor Deep Ones

There is no extended Deep One culture as humans understand the word. Instead individual Deep One settlements spread throughout the world's oceans, organized in rough clans descended from a singularly powerful Greater Deep One like Dagon, Hydra, Shaurash-Ho, or Byatis, called a Progenitor.

Deep One "cities" comprise a series of caves and large coral-like structures centered on the resting place of their Progenitor, which is usually at the bottom of a submarine canyon a mile or more down. Some settlements have no Progenitor, instead founded by hybrids or outcasts. Even these outposts perform rituals in the hopes of drawing unaffiliated Progenitors to them.

Progenitor Deep Ones are multi-ton creatures, 20 feet or more in length. They are not Godzillas, but thinking demigods familiar with human weaponry.

Progenitor Deep One

Abilities (on land/in water): Athletics 25/35, Fighting 27/41, Health 29+

Hypergeometry: 30+; for them, all spells connected with Cthulhu or their own race have a Cost of 1; all others have a Cost of 3.

Hit Threshold: 3/4 (enormous)

Alertness Modifier: -1/+2

Stealth Modifier: -3/+1

Attack: talons (L2*H)

Armor: -4 vs. any (scales and skin); Resilient (bullets, stabbing weapons) [L-2]

Stability Loss: +1; +2 to any Sanity loss

Dimensional Shambler

Resembling a hulking, insectoid ape, the dimensional shambler (the term comes from Ludwig Prinn) infests the vortices and eddies of nine-dimensional spacetime. Its skin is tan, red or ebony-black, and loose, hanging in folds all over its body and its stumpy head. Its skeletal system turns and moves in unnatural ways, allowing it to spin its head like a top, for instance, or reverse its knobby limbs and suddenly attack a foe behind it.

The shambler's relatively low intelligence and ability to travel through four-dimensional space makes it a favorite servitor for sorcerers of all species.

Dimensional Shambler

Abilities: Athletics 11, Fighting 18, Health 14

Hypergeometry: 4+ for the servant of a magus, who might have provided it any spell.

Hit Threshold: 4

Alertness Modifier: +1

Stealth Modifier: +2 (to surprise apportation attacks only)

Attack: flailing smash (d+1); the shambler may attack the same target twice in a round

Armor: -3 vs. any (thick rugose hide); Transcendent (any attack by its current target); all other attacks do half damage

Stability Loss: +0

Apport: For 1 pool point of Athletics, the shambler can teleport anywhere within 50 yards, stumbling and shuddering silently in and out of reality.

Grasp: The shambler can use Monstrous Grappling (p. 222) against a prone target. (Against any target by paying 2 Athletics.) If the grappled target is bleeding, the shambler slurps up 1 Health per round until the target dies or escapes. Otherwise, the shambler carries the target out of Euclidean space-time, never to be seen again.

Loping: The shambler moves like a double-jointed great ape; it has contest advantage in any foot chase.

Investigation

Criminology: Blood spatter indicates that the attack happened right here in the middle of the room, but there aren't any other spots, or a trail to indicate the victim was moved anywhere. And you'd see it on that carpet or those white walls.

Sense Trouble: The mirrors and windows in the room reflect a shimmering light that you don't see in the room itself.

Feaster from the Stars

This loathsome, hovering thing is normally invisible, its presence signalled only by a sort of ghoulish tittering. A feaster is roughly ovoid, a pendulous stomach surrounded by tentacles, each tipped with needle-toothed suckers. Two cartilaginous stalks hold razor-sharp talons, with which it grasps and slashes open its prey. It then maneuvers its large central mouth to drink the spurting gore. As the feaster feeds, the blood it drinks or splashes on itself remains visible, revealing the form of the bloated obscenity.

Feasters are very strong, capable of smashing through window-ledges and snapping a human spine in two in mid-air. They travel on a cold wind, presumably from interstellar space, often in response to a hyper-geometric summoning.

Feaster From the Stars

Abilities: Athletics 9, Fighting 20, Health 12

Hypergeometry: Hypergeometric operators who repeatedly summon the same feaster run the risk of allowing it to learn spells. A feaster who takes advantage of its opportunities has a Hypergeometry rating of 4 to 10, and a spell for subtle revenge like Exchange Personalities.

Hit Threshold: 6 (invisible but tittering); 3 (slow and visible while feeding, and for 3 rounds thereafter)

Alertness Modifier: +1

Stealth Modifier: +0

Attack: taloned limb swipe (d+1), bite (d-1); the feaster can either bite, feed on a target, or make two limb swipes per round.

Armor: -1 vs. any (slippery skin) [L-1]

Stability Loss: +1

Blood Hunger: If not actually feeding, the feaster must make a Difficulty 3 Athletics test to avoid moving toward the largest quantity of spilled, open, or spurting blood available.

Exsanguination: On a successful bite attack, the feaster adds the Health lost by its target to its own Health or Athletics pool. Successive bite attacks automatically succeed. The target is held by the feaster's motile mouths as by a Monstrous Grapple (p. 222), although she can attack without spending Athletics.

Investigation

Chemistry: The body is slightly cyanotic — the thing's own blood may rely on hemocyanin instead of hemoglobin. That lets it process oxygen far better than we do — but it's more vulnerable to heat than we are. *(1 point spend)* (Biology)

Cop Talk: The whole estate was guarded. Nobody saw anyone cross the lawns, no dogs barked. Right around 2 a.m., the time of death, one of the girls thought she heard him sniggering or tittering to himself in the room.

Forensics: The body was found almost folded up, the joints so bloodless as to be loose and slack. There was not a trace of blood anywhere in the corpse, despite the deep, jagged wounds under the arms, across the throat, and in the back. The skin and flesh were stark white — even the capillaries were drained, so there was no postmortem lividity. The bones were hollow; the marrow gone. The spine, humerus, and femurs were snapped like pencils.

Physics: These things must be transparent, not truly invisible, or else we couldn't see the blood inside them. If we can hit on the proper combination of colored light beams, their matter *must* refract: we might get an after-image, or a highlight, or better yet a halo. *(1 point spend per each -1 to Hit Threshold)*

Ghouls

Rubbery, loathsome, foul-smelling humanoids with semi-hooved feet, pointed ears, and claws, ghouls dwell in graveyard warrens, subway tunnels, and the like beneath many human cities. Their greenish or grayish skin is matted with grave earth or flecked with leprous lesions and leathery dead spots. They move in a low, hunched posture, almost semi-bipedal; they climb, leap, and lope at prodigious speed. Their eyes are red or yellow, and glow in pitch blackness or when hungrily attentive on something or someone. Ghouls can see into both infrared and ultraviolet; in utter darkness, they can find a foe by smell or sound.

Ghouls eat dead flesh, especially human corpses. Some heretical ghouls consume very fresh corpses — transients, the lost and curious — but most ghouls restrict themselves to rotting flesh for religious reasons. They also know that too much predation on the living invites human investigation. Ghouls can digest almost anything; flesh soaked in formaldehyde and other embalming fluid goes down as easy as flesh left rotting in the sewer for a month.

They speak their own language, one of gibberings and meepings, although some recall or have learned human tongues. These ties to humanity extend past diet and language: ghouls associate with human witches as go-betweens, and with human necrophiles, serial killers, and other unwholesomely death-obsessed sorts. Indeed, a human of particularly thanatophilic tendencies can transform into a ghoul over a prolonged period of time.

Most significantly of all, ghouls regularly exchange human and ghoul infants, raising and nursing the kidnapped human child as a ghoul and leaving the ghoul changeling to ignorant human parents. Some human children interbreed with their ghoulish warren-mates to produce hybrids or mongrels; some human cultists or degenerates mate with ghouls for their own purposes, likewise. And of course many ghouls brought up as humans never reconnect with their true species and marry humans. Like Deep One hybridism, ghoul hybridism can turn recessive and pass through several human generations before reverting to type, usually upon exposure to some ghoulish stimulus or infection vector.

Human-Ghoul Changelings

Humans raised by ghouls might metamorphose into ghouls or remain human to serve as interlocutors and ghoul agents in the surface world. In addition to likely high scores in Unarmed Combat and perhaps Conceal, they have a +1 Alertness Modifier, and suffer no penalties for darkness.

Ghoul changelings or hybrids raised as humans have the same adjustments to their statistics.

Ghoul

Abilities: Athletics 12, Fighting 14, Health 13

Hypergeometry: 5-9 for pure-born ghoul priests of their dark gods; 10+ for once-human ghoul-lich sorcerers. Liches may have Raise From Essential Saltes; both liches and priests may have Charnel Meditation for negotiations in strange cemeteries.

Hit Threshold: 4 (5 underground)

Alertness Modifier: +2 (+0 in daylight)

Stealth Modifier: +3

Attack: claws (d+1), bite (d+0); ghouls can engage in two claw attacks and a bite against the same target in one round.

Armor: Resilient [L-3]

Stability Loss: +0; +1 if the ghoul was known to the witness when alive

Charnel Feast: Consuming rotten human flesh immediately restores 3 Health to an injured ghoul. This may be done once per 24 hours.

Charnel Visage: A ghoul that eats a corpse can take the appearance of the devoured human. This ritual costs 2 Hypergeometry pool points. Many ghouls can transform rapidly between their native form and any of a dozen previously consumed human forms.

Diseased: Even if ghouls don't spread supernatural ghoul-virus, there is nothing more infectious than a mouth full of teeth clogged with rotting human flesh. A few (2-8) days after a ghoul bite, the victim must make a Difficulty 8 Health test to avoid horrible infection. If the ghoul bite was *immediately* treated with First Aid, her Difficulty is 4; if medical treatment waited until after the battle or the next day, her Difficulty is 6. (Claw wounds are -1 to those Difficulties.) On a failure, the victim becomes Hurt and takes +3 damage to Health. She loses 3 Health and 3 Athletics thereafter each day until cured or dead.

Inhuman Agility: By spending 2 Athletics, a ghoul can leap 5 yards in any direction from a standing position, scale and cling to any surface including ceilings, run up to 35 mph, or drop up to 50 feet without damage.

Mephitic Memories: A ghoul that eats the brain or sensoria of a corpse can "imbibe" the memories of the deceased. This works for all vertebrate flesh, not just for humans. The memories last forever, or at least until the ghoul would normally forget them.

Pack Attack: Up to three ghouls may attack a single target in one round. The foe's Hit Threshold drops by 1 against the third ghoul.

Tunneling: Ghouls can tunnel through soil, brick, concrete, or solid bedrock in minutes, hours, or days.

Worrying Bite: If two bite attacks in a row succeed against the same target, the ghoul worries the victim with its mighty canine jaws, and the second attack thus does double damage. The ghoul continues to do normal bite damage to the victim automatically each round until killed or driven off. The target can attempt an Athletics test (as with *Monstrous Grappling*, p. 222) to pull free.

Investigation

Biology: The flies in the Wensdon house have the characteristic hunched thorax and scuttling movement of *Megaselia scalaris*, the coffin-fly. There's a dead body hidden somewhere in there – from the number of flies, possibly a good many bodies.

Forensics: The entire body is covered in bite marks. Oddly, although the marks are clearly canine, the jaws are unusually short and wide. From the marks, we estimate three or four of the animals. The eyes were plucked from their sockets, and are missing, as are the kidneys, spleen, liver, thymus gland, pancreas, and intestines. The large wound in the belly was a tearing wound. The skull, on the other hand, was smashed open postmortem on the gravestone, and the gray matter scooped out with some kind of clawed utensil and taken. Also postmortem, the long bones of the limbs were cracked and pried open with a four-pronged, sharpened tool, and the marrow removed. Extensive saliva traces were found in and around the bone cavities.

Notice: The "newly dug grave" over in the next plot has a marker on it labeled 1949.

Occult: It's probably just a coincidence, but the Greenyear and Detiller families we've been investigating could be descendants – perhaps refugees who changed their names in the New World – of Jean Grenier and Pierre de la Tilhaire, accused werewolves in Bordeaux in 1603.

The Ghouls of New York

In the 1636, a religious order run by a heretic named Mogens Dekker fled from the Holy Roman Empire to New Amsterdam (later New York), and there set about the secretive worship of an unknown god. Dekker and his followers — known as the Keepers of the Faith — were ghouls in the making, once-human monstrosities who dug into the earth and fed on dead human flesh.

After a 1925 police raid in Red Hook, Brooklyn nearly exposed the ghoul colony, most of the ghouls migrated outward to cemeteries in New Jersey and Queens. The remaining fanatical Keepers grow lean as the cemeteries in Manhattan (all closed in 1851) empty. Heretical new-fledged ghouls hunt transients and bums in the sewers and alleys, risking exposure to DELTA GREEN.

Ghouls in Old Europe

Ghouls once infested all of Europe, and warrens still persist beneath industrial cities with regular influxes of the dead. World War II provided a rich bounty that boosted the ghoul population; individual ghouls haunt cemeteries all over Western Europe. Even with all that, London, Paris, Rome, and the other ancient capitals are as hunted out as New York.

The largest and most dangerous recent ghoul outbreak occurred in Russia during the reign of Josef Stalin, whom Russia's ghouls called the "Great Provider." The Soviet counter-unnatural agency GRU SV-8 (p. 291) still hunts the Cult of the Great Provider in the gulags and charnel pits of the Workers' Paradise. Thanks to GRU SV-8, the ghoul populations behind the Iron Curtain have been culled, or at least driven into hiding.

Gnoph-Keh

This "hairy myth-thing of the Greenland ice" has six legs and a horn, though at a glimpse it resembles a misshapen polar bear more than anything else. It may be a Pleistocene survival, or a construct built by some elder race such as the Mi-Go. It can travel on one, two, or three pairs of legs; it is a fast swimmer and often lurks under the ice of a lake or river waiting to erupt and ambush its prey. Under the name *kokogiak* it appears in Inupiak legend as a tricky monster in the form of a ten-legged polar bear. According to the legend, to see the kokogiak is to die.

That said, gnoph-keh sightings have been reported from Alaska to Greenland as far back as 1870. The natives blamed a particularly bloody massacre in the Yukon on the gnoph-keh in 1929, just before a spate of wendigo attacks and Itla-shua cultism manifested in Saskatchewan and Manitoba. The Pnakotic Manuscripts associate the gnoph-keh with Rhan-Tegoth, ancient enemy of Lomar.

Gnoph-Keh

Abilities: Athletics 15, Fighting 21, Health 15

Hypergeometry: 15 for a (exceedingly rare) gnoph-keh shaman; it can summon the Wendigo or possibly Itla-shua itself at Cost 4.

Hit Threshold: 4 (5 in Arctic against non-Arctic dwellers)

Alertness Modifier: +1

Stealth Modifier: +2 (in snow or ice)

Attack: claws (d+1), horn gore (d+3); the gnoph-keh can attack with its horn, or with one or two pair of claws. It cannot make a horn attack on the round after it makes a two-pair claw attack, as it has to drop to its feet again.

Armor: -5 (thick furry hide), Transcendent (cold, drowning)

Stability Loss: +0

Blizzard: By spending 1 Health every hour, the gnoph-keh can howl up a blizzard, restricting human visibility to point blank (the gnoph-keh can still see fine) within a 140-yard radius. (Difficulties for visual tests past Point-Blank increase by +4. This includes Hit Thresholds and Sense Trouble tests to avoid surprise.) Alternately, it can spend 1 Health point to drop the air temperature by 25°F for an hour. Each additional Health point increases the blizzard radius by another 140 yards or drops the temperature another 25°F; multiple gnoph-keh can howl up glacier-clearing storms.

Agents caught in a blizzard likely begin *Freezing* (p. 111). At -50°F even Arctic gear is the same as being Somewhat Prepared.

Paired Claw Attack: When the gnoph-keh swipes a foe with a pair of claws, roll one Fighting test, but two separate damage results. For a two-paired claw attack, roll one Fighting test, but *four* separate damage results.

Investigation

Biology: The end toe on these polar bear tracks is unusually distended, and the claws are remarkably long. (Survival)

Forensics: The body died not from blood loss, or even from the trauma of being impaled through the chest, but from hypothermia, despite being clad in a parka at the time of death.

Sense Trouble: That snow is blowing against the wind.

Inukgaklinut

The Noatagamut Eskimos in northwestern Alaska tell stories of a tribe of dwarfish cannibals far upriver, the Inukgalklinut, who hold the gnoph-keh as a totem animal or spirit. The Inukgalklinut ambush interlopers during snowstorms. The grinning, flat-faced savages hurl their spears and then close in with knives to eat their foes.

Inukgaklinut

Abilities: Athletics 6, Health 6, Melee Weapons 7, Unarmed Combat 7

Magic: 5+ for an Inukgaklinut shaman; he can summon the Gnoph-Keh at Cost 4, whistle up a blizzard (as Gnoph-keh power) at Cost 2, and knows rituals concerning Rhan-Tegoth and Itla-shua.

Hit Threshold: 3 (4 at night; 5 on ice or snow)

Alertness Modifier: +2 (in snow or dark), -1 (in sunlight)

Stealth Modifier: +2

Attack: knife (d-1), barbed spear (d+0), bite (d-1)

Armor: -1 (thick furs)

Stability Loss: +0

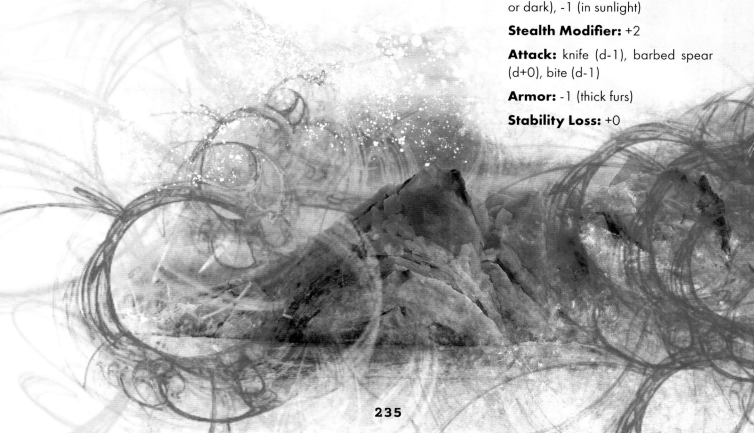

Great Race of Yith

The Great Race, a purely mental species, took over the minds of a conical, quasi-vegetable species in the Ordovician era when they fled the destruction of their own world, Yith. In their new bodies, the Great Race drove the spectral, whistling polyps that fed on the cones underground. In the early Triassic, after a period of external and internal wars, they built a fascist empire centered on a Great Library complex in Australia (see *Pnakotis*, p. 213). They filled their libraries with the knowledges of all eras, gathered by sending their minds throughout time to possess sentient beings across the solar system.

When the polyps erupted again at the end of the Cretaceous, the Great Race left the cones to their fate and jumped ahead to our far future, where they possess the co-leopteran bodies of Earth's by-then dominant race. Their final stop in this solar system is the bulbous vegetable entities of Mercury, a billion years hence.

DELTA GREEN has not yet encountered one of the Great Race in its cone-shaped Mesozoic body. The "Strange Men" (and Strange Women) possessed by Yithians in the present are bad enough.

The Strange Men

The Great Race of Yith flings its agents forward to the Holocene, occupying certain human vessels during this period. No more than a dozen in number, these infiltrators act in furtherance of the Great Race's unknowable plans to nudge, alter, or downright bludgeon the timeline towards something they call "the Construct." They command and operate a human cult known in this era as the Motion (p. 296).

When the alien intelligence takes over a human mind, it is always the same: an otherwise normal human collapses, and when they wake they are not themselves. This alien being uses the body to travel, collect unnatural information, and most of all to study its "peers". It slowly becomes acclimatized to its host body and era, while the mind that the Great Race has displaced remains imprisoned in a cone-shaped body, 150 million years in the past.

Although the human brain cannot contain the entire Yithian intellect, a Yith-possessed human stands out as profoundly more intelligent and strong-willed than any normal person. Often they seem off-putting or dangerous, inciting vague fear and aversion in the sensitive. An Agent who has encountered a Strange Person before can spend HUMINT to identify a Yithian-possessed individual by observing the unconscious shying behavior of the regular humans around her.

The defeat of a Strange Woman may be no defeat at all, if it provides the Great Race information about its opposition in this decade. With access to the entirety of time, there are only momentary setbacks. The Yithian can jump into a previous moment and re-run a confrontation, or the next week and lay an ambush, or back a hundred years and win by default. Even killing a Strange Man means nothing. The Yithian retreats back to the Mesozoic, free to start again – or the "death" of their agent may be just the link the Great Race intended to establish their future.

Strange Person

A Yithian's ability scores vary depending on its host body's abilities, and on how long the Yithian has spent familiarizing itself with its Strange Person form.

Abilities: Athletics 6, Firearms 6, Hypnosis 8+, Preparedness 10+ (see *Future Sense*), Unarmed Combat 6, Yithian Technology 10; any other needed General Abilities at 6 or 7

Hypergeometry: 12+ and any of a wide variety of rituals, especially those found in the *Pnakotic Manuscripts*.

Hit Threshold: 3

Alertness Modifier: +2 (time sense)

Stealth Modifier: +2 (instantaneous sight-line calculation)

Attack: electric gun (d+1 or L1H)

Armor: none

Stability Loss: +0

Future Sense: Even in primitive human sensoria, Yithians can sense the flow of time in their vicinity, and see future events. The Strange Man has a Preparedness pool of 10+, which works as normal. But the Yithian can also test and spend its Preparedness to get surprise, disappear in the moment nobody is watching, avoid ambushes, be not standing where the gun pointed, etc. Difficulties are either 4 or the total of the Agents' spend and roll, if the Yithian is pre-evading direct Agent action like gunfire.

Hypnosis: The superior minds of Yithian-humans let them "influence the thoughts and acts of others," modeled with a Hypnosis ability pool (**Trail of Cthulhu,** p. 043)

usually at 8+. Yithian Hypnosis can work on the unwilling, and includes simple commands ("open the door") and even alters thoughts ("you never liked policemen" or "these machines seem normal"). Model hypnotism used on the Agents with Psionic Attack (p. 221); hypnotism used on GMCs succeeds automatically with a spend of 2 Hypnosis (or 3 for strong-willed GMCs).

Never Sleep: Although the human body needs some rest, the Yithian brain requires no sleep. This provides yet more time to study unnatural tomes or conspire to redirect history.

Perfect Calculation: Yithians can perform rapid, complex mathematical analysis. A Yithian who applies perfect calculation to bullet trajectories gets +2 on aimed Firearms rolls; one who calculates tensile strength and angle of approach perfectly gets a similar bonus to Mechanics tests to set traps; the possibilities are endless.

Temporal Immortality: To a temporal being, death is only an inconvenient "blank spot" in the otherwise limitless expanse of four-dimensional timespace. Even if the human shell of the Great Race appears to perish, that entity persists on, somewhere in time.

Total Knowledge: Yithians can memorize text at sight, and as time travelers, they thoroughly research their target era in the Great Library. This manifests as complete knowledge of all history, science, languages, geography, and technology – the equivalent of a smart phone in 1965. That said, the vagaries of causality (and Yithian arrogance) may lead them to make slight errors, especially in slang or topical references.

Yithian Technology: This catch-all ability covers building and using jury-rigged Yithian technology in the present.

Yithian Equipment

Yithian time-travel depends on hyper-scientific machinery, much of which exists in a purely mathematical state, since it can be constructed with virtually any level of technology, no matter how primitive. Even given the pathetic components available in the temporal backwater that is the 1960s, it takes only a few minutes to jury-rig something unimaginably in advance of human science. And only a few seconds more to rig it to self-destruct in a puddle of slag and alpha particles.

If an Agent somehow captures a piece of Yithian equipment intact, puzzling it out takes either a 1-point Physics spend (sometimes for each use) or a Mechanics test, at Difficulty 8. Each successful use lowers the Difficulty of the test by -1, to a minimum of 4.

Electric Gun: This hand-held tube-shaped device projects a gout of electricity (d+1 damage) at Long range (100 yards) with a specific charge that annihilates spectral polyps. At minimum setting, it stuns organic matter (Difficulty 6 Health test to remain conscious; even on a success the target cannot act for four rounds without paying 3 Athletics per round). At maximum setting, it unleashes a bolt of lightning (L1H). A non-Yithian using it blows up the gun (L2H) on a failed 1.

Memory Eraser: This small copper box erases the memories of the kidnapped minds before they are sent back. The operator connects it to the cranium with thin wires and probes, then creates a conceptual vacuum in the copper that siphons off memories. Yithian operators (or their trained agents) can also use it to implant memories, transfer memories to other minds, and make memory copies without draining them. Non-Yithians must spend 1 Unnatural and make a Difficulty 7 Psychotherapy test to operate it as an eraser; they cannot access its other functions.

Temporal Mine: Activating this device causes everything within its field effect to freeze in time, isolated from the matrix equations of space-time. Mine effect fields range from the size of a large book to the size of a large tyrannosaur. Programming the mine is impossible for non-Yithians, but simply activating or deactivating it sometimes requires only the push of a contact – or a 3-point Physics spend, depending on the drama.

Time Projector: This resembles a jumble of rods, wheels, and mirrors, though only about two feet tall, one foot wide, and one foot thick. The central mirror is circular and convex. When activated (Difficulty 5 Mechanics test or 1-point Physics spend) it translates the viewer back into a Yithian cone-body in the Mesozoic, replacing her mind with the one in that body. (Re-setting its coordinates is impossible for non-Yithians.) With a 2-point Physics spend and a Difficulty 7 Mechanics test, a non-Yithian can alter the foci of the mirror and turn the projector into a holographic-telepathic cross-time communicator.

Investigation

Cryptography: This code simply can't be broken, even with one of the new super-computers, not unless you had a team of mathematicians working in parallel for a decade. And yet he plainly deciphered it overnight, despite having no background and no training we can uncover in math or codes.

Forensics: His hair is singed, there are fern-pattern burn marks on both his chest and coat, and lesions extend deep into the muscle. The coins in his pocket show "arc marks," and heated enough to burn his skin, as did his pen and ring. Cause of death appears to be cardiac arrest induced by lightning stroke.

Fringe Science: The creature the professor drew in his dreams – cone-shaped torso, tall, claws on tentacle arms, glowing eyes in a round head – eerily resembles the Flatwoods Monster spotted in Braxton County, West Virginia after a UFO crash on 12 September 1952.

Sense Trouble: The man staring at you seems not to know what to do with his hands; he's just holding them straight out at an angle. (HUMINT)

Haedi Nigritiae

Their name, corrupt Latin meaning roughly "young goats of darkness" comes from a passage in Ludwig Prinn's *De Vermis Mysteriis*. Their description comes from a few mad-dened survivors or captured cultists: a black, ropy tree-thing, squatting and crawling on its hooves, covered in mouths and snaky arms. MJ-8 covets larger samples of its thick, woody, resinous flesh, and of its bizarrely mutophilic sap or "milk." DELTA GREEN has only these frag-ments of legend and intel to go on, that and the ancient chant that hails the presence of the haedi nigritiae: "Iä! Shub-Niggurath! Black Goat of the Woods with a Thousand Young!"

The old witch-haunted groves of Europe and New England may have been cleared and tamed centuries ago, but the program enters new forests this decade. Not just mis-sions in the jungles of the Congo, Colombia, and Indochina, but the cyclical "back to nature" impulses of the American counter-culture, lead DELTA GREEN's investigators of the unnatural deep into the woods.

Haedus Nigritia

Abilities: Athletics 23, Fighting 26, Health 18

Hypergeometry: 8+. Haedi nigritiae are pregnant (sometimes literally) with magical force. They can summon fellow haedi nigritiae at Cost 3, and call Shub-Niggurath on nights of the new moon at Cost 13. They eagerly sacrifice humans to pay that cost.

Hit Threshold: 3 (large)

Alertness Modifier: +1

Stealth Modifier: +2 (in forests or jungles)

Attack: trampling hooves (d+6), tentacle (d+3), horrible sucking mouth (d-2); after a successful tentacle attack, in lieu of doing damage the haedus nigritia may pull its victim inexorably toward a mouth for an automatic blood drain each round thereafter. (See *Monstrous Grappling*, p. 222)

Armor: [L-2]; Resilient (firearms, explosives) and Transcendent (fire, blast, corrosion, electricity, organic toxins); cutting weapons (including Primacord) do normal damage, and inorganic herbicides might be effective.

Stability Loss: +2

Multiple Attacks: In its masses of tentacles, a typical haedus nigritia has four thicker sinuous tentacles with which it attacks. Each of these thicker tentacles can strike out to injure or to grab and capture once per round, conceivably at four different targets. Instead of making a tentacle attack, the haedus nigritia may trample one victim with its massive hooves, typically hooting and bellowing the while.

Stench: "As a foulness shall ye know them." All unprotected breathers around a haedus nigritia must make a Difficulty 5 Health test or be Hurt until they return to clean air.

Investigation

Forensics: The knife wounds didn't kill him — they were superficial cuts at best — although the blood loss was serious even before whatever happened. The face and mouth cavities are full of blackish-green pus. Ulcerated open sores are on the anterior of the body, though that clear grease has dried by now. The expression on what's left of the face is... well, if you didn't know better, you'd say it was religious ecstasy.

Law: Look, if we can just prove this horrible thing is on Calvert's land, we can have him charged under Michigan law (Act 91, P.A. 1905) with keeping infectious plants on his property. Maybe he bought the local cops, but did he buy the State Agricultural Control Board? At worst, it makes a great diversion.

Sense Trouble: Although the wind doesn't shift, it picks up — and it must have uncovered something dead for a week. And there seem to be more trees there than there were just a minute ago.

Survival: Those prints are like enormously splayed goats' hooves, as though a goat weighing several tons stood here. But there's no room among these trees for something like that to have passed — look, all this lush, new foliage is completely undisturbed. Strange for it to have grown up this thickly without any rain, though. (Biology)

Hounds of Tindalos

These terrifying, geometric entities boil and emerge into our four dimensions from sharp angles and edges. Some forbidden texts refer to them as the "dogs that howl in the maelstrom of Azathoth," harrying and hunting at the beck and call of the Daemon Sultan and its dancing attendants. Others say they emerged at the beginning of time, coming from some source beyond it, and leap from time to time to sate their cosmic hunger on anyone so unfortunate as to perceive them.

And indeed, perceiving them horrifies. Their bodies refract a thousand glittering, razor-sharp shards of space-time that move and reform in the vaguest outline of a quadru-pedal predator. They do not so much resemble hounds or wolves as they convey to their unlucky viewer an inescapable sense of *being hunted*.

Hound of Tindalos

Abilities: Athletics 13, Fighting 23, Health 13

Hypergeometry: 12+; rituals always include Contact Hounds of the Angles, with a Cost of 1.

Hit Threshold: 4

Alertness Modifier: +3

Stealth Modifier: +1

Attack: shard "limb" sweep (d+1), engulfing shard swarm (L1*); cannot engulf a target in the first round.

Armor: Transcendent

Stability Loss: +2

Angular Apport: The Hound can flicker in and out of existence to "skip" a round of combat and re-enter anywhere in the action sequence (before or after a foe, for example) it wishes. This flickering in-and-out costs 2 points of Athletics. When it flickers, it leaves and enters through any sharp, physical angle — the corner of a room, the edge of a table, the hinge of a pair of glasses — teleporting between those points instantly no matter the distance between them. Thus, outrunning a hound is unlikely.

Held Back By Curves: A Hound must make a successful Athletics test against a Difficulty of 8 to cross a curved line or surface, and a Difficulty 8 Health test to spend a whole round in a large area composed of curves or spheres.

Inconstant Form: The hound can fold, change, stretch, extend and warp its form in amazing ways, altering its size as needed from moment to moment. It can effectively attack anyone within 10 yards by directing its form to a new location.

Investigation

Anthropology: This is a "tindalo" boomerang, probably carved on the island of Tulagi around 1900. Note the angled geometric design contrasting with the smoothly curved wood – you can see this same work on clubs, paddles; other curved wooden items. This boomerang is splintered, of course, meaning the tindalo's power has escaped.

Forensics: The body was found flat on its back, sliced by hundreds of wounds; the worst of the damage was to the face and eyes, but there are cuts all over the corpse. The weapon must have been unimaginably thin and sharp, like a hundred razors made of mica. The cause of death was a massive coronary. The body showed old needle tracks indicating drug use, but none were found in the system.

Intimidation: The cleaning woman has a family to feed. She didn't know that taking money to leave a bent hairpin in the room would do any harm, but she'll describe the man who paid her as long as we keep her out of it. (Reassurance)

Notice: I don't think the round furniture was just a mod fashion statement. There's nothing but eggs, sausage links, and oranges in the refrigerator. Whoever lived in this room filled in all the corners with plaster. They even puttied over the corners of their windows and the electrical outlets.

Hunting-Horror

Those trapped in nightmare see these mindless, flying hulks, and when waking half-remember the mocking laughter of Nyarlathotep urging them to attack. The *Liber Ivonis* describes them as the larvae of Nyarlathotep's masters, the mindless Other Gods.

Hunting-horrors resemble enormous ropy black serpents or worms with one or two bat-like or sail-like wings. Their writhing, slithering forms shift and change, like a cloud of thick, black smoke. Some are blind, locating prey by extrasensory ability or preternatural smell; some have one or three burning eyes.

They derive their strange instincts from their master Nyarlathotep, or from the one who foolishly summons them. On their own they hunger; they seek to devour flesh or hope.

Hunting-horrors manifest only in deep darkness.

Hunting-Horror

Abilities: Athletics 18, Fighting 30, Health 23

Hypergeometry: 13+; all its rituals related to Nyarlathotep have Cost 3; it can also manifest attack rituals such as Withering.

Hit Threshold: 3 (large)

Alertness Modifier: +2

Stealth Modifier: +2 (rapid flight)

Attack: bite and rend (L2*), seize (d+2; ignores worn armor)

Armor: -5 (bubbling scales) [L-4]; no armor against light

Stability Loss: +2

Aberrant Flight: The hunting-horror can "fly" through any environment from the ocean to outer space. It can outpace a fighter jet or hover over a churchyard.

Damaged by Light: The full light of day sears a hunting-horror to dust. Focused light beams and bright light explosions calve off portions of the horror's infra-flesh.

All damage drops by -1 at each range increment greater than Close. Light damage ignores the horror's Armor. "Firing" a light beam resolves as a Firearms attack, at -1 to Hit Threshold. Shining a light at a hunting-horror is a great way to get attacked by it – and your Hit Threshold also drops by -1, being so well illuminated.

Held Back By Light: A hunting-horror must make a successful Health test against Difficulty 8 to cross a lighted area (torches or street lamps count). It can spend Hypergeometry points on this test.

Seize: The horror uses *Monstrous Grappling* (p. 222) to seize a target; once within the horror's writhing

Hunting-Horror Light Damage

Light Source	Damage
Flashlight	d-1
Headlights	d+0
Floodlight, flare gun	d+1
Arc lamp, WP grenade, parachute flare	d+3
Star shell round (up to 75mm)	L1*
Star shell round (76mm or larger), bombing run	L2*

grasp the target must spend 3 Athletics to attack it. The horror can automatically squeeze a target in its grasp for seize damage; this does not count as an attack. The horror can grasp and seize up to two targets.

Investigation

Forensics: The corpse was mauled and mutilated, showing severe blunt trauma as well as ligature marks on the limbs (indicating thick, looped cable was used to suspend the body and possibly slam it into a wall) and wounds made by at least five different shapes of blades, mostly hatchet-like. The left foot, heart, and at least three inches of the trachea have not been recovered from the crime scene.

Fringe Science: A forty-foot column of smoke flew over the abandoned Starry Wisdom Church in Providence, Rhode Island the night of the great storm of 9 August 1935. Witnesses described seeing "three burning eyes" in it.

Notice: Somebody smashed the streetlight that ordinarily shines on this courtyard. These bullets hit something, though, something that flattened them out. (Criminology)

Ifrits

These beings resemble balls or columns of fire that grow from pinpoint sparks to man-sized or larger infernos. They can potentially combine into enormous firestorms. They appear to be sentient, even intelligent, plasmas. Their true "self" likely resides in a tangent dimension, and extrudes into ours with incendiary results. DELTA GREEN operatives first encountered ifrits in Iran in 1943, but they seem to be favored servants of hypergeometric operators in America and Africa as well.

They likely have some connection to Qu-tugkwa, and may be the "bringers of elder wisdom" known in Theosophical lore as "Children of the Fire Mist." If the latter, they can communicate with cultists, implying a psionic capability that DELTA GREEN has fortunately yet to encounter. This might tie in with reports that one Kurdish cult of Kheshthogha calls on ifrits to burn unnatural knowledge out of enemies and madmen.

Ifrit

Abilities: Athletics 1-8, Fighting 2-17, Health 5

Hypergeometry: 0 or 7; if an ifrit knows any rituals, it knows how to summon more of its kind at a Cost of 3 per ifrit. An ifrit may learn any ritual by burning someone who knows it, or a book containing it.

Hit Threshold: 5 (quick)

Alertness Modifier: +1 (flammables, e.g., ammunition, paper, gasoline)

Stealth Modifier: +1 (in spark form only)

Attack: fiery touch (d-2 or d+0); flame immersion (L1*)

Armor: Transcendent (material weapons, fire); can be extinguished

Stability Loss: +0

Extinguishing: To extinguish an ifrit is like putting out a very stubborn fire. Water costs an ifrit 1 Health per gallon; a bucket of sand does d-2 damage to it; a hand-held fire extinguisher does d-1. If the ifrit has even 1 Health remaining at the end of the round, the ifrit immediately returns to 5 Health the next round.

Fiery Touch: On a normal Fighting attack, the ifrit sets its target on fire with Minor Exposure (d-2 each round until put out); on a successful

Ye Liveliest Awfulness

The ritual known as Raise from Essential Saltes (p. 207) resurrects the dead. But if a corpse has been so destroyed or eaten away as to be incomplete, what returns is a grotesque, immortal monstrosity that one witness called "ye liveliest Awfulness."

The awfulness is essentially human in structure but horribly malformed and misshapen, darkly discolored and stained – the marks of the infusion of Outside powers that gave it life.

Its nauseating fetor and dismal whining announce its presence long before the awfulness appears in sight. It lurches and flops clumsily across the ground, or flings itself in spasmodic leaps, reaching with twisted limbs.

Those who know the Raise from Essential Saltes ritual can return the awfulness to ash in the same manner as anyone more fully resurrected by it. Cruel sorcerers keep these remnants as victims for ritual sacrifice, as guards for forgotten passages, and as a way to dispose of those who trespass in such passages.

Awfulness

Abilities: Athletics 13, Health 12, Unarmed Combat 8

Hypergeometry: None

Hit Threshold: 4

Alertness Modifier: +2

Stealth Modifier: -2

Attack: fist (d+0), bite (d+1) only after a successful grapple

Armor: Resilient (weapons) [L-1]; vulnerable to fire

Stability Loss: +1

Ravenous Mob: The awfulness can attack with Monstrous Grappling (p. 222); any other awfulness in Point-Blank range of the same target can spend Unarmed Combat pool points to assist the attack or Athletics to raise the Difficulty for any of the target's tests to escape. Spending counts as an attack by that awfulness. The round after a successful grapple attack, any awfulness who spent on that attack (or who spends on the escape test) automatically succeeds with a bite attack. If the awfulness has taken damage, it heals 1 Health for each point lost by the target to its bite.

Mi-Go

This interstellar race call themselves the Outer Ones, and their main colony in the solar system is the planet Yuggoth, called Pluto by Earthly astronomers. They resemble huge, pinkish-gray, spongiform crabs, with two nippers and myriads of twitching smaller limbs. A bulbous, frond-covered head and two membranous wings complete the picture. Their multiple legs leave strange footprints resembling pronged wedges; it can be difficult to tell which direction they traveled from such spoor.

Green, sticky ichor permeates all their tissues; they have no skeleton or internal organs. They can reshape their basically fungoid anatomy at will, but are unable to eat terrestrial food as their biochemistry is fundamentally alien. Indeed, they exist in manifold dimensions above and below those observable by the human race and vibrate at a different frequency; they cannot be photographed or filmed.

Even their movement and modes of thought are macro macrodimensional, allowing mi-go to see short stints of the future, or to cross otherwise impassable barriers by taking a dimensional shortcut. This macrodimensionality even allows them to "fly" and "breathe" in open vacuum. They may be an extrusion into our four-dimensional space of some greater entity in a higher dimension.

Complex patterns of colors flash between mi-go, conveying detailed messages in short bursts. Communication in this fashion is much more rapid than verbal intercourse, is completely silent, and can be used in the void of space. They can speak human tongues in buzzing, insect-like voices. The mi-go surgically and genetically graft their own and other life-forms into constructed beings for their own unknown purposes. Their surgical skill extends to removing a living human brain and emplacing it in a life-supporting metal cylinder that can withstand the rigors of interstellar space.

Mi-Go

Abilities (on land/in air): Athletics 4/10, Energy Weapons 6, Fighting 7/10, Health 8

Hypergeometry: 1-2 for normal/worker mi-go; 8+ for sorcerer/priest caste mi-go. Casters can contact Nyarlathotep; other common rituals include Create Hyperspace Gate (faster and more effective than Create Stone Gate) and versions of Call Forth Those From Outside for haedi nigritiae and hunting-horrors. Mi-go need no rituals to contact their fellow mi-go.

Hit Threshold: 3/4

Alertness Modifier: +1 to +3 (alien surveillance technology or implanted sensoria)

Stealth Modifier: +0/+1

Attack: nippers (d-1), electric wand (1 to L1H), cold web (d+4); mi-go may attack in hand-to-hand combat with two nippers at once; if a mi-go succeeds in two nipper attacks in a row against the same target, it can use Monstrous Grappling (p. 222) to inject him with an eraser, or carry him into the sky until his lungs burst or it drops him on something painful.

Armor: Out-of-Phase; Transcendent (toxins, cold)

Stability Loss: +1

Cannot Be Photographed:
An Agent could create a suitable combination of lenses and emulsions to capture the mi-go on film with a 2-point Photography spend – but only after many tests and observations of the things.

Etheric Flight: Mi-go can "fly" in any environment from underwater to outer space, but thick atmosphere or water slow them down. (Rapidly rushing water can even drown them.) They can "walk up" walls and ceilings like enormous spiders, hover in place, and outpace a car. In the upper atmosphere, they can fly as fast as a jet and maneuver ignoring gravity and momentum.

Shortcut: A mi-go can bypass a physical obstacle or blink across up to 100 yards of space in a round with a Difficulty 4 Athletics test. On a failure, they do not accomplish the shortcut and any attack that round can damage them regardless of their Out-of-Phase ability.

Mi-Go Equipment

For a human to use mi-go equipment requires a Mechanics test against Difficulty 6; on a failed 1, the device injures the human user.

Cold Web: This hypergeometric arrangement of dipolar fibers transposes the cold of interstellar space to an area about 10 feet across for about 3 minutes (d+4 damage followed by loss of 1 Athletics every minute). Agents who have seen the cold web in action may try to dodge its slowly expanding field with an Athletics test (Difficulty 4).

Electric Wand: This 18-inch wand-like object is made of a black, non-reflective metal not found on Earth. It inflicts either a Mild, Moderate, or Extreme shock (p. 111); the mi-go can change the setting at any time.

Eraser: Developed for use on humans, this serum prevents the creation of short-term memories for 12 hours. The victim "comes to" 12 hours later and makes a 2-point Stability test (Unnatural). Any Stability or Sanity lost during the initial attack scene refreshes; the loss only recurs if the victim discovers what happened during the missing time or otherwise recovers her memories.

Gravity Weapon: The mi-go use this deadly macrodimensional device only as a last resort. Hinges

KEEPING THE MI-GO SCARY

The mi-go may feel familiar; the Greys might even seem campy. The Handler should fight both of those impressions, and keep the Outer Ones unknowable, unpredictable, and terrifying.

Change salient features in the mi-go description: add trailing cilia or chitin shells or cartilaginous lattices or visible mold and rot, mess with human perspective by describing them as impossibly small and faraway seeming even when up close, herald their coming with heat distortion or Doppler sound, surround them clouds of dancing spores or waving hairlike villi refracting unknown wavelengths of light. Their forms don't exist here: they might intersect each other, vanish and reappear like images in a frame-dropped film, fly and move at stuttering impossible speeds. They are utterly alien.

They transcend terrestrial physics, and can change or ignore the physical world in inexplicable and maddening ways. They might be able to access a sealed facility, or reverse local gravity, or shift forward and backward in time as apparition and premonition. Take the terrifying experiences of UFO abductees not as fodder for psychoanalysis, but as true narratives of a starkly impossible world.

Screen memories, "missing time," strange marks and burns - the mi-go and the Greys can cut and paste human thought and memory as easily as they can organic flesh. And they do so with as little regard for human aesthetics and consistency. Their poor understanding of linear time as experienced by humans leaves sloppy holes and edges in their victims' minds - including, perhaps, the minds of the Agents. Remember, the narrative of what an Agent experiences is under the Handler's total control. Play out the mental trauma of mi-go contact in shards and flashbacks, or leave unknowable holes in the story. Let the Agents uncover the truth on their own - or the void left when the truth is excised.

---

connect two six-inch sections of black stone-like material folded in on each other. When opened it unleashes a force in excess of 100 gravities in a cone emanating from the center of the sigil (L4*H). The cone affects everything in its path, knocking down buildings, breaking bones, and tearing structures to pieces with tidal forces. The weapon generates no counter-force.

Macrodimensional Scalpel: Although it resembles a short, shiny black baton, this foul-smelling device is actually a fifth-dimensional scalpel-suture-forceps-implant multitool. At Point-Blank range, it slices through (or unfolds, or cauterizes, or sews up, or drains of fluid) any organic tissue (L1* if used as a weapon). Its operations look and feel like torture, not least because mi-go don't use anaesthesia (preferring to delete the memory of the pain afterward if need be). Seeing it used on humans always costs 1 Stability, even if the witness succeeds at the Stability test.

Investigation

Anthropology: The moth-demon motif shows up on the pottery of Puaray pueblo, in the New Mexico mining country settled in the 12th century by Anasazi moving south from their cave cities. Some Hopi artists still paint moths delimiting and surrounding the world from outside. (Art)

Chemistry: The "cheese" you found is composed of dextroproteins — but everything organic on Earth except a few very ancient and extreme bacteria is composed of levoproteins. (Biology)

Forensics: The chest and abdomen bear dozens of tiny wounds and incisions, made by delicate blades. The wounds were delivered from an oblique, upward angle. Aside from the sharpness of the implement, however, they had little penetrating power. The victim ran a great distance, was attacked, and then bled to death.

Sense Trouble: You hear a noise halfway between a cicada chirp and the blurred flutter of a trapped moth. But the regular night-noises of the forest creatures have vanished.

Survival: Even the animal trails point down and away from this hillside. Literally nothing on earth goes here. (Biology, Notice)

Greys

These mi-go constructs appear as slender, noseless humanoids with large heads, long limbs and fingers, and liquid black, almond-shaped eyes. As their name indicates, they are grayish in color, ranging from pale gray through yellow-gray and green-gray to brownish-gray. They are photosynthetic, with a vestigial digestive system; they enter torpor if isolated from their own kind or environment. A single mi-go can teleoperate up to six Greys as well as its own body with no difficulty.

Some of their spacecraft are illusions or mobile hyperspace vortices projected by the mi-go; others are constructed saucers intended to lure MAJESTIC into further obsessive excesses. Grey technology is reskinned mi-go technology, made more primitive and "science-fictional" to conform to human expectations. Much of the Outer Ones' work as Greys involves conducting experiments in human intuition under the cover of UFO abductions.

The mi-go subject each abductee's mind to bizarre stimuli while monitoring their reactions. They return some subjects with the memory of the experience suppressed. Sometimes

the fungi take a particularly promising subject (or just their brain) back to Yuggoth and subject her to further unspeakable horrors. In communication with human abductees, the Greys tell any sort of story the mi-go devise, but their common legend involves the dead planet Zeta Reticulum III and a mission of exploration and eventual contact with Earth.

Grey

Abilities: Athletics 6, Energy Weapons 8, Health 5, Unarmed Combat 3

Hypergeometry: The controlling mi-go can use Greys to perform any ritual it knows, and spend up to 4 points of a Grey's Health on the Cost.

Hit Threshold: 3

Alertness Modifier: +1 to +3 (alien surveillance technology or implanted sensoria)

Stealth Modifier: +0

Attack: pinch (d-2), eraser beam, paralysis ball

Armor: none

Stability Loss: +0

Eraser: The Greys use this mi-go technology (p. 245) as a beam (Close range or nearer) rather than an injected serum.

Paralysis Ball: This silvery sphere increases the local inertia of all particles surrounding the target, creating a "bubble prison" in which time seems to stop for 10-60 minutes per Energy Weapons point spent. It takes a Sense Trouble test (Difficulty 6) to not be where the bubble focuses. Coming out of a bubble causes a 2-point Stability test (Difficulty 5).

Telepathy: The mi-go have outfitted some Greys (including the Roswell "survivor" held in the ICE CAVE) with telepathic modules for scanning human thoughts and sending messages. Treat a telepathic invasion as a Psionic Attack (p. 221) using a Psi pool of 12.

Metoh-Kangmi

The "abominable snowman" of the Himalayas is another mi-go construct, this one based on the yeti, a Voorii survival from the Pleistocene. The mi-go mining colony in Central Asia built the metoh-kangmi as a host body that could process terrestrial food — keeping the Gate that supplied it open was too dangerous so near Leng.

It resembles a bipedal, pale creature sprouting whiplike tendrils of hair and sinew. It has no wings; its head can unfold back from its face to expose the mi-go "brain" within. It moves in yards-long, hovering steps and can bilocate — the *lung-gom-pa* and *shespa-po* of Tibetan mysticism. Metoh-kangmi can and do use regular mi-go technology, in different forms.

The DELTA GREEN operatives who have encountered the metoh-kangmi in Nepal and Tibet have no idea that they are the same beings as the winged terrors of Vermont and the deeper Appalachians.

Metoh-Kangmi

Abilities: Athletics 8, Energy Weapons 8, Fighting 8, Health 8

Hypergeometry: As regular mi-go.

Hit Threshold: 4

Alertness Modifier: +2

Stealth Modifier: +1

Attack: kick (d+0), tendril (d−1); two tendril attacks in a row allow Monstrous Grappling (p. 222) to inject the target with an eraser (p. 245).

Armor: −3 (ablative coating); Transcendent (cold)

Stability Loss: +0

De-oxygenator: This ray burst removes the oxygen from the air in a 10-foot radius around the target, triggering immediate suffocation (p. 110) in anyone not wearing oxygen gear.

Lung-gom-pa: The metoh-kangmi can move two range increments (e.g., Near to Point-Blank or Close to Long) in one round by spending 1 Athletics.

Shespa-po: By spending 1 Health or Hypergeometry, the metoh-kangmi can create a convincing illusion of itself up to 12 miles away, or more if the witness has already seen the metoh-kangmi. The illusionary double can speak and sense its surroundings, but cannot be affected by physical force. (For 2 Health or Hypergeometry, the metoh-kangmi can project its double invisibly to that location.) The metoh-kangmi can spend 3 Health or Hypergeometry to instantaneously (and indetectably) switch places with its bilocated double.

Yeti

Abilities: Athletics 8, Fighting 16, Health 9

Hypergeometry: A very few yeti shamans might still survive, holding to the ancient Voorii magics of Hyperborea. Their Hypergeometry ratings are likely in the single digits, focused on rituals devoted to Tsathoggua or Itla-shua.

Hit Threshold: 4

Alertness Modifier: +2

Stealth Modifier: +1 (+2 downwind)

Attack: fist (d+0), thrown rock (d+0)

Armor: −3 (very thick fur)

Stability Loss: +0

Muuruup

The Gunditjmara of Australia's western Victoria state tell stories of the Muuruup, an enormous demon or ghost who lives underground and sends storms to kill his enemies. His servants are invisible spirits who screech like owls. These legends describe the spectral, polypous flying race that drove the Great Race of Yith fleeing into the future 70 million years ago, and that still lurks in primordial stone chambers beneath Australasia. Their true name is unknown; the Great Race called them the Elder Things and shuddered in terror at the whistling sound of their winds.

Gigantic blots of otherspacial un-matter, the spectral polyps infected the Earth and three other worlds of the Solar System billions of years ago. They carved stupendous, windowless basalt buildings and hunted the planet's primitive life forms until the Great Race arrived and, after millennia of war, penned them up in underground prisons.

They appear as huge, undulating, multi-colored tubelike beings. Their humps, tentacles, and organs peer and roil in and out of our visible dimensions. They screech and howl in the darkness, annihilating the few beings who chance across them.

Unfortunately, the upthrust basalts in which they dwell often contain vast mineral wealth: it is only a matter of time before newly drilled deep mines open up the ancient Yithian prisons again.

Muuruup

Abilities: Athletics 22, Fighting 17+, Health 44, Wind 10+

Hypergeometry: Some of these mysterious beings might worship one or more deities of the subterranean realm such as Tsathoggua or Nyogtha. Such worshippers have Hypergeometry ratings between 8 and 12, and appropriate rituals.

Hit Threshold: 4 (large but only intermittently visible)

Alertness Modifier: +2 (hyperdimensional senses, can see through cover)

Stealth Modifier: −1 (whistling)

Attack: tentacle whip (L1, ignores armor), un-matter touch (L2*)

Armor: Transcendent (all non-Lethality attacks and L1 attacks except electricity); all Lethality attacks above L1 do normal (non-Lethal) damage; suffers double maximum damage from electrical attacks

Stability Loss: +2

Invisibility: Although its body is always rotating through visible space and fading in unsettling fashion, a spectral polyp can become entirely invisible for one round by spending 2 Health points. It continues to emit its nauseating whistling noise, however, so its Hit Threshold rises to 6 rather than vanishing altogether.

Un-Matter Infection: The strange un-matter that composes the giant polyp is completely inimical to Earthly life. A simple touch from the visible portions of the polyp (with a Fighting test) is enough to disrupt living material, consuming it like a fire turning wood to ash.

Vacuum Burst: Muuruup can suddenly evacuate huge areas of atmosphere, causing a thunder-like explosion as the air rushes back in to fill the empty space. When targeted at a human, this attack is treated as an explosive (L1H; Lethal Radius Close; Damage Radius Near). When projected at a vehicle, on a successful Wind ability test, it blows open every sealed surface within it, completely disabling it (and causing aircraft, of course, to crash).

Windblast: Using its Wind ability, the Muuruup can emit a blast of desiccating wind to strip the flesh from its target's bones and blow him across the room. Damage modifiers depend on what he hits on his way across the room, and on the range, as follows: Close or Point-Blank (d+4), Near (d+2), Long (d+0).

Investigation

Forensics: The skin at the wounds is deeply but irregularly pockmarked, with some abrasion in no discernible pattern. Death was caused either by the suffocation or possibly by the contusions. The whole body is reddened slightly, and there is particulate matter in the skin and hair, some embedded quite deeply. The flesh is somewhat desiccated, as though it had been sun-dried or baked. The eardrums are split.

Survival: That wind came up from the ground, and the weather has been clear all week. (Sense Trouble)

Rat-Thing

Rat-things resemble ordinary rats, and are easily mistaken for them at a distance. Their heads are nonetheless evil caricatures of human heads, and their paws are like tiny human hands. They have extremely strong, sharp teeth, canines grown forward to resemble incisors. They nuzzle and nurse on human blood from their witch companions or from convenient sleepers. Though they do not die naturally, they are now thankfully rare.

Malign sorcery creates these unnatural hybrids of rat and human. This foul transformation allows deceased cultists or stillborn witch-children to be transformed and thus continue to serve their master Nyarlathotep.

Rat-Thing

Abilities: Athletics 9, Fighting 8, Health 3

Hypergeometry: A rat-thing might have a Hypergeometry rating as low as 3 or 4, or more likely one in the double digits like the human wizard he once was. All rat-things know at least two other rituals in addition to those for contacting Nyarlathotep and their fellow rat-things. The canonical rat-thing ritual creates a hyperspace gate.

Hit Threshold: 6 (small and incredibly nimble)

Alertness Modifier: +2

Stealth Modifier: +2

Attack: bite (d-2, infected with plague (p. 112)); drained Health lost to rat-thing bite refreshes its own Health (up to 6).

Armor: none

Stability Loss: +1

Familiar: A rat-thing can act as an assistant in any ritual that its master or mistress knows, even one that requires assistants to know the ritual. Because a rat-thing knows all languages, it can help its master or mistress learn a ritual even without knowing the language of its source.

Internal Attack: If a target has ever participated in a ceremony with a rat-thing (even involuntarily during a dream) the rat-thing can teleport to the target's insides and chew its way out. Its internal attacks begin at Hit Threshold 0 and increment up by 1 for each attack; the first two do two instances of bite damage. When it reaches Hit Threshold 2, it emerges from the target's skin and can be attacked in turn – assuming the

target has any Stability left. (Being chewed through costs 1 Stability per Health point lost; seeing the rat-thing burst from one's body is a 7-point Stability test.) Truly horrible Handlers can allow the rat-thing to target anyone it's bitten, or anyone it's seen near a Gate, or smelled.

Investigation

Biology: The skeleton is obviously that of a huge, diseased rat. That said, the bones of the paws almost seem prehensile, with joints so well developed and used as to have become arthritic. The skull is queerly flattened in front, and distended in the cranial region.

Chemistry: Testing the rat urine from the dead man's clothing revealed high levels of uric acid – a compound that only appears in the urine of humans and higher apes. Must have been some contamination – some *further* contamination – of the sample. (Biology)

Criminology: Two of the bloody rat prints almost resemble human hand prints, except for the size, of course. (Notice)

Forensics: The body was cored out and gnawed from the inside as by the teeth of an enormous rat. The path ran from the abdominal cavity up through the liver and heart and out through the base of the throat. No indication has yet been found as to how the rat got into the body cavity in the first place, however.

Rat Swarm

These statistics are for a swarm of 10 non-supernatural rats. Increase Fighting and Health by 2 for every 10 additional rats; increase damage by +1 for each 30 rats. Every hit against a rat swarm kills 2 rats and disperses 8 others; if the fight continues for more than two rounds, dispersed rats rejoin the swarm.

Abilities: Athletics 5, Fighting 3, Health 3

Hit Threshold: 3 (target-rich environment)

Alertness Modifier: +1 (keen smell)

Stealth Modifier: +0 (numerous)

Attack: bite (d-1); may be infected with plague (p. 112)

Armor: none

Stability Loss: +0 unless the character has a specific phobia

Serpent Folk

The squamous serpent folk resemble upright, bipedal snakes, with wedge-shaped heads and taloned arms. They can sense motion, have a keen sense of smell thanks to their forked tongues, and sense heat like a pit viper. They range in color from green and brown to pale yellow or gray, often spotted or streaked with darker markings.

Their civilization flourished on the subcontinent of Valusia (roughly where Europe, Egypt, and the Mediterranean basin are now) before even dinosaurs walked the earth. There they uncovered and attempted to exploit the ancient technologies left behind by other alien cultures that had colonized the Earth. With these secrets, these sorcerer-scientists learned to change and manipulate space, life, and time.

After the destruction of Valusia, the serpent folk scattered to red-litten Yoth and lost Atlantis. The cataclysms sent them back down the evolutionary ladder to interbreed with humans and lurk in the shadowy caves and desolate moors above their former empires. A few of the pure breed survive in human disguise, working inscrutable plans to return their kind to supremacy over Earth.

Valusian (Pure-Bred or Atavistic)

Abilities: Athletics 10, Health 6, Unarmed Combat 11

Hypergeometry: 10+; any ritual is possible; Infallible Suggestion and Withering are common.

Hit Threshold: 6 (preternatural reflexes; Hit Threshold 4 against explosives)

Alertness Modifier: +2 (for motion and smell, not sound alone)

Stealth Modifier: +1

Attack: bite (d-1 plus snake venom (p. 112) L1H), joint lock (d+0), Sign of Power (d+1)

Armor: -3 vs. any (scales and inhuman toughness); Transcendent (toxins)

Stability Loss: +1; +2 to see someone you know well transform into one of the serpent folk

Blood Feast: A serpent-man must make an Athletics test (Difficulty 7) to resist grappling a bleeding target using *Monstrous Grappling* (p. 222). If the grapple succeeds, the serpent-man drains 2 Health per round automatically from his target. (Successfully pulling free of the grapple costs 1d-2 Health in ripped flesh and spurting blood.) Any successful attack on the serpent-man ends the blood feast; until it ends, the serpent-man can take no other action.

Charnel Visage: A serpent-man that eats a corpse can take the appearance of the devoured human. This ritual costs 2 Hypergeometry pool points. Many Valusian sorcerers can transform rapidly between their native form and any of a dozen previously consumed human forms.

Sign of Power: With a gesture, a serpent-man can cause a single target to be flung backwards with extreme force, inflicting d+1 damage. It is unknown if this ability is a ritual or an inherent ability of the serpent folk.

Investigation

Accounting: The signature on this form is a bad forgery, but to get at the safe deposit box, he would have had to appear in person – and the bank manager would definitely have recognized an imposter.

Biology: Snakes become torpid after a large meal – it sounds horrible, but now might be the best time to rush the thing. (Survival)

Forensics: There were two large punctures in the throat, with only a trickle of blood near them. The blood remained tacky for an unusually long period post mortem. The skin around the punctures is friable, almost necrotic, and emits a greenish oily liquid. (The examining assistant got some on his hand, and it tingled for several minutes.) The extremities were bluish, and the face engorged with blood and bright blue. The protruding tongue was swollen and black, and the eyes purpled. Cause of death was paralysis of the chest muscles.

Sense Trouble: This apartment smells like the snake house at the zoo.

Degenerate Serpent Folk

Most serpent people remaining in the modern world are the degenerate descendants of interbreeding with Neanderthals, Voorii, and isolated human groups over the last few million years. They live in barrows, caves, and waste places – or in sewer and subway systems in metropolitan anonymity. They live by cannibalism, kidnapping human brides when they can to replenish their dwindling genetic stock.

They come in two main varieties, a dwarfish and stunted humanoid form ("Children of the Night") and a bloated snake form ("Worms of the Earth") with vestigial limbs. By and large the snake form is more debased and less intelligent than the humanoid form, but the genetic lines are so twisted and coiled that any sort of atavism or progression is possible.

Child of the Night

Abilities: Athletics 6, Melee Weapons 6, Health 6, Unarmed Combat 7

Hypergeometry: 5+ for an ollave of the Children

Hit Threshold: 3 (4 in shadows or at night; 5 in pitch darkness)

Alertness Modifier: +2 (in darkness), -1 (in bright light)

Stealth Modifier: +2

Attack: flint knife or axe (d-1), arrow (d-1 plus snake venom (p. 112) L1H), bite (d-2 plus snake venom (p.112) L1)

Armor: -1 (squamous skin)

Stability Loss: +0

Worm of the Earth

Abilities: Athletics 6, Fighting 10, Health 8

Hypergeometry: 5+ in rare circumstances; uses Hypergeometry for natural effects (1 point each): cave-ins, floods, controlling water and wind, or creating a will-o-wisp light to lure prey into the cavern.

Hit Threshold: 4

Alertness Modifier: +2 (motion and smell only)

Stealth Modifier: +1

Attack: bite (d+0 plus snake venom (p. 112) L2H), talon (d+1)

Armor: -3 (reptilian hide)

Stability Loss: +1

Children of Yig: For the enormous snakes that serve as Yig's harbingers and attendants, use these statistics with no talon attack or Hypergeometry. Anyone who fails a Stability test because of the Children of Yig receives Nightmares (p. 124); anyone who kills a Child of Yig and fails her Stability test receives Nightmares and the personal attention of Yig.

Shoggoth

This species of giant, plastic, ever-changing acellular life gained sentience and rebelled against its crinoid elder masters long before mankind rose to prominence. Barely defeated in a world-sundering war, the surviving shoggoths are semi-intelligent, malevolent, and incredibly dangerous. Seemingly immortal and nearly indestructible, shoggoths make perfect weapons; informants speak of shoggoths deployed by the Deep Ones and by individual hypergeometers.

A shapeless black blob fifteen feet in diameter or larger, the shoggoth boils with green eyes and iridescent bubbles, making and unmaking any organs or tendrils needed for a given task. It can exert prodigious strength or ooze through the tiniest cracks.

Their protoplasmic matter is neither plant nor animal, at base somewhat like fungi or algae but capable of mimicking or adapting any organic form needed or desired. They are the ultimate problem solvers, seemingly designed to overcome, construct, or *destroy* any obstacle. More than any other species in this book, the Handler should change and add abilities to shoggoths to make them more horribly hazardous to the Agents.

Shoggoth

Abilities: Athletics 28+, Fighting 23+, Health 38+

Hypergeometry: A shoggoth that had somehow absorbed (or perfectly imitated) the rites of its masters might have a few points in Hypergeometry and one or two rote rituals.

Hit Threshold: 3 (large)

Alertness Modifier: +3; shoggoths suffer no penalties for darkness, fog, etc.

Stealth Modifier: -1

Attack: pseudoposcis strike (d+2), smash (L2)

Armor: Resilient (everything), Lethality attacks above L2 do d+2 damage; shoggoths are never Hurt or suffer any damage penalties

Stability Loss: +3

All Along the Shoggoth: In combat, a standard (15') shoggoth can attack two beings at Close range per round and all beings within Point-Blank range simultaneously, although its targets' Hit Thresholds increase by 1 for every three separate targets it attacks. After successfully attacking a target at Close range, that target counts as Point-Blank — the shoggoth has oozed some part of itself even closer. A shoggoth may stretch or shape its bulk to bring itself into Point-Blank range of as many targets as possible, spending 2 Athletics to do so per target (3 points for Near targets).

Locomotion: A shoggoth can roll along the ground, disperse its density to rise lighter than air, or pull water or air through itself like a jet. No one has survived an encounter long enough to measure a shoggoth's maximum speed, but some victims have escaped shoggoths by speeding away in an automobile, motorboat, or airplane.

Mimicry: The shoggoth can imitate any human voice (or indeed any sound) it hears for 2 Health per scene. Listeners who suspect that they are hearing monsters instead of friends must make a Difficulty 6 Sense Trouble test to convince themselves.

Oozing: A shoggoth can ooze, grow, shift, or change its shape to fit through any gap that air can penetrate.

Pseudoposcis: The shoggoth suddenly extrudes a hollow, razor-sharp pseudopod that impales its target (d+2) and begins slurping up nutrient protein. The shoggoth gains all Health points lost by the target.

Regeneration: A shoggoth with at least 1 Health left can regenerate d+1 Health every turn in which it neither moves nor attacks.

Snare and Crush: With *Monstrous Grappling* (p. 222), a shoggoth may loop an increasingly muscular tendril around a character (d+0). Each round thereafter, the shoggoth hits automatically and does +2 more damage each time. (It might also make a second attack and bite down with a suddenly-grown mouth for d+5.) Characters snared by the shoggoth also automatically hit the shoggoth. When a crushed character dies, the shoggoth adds her Health rating to its own; she has been broken down into nutrients and digested.

Unstoppable: If reduced to 0 Health, a shoggoth collapses into inert, hardened, desiccated bits of organic matter. However, it is not dead. If left in this state in an environment with access to oxygen and water, even trace water in the air, it reconstitutes to half strength in 18-23 hours. If this desiccated matter is burned or subjected to other destructive forces (even ones which would not usually affect the shoggoth), the shoggoth is permanently destroyed.

Investigation

Biology: The slime is pure protoplasm, much like the matter of an amoeba. There is no cell structure visible. Its chromatin is fragmentary and evenly mixed throughout, rather than being differentiated into nuclear bodies or organelles.

Forensics: Blackish putrescent slime covered the heavily contused body. The spine was partially detached, and what was left of the head hung by ragged fragments of skin and tendon. There were ten or a dozen different types of bite and claw marks on the body.

Notice: The bricks on the south wall are just piled up against each other, as though the mortar was dissolved in place by something that flowed through the wall into the room. (Architecture)

Sense Trouble: From down the tunnel comes a sort of anechoic roaring or rumbling. It almost sounds like a crowd of people or birds.

Spawn of Yog-Sothoth

These are the beings formed when Yog-Sothoth mates with a human, creating a hybrid creature. No two Sons (or Daughters) are alike. All such hybrids grow and mature rapidly, requiring great quantities of fresh, raw flesh for sustenance. For a while, the lesser of such progeny can pass as human without close inspection. It reaches apparent adulthood in 10 years. By age 15, such a monstrous hybrid may be so tall and deformed as to seem human only by stooping in all-covering, loose clothing.

But nothing can mask its stench, foul and unrelated to anything produced by humanity. Dogs hate the impure spawn of Yog-Sothoth and attack with little provocation. The hybrid must avoid humanity whenever possible, risking contact only when necessary to fulfill its purposes. The spawn of Yog-Sothoth are driven to open ways into the world for their sire and their unseen, purer cousins.

Humanoid Spawn

Abilities: Athletics 10, Fighting 13, Health 11, Melee Weapons 5

Hypergeometry: 1 for each year since its birth; Call Forth Those From Outside (Yog-Sothoth), Voorish Sign, and as many more rituals as it can learn.

Hit Threshold: 4

Alertness Modifier: +2

Stealth Modifier: +1 (-3 against dogs)

Attack: inhumanly strong fist (d-1), sacrificial dagger (d-1), vampiric suckling (see below)

Armor: Resilient (bullets and puncturing attacks)

Stability Loss: +0 (clothed or relatively human), +1 (naked, dead, or relatively inhuman)

Jumping, Climbing, Loping: The impure spawn can leap, climb and lope in a manner wholly unlike a human. By spending 2 Athletics, it can cross vertical distances and impassable obstacles that would stop a normal human, but otherwise moves at human speeds.

Vampiric Suckling: In any round after the impure spawn has a victim pinned using *Monstrous Grappling* (p. 222), the red, sucking mouths of its (usually concealed) tentacles greedily suck blood from the victim's veins. This attack automatically hits, doing d+1 Athletics damage; each point of lost Athletics heals 1 Health for the spawn. At Athletics 0, the victim passes out and the spawn's suckling does Health damage. (If the target survives, he regains 1 Athletics for each day of bed rest.)

Pure Spawn

Abilities: Athletics 13, Fighting 25, Health 21

Hypergeometry: 2 for each year since its birth; same rituals as the humanoid spawn. If it and its sibling each spend 1 Hypergeometry point casting a ritual, those 2 points count as 3 toward the Cost.

Hit Threshold: 7 (while invisible), 3 (large, while visible)

Alertness Modifier: +1

Stealth Modifier: +2 (while invisible), -3 (while visible, against dogs)

Attack: trample (L1H), trunk (d-1); after a successful trunk attack, the spawn grasps the target with Monstrous Grappling and begins Vampiric Suckling (see above).

Armor: Transcendent (while invisible), Resilient (all but enchanted weapons, only while visible)

Stability Loss: +1 (invisible), +3 (visible)

Investigation

Forensics: The torso and one leg were smashed flat by the rapid descent of a roughly barrel-shaped mass. (If this were India, not Oregon, I'd say it was an elephant track.) The black, ropy tar on the body sublimed away into a whitish gummy residue. There was surprisingly little blood or bruising. The large, circular black mark on the upper back proved, on further inspection, to be composed of dozens of small, suppurating punctures.

HUMINT: Pore ol' Elspeth. Got knocked up on Roodmas an' los' the chile on Midsummers, and still pretends to go 'feed her babe' down in Devil Glen when she thinks no-one's a-watchin.' Runs in th' family, I expect; her mammy used to put out calf's brains for whippoorwills, of all things.

Notice: The trail of the thing goes vertically up the side of the shale cliff, despite weighing more than a moose from the depth of the tracks. (Survival)

Star-Spawn of Cthulhu

This is Cthulhu's quasi-saurian, quasi-octopoid species, which seeped down from his green binary star unguessable aeons ago. He is the largest and the mightiest of them, but they are still titans, each weighing over 100 tons. The *Necronomicon* calls them "the star-spawn of Cthulhu," under which name most occultists know them.

They fought for supremacy agains the Elder Things in ancient times, forcing them from the surface world. Perhaps that defeat was the precursor to the Elder Things' creation of the shoggoths. Not all the inhabitants of R'lyeh were trapped when it sank. Some still live on in the deep trenches beneath the ocean, tended by Deep Ones and guarded by sea-shoggoths.

Five great Star-Spawn, the "Five Watchers," reputedly slumber in subterranean gulfs beneath the Bayan Kara Shan mountains in China, the Nameless City in the Arabian desert, the Greenland glacier, New England, and the Amazon Basin. Related entities dwell in the stars, such as the beings said to infest the Lake of Hali on or near Aldebaran.

Star-Spawn of Cthulhu

Abilities: Athletics 23, Fighting 27, Health 51

Hypergeometry: Ranges from 15+ for normal star-spawn to 300+ for the "Five Watchers." Their rituals include Call of Dagon, Call Forth Those From Outside (Star-Spawn), and rites to contact dread Cthulhu in dreams.

Hit Threshold: 2 (titanic)

Alertness Modifier: +2

Stealth Modifier: -2 (except in deep ocean or subterranean abyss)

Attack: claw swipe (L1*H), grab and consume (L2*H)

Armor: Resilient (weapons) [L-3]; weapons L4 and above have full effect

Stability Loss: +0

Ballistic Flight: With a spend of 3 Athletics, a star-spawn launches itself into the atmosphere at Mach 2. It lands with an unceremonious impact similar to an explosion (L1H, Lethal Radius Close, Damage Radius Near).

Grab and Consume: The star-spawn attempts to grab and consume any target that hit it with a Lethality attack of any level. The star-spawn smashes a limb down (Difficulty 4 Athletics test to evade), and seizes the target using Monstrous Grappling. The next round (if the target fails to escape) it drops the target into an orifice for digestion (L2*). Nutrients from the shredded target restore d+1 Health to the star-spawn.

Psychic Shout: Some characters who fail the Stability test when encountering the star-spawn feel more than its awful physical presence. A character who fails the Stability test and is exceptionally sensitive (rating of 2+ in Art, Fringe Science, Occult, or Psychotherapy) is overwhelmed by a psychic "shout." It can only be approximated as a voice shouting or babbling what should be nonsense if it were a voice—yet it is clearly filled with utterly alien meaning. The hearer can do nothing while in the presence of the star-spawn.

Tcho-Tcho

No one knows where the "Tcho-Tcho" people hail from, or even, indeed, if that is their name. To the Greeks they were the Tochoa, and they swept in and violently ruled much of what is today Afghanistan before being pushed back to the Asian wilds in the 3rd century B.C. by the Sassanid Persians. The Chinese called them the Hsiao Yueh-Chih, and shunned "those with the knife smile" as cannibals, whispering that they traveled between the known world and hidden Leng.

The British followed rumors of hidden cities of the Khyo-Khyom on the plateau of Singu in Burma and in Gelanggi in Malaya. To the French missions in Indochina, they were the Chauchas, little, withdrawn tribes-people who at first seemed friendly, but who showed a propensity for sudden ambush and violence. The American cultural anthropologists identified them as Tcho-Tcho, a name derived from the Khmer "glowing"... or from the Yi word meaning "those who eat."

All of these things, and names, can be said to be true, or at least, not false. What do the Tcho-Tcho people say about themselves? Noth-

ing, though if asked, they will smile, and laugh through black, sharpened teeth. They may even offer a pipe stuffed with aromatic, nighted *khmaw chhouk* petals. The one thing known by all parties is that the Tcho-Tcho, in addition to being somewhat dangerous, are capable liars. They are not to be trusted.

Other Americans didn't care about their name or their reputation – the CIA knew them as ruthless, even brutal, fighters who hated the Communists and begin arming them in 1961 for the secret war in Laos. By 1965, DELTA GREEN has some questions about the Company's unsavory allies: the Tcho-Tcho are unfathomably sadistic, and avowed cannibals. In 1969, the Tcho-Tcho begin to turn on the Americans, luring them into ambushes and stew pots; in 1970 DELTA GREEN repays the favor with an annihilating bombing campaign.

Tcho-Tcho

Abilities: Archery 6, Athletics 8, Firearms 6, Health 6, Melee Weapons 5, Unarmed Combat 7

Hypergeometry: 5+ for shamans, 10+ for sorcerers; rituals always include a means of contact for the relevant deity and Call Forth Those From Outside for its servitors, as well as Voorish Sign, Withering, and anything else unpleasant.

Hit Threshold: 4

Alertness Modifier: +1

Stealth Modifier: +2 (in native countryside), +1 (elsewhere)

Attack: fist (d-2), bite (d-1), blowgun dart (d-2 plus poison), kris (d-1 plus poison), arrow (d-1 plus poison), M1 Garand .30 caliber rifle (d+2, plus poison)

Armor: none

Stability Loss: There is no Stability loss for seeing a Tcho-Tcho, until you get to know them better.

Hollow-Point Ammo: Guess what – with a tiny hollow needle, a small awl, a fire, and some patience, you can fill the hollow tip of a bullet with poison! Hollow-point bullets increase damage by +1 and increase armor effectiveness by -1 (e.g., Armor -1 becomes -2). And deliver poison.

Paralytic Poison: Any Tcho-Tcho attack that breaks the skin (or a covert application of khmaw chhouk to an Agent's food or clothing) delivers a toxin (p. 111):

△ Onset: 1-3 rounds (3-6 minutes out of combat)

△ Test: Difficulty 7 Health

△ Minor: d+1 damage, Hurt, -1 to Hit Threshold for a day; d-1 only if treated immediately with Pharmacy or First Aid.

△ Severe: L2H, total paralysis and -1 to Health and Athletics every 30 minutes until dead or hospitalized.

Tcho-Tcho herbalists can handcraft any number of symptoms from khmaw chhouk tar: Dreaming quests, ecstasy, sleep, berserk rage, shamanic contact with a deity, aphasia, panic fear – anything the Handler can imagine. They can also develop toxins for (and from) anything organic, quicken the onset of poisons, replicate seemingly innocent symptoms, or make use of other unnatural creatures' innate poisons.

Investigation

Biology: The stems and fragments of leaf matter we found in the gutters of the warehouse are definitely from lotus plants, and probably from south-east Asia. But it's no variety of genus Nelumbo I know of, and that sap is so toxic that it bleached the rotten wood where it rested.

Forensics: The victim died in horrible agony, the back arched almost into a circle, the fingers and toes ankylosed almost into claws, and the face twisted into a sardonic rictus of unimaginable gruesomeness. On the third search, we found the puncture wound in the palm of his left foot – the dart was apparently hidden in his shoe while he slept.

Medicine: Miss Delahunt isn't flirting – her eyelid is drooping involuntarily. Such ptosis is a symptom of opiate use; perhaps Miss Delahunt knows more about these matters than she lets on. *(0-point spend)* Ptosis is also triggered by over-exposure to nuciferene, an alkaloid found in lotus leaves and flowers. *(1-point spend)*

Sense Trouble: You hear a chuff of breath off to your left, down low.

Those Beyond

An unseen world exists in tandem with our own, invisible to normal humans, due to our inability to sense at the strange frequencies which illuminate the liquid aether of this other realm. The creatures which exist in the liquid world beyond cannot "see" us, although they slither over us and through us constantly. Our atoms vibrate a very tiny bit out of phase with the atoms of this other world, and so we pass each other while occupying the same space.

Until Crawford Tillinghast invented his resonator in 1920, mankind was safe, although other hypergeometries may have opened the way beyond before then. The Tillinghast Resonator not only awakens ancient atrophied sense organs within the human brain which can see this other world, it also brings the quantum structures of both worlds into alignment, until physical interaction becomes possible.

The creatures that exist beyond come in a multitude of horrific forms, as various and endless as those found on Earth: an array of swirling bony, razor-sharp disks; a lamprey-like thing that moves by turning itself inside out; a thing built of mantises and anglerfish and piranhas covered in wide, spiral mouths; a mauve-glowing jellyfish radiating barbed cartilaginous hooks.

All of them seem to swim through the air and through solid things in this world. They hunt in the higher dimensions utilizing senses not generally found on Earth, consuming each other in a violent and never-ending interplay of predators and prey.

The Tillinghast Resonator (and other unnatural processes) can illuminate our physical world to the strange senses of the predators, allowing these dangerous creatures to see us and interact with us within the T-Field effect. Movement within the field, and to a lesser degree those things imbued with Tillinghast radiation (T-Radiation), draw devourers towards them, usually with catastrophic results.

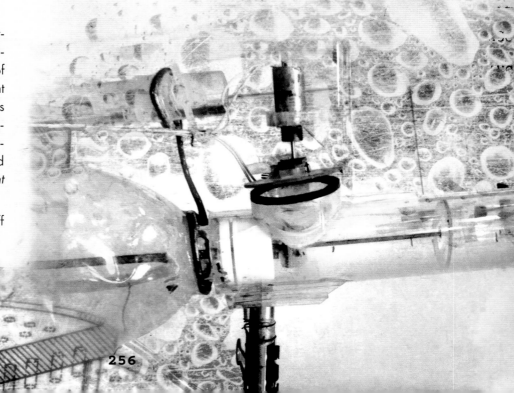

Ultraviolet Devourer

Abilities: Athletics 7, Fighting 6, Health 5

Hypergeometry: 0

Hit Threshold: 4 (flickering)

Alertness Modifier: +2 (in the T-Field); +0 (against unmoving targets)

Stealth Modifier: +1 (noiseless)

Attack: cutting blades (d+0), tendril hooks (d+0), slurping mouths (d+0)

Armor: Out-of-Phase

Stability Loss: +1

Out-of-Phase Attack: On any attack roll of a natural 1 or 2, those beyond do no damage as they are not "in phase" with their target. Instead, they interpenetrate him bodily, flowing visibly through him; this triggers a 6-point Unnatural Stability test the first time it happens.

Swarm Attack: Ultraviolet devourers attack as a swarm. Each additional devourer adds +2 Health and +2 Fighting. Each two additional devourers increase the damage by one increment: three bite for d+1, five for d+2, etc. There is no practical limit on the number of devourers that can swarm a single human.

Investigation

Forensics: The pile of clothing seems to have been shed all at once, underclothes still hooked and entirely within the buttoned and tucked outer garments. It's as though the body within simply vanished. The only possible clue: damp sweat and urine stains in the clothing, recent and copious.

Notice: Light from the lamps in this room has a queer purplish tint to it. The air still smellsy faintly of ozone, as if heavy electrical equipment had been at work here. (Mechanics, Physics)

Sense Trouble: You hear a sound slowly come up around you: faint, a musical vibrato to it, but somehow dissonant. Your flesh creeps and your teeth sting with a cold draft, rushing past you from the direction of the sound, the direction of that purplish light.

Wendigowak

These cannibal-ogres of Algonquin legend manifest an infection among those in the northern reaches who have partaken of the communion of Itla-Shua and eaten human flesh. The wendigo's strange-smelling hair bristles from frozen, blue-white corpse-flesh. Its eyes blaze red or purple, and a long tongue emerges from between its protruding, fanged teeth. Despite its deformed or animalistic feet, the wendigo travels in enormous leaps.

Wendigo

Abilities: Athletics 12, Fighting 16, Health 13

Hypergeometry: 8; can summon Itla-Shua for Cost 5.

Hit Threshold: 4

Alertness Modifier: +2 (+4 to track wounded prey)

Stealth Modifier: +2 (+3 while snowing)

Attack: claw (d+1), bite (d+0, plus possible wendigoism), howl (special); the wendigo can attack twice in a round, either claw-bite or claw-claw. If two claw attacks hit in succession, its bite attack succeeds automatically until forcibly separated from its prey.

Armor: -4 (thick and frozen hide); Resilient (all attacks except fire below L2) [L-1]; takes double damage from fire, which ignores its armor.

Stability Loss: +0; +1 if the wendigo was known to the witness when human.

Giant Steps: For 2 Athletics points, wendigo can bound or "step" up to 20 yards vertically or 40 yards horizontally (from Near to Point-Blank, for instance) in one round.

Howl: The wendigo's howl costs it 2 Hypergeometry; hearers make a 5-point Stability test (Unnatural). Those who fail become Shattered for the duration of the scene; those who succeed lose only 2 Stability.

Wendigo Bite: After the combat, surviving bitten Agents must make a Stability test (Difficulty 5, +1 for each additional wendigo bite, +5 if he has ever eaten human flesh). On a failure, the Agent adds +3 to Athletics and Health, doubles his Unarmed Combat, and does d-1 (and communicates wendigoism) with a bite. He has an Addiction (Human Flesh). His feet begin to deform and his eyes change color (Difficulty 5 Sense Trouble to spot). At the end of the operation (or later at the Handler's discretion) he transforms into a wendigo and runs out into the Arctic.

Investigation

Anthropology: The best compendium of wendigo beliefs and wendigo encounters, as well as other spirit lore of the Cree and Ojibwa, appears in the 1823 journal of the Hudson's Bay Company trapper George Nelson, kept during his sojourn at Lac la Ronge, Saskatchewan.

Forensics: The body is frozen solid, as though it spent days in a deep freeze or in the Arctic winter wilderness. Or on a mountaintop, or in the upper atmosphere: the bleeding visible around the eyes may have been caused by depressurization. The frozen blood around the throat and belly comes from the deep bites, of course; the liver is missing.

Sense Trouble: A weird smell carries through the freezing air: acrid, with hints of decaying leaves, rotting wood, and blood. The closest you can come to summarizing it is "the odor of lions."

White Apes

Turned into ritual tools by the Great Race over a million years ago, the early hominid Tchadanthropus clustered in Central Africa and thus separated itself from the primary evolutionary lineage that eventually became Homo sapiens. However, interbreeding between Tchadanthropus and both man and apes remains possible down to the modern era – a possible legacy of Yithian genetic tinkering.

The result: a race of white apes with the cunning of savages and the ferocity of baboons. They are approximately as tall as men, but their ape muscles knot around thicker limbs and torsos; wide jaws full of razor-sharp teeth split their low skulls. Their eyes are not albino red, but pale blue or green. They carry primitive stone weapons; trophies of their kills, carefully dried in the tropical sun, dangle from their knotted fur or from lanyards of sinew or rawhide.

The British explorers Sir Wade Jermyn in the 18th century, and Samuel Seaton in the 19th, both reported a gray city of white apes deep in the Congo, a likely reference to Itoko/Thule (p. 213). A Soviet expedition under P.E. Zvery encountered the apes in 1930. Since Thule's violation in 1943, white apes have appeared on battlefields in the Congo, Biafra, Angola, Rhodesia, and other African wars – sometimes fighting, always scavenging the dead. The white apes are migrating, possibly seeking some new lost city to call their own, possibly following the ancient call of Yith bred into their genes before the Ice Age.

White Ape

Abilities: Athletics 10, Health 8, Melee Weapons 7, Unarmed Combat 16

Hypergeometry: 0

Hit Threshold: 4

Alertness Modifier: +2 (in jungle)

Stealth Modifier: +2 (in jungle)

Attack: fist/bite (d+1), gorilla hug (see below), club/sharp rock/stone axe (d+0), spear (d+1)

Armor: -2 (hide)

Stability Loss: +0

Climbing, Leaping, and Swinging: By spending 2 Athletics, a white ape can near-instantly shinny to the top of a tree or 7 yards up a cliff, leap up to 7 yards with a running start, or swing across a 15 yard gap. Swinging on vines or brachiating between jungle tree limbs, they can outpace running humans.

Gorilla Hug: After a successful monstrous grapple attack (p. 222), the white ape's squeeze automatically does d-2 per round, but the ape can spend Athletics to increase the damage at a rate of 2 Athletics per +1 to damage.

Investigation

Biology: This tuft of white fur resembles ape hair – it's thicker and more opaque – but look how long it is! Ape hair doesn't grow that much.

Forensics: At first glance, he was torn to pieces by a baboon: note the bites on chest and throat, the broken limbs, and the fact that he was hurled across the clearing. But those tooth marks are too close together to be baboon fangs, and the bruises on the arms too large to be baboon hands.

Sense Trouble: All the bird sounds have just stopped: an ambush? But you don't smell gun oil, or cigarettes, or anyone's sweat but your own.

Worm That Walks

A wizard walks the earth in a town. He dies, and is buried. The worms eat his flesh, and grow fat. They also grow large, and gravid with sorcerous power. They breed more worms, and the clat swells to human size and crawls up out of the grave, or is dug up by another cultist, or by a seeker after wizardly power. The clat of worms emerges from the soil and dons an all-concealing robe and mask. A wizard once more walks the earth in a town.

After its blasphemous resurrection, the worm-wizard either mates with a human woman and breeds his own shuddersome lineage of pupils, or seduces would-be sorcerers with its grave-won lore. Eventually, it converts its descendants or students into worm-cultists, through hypergeometry or by subtle adulteration of their food or blood. When and if these cultists die, they too resurrect, bloated clats of grave worms wearing long coats and masks to move about the city.

Worm That Walks

Abilities: Athletics 4, Health 8, Melee Weapons 4

Hypergeometry: 4-10+; worm-wizards usually have at least one version of Call Forth Those From Outside for a flock of ai-apa, a dimensional shambler, or a feaster from the stars. They also use attack rituals such as Withering, Infallible Suggestion, or Exchange Personalities.

Hit Threshold: 3

Alertness Modifier: -1

Stealth Modifier: +1

Attack: dagger (d-1)

Armor: Resilient (physical weapons)

Stability Loss: +2

Crawling and Chaotic: It is not one monstrous Worm but many, its body built out of a mass of writhing, squirming worms. Such a Crawling Thing can ooze through any space the size of a worm's body or smaller: window cracks, mail slots, virtually any wooden or cheap construction.

Investigation

Forensics: The expression on the face was one of the sheerest insane terror. When we pried open his clenched fists, his hands were covered with slime and dirt: crushed worms and soil. The actual cause of death was massive heart failure, combined with a cascading series of brain aneurysms and miniature strokes. It's as though his neurological and cardiac systems both suffered an immense, simultaneous shock.

Notice: There are a number of odd holes in the soil over Abednego Stark's grave. It's almost as if worms were tunneling there repeatedly, but after 200 years there just can't be that much of him left. (Biology)

Occult: "Wisely did al-Shakashik say, that happy is the tomb where no wizard hath lain, and happy the town at night whose wizards are all ashes. For it is of old rumour that the soul of the devil-bought hastes not from his charnel clay, but fats and instructs *the very worm that gnaws;* till out of corruption horrid life springs, and the dull scavengers of earth wax crafty to vex it and swell monstrous to plague it. Great holes secretly are digged where earth's pores ought to suffice, and things have learnt to walk that ought to crawl." This Alhazred quote is well known enough to appear in other collections of Islamic occult lore.

Sense Trouble: One or two worms just dripped from that man's hands.

Xin

Also transliterated as *shen*, xin is the traditional Chinese name for various earth, weather, and celestial spirits: a rough equivalent (and possible cognate, perhaps via the Chinese *hsien* or *xian*, meaning immortal bodiless sorcerer) to the Arabic djinn. Like many creatures of traditional folklore, however, they have a darker, unnatural truth behind them.

A malign energy field reached earth from Andromeda or Aquila some time in the late Pleistocene and dominated the humans of the last empire of Mu. The xin field distorts potential energy, gravity, kinetic force, and even time down to the quantum level. At fullest extension, xin telekinetic force tears matter to fragments. They can also manipulate ambient molecules (especially in fluid or gas form) to create a material "dragon form," the lung-xin.

Ruling through suicidal terror, alien discipline, and the gift of unnatural life – or chancreous death – the xin flowed or conducted across the Earth, carried in xin-conductive stones (especially jade) and intricate hypergeometric patterns of metals. Fortunately, Earth's lower entropy and higher Boltzmann constant weakened the xin; too, they began to exhaust themselves destroying rebel cities and warring with Lomar and Hyperborea.

Eventually, the entropic xin energy dimmed and flickered out into random uncertainties in all but a few remote locations. There, survivors of Mu or aberrant cults protected the xin-charged focus stones from their enemies, and learned to recharge the xin fields with hatred and despair. Occasionally, the xin resurge, usually leaving terrified cults and more ruined cities surrounded by brackish blue-green water: Liangchu crushed and drowned in Taihu Lake in 2250 B.C., Ugarit on the Mediterranean cracked and burnt in 1190 B.C., Corbenic devastated in 535 A.D. and drowned beneath Llyn Safaddon in Wales.

Xin cults continue to the present day, huddled around pools of xin charge and guarding their stones, often now in the form of antique jade bi disks and tao t'ieh vessels. The xin control their slaves by life extensions and cruel punishments, such as amputating limbs or causing cancer-like tentacular growths to sprout on them. The xin communicate telepathically, an experience that often leads to suicidal depression or pessimistic fatalism. Their current cult, the Kuen-Yuin (p. 294) harvests the pain and chaos of China's Cultural Revolution, despite being endangered by it politically.

Xin

Abilities: Health 22

Hypergeometry: 21+. The xin are not individuals, but rather local concentrations of field strength. A more intense xin field uses higher Hypergeometry values, into the three digits. They may have any ritual, in addition to their powers.

Xin powers are Hypergeometric rituals; they can also spend Health to power them at 2 points per 1 point of Cost. Xin pay 2/3 Cost for all powers and rituals when using them in a subsurface but open area such as a canyon, riverbed, or depression; xin pay 1/3 Cost when using them underground, e.g., in a basement or cavern. Minimum Cost is always 1.

Hit Threshold: 7 (invisible)

Alertness Modifier: +1 (+2 vs. any electrical field or music)

Stealth Modifier: +2

Attack: telekinesis or spiral attack (see below)

Armor: Transcendent (matter)

Stability Loss: +1 for impinging on the xin field; +3 for communication or mental contact

Cancerous Growth: Xin can cause cancerous growths on their human servants at will, picking a given organ or part (eye, liver, hand, leg) to transform into a tentacle-shaped tumor. Xin can work such transformations on anyone who has been reduced to -5 Stability or below in the presence of xin. The cancer may develop instantly (4-point Helplessness Stability test), or over a period of weeks, months, or years: xin ignore time. (Cost 1 per Health point replaced with cancer; once half the target's Health is replaced with cancer, the target remains permanently and terminally cancer-ridden.)

Depression: Contact with the pure, overwhelming pessimism of the xin imprints that pattern on human minds. The disorder gained from xin contact is always Depressive Reaction. Xin contact automatically turns a pre-existing Depressive Reaction condition acute.

Drain Energy (Mass Population): Xin refresh ability pools only by draining energy from sleeping intelligent beings, or from humans if need be. Affected humans awaken normally, but feel flu-ey and unrested; they are Exhausted (p. 085) and cannot refresh pools (p. 126). (Cost 1 per d+0 points of Athletics, Health, Hypergeometry, or Stability drained from a sleeping human within 6 miles)

Drain Energy (Single Target): To recruit or kill a specific human, xin put her into a coma and drain d-2 Stability or Health as above. Each morning, the sleeper can make a Health test at Difficulty 4 to awaken and refresh 1 Stability (or up to Stability 1, if she was at negative Stability). If not, she continues to slumber until she reaches -12 Stability *and* -11 Health. At that point, she awakens a slave to the xin, seemingly normal but at Sanity 0. (Cost 4 per night per target)

EMF: Xin can emit or manipulate electromagnetic energy for effects including: fogged film, degaussed compass needles, wiped audio or computer tapes, fried electrical components in vehicles or gear, radio interference, and so forth. (Cost 1-3, depending on the scale of the effect and the hardness of the target)

Fog: Xin can manifest a concealing fog by altering the local air's physical properties. (Cost 2 per +1 to visual test Difficulties (Piloting, Driving, Hit Threshold, Sense Trouble, etc.) within 100 yards)

Intangible Entity: Xin are intangible, and cannot be harmed by any material weapon or substance. Xin can both sense and move/radiate through solid matter.

Psychic Surgery: The xin can seamlessly and instantaneously remove or alter any part of their human slaves' bodies without shock or blood loss. They can do the same to humans who touch a xin-stone. (Cost is half the target's Health for terrifying but minor surgery (e.g., removing a foot) doing d-2 damage; equal to the target's Health for a terrifying major surgery (e.g., removing a leg or a lung) doing d+0 damage; twice the target's Health for terrifying fatal surgery (e.g., removing the heart, turning inside-out) doing d+4 damage and killing in 1 round per remaining Health point. The target may make a Difficulty 8 Health *or* Stability test to resist, thus taking only d+0 damage to the organ in question.)

Spiral Attack: It's not manipulating matter that xin find taxing, it's maintaining that matter's integrity. Without such maintenance, xin telekinesis rips matter to shreds, imploding along invisible, spiraling fault lines in its energy patterns. This explosion has damage L2*; Lethal Radius Point-Blank; Damage Radius Close. It ignores armor, exploding targets using the forces within their molecules. The blast leaves even the ground splintered, dry, and discolored, with bluish-green water pooling in divots and crevices. The spiral takes a few seconds to build, making a low rumbling sound like distant thunder. An alert Agent can attempt (Difficulty 5 Sense Trouble test; Difficulty 4 if she has encountered xin before) to dive out of the blast radius. (Cost 10; each 10 after that expands the Lethal Radius by 10 meters or adds 1 to the Lethality.)

Suicidal Depression: This amplifies Depression, above. Xin can drive most GMCs to suicide by three nights of unfiltered xin contact. Characters with Stability ratings must make a 6-point Stability test (Difficulty 5) every night; when they reach -13 Stability, they commit suicide. Leaving the xin vicinity ends the attack. (Cost 2 per night)

Tearing Frenzy: Xin can inculcate a kind of wolfish frenzy in their servants at will: they double their Unarmed Combat pool and immediately bite and tear at their foes (d-1 damage for mania). Against other humans, xin make a Psionic Attack (p. 221). On a failure, the target doubles her Unarmed Combat pool and must immediately attack the nearest human (or the weakest in a nearby group). This effect lasts for a number of rounds equal to the target's margin of failure. After that, the target may make a Difficulty 7 Stability test to snap out of the frenzy every round. (Cost 2 plus spend, per target)

Telekinesis: Xin can discretely affect the material world where their field strength is most intense. Xin must be "directly present" (focused both perceptually and energetically) to do so; ideally, less than 10 yards from a xin-stone "battery." This telekinesis can move or manipulate matter: anything from shoving a spelunker into a crevasse, to diverting a gun barrel, to opening a safe. (Cost 10 for 7 lb. of force or 1 Athletics point for contests; for each additional 10 the force doubles)

Temporal Doldrums: Xin can alter the passage of time for a perceptually linked group of up to 6 humans.

A sentry might believe he patrolled for two hours and come back to find eight hours elapsed; an ambulance might spend 10 minutes driving and arrive 40 minutes after departing.

Recognizing such a time-slip requires a Difficulty 7 Sense Trouble test: easier to believe you dozed off or got lost. (Cost 4 per extra increment of time missed; both examples add 3 increments (of 2 hours and of 10 minutes, respectively) and thus have Cost 12; double costs for up to 60 humans, triple costs for up to 600 humans, etc.)

Investigation

Architecture: If I didn't know for sure there hadn't been any earthquakes in this part of the country for the last 500 years, I'd swear these cellar stones had been twisted and pulverized by an earthquake about 80 years ago – and then put back up in their old position. (Chemistry)

Bureaucracy: This goes beyond the simple runaround. Literally nobody in either the police department or the hospital has taken any action on these cases, some of them for years. This is either a massive conspiracy – or what's worse, a subconscious, conditioned reaction.

Forensics: The explosion fragmented every living creature in the clearing. Disfigured chunks of flesh and bone, stretched like taffy, littered the site. Even the dog tags were warped, snapped, and pulverized. No charring, no shrapnel; just pure blast effects, but with no real center either. The hand at the edge of the field was the largest intact segment, but it was not hers. (Demolitions)

Sense Trouble: The air seems to be overlapping itself in a sort of moiré pattern of swirling lines. There's a kind of half-heard throbbing, as though you're only hearing the very low notes of an arrhythmic dirge, but you don't know if it's in your head or coming from somewhere. Maybe underground?

Lung-Xin

Xin manipulate local matter, often along pre-existing psychic blueprints, to create bodily shells. In China, Wales, and elsewhere, the shell most often takes the form of a dragon or enormous serpent.

To take form from heavy fog and ambient molecules the xin must expend a ritual Cost equal to the lung-xin's Fighting pool. This cost is halved if the xin spends an entire night forming the body. The lung-xin can maintain its form indefinitely or dissolve it at will. If the lung-xin goes to Health -12, it dies permanently. A lung-xin is not intangible or invisible, but possesses all the other powers of the xin.

Occasionally, a manifesting lung-xin spalls off acrid-smelling, hairy vermin called *mo yü-hsieh* ("demon jade crabs") resembling a cross between a spider-worm and a sea urchin. Mo yü-hsieh may be prehistoric or infradimensional beasts pulled into our space-time, incidental sub-creations, or something else. They may be poisonous, as well.

Lung-Xin

Abilities: Athletics 7, Fighting 17, Health 22

Hypergeometry: A "single" xin charge must trade Hypergeometry for Fighting; a more energetic xin field ("multiple xin") can keep the lung-xin's Hypergeometry rating up at 21+.

Hit Threshold: 3 (large)

Alertness Modifier: +1 (+2 vs. any electrical field or music)

Stealth Modifier: +2

Attack: claw (L1*H), bite (L2*), tail sweep (see below)

Armor: -5 vs. any (reptilian hide) [L-5]

Stability Loss: +0 as reptile; +3 for communication or mental contact

Tail Sweep: With a Fighting test, the lung-xin can sweep all characters in a broad arc behind it. Those behind the lung-xin must make an Athletics test against a Difficulty equal to the lung-xin's total result on the tail sweep. On a successful 6 the Agent dodged the sweep entirely; all others take d+1 damage; those who failed the Athletics test are knocked prone.

Zombies

Many kinds of unnatural formulae can restore a corpse to a semblance of life. We call them all zombies, but they may have very different features. Some hunger mindlessly for living flesh, some are impelled by desperate urges, others have barely even animal consciousness. The powers that give energy to dead tissue usually make zombies stronger and hardier than they were in life, perhaps immune to pain and shock altogether. Adjust a zombie's stats and powers to reflect the technique that reanimated it.

Zombie

Abilities: Athletics 5, Fighting 10, Health 8

Hypergeometry: none

Hit Threshold: 2 (slow and clumsy) or 4 (fast and skittery)

Alertness Modifier: -1

Stealth Modifier: -1 (rotting stench)

Attack: bite (d-1)

Armor: all weapons do half damage; [L-2]

Stability Loss: +0

Infectious Bite: The bite of some zombies turns the bitten victim into a zombie. After the combat but before First Aid or other healing, a bite victim must make a Health test against a Difficulty equal to the total zombie damage she suffered in any one round. *Spending herself negative on this test means failure.* If she fails, she becomes a zombie in 2d6 hours. Keep this roll secret from the other players!

Postmortem Infection: In some cases, those who die – or even get reduced to below 0 Health – by zombie bite automatically rise again as (or transform into) zombies within 1-6 hours (or rounds if drama calls for it).

Ravenous Mob: A zombie can attack with Monstrous Grappling (p. 222); any other zombie in Point-Blank range of the same target can spend Fighting pool points to assist the attack or Athletics to raise the Difficulty for any of the target's tests to escape. Spending counts as an attack by that zombie. The round after a successful grapple attack, any zombie who spent on that attack (or who spends on the escape test) automatically succeeds with a bite attack. If the zombie has taken damage, it heals 1 Health for each point lost by the target to its bite.

Striking the Brain: If a zombie needs its brain to function, a Called Shot to the head (+2 to Hit Threshold) de-animates it.

Investigation

Forensics: The body was bitten and chewed, probably while being restrained – the muscle bruising and tearing indicates as much. Cause of death was probably blood loss and hysterical shock from the wound trauma. The bites are full of necrotic tissue, which seems very advanced given when you said the attack happened.

Occult: In Haitian tradition, if a zombie tastes salt, it returns to the grave. Load up with rock salt in the shotguns, I guess. If these aren't Haitian zombies, well, I don't know what to tell you.

Sense Trouble: You smell a rotting corpse somewhere – perhaps where that shuffling sound is coming from.

Customizing and Creating Unnatural Beings

Lovecraft believed that by the 1920s and 1930s it had become virtually impossible to wring new horrors out of the tired pulp staples: vampires, werewolves, ghosts, and so forth. Thus, he created his own "shadowy congeners" – creatures designed to express horror on a newly cosmic scale, creatures from the immense depths of geological time or astrophysical space. In the decades since, horrorists have occasionally discovered that originality in treatment could rescue even traditional monsters. This even as Lovecraft's would-be successors have amply demonstrated that simply repeating Lovecraft's bestiary ad nauseam reduces his modernist monsters to the same tired state in which he found the medieval werewolf.

Customizing Creatures

When presenting such threats as a Handler, move through the Lovecraftian modern and into the postmodern: rather than aim for a unified effect over many games, embrace contradiction. Humans can never know, never understand, the simplest and closest of these intelligences: even the once-human ghouls and Deep Ones present as starkly alien. In a single operation, a ghoul might reflect the unseemly Faustian desires of the corpse-farming FBI pathologist, but the next ghoul should look, act, and attack entirely differently.

Snake it Up Baby

For an example, let's take a normal, natural creature: the snake. (If you wish, go ahead and think about serpent folk here, too.) What color is a snake?

A snake is green. Or red. Or red-and-white. Or bright yellow, like a fatal Sign. Or the color of the dead earth. Or nighted ebony. Or you never saw what color it was, because it was out of your field of vision and it already bit you and now you're hallucinating purple snakes because its venom has burned through your bloodstream and plays your nervous system like a harp from Hell.

Speaking of venom: you can do a lot with snake venom besides force a Health test. Some species' venom induces multisensory hallucinations, or epileptic seizures, or muscular paralysis, or aphasic word-salad. Cytotoxic venom can swell a limb like a gigantic blister. Viper venom can restart bleeding even from old, healed wounds – and from internal injuries. It can also necrotize flesh or internal organs.

And that's just for normal, terrestrial snakes. Tcho-Tcho toxins, mi-go spores, or the conceptual contagion of a Yog-Sothoth cult should be able to deliver still worse debilities.

Contradiction and Drama

Embrace contradiction: the world of the unnatural should be arbitrary and even incomprehensible. Look at your creatures from unusual angles, and change up physical descriptions (insects instead of crustaceans for the Mi-Go), emphasize different impressions at the table (gait rather than face), and even extrapolate new powers merely hinted at in the source material. A ghoul that seems maggot-like instead of canine allows you to evoke the fear of the unknown, even if it still lurks in graveyard warrens. If the ghoul stalks the Agents through stifling tunnels cored out of the Dreamlands rather than burrowing up from the cemetery soil, or slurps the fatty deposits from a living body rather than cracking corpse bones for marrow, that adds surprise to the mix.

Drive creature details – attacks, motives, powers, forensic evidence left behind – to serve the needs of this scenario, or even the needs around your gaming table this night or this minute, rather than hewing to some imaginary Linnaean master ghoul template. Absolutely allude to the original fiction, or to the "default" version of the monster in this game, but while you do so, shift the familiar pattern to unveil something new.

The ideal result of this blend of unknowability, surprise, and the shadow of the original creation is the uncanny: the recognition of the weird in the familiar.

Variant Creatures

Establishing different angles on, perceptions of, or powers for, a familiar creature only gets you so far. The next stage is new versions of the creature: make aquatic Mi-Go, or devolved and stunted Elder Things, or alien "rat-things" on a centauroid body pattern ringed by a ridged mouth. Associate them with different Great Old Ones: a Deep One spawned from Tsathoggua blends toad and bat, not fish and frog, and emerges from deep caverns rather than deep oceans. Mi-Go who reshape themselves in worship of Ghatanothoa might extend their cilia into short tentacles and wrap their body in a tubular carapace, paralyzing rather than mesmerizing with their buzzing drone.

Many of Lovecraft's species explicitly incorporate human ontogeny: Deep Ones, ghouls, spawn of Yog-Sothoth. Do Deep Ones become walrus-like, bloated, tusked monsters if the batrachians mated with the sasquatch-like Voorii? If a serpent woman turns to obsessive, ghoulish necrophagy does she morph into a hideous blend of albino salamander and ... what? Go back to basics: ghouls take their canine appearance from corpse-eating graveyard dogs. Tunneling land crabs devour dead snakes, so add crab features to our serpent-ghoul. She slowly grows a thick shell, her forefeet ossify into claws, and her jaws overlap into mandibles flanked by greedily waving maxillipeds.

As our two ophidian examples demonstrate, there's plenty of fresh horror waiting to be repurposed in the natural world. But Lovecraft didn't content himself with the zoological, and neither should we. He took his ghouls from Beckford and Burton's arabesque imaginings, drew elements of the Mi-Go from the yeti, the Abenaki bmola, and the Greek kallikanzarai, and inverted mermaid legendry for the Deep Ones.

Reinterpret Lovecraft's monsters through the lens of their folkloric distortions: if the shoggoth gave rise to the myth of the Hydra, give your shoggoth toothy regenerating heads instead of mere pseudopods. Or go the other way: take a myth and invent an unnatural origin for it. Perhaps the Hydra story derives from a particular Yig-spawn, resembling a dozen snakes tangled together in a protoplasmic bulb, unkillable until the true head is isolated.

New Creatures: Theory

This raises the question of new creatures, rather than reinterpretations or tweaks to existing ones. The advantage to a new monster or threat is customization: you can tailor its attacks, spoor, and so forth directly to the mood or storyline of your operation. Press this advantage to the fullest — you're not constrained by H.P. Lovecraft or biochemistry or anything but the dramatic imperatives of terror, shock, and wonder. Your new creation has to hit harder, and horrify more completely, to make up for its disconnection from the Lovecraftian background in the players' minds.

Solitary Cases

Fortunately, you have plenty of options for one-off creatures. They may simply be extrusions from the ultraviolet, or alien infections like the colour out of space. A sorcerer can summon literally anything from the farther angles of dimensionality: a rain of mirror-like threads that liquefy carbon, a suspended-gas lattice that refolds the human pulmonary system into its own non-Eudlidean pattern, a sphere of fur and mucus membranes with seven hyper-extended chitinous arms.

Rather than being summoned, someone (or something) might have constructed a new singleton species. Mi-Go, Elder Things, Xin, and the inhabitants of K'n-Yan all practice genetic engineering, advanced surgery, and other monster building techniques — as do any number of MAJESTIC-funded labs. Finally, Shub-Niggurath and the thousand forms of Nyarlathotep likewise offer an excuse or a template for any monstrosity you can shape with your mental clay.

Senseless Words and Unseeable Images

When it comes time to present your new-fledged horror, there's no better approach than Lovecraft's. He described such things using two techniques, which we might term *catachresis* and *cubism*. Catachresis is a poetic technique in which a deliberate misuse of language or impossible metaphor inspires a response: a solid creature "filters" or "seeps," a god resembles a "shining darkness," and so on. Here is where Lovecraft gets his angles that are "both acute and obtuse," his elements unknown to science, and the "indescribable" in general. You can also approach catachresis through negation: "a voice that was not a voice," or the Leng-sailors who were "not unlike men." Try describing something as "not quite a rat" or having "a fluid carapace."

To catachresis, Lovecraft adds cubism: drowning the image in details, often invoking other images until the result is just as impossible as the acute-obtuse angles on R'lyeh. Cthulhu resembles "simultaneous pictures of an octopus, a dragon, and a human caricature." The dissected Elder Things and the disintegrating Wilbur Whateley have so many "surfaces" — scales, barrels, tendrils, wings, tentacles — to examine that they become completely fluid and chaotic. Introduce contradictory imagery to describe your creature: "a face not unlike a scarab-beetle or a rabid baboon, with something feathery in the outline" evokes Nyarlathotep without ever really looking like anything understandable.

New Creatures: Practice

After you've determined what the entity's concept is, find one defined in the list of pre-established entities that feels closest to what you are trying to build. Is it huge and destructive? Start with the stats of a shoggoth. Is it humanoid but difficult to kill? Start with a dimensional shambler. Is it a human altered by the unnatural? Start with a Deep One's stats.

Athletics and Hit Threshold

Once you have the starting abilities, determine which ones need to change. Add more to Athletics if it seems particularly strong or fast, or needs to win a lot of Monstrous Grappling constests. Lower its Athletics if it's weak and spindly like a mi-go.

Base a creature's Hit Threshold on its Athletics, just like for characters. If it's remarkably large or slow, subtract one; if it's remarkably fast or small, add one; if it's invisible give it Hit Threshold 6 (if Agents can guess where it is based on sound or smell) or 7+ (if it's truly impossible to locate).

Health

Increase or decrease Health based on the creature's mass, and on how long you want it to stay in the fight: calculate the average damage that could be done to it in a round (three Agents armed with Colt .45 pistols do 12 points in a round if all of them hit) and multiply as needed. Of course, Armor affects this calculation (*Armor and Immunity*, p. 267); if those pistols hit a Resilient creature, the Agents wind up doing 6 points per round instead.

Fighting

Base Fighting on its ferocity: each 3 points of Fighting (or other combat ability) can produce one guaranteed hit on an Agent; each 2 points produces a pretty-sure hit. How many hits do you want the encounter to last? Is this thing designed to kill the whole team, or just one of them?

Stability Loss

Unless the thing is *particularly* unnatural in appearance or effect, stick to the table suggestions for extra Stability loss. Most of the Stability cost of dealing with the thing should come from failing the test upon seeing it, being attacked by it, or witnessing the horrors it perpetrates upon one's friends.

Hypergeometry

If its race practices hypergeometry or is fundamentally hypergeometric like the Xin, give the creature a Hypergeometry rating. Pick rituals that seem right for it, or invent your own.

Even without rituals, it might fuel its special powers using that rating. Innate powers are usually cheaper than rituals, with a Cost between 1 and 4 per use.

Alertness and Stealth

Assign Alertness and Stealth modifiers based on parallels, not just to the monsters already statted out, but on your intent for your beast. +2 Alertness is about the limit for trained humans or natural entities: eagles' eyesight, dogs' smell, and so on. Save +3 for unnatural abilities: can it see in all 360 degrees? Do its cilia detect vibrations?

Likewise +2 Stealth is almost the highest anything that actually has to move on ground can get: cats and other solitary predators. +3 Stealth is for immaterial beings or those who fade in from other dimensions.

Consider increasing the modifiers only in certain conditions: super-stealthy only in its home environment, only alert to EM radiation

Creature Design Parameters

Type of Entity	Start With This	Size	Stability Loss
Alien parasite	Those Beyond	Cat or Cobra (10 lbs.)	+0 or +1
Unnatural-infected Human	Lesser Deep One, Ghoul	Human (100-250 lbs.)	+0 or +1
Insubstantial Being	Colour Out of Space, Xin	Any (no mass)	+1
Resilient Alien	Dimensional Shambler	Gorilla (350 lbs.)	+1
Horror From Beyond	Ai-Apa, Hound of Tindalos	Tiger Shark (1,000 lbs.)	+1 or +2
Horrendous Killing Machine	Shoggoth, Haedi Nigritiae	Allosaurus (2,000 lbs.) or Great White Shark (4,000 lbs.)	+1 or +2
Gargantuan Monstrosity	Star-Spawn	Godzilla (20,000 tons)	+2

THE MONSTER MASH

Feel free to beef up abilities on one creature in a pack or flock: the alpha or master creature provides variety and a target to inspire players to action. Likewise, feel free to drop Health to 2 or 3 and triple or double the number of creatures in the scene: a horde of mook monsters can still be very deadly, and a sudden, huge wave of attackers combines fears from both Lovecraft and the Vietnam War.

Want a teleporting shoggoth, or a flying Deep One? That's easy. Just grab the shoggoth stat block and slap on the Apport ability from the dimensional shambler, or take the Deep One stat block and say it can fly like a black winged one. There are no restrictions. Not only are you encouraged to mix-and-match, as you begin to create your own catalog of new special abilities, it gives you a rich list of ingredients to pull from when you design new creatures.

Look at the various powers and abilities in the existing monster stat blocks as inspiration, not as confinement. As Handler, do your own Thing.

or human heartbeats. Just removing the negative modifier for darkness (p. 084) gives creatures a huge advantage: Deep Ones, ghouls, haedi nigritiae, rat-things, and any Outside entities might easily have such ability.

Here are six more special Alertness and Stealth-related powers for your new creature. Feel free to add them to the existing monsters as well; some suggestions to that end appear in the entries:

△ **Chameleon:** The creature can shift its color to match its background. Increase its Stealth Modifier by +2 vs. visual detection, including Sense Trouble tests against ambush. Increase its Hit Threshold by +1. Shoggoths should use this capacity; it also fits haedi nigritiae, serpent folk, and Tcho-Tchos.

△ **Discriminatory Smell:** Raise the Alertness Modifier to +3 for odorous targets like living humans, gun oil, old parchment, etc. Worse yet, once the thing smells a human, it can always recognize that person in any disguise or environment. Suitable for ghouls, Hounds of Tindalos, and serpent folk especially.

△ **Echolocation:** Like dolphins or orcas, the things can map and track objects by sound underwater. Their Alertness Modifier goes up to +2 underwater, and +1 on land for noisy targets. This power is ideal for Greater Deep Ones and star-spawn; shoggoths can grow a sonar sense.

△ **Heat Detection:** The things see heat signatures, even through brick or wooden walls. Add +2 to their Alertness Modifier against warmer targets such as living people, vehicles, or recently fired guns. A monster with both smell and heat senses might have Alertness Modifier +5 for human intruders! Give this ability to your beast and to thirsty feasters from the stars and haedi nigritiae, viperine serpent folk, and to infrared-sighted ghouls and ifrits.

△ **Hypersight:** The thing can see around corners, through walls, and into closed containers. Add +1 to its Alertness Modifier. Possibly already true for Hounds of Tindalos, mi-go, those beyond, and Yithian Strange Men; consider it for exodimensional creatures in general.

△ **Tracking:** The creature can track anyone it has bitten, or whose blood it has smelled, or who summoned it, or its chosen (or assigned) target. Add +3 to its Alertness Modifier for that target. This seems apropos for black winged ones, feasters from the stars, ghouls, Hounds of Tindalos, hunting-horrors, Tcho-Tcho, white apes, and many more.

Attacks

How much damage should your creature do? Again, be guided by the pre-statted monsters, and by how many kills you want to see. If your creature reliably does 4 or 5 points per round (d+1) then it likely incapacitates one Agent every two rounds.

For Lethality, compare deadliness: is your creature as deadly as a fully automatic assault rifle [L1], a lightning bolt [L1H] or a grenade

[L1*]? If moreso, increase Lethality, but consider capping all but the most horrendous monster attacks at L3 (artillery shell) or thereabouts. Even if the target technically survives Lethality, that attack does d+15 damage, plenty to kill an Agent.

Even adding one extra attack per round is fairly dire, given the amount of damage most creatures can do compared to the average Agent's Health.

If your creature has tendrils, tentacles, or constricting coils; or if it's an ooze, a long-limbed ape-thing, or giant Venus flytrap, give it Monstrous Grappling (p. 222). This can also cover a paralyzing grasp for ghouls, entangling vines for the haedi nigritiae, or other variations on the theme.

Similarly, consider adding Hypnosis (p. 236) or outright Psionic Attacks (p. 221). A mind probe, mind wipe, dazing stare, or a simple "you kill your friend now" impulsion or "you come here now" compulsion; all are fair game. Add them to any intelligent monster, as well as to Deep Ones (dolphin telepathy), haedi nigritiae (hallucinogenic or pheromonal spores), serpent folk (mesmerism), and the spawn of the various gods and titans.

Here are six more special attack powers for your new creature. Feel free to add them to the existing monsters as well; some suggestions to that end appear in the entries:

△ **Acid:** Acidic slime coats the creature (add +1 damage to its blows) or it spits acid (d+1 up to Near range); lingering acid does damage as on p. 108. Easily added to Hounds of Tindalos, hunting-horrors, or shoggoths.

△ **Berserk:** If it loses more than 5 Health in a single round, the thing goes berserk. It adds one more attack per round and does +2 additional damage with each attack until killed. A likely condition for black winged ones, ghouls, ye liveliest awfulness, and white apes.

△ **Diving Attack:** A raptor-like creature can dive from hundreds of feet high to Point-Blank in a single round, or vice-versa. A diving monster spends Athletics points on Fighting tests or to increase attack damage by 1 per point spent. (It must still spend all points before rolling.) Even deadlier creatures can spend 2 more Athletics points to fly back out of range immediately after attacking. Add this to the black winged ones, ai-apa, hunting-horror, mi-go, or any other flying monstrosity.

△ **Drain:** Health lost to this attack refreshes the thing's Health pool. For particularly vampiric creatures, draining might even add more Health above its rating. Consider this ability for haedi nigritiae or anything else you want to add vampirism to as a leitmotif.

△ **Parting Shot:** Even after going to 0 Health (or even -12), one of the creatures can make one last attack with energy stored in its muscles or a last flicker or temporal drift. It makes this attack with all remaining Fighting points, at -1 to Hit Threshold. Good for dedicated killers like black winged ones, and for unnaturally animated things like ghouls, zombies, and ye liveliest awfulness.

△ **Scorpion Sting:** In addition to claws and jaws, the creature has a scorpion-like tail. When it stings, that is the creature's only attack for the round. Its tail can strike foes at up to Close range and does d+1 damage. Every round after that, the target must make a test of Health or Stability (Handler's choice) with a Difficulty equal to the total damage done by the strike as the agonizing pain burns through his veins. Only blessed unconsciousness ends the torment. A useful adornment for ai-apa, black winged ones, a mi-go warrior caste, and those beyond; a natural outgrowth for a shoggoth.

Armor and Immunity

In the first place, can your entity be damaged by physical attacks? If not, it is Transcendent (p. 223). If it's only immune to some things, it's Transcendent (those things); if it just takes minimum damage from bullets it's Resilient (bullets) and so on. In short, check the special defenses on p. 222 to see if they apply to your creature.

For Reduced Lethality, ask the reverse of the same question as you did for Attacks: is it tougher than a fully automatic assault rifle, lightning bolt, or grenade? If so, it has [L-1]. Note that the example creatures only go up to [L-3] or so; shrugging off (or rather, taking "only" d+15 damage from) an artillery shell. A B-52 airstrike is [L5*] (one bomb is [L4*] so a barrage is [L5*] per p. 099), and if your creature can survive a bombing raid, it's probably Transcendent.

Unless otherwise noted, unnatural entities generally suffer no damage from environmental effects

Armor Equivalents

Armor Roughly Equivalent To	Armor Value
Tough skin, scales, fur (wolf)	-1
Leathery or mummified skin, hide, bone, thick fur, APC armor	-2
Shark skin, thick hide, hide and fur (gorilla), very thick fur (bear, yeti)	-3
Chitinous exoskeleton, polypous matting, unearthly integument	-3 or more
Hard wood (1.5"), alligator hide, brick wall	-4
Rhinoceros hide, concrete wall (4")	-5
Triceratops skull bone, brontosaur hide, stone wall, thick hide plus blubber or fat (whale)	-6
M60 battle tank armor	-7

like gravity, radiation, heat, cold, and the like. But adding an explicit note never hurts, especially if you wish to emphasize the thing's origin or nature: a metalloid being ignores metal weapons, a star-birthed entity cannot even feel heat or electromagnetism, creatures from a gas giant suffer no pressure damage at the bottom of the ocean, etc.

For specific armor equivalents, look at the monsters provided, or check the table. By and large, bigger creatures have thicker armor.

Here are six more special defense powers for your new creature. Feel free to add them to the existing monsters as well; some suggestions to that end appear in the entries:

△ **Fugue:** So-called "packs" or "flocks" of the things are just reiterations of the same creature, moving back and forth in time or between dimensions. Only one creature of any pack can be injured in any way, as the others have "already" escaped harm. Add this to ai-apa, Hounds of Tindalos, ifrits, mi-go, those beyond, and any

other ultra-, meta-, hyper- or transdimensional monster.

△ **Movable Heart:** Snakes can move their hearts out of the way when they ingest a large meal. The creature has a similar ability, honed for use in combat. Once per scene, it may refresh half its lost Health to indicate those vital hits... weren't. Possibly standard for serpent folk warriors, as well as mutable anatomies like ai-apa, mi-go, spawn of Yog-Sothoth, and (of course) shoggoths.

△ **Regeneration:** The thing refreshes 1 (or 2) Health per round until dead. For more danger, the creature heals all Health lost to one wound per round. This ability matches the folkloric ghoul, and the unnatural liveliness of haedi nigritiae and the Worm That Walks.

△ **Smoke Form:** The thing can turn to smoke, making it Transcendent (material attacks); energy attacks like lightning or heat might still affect it. It can flow through cracks, small windows, etc. Changing forms

costs 3 Hypergeometry (or Health). This is practically canonical for hunting-horrors and vampires; it might apply to feasters from the stars, shoggoths, or even a star-spawn.

△ **Stony:** The thing is made of stone or the like; small pieces might spall or chip off. Immune to any weapon doing less than d+1 normally; -2 armor against heavier weapons. Immune to fire and electricity; -5 armor against impact. Xin might animate statues with this feature.

△ **Uncanny Reflexes:** The creature can spend 1 point of Athletics to dodge any blow or missile, including bullets. For an even more terrifying creature, this dodge ability is free; only high-velocity (3,000+ fps) rifle bullets (.220 Swift, NATO 5.56mm, etc.) can hit the things, and only at Near range or closer. An excellent benefit for black winged ones, ghouls, and other preternaturally murderous beings.

Unnatural Powers

In addition to hypergeometric formulae, many unnatural creatures have innate powers requiring no casting or other special actions. For mechanical simplicity, they usually pay the power's Cost with Hypergeometry, or with Health if they have no rating in that ability. A few creatures pay with Athletics if the power clearly relates to physical skill, although some powers are free.

Even more than the other types of ability, check the existing monsters for more powers to recycle. Here are six new eerie powers suitable for your entity, or for entities already listed:

△ **Call Storms:** A standard of Lovecraftian magic, this might be a hypergeometric ritual or an innate ability. Assign a value to the storm (the Difficulty number for a Piloting test to escape it, or for a Sense Trouble to see anything in it); Cost 1 per point of Difficulty. Really awful things might be able to call lightning out of the storm (L1H) and attack foes with it (-1 to Hit Threshold), spending Hypergeometry to attack. This works thematically for Deep Ones, haedi nigritiae, and xin.

△ **Cling to Walls:** The thing can walk on walls or ceilings, due to polarized gravity or tiny suckers. An attack from the ceiling is Sense Trouble Difficulty 6+ to spot. Many creatures already have this ability, but it makes sense for black winged ones, Hounds of Tindalos, and shoggoths as well.

△ **Dream-Chase:** The creature can enter the dreams of those it hunts. From there, it can discern their target's whereabouts, create nightmares (5-point Stability test), carry the sleeper into the Dreamlands, or even emerge into the dreamer's room if it abuts a suitable environment (open window, basement, ocean view, graveyard, woods, etc). Cost 3 for black winged ones, ghouls, hunting-horrors, and other things of nightmare.

△ **Frostbite:** Encountering the creature causes accelerated, dangerous frostbite. Everyone within Point-Blank range of the thing loses 2 Athletics, and 1 more for each time the monster touches them. These points (as well as fingers, toes, chunks of flesh) are lost *permanently* unless the victim receives medical treatment (First Aid, treat lost Athletics as Health) in a warm room within 12 hours. Good for creatures of the ice or of interstellar space: ai-apa, feasters from the stars, gnoph-keh, metoh-kangmi, etc.

△ **Hive Mind:** For every additional hive-creature in a combat, one foe's Hit Threshold diminishes by 1 against them. Also, any individual can perceive what any other does and senses. Useful for black winged ones, Hounds of Tindalos, ifrits, mi-go, those beyond, and other insectile monsters.

△ **Howl:** The thing utters a howl, screech, or bull-roar that shorts out or blows out all recording devices and does d+1 damage to both Health and Stability to those who hear it (Near range) as they bleed from the ears and nose, and know themselves utterly and completely alone in the cosmos. For dramatic purposes, the thing can only howl once per scene. Thematically suits hunting-horrors and Hounds of Tindalos. For a variant Howl, see the wendigo (p. 257).

Weaknesses

All unnatural creatures are vulnerable to hypergeometric rituals, and possibly to enchanted weapons if such things exist.

Others may have specific weaknesses worth noting: cold iron, Antarctic cold, microwaves, sunlight. Weaknesses can be related to the creature's nature (a flame being probably reacts poorly to Halon gas), to traditional folkore (the Haunter of the Dark flies the light), or completely arbitrary (it will not enter an area with bee colonies in it). All are true to Lovecraft, and to the malign universe of DELTA GREEN.

Types of weakness include:

△ **Dread:** The thing must make an Athletics or Health test (Difficulty 5+) to enter or remain in the presence of a dreaded item or effect. An Elder Sign should force a Difficulty 8 test on an affected creature, at least. In Lovecraft's stories, the mi-go avoided dogs and light; Wilbur Whateley rightly feared dogs; Deep Ones reportedly fled the swastika-shaped Elder Sign. Night-adapted creatures may dread direct sunlight.

△ **Vital Point:** The creature has a single vital point: its dimensional anchor, the organ that transmutes human blood, its anterior brain. If struck there (+3 to Hit Threshold; only those who have read the right tome know the right point) by a specific weapon (silver bullet, radioactive pellet, electric arc), it takes double damage (or maximum double damage!) without armor or other mitigation.

△ **Vulnerability:** The thing might be vulnerable to a specific wavelength of radiation, type of gas, or environmental condition despite everything else. A vulnerability might do extra damage, or ignore its armor, or merely be the only thing that can damage the creature at all. That's what the Agents have to find out.

The Great Old Ones

"THEY WORSHIPPED, SO THEY SAID, THE GREAT OLD ONES WHO LIVED AGES BEFORE THERE WERE ANY MEN, AND WHO CAME TO THE YOUNG WORLD OUT OF THE SKY. THESE OLD ONES WERE GONE NOW, INSIDE THE EARTH AND UNDER THE SEA; BUT THEIR DEAD BODIES HAD TOLD THEIR SECRETS IN DREAMS TO THE FIRST MEN, WHO FORMED A CULT WHICH HAD NEVER DIED. THIS WAS THAT CULT, AND THE PRISONERS SAID IT HAD ALWAYS EXISTED AND ALWAYS WOULD EXIST, HIDDEN IN DISTANT WASTES AND DARK PLACES ALL OVER THE WORLD."

— SUMMARY OF PRISONER TESTIMONY FOLLOWING THE ST. BERNARD PARISH RAID (2 NOV 1907)

There is no definition of a "Great Old One." The Cthulhu cult described the peers and paladins of their priest-god as "Great Old Ones." In his Antarctic report, William Dyer mentions "primal myths about Great Old Ones who filtered down from the stars and concocted earth life as a joke or mistake." In each case, a terrified human brain reaches for a descriptor associated with the sublime unnatural entity it has unwittingly brushed against.

Defining one set of field-strengths and organic realities as "Great Old Ones" in the first place remains at best rough taxonomy, no more scientific or truthful than a medieval bestiary. And indeed, in practice DELTA GREEN's classification of these unimaginably vast entities follows medieval demonology – specifically that of Abdul Alhazred's *Necronomicon*. The "mad Arab" divided the *al-Qadimat Kabira* into three categories, the *al-Najmay* ("ones of the stars"), the *al-Ard* ("ones of the earth"), and the *al-'Ahlam* ("ones of dreams"). Alhazred's categories were fluid, or he was distracted while composing this section of his grimoire, as Cthulhu winds up both "of the stars" and "of dreams," for example.

Other sources, unsurprisingly, contradict Alhazred and each other. The Mayan Codex Borgia hints that Yig may have come down from the stars; parts of the Pnakotic manuscripts suggest that Cthulhu and Tsathoggua are brothers, which is to say that they are both extraterrestrials. In short, these unknowably vast beings are also unclassifiable.

Do not assume DELTA GREEN knows everything about them. Do not assume DELTA GREEN knows anything about them.

Star Gods

The cult-pattern of most of the "Ones from the Stars" resembles that of Cthulhu, albeit usually on a smaller scale. The entity "fell from Heaven," ruled terrifyingly (or wisely, in later sanitized traditions), and now dwells apart from humankind in the underworld or the stars, to return at the End Times. Star-cults tend to worship outdoors, punish outsiders and traitors harshly, and blame non-human or magical actors for rapes or murders committed in the god's name.

The individual emanations, manifestations, and spoor of the "extraterrestrial" Great Old Ones vary more widely. DELTA GREEN tentatively classifies the following Great Old Ones among Alhazred's *al-Najmay*.

Cthulhu

The first Great Old One encountered by DELTA GREEN, back in the P4 days of the raid on Innsmouth, Cthulhu's influence remains pervasive and ubiquitous. In 1908, documented Cthulhu cults existed in Greenland, Louisiana, Massachusetts, New Caledonia, Ponape, and Singapore. Whether Cthulhu is actually the greatest of the Old Ones, or simply the one closest to awakening, DELTA GREEN has run across its tendrils more often by far than any other unnatural entity.

According to the Innsmouth and Louisiana interrogations, Cthulhu rests in some sort of torpor beneath the South Pacific in the "corpse city of R'lyeh," imprisoned by a chance cosmic alignment or tectonic disturbance. Its occasional stirrings as the stars slowly "come right," combined with its omnipresent telepathic dream-sendings, inspire both localized riots (as in March 1925, when its brief awakening drove thousands mad and sparked magical rebellions from Haiti to the Philippines) and an age-old global cult (p. 284).

Cthulhu "seeped down" from the green star Soth (most likely either Zubeneschamali (Beta Librae) or Sothis (Sirius)) during the Paleozoic Era. Mountain-sized and protean, it most commonly appears in human art and dreams as a tentacled monster resembling an octopus, dragon, and human being combined. Human myth often represents Cthulhu as a "chaos dragon" such as Tiamat, Vritra, or Typhon, driven into the underworld. As Tutula in Tonga, Clulu or Nkulu in Uganda, Alalu to the Bronze Age Hurrian peoples, Tlaloc to the Aztecs, Iku-Turso to the Finns, and many similar names, its connection to water or the sea remains, the monstrous inhuman truth painted over with pious rationalizations.

Cthulhu's servitors and creations the Deep Ones have their own versions of such myths, perhaps no more reliable than the human distortions: the texts and scriptures recovered from Innsmouth, Ponape, and other Deep One centers use the same exalted language to describe their creator. Human myth, intermin-

DEEP R'LYEH

The traditional location of R'lyeh (49° 51' 0" S, 128° 34' 0" W) is well known by DELTA GREEN, which monitors that hotspot of disappearances using the Navy's SOSUS underwater listening posts. Despite precautions, some vehicles have wandered into the zone, some never to return. Twice such vehicles (a Navy PBY scout plane in 1943, and a Russian freighter in 1963) have reported an island in the ocean where there should be none. Since 1925, no one has landed on such an island — at least, as far as DELTA GREEN knows.

DELTA GREEN is extremely interested in the hypergeometry behind the torpor that renders Cthulhu and his minions inert. No one knows if this is a natural result of Cthulhu's biology, or perhaps a weapon utilized by another species on Cthulhu to "trap" it. Factions within the program believe that the math needed to keep Cthulhu permanently interred at R'lyeh is contained within the angles and structures of R'lyeh itself.

R'lyeh seems to rise and fall out of existence at intervals perceptible and sometimes predictable to those with both deep-ocean seismic records and knowledge of the unnatural. As such, an expedition to the island is possible, though obviously ill-advised, when the time is right.

gled with the teachings of the Deep Ones, ascribes the names Dagon and Hydra to two of Cthulhu's spawn or kindred; they may or may not be the same entities as the Progenitor Deep Ones (p. 230) called by the same names.

R'lyeh slowly congeals into our space-time, moved by otherworldly realities for reasons unfathomable to humanity. One day, it is foretold, the city will appear, and remain, and Cthulhu will fully awaken. Then, the legends say, humanity will rise up in an orgy of violence and death, to become one with the Great Old Ones.

Ghatanothoa

According to von Junzt, this horrific being ruled the Pacific continent of Mu, transforming those who gazed upon it into living mummies. A 1932

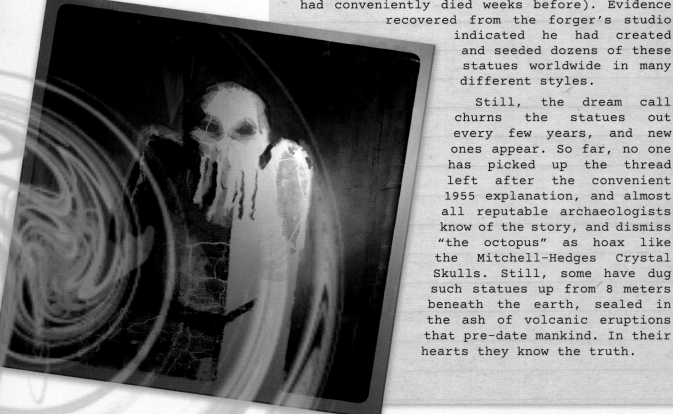

THE IDOL

When an artist hears the dream call, it compels the sufferer to carve an image of Cthulhu. The true statue is almost always the same, regardless of culture and time period. A squat, toad-like being, with a tentacular face and stubby wings, perches on a cube incised with alien runes.

The 1907 St. Bernard Parish raid in Louisiana recovered the most famous of these, the LeGrasse statue, photographed repeatedly before being lost. But others have been found. So many, in fact, that in archaeological circles, "the octopus" or "the monster erratic" is a well-known oddity. From 1925 to 1955, several papers attempted to explain away the seemingly identical statues recovered from the ruins of a 9th-century Japanese shrine, an Iroquois longhouse, and an Inca burial site.

In 1955, with the archaeological community on the verge of admitting the connection, the program enacted counterintelligence Operation LANCASTER. Modern sculptors working on CIA grants produced obvious fakes of the statue, and DELTA GREEN operatives salted them into auctions to be revealed as the work of a forger (who had conveniently died weeks before). Evidence recovered from the forger's studio indicated he had created and seeded dozens of these statues worldwide in many different styles.

Still, the dream call churns the statues out every few years, and new ones appear. So far, no one has picked up the thread left after the convenient 1955 explanation, and almost all reputable archaeologists know of the story, and dismiss "the octopus" as hoax like the Mitchell-Hedges Crystal Skulls. Still, some have dug such statues up from 8 meters beneath the earth, sealed in the ash of volcanic eruptions that pre-date mankind. In their hearts they know the truth.

incident at the Cabot Museum in Boston tends to bear him out. Ghatanothoa cults appear all along the Pacific littoral from Peru to Malaya, and even in Burma, Ceylon, and Yemen. Von Junzt places Ghatanothoa in opposition to the Mi-Go and to Shub-Niggurath, implying a ferocious independence exemplified by its fanatical modern-day apocalypse cultists.

Giliszta

Named "the Worm" in Hungarian, this monstrous, slug-like entity dwells at the bottom of the Black Lake in the Hungarian Carpathians. Its "dream pull" calls seekers and madmen to its shores to be enslaved, impaling them with its quasi-metallic spines. These undead slaves live decades or centuries until they rot in the sun, leading to a minor Cult of the Worm wherever wizards seek immortality. It manifests below many lakes, from the primordial lakes of Nabta and Tushka in Stygia and predynastic Egypt to a medieval meteoric lake in Gloucestershire and an artificial reservoir (North Fork Lake) in Missouri. It connects itself to itself across space and time, possibly through the Lake of Yath in the Dreamlands.

Noth-Yidik

An exceptionally repulsive entity associated with "the dogs that howl in the maelstrom of Azathoth," i.e., the Hounds of Tindalos. As such, it may come not from out of space, but from out of time. Known cults have manifested in Turkestan and the Marshall Islands.

Qu-tugkwa

Its name comes from the Southern Paiute meaning "night (or darkness) from fire," and it appears as an immense ball of flame or as a congeries of smaller sentient plasmas. In North America, its ritual home is the star Fomalhaut, to which the Bighorn Medicine Wheel in Wyoming has been aligned since at least 1050 A.D. In Mesoamerica, it was known as Xiuhtecutli, "Lord Xiuha."

The so-called "fire worshipers" of the pre-Islamic Middle East may have included some cultists of Kheshthogha, possibly directed by the "beings of smokeless fire" known to them as djinn or ifrits, and to the Theosophists as the Children of the Fire Mist. Most of its modern apparitions can be traced to individual sorcerers, not to continuous cult activity, although the program keeps assets in the Middle East and the Midwest to see if that should change.

Rhan-Tegoth

A congeries of globes, eyes, and snakelike filaments, Rhan-Tegoth ruled west of Lomar during the Ice Age. According to PISCES' best guess, after it fell into suspended animation, occultist and showman George Rogers discovered its body and shipped it to London. Following Rogers' disappearance, at least one death, and numerous complaints, it vanished in 1932. Von Junzt claims the Mi-Go brought Rhan-Tegoth to Earth, possibly along with Ghatanothoa for use as a superweapon. Like Cthulhu, its cult (surviving in the upper Noatak River valley) demands human sacrifices.

Gods of Earth

Where Cthulhu and the "Starry Ones" often accumulate apocalyptic sects, Tsathoggua and the "Earthly Ones" tend to attract individual wizards or madmen. Occasionally a social cult of Tsathoggua or similar spreads through a community or district, but it tends to burn itself out as the various lunatics granted unnatural abilities can't resist showing off and inviting reprisals from rival cults or the dominant religon. Only in rare cases such as the Hittite mining cults of a-Abhi or the Auvergne witch-cult does a cult remain stable over centuries.

In anthropological terms, Tsathoggua and the "Earthly Ones" resembling it are culture heroes, totems, or quest objects: givers and withholders of knowledge or boons with which one visionary can alter the world. In shamanic cultures such as the Eskimos and Siberian or American Indian tribes, such a "transactional" entity can become widely worshipped, or at least widely feared: Itla-shua and Yig, for example.

Most of Alhazred's *al-Ard* are either closely associated with one or two terrestrial creatures, or take on Tsathoggua's black formlessness as their iconic semblance. The program tentatively believes the following Great Old Ones are "of Earth," and may therefore be slightly more susceptible to material weapons, or those using the conventional energies of our own space-time.

Tsathoggua

DELTA GREEN believes Tsathoggua's current resting place to be the cavern-vault of N'Kai approximately 3.5 miles below Oklahoma, assuming N'Kai can be mapped to terrestrial locations at all. The physical presence of a Great Old One inside continental U.S. territory is more than enough to raise Tsathoggua's threat profile, but it gets worse: the entity has a reputation (in von Junzt, and especially in the Hyperborean *Book of Eibon*) of sharing (or calving off, or sporulating) hypergeometric knowledge with deranged seekers.

The *Book of Eibon* claims Tsathoggua arrived on Earth before Cthulhu, possibly from the planet Saturn. Alhazred classes Tsathoggua as one of the "earthly" Great Old Ones and describes its conjuration by black, "worse than formless" alien "star-spawn" after their arrival in N'Kai from the planet Kythamil.

N'Kai follows the pattern of many mythological "deepest underworlds," being beneath a lesser hell, in this case below "red-litten Yoth." Occult lore locates Yoth and N'Kai beneath everywhere from Guanajuato to Germany, implying either an unprecedented natural fissure system reaching through the crust of the Northern Hemisphere or a hypergeometrical component to N'Kai's architecture. The result in either case is that Tsathoggua's cult, like that of Cthulhu, is global.

Tsathoggua has manifested to witch-doctors in Uganda (as Tsadogwa), for the Greenlandic and Algonquin shamans (as Saaktoq and Sadogowah respectively), and

to the Pawnee medicine men (as Tiráwa). All these peoples' lore describes the god as a formless, protean mass, usually pitch black or (to the Pawnee) invisible. This broadly comports with the nature of the Kythamila "spawn of Tsathoggua" and with the entity's description in the *Necronomicon*.

Statues of the Gallo-Roman god Sadoqua and the Auvergne witch-cult deity Sadoguë instead follow the Hyperborean tradition and depict a squat, toad- or bat-like entity coated in thick fur. This matches the Aztec Tlaltecuhtli, "Lord of the Earth," descended from the Olmec toad-god of eternity and the earth, often depicted with two large, batlike ears.

Like Cthulhu, Tsathoggua has a number of spawn or lesser avatars, about which little is known: Yabou, Ossadagowah, Zuilphagua, and so on. Unlike Cthulhu, there is some evidence that the Mi-Go worship – or at least seek to placate – this being while on Earth.

A-Abhi

The name of this Hittite god of the underworld (also called al-Abhi) literally means "the sacrificial pit." Its name shares a root with the Hebrew 'Obhoth ("necromantic pits" or "ghosts"), implying a connection to the dead and more specifically to necromancers. Worship of a-Abhi logically connects itself with plague pits and disease, along with the foulness and corruption of decay. Cultists represent a-Abhi either with a black block of stone, or as a gray-black slime from which reanimated corpses may rise.

Crom Cruach

The "bent bloody one" or "crooked one of the mound" kept its local worship in Ireland until the 5th century, propitiated by blood sacrifice to grant victory in war. Crom Cruach and the Cimmerian war god Kagh (or Kaghya) may be connected; both entities' rites include blood spilling on sacred stones. Crom-Kagh could be a mineral intelligence or silicon-based distributed consciousness haunting European geology from Ireland to Azerbaijan.

Itla-shua

Its name means "Sky-Owner" in Greenlandic Inuktun, but this Great Old One is better known in North America as the Wendigo, Arctic spirit of the wasteland, terror, and cannibalism. It appears in Babylonian lore as Enlil, to the Canadian Inuit as Sila, to the Siberian Koryak as Ina'hitelan, and to the Delaware as Pethakhuweh. Tradition depicts Sky-Owner as a terrifying or powerful beast: a bull in the Middle East, a moose or an antlered man in the Canadian North.

Supposedly confined to the Arctic by the Temple of Winds, Itla-shua has abducted unfortunates as far south as Wisconsin and Iran, carrying them into the sky, to some unknown boreal realm, or to the Plateau of Leng. Sometimes these unfortunates reappear, frozen solid and seemingly dropped from a great height, their feet burned and melted by the speed of re-entry. After a spate of mass disappearances and predation in Manitoba in the 1930s, Itla-shua's activity dropped significantly, possibly correlated with the return of colder weather in the Arctic.

Mormo

The occultist and kabbalist Robert Suydam attempted a magical marriage and resurrection with this entity beneath Red Hook, Brooklyn in 1925. Research in classical grimoires and magical papyri could reveal similar rites; "she" was well known to the Greeks as a child-killing vampire demon, described by the poet Erinna as a shape-shifter, perhaps a wolf. "She who rejoices in the baying of hounds and spilt blood" is associated with crossroads and the "thousand-faced Moon," and sometimes identified with Lilith, Hecate, or other baleful goddesses. The Moon-Beasts of the Dreamlands worship her. She may be an avatar of Nyarlathotep.

Nug and Yeb

The "twin blasphemy" is depicted as two featureless ovals or as twin dragons (probably taken from Welsh or Chinese lore). Supposedly the spawn of Yog-Sothoth and Shub-Niggurath, Nug and Yeb remake matter in "subtle and orgiastic rites." Shrines to Nug and Yeb lie underground in Arabia, New Guinea, and K'n-Yan. The Tcho-Tcho worship Nug-Yeb under secret names, forbidden to repeat to outsiders.

Nyogtha

Supposedly the spawn of Tsathoggua, Nyogtha takes the form of a black, amorphous, worm-like thing with crescent horns. The "Thing That Should Not Be" opens hypergeometric tunnels for its worshipers, including the Salem witch-cult and many ghoul populations.

Tleche-Naka

The Great Spider, supposedly a companion or rival of Tsathoggua in the Hyperborean myth-cycle; its name recalls the Pueblo "Spider Grandmother" Tseche-Nako. The classical Phoenicians and Lydians worshipped Tleche-Naka under the name Omfalé, possibly related to the Greek *omphalos,* or "navel of the world." The purple spiders of Leng may be its spawn, and it may dwell beneath that plateau. Its webs supposedly connect all dimensions; its "spider form" may simply be occult code for (or ignorant mythmaking about) a hyperspatial entity.

Yig

Worship of the Father of Serpents surfaces among all the Plains tribes of North America, likely descended from the Yig cult in K'n-Yan. K'n-Yan may also have spawned the serpent-god cults of Kulkulkan and Quetzalcoatl in Mesoamerica. Differentiating "conventional" snake rituals such as possession by Damballah in Vodou or snake-handling Pentecostalism in Tennessee from intentional cultism of Yig is difficult without deliberate infiltration and long observation.

If even a fraction of the snake cults and serpent gods throughout human history represent Yig worship, then Yig is by far the most ubiquitous of Great Old Ones. Yig may be a soul-symbol of the serpent-folk, raised to cosmic power by their sorceries, or a gigantic self-aware weapon deployed by the Mi-Go or Lemurians against Ghatanothoa. Regardless of its origin, it exacts gruesome revenge on those who trespass against its serpent avatars.

Gods of Dream

The Headless One appears in visions and in warped art and debased scriptures, but must alter a human instrument to act in the world. It shares these qualities with the "Dreaming Ones"... in the waking world, at least. In the Dreamlands, these beings function as actual gods, patronizing cities and priesthoods, wielding banes and granting boons. Some of them can even, very briefly, protect their worshippers from the truly cosmic gods such as Nyarlathotep or Yog-Sothoth.

That is likely why Alhazred bothered to categorize the *al-'Ahlam* at all. It is certainly why DELTA GREEN continues to search out the "weak gods of dream" in archaeological inscriptions, Swiss diaries, and even the occasional opiated mission.

The Headless One

The Headless One actively seeks to corrupt and influence humans, laying trails to attract degenerates to its service. Reading its scriptures, using its rituals, or even "suffering its embraces" opens one up to possession and eventual replacement by a headless monstrous Avatar (p. 224). The prospect of a depraved sociopath with the powers of a Great Old One potentially at his disposal is literally apocalyptic.

The Graeco-Egyptian magical papyri refer to the "Headless One" Osoronnophris as the ruler of all demons, imprisoned or fettered in "the void air" behind a wall or inside a labyrinth. Modern ritual magicians of the Golden Dawn and Crowleyite traditions refer to him as the "Bornless One". Other texts refer to the magical phrase IA-GOLOG-AI, like many such voces a palindrome concealing a secret name. Golog, or Golen, as described in *The Sacred Magic of Abramelin*, is a demonic servant of Ashtaroth whose name means "cavern dweller."

The Headless One also surfaces in the guise of the bloody and headless Hindu goddess of unrestrained sexuality Chinnamasta and the Chinese giant-musician Hsing T'ien who wars against the Heavenly Emperor even after being decapitated. DELTA GREEN has encountered cults of both gods showing the characteristic depraved behavior and shape-shifting tendencies inculcated by the Headless One in its slaves and abject worshippers.

The archetypal figure of the Great Old One appears throughout human art, from the headless petroglyph figure with a distended penis found in the Kalabera caves on Saipan in the Marianas, to the savage Akephaloi of Herodotus and the headless Blemmyes representing gluttony in medieval Christian art, to the Acéphale icon of the Surrealist Georges Bataille. Program analysts believe such a widespread image-pattern can only be the result of dream-transmitted lore, as with the global Cthulhu cult.

Great Ones of Sarnath

The triune gods of Sarnath, the doomed city of Mnar, still appear in the Dreamlands, especially to those who fall asleep and dream within them. They offer what protection they can, sometimes locating a hidden star-stone or other treasure. Following the work of Dumezil, program ARCHINT tentatively identifies the Great Ones with the gods of Mitanni, the "lost civilization" that briefly ruled what is now Kurdistan around 1400 B.C.

△ **Lobon:** His symbols are the waking eye, the spear, and the color white. Identified with the Mitanni god of truth and oaths Mitra.

△ **Tamash:** Likely a ruler god of thunder and altered consciousness; his color is red or gold. Identified with the Mitanni solar-archer god Indara.

△ **Zo-Kalar:** His color is black; he carries a whip or rope. He may be a twin. Identified with Nashatiyana, the Mitanni god of cattle, horses, and the earth.

Hypnos

The Greek god of sleep dwells in a sunless cave by the banks of the River Lethe, guarded by poppies. This entity enters the mind through narcotics or the active search for transcendence, luring its partner deeper into both. For unknown reasons, Hypnos fears the constellation Corona Borealis.

DELTA GREEN friendlies recovering in hospitals have seen Hypnos while on morphine, for instance; their descriptions of "him" resemble Edgar Allan Poe. They often confabulate memories or entire histories explaining "his" presence in their lives.

Nath-Horthath

The patron god of Celephaïs in the Dreamlands, attended in a turquoise temple by 80 immortal priests wreathed in orchid, responds on rare occasion to human invocation in Dream. It offers protection and illumination – by shifting personal memories, or even freezing or altering whole subjective time-streams. Its temple and priests exist outside time, not inside it.

Nodens

Nodens governed healing, hunting, and the sea for the Britons, Irish (as Nuada), and Gauls (as Noadatus). The Britanno-Romans may have worshiped Nodens as Pan, under the title "Lord of the Abyss." A major temple to Nodens flourished in the 4th and 5th centuries A.D. at Lydney Park in Gloucestershire, on the Severn Estuary. Here, sufferers slept in *incubatio*, sacred chambers designed to attract dreams of Nodens and effect a cure.

While "hoary and primal Nodens" seldom appears in the waking world, the god remains a powerful force in the Dreamlands and in overlapping "soft places" of the unnatural such as Kingsport, Massachusetts. Nodens commands the night-gaunts, who fear not even Nyarlathotep. Those touched by Nodens often undergo personality-shifting neurological events, possibly triggered by exposure to the true geometries of Dream, or of the Abyss.

Alien Dream Gods

Not all dream gods protect humans.

△ **Bokrug:** In the form of a water-lizard, Bokrug protects the slimy, amphibian humanoids of Ib, implying that it may be an avatar of dreaming Cthulhu. Green, soapstone amulets of Bokrug have been uncovered in the Congo basin and in Mesopotamia, the latter possibly depicting the Babylonian fish-demons called kulul<l>û.

△ **Nameless Mist:** The "Nebulum Innominandum" protects the gugs of the Dreamlands. It may be the spawn, or merely the side-effect, of Azathoth.

Customizing Great Old Ones

Lovecraft only really used four gods in his major fictions, borrowed one more from Clark Ashton Smith, and kept three more in the minor leagues of his revision work, plus a smattering of dropped names. Even if you add the gods he borrowed from previous myth – Nodens, Dagon, Hypnos, and Mormo – you barely pass a lucky thirteen deities for the malign Olympus of this pitiless hyperphysics.

In these pages, we've added one or two more in forms that placate the blind apes of copyright law. That's more than enough. The Great Old Ones extend far beyond any single human's vision. Consider everything you can do with a truly cosmic entity, everything it might mean or symbolize, especially to the deranged apopheniacs who write grimoires or ritually murder school kids.

Cthulhu is the oceanic titan-kraken slumbering beneath the Pacific, but it is also the dead god of deserts and Chinese mountains, the winged incarnation of the poisoned skies of the Paleozoic and of the apocalypse, the iridescent abyss of chaos and hallucination, made manifest in unknown stone and metal and superstrings. Cthulhu is the begetter of rapist mer-spawn, the author of dreams, the inspiration of assassins, and the avenger of the wretched of the earth.

That's just one god.

If you really need a specific, customized entity for your operation, and none of Nyarlathotep's thousand forms seem to fit, then go ahead and make one up. Hit a theme or symbol hard: the ocean, the north wind, a tattered robe, a pharaoh. Extend its scope in space-time until only its distorted image remains visible. Since you've already got a scenario you're fitting the deity into, you already know who might call up or call on such a thing. Then decide why your cultist, sorcerer, government contractor, or rogue physicist sees Cthulhu or Tsathoggua or Ghatanothoa *that* way, through *that* lens. This will also save you from having to invent a deity name that doesn't sound stupidly derivative.

Or pick a "regular" human deity out of the mists of myth or anthropology and decide which of the Great Old Ones she *really* represents. Is the virgin huntress Diana a desperate "whitewashing" of Shub-Niggurath or 'Obhoth? A misunderstanding of the eternally youthful, skin-shedding Yig? A female aspect of Nodens of the Hounds? Every mortal faith, after all, from prehistory to postmodernism, ultimately derives from frantic denial of cosmic truth. The Great Old Ones are already vast enough to touch any imaginable human belief, so go right ahead and hook your cult up to the thrumming dynamo that is a Great Name straight out of Lovecraft.

The Cosmic Gods

Alhazred also drew a seemingly arbitrary distinction between the Great Old Ones like Cthulhu and Tsathoggua and the *al-Alihat al-Kuniya*, or "gods of the cosmos" – Azathoth, Yog-Sothoth, Shub-Niggurath, and Nyarlathotep. Unlike the mere Great Old Ones, these gods receive worship and veneration – or at least very delicate recognition – from alien species such as Mi-Go, Deep Ones, and so forth.

Alhazred also connected the four cosmic gods to the four elements (water, air, earth, and fire), more likely as part of an abstruse alchemical code than as a deliberate attempt to reify these unknowable forces. MAJESTIC physicists have, however, reported surprising results from experiments mathematically mapping the four cosmic gods to the four fundamental forces (gravity, electromagnetism, strong and weak nuclear interactions) so perhaps it is possible that the entire energetic universe is in fact actively composed of malign sapiences.

Azathoth

Azathoth dwells "at the center of the Universe," the idiotic and meaningless solution to every hypergeometrical equation. Surrounded by amorphous dancers and shrill flautists – possibly a medieval symbolic image of fractal patterns and quantum wave forms – it roils and shrieks or gnaws hungrily in the dark.

In some traditions, Nyarlathotep lulls the Daemon Sultan to sleep, the better to arrogate Azathoth's power to itself. The name "Azathoth" is likely an occult fiction, possibly derived from the Egyptian User-Thoth ("strength of Thoth," i.e., the power behind Nyarlathotep). The true Dread Name of Azathoth is something, literally, to conjure with.

The good news is that only a very few isolated madmen seek communion with Azathoth, the Daemon Sultan, the Idiot Chaos at the heart of the Universe. Even the few cults of Azathoth tend to come apart in appropriately idiotic chaos. The highest leaders of the Cult of Transcendence seek admission to Azathoth's Court, but while waiting to get there they play petty politics with each others' protégés and meaningless terrestrial power. The witch-cult signed "the Booke of Azathoth" but worshiped Nyarlathotep.

The bad news is that even the briefest communion with Azathoth on this plane of existence is the rough equivalent of a 15-megaton atomic burst, as the "monstrous nuclear chaos beyond angled space" energetically disrupts space-time around it. Program analysts have long considered the Tunguska blast of 1908 the result of some previous Azathoth-worshiper's distracted exaltation.

A similar "miscalculation" by the Karotechia in January 1945 blew the top off a Bavarian mountain and obliterated Naudabaum Castle. The Naudabaum accident was some sort of inter-dimensional "rip" in space, created through unnatural science. Something incomprehensible began to pour into our world, flattening the castle and the surrounding forest and poisoning the lake, before the rift snapped shut. Hitler ordered Aktion GÖTTERDÄMMERUNG, commanding the Karotechia to again attract "the Eye of the Daemon Sultan" but this time to leave the rift wide open, destroying the victorious Allies – along with the planet. Fortunately, DELTA GREEN's desperate Operation LUNACY in the summer of 1945 prevented that existential disaster.

Nyarlathotep

By contrast to the blind idiot god it serves, Nyarlathotep constantly acts to corrode humanity – or perhaps to evolve it to be worthy of the Great Old Ones. The Crawling Chaos awakened the Cult of Transcendence, founded the Fate, and egged on the Karotechia – and that was just in 25 years.

In the 19th century, Nyarlathotep sparked the Starry Wisdom cults in Providence and elsewhere as the Haunter of the Dark; in the 17th century, the Black Man led witch covens on two continents; in ancient Egypt it reigned as Nephren-Ka, the Black Pharaoh who did "that which caused his name to be stricken from all monuments." Nyarlathotep's thousand forms appear all over the world, wherever human misery or hubris grow so great as to welcome the inhuman.

Nyarlathotep is the Mighty Messenger, the soul and herald of Azathoth, translating the Daemon Sultan's thrashings into vile action. It commands the Mi-Go, who consider themselves among Nyarlathotep's "Million Favored Ones," and unleashes its hunting-horrors against those who oppose its whims. According to the most complete description of the Nyarlathotepic faith, Ludwig Prinn's De Vermis Mysteriis, at the End Times Nyarlathotep will come among humanity, work wonders, inspire mobs, and then raise sunken continents as "mad auroras" destroy cities.

DELTA GREEN doesn't necessarily believe every stanza of Prinn, but considering what Nyarlathotep can accomplish while lurking in secret, the open return of the Black Pharaoh must be considered nothing short of an apocalyptic, civilization-ending threat. And the program has no idea how to stop it.

Shub-Niggurath

The spawn of Azathoth and the Darkness, beings across the cosmos venerate Shub-Niggurath in words that translate to human ears as "The Black Goat of the Woods with a Thousand Young." The cry "Iä! Shub-Niggurath!" rings out at ceremonies and rituals to every god and Great Old One, and even imprints itself on their victims. The name thus has some deeper connection with sentience, or perhaps with perception.

The program has no ARCHINT before the 10th century B.C., when Babylonian magi desperately carved summons for the "Shining Terrible Secret One of Earth," Shu-ba-Nígùr-Urash, in Sumerian, a language forgotten for a millennium. Sumerian texts from before the time of Gilgamesh name a terrible being called Másh-Ngi, words meaning both "black goat" and "prophetic dream." It was later disguised as the goddess Ningal ("Great Lady").

Shub-Niggurath has also been present, acknowledged openly or secretly invoked, at ceremonies for every fertility goddess in human history, or indeed in the history of the planet. (And off the planet; the Mi-Go maintain a great shrine to Shub-Niggurath on the Moon.) The priests of K'n-Yan and Mu worshiped it; Astarte, Cybele, Freyja, Durga, Coatlicue, Haumea – all of them have been masks for Shub-Niggurath, as have a number of gods, from Osiris to Voltumnus to Makemake. As the incarnation and embodiment of the decay and poison known as life, Shub-Niggurath transcends gender: "The Black Ram of the Forest with a Thousand Ewes" translates the god's title in valid grammarye.

Shub-Niggurath's toxic and distorted fertility incorporates psychoactive organics, growth hormones, and all manner of exotic biological substances. Both MAJESTIC researchers and various modern cults shyly (or eagerly) suckle at Shub-Niggurath's teat for access to such weapons, elixirs, or gateways into inner space.

Once Shub-Niggurath's spores, milk, or sweat enter a human, that human becomes part of the god's garden, to be grown or harvested at will. Given that at least half a dozen Shub-Niggurath cults have gone into the health food business over the last century, the Black Goat of the Woods may have millions of Young who just haven't gotten the reunion invitation in their blood yet.

Yog-Sothoth

Yog-Sothoth, the All-in-One, dwells in the interstices between the dimensions; hyperspace curves around its congeries of spheres. The Necronomicon describes this entity as "the Key to the Gate, whereby the Spheres meet." Thus Yog-Sothoth guards and controls all passages from one plane of existence to another, both the Key and the Gate.

This role combines the occult concepts of the Watcher on the Threshold and the Opener of the Way, implying that to attain true hypergeometric knowledge one must both supplicate and defeat Yog-Sothoth. In its infinite combinations, Yog-Sothoth can be invoked to oppose Nyarlathotep, for instance.

For human sorcerers, Yog-Sothoth offers power over life and death: the magus Joseph Curwen summoned Yog-Sothoth to learn not only how to resurrect the dead, but how to preserve his life-force within his essential salts and orchestrate his own return from the dead. This was only part of the possible harvest of knowledge Curwen's circle sought; other Yog-Sothoth cultists have obtained access to the past or to completely impossible realms through rose windows, skrying balls, and the like.

Yog-Sothoth exists in all times and spaces, leading to its Arabic cognomen Tawil at-'Umr, "the Prolonged of Life." Nevertheless, at least here and now, its quasi-material presence on Earth remains limited to a few minutes and miles: May Eve and Halloween of certain years, inside a few megalithic circles.

Like all the cosmic gods, Yog-Sothoth has an active cult among the Mi-Go, and among other alien beings such as the vaporous egregores of the spiral nebulae. The Elder Things, however, feared it, possibly connecting its iridescent globes with their own spherical nemeses the shoggoths. Or perhaps at some point in their eons of experimentation they reified an avatar of Yog-Sothoth near the South Magnetic Pole.

Elijah Whateley did much the same in 1912, and bred Yog-Sothoth with his daughter Lavinia during a brief moment of tangency between the god and Sentinel Hill near Dunwich. Only quick action by a coterie of academics prevented Lavinia's twin sons from entering the invisible cities of Dho-Hna and invoking their father to scour the planet clean of mere material life. Had they not acted, the folk of Dunwich planned to invoke Yog-Sothoth to defeat itself — it's probably for the best that the Key and Gate never met in apocalyptic combat over rural Massachusetts.

Creating the Cosmic

By and large, the advice on Great Old Ones applies here, only even moreso. The cosmic gods are even vaster than the Great Old Ones, containing even more contradictory multitudes. Nyarlathotep has his thousand forms, but the others are similarly multifarious. Shub-Niggurath extrudes all life, and Yog-Sothoth is after all the Key and the Gate to every dimension. At the end and beginning of all of them, of course, lies Azathoth, the howling void where everything ceases to be.

But outside Lovecraftian physics, it's not impossible that you might want to explore other literary dimensions with your horrors. In a simplistic reading, we might code Lovecraft's cosmic gods as overarching fears: Azathoth as the meaninglessness of the scientist cosmos, Nyarlathotep as civilizational destruction, Yog-Sothoth as Faustian hubris. Lovecraft barely mentions Shub-Niggurath, but casting "her" as his well-known terror of miscegenation works for this model, and in our version of the myth Hastur embodies despair itself.

So what else terrifies you? Not just a shudder or even a phobia, but something existential. Loneliness? Emptiness? Consider a blind god, a silent god, a god even its maddest devotees are never sure exists. Its face or Sign appears and disappears at random. It is a god of uncertainty, of deconstruction, of nothing. It destroys human relationships indirectly, inculcating obsession or doubt or callousness in its believers. That doesn't feel like any of our current gods or titans. In a pinch, you could cast it as Hastur or Hypnos or perhaps even the Headless One behind the wall, but it feels like its own sort of thing.

If you can come up with one strong horror story about your god's effects on a human being, then you have a reason to come up with your god. You'll need a name, though. Avoid apostrophes: Lovecraft doesn't use them for his gods' names. Instead look through lists of goëtic demons or rakshasa princes and play with the syllables until you have something that feels right: aim for "believably distorted," not "B-picture monster."

Ideally, add a few completely random details to the god's cult or symbology to throw chaff at any temptation to allegory, and to blunt the kind of facile one-note interpretation I just engaged in two paragraphs back. Try to provide your new god with individuality or even idiosyncracy, while still leaving it amorphous enough to provide challenges in all sorts of settings. After all, you may come up with another horror story about it.

The Hastur Mythos

Hastur has no personality, no individuality, no sentience. Hastur is the force of entropy, the cosmic principle which destroys order. Because this destruction of order happens at every level from the atomic to the cosmic, the "deity" Hastur has influence at all levels of reality. Exposure to the Hastur-force, often in the form of the Yellow Sign or in the malign poetry of the play *The King in Yellow* (p. 195), can inspire cults or undermine perception of fundamental reality. Or both.

Hastur cannot be met but it can be encountered, and perhaps even understood, as far as human brains can tolerate it. When humans cause entropy, they resonate with Hastur, and vice versa: our despair gives it a voice, our devastations give it form, our self-destruction gives it a name. When human cultists envision a deity with properties resonant with the principle of entropy, they can commune with their vision directly, fostering a greater – albeit insane – understanding of it than mere physicists can grasp.

In brief, Hastur can be described as a sublimely subtle force for, or of, insidious destruction. It breaks things down not from without, but from within. Hastur operates on and within the human mind: the manifold subtleties of thoughts and chemicals that compose our personalities are the fields in which Hastur is at play. Its molecular micro-adjustments produce insane, destructive – often self-destructive – tendencies.

Hastur's influence spreads along a vector of infectious mental illness, passed as easily through speech or imagery as through the printed page or musical score. The entropic fever burning in this influence breaks down human perception of reality, and on a quantum level reorganizes (or disorganizes) the reality around them. Buildings shift, paintings change, lights flicker, statues mutate, but only in the presence of those Hastur has touched. Around them, order is the Joker and chaos the King.

The King in Yellow

The taciturn and malign avatar known as the King in Yellow manifests where Hastur's field intensity heightens: vice and melancholy, the social entropy disintegrating human order. The King stochastically presides over the terrible alien city of Carcosa (p. 214), an embodiment of despair and paranoia, further elements of entropy at the level of everyday human experience.

He might well have once been an ordinary person whose understanding of entropy approached the cosmic level, and who acquired some form of immunity to entropy as a result. Thus distanced from the rest of reality, he acquired peculiar powers and understanding and thereby became the King in Yellow.

Alternately, it could be that all of the faith and strength of will possessed by followers of Hastur has drained from their despairing minds and into the living shadow of the King in Yellow. Explanations are many: facts are few. Perhaps only barely sentient, the King needs only his nature as incarnate despair. Personality is only inferred, and is all but irrelevant.

The Phantom of Truth

This strange being – dressed in robes and wearing a Pallid Mask that is not a mask – travels to cities teetering on the brink of being consumed by Carcosa. The Phantom determines whether the city shall be consumed or not based on the city's state of melancholy and despair. Each time, the Phantom possesses someone in the city and uses his body as its vessel.

Encountering Entities

Encountering (in rituals, dreams, or worse yet some weed-covered Pacific islet) a Great Old One or Outer God imposes a still-greater Sanity and Stability loss than merely seeing some other sort of immense, horrible monster. These entities exist on more than just the normal human levels of perception. They invisibly radiate wrongness, disconfirming every cherished belief in logic, observation, or decency. In general, given these beings' vast psychic powers, seeing them in dreams is no safer than seeing them in the liquescent, protean flesh, but dreams or visions can at least be denied (see p. 122).

Entity Effects

The effect of encountering a cosmic god or titan cannot be fully quantified. They have no Health levels or ability pools; they are arbitrary and immense. But they definitely have an effect on those who witness them, and some Agents may be able to have an effect on them.

Interpolate values for other entities based on the Entity Effects Table on p. 283.

Stability and Sanity Losses

Stability pool point losses from seeing such entities are *in addition* to the loss risked by an encounter indicated on the Unnatural Stimuli Table (p. 119). Some entities are so horrific that they impose automatic losses even if the Agent makes her Stability test; those losses are indicated in parentheses after the first number.

Some also deplete Sanity pool points as well as Stability. Automatic Sanity pool losses also appear in parentheses after the first number.

The Handler should tailor specific losses for a given entity to the degree of horror it presents in that encounter: Nyarlathotep has a thousand forms, some human and some unutterably monstrous.

Aura of Power

Entities on this scale simply defeat human perception and will to act. Every human present when an entity manifests suffers an increase to the Difficulty of all her actions given on the table.

In addition to any other effects, characters who fail a Stability test due to the presence of an entity cannot act at all for 2d6 rounds, save to stare in mad wonder at the transcendent horror of it all.

Attacks

If you are so unwise or unfortunate as to draw an entity's attention, it may deign to smite you. It automatically hits. Use this entry as a guideline.

Dismissal

This is the *additional* sacrifice of Sanity *rating points* needed to dismiss an entity, using the Closing of the Breach ritual or another. It can be spent by any witness who knows the ritual, or in some cases by any witness who also sacrifices double that amount of Health in blood. (At least one witness must know the proper ritual.) The Handler may vary this depending on the ritual, but don't count on it: touching these horrors, even mathematically, strips human minds to their bare threads.

Cthulhu, at least, can be physically dismissed while the stars remain wrong. Any attack doing L4 or higher damage to it (such as being struck by a 300-ton or larger object at full speed) discorporates it and returns it to R'lyeh. Other entities may be similarly "vulnerable" at the Handler's discretion.

Entity Effects

Entity	Additional Stability and Sanity point loss	Aura of Power	Attacks	Dismissal	Special
Azathoth	+6 (5) Stability +5 (3) Sanity	+3	Manifest (L1), 10 yd radius; double radius and +1 Lethality each round	4 Sanity	
Cthulhu	+5 (3) Stability +3 (2) Sanity	+3; Psychic Shout (p. 254)	claw swat (L3*) up to three clustered targets	3 Sanity	Those who fail Stability tests receive Nightmares (p. 124)
Ghatanothoa	+4 (2) Stability +2 (1) Sanity	+1; +3 Diff to all physical tests	-2 Athletics per round for all eyewitnesses; mummified at 0	1 Sanity	
The Headless One	+3 (2) Stability +2 (1) Sanity	+2	Biting hands (d+5); two attacks per round	1 Sanity	No mandatory loss or Aura to behold its avatar
Itla-Shua	+4 (2) Stability +3 (1) Sanity	+2	Swipe (L1); Diff 7 Athletics to dodge also being carried into the sky and frozen solid	2 Sanity	Accompanied by dozens of wendigowak (p. 257) and ice-cold winds
Nyarlathotep (Black Man form)	+1 Stability +0 Sanity	+4 (only for attacks on Him)	Summons a hunting-horror (p. 240)	1 Sanity	
Nyarlathotep (Monster form)	+5 (4) Stability +4 (3) Sanity	+3	claw (L2*H)	3 Sanity	
Qu-Tugkwa	+3 Stability +1 Sanity	+1	fireblast (L2*H), 20 yd radius	1 Sanity	
Tsathoggua	+2 Stability +2 Sanity	+2	Diff 9 Athletics to dodge being eaten	1 Sanity	Can grant any ritual or any Investigative Ability at 2
Yig	+3 (2) Stability +2 Sanity	+2	Bite (d+2 and L3*H venom)	1 Sanity	Accompanied by Children of Yig (p. 251)
Yog-Sothoth	+6 (4) Stability +4 (3) Sanity	+3	Sphere touch (d+0 Health *rating* points); blast (L4)	4 Sanity	no extra loss for cloaked Tawil at'Umr form

Targets of Opportunity

"THEN, TOO, IT IS UNDENIABLE THAT A FRESH AND EVIL WAVE OF UNDERGROUND CULT ACTIVITY SET IN ABOUT THE TIME OF MY ODD MUTATION."

— H.P. LOVECRAFT, "THE SHADOW OUT OF TIME"

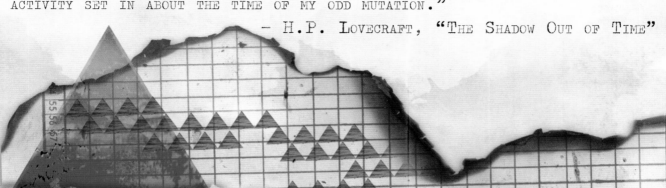

The first, and usual, response of humanity to the unnatural is to shatter. But occasionally, our species' great gifts for greed, hatred, and curiosity provide a certain resilience: a few of us come together after the shock and seek to use and understand what nearly killed us to kill our enemies.

Not every cult remains a backwater family of inbred hill people, or an isolated monastery tangent to Leng. Some unnatural cults reach their tendrils out into the world, conduits for the poison of their maltheology. Some cults corrode the old order to empower themselves; others just embrace entropy. Some cults even try deliberately to shift the world faster in the direction of the foredoomed apocalypse: in this decade especially, perhaps.

In this decade, at least, DELTA GREEN stands watch to prevent that. The program buries isolated cults: where none can see, it leaves no witnesses. The program chops off cult tendrils, burns out corrosion, fights for order and for our illusionary moment of stability. DELTA GREEN stands against the apocalypse, and shoots back whenever a target of opportunity presents itself.

CAN THIS REALLY BE THE END?

Most of the cults in this section were created for the original **Delta Green** material in the late 1990s. In "official **Delta Green** continuity" they survive at least that long until a spate of action by the cowboy-era conspiracy clears the decks for the new millennium.

None of which should have anything to do with how you investigate, attack, or even eradicate them in your 1960s **Fall of DELTA GREEN** campaign. Destroy anything listed here if its destruction makes your story more terrible and glorious. Some of these figures – Stephen Alzis, the Kuen-Yuin, the Motion – may be essentially invulnerable to even the unleashed might of the United States government. (Why shouldn't at least one or two unnatural cults have the staying power of Castro and North Vietnam?) But even those eerie entities can suffer setbacks at the hands of your Agents, setbacks that went unrecorded after the final fall of DELTA GREEN.

Unfinished Business

Despite decades-long campaigns, foes from the program's early days still haunt the nighted places of the world. Admittedly, DELTA GREEN has driven them into hiding – but a foe you think is gone is often the most dangerous.

The Cthulhu Cult

DELTA GREEN first encountered the Cthulhu cult in the decayed fishing village of Innsmouth, Massachusetts, but expanded that battle all over the world in the next decades. In 1930, Operation TALCUM smashed a Deep One colony on Piedra Negra, an islet in the Philippines near Mindanao. January 1933 saw

Operation BAKELITE play catch-up after too-enthusiastic Nicaraguan national guardsmen torched the village of Agua Verde and massacre its Dagon cult before the program could plan the assault. P4 officers repeatedly contacted Deep Ones using a ritual recovered in their raids, to acquire more specimens for study and to discourage the batrachians from responding to such "summons."

The war on Cthulhu took a back seat to the war on the Axis, even for DELTA GREEN, but individual agents supplied local anti-cult forces with sonar maps, guns, and even the occasional offshore bombardment. This pattern continues in the shadow of the Cold War. Local tribes and townsfolk have driven the old Cthulhu societies to extinction in Greenland and the Philippines; DELTA GREEN has mounted direct assaults on a dozen Deep One colonies. This campaign continues with Operations RIPTIDE (p. 179) and GOBLIN MARKET (p. 181), along with other direct actions on lonely shores. But this decade, the real war against the Cthulhu cult moves into the tropical capitals of the newly independent colonies.

Program operatives finger Cthulhu cultists for reprisals by new governments or pliable mobs: the Zanzibar Revolution of 1964, the Indonesian massacres in 1965, the tribal purge in Uganda in 1966, and scores of riots and skirmishes from Santo Domingo to Singapore just "happen" to sweep up Cthulhu cultists in the fires and lynchings. The program follows behind CIA secret warriors not just in Indochina but in Guatemala, Colombia, and Peru, burning out cult compounds and burying the action in other atrocities.

A few centers of the old 1920s-era "dockyard cult" remain: Buenos Aires, Valparaiso, Acapulco, Istanbul, Lourenco Marques, and quite likely Shanghai. The cult wreaks vengeance on those who directly cross or expose it, but its reach weakens as ocean trade concentrates in a few ports policed by unfriendly forces, and as its Kuen-Yuin sponsors become ever more distracted at home (p. 294).

The most effective remaining Cthulhu cult is the Exalted Circle (p. 301) in America. Even the Circle, however, seems to value its profits over Alhazred's prophecies. Cthulhu still dreams in the deep, but its sendings now inspire mostly isolated artists or madmen.

The Genyosha

Part political party, part secret society, and part unofficial espionage arm of the Japanese military, the Genyosha, or Black Ocean Society, began in 1881. It infiltrated secret societies, criminal organizations and occult brotherhoods across Asia, and avidly pursued contact with the Deep Ones. The inner core of the Genyosha exercised power through their official positions in the Japanese military, government ministries, and secret police. Although the program uncovered individual Genyosha fronts and assets, only when war with Japan led to the breaking of the IJN naval codes did DELTA GREEN discern the full scope of their opponents' operations.

In February 1944, DELTA GREEN launched Operation BROWN STUDY, a landing on Eniwetok atoll ahead of the main Marine assault to disrupt Black Ocean sorcerous defenses in place. The ensuing bloodbath nearly wiped out the DELTA GREEN detachment and its support Marine company. As a result, DELTA GREEN prevented the planned landing on Ponape, the major Black Ocean fane in the Pacific. Instead, Operation MERITORIOUS pulverized every possible unnatural feature with flights of B-24 and B-25 bombers and a lengthy shore bombardment by USS *Iowa* and USS *Massachusetts* on Walpurgisnacht 1944. A DELTA GREEN analysis identifying the Cabinet of Confiscated Foreign Books in Nagasaki as the Black Ocean's primary research center did nothing to dissuade the USAAF selection of that city as a nuclear target.

The atomic bombing of Nagasaki scorched the heart out of the Genyosha and its political wing, the Kokuryukai (Black Dragon) Society. It also obliterated any chance DELTA GREEN had of finding a membership roster for this sorcerous-minded sect of ultranationalists. Many members of far-right movements joined the Yakuza criminal underworld after the war, funding Japanese industrialists and the ruling Liberal Democratic Party (LDP) — it's quite likely that any surviving Genyosha cultists nest quite high and comfortable in the Japanese establishment.

The Yakuza also maintains a special relationship with the CIA, as a funding channel for the LDP and a weapon against Communist unions in Japan. These ties, and the importance of Japan to the logistics of the Vietnam War, make DELTA GREEN's task of rooting out Genyosha survivors extremely difficult. Genyosha, for its part, has extended its own researches from Ryujin (Cthulhu) and the kappa (Deep Ones) to Mara-Soto ("Outside Evil," or Yog-Sothoth) and the Tokoyo-no-Kami ("God of the Eternal World," a worm-entity that briefly manifested in Shizuoka prefecture in 644 A.D.).

Omori Sogen, the highest-ranking known member of the Kokuryukai to survive the war, refounds the society as a student club in 1961. Now a Zen Buddhist priest, he remains active in right-wing politics and unnatural studies. Nori Onishi, a former Black Dragon operative arrested by the FBI in 1942 at the age of 16, was released from internment in 1945. He now leads a renewed Genyosha cult with its fane in his Tokio Club in San Francisco. Onishi uses criminal and legal means to acquire books, papers, and artifacts from the estates of dead or vanished Genyosha members in the Americas, and from anyone else he thinks he can muscle. He also runs a gambling and prostitution network in the Bay Area, protected by his unnatural enforcers the ki-yamma (Black Winged Ones).

The Karotechia

The occult-obsessed head of the SS, Heinrich Himmler, established the Ahnenerbe in 1935 as an "Ancestral Heritage Research Bureau" to investigate everything from ley lines to Atlantis. While the Ahnenerbe were mostly dilettantes and cranks devoted to measuring skulls and recording folk songs, others were more serious. Within the Reichs Security Office (RSHA) a small group of researchers into the medieval witch-cult uncovered hypergeometric rituals, tried them out in the spirit of Nazi crank science – and found that they worked.

In 1939, Himmler formalized this new group as a special SS command called the Karotechia. During the war, they attempted to commune with alien entities, command unearthly energies, and unlock the secrets of life after death. DELTA GREEN blocked them everywhere it could as America ramped up its war effort. In late 1942, for example, DELTA GREEN worked with French partisans and the British occult special operations group PISCES (p. 174) to disrupt a planned mass sacrifice by the Karotechia in Cap de La Hague, France.

The final Karotechia operation was to be Aktion GÖTTERDÄMMERUNG, the intentional summoning of Azathoth using a ritual taken from the Gothic-language version of the *Necronomicon* (p. 194). During the summer of 1945, DELTA GREEN devoted its energy to a counter-operation called Operation LUNACY: the hunting down of every surviving Karotechia cell in Europe. By September, Cook's commandos had obliterated Aktion GÖTTERDÄMMERUNG in a series of covert actions that cost the lives of many agents – and of many more Karotechia members.

Several high-ranking Karotechia operatives and researchers escaped Germany on the ODESSA "rat lines," fleeing to Africa, Spain, and South America. DELTA GREEN launched Operation SOUTHERN HOSPITALITY to track, infiltrate, and eliminate these remnants of Himmler's occult bureau. Initially an informal (and illegal) ongoing investigation, SOUTHERN HOSPITALITY climaxed in April 1952 with a final showdown in Antarctica, and shut down completely in 1956.

DELTA GREEN believes that Operations LUNACY and SOUTHERN HOSPITALITY destroyed the Karotechia. They are almost right: of the original 164 members of the group, only three survive. Even those three barely communicate: Galt and Frank sometimes cooperate; Galt has encountered the new Läufern (as have Frank's operatives) but not Bitterich; Bitterich so far believes himself to be the sole survivor. One link between the three is the former commando SS Obersturmbannführer Otto Skorzeny, who splits his time between Spain, the Middle East, and Argentina – but Skorzeny considered the Karotechia more of Himmler's occult idiocy and only knows the three as fellow war criminals.

Dr. Olaf Bitterich (b. 1902)

The spirit medium Bitterich spent WWII communing unknowingly with Nyarlathotep, who appeared in the guise of Frederick the Great, Arminius, Heinrich the Fowler, and other German heroes. Now based in Spain, Bitterich serves the spirit of the Ascended Master Adolf Hitler – Nyarlathotep again. "Der Führer" sends Bitterich far and wide, collecting the tools, knowledge, and followers he needs to elevate the Aryan race to their place as Enlightened Masters. Bitterich recruits twelve pure Aryan pupils in the black arts, whom he has christened his *Läufern* (Bishops).

SS Oberführer Reinhard Galt (b. 1911)

Galt looted libraries and laboratories for the Karotechia during the War, killing two DELTA GREEN agents personally in Algiers. In 1945, Galt encountered the Anzique tribe in the Belgian Congo and by sacrificing his men to their cannibal feast learned the secret of immortality. He returned to Europe in 1951 and began a career as a mercenary soldier,

torture instructor, and military advisor. He spends most of his time in Egypt working for Nasser's military; during the war in Yemen (1962-1970) he mounts several expeditions into the desert searching for the tomb of Alhazred.

Dr. Gunter Frank (b. 1896)

During the War, Frank studied technological necromancy, masterminding Aktion DRAUGR, the "Resuscitated Casualties" project that used the re-animated dead as soldiers. (SMERSH captured his assistant, Erwin Peis, in 1945.) Frank smuggled a fortune in art out of the collapsing Reich and purchased an immense rubber plantation in the Brazilian rain forest, La Estancia. He continued to study re-animation, combining his prior work with the chemical-pharmacological-occult methods of the renowned Spanish physician Dr. Javier Muñoz. This came in handy when he died of cancer in 1958.

Frank now exists in a ghastly sort of half-life; his mind remains intact, although only meat remains of his eviscerated body. (He cut out his cancer-ridden internal organs to halt the disease's spread.) As a side effect of his "condition," Frank's body must remain constantly below 50°F or putrefy and deliquesce. His higher brain functions, cognitive abilities, and memories are intact, despite the death of his body and the excision of his cancer-ridden internal organs. A prisoner of his ice-box hacienda, Frank seeks the secrets of mind transfer, bodily resurrection, or anything else that will let him escape his refuge. He funds thieves and criminals — and the occasional clandestine operation — all over the world in his quest.

The Fate

In 1927, the clairvoyant Madame A and her parapsychologist spokes-man Dr. Otto Schmiddt founded the Fate, a self-help cult for rich and desperate New Yorkers. Six years later, after a vicious murder scandal drove the original Fate underground, Madame A revealed to the few loyal members that they were Nyarlatho-tep's chosen sentinels, harbingers of the Apocalypse. The Fate ac-quired books and artifacts cheap, on Depression auction blocks and from frantic refugees from fascism and Communism. Madame A used her new acquisitions to do magical favors for the New York City un-derworld — favors that became de-mands.

When Madame A renewed her demands after a brief surcease during WWII (to avoid federal attention) the Five Families struck back. Fifteen men emptied subma-chine guns into Madame A's car in 1951, and although only two sur-vived with their sanity, Madame A was gone. Two years later, Stephen Alzis took control of the Fate. Faith-less members of the Fate met grisly accidental deaths — and then the Families followed. Albert "the Exe-cutioner" Anastasia is executed in a barber shop in 1957, Joseph Profa-ci dies of cancer in 1962, Anthony "Tony Bender" Strollo simply vanish-es the same year, and Tommy "Three Finger Brown" Lucchese dies of a brain tumor in 1967.

And those are just the ones that make the headlines: over the ten years from 1957 to 1967 over two dozen key underbosses and consiglieri vanish, go mad, get eaten by wild animals, and in at least one case spontaneously combust. The bosses see horrifying visions, and then they see the light. In the 1960s the Fate becomes the Network: the secret ex-tortionists who extort the Mob. The Network makes and unmakes capos and Congressmen, ruling from deep in the shadows. Alzis returns the Fate to its old business of sorcery for hire, but also uses the New York mob as his own personal hiring hall. So a Gambino soldier "just decides" to rob a library reference room, or a Colombo made man "accidentally" runs down a folklore scholar. Deni-able, unknowable, and inevitable — it must be Fate.

Organization

At the top of the Fate stands Stephen Alzis. Below him is his second-in-command Robert "Belial" Hubert. In a sense, only Alzis and Hubert are truly the Fate: everyone else is just Fated. All of them bear the Mark of the Fate: a birthmark resembling the Eye of Horus. (Although Alzis' Mark comes and goes at his whim.) As Alzis accumulates more Lords this decade, he promotes Agdesh and Hutchins to full Fate membership, although they still engage in the occasional Lordly commission.

Stephen Alzis

Like the Comte de Saint-Germain, Stephen Alzis has seemingly always been around. The documentary record goes back at least as far as his death on the *Morro Castle* on 8 September 1934. He has also died in a car crash on the Triborough Bridge in 1938, and was reported killed four times during World War II. Most recently, he died in a fire in Queens in 1950, and over the Yellow Sea in 1964 (see Operation PARIAH, p. 180). People who dig up details about Alzis' various deaths often die in remarkable ways them-selves, albeit only once.

Alzis always reappears after a few months, looking the same as ever: a slim, good-looking Arab man in his thirties wearing a habitual smile and a designer suit. He is rarely seen coming or going; he's simply there. He has no true address, frequenting dozens of town houses, mansions, and apartments all over the world. Documentation of his properties, like that of his existence, is usually sketchy, but somehow avoids official scrutiny.

Alzis collects odd things, espe-cially odd information. He deals in knowledge, and the books and items that can grant it. He brokers for the Vatican and for serial killers — and even for DELTA GREEN agents, if the price is right. He doesn't denom-inate his prices in curre210ncy, but in barter: for curious relics or certain obligations. Those who deal with him get what they want, but he gets more: his web of favors, whispers, and trades always redounds to his benefit. He reads lives at a glance, and knows his customers better than they know themselves.

The only thing Stephen Alzis doesn't know is... Stephen Alzis. He knows he has a part to play in the Apocalypse, but he doesn't know why. He walks the streets and corri-dors of his city, seeking answers and selling them, trying to fit himself into the pattern of destruction he weaves.

Those who claim to be in the know consider Stephen Alzis an avatar of Nyarlathotep. Those really in the know... know better than to speculate about Stephen Alzis.

SECRET

COUNTRY: NORTH VIETNAM/USSR

DOI: EARLY FEBRUARY

SUBJECT:

The Unnatural

DIST 18 FEBRUARY 1968

CONVENTIONAL OPPOSITION

As part of the U.S. intelligence community, DELTA GREEN may find itself the target of - or targeting - foreign intelligence agencies.

Communist China: The "Organs in the Western Garden" (synecdoche for the Central Investigation Department (CID) or Chungyang Tiao-ch'a Pu) handle foreign intelligence and domestic security. Powerful rivals purge CID director Kong Yang in 1967 (to weaken his patron Teng Hsiao-ping) and Mao (or General Lin Piao) dissolves the CID in 1969 during the Cultural Revolution. Ruthless WWII-era spymaster Kang Sheng takes over its counterintelligence functions; the rest fall to the Second Department of the People's Liberation Army General Staff, China's military intelligence department.

Cuba: Castro and the KGB create the DGI (Direccion General de Intelligencia) in 1961. In addition to foreign and domestic intelligence, the DGI oversees four Liberation Committees (Caribbean, Central America, South America, and Africa). The KGB disbands Cuba's African CL in 1968-1969 while reining in the DGI and purging its director, Manuel Piniero.

East Germany: The Ministry for State Security ("Stasi") headed by Erich Mielke keeps its citizens under nearly complete surveillance. Legendary spymaster Colonel Markus Wolf runs the HVA (Main Directorate for Reconnaissance) that penetrates West German politics as well as NATO and American operations in Europe.

Egypt: Until 1967, the energetic and effective Salah Nasr runs the Gehaz el-Mukhabarat el-Amma (General Intelligence Directorate, "Mukhabarat" for short), which spies on Israel and assists pro-Nasserite forces all over North Africa and the Middle East. The Mukhabarat maintains good relations with many regional and European spy agencies, especially including the KGB. Following the Six-Day War, Nasr retires for "health reasons"; his replacement is the ambitious Amin Howeidi.

North Vietnam: Minister of Public Security Tran Quoc Hoan controls domestic intelligence, purging the Vietnamese Communist Party in 1963 and 1967, and investigating the activities of the KGB and GRU in Vietnam. Foreign intelligence falls to the Military Research Department (Cuc Nghien Cu) of the Ministry of Defense.

Soviet Union: The KGB runs foreign intelligence (First Chief Directorate) and domestic surveillance (Second Chief Directorate). Its Third Chief Directorate monitors the Soviet armed forces for subversion; the KGB has veto power over the staffing and foreign assignments of the Soviet military's Main Intelligence Directorate (GRU). Brezhnev forces out the relatively colorless functionary V.Y. Semichastny as KGB Chairman in 1967, replacing him with Yuri Andropov.

Robert Hubert

Hubert begins the decade as a would-be somebody on the occult make and ends it as Belial to Alzis' Satan. In 1960 Hubert arrives in New York after graduating from Bard College, eagerly seeking unnatural lore. He discovers the Fate while compounding specialized amphetamine formulations and disposing of bodies for the Genovese family. Alzis recognizes Hubert's inhuman drive and adopts him as his consigliere, making him a Lord (the Lord of Life) in 1963, and nicknaming him "Belial." Hubert spends most of the middle 1960s managing the Fate for Alzis, hanging out at Andy Warhol's Factory, and managing a number of failed or one-hit bands.

After a bitter argument with Warhol over the Velvet Underground (Hubert tries and fails to sign them) in 1968, he leaves the Factory for the nascent metal and proto-punk movements. (Valerie Solanas shoots Warhol three days later.) On 30 October 1969, Hubert opens Club Apocalypse on 98th and Lexington in silent partnership with Stephen Alzis.

Unknown to everyone except perhaps Alzis, Hubert is actually a former Karotechia savant, SS Hauptscharführer Dieter Scheel. In 1944, with the Red Army on the horizon, Scheel dove into the Black Lake in Hungary, communing with and offering himself to the entity Giliszta in its depths. He emerged, eventually, in Missouri in 1954. He drowned and replaced the real Robert Hubert in 1960; other blond boys who awaken his inner monster he merely drowns in Long Island Sound. Some day, he will find another Lake worthy of such sacrifices. Until then, he avoids sunlight when possible and grooms himself fastidiously against any sign of decay or age.

The Lords

Below Hubert are the other Lords, master hypergeometers whose services command fear and tribute from New York's criminal underworld. They represent the Fate at any outside meeting – unless Alzis decides to make an appearance himself.

△ Emir Agdesh is an Egyptian cotton heir now living a placid investor's life in Central Park West. He is also the heir to – or rather, the latest incarnation of – a lineage of Nyarlathotep worshipers reaching back to Nephren-Ka's reign.

△ Emmanuel Hutchins appears to be a Hispanic teenage boy, but commands surprisingly varied hypergeometries. Nobody sees him by day, he smells like chlorine and is immensely strong, and he seems to understand neither grooming nor emotions, engaging in both at random. He acts as Alzis' lap dog and attack dog by turns.

△ "Queen Marie" began as a teenage Voodoo mamaloi in Harlem but soon discovered the older and more terrible Invisibles of the unnatural world. An attractive Black woman, she has a romantic attachment to Joseph Anthony Colombo that discomfits his more old-fashioned fellow mobsters. This, some think, accounts for much of her attachment.

△ Otto Schmiddt might miss the simple days of hustling mobsters if his new researches weren't always so fascinating. A consummate scholar and still spry in his eighties, he takes jobs only when he wants to – usually if the client adds a valuable tome or unicum grimoire to the price. There's always something new to learn from an old book, Otto says, in a German accent that hasn't lost its stutter in forty years.

The Lords are always open to any ambitious and amoral person willing to risk total destruction for unnatural knowledge. And willing to follow the whims of Fate, of course. Each Lord has one or two Neophytes in training at any time: expendable but capable students of the unnatural.

GRU SV-8: THE ENEMY OF OUR ENEMY

In the winter of 1918 during the Russian Civil War, Lieutenant Gregor Studnikov of Red Army intelligence investigated rumors of cannibalism in his sector of the Siberian front. He discovered the existence of *nekrofagiyisti*, or ghouls. Studnikov entered the GRU in 1927 after rooting out a cult of Kotura, Lord of the Winds. By 1931 Major Studnikov headed Spetsialni Viedotstvo 8 (SV-8; Special Department 8) of the GRU. His mission: spy on Stalin's secret occult experimentation unit within the OGPU, later the NKVD. Unsurprisingly, the NKVD purged Studnikov in 1938 along with the rest of the GRU leadership.

In 1940, the GRU reactivated SV-8 for the occult war against the Ahnenerbe and Karotechia. In 1942, SV-8 again hunted ghouls during the Siege of Leningrad; in 1945 it encountered "resuscitated casualties," or *poyavlyatsya*. Under its chief, General-Major Sergei M. Shtemyenko, it also fought Stalin's occult directorate inside SMERSH, going so far as to ally with DELTA GREEN against SMERSH during the chaos in occupied Vienna during Operation SUMMER BREEZE. SV-8 renewed the alliance in 1952, allowing a DELTA GREEN team to destroy the SMERSH life-extension laboratory and doom Stalin's occult immortality. In June 1953, the GRU purged SMERSH, and SV-8 executed or absorbed its occult researchers and assets.

When Soviet intelligence learned about the Roswell crash, Shtemyenko (by then head of the whole GRU) convinced Stalin to assign the investigation to SV-8. The department began a full espionage campaign against MAJESTIC, while Shtemyenko simultaneously removed all evidence of SV-8's continued existence from army and intelligence files. After 1947, the personnel of SV-8 would officially not exist, even in the all-seeing State. Even its funding came from fictitious projects, approved by Shtemyenko and his successor as GRU head, SV-8 veteran Colonel-General M.A. Shalin.

In MJ-3, the GRU has met a foe as deadly and ruthless as itself. MJ-11 sends its own spies into the Soviet bloc to find out what Russia and SV-8 know, about MAJESTIC and about the unnatural in general. Under its current chief, the affably brutal Lieutenant General G.F. Ivanov, SV-8 works to extract such knowledge from its crop of Karotechia "recruits," from active measures against MAJESTIC, and from its ongoing operations: investigating the magical murder of a Cuban DGI colonel in 1964, burning through North Vietnamese Army cannon fodder to destroy a Dao Sâm cult stronghold on the Ho Chi Minh Trail in 1966, rounding up unusual suspects during an occult serial killing in Kiev in 1968. And, of course, penetrating their old friends in DELTA GREEN.

The Adepts

The Adepts are misfits, bums, junkies, the downtrodden: those broken by New York City. When they break just right, they hear the call of the Fate and respond. They carry messages, pick up protection money, answer pay phones, and follow the hints and orders in their dreams. They tend to show up whenever and wherever something of occult or unnatural significance happens in the city. If the Agents have an operation in the tri-state area, one of them sees an Adept in his peripheral vision – and again, two days later.

Each Adept has an assignment handed out by her personal demons, by the voices in her head: feed only the pigeons on the west side of Washington Square Park, follow a ten-dollar bill wherever it goes, take a picture of a certain wall in Tribeca every Saturday at dawn, tear pictures of Elizabeth Taylor out of the *Post*. If an Adept needs something for his "mission" the Network provides it: a camera, a library card, more purple markers.

The Network keeps around fifty Adepts in active service. They may turn up anywhere, at any time, the invisible in pursuit of the incoherent. In addition to standing their strange watches, the Adepts insulate the Network from provably criminal activity. A complete airlock of secrecy exists between the already shadowy Fate and organized crime. No solid link, written, recorded, or photographed is detectable between the crime families and the Lords of the Fate. The Adepts provide this security with their utter anonymity and insanity.

Assets

The Fate, in the person of Stephen Alzis and various legal fictions, owns a great deal of real estate scattered all over the five boroughs, Long Island, and New Jersey. Choice locations include Perry Court in Manhattan, the old Suydam mansion in Flatbush, and a stretch of Red Hook condemned in 1925 after a freak accident collapsed the buildings.

Its crown jewel, and the headquarters of the cult, is the Moritaum Estate in Southampton, Long Island. In 1957, shortly before his death, the dilettante and former Fate cultist Arthur Moritaum willed his mansion and fourteen acres of grounds (including Ilium Island about four miles off shore) to Stephen Alzis. It serves as a repository for books and artifacts, a residence for Lords and promising Neophytes in training, and a ritual (and burial) ground during the solstices.

Guarded and staffed by platoons of intelligent and brutal cultists of the Black Pharaoh – Egyptian immigrants hand-picked by Emir Agdesh – it has the best security money and magic can procure, including the Southampton town police chief. That said, as the only place the entire Fate meets at once, it is paradoxically the only place the organization is vulnerable.

Whole Earth Enterprises

In 1961, Stephen Alzis moves his investment firm Whole Earth Enterprises (WEE) into offices in the McMahon Building on Central Park South. Alzis remains the only stockholder, and WEE continues to operate behind the scenes: buying minority shares of growing corporations, providing investment capital or bridge loans to desperate companies, and gathering up a few unnoticed subsidiaries around the world. Its highest-profile deal got four column inches on an inside page of the *Wall Street Journal* in 1959: the complicated three-sided purchase of the Agdesh-Shaqti cotton plantations in Egypt via a West German avionics company and a Swiss bank.

Even with the lowest of public profiles, 200 employees in New York and 9,000 around the world leave tracks: DELTA GREEN assets within the IRS tipped off the Executive Committee, and a few accountants now diligently map Alzis' surface business dealings. WEE has fingers in a lot of pies: napalm, synthetic opioids, television production, computerized switches, corn syrup – a seemingly random portfolio with only profitability in common. Overseas, WEE manages factories and plantations from Taiwan to Guatemala, but sells their production mostly to other foreign countries – a business decision that makes more sense if you consider any U.S. government attention a dead loss.

Club Apocalypse

In 1951, Whole Earth Enterprises built a modest apartment building on top of the infamous Doolittle Sinkhole, which was responsible for the collapse of four buildings and the death of fourteen people a decade earlier. On 30 October 1969, acting on behalf of an unnamed owner, Robert Hubert opens Club Apocalypse in its basement. It rapidly becomes a hub for the larval punk and metal scenes in the city, and (due to the Club's *extremely* strictly enforced "no reporters, no cameras" policy) the famous flock to its inner and exclusive "Green Bar" or the even more exclusive "Hell Lounge" in the second sub-basement.

The Club allows the Fate's occult elite to mingle with Mafia princes and Hollywood stars, and provides petitioners (and Agents) their most likely meeting with Stephen Alzis. If any guests overstep their bounds, of course, Alzis or Hubert invites them further downstairs to discuss matters with "the Manager." Downstairs, below the third sub-basement and past a red silken rope, the levels and chambers continue: colonial cellars, Dutch smuggling tunnels, still older pits and passages in a black labyrinth with no end and no bottom.

Kuen-Yuin

The Kuen-Yuin have been the pre-eminent society of sorcerers in China for at least a millennium. According to their own legends, they date back to the first Yellow Emperor, Huang-ti. Since the Yellow Emperor is also the Yellow Dragon (Huang-Lung) this may refer not to the historical period ascribed to Huang-ti (c. 2650 B.C.) but to some antediluvian immanentization of a Great Old One. Certainly their symbol, a golden globe engraved with reptiles and Chinese hieroglyphs, implies as much.

Their name roughly translates as "Those Who Cause and Follow Power," which describes their traditional relationship with the Chinese state: for centuries, they strengthened the Emperor as long as he supported their aims. If not, they conspired against him or suborned and debauched his successor. The Kuen-Yuin intervened in imperial marriages and politics, sometimes inserting mandarins or eunuchs at court and sometimes manipulating affairs remotely by hypergeometric means. During warlord eras, the Kuen-Yuin vented their appetites for sadism and power, looted imperial libraries, and laid the foundations of their next dynasty.

The Communist revolution in 1949 upset this ancient practice more than any development since the Mongol invasions. The Communists declared traditional magic counter-revolutionary and ruthlessly purged anyone suspected of such beliefs. While the Kuen-Yuin practice perversions of Taoist and Confucian magic, these distinctions were lost on the commissars enforcing Mao's edict. Bombers and railroads brought destruction even to the remote monasteries and palaces where the Kuen-Yuin habitually retreated in times of persecution. When the Cultural Revolution begins in 1966, purges become mass executions.

Even the immortal masters of the Kuen-Yuin feel the threat. Increasingly since 1949, they reinforce their efforts outside China: Taiwan, Southeast Asia, India, Europe, America, anywhere they can establish a base amidst a terrified Chinese population and take over. The Kuen-Yuin tend to bridle or even eliminate other unnatural cults in cities they infest. For this reason, PISCES has been reluctant to pursue the Kuen-Yuin in Hong Kong, their new center of operations outside their mystical capital Yian-Ho (p. 213).

Organization and Aims

Each sect of the Kuen-Yuin operates under its own governor, called a kwan, as part of a bureaucratic whole. Communication up and down the ranks occurs overnight in dreams. The emblematic cult orbs also allow instantaneous transmission of orders and reports, and change color to indicate dissent or signal emergencies. Enforcement of the hierarchy's decisions is cruel and immediate, and seldom needed given the detailed and explicit institutional memory within the Kuen-Yuin.

Yue-Laou

The leader of the Kuen-Yuin is Yue-Laou, the Dzil-Nhu, the Maker of Moons, who dwells in Yian-Ho as he has for millennia. Yue-Laou may not be human, even if he once was: he may be a renegade Mi-Go torturer, a Moon-Beast sorcerer from the Dreamlands entering our dimension,

the Yellow Lama of Leng, or some other eldritch figure. Chinese mythology calls Yüeh Lao the "Old Man Under the Moon," a god of true love who "unites with a cord all predestined couples." This alludes to Yue-Laou's command of destiny, and possibly to the Kuen-Yuin's history of interfering with Imperial and other bloodlines to achieve their goals.

Goals

The short-term goal of the Kuen-Yuin is survival, and the extension of their own power to lands less dangerous than Mao's murderous paradise. Like most cults, they also accumulate unnatural lore and magical artifacts, although in Yian-Ho they have the ultimate weapon in the *Ghorl Nigral*. Many Kuen-Yuin kwan breed deadly poisonous plants or bloated and vicious moyü-hsieh (see *Lung-Xin*, p. 261), demonstrating the cult's interest in bloodlines.

Sadism for sadism's sake appears to be a key tenet of the cult's actions. They inflict not mere torture but heartbreak and despair and loss, often with a calligraphic touch as if creating lasting art in the medium of pain. Like many imperial masters, they employ Tcho-Tcho allies; unlike those others, they do so knowingly.

The ultimate goal of the Kuen-Yuin is the nurturing and creation of the cruel Empire of Tsan-Chan, destined to reign over Earth three thousand years from now. Every marriage alliance between two strange families, every child born to the genetically and astrologically correct parents, every memory of cruelty or history of terrible wonder, lays one more stone in Tsan-Chan's foundation. In the eon of Tsan-Chan, humanity finally casts good and evil aside and

becomes like the Great Old Ones, shouting and reveling in a holocaust of ecstasy.

The Kuen-Yuin and DELTA GREEN

The federal government has encountered the Kuen-Yuin numerous times, beginning at least as far back as the 1896 "Shiner" gold-counterfeiting plot in New York. Intelligence from Louisiana and the Philippines pointed to a sect of deathless Chinese priests guiding the Cthulhu cult; a 1933 reconnaissance in force by P4, Operation THIMBLE, ended in disaster (p. 214). Other ONI and P4 operatives on the U.S. Navy's Yangtze River Station had run-ins with the Kuen-Yuin, although they didn't always recognize the opium-traffickers, murder rings, or child-nappers they battled as such.

The OSS had a major presence in China during WWII, as did DELTA GREEN; Martin Cook ascribed at least two missing aircraft, four firefights, and three major occult manifestations to the cult's operations. Stephen Alzis' house in Tsingtao showed up on the program's radar thanks to a Kuen-Yuin racket that went noisily (and uncharacteristically) awry in 1947. In the 1950s, the Kuen-Yuin attempted to worm their way into the Communist hierarchy, beginning with the intelligence and security apparat.

As a result, the cult crossed paths with DELTA GREEN repeatedly in Korea and again in Vietnam until Chinese forces withdraw (and Mao purges the Chinese intelligence services) in 1968. Kuen-Yuin wushi especially seem to consider Laos vital or at least worth actively sabotaging the DELTA GREEN presence in that country. They expend considerable resources guiding and protecting the "Chinese Roads" in Laos in 1962-1963 and 1966-1971, and conduct rituals on the Plain of Jars.

DELTA GREEN analysts keep a very close eye on Chinatowns in San Francisco, Los Angeles, New York, and Chicago for signs of Kuen-Yuin infiltration. The program cultivates informants and friendlies within America-based tongs such as the Hip Sing and On Leong, hoping that any resulting tong war with the Kuen-Yuin provides DELTA GREEN with an early warning.

The Secret of the Kuen-Yuin

DELTA GREEN analysts have two theories about the cult:

△ The Kuen-Yuin are the "deathless ones in the mountains of China" who control the worldwide cult of Cthulhu, or perhaps are controlled by Cthulhu itself. P4 launched Operation THIMBLE on this basis, which does not necessarily disprove the theory.

△ The Kuen-Yuin are the human face of the Xin (p. 259). This minority view appears in the files of Col. Franklyn Barris, who thwarted the cult in 1896 in New York. The cult's appetite for certain antique jades and its presence deep inland tend to support this possibility.

The Kuen-Yuin, however, make use of a wide variety of unnatural entities in their activities. Almost as many files report the Kuen-Yuin operating with Deep Ones or Black Winged Ones as there are cases that fit the program's fragmentary Xin profile.

The truth is a combination of both views. The Kuen-Yuin are the descendants of the Xin's ruling elite from the fallen empire of Mu. Xin surgeries and temporal cysts made the Kuen-Yuin masters immortal millennia ago; they wish to remain so. They guard the Xin jades in their possession not merely in obeisance to this ancient fealty but because the destructive power of the Xin often proves useful.

The Xin likewise seek the rise of cruel Tsan-Chan, believing it the true successor to Mu. And the Xin believe that awakening Cthulhu is the most efficient way to achieve their ends: not only will It sweep away masses of undomesticated humans, but Its lambent power will transmute the remnant of the species into ideal bricks for their inhuman empire.

The Motion

No human can comprehend the landscape of time as seen by the Great Race of Yith – even "landscape" is too limiting a term for a dimension the Yithians can move into, over, out of, and through on any trajectory and at any interval. However, even the Great Race have goals, or seem to: they must contain their spectral, polypous nemeses long enough to escape them; and they *must* escape them, finding refuge occupying the giant coleopterous beetle-things that scuttle in the distant radioactive future after the death of mankind.

Their escape is at once inevitable and always at risk. Powers as contemptuous of the Yithians' Construct as the Yithians are of human causality operate too near – and sometimes within – the architecture of the Yithians' chosen future. Chaos unleashes, entropy shifts, and suddenly even human history becomes a relevant factor in the Great Race's chronal ballistics.

Motion and Lamplighters

At hinge points in time, the support network for Yithian temporal scholars becomes something else, something capable of moving history a few radians in the necessary direction. It becomes the Motion. In ancient Greece, the Kinesis guarded Pythagoras and exiled Carnamagos; eight centuries later the Cultus Motionis kept certain texts in a darkened library in Ravenna and altered others they left in the light; the Tung Sheng whispered in the ear of Kublai Khan and sent ships to new coasts under the Ming dynasty.

In the Victorian era, they took the name of the Lamplighters as a recruiting tool – a new empire needed many more servants for its secret masters – and as an arcane reference to Georg Simon Ohm's discovery that electric current (motion) equals power over resistance. When the Cult of Transcendence (p. 298) wrested control of the Lamplighters' European and American chapters away in 1928, the cult simply reincarnated under its oldest name: the Motion.

Organization and Distribution

The Motion depends entirely on Yith for its organization: the Great Race appoints a local cell leader across a specific span of years, and her recruits carry out her instructions. Yithian travelers possess the recruits if their brains are suitably robust, and direct matters while present.

The Lamplighters, needing to maintain a worldwide cult system themselves once communication and transportation between continents became practical, created a global structure of Academies, their term for the Lamplighter chapters in a given city. All the Academies on a continent make up its Lodge, directed by three Shining Ones, usually the heads of the most successful Academies (or those with an indwelling Yithian at the moment). Below the Shining Ones are the Humble Ones – targets for Yithian possession and capable occult agents in their own right – and below them the Learned Ones, chosen for their wealth or access.

The Motion still controls the entire Lamplighter Lodges in Australia and Asia, and a few Academies in other cities: Boston, Denver, Richmond, New Orleans and Mexico City (both retaken during a Cult of Transcendence vendetta in 1947), Pretoria, Stanleyville, Algiers, and Moscow. Elsewhere, the Motion has returned to a decentralized structure, its cells (and the remaining Academies) now linked by a cryptographically secure telex system. Any Yithian present in the current time who can communicate with any Motion servant can communicate with all of them without diving in and out of time, which is not always convenient.

Techniques and Goals

The Great Race provides its servants not just ritual fulfillment but practical rewards: knowledge of the future, and advanced technological devices. Only the Shining Ones receive the first, as knowing the future tempts less disciplined minds to change it, and even then some events wind up edited out of the oracle. However, even redacted prophecy can allow a Motion cell to make wise investments or avoid dangerous political commitments. It is in the Great Race's interest for its tools and potential hosts to be wealthy and safe, after all.

Advanced Technology

A Motion cell with an indwelling Yithian has its choice of Yithian Equipment (p. 237) and even time-bound cells often have a Memory Eraser. All Motion agents (and Lamplighters of Humble One rank or above) know how to build a Time Projector (p. 238). Often, Yithians implant deep aptitudes in their agents: they "remember" how to construct advanced technologies but cannot consciously analyze their knowledge or the devices. Sometimes the Yithian simply spends three or four days and builds enough gear for its projected needs and those of its protectors.

Perfect wireless communicators, compressed data storage devices, super-strong fibers, bullet-proof street clothes, EM pulse projectors, near-omniscient sensors — anything that might exist fifty or a hundred years in the future can show up in a Motion agent's closet or a Lamplighter Academy attic. The Motion places a very high priority on keeping such devices out of profane hands: they build self-destruct mechanisms, trackers undetectable on conventional frequencies, and remote controls into everything.

The End of the Line

The Motion knows that the Great Race has enemies: not just meddling mayfly governments, but the unceasing pressure of the spectral polyps and the chaotic lurches of the Outer Gods. In this eon, Yith finds itself locked in a relentless contest against the immaterial forces of the Xin and their Kuen-Yuin accomplices. The Xin seek to awaken degeneration and horror in mankind, even to unleash or incarnate the Great Old Ones in pursuit of the grim future of Tsan-Chan. Such a manifestation threatens to derail the Construct entirely, and so the Great Race opposes it.

From our limited human perspective, and to the Motion, it appears the Great Race attempts to protect humanity: keeping it on track, and away from occult catastrophe. While this is true, the vaster and less sympathetic truth overshadows it: the coleopterous species into which the Great Race escapes only exists in its irradiated future because mankind, eventually, has destroyed itself. One set of lemmas popular in the latter centuries of Pnakotis argues that allowing Homo sapiens its final allotted millennia wastes the current decades' valuable potential for nuclear destruction, in the name of a needless conservatism.

The Cult of Transcendence

A handful of debased and degenerate adepts consecrated to Nyarlathotep rule this peculiar group, a globe-spanning conspiracy in the Illuminati mold. It began in the 13th century as the Alta Vendita, a cabal of Italian bankers seeking alchemical lore and sorcerous advantage. After their agent André de Tours discovered the "shining text" *P'Dwahr M'Ankanon Nyarlathotep* while on Crusade in Egypt, the Alta Vendita gingerly used its spells for centuries in an ultimately failed attempt to rule Europe.

In 1919, their plans shattered, the lords of the Alta Vendita roasted their families and abased themselves before Nyarlathotep. He heard their plea and granted them his guidance. Since then, the Cult's Transcended Masters no longer gather power for the sake of power, or wealth, or status. They seek admission to the Court of Azathoth at the center of the universe. Their still earth-bound Bishops direct a dizzying array of front groups with common goals: the erosion of humanity, the corrosion of society, and the promotion of sociopathy.

Cult initiates constantly attempt to divorce themselves from their humanity spiritually, intellectually, morally, and physically. They show no mercy to themselves or to others. Good and evil are null concepts to them; suffering is an illusion, morality is an illusion, love and hate and joy and pain are illusions; only power is real, and its only use is to break humankind into the image and pattern of our true gods.

Cult Hierarchy

The Transcended Masters dwell in the hypergeometric nightside of Vagnoptus Manor, an 18th-century chateau built in Stockholm as the antechamber to the Throne Room of Azathoth. After their Final Marriage to Nyarlathotep, alien forms grow from their severed genitals and their human flesh slowly sublimes or evolves as they beseech the Daemon Sultan to subsume them entirely. Their infrequent, and usually indecipherable, orders come in dreams, magical compulsions, and occasionally mundane communication.

Bishops

Below the Transcended Masters, the four Bishops direct the Cult and conspire against each other: inculcating sociopathy has its drawbacks. The Bishops have undergone the Greater Marriage (sexual congress with the severed head of a human sacrifice) and as a result expand psychically, with idiosyncratic and uncanny effects on those who perceive – or sometimes, even think about – them. This, likewise, doesn't encourage smooth Cult operation.

Acolytes

Each Bishop has two Acolytes, except when one or both of them have killed each other, incurred a Bishop's wrath, or suffered the notice of a Transcended Master. In this centuries-old cult founded by centuries-old men, only men may become Acolytes.

The human sacrifice performed in their Lesser Marriage binds Acolytes to Nyarlathotep but also unmoors them dimensionally: they possess limited precognition and can apport through acute angles within a mile. Even an Acolyte counts as one of the deadliest and most capable sorcerers in the world. They have to be – their worst enemies are their fellow Acolytes.

Fronts and Dupes

Each Bishop oversees a See, a hook baited with what the Cult knows as one of the fundamental motivations of humanity. The Sees of Fear, Flesh,

Greed, and Hate spread their rot through numerous front groups and puppet organizations. They create some fronts and take over others that seem promising. These organizations appear to be independent entities – but together they furnish funds, supply field agents, gather information, and (above all) increase the common woe of humanity by exploiting human failings.

The dupes taken in by these fronts – and even their leaders – very rarely uncover the larger presence of the Cult. Some do pass beyond the outer ranks, however, and aspire to the true Cult. If such an aspirant survives his ambition, he may become an Acolyte if there is an opening. If not, he just needs to wait a while.

See of Fear

The See of Fear draws those who are motivated by aversion to something: real threats, perceived threats, or even responsibility. Since 1948, the Bishop of Fear has been Dwight Reynolds, a Dreamlands tyrant who rules from the Basalt Throne of Dylath-Leen. His comatose earthly body (a former gas station attendant) lies in the Lamplighter Academy in Detroit, protected by a retinue of Moon-Beasts incarnated in human hypergeometers.

His Acolytes, Matthew Hanna and Tadeusz Mazurkiewicz, have a relatively free hand to run the See. As long as they don't sleep a lot.

Americans Against Covert Communism

A group of businessmen devoted to defeating Henry Wallace, and by extension Communism everywhere, formed AACC in Leyland, Illinois in 1948. In 1956, Tennessee distillery owner and Exalted Circle member Hugh Brandt became president of AACC and turned it over to the Cult. The Cult uses AACC for short-term political pressure in the U.S., especially at the state level and in the Midwest and West.

Protecting America from subversion means spying on your neighbors to make sure they're not Communists. Many AACC chapters run their own local COINTELPRO (p. 179) on area hippie and peace movements – a lot of AACC members have private investigator licenses. This tranche of information flows up to the Cult, which is especially interested in any unnatural actors they can recruit.

Amici Domitiani

This globally distributed police conspiracy takes its name from the Roman Emperor Domitian, who famously said "I care not for their hate, so long as they fear." The A.D. (or "Friends of Dom" in some U.S. precincts) provides backup, cover, funding, alibis, and protection both legal and extra-legal for cops who go outside the law to terrorize or murder criminals. The Amici use Interpol connections, coded police alerts and bulletins, and informal "retreats" to maintain communications.

Former Bishop of Fear Alphonse Markham began the Amici as a murder cult within the British Special Branch in 1924, and in 1925 it annexed a suddenly headless cult of Mormo operating within the New York Police Department. Its "independent but fraternal" rings spread through "Red Squads" in America and elsewhere, metastasizing after the postwar rise in crime. Some of its individual death squads dedicate their kills not to Mormo but to Nodens, god of hunters, which may attract unfriendly Cult attention.

Skorlupa Koshcheiya

This cult ("Koschei's Eggshells") began in the Soviet Union in 1918 among a group of corrupt Cheka officers selling protection from Lenin's first purges. When they were in turn purged, some of them turned to a dark hypergeometrical entity they called Dal'Likho to hide them from the universe. Dal'Likho stripped them of their very identities: eyes only saw their outlines, no one remembered them, they could not be recorded, they walked the streets as ghosts.

The Bishop of Fear Lobsang Prinahu discovered them in 1936 when one Skorlupist tried to rob the Lamplighter Academy in Leningrad. He recruited them in 1936 by extortion – if he could find them, so could Stalin – and ever since then they induce those who fear the Soviet state (or its client regimes) to give up their humanity to save their lives. Its victims give the Skorlupa not just their money, but their families and finally their souls, serving Dal'Likho and the Cult as "invisible men."

See of Flesh

The See of Flesh tempts with physical or aesthetic luxury and pleasure. Its Bishop, Carlos Sanriki, a worshiper of Shub-Niggurath as Pan, began as a sex-den manager in silent-era Hollywood. Even after his investment as Bishop in 1947, he keeps a very "hands-on" approach to his See, which nearly exposes the Cult as the studio system breaks down and the gossip press rises this decade.

His Acolytes manage the See outside America: Olle Einarsson runs heroin in Europe and Jinji Kouzuki fosters the "new decadent" school of Japanese literature and film.

Delightful Heavenly Banquet Society

The first Bishop of Flesh, John Tyler Oringo, founded this front in Shanghai in 1923 as an attempt to contact the local Nyarlathotep cult of Heng Fu-Nu, the Swollen Lady. It relocated to Hong Kong in 1949 – a society for rich, decadent gourmands had no appetite for Communist rule. It now attracts wealthy British, Japanese, and American gluttons to its obscenely Lucullan feasts, making it a superb channel for information and influence all over the Pacific world. It has not yet attracted Heng Fu-Nu.

Dorian Gray Society

Beginning as a brothel for rich perverts in the 1880s, it drew in members of Aleister Crowley's sex-magical entourage. From there, short steps took the Society to invocation of the Headless God and the eventual notice of the Cult. Sanriki taught the Highest Members of the Society the Road of Souls ritual, allowing the user to possess and puppet any body in history. The unmatchable potential of this debauchery cemented the Cult's hold over the Society.

However, without the rare gaturia plant (which grows only on one very heavily defended Society-owned acre in South Africa) the Road is random: with gaturia, the user can guide his astral clairvoyeurism. The Society provides not just gaturia for the Cult, but money and favors, and not just from high society. Rape cults make friends in very low places as well: human traffickers, drug kingpins, and worse.

The Sylph Group

This front exists solely to run exclusive "no request refused" brothels in Paris, London, Tokyo, Hong Kong, Bangkok, Washington, and the elite Communist Party resort on Lake Balaton in Hungary. It operates under a dizzying variety of names and covers. It loses money (constant moves and high overhead) and has no unnatural involvement, but provides unbeatable blackmail material on government employees and elected officials.

Sylph Grand Mistress Verecondia Vampata is the highest-ranking woman in the Cult. Refused an Acolyteship, she rankles at her chauvinist overlords and seeks power through Shub-Niggurath this decade, funding her own "Amorati di Undini" sex cults (mostly among poor students in warm Western cities) to find it. She also starts an arm's-length relationship with MI-6, looking for insurance in case the Cult goes after her.

See of Greed

The See of Greed ministers to those who are dominated by a desire to obtain something: power, money, or influence. Its new (since 1956) Bishop, Italian dry-goods magnate Vincenzo Cervelli, falls under the increasing sway of his obsessive Acolyte Lionel Glass this decade. Glass' rival Acolyte, American financier Andrew St. Claire, begins looking for outside power bases, recruiting more new fronts for the Cult such as the White-power Operation New Day cadre in 1970.

Brotherhood of Dion

In 1829, appalled at the election of Andrew Jackson, a society of New England blue-bloods named themselves after Dion of Syracuse, a 4th-century B.C. tyrant who attempted to apply Plato's theories of the "ideal republic" to the rule of Sicily. They sought to create a moral and intellectual elite to govern America by secrecy if need be, to save it from the consequences of mere democracy. Their "old boy network" completely infiltrated law firms, mainstream churches, universities, and the press, recruiting willing tools and developing eager chapters even in mere state universities.

Most Dionites remain dedicated to nothing more than their own aggrandizement in the name of knowing what's best for the country. But in 1894, two Harvard Brothers pursued Platonic mysticism as far as the Widener Library's copy of the *Necronomicon*, and ever since an inner core of the Brotherhood has served Nyarlathotep. Bishop of Greed Ian Roehl offered them even closer communion with Nyarlathotep in 1922, and after that the Dionites have also served the Cult.

The Exalted Circle

Boston merchant and slave-trader Nathan Warrick founded the Exalted Circle as a Dagon cult in 1838. His rich friends got richer from Deep One gold, and helped build America's military-industrial complex. The Circle conducted their rituals not in towns but on isolated islands, which (along with their increasingly vast wealth and political power) protected them from P4 investigation – but not from the Cult. Determined to defeat the group they thought were America's "occult overlords," the Cult decapitated the Circle in a body-switching ambush in 1929.

Now the Circle provides power, influence, wealth, and Deep One connections to the Cult while milking America and the world for its own enrichment. Its thirteen Guardians live on private islands around the world, protected by wealth, position, and a dozen or so Sentinels each who crave more of both. Below the Sentinels, mere millionaires and senators serve the Circle as Watchmen. Promotion within the Circle is by three-day auction after a position opens, as positions tend to do with brutal suddenness.

Lamplighters

The Cult snatched two Lodges and two dozen other Academies of this Victorian occultist front for the Great Race of Yith (see *Motion and Lamplighters*, p. 296) in two coups d'etat in 1928. With the dawning of the Age of Aquarius, credulous would-be "magical explorers" flock to the Lamplighter academies, many of which now operate under other guises: martial arts dojos, meditation workshops, "Eastern Wisdom" study groups, and so on.

The Lamplighter chapters under Cult control still invite alien (just not Yithian) possession, or send acolytes on the Road of Souls. The Cult uses the Lamplighters as a strip mine or a puppy mill for harvesting ritual knowledge or creating hypergeometers. About one in twenty experimental possessions or random trips on the Road of Souls produces a useful ritual. The same percentage of trips kills or permanently deranges the Humble One undergoing it. The survivors get better at it, and then they go back in.

See of Hate

The See of Hate calls to those who are motivated by an urge to destroy, or by an all-encompassing loathing for humanity and the world. Its Bishop, Vichy propagandist and crank historian Guillaume Broche, underwent the Greater Marriage in 1945 mostly to avoid French retribution. Broche remains primarily dedicated to tracing the True Bloodline of Nyarlathotep (which might lead him to Emir Agdesh and the Fate, p. 288) and to containing his ambitious subordinates.

Of Broche's two Acolytes, Nathan Harmati, the Bombay-born head of the Church of Interlife, poses by far the bigger threat. Cruel and ruthless even by the standards of the Cult, he slaughters enemies and purges supporters to expand his power. In Johannesburg, Cees Van Niekerk combines former Bishop Egbert Sharpe's policy of retail hatred — murder rings, colorful massacres to be blamed on "the other side," and political gangs — with propaganda across Africa.

Church of Interlife

Former missionary Angelo Hidalto founded the Church of Interlife in San Francisco in 1844 after a peyote trip showed him the Dreamlands. Ingesting the wrong button led Hidalto to the nightmare countries of dream; his unnatural quest eventually devoured him. His successor, Charles Knightsbridge, took the Church deeper still into the unnatural, using the Dreamlands as leverage on the waking world. In 1933, Nathan Harmati took control by killing the waking bodies of his rivals and emphasized the hard core of Hidalto's vague Gnosticism: hatred of the waking world, and hatred for people too blinkered or repressed to believe in an inner life.

The hippies and Hesse-readers who flock to the Church don't get the pure Hate from their Teachers at first: just a vague smugness and confirmation of their superiority to the "sleepers and squares." They read *The Inward Turning Mirror* (a psychedelic paperback available in all good head shops) and learn of "capability expansion" and the importance of awakening the Deep Self by breaking waking taboos and rules. They enter the "Inner World" and dream of building a fortress — the city of Sarkomand, the Interlife power base in the Dreamlands. Those who show real gifts for both sociopathy and Dreaming get promoted to Teacher, and eventually Elder, and master the true power of the Dreamlands.

THE ANNEALED

Not all unnatural cults are made up solely of isolated hermits and inbred hill folk. Some cultists have initially uninvolved spouses or romantic partners, close friends, even children. These unfortunates encounter the unnatural by proxy and find it poisoning their lives. Then, something happens: a summoning, a possession, an irruption of insanity that cannot be denied.

A very few bystanders escape into amnesia or even a semblance of normalcy, perhaps moving across the country and completely severing their ties with the past. Most go mad or die in blind shock. A very few emerge on the other side — not sane, but not utterly destroyed. They hunger for more contact with the very thing that nearly destroyed them.

Bishop of Hate Egbert Sharpe called these last the Annealed. They served as his occult hatchet men, once they'd been easily remolded into whatever the local agents of the conspiracy needed: cold-blooded assassins, passive channelers, or even recruiters to breed future Annealed victims. In the confusion and wreckage of postwar Europe, the See of Hate lost track of Sharpe's network of Annealed scattered across orphanages, asylums, prisons, and dank basement apartments. How many Annealed wander the world, believing that they work for the See of Hate? Nobody knows, least of all Guillaume Broche.

Lavrenti Beria Tendency

One of the few fronts founded by Broche, since 1962 the TLB exists to keep the European Left tearing at its own liver. Cult funding, weapons, and propaganda offer the worst radicals and power trippers in the European student movement the means, leverage, and ideological justification for anything up to and including murdering their enemies and framing the police for it. *Rien à droite de Beria,* they graffiti the walls: "Nothing to the right of Beria." Every so often the TLB encourages one of its more excitable cells to go public under a new acronym announced with a bombing or an execution.

The TLB does not just provide the Cult with deniable murder squads and clouds of irritating protesters to unleash on their enemies. True to its namesake, the Tendency also infiltrates other student and Left movements, gathers information, and suborns assets all over Western Europe, and even in the "soft Khrushchevite East."

Two Lanterns

While on an outreach tour of America in 1963, Van Niekerk gives an ambitious South Boston bomb-thrower named Michael "Rags" O'Gara a pair of human corneas that had seen Ghatanothoa. When worn as contact lenses, they paralyze the beholder. O'Gara turns them into the secret weapon of his gang, Two Lanterns. Named not just for the two "lanterns of the soul" in his eyes but for the two lanterns hung by Paul Revere in 1775, O'Gara means to warn White America of the threat "coming by sea" – namely Blacks, Puerto Ricans, and (non-Irish) immigrants.

Funded by the Cult (and by pill dealing), Two Lanterns branches pop up all across the northern tier of the States: New England, New York, Minnesota, the Pacific Northwest. By 1967, Two Lanterns bikers rumble with the Klan over White-supremacist recruiting turf. O'Gara actively searches for more "White Witchcraft" like his death-gaze and for "White Brotherhood" lore from Mu and Lemuria: he finds any number of leads in Arkham, and makes contact there with Bitterich's Läufern in 1968.

Other Cults

Whether or not this decade marks the dawning of the Age of Aquarius, it absolutely sees a sunburst of cult activity. Hundreds of communes "get back to the land," scores of fringe and manic political sects shoot up, UFO contactees and dodgy gurus reveal unlikely truths in unreadable pamphlets. From Timothy Leary's League for Spiritual Discovery to the Church of Satan, from the Hare Krishnas to the Manson Family, a thousand strange new flowers bloom in the spiritual landscape. DELTA GREEN has to find the poisonous ones and pull them up by the roots.

11th District Police Station

On Chicago's West Side, an island of stability holds out as the city slides into a war zone. The Chicago Police Department's 11th District keeps the peace, clears its cases, and works with the community. Only the Division Street Riots in 1966 leave a blot on the 11th's record – but 500 cops were there, and you can't pin every complaint on the hard-working police personnel at 801 N. Homan Avenue in Humboldt Park. Sure, self-appointed Puerto Rican "activists" claim that arrest records were woefully incomplete and that some people never reappeared, but if you ask around the neighborhood, you'll hear no complaints, and maybe even an occasional "good riddance."

Built in 1960 on the site of a Capone-era warehouse, the 11th District Police Station gleams with modern legal professionalism – above ground. In the basement, the standard complement of interroga-tion rooms, metal sinks, and "tempo-rary" holding cells sits ready for the "wrong element." A large brick-lined cellar lies below that basement, with grates in the floor and walls, and metal rings in the immense pillar in the center. Below the cellar, tunnels run.

If in the considered judgement of 11th District officers, you are not fully cooperating with your Chicago Police Department, you receive a "fair trial" in the basement: beatings with phone books and truncheons, the water cure for poor memory, and a car battery to spark civic pride. If you wish, you can "appeal" to the rats in the brick cellar; manacled wrongdoers often make a full confession to them. Inside the tunnels is the "court of final appeal" – the hyperdimensional realm of Nyogtha. The Dweller in Darkness grants His guardians certain abilities: true sight in His darkness, and aura sight to find those whose criminal souls fit them for His maw.

Most of the cops in the 11th only know about the basement and the cellar. Only those awakened to His darkness and given His true sight know about the tunnels, or can even find their hypergeometric entrances. Two such officers of the 11th have put in for transfer to the 7th District, in "Bloody Maxwell" on the South Side. The station was built in 1888, so it's sure to have some interesting architecture in its sub-basement.

Children of Chorazin

In the Haight and Chelsea and the places where the shocking gather, the hippest magus of them all is tall and hideously ugly, dressed in "Jacobean chic" of a black cloack and old-fashioned broad-leafed hat. This charismatic impresario, guru, sorcerer, and so on goes by the name of Chorazin; the pale and black-clad Children of Chorazin swarm through the tie-dye sea like so many black mollies and damselfish. He appears in art-house movies and on album covers accompanied by his robed and hooded dwarf assistant, utters cryptic pronouncements, and then sails his yacht *Pontus Gardie* off to the Kingsport Jazz Festival.

Fragmentary records place Chorazin in England since 1863, although the Pantechnicon fire of 1870 destroyed the really crucial ones, it seems. He mostly splits his time between London and San Francisco – and Stockholm. Which makes sense, because "Chorazin" is the resurrected Swedish necromancer Count Magnus de la Gardie. He made a pact with the "Prince of the Lower Air" in 1599, a pact Yog-Sothoth has honored ever since. He seeks powerful artifacts associated with the god: the Silver Key, the Orb of Borellus, the De Marigny Clock, and similar puissant items.

In addition to his own sorcerous powers, he has his unnatural familiar, The One Who Hunts. A stunted, bloated figure with tentacles for arms, it provides Chorazin with unnatural lore, whistling flute music, and ritual assistance. The One Who Hunts helped Chorazin re-animate his true children: an undersea Nazi army taken from the wrecks of the *Wilhelm Gusthoff* and *General von Steuben*, sent to the bottom of the Baltic Sea in 1945 by Soviet submarines with 14,000 evacuees from the Courland pocket aboard. In several trips, Chorazin has stocked the Thames estuary and San Francisco Bay with battalions of waterlogged

Nazi zombies; the less decayed specimens crew his yacht, and the rest await his orders.

Dao Sâm

During Operation SEVEN in Singapore, DELTA GREEN encountered the "Order of the Black Buddha." As such encounters tended to, this one ended in gunplay and occult destruction in September 1955. Rear Admiral Cook believed it was just another one-off manifestation, or possibly a splinter group of the Kuen-Yuin, and closed the file.

By 1966, reports of a new religion called the Dao Sâm ("black" or "dark" Dao) appear in internal Army Intelligence memos. This band of indoctrinated fighters serves in the People's Army of North Vietnam, and with the Khmer Rouge rebels in Cambodia. Publicly they espouse "revolutionary Buddhism," hailing the Buddha who "strips the world of lies" such as imperialism. Like the Viet Cong, the Dao Sâm has cadres all over South Vietnam, and also in the rest of Southeast Asia.

However, the Dao Sâm believe that the truth of the world is suffering, death, shame, and pain: their Phat Sâm, or "Black Buddha," strips away lies by revealing this truth. Thus betrayal, torture, ritual flensing, and self-mutilation become acts of worship. (Butcher knives and extreme scars are two signifiers of cult membership.) Without lies there can be no betrayal, and so the Dao Sâm integrate and ingratiate themselves into Western military and media circles in Indochina.

Phat Sâm is a humanoid intelligence – possibly an aspect of Nyarlathotep, Yog-Sothoth, or something less well known – summonable at certain times and places. The Dao Sâm cult center at Ban Talat deep in northeastern Cambodia is such a place. In 1969 DELTA GREEN launches the doomed Operation OBSIDIAN against the cult stronghold and then destroys it, and perhaps the Black Buddha, from the air (p. 186).

The Maryland Skoptsi

After surviving persecutions by Shi'a Persians and Orthodox czars, the heretical self-castrating Russian cult called the Skoptsi fled the Bolsheviks in 1918. In 1935, a community of Skoptsi fetched up in Maryland on the eastern shore of the Chesapeake, building their Basilica of Our Virgin Mother in 1938. In 1948, a leading Skoptsi named Yelena Kalamatiano founded Families Without Frontiers, an adoption program for orphans from behind the Iron Curtain; many of them live on the community's farm, the Cornucopia. Old-fashioned and law-abiding, the Skoptsi are model immigrants.

And they will continue to so abide, until they can find the Black Icons seized from them by the hated Cheka and once more worship the Magna Mater, Shub-Niggurath, as she truly deserves: with ceremonies of unnatural and inhuman rebirth. (Those ceremonies will also allow them to replenish their slowly dwindling membership, down to about 350 now even with brainwashed orphan recruits.) Until then, they must sate themselves with mere animal and human sacrifice in the immense temple beneath the basilica. The High Priest of the sect, Jermija Bogdashkavich, has been waiting since the Goddess' womb spat him out in 1870: his patience is not infinite.

True Love Study Group

Founded in 1965 by former Stanford classics professor Richard Waugh, the TLSG is a pagan free-love commune. They operate on a large forested plot in the heart of California's northern Sierra Nevada range, worshipping "the Goddess." Numerous layers of initiation veil the Goddess' true form. Stripping away each veil strips away the initiate's compunctions against anti-social behavior, freeing her from the shackles of conventional society.

The final veil to part is that of human sacrifice to the Goddess; by then, the initiates have freed themselves so fully of internalized taboos and social mores that they never object. If they do object, well – the Goddess' trees gratefully accept one more body. When the final veil parts the Goddess announces Her true name, Shub-Niggurath, and grants Her pheromonal blessing to an animalistic orgy that may leave one or two weaker souls among the trees.

Waugh's fellow votaries Joshua Freese and Chester Marsh handle recruitment and security respectively: Freese drives a bus to San Francisco or Sacramento or San Jose most weekends in the fall for the "harvest" – when the street children start needing a warm place to crash. Marsh (who used to handle such tasks for his father in Chicago in the 1920s) pays off the county sheriff in money and girls, ensuring that nobody disturbs the group's study of true love.

NO. 2, 3, 4 NUMERALS 1-1/2 INCHES WIDE X
1-3/4 INCHES HIGH 1/8 INCHES THICK. NO. 5
NUMERAL, 1-3/4 INCHES WIDE X 2 INCHES HIGH
1/4 INCHES THICK.

Figure 66. S target.

AGO 6431B

140

PROVIDENCE,

OF CUJENT

SSUN OF THE

MADE AVAILA

VIDENCE:

dding MACHINE 1260

BINOCULARS 13866

opane TorcH

tebasket, Ligu

tle

WIRE, PACK OF CA

2 EXTENSUNS, Res

s,

t

us HARDWARE

ers, 2 condenso

re

1 Hallicrafter Radio 87402
1 Phono Amplifier
I authorize the Dispos
other material that was
f.p. A

THE HANDLER'S HANDBOOK

DELTA GREEN Agents carry out lethally dangerous operations, suffering unimaginable stress as they confront unnatural terrors to protect the world around them. As a Handler running *The Fall of DELTA GREEN*, your job might be even harder. You have to set up the operations, portray and provide the stress and terror, and remind the Agents of the world around them.

Being a Handler requires preparation, imagination, and an unwavering vision of the apocalypse in wait around the next angled corner. It also requires an indifference to the outcome. You might want to alter a die roll to save an Agent, or give them one last chance to avert catastrophe. Resist these urges. *The Fall of DELTA GREEN* is not about victory, or comfort, or narrative closure.

It is about the hard truth: mankind means nothing to the universe, and much worse things wait outside and in the future. The truth kills. It doesn't set anyone free, except the Great Old Ones. It certainly doesn't step aside for a handful of GS-10s with forged badges — unless they fight to the last drop of blood to make it step aside.

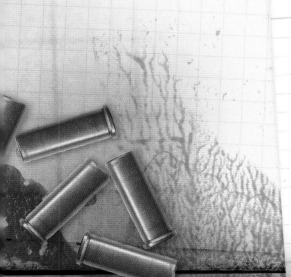

You had to get on the ground with your troops to see and hear what was happening. You have to soak up firsthand information for your instincts to operate accurately. Besides, it's too easy to be crisp, cool, and detached at 1,500 feet; too easy to demand the impossible of your troops; too easy to make mistakes that are fatal only to those souls far below in the mud, the blood, and the confusion."

— Lt. Gen. Harold G. Moore, <u>We Were Soldiers Once ... And Young</u>

How Does It Feel?

Every Handler builds her own **Fall of DELTA GREEN** campaign from the materials provided by history and its horrors, by Lovecraft and his successors, and by this book and its kindred works. She picks details and themes based on her own interests and aptitudes, and ideally summons up personal nightmare scenes she can't get out of her head any other way.

But before we talk about making this game your own, let's look at the aspects of cosmic horror and of the Delta Green setting that should never change.

Although the title (and the history of well-meaning government action in the 1960s) should mitigate it, the temptation remains to make **The Fall of DELTA GREEN** games upbeat and winnable. This game, centered as it is in both Lovecraftian horror and the wider Delta Green mythos, is not about that.

Such a choice turns the game into alternate history, or a thriller, or a conventional military or spy-centric RPG. Those choices can make for great games, and indeed they do — in other games than this one. **The Fall of DELTA GREEN** without the hopelessness of Lovecraft echoed by the doom of Indochina misses the point — and loses the horror.

Horror: The High Notes

What makes **The Fall of DELTA GREEN** horrific? Three core tones: uncertainty, risk, and lack of control. Without these essential elements, any operation, no matter how terrible the creature involved, devolves into a bug hunt or a dungeon delve with crumbling tomes (or, at best, restored Sanity) standing in for treasure.

Uncertainty

"Deep Ones only have 9 Health and -1 Armor. Switching to full auto." Statements like this impose a death sentence on your horror game.

Lovecraft correctly called the "fear of the unknown" the strongest kind of fear. Agents must never feel certain of their situation, what they're facing, or why. They should never be able to figure the odds tactically or on the dice: threats should pose dire and obscure dangers, attack under cover of darkness and other favorable conditions, and never leave their real name (or ideally anything identifying) behind. Don't (necessarily) lie to the players, but remember their Agents' senses are only human, and are flawed and fallible. Never tell them anything they haven't earned with blood, and even then just tell them what the sticky traces look like.

Especially keep monsters mysterious and therefore frightening for as long as you can. Never give them a name; don't begin the combat with "five ghouls attack you." Instead provide the sign or the scat, the fetid smells and uncanny distorted effects of their presence. Look at the Sense Trouble entries in the creatures' Investigation headings and craft your own versions:

△ "The trees hide most of the flickering shadow and strobing lights from you."

△ "The smell of open grave earth overpowers you, like it's climbing into the back of your throat."

△ "The sounds of the tide don't quite hide the hoarse susurrus of something breathing under the dock, something that has to work to breathe air."

Then, you can spring the attack. "Four or five shapes appear among you, you're not sure where exactly they came from or how many of them they are, they're striking so fast." Or if the Agents made their surprise test, you can give the actual number of foes as you milk the terror of their appearance: "Five of the violet glows stutter and blink into place around you, and you hear baritone clicking noises like something made by enormous, slow-motion cicadas."

During the encounter, provide brief, snapshot impressions: ice-crusted crablike claws, waving tendrils, unblinking yellow eyes, a fanged mouth blowing rotting flesh-smell. And of course: "Its talons rip through your side, you can see blood mixed with human fat pooling in your jacket." Agents might not even know what hit them: "It feels like a piledriver, your ears ring and breathing hurts, maybe a broken rib" or "Your whole lower torso goes numb and you topple toward the floor."

Eventually, by interrogating deranged cultists or reading stained field notes, the Agents may learn that their attackers were "Outer Ones" or "the Biters of Shady Lawn" or "children of Dagon" or something. The DELTA GREEN program barely knows even loosely what half the things it fights might be called: the *Necronomicon* isn't an encyclopedia or a biology textbook.

Freely contradict this rulebook or Lovecraft: maybe the witness or the cultist was wrong or crazy, or maybe the Thing is no longer the same as it once was. Accumulating contradictory and unreliable details and descriptions builds unease better than even the most terrifying "official" monster name.

Risk

If the players feel confident that you're looking out for their Agents, and know their Agents can't die or go insane until the dramatically perfect moment, you have stopped playing a horror game. Fear involves risk and consequences. The players should feel that any mistake can begin a spiral of events ending in exposure or death for their team. They should know in their bones that putting an Agent in danger has real consequences. When they do it anyway – then you're playing a horror game again, and one with real heroes in it this time.

If the Agents treat the CIA or the FBI (or the Boise Police Department, for that matter) as stage scenery and spear-carriers, disabuse them of that illusion. Put an Internal Affairs audit team on their case, or two guys in bad suits and a black car on their tail. Add a good-hearted, patriotic investigator GMC who for excellent

reason believes the Agents are up to something shady. Make them risk their souls by killing her, or risk the mission by evading her.

And above all else, pull no punches when a monster attacks. Use all its powers to the utmost, unleash every extra attack or unfair ritual. Start with 3-point spends on the Fighting die in the first round or two. These creatures' intelligence often exceeds humanity's; their hostility and cruelty always do. Even a single Deep One or ghoul should be a real and deadly threat: attacking by night, doubling back and ambushing pursuers in neck-deep water or pitch-black tunnels, striking hit-and-run style to drain the Agents' ammo, Stability, and Health.

Monsters don't attack in the open, in sunlight – unless that's when the Agents are asleep and unprepared.

Lack of Control

DELTA GREEN strategy is fundamentally reactive: the unnatural breaks out, and then the program contains it. They know nothing of the truth, and could frankly do nothing to avert it if they did know. The biggest win is only a tactical victory, or at best a spoiling maneuver like Operation RIPTIDE (p. 179). But DELTA GREEN cannot change the tempo or win the war.

Reflecting this reality in the game walks a fine line. Agents can and should try to alter the tactical outcome: prepare loadouts, research manifestations, make plans, secure an exit or an air strike. All these are healthy and sensible reactions that show the Agents are thinking, and that the players are worried. But all the preparation possible should never let the players feel certain of

the outcome. They cannot control the battle, much less the battle space.

Like certainty, control washes out horror. Most players seek control. This game subverts that desire: control of the unnatural corrupts and destroys those who seek it, and even moreso those who achieve it. Players should taste some of their Agents' sweat and desperation. They should feel tingles of their Agents' nervous scrambling, their grasping for balance, in their muscles and in their gut.

This game should provide that. At its mechanical core, **The Fall of DELTA GREEN** produces stories of Agent deaths interspersed with the occasional miraculous escape. As the name makes clear, this game foregrounds decline: moral, mental, physical, and social, into a pit of horror and death. It is not about winning anything but fleeting victories as certain doom closes in.

That is the real question you answer in play: not "How do we win?" but "Why do we still fight?"

Delta Green: The Low Notes

So much for the elements of horror. What elements show up in the spectrograph for Delta Green?

Humanity is the Threat

DELTA GREEN may focus on the unnatural, but its operations target humans. Power, as the program discovers anew this decade, corrupts – and the promise of literally unearthly power creates unimaginable corruption. People who crave power, control, and immortality gladly pry at the locks of the world, heedless of what they keep shut out. DELTA GREEN exists to slam the doors of reality back shut on those people's fingers.

Note that humans, unlike extradimensional alien intelligences vigintillions of years old, are something DELTA GREEN can investigate, understand, and beat.

Mundanity is the Setting

Root the game in the mundane, in the real world of 1960s history and geopolitics. The more you cement the story within things the players know,

believe in, and comprehend, the more vivid the outbreak of unnatural terror appears. A dimensional shambler manifests in a supermarket; greenish slime coats a copy of *Look* magazine with Goldie Hawn on the cover; it's a Volkswagen Beetle that sits frozen on the Greenland ice cap. The unnatural horrifies because it haunts our real world.

It haunts it, but does not define it. The unnatural appears in flashes and sparks, it doesn't light the set. Consider your game a symphony: the crescendo occurs at the crucial moment, not throughout the performance. Build up and reinforce the reality of the world, so that when unreality breaks through it terrifies and hurts.

Certainty is Impossible

If your players feel confident that they know what's happening, either they or you are doing it wrong. The Agents should live in fear of being double-crossed or set up, of making the wrong move or trusting the wrong cop or just of getting caught. They commit felonies and war crimes and possible treason, or so it would appear to people they can never explain anything to. Anyone could be compromised: by MAJESTIC, or by the Russians, or by some inhuman intelligence wearing their skin like a puppet. Any record could be disinformation or denial, any testimony could be a lie or a hallucination, any lead could be a trap.

If their clandestine world lacks certainty, the unnatural world lacks sanity. The Agents may never get answers or explanations. How did our faces show up in that tomb paint-

ing? How can a toddler gesture a man into orbit? Why did that oblong swimming Thing appear, and where did it go, and will it come back?

Fatality is Normal

Death is not only part of the Delta Green universe, it is its foundation. Not for nothing are so many of the setting's villains broken, twisted shells clinging to unnatural immortality. The game dictates its own outcome: let the circumstances set the boundaries and the consequences play out without malice or mercy.

Your Agents show up for operations knowing the price in death and mental trauma. Surviving just means fighting another day. Any operation that doesn't leave any agents dead, crippled, or insane counts as a red-letter day. They write their report in the negative space left by the disaster that everyone expected.

Alternity is Worse

And after all, there are much worse things than death. Creatures that hollow out your mind or just work your body as a puppet, nightmare forces that scrape thin your soul to facilitate an inhuman longevity, experiences that rewire your brain until you too love Dagon or Shub-Niggurath, places where all rules vanish forever.

Dangle those monstrous rewards, show their destructive price. Agents should live in terror of seeking such an outcome, even as they patrol the unwholesome districts where such things fructify. Around every corner they may face an unholy bargain for power that betrays the very thing they fight for: normal human existence.

DISTANT COUSINS (BUT NOT TOO DISTANT)

The Fall of DELTA GREEN bears some family resemblances to its GUMSHOE horror cousins. By and large, this game inter-operates with *Trail of Cthulhu, Night's Black Agents, Fear Itself,* and *The Esoterrorists.*

If you want to use monsters, mechanics, or rules from those GUMSHOE games here, you should find it little trouble to slot them into your campaign. You could even introduce alien tech from *Ashen Stars* in a Mi-Go or MAJESTIC laboratory, or give a magus a hypergeometrical super-power from *Mutant City Blues.* But the GUMSHOE-experienced Handler should keep these games' differences in mind as well.

As noted on p. 062, this game has no Library Use or Research ability, so Handlers need to keep the subject matter of the clue at the forefront, not necessarily how it's delivered. Also, the HUMINT and Stealth abilities occupy much broader remits than their more subdivided parallels in other GUMSHOE games. This not only models the mechanics of *Delta Green: The Role-Playing Game,* but also allows player Agents to "concentrate their fire" on the core activities of the game: investigating strangers and sneaking up on (and into) danger.

The Stability economy in this game may seem parched and tight to players used to the more forgiving full Stability refreshes in other GUMSHOE games. This is fully intentional. DELTA GREEN Agents burn their bridges, then they burn out or burn up; they scrabble for purchase on their humanity as it corrodes around them. Consider providing more free Stability rating points during character creation, or even playing on Bright and Shining mode (p. 130) if you wish to soften the blows of reality.

The Fall of DELTA GREEN occupies the Purist end of the *Trail of Cthulhu* spectrum, but without Pillars of Sanity or Anagnorisis, it privileges steady erosion of the protagonist's Stability over the sudden, Lovecraftian collapse. As noted on p. 223, the monsters in this game are by and large more dangerous than their Depression-era equivalents, a dramatic necessity given the increase in investigators' firepower over the decades.

Even with M16s, DELTA GREEN Agents seem underpowered compared to the badass vampire-hunters of *Night's Black Agents.* In that game's terms, *The Fall of DELTA GREEN* starts with Burn and Dust baked right in. By contrast, *Fear Itself* characters (psychic powers aside) feel physically weaker but psychologically perhaps more complex (albeit often damaged). Much of this comes down to the difference between player characters who came of age before the 1970s and those who came of age afterward.

If *The Fall of DELTA GREEN* feels like any pre-existing GUMSHOE game the most, it's likely *The Esoterrorists.* Both games feature government conspiracies against the unnatural, and both assume a cover-up or veil-out as the final act of a scenario. Given the slightly different shakeout of abilities and backstories, *Fall of DELTA GREEN* Agents have more investigative options than the standard Ordo Veritatis police-work model. But the combats should feel similar, with the occasional terrifying spike of Lethality in this game.

Furnishing The Madhouse

The Handler builds the game using horrible events and worse people as motors and girders, like some hellish Erector set. Many such events and people appear earlier in this book, but every Handler wants to add her own pieces to the construction.

Constructing a Crime

At its heart, **The Fall of DELTA GREEN** is a game not just of horror but of mystery. And every mystery can use a few good crimes. Crimes provide DELTA GREEN Agents the thin excuse they need to investigate the unnatural core of the event, and provide the best leads to uncovering the human culprits trying to do the same for less noble purposes.

A crime story needs four elements to work at the table: the victim, the deed, the culprit, and the puzzle to explore.

The Victim

The victim might have been a target, or just have been in the wrong place at the wrong time. He might be the first (or fifth) in a series, or the only mistake in an otherwise invisible plan.

Consider providing some or all of these elements for your victim:

Δ A reason for the Agents to sympathize: Was the victim young and pretty, or noble and good, or a friend or squad mate?

Δ A hook for federal action: Was the victim a federal employee, or a member of the U.S. military, or killed on federal property, or a witness or dignitary under federal protection?

Δ An interesting story: Perhaps the victim is still alive after a narrow escape, or belongs to an interesting group such as organized crime or a fringe religion, or left a diary or notes of her own investigation into the weird goings-on, or his corpse sports very peculiar wounds.

Δ People who knew him: This is less important if the crime is merely a chance kill or the starter gun for a larger mystery, but if the culprit targeted the victim, the victim's friends and family provide the richest veins of information.

Δ A secret: This simply gets in the way for a chance kill, but the target's secret can provide insight into the culprit's motive, or leverage to use on witnesses or friends, or a lurid setting to break up a long sequence of interview scenes.

The Deed

The crime itself should have some spoor of the unnatural that explains why the Agents get called in. If the Agents are the first on the spot, provide forensic details and other crime scene arcana – time and cause of death, at least (even if both turn out to be wrong or misleading) – because players rightly expect it. If others – journalists, local law enforcement, weird death cultists – have gotten there first, the evidence might be muddied, missing, neglected, covered up, or misinterpreted. Provide GMC coroners, cops, or criminologists for the Agents to question, rely on, and suspect.

In your own mind, at least know *what* happened at the scene, even if nobody including you knows *how* it happened. That way you can extrapolate answers to inevitable player questions.

Remember the crime might not be a murder or missing person. It might be a seemingly impossible robbery, a strangely colored arson, trespassing on a federal installation, a missing blueprint, a suspected double agent, a Viet Cong ambush, a UFO encounter, or anything else the federal government could horn in upon.

The Culprit

Think outside the standard evil sorcerer or mad scientist, unless you have a truly excellent or original variation on those themes to play. At the very least, recast them in period clothing: a hippie guru in the Haight instead of a gnarled crank on the hill, a tenured professor larded with honors and government contracts who explores the unnatural out of mid-life ennui instead of a megalomaniac German out for revenge.

The culprit defines, shapes, and kicks off the story: he has a good, if insane, reason for harming the victim or doing the deed. If he continues his malign actions, or if they spiral out of his control, he continues to shape and drive the adventure throughout it. He might even have died before the mystery began: Killed by his own monster? Setting vengeance in motion from beyond the grave?

Blown up in Vietnam before he could perfect his scheme? In any case, investigating his actions and his past likely provides the Agents needed clues to stop whatever Thing or Power he let out.

The classic lines of investigation remain the best ones for you to consider and lay clues along:

△ **Means:** How did the culprit find and unleash the unnatural? How did she control it, or how did she think she was going to control it? How did she learn about the unnatural in the first place? What clues did she leave behind in her haste, or hubris?

△ **Motive:** Why did the culprit kill the victim or commit the crime in question? How and why did the culprit pick that victim? Why commit the crime now? How does the culprit benefit? If the victim died accidentally or collaterally, what was the culprit trying to accomplish? For clue-laying purposes, think in terms of his concrete goals here, not his psychological motivations.

△ **Opportunity:** What else has to be true for the culprit to have committed the crime? Was she outside under the gaze of Fomalhaut that night, trained in Aklo, or within seven leagues? While the investigation might not pivot on an alibi, think about what the culprit might say if accused.

Finally, think about the culprit's next moves. Does he have a deeper plot? Was this the first (or sixth) of the Nine Necessary Murders? Or, like genuine murderers, does he find the temptation to commit more growing, now that he has broken the taboo? Does the charnel gravity of the un-natural warp his mind, control his actions, or simply pull him ever deeper into psychopathy? Is he part of a cult or conspiracy that might protect him, or that might try to eliminate him before the Agents uncover their tracks?

The Puzzle

For all those questions, provide clues and traces and perhaps witnesses. Think of strings running from the crime scene to the culprit, from the victim to the culprit, and from the culprit to the unnatural. Every one of those strings crosses something – a witness, an archive, a soft patch of mud – and leaves a trace. That trace is a clue.

Reconstruct the crime in your mind and ask: what evidence do these actions leave behind, what ripples out from the unnatural stone the culprit just threw? Be alert for player questions – "are there any footprints?" "any relation to the Innsmouth Marshes?" "did the news vendor see something?" – and try to answer them both logically and productively: with a "yes" and a clue, unless the villain absolutely would have covered her tracks in this one instance.

Game Master Characters

Witnesses have their own means and opportunity – to see those weird lights, to overhear a threat, to smell something strange that night. What's their motive to tell the Agents? Patriotism or law-abiding decency? Fear? Petty revenge on whomever they think they're fingering?

Ideally, you want about five to seven well-defined GMCs who provide specific clues or specific avenues of investigation. You've probably already introduced police or other federal agents. Now riffle through the victim's family, colleagues, rivals, and anyone the police already consider a suspect. Who are these people? What are their motivations, loyalties, secret lovers or allegiances? What will they do for those things? Go through the Interpersonal abilities and decide which ones your witnesses and other GMCs respond to.

Red Herrings

Red herrings appear in mystery stories because the author wants to mislead readers and prolong the mystery. Players are perfectly capable of misleading themselves and prolonging the investigation without your help. Keep red herrings, and complications of any kind, to an absolute minimum. If the players start reliably solving your mysteries too easily, only then should you introduce twists.

When the players investigate a false lead, whether you or they put it in their minds, give them opportunities to use their Investigative Abilities to disprove their erroneous theories. Make sure the red herring leads somewhere thematically interesting, or into a fun scene to play. Close off the red herring without making players feel like they wasted their time; ideally let them feel satisfied that eliminating that false lead still means progress.

Alternatively, you may be able to turn a red herring into an alternate core clue with a moment's thought – when the Agents head off to interview the wrong suspect, check your list of prepared clues for any information you can introduce into this unplanned scene.

Constructing a Cult

The Delta Green setting already has plenty of global cults and conspiracies: the Cult of Transcendence (and inside that, the Exalted Circle, Lamplighters, and Amici Domitiani), the Kuen-Yuin and the Motion, even Whole Earth Enterprises or the remnants of the Cthulhu cult and the Genyosha. Try tying your would-be global conspiracy into one of those.

But local cults can arise anywhere and everywhere. A small town might have (or be) one cult, or two feuding ones. In toxic waste dumps of the unnatural like the Miskatonic or Severn valleys, the taint breaks out into six or a dozen cult vectors. Cults can appear inside hospitals, air cavalry brigades, Third World prisons: anywhere that pressure and death are constant factors. A single powerful artifact like the Shining Trapezohedron spawns a new cult every few centuries as it moves around the globe; the lineage of a forgotten Great Old One's worshippers holds out in a desert ruin or on a tropical island.

Huge cities like London, New York, Tokyo, and Chicago support literally hundreds of sects, hippie squats, Voodoo societies, Eastern Wisdom study groups, hallucinogenic scenes, revival tent churches, storefront covens, ethnic brotherhoods, artistic circles, quasi-Masonic guilds, occult fraternities, and murderous inbred families, any or all of which could be influenced or corrupted by the unnatural.

Naming the Nameless

The first thing to decide about your new cult is its name. That name can give you insight and guidance into your cult's nature and perhaps even its rituals. If you can't come up with a creepy name, maybe don't bother coming up with a new cult. At the last extremity, take a page from von Junzt and leave your cult nameless rather than give it a lame or silly name.

But then you have to build the cult's ingredients separately: Which entity does it serve? Wittingly or unwittingly? What do its members believe? Is there a secret lore that key members know? Do they practice vile rituals, or simply aid each other with call-signs and passwords against the Day? What will they do to protect themselves? What's their signature means of murder, their warning sign, their venerated symbol? From that, you can probably figure out who founded the cult, its local (or global) history, and whether it has always been like it is now.

But if you start out with something like, say, the Spine of Apep, you've got a framework. It serves Yig or Nyarlathotep (Apep was a snake god and the enemy of Ra in Egyptian myth), probably wittingly with a name like that. Its members believe that they are the literal spine of Apep, the line of transmission of anti-Ra wisdom. There might be a secret lore, if the head priests know they actually serve Nyarlathotep but the rank and file worship Yig.

The Spine of Apep practices groovy Tantric rituals awakening that Kundalini serpent in the spine. They slink into the darkness by preference, but set the sacred skeletal snakes on you if they must. Their warning sign is a hatched spiral, representing a snake's spine. Their venerated symbol is a snake spine wrapped around an ankh. It was founded either by ancient Egyptians or by crazed Egyptologists, it's been in Cairo forever but just recently came to Florida, and it has pretty much always been creepy sex murderers.

RIPPED FROM THE (HISTORICAL) HEADLINES

The Fall of DELTA GREEN takes place in a historical era immediately evoked by a hundred greatest-hits soundtracks, by dozens of movies about the Vietnam War or the Beatles or the loss of the American dream, and perhaps by the memories and reminiscences of the players or their parents. "The Sixties" has entered into legend, although the legend really only gets going in the High Psychedelic Age from 1967 through 1973. That legend gives players touchstones to the period, so be wary of debunking it for debunking's sake. In keeping with the grounded core of the Delta Green setting, try to blur the distinction not between the legendary Sixties and the real decade, but between the real history and the esoteric horrors of the unnatural.

Scan history books, biographies, collections of weird phenomena, cultural compendia, and period movies and television for the most peculiar, anomalous, or outrageous events of the era, or of your campaign month and year. Add an additional layer of backstory, explaining the migo involvement in the Falcon Lake UFO abduction in 1967, or that a summoned bhole caused the Ishikawa prefecture earthquake of 1961, or that Stephen Alzis stole Caravaggio's *Nativity with St. Francis and St. Lawrence* from Palermo in 1969 because he appears in it. How did the unnatural or its adherents influence, exploit, or create the event? Use the event or its aftershocks as the hook for a scenario, and half your adventure is already done.

The Inciting Event

If the player wants to explore the inciting event that brought his Agent to the attention of DELTA GREEN, the Handler should have some possibilities ready. She doesn't have to play it out immediately. In fact, it's best saved for later in the campaign when it can reinforce, or cast a terrifying highlight on, an ongoing development, an suddenly-hot cold case, or a recurring GMC.

Whenever you and the player prepare the Agent's backstory, keep a few guidelines in mind.

Shorter is Better

The Agent should be able to relate her origin story in character to other Agents without their players checking out. That means one or two sentences, or a short paragraph at longest.

Unnatural Not Required

The program recruits to fill its numerous and recurring personnel vacancies on the ground. Not every recruit comes in through the side door of the unnatural; some walk in from the front. Vietnam veterans, CIA hard-cases, FBI cynics – they've all seen, and sometimes done, enough horrible things that they've passed the DELTA GREEN audition.

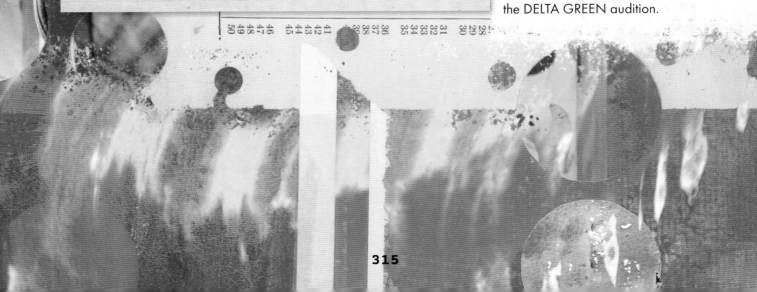

Don't Explain the Unnatural

An Agent's unnatural inciting event should be scary and plausible, but mostly it should be weird and mysterious. No Agent shows up exclaiming "That mi-go almost abducted me!" She might say "I followed up on a UFO case, but the witnesses had all been trepanned or lobotomized. Then I saw a glowing purple orb." Keep it vague, not least because you might want to tie it into the ongoing campaign.

Consider Running Away

The story doesn't have to be involved: The Agent glimpsed or brushed against something unnatural in the course of his duties, or while on patrol, or by coincidence. He ran away, or beat an intelligent tactical retreat, or was told to leave it alone, but the mystery has nagged at him ever since. The End.

Some stories can be deeper or more personal, if the player and the Handler think they can handle them. But don't let the backstory swamp the main action, or warp a character into a one-note cutout or just into someone boring to play.

And Then DELTA GREEN Found You

How did the program hear about the incident? Did the Agent's report make its way through channels to the analysts searching for unnatural spoor? Did DELTA GREEN rescue him from the unnatural, or from bureaucratic oblivion? Did she resolve the situation well enough to impress the program recruiters?

OPTIONAL TEAM BUILDING

For Handlers who want to emphasize interpersonal relationships and roleplaying, consider building the Agents' backstories together. Maybe two Agents were partners for the same Inciting Event, or one investigated the other's report. It's unlikely that their case officer assembled a whole team of rookies for their first mission: who's the grizzled program veteran?

Ask one or two pairs of Agents to collaborate and describe a backstory operation, a previous mission they've been on together. Use the guidelines for Inciting Events: quick, unexplained, no closure necessarily. Agents who take a backstory operation get a floating pool of 2 dedicated Investigative pool points for use against one specific element of their backstory operation: e.g., Deep Ones, hypergeometers, the Kuen-Yuin, UFOs, MK-ULTRA.

The Agent with the lowest Sanity is the **grizzled veteran** of the program. (In case of a tie, it's the oldest Agent.)

- Give the grizzled veteran an extra Bureaucracy 2 and an extra Unnatural 1.
- Replace one of her Bonds with another Agent, or with a DELTA GREEN GMC: her former partner, perhaps, now a case officer.
- Increase her floating pool by 2 more points: "This reminds me of that case in Houston."

The Agent with the highest Sanity is the **new meat** on the team. (In case of a tie, it's the youngest Agent.)

- He gets no backstory operation (and thus no floating pool), although he may have an Inciting Event.
- If the Handler allows him to buy an Unnatural rating during character generation, it is capped at 1; if he wishes, he can trade that 1 point for 2 rating points in Interpersonal abilities.
- Increase his Stability by 2.

This also gives the Handler a great opportunity to seed elements she knows she wants to use during the campaign - the Greys, the Headless God, the reviving Karotechia - into one or more of these backstory operations.

Creating an Operation

At its most basic, consider an operation a series of scenes arranged in a straight line, from the first scene hook to the final coverup or debriefing. Each scene provides the information (the core clue) or the impetus for the Agents to move into the next scene, until they reach the climactic confrontation and escape out the other side. This proves a little too basic for most groups, so hide that structure! Instead, provide multiple exits from each scene to the one following it, or multiple scene paths to the climax, or both.

It's entirely possible to improvise an operation, with a strong enough idea of the target (see *Operations on the Fly*, p. 326). The Agents are trying to solve the mystery or stop the outbreak; therefore they move toward your confrontation scene anyway. Your job is to be ready along their route with horror and information – and if either of those nudges them in a given direction, that just makes for better, more focused play.

The Spine

In this investigative line, designed or improvised, the Agents pursue a series of core clues until they achieve a resolution of some sort. This is called the **spine.** In your notes, it can consist of large sections of fleshed-out narrative, or a bare-bones list of the elements that need to occur to create a minimally satisfying horror experience. See the introduction to the operation included in this book, *Operation ALADDIN'S CAVE*, for a sample spine (p. 329).

A skeleton of individual scenes surrounds the spine and gives it body. Most of those scenes deliver either information or horror or both. Some of them might just be quick investigation scenes: bluff your way into the building, check the records in the weirdly echoing file room, get a core clue, and you're gone. Some might be slightly longer interactive scenes: either an Interpersonal ability moment with an GMC, or a quick action beat.

A General Ability test or two advances the story or gets a plan rolling: fight scenes and chases, mounting and slipping surveillance, a break-in or a mugging: the goal might be to escape, or the opposition might have useful information on them. Make sure any core clues from a fight scene are available (possibly elsewhere) without a win!

Some scenes provide information useful in understanding and solving the central mystery, but not strictly necessary to reach the conclusion. These scenes provide context and detail, or involve theme and flavor elements you wish to emphasize.

The Horrible Truth

Decide what is actually going on. This can be weird and impressionistic, as long as you have some idea how it affects the mundane world, and what clues or other spoor it might leave.

If it's an anomalous incursion by the unnatural ("The Colour Out of Space," "Out of the Aeons"), an ongoing infestation ("The Whisperer in Darkness," "The Shadow Over Innsmouth"), an unfortunate discovery (*At the Mountains of Madness*), or something in between ("The Shadow Out of Time"), determine what the entity is, how it got there, what it wants, and where it's going.

If it's a crime or plot by cultists ("The Haunter of the Dark"), a solitary madman ("The Dunwich Horror"), or an unfortunate experimenter (*The Case of Charles Dexter Ward*), do the same for them. Decide how they fit into the larger unnatural theosystem, or with the other cults in the setting, if at all.

In any case both cases, figure out how the hook (p. 319) fits into the overall story. Was it triggered accidentally, coincidentally, deliberately, or carelessly? And why?

End State

Determine what happens if the horror goes unchecked. Do the mi-go keep mining Vermont, does Simon Orne raise an army of revenants, or does Yog-Sothoth wipe the globe clean? If you short-circuit that last one with "just" an electrical blackout over five states, a disappeared B-52 with its full bomb load, the mysterious destruction of a small town, and a thousand deaths in rioting, your players shouldn't object too much. Did a different team of Agents resolve the situation at the last second, or were the stars not quite right?

Along those lines, determine what has to happen to solve the problem or resolve the situation, if only here and now. Some operations have no solution: the entity simply moves on, as in "The Colour Out of Space." In other cases, the unnatural is here to stay, and the best the Agents can do is post Keep Out signs around it.

317

Core Clues

Most scenes present at least one piece of information necessary to figure out the opposition plot, leading to the climactic scene. As noted on p. 317, that piece of information is the **core clue.** A core clue typically points the group to another scene, often another core clue scene.

Avoid hard sequenced core clues, which can only lead to one another in a single order. You're constructing *one* way to move through the story to another core clue, not the *only* way. In play, you may find yourself placing the core clue from one scene in another, improvised scene inspired by the logical actions undertaken by the players. (This is also true of published scenarios, by the way.) Planning a spine ahead of time guarantees that there's at least one way to navigate the story, but should not preclude other scene orders.

Likewise, ensure that any clue, especially any core clue, is available not only to players using the ability specified in the scenario, but to *any player who provides a credible and entertaining alternate method of acquiring that clue.* The scenario is a foundation to work from, which ensures that there is at least one way to move through the story. It should never be regarded as the only way to get to the resolution. A group of players will often come up with better ideas than one Handler or writer ever could. Give yourself permission to go along with them.

If you like, try mapping out your operation, putting scenes in boxes connected by clue arrows. A good, robust adventure has more than one arrow into any scene, and more than one route from hook to climax.

Floating Core Clues

It can be useful to structure an operation with one or more free-floating core clues. These typically advance the story from one distinct section to another. Where an ordinary core clue is linked with a particular scene, the Agents can glean a floating clue in any one of several scenes. The Handler determines during play which scene gives up the clue.

Floating clues allow you to control the pacing of an operation. They allow the players to enjoy all the interesting or soul-freezing experiences in one section of the operation before the story takes a dramatic turn. For example, you might want them to separately meet all of the suspected ghoul changelings before they, and the Agents, get trapped at night in the abandoned cement factory. To achieve this, withhold the core clue that moves the Agents to the cement factory until after they've met all of the relevant supporting characters. That way, you prevent them from leaping ahead into the narrative without getting all the information they need to fully enjoy what follows.

Likewise, a floating clue allows you to perform like a ruthless editor, skipping unnecessary scenes when you need to kick the narrative into a higher gear. Let's say you've chosen five possible scenes in which the Agents might logically get a necessary core clue. You figure that this phase of the adventure should take about an hour. If the players breeze through the scenes in ten minutes apiece, you can save the core clue for the last scene. If they linger, taking twenty minutes per scene, you'll want to make the core clue available after the third scene.

LEVERAGED CLUES

A standard feature of the policier and the spy story is the crucial fact which, when presented to the interrogation subject or tight-lipped contact, causes him to suddenly break down or open up. In GUMSHOE, this is called a leveraged clue.

This clue comprises two sub-clues: the use of an Interpersonal ability on a GMC, and the mention of another, previously gathered, prerequisite clue. When using leveraged clues, stay alert for any player mention of the prerequisite clue during the Interpersonal scene; players don't always think of using all the leverage they have. Or, hint to the player with Interrogation that the mobster might soften up if you hit him with the result of that Accounting clue you gathered earlier. "Well, since we already know about Vinnie's gambling boat, you're not really protecting anyone any more..."

Player frustration level usually serves as a better trigger for a floating core clue than a predetermined time limit. If they're having obvious fun interacting with the vivid supporting characters you've created, or being creeped out by lights in the sky, you can give them more of what they want by saving the core clue for the final scene. On the other hand, if you see they're getting bored and frustrated, you can slip in the floating clue earlier.

The Operational Skeleton

Here's a "standard" **Fall of DELTA GREEN** operational skeleton, with a few possible specific scenes for each element. Never be afraid to let any of these scenes involve a fight, chase, contest of Stealth, or other confrontation.

The Hook

An event, problem, or opportunity attracts the Agents. Likely an unnatural incursion intersects with mundane (if disturbing) humanity. Follow the leads and ramifications out from the inciting event. Imagine the hook as something solid, a thing to which all the leads attach.

△ A UFO abducts two teenagers.
△ A CIA patrol uncovers a weird idol in the Laotian hills.
△ A research scientist dies of sudden onset anemia.

The Curtain

The Agents check out the hook based on their initial suspicions. The investigation yields a core clue (and possibly various red herrings) but no confirmation of their suspicions.

The investigated individuals present a credible front of innocence; the opposition begins to respond. A good place for a chase or infiltration.

△ The Agents check with the Air Force and interview the teenagers.
△ The Agents research the idol in various archives to little effect, and plan their cover in Laos with the (too helpful?) CIA station.
△ The Agents poke around the research facility's murky government funding.

The Wakeup

The Agents suffer a jolt of horror, most often a horribly mangled victim or attack by unnatural forces. If you haven't had a fight scene yet, here's a good place for one. Or consider a few creepy touches of the unnatural: embed something memorably weird in the scene.

△ The Agents see a UFO and rule out conventional aircraft.
△ Tcho-Tcho ambush the Agents on arrival in Laos.
△ Investigating the lab at night puts everyone on edge.

The Stall

One line of inquiry goes cold, and usually dead. *This is an optional floating element; only deploy it on B-plots or when the Agents have enough clues to start another line of inquiry.*

△ The family refuses to let anyone speak to the teenagers, who change their story.
△ The CIA refuses to provide an armed escort to the idol.
△ The lab supervisor turns up dead in his car, an apparent suicide.

The First Reveal

Possibly as a result of the Wakeup, the Agents gain information leading them closer to the true or main opposition. This likely leads to more investigative scenes, surveillance of a target, or an infiltration.

△ The Agents examine the second landing site and identify a specific radioactive signature.
△ The Agents infiltrate the Tcho-Tcho compound in the CIA training camp.
△ The lab turns out to be funded by MAJESTIC.

The Blowback

The antagonists move directly against the Agents, as a consequence of the investigation so far. *This is an optional floating element, which can be inserted as needed into the action, often more than once.*

△ An Agent is abducted and interrogated by Greys.
△ The Agents flee into the Laotian hills.
△ An MJ-3 Man in Black gets the drop on the Agents, and warns them to back off.

The Twist

Further investigation leads to an upending of the Agents' assumptions, and a switch in the chessboard. A common Twist scene eliminates a red herring. While not a core clue in itself, it helps clear the board for the true solution, and often adds in more bloody death.

△ The Agents discover a local Crow tradition of "flying wolverine fish" centered on the UFO sites.
△ The Agents travel through a time-slip to the final days of the Muvian colony.
△ The dead scientist reappears and kills his wife and son.

The Relief

The agents gain unexpected aid or information, putting them back on the path to discovery. This may be as a result of their investigation or as a result of the blowback. ("Only Captain Lansing knew when our plane was due.") *This is an optional floating element, which can be inserted as needed into the action.*

- △ The abducted Agent gains the sympathy of one of the teenagers.
- △ The Agents witness the erection of the idol in the past.
- △ The Agents examine the murder scene and notice the television set is burned out.

The Final Reveal

The Agents learn what's really going on — and it's worse than they imagined. This reveal may happen during a running fight, or through a series of confrontations.

- △ The Greys have some connection to the Earth's alien past.
- △ The idol compels obedience to the cruel gods of Mu.
- △ The scientist was translating bioelectricity to electromagnetism and back. This is insane, by the way, but somehow he had a Top Secret AEC biophysics grant for the research.

The Setup

The Agents carry out a necessary action before the confrontation can occur. *This element doesn't always occur; when it does, it's often driven by player ingenuity rather than Handler pre-planning.*

- △ The Agents find a Crow shaman and "borrow" his sacred meteoric-iron axe.

- △ The Agents find the temporal gate they fell through and return to 1964.
- △ The Agents re-create the experiment, attempting to magnetically draw the scientist back to the lab.

The Confrontation

The Agents decisively act against this manifestation of the unnatural, hopefully defeating it, sealing it away, or banishing it... for now.

- △ The Agents follow the radioactive signature and ambush the Greys with their axe.
- △ The Agents blow up the idol.
- △ The Agents trap the scientist in a magnetic coil and melt it down in a furnace.

The Cover-Up

Reducing human exposure to unnatural contamination is the purpose of any DELTA GREEN operation. What steps must the Agents take to explain everything away so nobody else investigates it? How far must they go to obscure any crimes they committed while trying to save lives? Who is most likely to challenge their story? This might happen in the field or with a series of Bureaucracy tests back in Washington.

- △ The surviving Agents leave the scene to BLUE BOOK to cover up.
- △ The Agents kill the CIA officer who fell under the idol's influence, but make it look like a Pathet Lao ambush.
- △ The Agents provide a plausible "FBI report" on the various crimes and deaths, and resolve to take another look at the AEC's grant-writing methods.

Mix it Up

This is a framework to fall back on when needed, not a blueprint you have to stick to. Any given element may encompass one scene, a number of scenes, or be only part of a scene. Relief may be needed earlier in the story; red herrings in the stretch may help you pace scenario events to match your time frame. Often, you can combine the First Reveal and the Twist into one development. Above all, you're responding to player initiative, nudging but not pushing plot developments into as much structure as seems mutually satisfying. It's helpful while planning the Hook to think ahead to what the Twist and Final Reveal might be.

Only rarely will the resulting operation precisely match this structure. However, using it to think ahead helps prepare you for the messier, but more vital and interactive, operation that does result when the players start engaging with your game.

Floating Events

One or more floating events can add structural flexibility to the spine. Insert them as needed into the action. The Stall, Blowback, and Relief are examples of such events; others include a scene involving an agent's Motivation, an interaction with a Bond, a crash meeting or other scene laying the groundwork for a future scenario, a delayed consequence of a previous operation, or an uncanny event tied to a location or specific date. The players may add their own elements to the scenario, often by venturing on a "mini-quest" to obtain some crucial intel, gear, or other resource to carry out their plan. The Setup is an example of a potentially player-added element.

Creating a Campaign

A campaign is a series of operations, focusing on a single group of DELTA GREEN Agents. Agents might come and go – they may die, go insane, or "retire" – but a central thread remains. That could be the team's case officer, an ongoing unnatural antagonist (Deep Ones or Kuen-Yuin), a specific area or base of operations (the San Francisco field office), or some other key concept.

Define the Threat

What threats will your agents see in your DELTA GREEN campaign? Some campaigns are a random walk of the unnatural with no connections except the particular Agents sent to investigate them. Others focus on one specific foe, such as the ghouls or the cult of Cthulhu. You're not locked into a limited scope: if the players pursue a lead that points them away from the heart of the ghoul mystery, follow them. Just be ready with something equally horrible for them to uncover.

Campaign Connections

Some campaigns shiver with correlated contents. Knowledge obtained during one operation provides the necessary hooks into the next, or into any number of potential scenarios. Sometimes, the connection to the next scenario is the "clue reward" for defeating the adventure's antagonist; sometimes it shows up during the initial investigation or only gains its importance in hindsight. You can even connect what were once disparate investigations into a single unbroken thread at a later time, if an idea strikes you.

Potential connections include:

△ Letters or cables from one strand of a cult to another

△ Business cards, matchboxes, or other leads to locations

△ Photographs depicting known villains in interesting or identifiable places, or with identifiable or enigmatic other GMCs

△ Brochures, pamphlets, letterheads, or other leads to organizations

△ Cult symbols on bodies, walls, figurines, hand-bound books

△ Case notes from previous (usually dead) investigators

△ Testimony, wiretap recordings, expert opinion, hearsay, rumor, references, cryptic phrases, or confessions obtained from GMCs such as officials, scholars, reporters, gossips, criminals, bystanders, allies, or cultists

△ Art or artifacts, in photographs, books, or collections; these might lead to the artist, the museum, the dig site, or the curio shop

△ Shipping manifests, invoices, packing labels, or railway schedules

△ Intriguing pins (or markings) on maps, especially maps of places with no seeming relevance to the current operation

△ Physical or electronic surveillance of cultists or targets ("Why is he going there? Doing that? Talking to her?")

△ Physical links, from secret panels to hyperspace gates

△ Newspaper cuttings of similar events or phenomena across the country or around the world, found in a scrapbook, a newspaper morgue, or a locked case

△ Leads in books (especially unnatural tomes), lectures, or unpublished doctoral theses; including hand-written marginalia by previous readers

△ Insane rantings, scrawled, typeset, howled, or recorded

△ Places, people, and events mentioned in diaries, reporters' notebooks, or grimoires.

Continuing Characters

Spend a little time coming up with "recurring guest stars," GMCs who may either drive the story or otherwise repeatedly interact with the Agents. This might include Bonds, their case officer, their opposite numbers in the actual CIA or FBI, sources in the local police, Network contacts, a too-helpful MAJESTIC contact trying to flip them, an annoying (or attractive, or both) activist or journalist who seems to show up everywhere they do, a local occult specialist or other DELTA GREEN friendly, their bartender, or the squad of hard-core Marine Recon types they send in overseas to really blow things up. The players might even play some of these GMCs, as backup characters or for variety's sake.

Brief the Players

Inform the players of any details they need to know to create their Agents. If all Agents need to be based out of NATO bases in Europe, or need to be law enforcement officers, let them know. If you're planning a game set in Vietnam or Latin America, give all the Agents a free point of Foreign Language to spend: don't penalize them for agreeing to your idea.

Answer any questions the players might have. Walk them through Agent creation, and make sure the Agents they imagine work in the campaign you're creating. If a player comes up with a great idea that doesn't fit, decide whether you can adjust the campaign or, more likely, the Agent needs to be adjusted. Discuss it with the players.

It's best to do this footwork for them ahead of time, and to have some notes on how, specifically, to make their Agent work in your campaign, before the players go through all the trouble of making Agents.

Custom Situations

You may want to create your own particular setting within the Delta Green universe. You may want to run a campaign set in the Ward, or a MACV-SOG or Project PHOENIX campaign, or move things back to the 1950s and play out Operation SOUTHERN HOSPITALITY Nazi hunts, or run a "sympathy for the Devil" game in which the players take the roles of MAJESTIC operatives and slowly realize the bleakness of the project's corruption.

Being Handler means shaping your **Fall of DELTA GREEN** game into what you want it to be. Sometimes you can explore the game as it already exists before bringing anything new to it. Sometimes you begin with a clear vision of something fresh, but try to keep it in line with the nihilistic core of Delta Green.

Running the Game

This section provides a few hints, tricks, and best practices for running GUMSHOE games. Use them or not as you feel comfortable: they aren't required, but they reliably produce horror and forward story motion.

Setting up a Scene

Every scene can be considered a miniature scenario. A scene presents a story nugget – a problem to solve, an opportunity for progress, a question to answer – which is why it's in the operation to begin with. Hook the players with something interesting: a question, a description, a small puzzle. Don't lead the players right to the core clue, but be ready and willing to hand it over when they ask or when the scene rhythm calls for it. Then end the scene as the clue points them to the next little story nugget, or to a whole stream full of them.

Feed Their Head

Players want information from the scene, often very badly. Provide the immediate impressions: the shape of the room, the clothing and face of the suspect, the layout of the bunker. Let the players lob you questions for a few minutes; don't turn a fire hose of details on them. Once the first impressions are made, engage the rest of the senses: mention the whirring helicopter blades, batter them with the heat radiating from the tenement concrete, evoke the sharp tang of ozone in the air. Smell and sound bring a scene alive; smell especially seems to act as a short cut to player imagination. Linger on telling details that act as a synecdoche for the surroundings: cicadas whirring, condensation on a Dr. Pepper bottle, and drifting pollen invoke the Southern summer without a whole paragraph of text. Use the

> ## A HANDLER'S TOOLKIT
>
> When running a game, have the following items at hand:
>
> - Dice, pens, pencils, scratch paper
> - A clock or watch for timekeeping
> - A list of names to use for GMCs on the fly
> - A list of interesting or atmospheric locations in the vicinity of the game setting, to use as backdrops in unplanned scenes
> - A few weird or horrific images and spooky encounters cued up just in case
> - The likeliest combat scene, statted up and ready to go if need be
> - The Handler's Agent Tracking Sheet (p. 349) to make sure everyone is getting screen time, and to point clues toward Agents with the most helpful abilities

Sixties for your benefit and mention the song on the radio, too.

Steppin' Out

Start moving the players out the door once they've got the core clue. Don't let them drain the scene to a husk; if need be hold up an index card with NOTHING MORE HERE or SCENE END or FADEOUT written on it until they get the hint.

If the players have the bit between their teeth and rush out of the scene, jump in front and lead them wherever they think they're going. A scene the players want to play beats a scene you've meticulously planned every time. If they look seriously lost, a few weird happenings or an informative Blowback scene can put them back in the groove.

Pacing

Every player has a different threshold for speed of play. One player's sensible caution is another's tiresome anal compulsiveness. One player's enjoyable roleplaying interaction is another's pointless babble. Your group likely evolves its preferred pace as an average of the players' tastes, but if you have a party full of *Mission: Impossible* fans, there's going to be more planning than a player group of James Bond aficionados.

Try to provide a taste for each player every few sessions: a long, important park conversation with an informant for the roleplayer; a quick, brutal interrogation for the time-pressured tactician. Overall,

AVOIDING THE RAILROAD

By its very nature, an operation with an actual goal, or one that actually accomplishes or resolves something, will resemble a "railroaded game." The Agents begin at one point, and wind up at another, regardless of who laid the track. But most players don't mind moving forward if they got to work the throttle and toot the whistle.

Here are some tips to keep the clatter of the rails down where your players don't notice them:

Don't read right from the scenario. Paraphrase things, put them in your own words; your colloquial diction sounds more organic than my canned text.

Riff off the players in interpersonal scenes. Respond to Agent dialogue, and respect the emotional content. As long as the clue comes out, don't worry about being true to your notes or the scenario.

Encourage the players to flesh out details of the setting. "What's the laboratory like?" "You tell me, you're the one with Physics 3." "Is there a boat at the pier?" "There is; describe it to me." "What time is it now?" "When did you leave the base?" Only very rarely do player contributions overwrite your clue trail; if so, gently contradict them and move on: "You'd think there would be a big mirror behind the bar, but it's actually a big painted yellow panel. Weird, huh?"

Tailor GMCs and situations to the Agents. If an Agent is a law-and-order type, have his contacts wind him up by setting the meet in a student hangout, or at a protest. If an Agent (or a player!) likes brunets with swimmer's bodies, have him meet just such a man at the haunted lake.

Introduce story elements giving players opportunities to **flesh out their Agents' backstories.** Weave old friends, shipmates, mentors, political protectors, and rivals from the Bureau into your supporting casts, even before the player invokes the Network ability.

however, keep the story moving: Preparedness and Agency between them eliminate a lot of the need for over-planning. Use the threat of the unnatural to keep time pressure on. If things slow down too much, as Raymond Chandler said, have two guys with guns kick in the door.

Six Flags Over Innsmouth

The best and most reliable model for horror pacing remains the roller coaster. It starts with a long, slow build of tension, climaxing in a sudden horrifying realization ("Oh God we're up high"), followed by a vertiginous and terrifying fall. Then a moment to exhale, and then the car ratchets up the track once more...

Not surprisingly, Lovecraft's stories also use the roller coaster structure: a build-up of verisimilitude increasingly larded with the uncanny or monstrous, a sudden horrifying realization ("my nightmares were real memories"), followed by a rapid descent into danger and mental breakdown. Sometimes he switches the fall for the realization ("My God, Eliot, it was a photograph from life!") and if you can get away with that, be my guest.

You can build tension with any number of weird happenings, uncanny effects, or paranoid hints. Déjà vu, a strange smell of lions, the whine of a mosquito but slowed down, a Doppler effect in the sky, a furtive stranger on the docks, a bloated spider, the word "Carcosa" out of context – the entire arsenal of the unnatural equips you to creep players out. The horrifying revelation comes with the Final Reveal, and the terrifying fall equals the shoot out or fiery explosion at the end.

Leapfrogging

Allow players to leapfrog scenes by acquiring information they're meant to get later any time that pacing permits. If you're early in a session when the threat of leapfrogging occurs, and you're not confident you can improvise enough new intervening scenes to make a full evening's entertainment, block the players' efforts with a fight or other diversion. If you're zooming toward evening's end, leapfrogging may prove a blessing — just be sure to squeeze in all of the necessary ancillary information the players might miss by skipping ahead.

You can often juggle around scenes in the middle of an operation with no ill effect to the storyline. When this is the case, it's always better to let the players dictate pacing than to force them back into the order of events envisioned by the scenario.

The scenario is only the blueprint. The building happens during play.

Intercutting

In horror movies, characters always make the huge mistake of splitting up in the face of danger. As Handler, you should always encourage players to make that same error.

You may also want to run solo scenes, or sequences with only a few Agents present, during mundane scenes that develop character and further their personal goals.

To do this, rely on the cutaway technique. Spotlight the actions of a few players while the others look on. In a properly bloodcurdling horror game, other players don't

get restless but grateful that they're not under the gun or the claw or the pseudopod.

The secrets to successful intercutting are:

△ Allow all players to observe cutaway scenes they're not involved in as spectators, as long as they separate their player knowledge from character knowledge. It's more suspenseful to know what horrible events might be in the offing than to be surprised. The exception to this: when you're trying to sow paranoia among the players.

△ Keep cutaway scenes short and snappy. Cut quicker than ensemble TV shows pop from one story thread to the next. Cut when the spotlight players need time to think up their next move, or when they slow their own action down. During action scenes, cut ruthlessly away on cliffhanger moments.

△ See that something interesting is happening to everyone at the same time. This may be challenging, as it is often the wary player's goal to make sure that nothing interesting ever happens to his player.

Montages

Some operations have a very long build-up indeed, enough to defeat the best roller coaster. Gaming out Operation KURTZ doesn't really get going until the Agents reach the interior of the Congo — a thousand miles inland through several insurgencies. Rather than bluntly narrating "Your planes take off from Andrews, refuel in Dakar, and then land in Leopoldville where you transfer to river barges" instead present an impressionistic montage.

Describe the sweating crew loading the C-130 transports, the bumpy flight over the Atlantic into a miles-high thunderhead, the brutal Belgian police on the docks beating the native longshoremen, crocodiles in the river, dead bodies after a firefight, suspicious bite marks on an unknown corpse, and finally the LZ for the helicopters deep in the jungle. You can run a quick combat against Cuban advisers or a "day on the river" scene to set the mood.

Montages not only move the players into the story, but allow you to set mood, foreshadow story beats, amplify themes, and build suspense. Consider using them for every long journey or even for an investigation that would realistically take weeks to complete. Nobody wants to play out a day by day federal case; don't punish the players for going along with you and you can lead them anywhere you like.

Play to the Medium's Strengths

A tabletop roleplaying game is not a movie or a novel. It has no editing room, no second draft. It is unpredictable and unscripted — which is why we play such games in the first place. However, this makes some classic horror elements harder to execute. Jump scares may startle without soundtracks and deceptive lighting, but they seldom truly scare. A roomful of people with cell phones find it hard to internalize the fear of isolation, and without a sudden zoom-in, players habitually miss the GMC's slip of the tongue that reveals all in the midst of an ad hoc conversation.

However, other horror tropes can leverage the nature of roleplaying games.

It Just Looks Wrong to You

Insert horror into the gap between player and character. You can tell the player that there's something *wrong* about a seemingly mundane object or individual in the scene, some indefinable sense of dread or malice, without having to actually determine why the object is so creepy. You can draw the player's attention to that one weird detail. You can add a sense of the numinous, of invisible powers and threats lurking behind reality, by playing with the gap between what the player knows and the character perceives.

The Slow Burn

Instead of giving lengthy descriptions of a horrific sight, make the players complicit in the horror by having them ask questions and take action to learn more. Instead of saying "you find your partner's corpse – and he's been disemboweled!", start off by telling the players they've found a face-down body, and wait for one of them to say "okay, I'll look at the face" before revealing that the dead man was her partner. Reveal information bit by bit in response to the players' actions – until a player declares she's examining the body, only then do her partner's intestines fall out. Give horrific responses to questions and to actions.

Everyone Looks Real

Bring in other players by getting them to play supporting cast members – or even shapeshifting monsters. (You don't have to tell them that, of course.) Players assume that they are all treated equally, and that no GMC "really" matters compared to their characters. Undercutting that pays dividends. Just give the GMC player her motivation and goal, run the dialogue for a few minutes, and you're done. If you plan for the GMC to go berserk and attack the Agent, you can tell her player that as it occurs, or give her a note: "You go berserk and attack Agent Collins' when he mentions Steve. Until then, you're shifty and almost naively cooperative."

Split Perception

Perception takes place in the mind, not in the "real world." Every Agent's mind is different, each warped and poisoned by slow exposure to the unnatural. When it feels right (or very wrong) provide different descriptions of the same thing to different players. "He seems sweaty and suspicious" to the FBI agent; "he seems lonely and scared" to the medic. Describe the weird light as a different color depending on who asks. One Agent doesn't hear the humming noise; all the others do, except the NSA officer hears it as a definite signal. Never provide an objective viewpoint: there isn't one, in Heisenberg's world or in the world of Delta Green.

Operations On the Fly

It's entirely possible to improvise your way through fun and exciting operations you create as you go. If you're wired to think on your feet, you may find it easier to build an adventure this way. Improvised games require you only to keep the backstory in mind: what this unnatural outbreak does here and now, where it came from, and why. Anything the Agents do while sniffing around can let them stumble over this backstory; trained, suspicious experts like the Agents can find any plausible clue. Player action creates the flow of investigative scenes.

You don't have to anticipate what the players will do. Instead, you wait for them to do it, and build scenes and dispense clues accordingly.

Notes on the Underground

When first teaching yourself to improvise mystery scenarios, start by jotting down rough notes, using the operational skeleton on p. 319. Later you may prefer to keep everything in your head, but at least a flow-chart style diagram is helpful. The longer the interval between your rough plotting process and the actual game, the more likely you are to forget crucial details.

Before you start, nail down the backstory in detail, and create your introductory hook scene. Then go on to create provisional ideas for the other elements of the skeleton. Follow these as written, or set them aside in favor of more interesting possibilities that arise spontaneously in play.

The first approach is easier to keep straight in your head and may be preferable for beginning improvisers. The second allows you to harness the spontaneous energy that flows from spur-of-the-moment group creativity.

Roll With It

First of all, don't sweat any uncertainty you may be feeling. It's common, and will go away once you plunge in. When in doubt, take a deep breath, break down your options, and ask yourself which choice is the most interesting at the moment. Once you've made that decision and brought it out in play, you can build on it to spur further interesting developments down the line.

Strong improvising is about reacting to input. Each choice you make builds on the previous ones. Soon your scenario will manifest a sense of momentum all its own.

Three Scenes Ahead, Or None

When running a mystery scenario, it helps to think two or three scenes ahead of the players. It's often useful to have a possible climactic sequence in mind, too. Think up a good Twist (see p.319) and a suitably horrific Final Reveal (see p. 320). That allows you to foreshadow enough to make the ending appear to be a logical outgrowth of the scenes that preceded it.

Don't let the possible plot forks you have in mind become too fixed in your imagination. Instead, keep them provisional, so that you can turn away from them and substitute new choices more in keeping with player input.

Never fall in love with your fallback. Mentally separate what has actually been revealed in play from the background facts you believe, at the moment, to be true. If player interest suggests it, always be ready to abandon facts not yet introduced, however vivid they may seem to you.

Say Yes to Coolness

Improv people have a saying: never negate. As Handler, your more long-winded version is "If their version is cooler than your plan, say yes and praise their cleverness." Embrace unexpected possibilities and build them into the storyline. If the players really hate a GMC, make him a cultist, or a messy victim. If the players worry that the oil tanker holds a hunting-horror, it probably does. If the agents decide to try calling in an ARC LIGHT strike on the Mi-Go colony, drop the bombs and then send MAJESTIC after them.

It's not necessary to turn the narrative on a dime with every piece of player input. The key is to avoid a scene in which nothing happens, or in which your scene is less interesting than the one suggested by the player. When a player says that there's probably a survivor of those experiments still living in the Karotechia experimental center, it's weak play to leave the laboratory empty, or keep the players out of the lab entirely because nobody has Foreign Language (German). Extracting useful information from a maddened pineal mutant through the language barrier is more fun, and more plot-advancing, than not. This doesn't mean, however, that she won't try to escape, or burn the place down.

Leading and Following

Improvisation is a technique, not an ultimate goal. Occasionally you may find that it's more entertaining for all involved if you seize the narrative reins and steer them in a particular direction. This tends to happen more near the end of a scenario, when you're trying to wrap all of the threads together into a coherent and satisfying conclusion.

Again this is a matter of responding to the mood and attitude of the players. When they're actively engaged in the story and throwing out fun suggestions, follow their lead. When their creativity hits the wall, pick up the slack. Improvisation is an organic process of give and take.

OPERATION ALADDIN'S CAVE

"Finally the sailors entered a massive stone crypt — judged to have been part of a much larger edifice, and to have originally lain far underground.... After a short period of virtual panic, caused partly by certain carvings on the walls ..."

— H.P. Lovecraft and Hazel Heald, "Out of the Aeons"

This is intended as an opening-gun operation to get a **Fall of DELTA GREEN** campaign underway. It introduces a possible recurring villain, drops the Agents into the 'Nam, and presents the dangers of the unnatural in stark terms.

In playtest, some groups considered it a too-deadly meat grinder. While this is appropriate both for the Vietnam War and for DELTA GREEN, Handlers who want a friendlier introduction may want to lower Armor and ability ratings for the zombies and even for the VC.

Operational Spine

The Agents each get **Invited to a Day at the Races** and meet up in Da Nang for a covert **Operational Brief.** Choppered into **Firebase Jonas,** they uncover the story of the tunnel complex, and pick up **The Trail of Brent Moorman.** From here, whether they go **Into the Tunnels** or **Back to Da Nang,** they are racing against time. If they succeed in **Recovering the Lamp,** they can go **Back to Firebase Jonas,** possibly dodge **Charlie's Ambush,** and go **Back Into the Tunnels** to try **Sealing the Jar.** If not, or if *they* foolishly bring the Lamp back to the States, **Mere Anarchy Is Loosed** upon Vietnam, America, and most points in between.

Invited to a Day at the Races

Scene Type: Introduction
Lead-Out: Operational Brief

Have each player introduce their Agent in a short beginning vignette depicting him at his usual government job: in a Saigon command center, at the FBI office in Dallas, in a cubicle on the fourth floor of the embassy, or wherever.

A message arrives: by courier, over the telex, through the inter-departmental mail system, on the phone. It is a single sentence:

You are invited to a day at the races.

The Agent recognizes the DELTA GREEN activation code.

The message (or the voice) provides one more piece of information: the time and place of a rendezvous.

Depending on the Agents' individual assignments or locations, provide a logical rendezvous point: if they are all inside the continental U.S., then Gate 13 at Los Angeles International Airport; if not, then a similarly busy and anonymous location in Manila, or Saigon, or (if all the Agents are in Indochina) Da Nang Air Base in Vietnam.

Operational Brief

Scene Type: (Further) Introduction
Lead-In: Invited to a Day at the Races
Lead-Out: Firebase Jonas

When the Agents have all made the rendezvous, they meet a woman in Navy khakis with lieutenant commander's tabs but no unit or ship ID who introduces herself as "Agent Carlson." She briefs them:

U.S. Marine Corps recently captured a Viet Cong tunnel complex in I Corps territory at Xue Than, in Quang Tri province near the DMZ. It is believed that they removed something from that tunnel complex, not least because Corporal Paul Lewis, the unit photographer attached to Firebase Jonas, died from an "accidental firearm discharge" two days later. That was three days ago.

Your mission: investigate this possible outbreak of the unnatural, and prevent it from damaging the war effort, or the world, any further.

THE HORRIBLE TRUTH

The VC found the Lamp when they extended the Xue Than tunnel complex into a Hoabinhian cave. Since it glowed, they removed it from the cave and used it elsewhere, which turned out to be a bad idea. The Hoabinhian Lamp is actually even older than this oldest known Vietnamese culture; it is also a Key, and an artifact of Ghatanothoa's reign in Mu. When the VC removed it from its Lock, they opened the way for a tendril of Ghatanothoa to enter our spacetime. The effects of the tendril drove them mad, and drove them to abandon the tunnel complex. Corporal Lewis' photographing of the Lamp began the corruption of Firebase Jonas, but unless the Lamp-Key is returned to the Lock (and the tunnel destroyed to prevent anyone else digging it up) the tendril will do the same to Indochina and eventually the world.

In Country

Carlson provides the Agents with travel papers and nebulous investigatory duty assignments within I Corps. Civilian Agents' papers describe them as "outside experts liaising with Naval support of I Corps" or the like.

If the rendezvous is not at Da Nang Air Base, Carlson puts the Agents on transport for Da Nang Air Base.

From Da Nang, their papers get them on a Huey helicopter to USMC Firebase Jonas in Quang Tri province.

Firebase Jonas

Scene Type: Core
Lead-In: Operational Brief
Lead-Outs: The Trail of Brent Moorman, Into the Tunnels, Back to Da Nang

Captain James Rickard

The firebase CO is Captain James Rickard. He can provide the basic briefing:

Six days ago, a platoon of Marines on night patrol under Lieutenant Gus van Ryn discovered a VC tunnel complex 18 klicks NW of the base and drove off VC forces in possession. A squad led by Sergeant Porter Jackson went into the tunnels, which were empty. They didn't appear to connect to a larger complex.

If the Agents ask Rickard:

He doesn't know about anything removed from the tunnels, and Corporal Lewis' death was an accident.

HUMINT knows he's lying about the last two points. 1-point spend of HUMINT, Agency (USMC), or Military Science tells you why:

△ he was ordered to keep quiet about anything removed from the tunnels

△ revealing that Lewis shot himself would be a disgrace to him and to the Corps, and would possibly endanger his wife's survivor benefits if it got out.

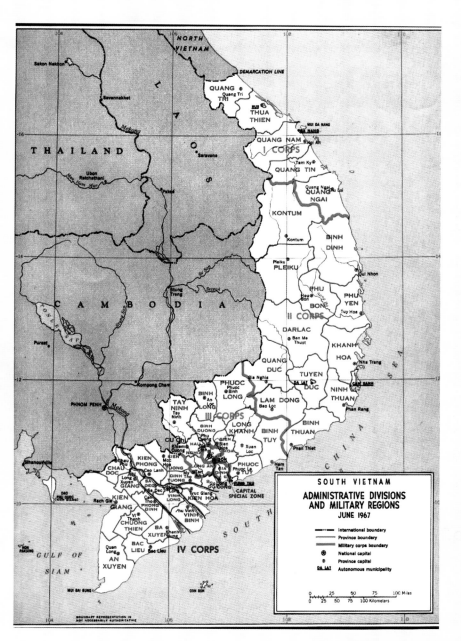

SOUTH VIETNAM

ADMINISTRATIVE DIVISIONS
AND MILITARY REGIONS
JUNE 1967

- - - - International boundary
——— Province boundary
▬▬▬ Military corps boundary
⊕ National capital
⊛ Province capital
DA LAT Autonomous municipality

0   25   50   75   100 Miles
0 25 50 75 100 Kilometers

Inspiration or similar 1-point spend gets Rickard to wink and reveal that he can't say anything about "any artifact that may or may not have been removed from those tunnels."

2-point spend: but if he does find something else he'll be sure to let you know: "You're out of Kirtland AFB, right?"

That might seem to come out of the blue, except that an Agent with any connections to MAJESTIC (AEC, CIA, Physics rating) or long experience with DELTA GREEN knows that Kirtland AFB in Albuquerque is a major MAJESTIC operational site. If no Agent background matches, give this intel to the Agent with the highest Bureaucracy rating as something she's heard.

Corporal Paul Lewis

Set the photography tent on fire three days ago, then shot himself. (This specific information is only available with **Reassurance** or a similar spend.) Specialist DiSalvo discovered the body.

No previous record of insanity or instability.

His body got shipped back to Da Nang yesterday "on the same helo that Air Force puke went back on"

Art: Lewis did have one or two gallery shows of his photographs in New York before being drafted.

With **Reassurance** that this isn't official, the men talk about Lewis coming unglued ("come to think of it, it did start after the men got back from that tunnel sweep") and talking crazy about light snakes coming through the cracks in time and you can't look away from it and well Nam affects everyone right?

Lieutenant Gus Van Ryn

Same story as Rickard, but more useless.

Routine night patrol, ran into VC in the bombed out zone where Xue Than used to be, drove them off with my tactical skills and the men's courage.

Captured one VC, took him back for interrogation. **HUMINT** spend detects Van Ryn's guilt here at letting a POW get killed.

Sergeant Porter Jackson

Jackson repeats Rickard's cover story, adding only the detail that "those VC didn't seem to want to hold on very hard. We only found the tunnel in the first place 'cause one of 'em came runnin' out of a hole in the ground right in front of me." **Military Science** (or an Agent with Vietnam combat experience) knows this is very unusual behavior.

He can describe the tunnel layout.

Reassurance (1-point spend) that this won't go any farther gets more details:

Tunnels were full of dead VC, killed in all kinds of ways; "something growing in them, like weeds."

There was a glowing piece of metal in the tunnel, like a lamp. Jackson's men took it out to keep the VC from coming back for it. Lewis took it to photograph it along with the rest of the intel haul (radio code books, etc.).

The patrol didn't try to collapse the tunnels because Van Ryn got spooked and called a retreat. To be fair, those tunnels *were* spooky, "even more than the normal VC ratholes."

Yesterday some honky Air Force REMF showed up, asked a lot of questions like you are, pulled rank on Captain Rickard, took the Lamp away with him back to HQ.

Military Science or **Agency (USMC)** knows the only way an Air Force REMF pulls rank on a Marine Captain is to call someone on the radio and get them to call his superior.

Specialist Anthony DiSalvo

A sapper who entered the tunnels with Jackson. He too can describe the tunnel layout.

The tunnel seemed recently extended into a pre-existing cavern; there were some shaped stone tools lying on the ground.

The glowing metal came from a different section of tunnels, farther back. It didn't exactly look like metal, more like metal-rich ore "but not really like that either."

Archaeology knows the Hoabinhian culture existed in Vietnam before 10,000 BC. They moved into caves around 8000 BC for unknown reasons and then vanished.

DiSalvo also discovered Lewis' body in the burned-out photography tent. With a 1-point **Reassurance** spend, he confirms that Lewis shot himself.

Specialist Dean Wemmer

Radio operator. Called Kirtland AFB for the REMF, who identified himself as Captain Brent Moorman, USAF, seconded to the Atomic Energy Commission (AEC). Moorman then ordered Wemmer out of the radio tent.

Reassurance or other suitable spend for gossip: Moorman called Rickard to the tent, Rickard listened to the radio on headphones, didn't like what he heard, the next thing we know Moorman is giving orders, shoots the VC prisoner, and takes the Lamp and Lewis' body and the interrogator's tape back to Da Nang with him.

If you'd like, maybe Wemmer overheard Moorman give the clearance code ("Tangent Pluto") identifying himself as MAJESTIC.

Specialist Raleigh ("Rolly") Dell

Interrogator. Didn't get much out of the VC prisoner "Nguyen Ca" to tell the truth, the guy just babbled about killing them and the light everywhere and something growing in a cave or whatever. "Probably went crackers down in that tunnel, I know I sure would."

With the least pressure, Dell happily rats out Brent Moorman for shooting the POW. Moorman took the recordings of the interrogation with him, though.

Dr. Andrew Smith

Medical officer. He examined Lewis' body, and to a fellow medical professional or a superior officer confirms that Lewis killed himself.

A 1-point spend of **Pharmacy** notices a large bottle of antihistamine eye drops on the doctor's back table. If asked about it, Dr. Smith confirms there have been more reports of eye irritation recently, "maybe an allergy or something the squad picked up in the tunnels."

Photography Tent

Looks very much like it was set on fire three days ago. **Criminology** or Investigative use of **Demolitions** can tell this fire is arson, not accident. Smashed and scorched pieces of camera lenses crunch underfoot; an Agent with **Photography** notices that there's no burned camera here.

Lewis' scorched and blackened camera is in a smaller "junk and repair" tent nearby, overlooked by Moorman. The Marine with the most reason to approve of an Agent says something like "Lewis' camera is still around somewhere if you want to see it."

Looking through the eyepiece, it at first looks like there's a scratch or a divot on the lens, but as you move the camera the scratch stays on the place you first saw it and seems to "stretch" or "grow" from there to the place it would appear if it were an actual flaw in the lens. This is creepy and horrid, and is the spoor of Ghatanothoa: 3-point Stability check (Diff 5). At suitable moments in the operation, the Agent who looked through the lens sees a similar scratch or divot on her spectacles, or through a windshield, or in any other clear or reflective surface. Successive viewings are only 2-point Stability tests.

The Trail of Brent Moorman

Scene Type: Alternate
Lead-Ins: Firebase Jonas, Back to Da Nang
Lead-Outs: Into the Tunnels, Back to Da Nang, Recovering the Lamp

MAJESTIC agent Brent Moorman removed the Lamp from Firebase Jonas. He flew back to Da Nang Air Base on a helicopter, and stored the Lamp in Building 237, one of the large cargo warehouses there.

Firebase Jonas was not Moorman's only mission in Vietnam; he's a roving troubleshooter for MJ-6 and keeps busy looking into weird ruins, UFOs, technical weirdness, etc. If the Agents can trace his movements (likely with Bureaucracy tests; Difficulty increases as he realizes DELTA GREEN has picked up his trail), the Handler can use that to feed them plenty of possible operations in Indochina.

Bureaucracy (Diff 6) or suborning a records officer gets Moorman's official record: White, Protestant. Born Bend, Oregon 1922, volunteered US Army 1942, OSS service in Pacific Theater 1943-1945, Army Counter-Intelligence Corps in Manila 1945-1947, joined USAF in 1947, pilot's wings, Atsugi AFB in Tokyo 1951-1953 intelligence support during Korean War, rotated to Holloman AFB 1954, then Kirtland AFB in 1958 and AEC secondment. Numerous postings in Philippines, Korea, Taiwan, Thailand, Vietnam.

Moorman is in great shape, checked out on sidearms and vehicles, but not a field combat officer.

His ability scores in general should be equal to or higher than those of the Agents. He is their opposite number in MAJESTIC.

Into the Tunnels

Scene Type: Alternate
Lead-Ins: Firebase Jonas, The Trail of Brent Moorman, Charlie's Ambush
Lead-Out: Back to Da Nang

Perhaps the Agents want to go see the tunnels for themselves. Rickard loans them a helicopter and pilot for a day mission; he won't authorize a night mission.

The land around the tunnels is a tumbled moonscape blasted out of the jungle canopy, bombed to perdition by B-52s. Evoke if possible the blasted heath from "Colour Out of Space" in your description.

Two or three orange flags flutter on metal spikes, marking the entrances the Marines found.

The tunnels are pitch black, accessible from many exits on the surface. They are narrow – 2 or 3 feet wide – and low, often requiring the Agents to crawl in places. The complex has four main chambers, connected by tunnels linked and engineered to avoid flooding. The drainage tunnel is what hit the Hoabinhian cave with the Lamp in it.

At least one tunnel from the surface has a spiked pit (d+3 damage) just after a sharp turn (Sense Trouble Diff 4).

The piles of dead and rotting bodies may lead to a Violence Stability check (Difficulty 3). Examining the corpses with **Forensics** indicates that they killed each other and themselves. Some of them bit or tore at the others' eyes. The bodies were riddled post-mortem (1-point **Forensics** spend) with M16 gunfire from Marines who encountered them, implying (**Military Science**) that the bodies were moving when encountered.

The smell is horrific, literally (2-point Unnatural Stability check). It's far worse than even the normal battlefield casualty smell: "As a foulness shall ye know Them."

A fire hot enough to burn all the bodies down here will use up the oxygen very fast, causing suffocation to set in immediately.

Any Agent who has looked through the viewfinder of Lewis' camera thinks he sees light glittering in the eyes of the corpses, like polished metal.

The Lock

The cavern does indeed have a few stone tools up against one wall that look Hoabinhian to Archaeology.

On that wall, petroglyphic art shows men fleeing fish-men uphill toward caves. The central cave icon has two interlocking glyphs in it, still showing flecks of what looks like glittering mica. **Anthropology** indicates that the interlocking glyphs might represent the boundary of the world or the interpenetration of the seen and unseen worlds. On a *1-point spend*: Such symbolism acts as cultural reassurance, that the unknown can be bounded and sealed off.

On the far wall, the Agents can see a weird pattern of striations and reflective patches. **Chemistry** thinks it might be metallic ore, but it seems more dendritic, like a solidified flow of liquid metal through rock cracks. A deep niche in the cave wall centers the pattern.

Any Agent who looked through the viewfinder of Lewis' camera does not see any pattern on the wall.

Back to Da Nang

Scene Type: Core
Lead-Ins: Firebase Jonas, The Trail of Brent Moorman, Into the Tunnels
Lead-Out: Recovering the Lamp

Either a radio call back to the air base or Rickard provides a helo back to Da Nang.

The port city of Da Nang hosts an enormous air base, the logistical center for all of I Corps and one of the main staging areas for the US presence in Vietnam. Near the runways, long lines of cargo warehouses hold military equipment, personal effects, and yes, dead bodies waiting to go home. The Agents can easily blend into the crowds of rear-area types looking busy while staying out of the actual war.

An Agent with Vietnam experience or an Army or USMC background (0-point spend of **Agency** or **Bureaucracy**) knows where to look for Moorman's trail: Bachelors' Officer Quarters (BOQ), Transient Officer Billeting, and the "mayors' cell" in the administrative offices generally.

Approaching these may require roleplaying or a spend (**Agency (Army, USMC)** or **Bureaucracy**) or both, depending on the Agents' approach, but the answer is the same: Moorman is still in country, but not on base at present. He's expected back tonight or tomorrow, though, because he left a cargo warehoused on base for shipment back Home tomorrow night.

The Body

Investigative use of **Bureaucracy** can trace the body of Corporal Lewis. He's stored in a morgue facility waiting to be shipped back to the U.S. Access to the morgue comes with First Aid ("I'm a doctor"), Disguise, or even Intimidate.

Lewis' body is badly burned, with the cause of death listed as "gunshot, accidental discharge"

Forensics: Lewis shot himself through the eye.

Which Warehouse?

In Da Nang the Agents need to find the Lamp in Building 237. This is a core clue, so any plausible plan succeeds, such as:

Agency (AEC) or an Investigative use of **Bureaucracy:** finds a warehouse where Moorman would have access, or where the AEC requirements for security and classification can be met.

Interpersonal asking around the air base: "Oh, you're friends with Captain Moorman? Sure, he parks his Jeep back by Building 237 when he's on base."

Using the overheard MAJESTIC ID code to impersonate Moorman on a radio call to Kirtland AFB (**Disguise**): "Just store it in 237 with the other find. Why are you bothering me with this trivia? Who is this anyway? How did you get this code?"

Or just **Notice** (with **Military Science**) a pair of USAF MPs on guard outside Building 237; the other MPs in this section of warehouses are all Army or USMC.

Recovering the Lamp

Scene Type: Core, Hazard, possible Conclusion
Lead-Ins: Back to Da Nang, The Trail of Brent Moorman
Lead-Outs: Back to Firebase Jonas, After Action

Recovering the Lamp involves breaking into Building 237, finding the Lamp, and successfully leaving with it. If they fail their **Stealth** tests at any point, the alarm brings USAF MPs: two at first, then a jeep full.

Breaking into Building 237

The warehouse is guarded by a two-man shift of MPs (**Notice**) when it's not being used to load and unload cargo. The Agents can try **Stealth** to break in at night, distracting or disabling the MPs in some clever fashion.

There is a closed-circuit camera set up over the main doors (**Notice**). Disabling it likely involves a bit of a tricky climb (**Athletics** Diff 4 to shinny along the roof line out of its vision) and a **Mechanics** test to disable it plausibly (Diff 4) or to loop in innocuous blank footage (Diff 6).

If the Agents have not done anything to alert Moorman to their presence (called back to the States or to Saigon or I Corps HQ to pull strings, used his MAJESTIC ID code, etc.) then the **Stealth** Difficulty to break in is 5. If they have somehow alerted Moorman, the Difficulty to break in is 6.

The Agents might also try to impersonate (**Disguise, Military Science**, perhaps **Drive** to borrow a fork lift) workers during a loading operation. Agents without Disguise can piggyback (p. 081) on their expert, if they're all dressed in fatigues or khakis appropriately.

Again, any sensible plan should be given a chance to succeed.

Finding the Lamp

The warehouse office (locked at night, up a set of wooden stairs: **Stealth** Difficulty 5 or Investigative spend of Mechanics to pick the lock) contains log sheets detailing who signed in which crates and where those crates are stored in the warehouse.

Flipping through those sheets takes some time, but **Traffic Analysis** picks out all AEC-tagged crates from the correct time frame: only four. (With a 1-point spend, narrow it down to 2 crates; 2-point spend, narrow it down to one crate.) Roll a die; on a 6, they've found the right crate... or it's the last one they try.

The Agents can reach and search each location in 15 minutes. Opening a crate just takes a crowbar and some muscle; opening it silently and re-closing it requires a **Stealth** test (Diff 4 or 5 depending on Moorman's awareness as above) by the Agent with the crowbar; she can spend **Mechanics** on this **Stealth** test.

The Handler may want to salt other leads to other MAJESTIC operations in Indochina in those crates – maybe Moorman isn't the only MAJESTIC troubleshooter in theater.

The Agents need to make a piggybacked **Stealth** test in 30 minutes (Diff 4 or 5).

If the Agents merely disabled the camera rather than hocusing it with a loop or some other chicanery, add +1 to the Difficulties to represent the possibility of someone in the security shack noticing the feed interruption and sending a couple more MPs to check it out.

The Lamp

The right crate is packed with newspapers around a surprisingly heavy metallic box and a sealed ammo can. The ammo can holds the tape recording of the VC interrogation, and a standard grid map showing the location of the tunnels.

The metallic box is lead (1-point **Chemistry** spend) or lead-lined, at least. Inside is the Lamp.

The Lamp glows brightly – in the darkened warehouse its light streams out and attracts anyone who might be patrolling; even during a busy work day its glow is noticeable in the dim building. Eventually its glow dims by itself, but not in response to anything the Agents do or don't do; in response to signals or stimuli coming from outside the world.

It is a weirdly twisted piece of metal, or perhaps metallic rock, but with a sort of lively feel to it like electricity or suppressed motion. **Chemistry** is baffled. It exactly resembles the crack-and-divot in the camera lens. Examining it intensely is both distracting and unsettling (3-point Stability test, Diff 5). Any Agent who looked through the camera sees the Lamp as somehow larger than the others do; their Lamp-shadow is larger, too.

It casts shadows very inconsistently, it must be said.

Perhaps it changes apparent weight or even floats in one Agent's hand, or rotates its geometry when nobody is looking.

Taking the Lamp With You

Removing a crate during a work shift is easier than sneaking out with one at night: after dark, MPs not just on this building but on the whole base are on watch for exactly that kind of behavior.

Removing the Lamp is easier, somewhat. It's too big to easily fit in a pocket of fatigues, but an Agent can unbutton his shirt and stuff it in.

One final **Stealth** test (Diff 4 or 5) to exfiltrate back to another part of the base where the Agents won't look so skulky, and they're clear.

The Tape

Holds a lengthy insane rant by the captured VC; a reel-to-reel tape player and **Foreign Language (Vietnamese)** are required to get the following:

△ The VC found the cave about a month ago, and pulled the Lamp off the wall like a sticky piece of chewing gum.

△ It glowed bright and dim, eventually its glow stuck to walls and metal and mirror and glass and eyes. (Agents might remember that the inside of the metal box seemed to glow, but they likely assumed that was a reflection of the Lamp.)

△ Shoots of shadow like rice shoots grow out of the wall and grow out of some of the dead.

△ Still growing! Growing in the cave! Growing inside the wall, in the dark! Shoots of rice! A glorious crop! The best ever year comes soon! Ocean waters the land, flooded like a big rice paddy!

△ Pull out their eyes! Kill them all! They have gazed upon His Light! They have profaned His Darkness!

△ Ga-thanh-a-tua! GA-THANH-A-TUA! *sound of rifle butt on skull*

In Deep

One hopes the Agents have realized they need to return the Lamp to the Cave. If not, see *Mere Anarchy is Loosed* (p. 339).

Back to Firebase Jonas

Scene Type: Core, Antagonist Reaction

Lead-In: Recovering the Lamp

Lead-Outs: Charlie's Ambush, Back Into the Tunnels

Lewis' action was brave and deliberate, but it wasn't quite enough. Little glints of light shine from rifle scopes, vehicle windshields (all of which seem to have developed a strange divot or hairline crack) and so forth. This effect works really well if the Agents get to Jonas by day and then at night start seeing the little glows of the Lamp.

The darkness from the cave has begun to grow in the shadows around the firebase; in fact, the Agents notice that the vegetation around the FB has been burned way back with napalm. **Military Science** identifies this as unusual and enthusiastic. **Psychotherapy** identifies the various manias growing in the Marines:

△ Rickard is clamping down on control; he suffers from obsessive-compulsive disorder or similar. He has the men report and sound off regularly.

△ Van Ryn vacillates between aping Rickard and secretly wishing to murder him.

△ Jackson barely holds it together. He may just break down completely or snap and tear out someone's eyeball.

△ DiSalvo stockpiles explosives, building "the ultimate Bangalore torpedo" for "the ultimate fireworks show." "Big light."

△ Wemmer is on the radio all the time, sending Morse or muttering, but (**SIGINT**) he is transmitting to an empty channel or possibly just broadcasting nonsense chunks of electricity into the Heaviside Layer or out toward the ocean.

△ Dell carves the glyphs from the cave into things, along with the letter G. (Dell wasn't in the cave, and nobody photographed them.) One of the glyphs kind of looks like the Lamp, says the Agent with the lowest Stability rating who has seen the Lamp.

Other Marine GMCs the Agents met are also weirdly exaggerated in behavior, like shadow puppet versions of themselves.

A **Psychotherapy** test (Diff 6) can straighten out a stricken Marine for at least one night or one day.

If the Agents left the burned camera behind and intact, it has become infested with the Lamp, and the firebase is that much worse. Maybe a couple of Marines have already shot themselves, or the squad dug up the dead VC and hung him on a cross with shell casings jammed into his eyes.

If the Agents display the Lamp or allow it to shine openly, the squad dissolves into mania, everyone trying to bury or steal the Lamp. Then the rest of the firebase joins in, first to try to suppress the craziness and then as they too see the shadows and the light, to join in themselves.

Charlie's Ambush

Scene Type: Antagonist Reaction

Lead-Ins: Back to Firebase Jonas, Firebase Jonas

Lead-Outs: Back Into the Tunnels, Into the Tunnels

Of course the Viet Cong plan to retake the tunnel. Cadre doesn't know it's a doorway to Ghatanoth-oa.

A team of VC (as many fighters as Agents, but if the Agents bring a squad of Marines along using Psychotherapy or a big Inspiration spend, the VC are outnumbered) tries to ambush the Agents on the march back to the tunnels. If the Agents manage to helo there despite the weird Lamp-divot in the windscreen distracting everyone, the VC hit the LZ.

The VC have AK-47s, so this is a great chance to try out the newer deadlier Autofire (p. 100) and Lethality rules (p. 093).

Viet Cong

General Abilities: Athletics 3, Firearms 4, Health 3, Melee Weapons 3, Unarmed Combat 3

Hit Threshold: 3

Alertness Modifier: +0

Stealth Modifier: +1 (+2 at night)

Attack: fist (d-2), machete (d+0), 7.62mm AK-47 assault rifle (d+0 [L1 on full auto])

Back Into the Tunnels

Scene Type: Core, Antagonist Reaction

Lead-Ins: Back to Firebase Jonas, Charlie's Ambush

Lead-Out: Sealing the Jar

Inside the tunnels things are even worse.

The VC corpses have become full-on zombies, though they look and move more like scarecrows or bundles of rice with skin stretched over them. They don't have and can't use guns.

Zombie VC

General Abilities: Athletics 3, Health 7, Unarmed Combat 4

Hit Threshold: 2 (slow)

Alertness Modifier: -1

Stealth Modifier: -1

Attack: bite (d-1)

Armor: Resilient (firearms); other weapons do half damage

Stability Loss: +0

Grab: Instead of a bite attack, a zombie can grab its target, using *Monstrous Grappling* (p. 222).

As the Agents tussle with the zombies, they see glints in the corpses' eyes, glints that float out of the corpse like glowing floaters in the Agents' eyes. They move back and forth across the Agents' field of vision in the tunnels. They are relatively enormous, because they seem to float directly in front of the Agents. (4-point Unnatural Stability test, Diff 5)

Anyone in the tunnel complex who becomes Shattered attacks the living and tears at their eyes.

If the operation still seems too soft, the tendril of Ghatanothoa oozes out of the cave wall.

Tendril

General Abilities: Health 8, Unarmed Combat 8

Hypergeometry: 18; the tendril can reanimate a killed zombie for Cost 3 instead of making a regular attack.

Hit Threshold: 3

Attack: penetrate (L1)

Armor: Transcendent (gunfire and reflective metals)

Stability Loss: +2

Sealing the Jar

Scene Type: Conclusion

Lead-In: Back Into the Tunnels

To end the horror, the Agents must destroy the tunnels with the Lamp pressed up against the far cave wall as it was originally.

Destroying a VC tunnel complex is very very hard: B-52 bombings sometimes can't do it, for instance. Fortunately the personal touch still works: if charges are hand-placed at each entrance, and carefully located (**Architecture** spends) throughout each main chamber, then the whole complex can be imploded. (Diff 7 **Demolitions**)

If the VC haven't attacked yet, or if any of the ambushers escaped alive, an attack as the Agents wire the tunnels for demolition is a great opportunity.

Specialist DiSalvo has Demolitions 8 but is unhinged enough to set off the Bangalore torpedoes early and collapse the tunnels onto the Agents if he loses it.

After Action

If the Agents have sealed up the tunnels and left the Lamp correctly sealing the breach inside the cave, every surviving Agent recovers 1 Sanity.

Mere Anarchy is Loosed

If the Agents or Moorman bring the Lamp back to the US, things aren't so nice.

If the Agents bring the Lamp to DELTA GREEN, the Handler decides whether it corrupts DELTA GREEN and contributes to the program's eventual manic self-destruction in 1970. Or perhaps DG destroys it on the "no artifact is a good artifact" principle.

MAJESTIC, of course, tries to weaponize it, recognizing its light and gravity and metallicity as sort of like the Roswell saucer, or at least something else just as good. This definitely contributes to their gleeful willingness to sell the human race down the river in the 1980s and 1990s.

(The Mi-Go, by the way, recognize the Lamp as a damping rod of sorts for Ghatanothoa and demand it from MAJESTIC at some point in the future.)

Firebase Jonas is reported overrun by enemy action; the B-52s fly again, more of the jungle becomes moonscaped. The cave collapses in the second (much worse) bombing, slightly slowing down the tendrils. Slowly the world goes mad, goes corrupt, becomes unable to recognize its own dark reflection in the madman across the cave, in the flickering light.

Use Other

DEPARTME

DELIVER TO

DATE

The Fall of DELTA GREEN

BACK MATTER

EXECUTIVE 9895
COMMITTEE

DG FORM 31
1 JAN 68

Conversion Notes

The following guidelines enable you to convert existing **Delta Green: The Role-Playing Game** scenarios (either your own, or published ones) and Agents for use in **The Fall of DELTA GREEN**. No game conversion is perfect, however, and if you run into something that your game should handle differently, feel free to tinker with it.

Round fractions up.

Agents

This converts Agents impressionistically, and likely results in characters that do not precisely match the result of using template builds. **Fall of DELTA GREEN** conversions privilege ability more than **Trail of Cthulhu** conversions from **Call of Cthulhu**, to represent the higher degree of training possessed by DELTA GREEN Agents compared to random 1930s Investigators.

Characteristics

- △ Ignore STR, DEX, CON, and CHA.
- △ If your Department template contains Traffic Analysis as a non-optional ability, divide INT by 6 to derive Traffic Analysis.
- △ Divide INT+POW by 4 to derive the Preparedness ability rating.
- △ Divide Willpower by 2 to derive Stability.
- △ Divide Sanity by 10 to derive the Sanity ability rating. If the result is higher than Willpower/2, use the result for Stability as well.
- △ Divide Hit Points by 2 to derive Health.
- △ Ignore Breaking Point.

Agent Abilities

- △ Reduce all skills below 6% to 0.
- △ Divide the following skills by 25 to derive the corresponding ability ratings: Accounting, Anthropology, Archaeology, Criminology, Forensics, History, HUMINT, Law, Medicine, Military Science (use the highest skill), Occult, Pharmacy.
- △ Divide all Science skills by 30, and assign the quotients to their corresponding abilities: Astronomy, Biology, Chemistry, Physics. For skills covered by one ability (Botany and Zoology both fall under Biology, for example), add the quotients together.
- △ Divide the following skills by 8 to derive the corresponding ability ratings: Alertness (becomes Sense Trouble), Bureaucracy, Demolitions, Disguise, Drive, Firearms, Melee Weapons, Psychotherapy, Ride, Unarmed Combat.
- △ Divide Unnatural skill by 20 to derive the Unnatural ability rating. Subtract this number from 10 and lower Sanity if necessary to match the cap.
- △ Divide Persuade by 10. Split these rating points among Flattery, Inspiration, Interrogation, Negotiation, and Reassurance as you wish.
- △ Divide Search by 25 to derive Notice, and by 8 to derive Conceal.
- △ Divide SIGINT by 15. Split these rating points between Cryptography and SIGINT as you wish.
- △ Divide Stealth by 6. Split these rating points between Filch and Stealth as you wish.
- △ Divide Bureaucracy by 20, and add the result to 2 to derive available Agency build points. Spend them as normal: second Agencies count double (p. 052).
- △ Divide Art (use highest skill) by 20 to derive the rating in Art. If the number of Art skills exceeds this result, use that number instead.
- △ Divide Art (Photography) by 25 to derive Photography.
- △ Take the highest of Athletics, Dodge, and Swim; divide that skill by 8 to derive Athletics. For each of the lower skills at 70%+, add 1 rating point.
- △ Divide Computer Science by 30 to derive Data Retrieval.
- △ Take the highest of First Aid and Surgery; divide that skill by 8 to derive First Aid. If the lower skill is at 70%+, add 1 rating point. If you have a Surgery skill, take it as a Special Training skill (p. 072).
- △ For each Foreign Language skill at any level, add 1 to Foreign Language. If you have a foreign language at 90%+, add 1 rating point. If you have three or more foreign languages at 90%+, add 2 rating points.
- △ Take the highest of Artillery and Heavy Weapons; divide that skill by 8 to derive Heavy Weapons. If the lower skill is at 80%+, add 1 rating point.
- △ Take the highest of Craft (any skill) and Heavy Machinery; divide that skill by 8 to derive Mechanics. Add 1 rating point for each of these skills above 80%.
- △ Divide Pilot (use highest skill) by 8 to derive the rating in Pilot. If the number of Pilot skills exceeds this result, use that number instead.
- △ Take the highest of Navigate and Survival; divide that skill by 20 to derive Survival. For each of the lower skills at 80%+, add 1 rating point.
- △ If you are an FBI Agent, U.S. Marshal, or other law enforcement agent, or if your

Department template contains Cop Talk as a non-optional ability, divide Persuade by 25 to derive Cop Talk.

△ If you are a CIA, DIA, ONI, or other intelligence agent, or if your Department template contains Tradecraft as a non-optional ability, divide HUMINT by 30 to derive Tradecraft.

△ If your Department template contains Fringe Science at all, you may move 1 to 3 points from any Investigative Ability or abilities into Fringe Science.

△ If your Department profile contains Streetwise at all, divide HUMINT by 40 to derive Streetwise.

Hypergeometry

△ Derive the Agent's Hypergeometry potential point pool based on the books or other materials she has studied, based on the values given on p. 197.

△ For each separate ritual the Agent has cast in play, add 1 to her Hypergeometry ability rating.

△ If her rating exceeds her pool, raise her pool to match it.

Bonds

△ Either re-derive Bonds using the rules on p. 045 or divide current Bond scores by 5 to derive Bond strengths.

Creatures

△ Divide the creature's STR by 2 to derive its Athletics.

△ Divide the creature's Hit Points by 2; add 1 to the quotient to derive its Health.

△ Divide the creature's highest native attack skill by 4 to derive its Fighting.

△ Divide the creature's highest weapon skill by 4 to derive its parallel Melee Weapons or Firearms ability.

△ The creature's Hypergeometry rating, if it has one, is roughly half its POW or WP.

△ Hit Threshold is 4 unless special circumstances obtain (size, speed, native advantages)

△ If the creature has an Alertness or Stealth skill, divide it by 40 to derive the relevant modifier.

△ If minimum Sanity loss for seeing the creature is 0, additional Stability Loss is +0 (+1 if the creature is clearly non-humanoid); if minimum Sanity loss is 1, additional Stability Loss is +1; if minimum Sanity loss is a die roll, additional Stability Loss is +2; additional Stability Loss is +3 or higher for gods or titans.

△ You may adjust these derived scores up or down by 1 or 2 points if necessary to clearly differentiate the various creatures from each other, or to pass the sniff test or create a desired mechanical effect.

Damage

Extrapolate damage from the following table, but remember that GUMSHOE damage is compressed. Damage in **The Fall of DELTA GREEN** should only go above +1 if the attack does over 2D6+3 damage in **Delta Green: The Role-Playing Game**.

Damage Conversions

Delta Green: The Role-Playing Game Damage	The Fall of DELTA GREEN Damage
1D3, 1D4	d-2
1D6	d-1
1D8	d+0
1D8+1, 1D10, 2D6	d+1
3D6, 4D6	d+2
5D6	d+3
6D6	d+5
10D6	d+12

Lethality

Divide an attack's Lethality percentage by 17 to derive its Lethality rating. Extrapolate * and H results from the examples in the rulebook.

Armor

Use the following table for Armor conversions:

Armor Conversions

Delta Green: The Role-Playing Game Points of Armor	Fall of DELTA GREEN Armor statistic
1	-1
2	-2
3-4	-3
5-7	-4
8-11	-5
12-16	-6
17-22	-7

Tomes

Only the *Al Azif* grants 4 Unnatural; only the *Necronomicon* grants 3 Unnatural. Major tomes grant 2 and minor tomes 1.

Except dedicated grimoires, most tomes grant only 1 or 2 Hypergeometry potential points. Generous Handlers may want to grant 1 Hypergeometry potential point for each three or four rituals listed in a text.

Rituals

Extrapolate Cost and other values for rituals based on the table on p. 202, and from the examples given in this book. In general, the Cost of a ritual roughly equals 40% of its cost in WP. Keep in mind that **The Fall of DELTA GREEN** compresses SAN, WP, and POW scores into ability pools that likely top out around 10-12 points.

Sources

The Progenitors

Begin, if you somehow haven't, with the seminal horror stories of H.P. Lovecraft. All of Lovecraft's fiction is in the public domain, and available in a number of formats in print or online. Here are the core texts to look for:

△ Short stories: "The Call of Cthulhu," "The Shadow Over Innsmouth," "The Shadow Out of Time," "The Whisperer in Darkness," "The Colour Out of Space,""Pickman's Model," "From Beyond"

△ Novels: *At the Mountains of Madness*, *The Case of Charles Dexter Ward*, *The Dream-Quest of Unknown Kadath*

Also read the two best Cthulhu Mythos stories of the 1960s, "Return of the Lloigor" by Colin Wilson and "The Deep Ones" by James Wade.

Delta Green

Delta Green has existed since 1992 when it first appeared in issue 7 of *The Unspeakable Oath*. In addition to **Delta Green: The Role-Playing Game**, from which **The Fall of DELTA GREEN** is adapted, many other books and game supplements for the setting are available, and provide much deeper mines for source material than this one corebook can.

With very few exceptions, you can easily translate nearly all the monsters, rituals, characters, and items therein to this rule set.

△ Game Supplements: **Delta Green, Delta Green: COUNTDOWN, Delta Green: EYES ONLY, Delta Green: Targets of Opportunity**

△ Fiction: *Delta Green: Alien Intelligence, Delta Green: Dark Theaters, Delta Green: The Rules of Engagement, Delta Green: Denied to the Enemy, Delta Green: Through a Glass Darkly, Delta Green: Strange Authorities, Delta Green: Tales From Failed Anatomies, Delta Green: Extraordinary Renditions*

James Ellroy

Finally, make every effort to read the "Underworld USA" crime trilogy by James Ellroy: *American Tabloid*, *The Cold Six Thousand*, and *Blood's a Rover*. Ellroy depicts the skeezy underside of the Sixties with brio and relish: seeing DELTA GREEN in the grimy window Ellroy peeps through should be unavoidable.

The Sixties

For better or for worse, the Sixties come with an indelible soundtrack, much of which I loaded into my iTunes feed for the duration. I found myself with a much greater appreciation for Bob Dylan and the Beach Boys at the end of this project. When the tambourines became too much I knew abject gratitude that the Velvet Underground recorded four albums between 1967 and 1970.

The best way to get your mind into an era is not necessarily to read history books about it, but to immerse yourself in works from that period. Look at clothes, buildings, cars, street scenes. The Handler looking for Sixties flavor as inspiration for **The Fall of DELTA GREEN** might look here:

△ Television: For spy stories, *Mission: Impossible, The Avengers, The Man From U.N.C.L.E., Danger Man*, and *I Spy* provide weird, grippy story hooks (a specialty of 1960s procedurals) and the limits of the plausible, along with period thrills and visuals.

△ Fiction: The first twelve "Parker" crime novels by Richard Stark are nearly perfect; crime novels in general provide the best grounding in a decade's mores and realities. Following the success of the James Bond films lots of spy stories filled the 1960s' spinner racks: at random I read some of the *Assignment* series by

Edward S. Aarons and the *Nick Carter: Killmaster* series. The first has better prose and characterization; the second more interesting plots.

△ Film: From an endless well of possibilities, try *Night of the Eagle* (Sidney Hayers, 1962), *From Russia With Love* (Terence Young, 1963), *The IPCRESS File* (Sidney J. Furie, 1965), *Blow-Up* (Michelangelo Antonioni, 1966), *Quatermass and the Pit* (Roy Ward Baker, 1967), *Ice Station Zebra* (John Sturges, 1968), *Rosemary's Baby* (Roman Polanski, 1968), *Performance* (Nicolas Roeg, 1970), and *The French Connection* (William Friedkin, 1971).

History

Mark Kurlansky's *1968: The Year That Rocked the World* focuses on the year everybody means when they say "The Sixties." Rick Perlstein's (leftish) political histories of Goldwater and Nixon, *Before the Storm* and *Nixonland*, are as good a place as any to start the domestic side.

The Vietnam War dominates the foreign side. Stanley Karnow's *Vietnam: A History* retails the mainstream consensus at length; my Vietnam veteran friends recommend Michael Herr's *Dispatches* as the best book about what it was like. Among the many Osprey Publishing books on the war, *U.S. MACV-SOG Reconnaissance Team in Vietnam* by Gordon L. Rottman seems particularly relevant.

If you don't your players already have, so watch *Apocalypse Now* (Francis Ford Coppola, 1979) for Mythic Vietnam. Your players might not have seen **Tour of Darkness,** the Vietnam "Weird Wars" setting for **Savage Worlds,** by Teller.

The Shadows

The American Intelligence Community, published in 1967 by Brigadier General Monro McCloskey, USAF provides a decent period overview. I also recommend Miles Copeland's *The Real Spy World* (1974) for an insider look at the CIA, along with Victor Marchetti's less positive *The CIA and the Cult of Intelligence* from the same year. Betty Medsger's *The Burglary*, about the 1971 burglary of an FBI regional office, provides a similarly dark glass through which to view the Bureau. Robert Gillespie's *Black Ops Vietnam* provides an in-depth look at MACV-SOG.

This is probably where I recommend *JFK* (Oliver Stone, 1991) as a period piece and an Erector set conspiracy model.

Where the Shadows Lie

If I had to recommend only one book of eliptony here, it would be *UFOs and the National Security State: Chronology of a Coverup, 1941-1973*, by Richard Dolan. Exactly the right tincture of UFO craziness and bureaucratic history gives persuasive gloss to your MAJESTIC.

The second book would likely be an occult overview such as *Turn Off Your Mind: The Mystic Sixties and the Dark Side of the Age of Aquari-*us, by Gary Lachman, although *The Morning of the Magicians* by Louis Pauwels and Jacques Bergier, which kickstarted the decade's occult revival in 1963 with its translation into English, would be a strong option as well.

Other rich period possibilities include:

△ *Flying Saucers – Serious Business*, Frank Edwards
△ *In the Wake of Sea Serpents*, Bernard Heuvelmans
△ *The Dragon and the Disc*, F.W. Holiday
△ *The Mothman Prophecies*, John Keel
△ *The View Over Atlantis*, John Michell
△ *Invisible Residents*, Ivan Sanderson
△ *Passport to Magonia: From Folklore to Flying Saucers*, Jacques Vallee
△ *The Occult: A History*, Colin Wilson

Read these books and those like them as inspirational period texts to sift for tone and theme, or as the outer shell of the inner secret kept by DELTA GREEN.

Other relevant modern works include Peter Levenda's *Sinister Forces* trilogy and *Weird Scenes Inside the Canyon*, by David McGowan.

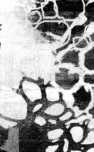

The Fall of
DELTA GREEN

AGENT RECORD SHEET

AGENT DETAILS

Player Name:	Service Record:
Agent Name:	Military Service:
Age and D/O/B:	Special Skill Training:
Nationality:	Special Weapons Training:
Branch/Department:	Hypergeometry:
Profession/Rank:	Potential: | Rating:
Education:	Adapted to:
Motivation:	Violence | Helplessness

SERVICE RECORD/BIOGRAPHY

INCITING EVENT:

SANITY

10	9	8	7	6	5	4	3	2	1	0

STABILITY				HEALTH			
-12	-11	-10	-9	-12	-11	-10	-9
-8	-7	-6	-5	-8	-7	-6	-5
-4	-3	-2	-1	-4	-3	-2	-1
0	1	2	3	0	1	2	3
4	5	6	7	4	5	6	7
8	9	10	11	8	9	10	11
12	13	14	15	12	13	14	15

GENERAL ABILITIES

Athletics*	
Bureaucracy*	
Conceal	
Demolitions	
Disguise	
Drive	
Filch	
Firearms	
First Aid	
Heavy Weapons	
Mechanics	
Melee Weapons	
Pilot	
Preparedness	
Psychotherapy	
Ride	
Sense Trouble	
Stealth	
Unarmed Combat	

*Default starting rating for Athletics, Bureaucracy, and Agency is 2.

INVESTIGATIVE ABILITIES

Academic Abilities		Interpersonal Abilities		Technical Abilities	
Accounting		Agency* ( )		Architecture	
Anthropology				Art	
Archaeology					
Astronomy		Cop Talk			
Biology		Flattery		Chemistry	
Criminology		HUMINT		Cryptography	
Foreign Language		Inspiration		Data Retrieval	
		Interrogation		Forensics	
		Intimidation		Fringe Science	
		Negotiation		Notice	
History		Reassurance		Pharmacy	
Law		Streetwise		Photography	
Medicine		Tradecraft		Physics	
Military Science				SIGINT	
Occult				Survival	
The Unnatural				Traffic Analysis	

The Fall of DELTA GREEN

| AGENT RECORD SHEET |

BONDS

Bonds	DELTA GREEN Bonds

DISORDERS

	Diff +

NETWORK CONTACTS

Name	Notes
Unspent Network Pool	5

GEAR/WEAPONS

NOTES

Beliefs, hobbies, obsessions, tastes in music or sports loyalties. What does your Agent drink? What does she smoke?

Something you admire about your Agent.

Something you dislike about your Agent.

Why does DELTA GREEN trust your Agent to confront unnatural threats and keep them secret?

Why does your Agent agree that helping DELTA GREEN and keeping its secrets feeds her Motivation?

The Fall of DELTA GREEN
HANDLER'S AGENT TRACKING SHEET

Player				
Agent				
Military Service				
Department				
Motivation				
Bond 1				
Bond 2				
Bond 3				
Bond 4				
Health				
Stability				
Sanity				
Mental Illness				
Network				
Contact 1				
Contact 2				
Contact 3				
Contact 4				
Accounting				
Agency				
Anthropology				
Archaeology				
Architecture				
Art (Specialty 1)				
Art (Specialty 2)				
Astronomy				
Biology				
Chemistry				
Cop Talk				
Criminology				
Cryptography				
Data Retrieval				
Flattery				
Foreign Language				
F Language 2				
F Language 3				
F Language 4				

Darkness

Darkness Level	Opponent's Stealth Modifier	Opponent's Alertness Modifier	Hit Thresholds	Visual Task Modifiers
Night	Up by +1	Down by -1	+1 at Near or longer range	+1 Difficulty
Dark	Up by +2	Down by -2	+1 at Close range; +2 at Near or longer range	+2 Difficulty
Pitch-Black +1 to Stability test Difficulty	Up by +3	Down by -3	+1 at Point-Blank; +2 at Close; +3 at Near or longer	+3 Difficulty

Weapons and Explosives

Weapon Type	Damage
Fist, kick	d−2
Blackjack, brass knuckles, small improvised weapon, pistol butt, nightstick, punji stake, knife	d−1
Machete, baseball bat, rifle butt, heavy club, large improvised weapon, crossbow bolt, light firearm (.32 pistol or smaller, 6.5mm rifle or smaller, assault rifle, 20-gauge shotgun or smaller)	d+0
Sword, fire axe, fixed bayonet, arrow, bed of punji stakes, heavy firearm (9mm pistol or larger, .30 rifle or larger, submachine gun, 12-gauge shotgun or larger)	d+1
Very heavy firearm (.50 MG, anti-materiel rifle)	d+2

For firearms, add an additional +2 when fired at Point-Blank range. All shotguns add an additional +1 to damage at Close range.

Lethality

If the attack has a Lethality rating (e.g., L2):

△ Roll a damage die.
△ If the result of the die is lower than or equal to the Lethality rating, the target dies.
△ If the result of the die is higher than the Lethality rating, apply Lethality x 5 plus the die result as damage to the target.
△ If the Lethality rating includes an asterisk (e.g., L2*):
△ Roll a damage die as above.
△ If the result is one higher than the Lethality rating, the target is Seriously Wounded (reduced to Health -6).

△ If the target was already Hurt or worse, the target dies.
△ If the Lethality rating includes an H (e.g., L2H):
△ Roll a damage die as above.
△ If the result is one higher than the Lethality rating, the target is Hurt (reduced to Health 0).
△ If the target was already Hurt, the target is Seriously Wounded.
△ If the target was already Seriously Wounded, the target dies.
△ If the Lethality rating includes both an asterisk and an H (e.g., L2*H):
△ Roll a damage die as above.

△ If the result is one higher than the Lethality rating, the target is Seriously Wounded (reduced to Health -6).
△ If the result is two higher than the Lethality rating, the target is Hurt (reduced to Health 0).

Example:

A damage roll of 2 means the target:
Takes 7 points of damage from a Lethality of L1.
Is Hurt by a Lethality of L1H.
*Is Seriously Wounded by a Lethality of L1*H.*
Is dead from a Lethality of L2H.

Weapon Type	Lethality Rating
Assault rifle or submachine gun on full auto, WP grenade	L1
Light machine gun or squad automatic weapon (.30 cal, BAR, M60), hand grenade, rifle grenade, M79 shot-shell, flamethrower	L1*
Heavy machine gun (.50 cal), RPG (M72 LAW, RPG-7), helicopter-mounted rocket (2.75-inch FFAR), light mortar shell (up to 60mm), autocannon (20mm or 40mm), WP shell	L2
Claymore mine, heavy mortar shell (61mm+), canister shell, automatic grenade launcher (M75, M129) burst, vehicle-mounted flamethrower	L2*
Tank main gun, recoilless rifle, satchel charge	L3
HE artillery shell, air-dropped napalm strike	L3*
Air-dropped general-purpose bomb	L4*

Explosives

Lethality Rating	Examples	Lethal Range	Damage Range	Debris Range
L1*	grenade, pipe bomb, stick of dynamite	Point-Blank	Close d+5	–
L2	RPG rocket, helicopter-mounted rocket, brick of C-4 or Semtex, 2 yd. of Primacord, light mortar (up to 60mm) shell, propane tank	Point-Blank	Close d+10	Near
L2*	Claymore mine, land mine, canister shell	Point-Blank	Close d+10	Near
	Heavy mortar (81mm) shell, gas main	Close	Near d+10	Long
L3	Anti-tank artillery shell, recoilless rifle shell, satchel charge, light air-to-ground missile (AGM-12, AGM-22)	Close	Near d+15	–
L3*	High-explosive artillery shell, cluster bomb, truck bomb	Close	Near d+15	Long
L4	Heavy air-to-ground missile (AGM-65)	Near	Long d+20	–
L4*	Air-dropped general purpose bomb	Near	Long d+20	240 yd

Combat Options Summary

Autofire

Three-Round Burst: Spend at least 3 extra Firearms points, which add to your roll. For each 3 points of margin over target's Hit Threshold add one more damage roll.

Full Auto: Spend at least 5 extra Firearms points, which add to your roll. You may spend Athletics and Stability to get to 5, but they do not add. Damage becomes L1 to all targets in your firing radius (2 yd. from aim point).

Walking Fire: Spend 2 Firearms (or 1 Firearms and 2 Athletics) to hit another target up to 3 yd. from your previous target. Your first result must hit all walking fire targets.

Shot Dry: On an unmodified roll of 6 you shoot the weapon dry and must reload. You can roll two instances of damage for two targets or three instances of damage for one target.

Jam: Two unmodified Firearms rolls of 1 jams a full-auto weapon. Firearms or Mechanics test (Difficulty 4) to fix in one round; Diff 3 in two rounds; Diff 2 in three rounds.

Heavy Weapons: Use Heavy Weapons instead of Firearms for machine guns. Machine guns fire on Full Auto without spending 5 extra points.

Critical Hit

Roll a successful 6, exceed Hit Threshold by 5+, do two instances of damage.

Disarm

Called shot to a weapon (+3 to Difficulty). Effect depends on ability used:

△ Firearms: Target disarmed.
△ Melee Weapons: Target disarmed if his weapon was lighter; on a successful 6, target disarmed even if his weapon was heavier.
△ Unarmed Combat against carried weapon: One-round Unarmed Combat contest, winner gets the weapon.
△ Unarmed Combat against holstered weapon: Spend 3 Filch or Melee Weapons to take weapon for yourself.

Evasion

Declare evasion, spend 2 Athletics to increase your Hit Threshold by +1, maximum +3. Your foes' Hit Threshold against you increases by +2 per spend, maximum +6.

Sniping

Prereq: Firearms 8+; using a rifle. Take at least one round to aim, decrease foe's Hit Threshold.

△ Aware foe: Hit Threshold -1.
△ Unaware foe: Hit Threshold -2.

Extended Range: spend 2 Firearms; free if your rifle has a scope.

Suppressive Fire

Make Firearms test at Difficulty depending on width of area suppressed (Diff 3 [doorway] to 6 [three lane road]).

Maintain fire for up to 2 rounds (semi-auto) or 5 rounds (full auto).

Cross suppressed area with Athletics test at Difficulty equal to result of suppressive fire Firearms test.

Called Shot Table

Desired Location	Modifier to Hit Threshold	Additional Damage
Large carried object (rocket launcher, suitcase, backpack)	+1	
Torso, *windshield*	+1	
Target in a crowd: at Near range, or in a small, dense group (3-6)	+1	
Chest (if attacker is facing target)	+2	+2 (weapon)
Gut, *specific window, tail rotor*	+2	
Head or limb	+2	+2 (weapon; head only)
Target in a crowd: at Long range, or in a large, dense group (7+)	+2	
Hand or foot, joint, groin, *tire*	+3	+2 (unarmed; joint or groin only)
Throat, mouth, or face	+3	+3 (weapon; throat only) +2 (unarmed)
Heart	+3	+3 (weapon)
Weapon or other hand-held object	+3	See Disarm, p. 104
Eye, *headlight*	+4	+2 (weapon, blind for 2 rounds) +3 (unarmed)

Ability Refresh Summary Sheet

Investigative Abilities

Completely refresh at the end of an operation, or at the end of a breakpoint in a long, multi-stage operation.

Health

Recoverable with First Aid:

△ 2 points per point of First Aid ability spent by others.

△ 1 point per point of First Aid ability spent by self.

△ 1 point per scene if healer's First Aid pool is empty.

Refreshes at 2 points per day of rest unless Seriously Wounded.

Seriously Wounded: Must spend 1 day hospitalized for each point lost below 0 Health. At the end of that time, refresh half of Health pool. Fully refresh Health pool the next day.

Sanity

Sanity does not refresh, although Agents can recover lost Sanity by *Denial* (p. 122) and *Fainting* (p. 122), and by *Destroying the Unnatural* (p. 122).

Stability

Recover 2 points per point of Psychotherapy ability spent by others.

Recover 1 point per 2 Bond points you spend *immediately* after a loss.

Once per session:

△ Refresh 1 or 2 points by following your Motivation into danger or story complication.*

△ Refresh 1d points of Stability by impressively spending points.* *Does not apply in a Harrowing game.*

△ Refresh points of Stability equal to the Sanity recovered for Destroying the Unnatural. *Applies in a Bright and Shining mode game only.*

Between operations:

△ Refresh 2 points by engaging in your Addiction, if any.

△ Engage in your Personal Life (p. 128).

*At the Handler's discretion.

Other General Abilities

Once per session:

△ Refresh 1 or 2 points in any pool by following your Motivation into danger or story complication.*

△ A Tactical Fact-Finding Benefit may allow a partial refresh, usually of a combat ability.*

△ Some Investigative Ability use during a chase contest may allow a partial refresh, usually of the chase ability.*

△ Fully refresh any three General Abilities except Bureaucracy, Health, Network, Sanity, and Stability after an hour in a safe Haven (p. 126).

Whenever 24 hours elapses since the last expenditure:

△ Fully refresh Athletics, Drive, Firearms, Heavy Weapons, Melee Weapons, Pilot, and Unarmed Combat.

Bureaucracy and Network cannot be refreshed during an operation.

Agents suffering from Exhaustion (p. 085) cannot refresh Athletics, Drive, Firearms, Heavy Weapons, Melee Weapons, Pilot, or Unarmed Combat.

At the end of the operation:

△ Full refresh of all General Abilities except Health, Sanity, and Stability.

*At the Handler's discretion.

Kickstarter Backers

A. Timothy Rogers, Aaron Burkett, Aaron Dykstra, Aaron Griswold, Aaron Larsen, Aaron Norman, Aaron Reimer, Aaron Schrader, Aasmund Fostervold, Adam Boisvert, Adam Crossingham, Adam Daniel Wayman, Adam Flynn, Adam Gal, Adam Lyons, Adam Maloon, Adam Marafioti, Adam Schroeder, Adam Tanaskovic, Adam Thornsburg, Adam Ward, Adam Whitcomb, Adrian Cable, Adrian Colbert, Alain Manguy, Alan Bundock (UKSM), Aleksandar Stossitch, Alex Hickman, Alex Kwong, Alex Thornton-Clark, Alexander Aplin, Alexander Garcia, Alexander Hallberg, Alexander Hanson, Alexander MacBride, Alexander Mew, Alexander Moore, Alexander Permann, Alexandre Delage, Alexis Godard, Allan Samuelson, Allan Sugarbaker, Allan T. Grohe Jr., Amber K Aguero, Analyn/Patricio Gonzaga, Anders Granström, Anders Håkon Gaut, Anderson Todd, Andre Bubel, Andrea Lo, Andreas Lundmark, Andreas Schnellbach, Andrew Borelli, Andrew Byers, Andrew Carey, Andrew Coe, Andrew Craker, Andrew D Gainer, Andrew Dacey, Andrew DeLorenzo, Andrew Gammell, Andrew Gray, Andrew Haines, Andrew Hermetz, Andrew James, Andrew Kasha, Andrew Kenrick, Andrew Laliberte, Andrew Lepperd, Andrew Light, Andrew Lloyd, Andrew Long, Andrew McCarty, Andrew Moreton, Andrew Pokorny, Andrew S. Collins, Andrew Schubert, Andrew Selkirk, Andrew Shultz, Andrew Smith, Andrew Southall, Andrew Stallings, Andrew Walker, Andy Kailhofer, Andy Leighton, Andy Raisovich, Angelo de Stephano, Antero Garcia, Anthony Ficano, Anthony Schocke, Anthony Stiller, Antoine Lenoir, Antony Brown, Antti Elomaa, Aonghus Kennedy, Arnaldo Lefebre, Aron Head, Aron Sandler, Arthur Boff, Arthur Breon, Arthur Wyatt, Arthur Young, Aser Tolentino, Atsushi Sakakibara, Austin Stanley, Balazs Foldes, Barac Wiley, Barbara Wilk, Barron Chugg, Ben Dinsmore, Ben Ferguson, Ben Heisler, Ben Kimball, Ben Mathis, Ben McFarland, Ben Short, Benito Santamaria de las Heras, Benjamin Bell, Benjamin Brown, Benjamin Dilworth, Benjamin Lyon, Benjamin Phillips, Benjamin Tortorelli, Benjamin White, Benson Gardner, Bernard Gravel, Bernarr Coletta, Bertrand Dehais, Bill Gibson, Bill Martin, Bill Sundwall, Björn Carlsson, Bob Fleck, Brad Bell, Brad Kane, Brad Kleinstuber, Bradley G. Wherry, Bradley Neil West, Brandon Bassile, Breck Stack, Brendan Power, Brendan Quinlivan, Brendan Wakeley, Brennan See, Breon Halling, Bret Kramer, Brett Dixon, Brian A Campbell, Brian Allred, Brian Covey, Brian Dorion, Brian Holt, Brian Isikoff, Brian K. Eason, Brian Koonce, Brian Lee Bethel, Brian Ridge, Brianna Wyn, Brien Corey, Bruce Ferrie, Bruce Geryk, Bruce Turner, Bruno Di Pentima, Bryan Holland-Minkley, Bryant Durrell, Bryce Perry, Bryce Robinson, Cairnryan Mower, Cameron Marschall, Carl-Niclas Odenbring, Carlos Daniel Muñoz Diaz, Carter Fliss, Casey Holcomb, Casey Link, Cesar Cesarotti, Chad Hughes, Chad K. Lewis, Charles Chapman, Charles D. Fitzpatrick, Charles Hill, Charles Litfin, Charles Little, Charles Myers, Charles Ulveling, Charles Wilkins, Chase LoVerde, Chase W. Beck, Chastity Blackwell, Chitin Proctor, Chris Boynton, Chris Butler, Chris Callicoat, Chris Cousen, Chris Eaton, Chris Halliday, Chris Hamje, Chris Harvey, Chris Masselli, Chris McNeil, Chris Miles, Chris Newell, Chris Parker, Chris Slazinski, Chris Spivey, Chris Sylvis, Chris Tutt, Chris Westbrook, Chris Womack, Chris Woodward, Christian Bull, Christian Givskov, Christian Kukli, Christian Lehmann, Christian Nord, Christian Odhner, Christian Rasmussen, Christoffer Hansson, Christoph Naefgen, Christopher Anderson, Christopher Avery, Christopher Church, Christopher Clark, Christopher Coulter, Christopher D. Brant, Christopher D. Nichols, Christopher Daniel, Christopher DeBatt, Christopher George, Christopher Haddad, Christopher Hauschild, Christopher M. Smith, Christopher Malone, Christopher Martzen, Christopher Nelson, Christopher Pickett, Christopher Reyes, Christopher Ryan Barnett, Christopher Sauro, Chuck Barbee, Chuck Reynolds, Claes Gerleman, Claire Connelly, Claudio Muraro, Clayton Oliver, Clayton Stanley, Clem Powell, Colen McAlister, Colin Beattie, Colin Kehm, Coman Fullard, Corey Fulton, Corey Liss, Cormac Russell, Cory Garcia, Cory Welch, Craig Bishell, Craig Gates, Craig Irvine, Craig Kellner, Craig Long, Craig R. Bickford, Craig Robertson Oxbrow, Craig Slee, Craig Tohill, Cris Merta, Cristin Chall, Cyril Puig, Dak F. Powers, Dale Elvy, Damon Dorsey, Damon Wilson, Dan Williamson, Dana Myers, Dana Thoms, Daniel & Trista Robichaud, Daniel Byrne, Daniel Corn, Daniel Fernández Rubio, Daniel Flood, Daniel Fristedt, Daniel Harms, Daniel Jacobsson, Daniel Krongaard, Daniel Ley, Daniel M. Kane, Daniel Moran, Daniel Ravipinto, Daniel Sharp, Daniel Speir, Daniel Stack, Daniel Thingvold, Daniel White, Daniel Yauger, Danny Dyer, Danny Hua, Danny Moody, Darcy Ross, Darin DuMez, Darren Buckley, Darren Henry MacLennan, Darren Howden, Darren Miguez, Darren Watts, Dashiell Anderson, Dave Desgagnes, Dave Olson, David A. Larkins, David A. Sokolowski, David A. Lavender, David Bagdan, David Clements, David Corrie, David Cutts, David Erickson, David F. McCloskey, David Farnell, David Goffin, David Hue, David Ingersoll, David J. Panseri, David John Buckley, David Karoski, David Lai, David M. Finch, David McKemey, David Millians, David Morris, David Nichol, David Paul, David Percy, David Post, David Rehbinder, David Rodemaker, David Shope, David Stephenson, David Thomas, David Tormsen, David Weidendorf, David Zurita Sánchez, Davy Claessens, Dawid Wojcieszynski, Dean Engelhardt, Dean Reilly, DeAnna Ferguson, Demian J. Morrisroe, Dennis Eggers, Dennis Matheson, Derek Grimm, Derek Guder, Derek Robertson, Derek Schmidt, Devin Binger, Devon Oratz, Dominic Mooney, Don Juneau, Donald Stark, Donna Howard, Donnie Cornwell, Douglas Cole, Douglas Fales, Douglas Lee Haxton, Dr. David McWilliam, Dr. Géza A. G. Reilly, Dr. Troy L. Sagrillo, Duane Kevin Turner, Duncan White, Duran Goodyear, Dylan Bach, Ed Kowalczewski, Eduardo Henrique Schaeffer, Edward Duggan, Edward Glasper, Edward Lopez, Edward McWalters, Edward Sagritalo, Egoitz Gago Anton, Elijah Dixon, Elof Ivarsson, Emeric Sarron, Emily Curtis, Emma Marlow, Enrique Esturillo Cano, Enrique Rivera De Lucas, Eric Betts, Eric Brennan, Eric Hansen, Eric M. Scallion, Eric Priehs, Eric Swiersz, Erik A Saltwell, Erik Hansen, Erik Isford, Erik Van Buren, Erlend Sand Bruer, Ernest Rowland, Ethan Mark Cordray, Eugene Doherty, Evan Franke, Everitt Long, F. Rusli, F. J. te Beest, Fabio Pires de Souza Santos, Fabio Zanicotti, Fahad Mustafa, Felix Girke, Ferenc Price, Ferrett Steinmetz, Frank Froemke, Frank Heller, Frank Jarome,

Frank M. Dickerson, Frank Pine, Frank Pitt, Frank Prassel, Franklin Jones, Frederick Foulds, Frédérik Rating, Fredrik Moen, Fredrik Wiklund, Friedrich Gerring, Frits Kuijlman, G. Bryan Miller, Gareth Jamieson, Gareth Livergood, Garret Aanerud, Gary Moore, Gary Achenbach, Gary Furash, Gary Mitchel, Gary Roe, Gavin Phillips, Ged Trias, Gene Lancaster, Genevieve Cogman, George Burruss, George Casper, George Freitas, George Gard, George R.Paulishak, George Tsemberlis, Gerald Saracco, Gian-Paolo Musumeci, Gil Cruz, Gil Trevizo, Glen Ilvey, Glen Taylor, Glenn Welser, Gonzalo Rodriguez Garcia, Graeme Price, Graham Kinniburgh, Graham Swanson, Graham Woodhouse, Grant Chapman, Grayson Richardson, Greg, Greg Cooksey, Greg Hartman, Greg Hickman, Gregg A. Helmberger, Gregory Bennett, Gregory Betchart, Gregory Davis, Gregory Kettler, Gregory M. Conant , Gregory Parsons, Grzegorz Koczyk, Guillaume Daudin, Guillaume Escrivant, Guillaume Tremblay, Guillem Gruartmoner de Vera, Gustavo Adolfo Diaz Sanchez, Hamid R. Peigahi, Hamish David Fitsell Campbell, Harold Berube, Hauguel Sébastien, Heath Delashmit, Henri Desbois, Henrik Arborén, Henrik Havemann, Henrik Hellbom, Henry Chow, Henry Lincoln, Houston Payne Newman, Hugh Guthrie, Hunter Ross Krenek, Iain Smedley, Ian Asha, Ian Barry, Ian Davidson, Ian Fabry, Ian Hart, Ian Jenkinson, Ian M. Ward, Ian McFarlin, Ian Noble, Ian Wyant, Ibon Presno Gonzalez, Ignacio Jesus Gallegos, Ines Noetzold, Isaac Betty, Isaac Brickett, Ivan Juric, J. H. Frank, J. Michael Bestul, Jack Anderson, Jack Gulick, Jack Kessler, Jackson Doyle, Jacob Ansari, Jacob Boersma, Jacob Carpenter, Jacob Derby, Jacob Engstrom, Jacob Leeder, Jacob Stocke, Jacob Tittle, Jacob Torgerson, Jacob Trewe, Jacques DuRand, Jake Bieber, Jakob Schilling, James B. Sullivan, James Barton, James Braswell, James Chang, James Christopher Reeve, James Clunie, James D'Alessio, James Francis Mackrell Dunne, James Herbert, James Holden, James Iles, James King, James LaRue, James Lister, James M. Brigham, James Muskett, James Pierson, James Silvers, James Smith, James Thierry, James Traino, James Trimmier, James W. Armstrong-Wood, Jameson Sampson, Jamie Wheeler, Janne Vuorenmaa, Jarod Jett, Jaron Bernstein, Jason Bean, Jason Beaumont, Jason Carter, Jason Corley, Jason Huck, Jason J. Middleton, Jason Janicki, Jason Mical, Jason Miller, Jason Sperber, Jason Turner, Jason Verbitsky, Jason Williams, Jassin Nasr, Jay Dugger, Jay Joyner, Jean-Christophe Demers-Caron, Jean-François Campourcy, Jean-Francois Roy, Jean-Paul Gourdant, Jeff Boles, Jeff Dixon, Jeff Erwin, Jeff Smith, Jeff Waltersdorf, Jeffery Dunkle, Jeffrey Chou, Jeffrey Dentzer, Jeffrey Fournier, Jeffrey Kahrs, Jeffrey Palmer, Jeffrey S. Moeller, Jeffry Rinkel, Jered Heeschen, Jeremy Bednarski, Jeremy Fridy, Jeremy Jagosz, Jeremy Skalin, Jerry Alexandratos, Jerry Ham, Jesper Andersson, Jesse Aponte, Jesse Garrison, Jesse Morgan, Jez Green, Jim Braden, Jim Causey, Jim Taylor, Jimmy Lovelace, Jimmy Tam, Joan A. Fontas, JoAnna Jones, Joe Adams, Joel Purton, Joel Sargent, Johan Ahlsten, Johan Englund, John Alexander Bell, John Anderson, John Ashenfelter, John Buckley, John Burgess, John Buse, John Christian Spainhour, John Cotter, John Dawson, John F. Rauchert, John Fu, John Hacker, John Hunter, John Hutson, John Kennon, John Larkin, John M. Kuzma, John McLaughlin, John Petherick, John Post, John Potts, John Reed, John Sheppard, John Tsang, John W. Taylor, John West, John Whitehead, John Willson, John Wilson, John Wright, John W. S. Marvin, Jon Backman, Jon K. Hendrickson, Jon Kimmich, Jon Preedy, Jon Sewell, Jon Stevens, Jonas Beardsley, Jonas Bolander, Jonas Karlsson, Jonas Schiött, Jonathan Bagelman, Jonathan H. Wilson, Jonathan Hsu, Jonathan Keim, Jonathan Korman, Jonathan Lapitan, Jonathan Man, Jonathan Sharp, Jonathan Westmoreland, Jordan Bowman, Jordan Millward, Jorge A. Torres, Jori Virtanen, Joseph Alexander DeSimone, Joseph Berriman, Joseph D. Walsh III, Joseph Gandee, Joseph Limbaugh, Joseph Noll, Joseph O'Toole, Joseph P. Craig, Joseph Wheeler, Josh Riggins, Joshua Brumley, Joshua C. Bishop, Joshua Clark, Joshua Ramsey, Joshua Sagaser, Joshua Whittaker, Juan Carlos Peralta, Juan Felipe Calle, Judd M. Goswick, Jukka Särkijärvi, Julian Breen, Julian Kluge, Jürgen Hubert, Jurie Horneman, Juris Purins, Jussi Kenkkilä, Justin Akkerman, Justin Howard, Justin Hukle-VanKirk, Justin Ramos, Justin Unrau, Kadin Hopko, Karen J. Grant, Karl Deckard, Karl Lloyd, Karl Parakenings, Kathleen Lambert, Keane Peterson, Keith Hartman, Keith J. Potter, Keith Marcks, Keith Nelson, Kelly Heffron, Kelly Reagin, Ken Boucher, Ken Doyle, Ken Finlayson, Ken Kersey, Ken Scroggins, Kenneth Labbe, Kenneth Ringwald, Kent Johan Johansen, Kerry Young, Kevin Empey, Kevin Flynn, Kevin Galton, Kevin Gray, Kevin Ham, Kevin Harrison, Kevin Heim, Kevin Lama, Kevin Lemke, Kevin Maroney, Kevin McHale, Kevin Newsom, Kevin Rolfe, Kiefer Paterson, Kim Andersson, Kimberly Malpertuis, Kirk Barrett, Kirk Foote, Kirk Henley, Kit Kindred, Koray Özbudak, Kory Hunt, Kreg Mosier, Kristian A. Bjørkelo, Kristopher L. Arseneault, Kurt McMahon, Kurtis Franks, Kyle Ayres, Kyle Cassidy, Kyle Miller, Kyle Takamoto, Kyle Ver Steeg, Kym Malycha, Lachlan Jones, Lance Schroeder, Lance Tracy, Lars Enzweiler, Lassi Seppälä, Laszlo Szidonya, Laurence J. Cornford, Laurent Tastet, Lauri Hirvonen, Lawrence C. Allen IV, Leandro Mena Ugarte, Lee DeBoer, Levi Whitney, Lewis Weaver, Liam Eyers, Lin Dale Wyeth II, Lindsay McLean, Lisa Padol, Lloyd Moore, Lonnie Harris, Lorraine Donaldson, Luca Lettieri, Ludovic Chabant, Lukasz Koczocik, M. Sean Molley, Magnus Nordin, Magnus Nordlander, Maher Leiland Sagrillo, Malcolm Harbrow, Marc D. Gibson, Marc di Lazzaro, Marc Margelli, Marc Schifer, Marcin Miduch, Marcin Rozycki, Marco Antonio Ramirez Garcia, Marco Menarini, Marco Subias, Marcus DeBoard, Marcus Ström, Mario Magallanes-Ribeiro Merino, Marisa Preciado, Mark Archer, Mark Bussey, Mark Caldwell, Mark DiPasquale, Mark Edwards, Mark Kirtland, Mark Margraf, Mark Rajic, Mark Richman, Mark Rinna, Mark Siefert, Mark Solino, Mark Thompson, Mark Turnage, Markus Plate, Martin Andersson, Martin Barrett, Martin Blake, Martin Cutbill, Martin Helsdon, Martin Hess, Martin Legg, Martin Oakley, Martin Tulloch, Marty Caplan, Mary Henry, Mary K. Johnston, Mateen Greenway, Mathew Weathers, Mathieu Lambron, Matt McElroy, Matt Willis, Matthew Barr, Matthew Bates, Matthew Campen, Matthew Darling, Matthew Hain, Matthew J. Mabry, Matthew L. Clarke, Matthew Lipparelli, Matthew Lippay, Matthew Moorman, Matthew Plank, Matthew Roberts, Matthew Sanderson, Matthew Silver, Matthew Tarplee, Matthew Wasiak, Matthew Wiseman, Matthias Hunger, Mattias Danielsson, Maurice E. Lane III, Max Kaehn, Melior Via, LLC, Micah Nielsen, Michael Barsness, Michael Bland, Michael Bowman, Michael C. Smith,

357

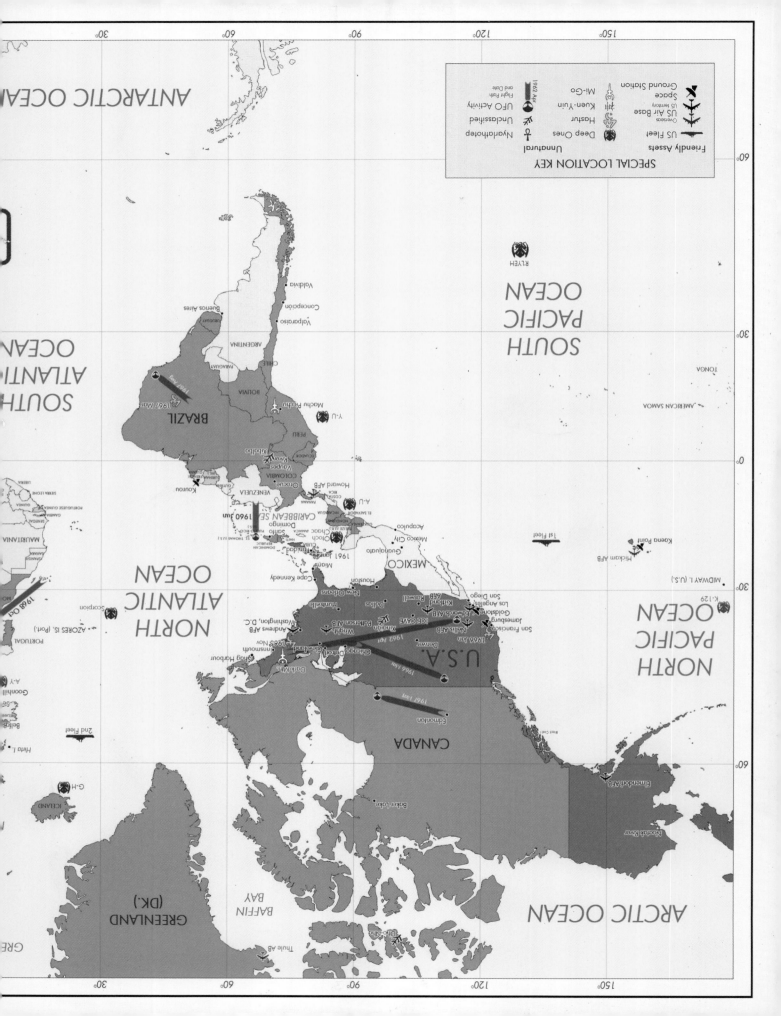